OCR
A LEVEL

ECONOMICS
FOURTH EDITION

Peter Smith
with Simon Dyer

2011

HODDER
EDUCATION
AN HACHETTE UK COMPANY

The teaching content of this resource is endorsed by OCR for use with specification AS Level Economics (H060) and specification A Level Economics (H460). In order to gain OCR endorsement, this resource has been reviewed against OCR's endorsement criteria.

This resource was designed using the most up to date information from the specification. Specifications are updated over time which means there may be contradictions between the resource and the specification, therefore please use the information on the latest specification and Sample Assessment Materials at all times when ensuring students are fully prepared for their assessments.

Any references to assessment and/or assessment preparation are the publisher's interpretation of the specification requirements and are not endorsed by OCR. OCR recommends that teachers consider using a range of teaching and learning resources in preparing learners for assessment, based on their own professional judgement for their students' needs. OCR has not paid for the production of this resource, nor does OCR receive any royalties from its sale. For more information about the endorsement process, please visit the OCR website, www.ocr.org.uk.

Hachette UK's policy is to use papers that are natural, renewable and recyclable products and made from wood grown in well-managed forests and other controlled sources. The logging and manufacturing processes are expected to conform to the environmental regulations of the country of origin.

Orders: please contact Bookpoint Ltd, 130 Park Drive, Milton Park, Abingdon, Oxon OX14 4SE. Telephone: (44) 01235 827827. Fax: (44) 01235 400401. Email education@bookpoint. co.uk Lines are open from 9 a.m. to 5 p.m., Monday to Saturday, with a 24-hour message answering service. You can also order through our website: www.hoddereducation.co.uk

ISBN: 978 1 5104 5840 6

© Peter Smith and Simon Dyer 2019

First published in 2019 by

Hodder Education,

An Hachette UK Company

Carmelite House

50 Victoria Embankment

London EC4Y 0DZ

www.hoddereducation.co.uk

Impression number   10 9 8 7 6 5 4 3 2 1

Year   2023 2022 2021 2020 2019

Cover photo © www.pelzinger.de

Typeset by Integra Software Services Pvt. Ltd., Pondicherry, India

Printed in Italy

A catalogue record for this title is available from the British Library.

Get the most from this book

This textbook has been tailored explicitly to cover the content of the OCR specification for the A Level qualification in Economics. The book is divided into sections, each covering one of the components that make up the OCR programme of study.

The text provides the foundation for studying OCR Economics, but you will no doubt wish to keep up to date by referring to additional topical sources of information about economic events. This can be done by reading the serious newspapers, visiting key sites on the internet, and reading magazines such as *Economic Review*.

Special features

Learning objectives
A statement of the intended learning objectives for each chapter.

Key terms
Clear, concise definitions of essential key terms where they first appear and a list at the end of each section.

Case studies
Case studies to show economic concepts applied to real-world situations.

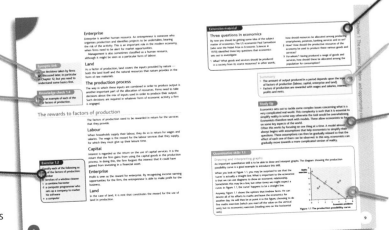

Synoptic links
Synoptic links showing the connections between the themes.

Knowledge check questions
Quick-fire questions to test your knowledge and understanding.

Exercises and questions
Exercises to provide active engagement with economic analysis, plus practice questions at the end of each chapter (except Chapter 28) to check your analysis and evaluation.

Extension material
Extension points to stretch your understanding.

Summaries
Bulleted summaries of each topic that can be used as a revision tool.

Study tips
Short pieces of advice to help you present your ideas effectively and avoid potential pitfalls.

Quantitative skills
Worked examples of quantitative skills that you will need to develop.

Answers are online at: www.hoddereducation.co.uk/OCREconomics

Contents

Section 2 Macroeconomics

Introduction

For teachers

The new OCR Economics A Level specification has been designed to enhance the co-teachability of the course in terms of AS Level and A Level. One of my biggest frustrations as a teacher of AS and A Level Economics, was that the AS course did not break at what I considered to be natural points in the course.

The new specification has a much more sensible split between the AS topics and the A Level topics, in an attempt to keep all the topics in discrete areas. So, for example AS Level includes the basic building bricks of Microeconomics and Macroeconomics without requiring any teaching of the more complicated A Level topics. This reduces the need to 're-teach' topic areas in Year 13 and makes the AS course a more user-friendly experience.

The real benefit to me, in the classroom, is twofold. First, I can teach my AS Level students in the same classroom as my A Level students. This makes timetabling easier and may have an impact on the number of students I have progress on to A level from Year 12.

Second, in years when I may not have any AS Level students, I can still teach the AS topics in Year 12, enabling me to use the AS Level examination papers as end of Year 12 exams for my A Level students. This saves me having to write my own assessment materials and gives my students a better and more realistic examination at the end of Year 12.

Each topic area within the AS is identical when it is also necessary for the full A Level. For example, 2.8 Government Intervention (AS Level) contains exactly the same content as 2.11 Government intervention (A Level), so teachers do not have to return to a topic area once it has been taught (except as revision).

Where A Level-only topics exist, these have their own section in the specification. Tables 1 and 2 map the AS Level topics to the A Level topics and the appropriate chapter in this textbook.

Table 1 Microeconomics

Topic	AS Level unit	A Level unit	Chapter
The economic problem	1.1	1.1	1
The allocation of resources	1.2	1.2	2
Opportunity cost	1.3	1.3	1
Specialisation and trade	2.1	2.1	2
Demand	2.2	2.2	3
Supply	2.3	2.3	4

Topic	AS Level unit	A Level unit	Chapter
Consumer and producer surplus	2.4	2.4	3 & 4
The interaction of markets	2.5	2.5	5
Elasticity	2.6	2.6	6
The concept of the margin	N/A	2.7	7
Market failure and externalities	2.7	2.8	8
Information failure	N/A	2.9	9
Public goods	N/A	2.10	9
Government intervention	2.8	2.11	10
Business objectives	N/A	3.1	12
Costs and economies of scale	N/A	3.2	11
Revenue and profit	N/A	3.3	11
Perfect competition	N/A	4.1	13
Monopoly	N/A	4.2	14
Monopolistic competition	N/A	4.3	15
Oligopoly	N/A	4.4	15
Contestable markets	N/A	4.5	15
Demand for labour	N/A	5.1	16
Supply of labour	N/A	5.2	17
The interaction of labour markets	N/A	5.3	18

Table 2 Macroeconomics

Topic	AS Level unit	A Level unit	Chapter
Circular flow of income	1.1	1.1	19
Aggregate demand	1.2	1.2	19
Aggregate supply	1.3	1.3	20
The interaction of aggregate demand and supply	1.4	1.4	20
The multiplier and accelerator	N/A	1.5	21
Economic growth	2.1	2.1	22
Development	2.2	2.2	23
Employment	2.3	2.3	24
Inflation	2.4	2.4	25
Balance of payments	2.5	2.5	26
Trends in macroeconomic indicators	2.6	2.6	28
Income distribution and welfare	N/A	2.7	29
The Phillips curve	N/A	2.8	33
Fiscal policy	3.1	3.1	30
Monetary policy	3.2	3.2	31
Supply-side policy	3.3	3.3	32
Policy conflicts	3.4	3.4	33
International trade	4.1	4.1	34
Exchange rates	4.2	4.2	27
Globalisation	N/A	4.3	35
Trade policies and negotiations	N/A	4.4	36

Topic	AS Level unit	A Level unit	Chapter
Money and interest rates	N/A	5.1	37
The financial sector	N/A	5.2	38
Financial regulation	N/A	5.3	39

Table 3 maps the chapters necessary for the AS course only.

Table 3 AS course only

	Chapters required
Microeconomics	1, 2, 3, 4, 5, 6, 8, 10
Macroeconomics	19, 20, 22, 23, 24, 25, 26, 27, 28, 30, 31, 32, 33, 34

Finally, for mark schemes for the practice questions featured at the end of the chapters in this book, please visit https://www.hoddereducation.co.uk/subjects/economics/products/16-18/ocr-a-level-economics-(4th-edition) and click 'Download answers'.

– Simon Dyer

For students

Prior learning, knowledge and progression

Most students who choose to study A Level Economics are meeting the subject for the first time, and no prior learning or knowledge of economics is required. The study of economics complements a range of other A Level subjects, such as history, geography, business, mathematics and the sciences, and the way of thinking that you will develop as you study economics will help in interpreting issues you'll meet in many of these subjects. Studying economics can provide important employability skills and is a good preparation for those wishing to progress to higher education. If you intend to study economics at university, you may wish to consider studying mathematics as one of your other A Level subjects.

Find out more about the OCR Economics offering at https://www.ocr.org.uk/qualifications/as-and-a-level/economics-h060-h460-from-2019/.

Economics in this book

The study of economics requires a familiarity with recent economic events in the UK and elsewhere, and candidates will be expected to show familiarity with 'recent historical data' — broadly defined as covering the last 7–10 years. The following websites will help you to keep up to date with recent trends and events:

■ Recent and historical data about the UK economy can be found at the website of the Office for National Statistics (ONS) at: www.ons.gov.uk
■ Also helpful is the site of HM Treasury at: www.hm-treasury.gov.uk
■ The Bank of England site is well worth a visit, especially the *Inflation Report* and the Minutes of the Monetary Policy Committee: www.bankofengland.co.uk
■ The Institute for Fiscal Studies offers an independent view of a range of economic topics: www.ifs.org.uk

For information about other countries, visit the following:

- http://ec.europa.eu/eurostat
- www.oecd.org
- www.undp.org
- www.worldbank.org

How to study economics

There are two crucial aspects of studying economics. The first stage is to study the theory, which helps us to explain economic behaviour. However, in studying A level Economics it is equally important to be able to apply the theories and concepts that you meet, and to see just how these relate to the real world.

If you are to become competent at this, it is vital that you get plenty of practice. In part, this means working through the exercises and case studies that you will find in this text. However, it also means thinking about how economics helps us to explain news items and data that appear in newspapers and on television.

Make sure that you practise as much as you can.

In economics, it is also important to be able to produce examples of economic phenomena. In reading this text, you will find some examples that help to illustrate ideas and concepts. Do not rely solely on the examples provided here, but look around the world to find your own, and keep a note of these ready for use in essays and exams. This will help to convince the examiners that you have understood economics. It will also help you to understand the theories.

Finally, for answers, commentary and explanations for the knowledge checks, exercises and case studies featured in this book, please visit https://www.hoddereducation.co.uk/subjects/economics/products/16-18/ ocr-a-level-economics-(4th-edition) and click 'Download answers'.

Enjoy economics

Most important of all, I hope you will enjoy your study of economics. I have always been fascinated by the subject, and hope that you will capture something of the excitement and challenge of learning about how markets and the economy operate. I also wish you every success with your studies.

– Peter Smith

SECTION
1

MICROECONOMICS

Part 1
How competitive markets work

Chapter 1

The economic problem and opportunity cost

Welcome to economics. Many of you opening this book will be meeting economics for the first time, and you will want to know what is in store for you as you set out to study the subject. This opening chapter sets the scene by introducing you to some key ideas and identifying the scope of economic analysis. As you learn more of the subject, you will find that economics is a way of thinking that will broaden your perspective on the world around you.

Learning objectives

After studying this chapter, you should be able to:
- explain what is meant by economic goods and free goods
- explain the basic economic problem, involving notions of scarcity, choice, needs and wants
- evaluate the problem of scarcity and choice and the requirement to make choices
- explain normative and positive statements
- explain the role of economic agents — government, firms (businesses) and households
- explain the factors of production (land, labour, capital and enterprise), and the rewards to each (rent, wages, interest and profit)
- evaluate rationality as a way of understanding the behaviour of economic agents
- evaluate the different objectives of economic agents in an economy
- explain opportunity cost and what is meant by a trade-off
- explain, with the aid of a diagram, movements along a production possibility curve (*PPC*)
- explain, with the aid of a diagram, shifts of a production possibility curve
- explain, with the aid of a diagram, the usefulness of the concept of opportunity cost

The economic problem

Key term

scarcity a situation that arises because people have unlimited wants in the face of limited resources

The basic economic problem faced by everybody is that of **scarcity**. This means that there are not enough resources in the world for everybody to have all of their wants and needs fulfilled.

In economic terms, we would say that societies have *finite resources*, but people have *unlimited wants*. A big claim? Not really. There is no country in the world in which all wants can be met, and this is clearly true at a global level.

Knowledge check 1.1

Thinking of yourself, give an example of a 'want' and of a 'need'.

Key terms

economic goods goods that are scarce

free goods goods such as the Earth's atmosphere that are not normally regarded as being scarce

poverty a situation in which individuals lack the basic necessities of life or have low incomes relative to their fellow citizens

There is a difference between *wants* and *needs*. Everyone needs to breathe and to eat, so air and food are necessary for human life. However, there are also things that people would like to consume, and these are known as wants. For example, people may want to eat an ice cream on a hot day, but this is not a necessity.

Economic goods and free goods

Goods that are scarce are known as **economic goods**. Most goods fall into this category. However, there are also some goods that may be regarded as **free goods**. An example might be the Earth's atmosphere.

Scarcity and poverty

Notice that talking about *scarcity* in this sense is not the same as talking about **poverty**. Poverty might be seen as an extreme form of scarcity, in which individuals lack the basic necessities of life — whereas even relatively prosperous people face scarcity because resources are limited.

Synoptic link

The meaning and causes of poverty will be examined in Chapter 29, where you will see that although absolute poverty exists in less developed countries, relative poverty also exists in advanced countries such as the UK.

Scarcity and choice

Key term

firm (business) an organisation that produces output (goods or services)

The key issue that arises from the existence of scarcity is that it forces people to make choices. Each individual must choose which goods and services to consume. In other words, everyone needs to prioritise the consumption of whatever commodities they need or would like to have, as they cannot satisfy all their wants. Similarly, at a national level, governments have to make choices between alternative uses of resources.

It is this need to choose that underlies the subject matter of economics. Economic analysis is about seeking to understand those choices made by individual people, **firms (businesses)** and governments.

Positive and normative statements

Key terms

positive statement a statement about what *is*, i.e. about *facts*

normative statement a statement involving a value judgement about what *ought to be*

value judgement a statement based on your opinion or beliefs, rather than on facts

Economics aims to look at the causes and consequences of choices in an objective way. However, some of its subject matter requires careful attention if we are to remain objective. To achieve this, it is important to be clear about the difference between **positive** and **normative statements**.

In short, a positive statement is about *facts*. In contrast, a normative statement is about *what ought to be*. Another way of looking at this is that a statement becomes normative when it involves an opinion or **value judgement**.

Suppose the government is considering raising the tax on cigarettes. It may legitimately consult economists to discover what effect a higher tobacco tax will have on the consumption of cigarettes and on government revenues. An economist might respond to this by noting that economic theory suggests that a higher tax will tend to reduce the consumption of cigarettes and generate tax revenue, and that the

Synoptic link

The effect of a tax on cigarettes will be examined in Chapter 10.

statistical evidence supports this. This is a positive statement, based on objective reasoning.

A very different situation will arise if the government asks whether it *should* raise the tax on cigarettes. This calls for an opinion to be expressed (a value judgement). For example, a response might say that the tax on cigarettes ought not to be raised because it discriminates against smokers. This would be a normative statement. There are some words that betray normative statements, such as 'should' or 'ought to' — watch out for these.

Positive and normative approaches are not always clearly separated. For example, if the aim of a policy is to stop people from smoking (which reflects a normative judgement about what ought to happen), then economic analysis may be used to highlight the strengths and weaknesses of alternative policy measures in a purely objective (positive) fashion.

Critics of economics often joke that economists always disagree with one another: for example, it has been said that if you put five economists in a room together, they will come up with at least six conflicting opinions. However, although economists may arrive at different value judgements, and therefore have differences when it comes to normative issues, there is much greater agreement on positive issues.

Knowledge check 1.2

Is the following statement a normative or a positive statement? 'The government ought to raise unemployment benefits.'

Evaluation of scarcity and choice

As you move further into studying economics, you will often meet the issue of scarcity and the need for choice. Why is it so important? Scarcity requires difficult choices. If you have limited pocket money, you cannot buy everything you would like. If a household decides to buy a new car, it may need to defer that planned foreign holiday. A farmer with limited land available has to decide whether to plant potatoes or onions. If he decides to grow onions, he has to forgo the opportunity to grow potatoes. If the government decides to devote more resources to the National Health Service, it must devote less to some alternative, such as roads or defence. You can see from this that scarcity lies at the heart of economics, which is about explaining how households, firms and governments take decisions and on what basis. It also provides a way of thinking that may enable better choices to be made.

Summary

- The basic economic problem faced by any society is scarcity, because resources are finite but wants are unlimited. As a result, choices need to be made.
- Most goods are economic goods because they are scarce, but there are also some free goods.
- Positive statements are about what is, whereas normative statements are about what ought to be.

Economic agents

In analysing the process by which choices are made, it is important to be aware of the various economic agents that are responsible for making decisions. In economic analysis, there are three key groups of decision-makers: households, firms (businesses) and government.

Households make choices about their expenditure. In this role, they are consumers who demand goods and services. However, in order to be able to buy goods, households need income, so they also make choices about the supply of their labour, which will be discussed in the next section.

Firms exist in order to produce goods or services. Firms also make choices, in particular about which goods or services to produce, and the techniques of production to be used. The prices at which they can sell are also important in economic analysis. Firms also have a dual role, as they need to purchase machines and raw materials if they are to produce goods and services.

Government fulfils several roles in society. It undertakes expenditure and influences the economy through its taxation and regulation of markets. It makes choices about which activities to support through its spending programme, and about how heavily it needs to tax households and firms to raise revenue in order to fund their expenditure.

The behaviour of economic agents

The way that resources are used in an economy is determined by the actions of the three key economic agents (households, firms and government) that operate in the economy. All take decisions that will influence the allocation of resources.

Think first about households, and the choices that they will make about economic issues. In their role as consumers, households take decisions about what goods and services they wish to consume. Of course, the range of goods and services that a household will consume is wide and includes food and drink, but also household goods, housing, leisure goods and services, education, healthcare — any number of different items. Even within these broadly defined categories, there are decisions to be made about what sorts of foodstuffs, what variety of drinks, and so on. This underlines the complexity of economic decisions.

Households also need to take decisions about their work patterns. What occupations should they pursue, which firms should they consider joining, how many hours of work should they offer?

Firms face decisions about what goods and services to produce, and about the technology and techniques of production that they should employ. How many workers should they hire? How much land do they need to rent in order to be able to conduct their business?

Governments also take decisions about expenditure, impose taxation and establish the framework in which the other economic agents take decisions — for example, by regulating economic activity in various ways.

Knowledge check 1.3

Give examples of the ways in which government spends its funds.

Synoptic link

The importance of incentives is explored in Chapter 2.

Objectives of economic agents

In order to begin to explore these decisions, it is important to understand what it is that economic agents are trying to achieve (their motivations and objectives). In turn, this will set the incentives that will affect their behaviour.

For example, when a household takes decisions about how to allocate its expenditure, what is it that they are trying to achieve by their spending on goods and services? Economists typically think of this in terms of the satisfaction (or utility) that households receive from consuming goods and services. In other words, if you buy an apple, you do not simply want to own it and know that you have it — you want to be able to eat it, because that is what gives you satisfaction.

Similarly, if you choose to work stacking shelves in the supermarket at the weekends, you do this not because you enjoy stacking shelves but because it provides you with income that you can use to buy goods that will give you satisfaction. So the decisions households make are influenced by the satisfaction they will ultimately gain from consuming goods and services.

Synoptic link

The differing objectives that firms may adopt are discussed in Chapter 12.

Firms also have objectives — and we will see later that different firms may have different objectives. For the moment, we will make the assumption that firms set out with the objective of making profits on their activities. They decide to produce particular goods or services, and to use labour, land and capital in order to receive a return on their efforts.

The government may have different objectives. It needs to raise revenue through taxation, pursue its expenditure programme and provide the framework within which the economy can operate. This incorporates the need to ensure the stability of the economy, meet environmental targets, avoid excessive unemployment and enable the economy to grow over time. It may also wish to influence resource allocation directly, for example by pursuing long-term plans or redistributing income to protect vulnerable members of society.

Synoptic link

Notice that many of the actions undertaken by government are relevant at the level of the economy as a whole, and form part of the subject matter of macroeconomics. Macroeconomics is the study of the economy as a whole, in contrast to the study of individual behaviour (microeconomics). Microeconomics is covered in Chapters 1–18, and macroeconomics in Chapters 19–39.

Evaluation of the behaviour of economic agents

An important consideration is whether economic agents will always make choices in a rational manner. And if not, how will this affect the way in which we try to understand their behaviour?

Synoptic link

What is meant by rational choice is discussed further in the next chapter (see pages 18–19).

Will households always act to maximise their utility? Looking around us, we have to admit that not all households do so. There are times when people do not seem to act in their own best interests. They may choose to donate money to charity, or to spend their time helping others. Or they may sometimes be enticed into spending on goods or services that they do not really want — or they may take out a gym membership at a high price but then not make full use of it.

Do firms always set out to maximise profits? Again, there may be instances where firms may pursue other objectives than just trying to make profit. They may sponsor a local football team, or encourage their workers to undertake volunteering activities or raise money for charities during working hours.

Do governments always act rationally or take the best possible decisions? Decisions may be taken based on imperfect information, or may sometimes be influenced by political considerations.

Exercise 1.1

Discuss the extent to which you think that economic agents take decisions in a rational manner.

Summary

- Three types of economic agents take decisions in economics: households, firms (businesses) and governments.
- Households take decisions about the goods and services that they wish to consume, and about the amount of labour they wish to supply.
- Firms take decisions about what to produce and how to produce it.
- Governments take decisions about expenditure, taxation and the regulation of the economy.
- Rational consumers may aim to maximise their utility (satisfaction).
- Firms may have differing objectives, but it is often assumed that they set out to maximise profits.
- Government decisions are sometimes based on imperfect information, or may be influenced by political considerations.

Factors of production

Key term

factors of production resources used in the production process, or *inputs* into production, including labour, capital, land and enterprise

It is clear that both *human resources* and *physical resources* are required as part of the production process. These productive resources are known as the **factors of production**.

Labour

The most obvious human resource is *labour*. Labour is a key input into production. There are many different types of labour, encompassing different skill levels and working in different ways, from unskilled labourers to web designers or brain surgeons.

Labour is a key input into the production process

Capital

The production process also needs non-human resources, such as plant and machinery, transport, equipment and factory buildings. These inputs are referred to as *capital*. They can be regarded as a stock of past production used to aid current production. For example, machines are used in the production process — they are resources manufactured for the purpose of producing other goods.

Enterprise

Enterprise is another human resource. An entrepreneur is someone who organises production and identifies projects to be undertaken, bearing the risk of the activity. This is an important role in the modern economy, when firms need to be alert for market opportunities.

Management is also sometimes classified as a human resource, although it might be seen as a particular form of labour.

Land

As a factor of production, land covers the inputs provided by nature — both the land itself and the natural resources that nature provides in the form of raw materials.

The production process

The way in which these inputs are combined in order to produce output is another important part of the allocation of resources. Firms need to take decisions about the mix of inputs used to produce their output. Such decisions are required in whatever form of economic activity a firm is engaged.

The rewards to factors of production

The factors of production need to be rewarded in return for the services that they provide.

Labour

When households supply their labour, they do so in return for wages and salaries. The wage is the reward for the labour services that they supply, for which they must give up their leisure time.

Capital

Interest is regarded as the return on the use of capital services. It is the return that the firm gains from using the capital goods in the production process. In doing this, the firm forgoes the interest that it could have gained from holding financial assets.

Enterprise

Profit is seen as the reward for enterprise. By recognising income-earning opportunities for the firm, the entrepreneur is able to make profit for the business.

Land

In the case of land, it is rent that constitutes the reward for the use of land in production.

Synoptic link

These decisions taken by firms are discussed later, in particular in Chapter 12, but you need to understand some basics first.

Knowledge check 1.4

Give an example of each of the four factors of production.

Exercise 1.2

Classify each of the following as one of the factors of production:
a timber
b services of a window cleaner
c a combine harvester
d a computer programmer who sets up a company to market her software
e a computer

Three questions in economics

By now you should be getting some idea of the subject matter of economics. The US economist Paul Samuelson (who won the Nobel Prize in Economic Sciences in 1970) identified three key questions that economics sets out to investigate:

1 *What?* What goods and services should be produced in a society from its scarce resources? In other words, how should resources be allocated among producing smartphones, potatoes, banking services and so on?

2 *How?* How should the productive resources of the economy be used to produce these various goods and services?

3 *For whom?* Having produced a range of goods and services, how should these be allocated among the population for consumption?

Summary

- The amount of output produced in a period depends upon the inputs of factors of production (labour, capital, enterprise and land).
- Factors of production are rewarded with wages and salaries, interest, profits and rents.

Study tip

Economics sets out to tackle some complex issues concerning what is a very complicated real world. This complexity is such that it is essential to simplify reality in some way, otherwise the task would be overwhelming. Economists therefore work with models. These allow economists to focus on some key aspects of the world.

Often this works by focusing on one thing at a time. A model almost always begins with assumptions that help economists to simplify their questions. These assumptions can then be gradually relaxed so that the effect of each one of them can be observed. In this way, economists can gradually move towards a more complicated version of reality.

Opportunity cost

Key term

opportunity cost in decision making, the value of the next-best alternative forgone

The need to face scarcity raises one of the most important concepts in all of economic analysis — the notion of **opportunity cost**. When an individual chooses to consume one good, he does so at the cost of the item that would have been next in his list of priorities. For example, suppose you are on a strict diet and at the end of the day you can 'afford' either one chocolate or a piece of cheese. If you choose the cheese, the opportunity cost of the cheese is the chocolate that you could have had instead. In other words, the opportunity cost is the value of the next-best alternative forgone.

Exercise 1.3

Andrew has just started his A Level courses, and has chosen to take economics, mathematics and French. Although he was certain about the first two, it was a close call between French and English. What is Andrew's opportunity cost of choosing French?

Knowledge check 1.5

Suppose your school or college wants to build a new sports hall. Identify possible elements of the opportunity cost of such a project.

This important notion can be applied to many different contexts because, whenever you make a decision, you reject an alternative in favour of your chosen option. You have chosen to read this book, when instead you could be watching television or meeting friends.

As you move further into studying economics, you will encounter this notion of opportunity cost again and again. Indeed, we already saw hints of it earlier in the chapter. A household choosing to buy a new car faces opportunity cost in having to forgo a foreign holiday. A farmer choosing to grow onions incurs an opportunity cost in not being able to grow potatoes. By spending more on the NHS, the government has less to spend on defence and roads. Economic thinking helps to explain how such choices are made, and how they could be improved.

Study tip

Opportunity cost is a key concept in economics, and will be important in a variety of contexts. In particular, it captures the way in which economists take decisions, which may be quite different from how non-economists approach choice. Make sure you understand it and watch for situations in which it is relevant.

The production possibility curve

Key term

production possibility curve (PPC) a curve showing the maximum combinations of goods or services that can be produced in a set period of time given available resources

Economists rely heavily on diagrams to help in their analysis. In exploring the notion of opportunity cost, a helpful diagram is the **production possibility curve (PPC)**, also sometimes known as the production possibility frontier. This shows the maximum combinations of goods that can be produced with a given set of resources.

First consider a simple example. In Exercise 1.1, Andrew was studying for his A Levels. Suppose now that he has got behind with his homework. He has limited time available, and has five economics problems to answer and five maths exercises to do. An economics problem takes the same time to answer as a maths exercise.

What are the options? Suppose he knows that in the time available he can tackle either all of the maths and none of the economics, or all of the economics and none of the maths. Alternatively, he can try to keep both teachers happy by doing some of each.

Quantitative skills 1.1

Drawing and interpreting graphs

An important quantitative skill is to be able to draw and interpret graphs. The diagram showing the production possibility curve is a good example to introduce this skill.

When you look at Figure 1.1, you may be surprised to see that the 'curve' is actually a straight line. What is important to the economist is that we can use diagrams to show an economic relationship. Sometimes this may be a straight line, but other times we might expect a curve. In Figure 1.1, the 'curve' happens to be a straight line.

Anyway, Figure 1.1 shows the options that Andrew faces. He can devote all of his efforts to maths and leave the economics for another day. He will then be at point A in the figure, choosing to do five maths exercises (which you read off the value on the vertical axis), but no economics problems (reading zero on the horizontal axis).

Quantitative skills 1.1 (continued)

Alternatively, he can do all the economics problems and no maths, and be at point *B*. The line joining these two extreme points shows the intermediate possibilities. For example, at *C* he does two economics problems and three maths exercises. Again, you can read off the values from the two axes.

The line shows the maximum combinations that Andrew can tackle — which is why it is sometimes called a 'frontier'. There is no way he can manage to be beyond the frontier (for example, at point *D*), as he does not have the time (i.e. resources) to do so. However, he could end up *inside* the frontier, at a point such as *E*. This could happen if he gives up, and squanders his time by watching television. That would be an inefficient use of his resources — at least in terms of tackling his homework.

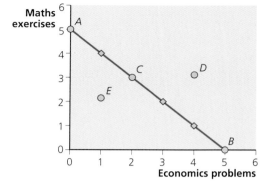

Figure 1.1 The production possibility curve

As Andrew moves down the line from left to right, he is spending more time on economics and less on maths. The opportunity cost of tackling an additional economics problem is an additional maths exercise not done.

Knowledge check 1.6

In Figure 1.1, which labelled points represent efficient positions?

Key term

trade-off a situation in which the choice of one alternative requires the sacrifice of another

A trade-off

In the example discussed in Quantitative skills 1.1, Andrew faces a **trade-off** between the time spent on economics and on maths. In other words, Andrew can only spend more time on economics by spending less time on maths. He must trade off one against the other. You will come across many instances of this notion as your study of economics progresses.

Opportunity cost and a movement along the *PPC*

Figure 1.2 shows how the *PPC* provides information about opportunity cost. Suppose we have a farmer with 10 ha of land who is choosing between growing potatoes and onions. The *PPC* shows the combinations of the two crops that could be produced. For example, if the farmer produces 300 tonnes of onions on part of the land, then 180 tonnes of potatoes could be produced from the remaining land. In order to increase production of potatoes by 70 tonnes from 180 to 250, 50 tonnes of onions must be given up. Therefore, the opportunity cost of 70 extra tonnes of potatoes is seen to be 50 tonnes of onions. There is a trade-off between the production of potatoes and onions associated with a movement along the *PPC*.

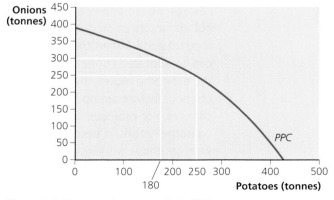

Figure 1.2 Opportunity cost and the *PPC*

Why might the *PPC* be curved?

Notice that the *PPC* in Figure 1.2 was drawn as a curve instead of a straight line. This is because the farmer's land varies in different plots, with some plots being ideal for potatoes but others being better for onions. The farmer can choose a balanced approach, using each plot of land for the use to which it is suited. However, if he were to choose to produce only onions (or only potatoes), overall the land would be less productive. In other words, the more onions that are produced, the higher their opportunity cost in terms of potatoes (and vice versa).

The *PPC* for an economy

Key terms

capital goods goods used as part of the production process, such as machinery or factory buildings

consumer goods goods produced for present use (consumption)

Suppose we have a simple economy that produces just two types of good: **capital goods** and **consumer goods**. Capital goods are used to increase the future capacity of the economy. For example, you might think of machinery, trucks or factory buildings that will be used to produce other goods in the future. Expenditure on such goods is known as *investment*. In contrast, consumer goods are for present use. They are goods that people consume, such as apples, televisions and private cars. This sort of expenditure is known as *consumption*.

Figure 1.3 illustrates society's options in a particular period. Given the resources available, society can produce any combination of capital and consumer goods along the *PPC*. So, point *A* represents one possible combination of outputs, in which the economy produces C_1 consumer goods and K_1 capital goods.

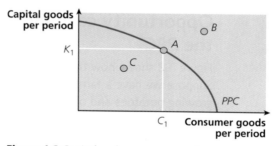

Figure 1.3 Capital and consumer goods

If society were to move to the right along the *PPC*, it would produce more consumer goods — but at the expense of capital goods. So, it can be seen that the opportunity cost of producing consumer goods is in terms of forgone opportunities to produce capital goods. Notice that the *PPC* has again been drawn as a curve instead of a straight line. This is because not all factors of production are equally suited to the production of both sorts of good. When the economy is well balanced, as at *A*, the factors can be allocated to the uses for which they are best equipped. However, as the economy moves towards complete specialisation in one of the types of good, factors are no longer being best used, and the opportunity cost changes. For example, if nearly all of the workers are engaged in producing consumer goods, it becomes more difficult to produce still more of these, whereas those workers producing machinery find they have too few resources with which to work. In other words, the more consumer goods are being produced, the higher their opportunity cost.

We can now interpret points *B* and *C*. Point *B* is unreachable given present resources, so the economy cannot produce that combination of goods. This applies to any point outside the *PPC*. On the other hand, at point *C* society is not using its resources efficiently. In this position some resources in the economy are being underused. By making better use of the resources available, the economy can move towards the frontier. However, at any point on the *PPC* production is efficient in the sense that all resources are being fully utilised.

Shifts in the position of the *PPC*

Figure 1.3 focused on a single period. However, if the economy is producing capital goods, then in the following period its capacity to produce should increase, as it will have more resources available for production. How can this be shown on the diagram? An expansion in the available inputs suggests that in the next period the economy should be able to produce more of both goods. This is shown in Figure 1.4.

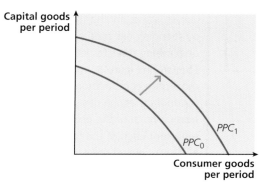

Figure 1.4 Long-run economic growth

Suppose that in the initial year the production possibility curve was at PPC_0. However, in the following year the increased availability of resources enables greater production, and the frontier moves to PPC_1. For example, there might be an increase in the number of people available to work. This is a process of **long-run economic growth**, an expansion of the economy's productive capacity through the increased availability of inputs. The *PPC* shifts outwards.

An increase in the availability of inputs is not the only way in which the *PPC* could shift outwards. An increase in the way in which the inputs are used would also allow the *PPC* to shift out. Such a change would be known as an increase in productivity. This could happen through technical advance, for example.

There could also be a shift inwards of the *PPC* if there is a reduction in the availability of inputs, or a fall in the productivity of inputs. For example, returning to the farmer's production of onions and potatoes, if part of the land is flooded and becomes unusable, then the farmer would have less land to work. If the land is over-farmed, it could become less productive. In either case, the *PPC* would shift inwards.

Potato farmers rely on their land to be usable

Knowledge check 1.8

Suppose that a firm devises a new and more cost-effective production method. How would this affect the *PPC*?

Exercise 1.4

Amy has been cast away on a desert island, and has to survive by spending her time either fishing or climbing trees to get coconuts. The *PPC* in Figure 1.5 shows the maximum combinations of fish and coconuts that she can gather during a day. Which of the points *A* to *E* represent each of the following:

a a situation where Amy spends all her time fishing?

b an unreachable position?

c a day when Amy goes for a balanced diet — a mixture of coconuts and fish?

d a day when Amy does not fancy fish, and spends all day collecting coconuts?

e a day when Amy spends some of the time trying to attract the attention of a passing ship?

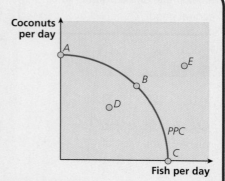

Figure 1.5 Fish or coconuts?

The usefulness of opportunity cost

The concept of opportunity cost is useful in decision making because it focuses on the true costs involved in making a choice. This can be seen using Figure 1.5. Imagine that you are Amy in the exercise. Yesterday, you chose to be at point *A*, but looking back you realise that you would have preferred more fish. Should you spend more time fishing today? The cost in doing that is not simply that you spend more time fishing, because the opportunity cost is not just the time you spend fishing but that you collect fewer coconuts (or are unable to prepare a beacon in case of a passing ship).

Summary

- The production possibility curve (*PPC*) shows the maximum combinations of goods or services that can be produced in a period by a given set of resources.
- At any point on the *PPC*, society is making full use of all resources.
- At any point inside the *PPC*, some resources are underused.
- Points beyond the *PPC* are unobtainable.
- Moving along the *PPC* shows that there is an opportunity cost because producing more of one good means producing less of another.
- In a simple society producing two goods (consumer goods and capital goods), the choice is between consumption and investment for the future.
- As society increases its stock of capital goods, the productive capacity of the economy increases, and the *PPC* moves outwards: this may be termed 'long-run economic growth'.

Case study 1.1

Plantains and tobacco

Jacob is a subsistence farmer who lives in Nangare, a village in the west of Uganda. He lives in a mud hut and owns two sheep, two chickens and one mattress for his household of 10 people. He farms a small piece of land, on which he grows plantains (a staple food crop in Uganda, related to the banana) and some tobacco. One of the key decisions that Jacob faces is how to allocate his land between plantains and tobacco. If he chooses to plant more tobacco in his field, he faces a cost, as growing more tobacco means growing fewer plantains.

A number of factors are likely to influence this decision. For example, the prices of plantains and tobacco may be important, and it may be that the costs involved in growing the two crops are different. Or it may be that some parts of the land are more suitable for growing one or other of the crops. There may also be additional types of crops that Jacob could grow on the land. All of these factors could affect his decision.

Plantains or tobacco? How will Jacob allocate his land?

Follow-up questions

a With reference to Jacob's choice between growing plantains and tobacco, explain the concept of **opportunity cost**.

b Draw a possible **production possibility curve** to illustrate Jacob's choice of producing plantains and tobacco.

c Identify a point on the diagram that you drew for part (b) to illustrate a situation in which:

   i   Jacob uses his land to produce only plantains.

   ii Jacob uses his land to produce a combination of plantains and tobacco.

   iii Jacob does not use all of the land available, but produces a combination of the two crops.

d Discuss how the notions of opportunity cost and the *PPC* help us to understand Jacob's choices.

A Multiple-choice questions

1 Scarcity is best defined as:

  a Limited needs in the face of limited resources
  b Limited wants in the face of unlimited resources
  c Unlimited needs in the face of unlimited resources
  d Unlimited wants in the face of limited resources

2 Which one of the following is not a normative statement:

  a The government should tackle unemployment.
  b Unemployment in the UK has increased.
  c Unemployment is not the most important government objective.
  d The government should not tackle unemployment.

3 What are the four factors of production?

  a Labour, cash, enterprise, land
  b Land, capital, enterprise, unemployment
  c Labour, capital, raw materials, land
  d Labour, capital, enterprise, land

B Stimulus response question

4 A group of students is running a school shop. They have a limited budget and need to decide what to stock in the shop. The group have narrowed down their options to cereal bars or bananas. Table 1 shows the combinations of cereal bars and bananas that the group could purchase.

Table 1 Possible combinations of cereal bars and bananas

	Cereal bars	Bananas
Option A	0	100
Option B	50	75
Option C	100	50
Option D	150	25
Option E	200	0

  a Refer to Table 1. Draw and label the production possibility curve.   [3 marks]
  b Calculate the opportunity cost of stocking one banana.   [2 marks]
  c Explain, with the aid of a diagram, how the production possibility curve could shift.   [4 marks]

C Essay

5 Evaluate the extent to which you made a rational choice to take Economics as an A Level/AS subject.

  [20 marks]

Chapter 2

The allocation of resources, specialisation and trade

The complexity of organising production, consumption, investment and government activity in an economy is extreme. Somehow, decisions need to be taken about what goods and services should be produced and by what technique. There are also questions to be resolved about how to distribute these goods and services to consumers. But how can this be achieved in a way that ensures the right things are produced in the right way and the right people get to consume them? This chapter explores some of the issues that arise in this context and looks at some different approaches that have been adopted to cope with the problem of coordinating the activity of the various economic agents introduced in the previous chapter. The notions of specialisation and trade will also be discussed.

Learning objectives

After studying this chapter, you should be able to:

- explain what is meant by incentives
- evaluate the effectiveness of incentives on the behaviour of economic agents
- evaluate the effectiveness of incentives on resource allocation
- explain market, planned and mixed economic systems
- evaluate the allocation of resources in the different economic systems
- explain what is meant by specialisation and the division of labour
- evaluate the role of specialisation and the division of labour in addressing the problem of scarcity
- explain barter systems
- explain money as a medium of exchange

Resource allocation

Key term

resource allocation the way in which a society's productive assets are deployed across their alternative uses

Synoptic link

The way in which resources are allocated will be discussed more fully in Chapter 7, once you have been introduced to some key economic ideas.

Chapter 1 highlighted the importance of scarcity as being the basic economic problem. This is because people have unlimited wants, but all societies have finite resources. This then forces people to make choices about how to make use of the resources at society's disposal. These choices are complicated because many of society's resources can be deployed in different ways or may have alternative functions. The choices about **resource allocation** are therefore choices about how to deploy society's available resources across their alternative uses, particularly in relation to society's productive assets. The way in which resources are allocated can have a major influence on the wellbeing of the members of a society.

As an example, think about a society that can use its productive assets (labour, land, capital and enterprise) to produce either food for people to consume today or machinery to improve its potential for producing goods in the future. If resources are allocated entirely to improving the potential for future production, people may starve today and not get to benefit from those future improvements. On the other hand, if all resources are used to produce food for today's consumers, society will not benefit in the future from gains in production.

In practice, the choices are much more complex in a real economy, where there are so many alternative options for allocating resources — and so many people involved in the decision-making process. Making sense of this is one of the key challenges of economics.

Rational choice

Given the objectives of economic agents as outlined at the end of the previous chapter, a next step is to take a view about how they will choose to pursue those objectives. At this point, economists have tended to make the assumption that economic agents behave rationally. In the case of households, this would be interpreted as saying that households not only set out to gain satisfaction (or utility) from their activities, but set out to get *as much* satisfaction as they possibly can, relative to the costs of achieving this. In other words, they set out to *maximise* satisfaction. Similarly, firms may be assumed to set out to maximise their profits.

This maximisation process underpins much of economic analysis, although some recent economics research has suggested that economic agents do not always act rationally in the sense of using maximising behaviour.

Incentives

Given the objectives of economic agents and the maximisation process, it is possible to begin to analyse how decisions are taken. Take the case of a household seeking to maximise utility from consuming a particular product. The decision will depend on the benefits gained from consuming a good relative to the costs involved. The costs here will depend partly upon the *price* of the good but also on the opportunity cost — the fact that in order to consume more of one product, some consumption of other products will need to be sacrificed.

In terms of resource allocation, the price of a product is especially important, as this will be seen as a signal from firms to households about the conditions under which they are prepared to provide the good, and a signal from households to firms about how much they are prepared to spend. This is crucial in helping to coordinate the actions of firms and households, as will be explained.

Of central importance is the idea that economic agents are seen to respond to *incentives*. Suppose a household realises that the price of a particular good has fallen. There is then an incentive to consume more of it, as the cost has fallen relative to the benefit. For example, if there is a decrease in the price of a haircut, you might decide to go to the hairdresser more frequently. Conversely, if a firm realises that the price of a good has risen, it has an incentive to supply more of it if this allows a higher return on selling it.

Knowledge check 2.1

What term do economists use to denote consumer satisfaction from consuming a good or service?

Knowledge check 2.2

How would you expect consumers to react to an increase in the price of a good or service?

If economic agents understand the incentives faced by other agents, they may be able to influence behaviour. For example, if firms know that consumers have an incentive to consume more of a good at a lower price, then they may be able to use this to encourage higher sales, and in so doing affect their own position in a market. Knowledge about the effect of incentives can also be crucial for government. For example, a government may wish to influence the consumption of certain products such as tobacco. Knowing the incentives that people face, a government may be able to influence their behaviour.

The effectiveness of incentives

How strong will these incentives be? Will the chance of a cheap haircut really encourage you to go when you don't really need one? Would a firm always try to increase its profit by dropping the quality of its product? Would a government reduce the size of the police force in order to be able to reduce taxes? This suggests that economic agents may not always respond to the incentives that they face. For example, they may face conflicting incentives, or they may choose not to respond.

Whether economic agents respond to incentives (and how they do so) is therefore important in allowing economists to analyse behaviour, which in turn allows us to understand how economies work. Indeed, we could not even begin to understand the behaviour of economic agents unless we can make assumptions about what they want to achieve and how they respond to economic circumstances and incentives. Whether incentives will always bring about the best possible results for society is another issue that will be explored in future chapters.

Market, planned and mixed economic systems

Key terms

market economy market forces are allowed to guide the allocation of resources within a society
centrally planned economy the government guides resource allocation within a society
mixed economy a combination of market forces and government intervention guides the allocation of resources within a society

With so many different individuals and organisations (consumers, firms, governments) all taking decisions, a major question is how it all comes together. How are all these separate decisions coordinated so that the overall allocation of resources in a society is coherent? In other words, how can it be ensured that firms produce the commodities that consumers wish to consume? And how can the distribution of these products be organised? These are some of the basic questions that economics sets out to answer. In reality, different societies have adopted different approaches to the coordination problem.

A **market economy** is one in which market forces are allowed to guide the allocation of resources within a society without intervention from government, whereas a **centrally planned economy** is one in which the government undertakes the coordination role by planning and directing the allocation of resources. However, in reality most economies operate a **mixed economy** system, in which market forces are complemented by some government intervention.

The working of a market economy

The role of prices is at the heart of a free market economy. Consumers express changes in their preferences by their decisions to buy (or not to buy) at the going price. This is then a signal to firms, which are able to respond to changes in consumer demand, given the incentive of making profit, which is related to price.

Synoptic link

The role of prices in influencing resource allocation is explored in Chapter 7.

This sort of system of resource allocation is often referred to as **capitalism**. The key characteristic of capitalism is that individuals own the means of production, and can pursue whatever activities they choose — subject, of course, to the legal framework within which they operate.

The government's role in a free capitalist economy is limited but nonetheless important. A basic framework of *property rights* is essential because it affects incentives. For example, a farmer who does not have the right to own property may not have an incentive to invest in improving his or her land. A basic legal framework is also needed if an economy is to be able to operate. However, the government does not intervene in the production process directly. Secure property rights are significant, as this assures the incentives for the owners of capital.

Within such a system, consumers try to maximise the satisfaction they gain from consuming a range of products, and firms seek to maximise their profits by responding to consumer demand through the medium of price signals.

As has been shown, this is a potentially effective way of allocating resources. In the eighteenth century Adam Smith discussed this mechanism, arguing that when consumers and firms respond to incentives in this way, resources are allocated effectively through the operation of an **invisible hand**, which guides firms to produce the goods and services that consumers wish to consume. Although individuals pursue their self-interest, the market mechanism ensures that their actions will bring about a good result for society overall. So, a solution to the coordination problem is found through the free operation of markets.

Centrally planned economies

Karl Marx (1818–1883) was a philosopher and economist who, together with Friedrich Engels, developed the theory of international communism. He argued that in a capitalist society in which there is private ownership of productive resources, the owners of capital would exploit their position at the expense of labour. This would eventually result in revolution. Although this did not work out in the way that Marx expected, in some countries there was a move away from private ownership of capital towards government control of resource allocation through central planning.

A centrally planned economy is one in which the government undertakes the coordination role, planning and directing the allocation of resources. Given the complexity of modern economies, reliance on central planning poses enormous logistical problems. In order to achieve a satisfactory allocation of resources across the economy, the government needs to make decisions on thousands of individual matters.

One example of this emerges from the experience of central planning in Russia after the revolution in 1917. Factories were given production targets to fit in with the overall plan for the development of the economy. The factory managers then had to meet these targets, and they faced strong incentives to do so. Factories producing nails were given two sorts of target. Some were given a target to produce a certain number of nails, whereas others were given targets in weight terms. The former responded by producing large numbers of very small nails; the latter produced a very small number of very big nails. Neither outcome was what the planners had in mind!

Micromanagement on this sort of scale proved costly to implement administratively. The collapse of the Soviet bloc in the 1990s largely discredited this economic approach, although a small number of countries (such as North Korea and Cuba) continue to persist with central planning. China has moved away from pure central planning by beginning to allow prices to be used as signals.

Evaluation of economic systems

Free market and centrally planned economies tackle the problem of how to allocate resources in very different ways, but both extreme forms are seen to experience problems. There are situations in which a free market system fails to produce an outcome that is good for society. Conversely, the logistical problems facing a centrally planned economy also create insurmountable difficulties in micromanaging such a complex economic system.

In practice, most countries now operate a mixed system, in which prices provide signals to firms and consumers, but the government intervenes by influencing the allocation of resources through regulation, and a pattern of taxes and expenditure. As this course progresses, you will see a variety of ways in which such intervention takes place, and you will come to understand the reasoning that underpins such intervention, especially in situations where the free market fails to produce the best possible allocation of resources.

Summary
- Resource allocation concerns the way in which a society deploys its productive assets among alternative uses.
- Alternative choices about resource allocation have implications for the wellbeing of society.
- If economic agents act rationally, they will set out to maximise achievement of these objectives.
- In setting out to make good decisions, economic agents respond to incentives.
- Changing incentives may influence economic behaviour.
- Society faces a coordination problem in seeking to find a good pattern of resource allocation.
- The coordination problem is tackled in different ways in market, centrally planned and mixed economies.

> **Knowledge check 2.3**
>
> Name an example of a mixed economy.

> **Synoptic link**
>
> Chapters 8 and 9 highlight some of the issues that arise when markets do not produce desirable outcomes for society. Chapter 10 explores how governments intervene to address these issues. Further tools of analysis are needed first.

> **Exercise 2.2**
>
> Discuss the relative merits of free market, mixed and centrally planned economies. Which system do you think is most appropriate for today's world? You might like to find two of your fellow students to join a discussion on this topic, with each of you setting out to defend one type of system.

Specialisation and trade

> **Key term**
>
> specialisation the process of concentrating on a task or activity in order to become expert in it

An important aspect of resource allocation is whether or not an economy is using resources effectively. This section explores the way in which specialisation and trade contribute to the problem of scarcity by making good use of available resources. **Specialisation** is the process of concentrating on a particular task and becoming an expert in that activity.

How many workers does it take to make a pin? The eighteenth-century economist Adam Smith figured that 10 was about the right number. He argued that when a worker was producing pins on his own,

Key term

division of labour a process whereby the production procedure is broken down into a sequence of stages, and workers are assigned to particular stages

carrying out all the various stages involved in the production process, the maximum number of pins he could produce in one day was 20 — given the technology of his day, of course. This would imply that 10 workers could produce about 200 pins if they worked in the same way as the lone worker. However, if the pin production process were broken into 10 separate stages, with one worker specialising in each stage, the maximum production for a day's work would be a staggering 48,000. This is known as **division of labour**.

The division of labour is effective because individual workers become skilled at performing specialised tasks. By focusing on a particular stage, they can become highly adept, and therefore more efficient, at carrying out that task. In any case, people are not all the same, so some are better at certain activities. Furthermore, this specialisation is more efficient because workers do not spend time moving from one activity to another. Specialisation may also enable firms to operate on a larger scale of production. You will see later that this may be advantageous.

Scientists perform specialist tasks in laboratories

This process can be seen in practice in many businesses today, where there is considerable specialisation of functions. Workers are hired for particular tasks and activities. You do not see Harry Kane pulling on the goalkeeper's jersey at half time because he fancies a change.

Chapter 1 argued that 'labour' is a factor of production. We will now develop this idea by arguing that there are different types of labour, having different skills and functions.

Although we refer to the division of labour, we can extend these arguments to consider specialisation among firms, or even among nations. For example, consider car manufacturing. The process of mass producing cars does not all take place within a single firm. One firm may specialise in producing tyres, another may produce windscreens, another may focus on assembling the final product. Here again, specialisation enables efficiency gains to be made.

Analysis of the division of labour

Specialisation means workers can focus on the tasks that they perform well and hence become more productive. Training can be provided more cost-effectively when it is focused on the specific tasks workers need to perform. Furthermore, working as a team allows more overall output to be produced. However, it is possible to take specialisation too far. A worker who spends all his time on a narrow and repetitive task may find that it becomes tedious, or he becomes bored and careless. Over-specialisation may also mean that a team of workers becomes inflexible: if a worker specialising in a key part of the production process falls ill, it may be difficult to find cover.

Specialisation also takes place at national level, simply because some countries are better equipped to produce some products than others. For example, it would not make sense for the UK to go into commercial production of pineapples or mangoes — there are other countries with climatic conditions that are much more suitable for producing these products. On the other hand, most Formula 1 racing teams have their headquarters in the UK, and there are benefits from this specialisation. In particular, the teams can draw on the skills and expertise available in the local workforce.

Analysis of specialisation

Everyone is different. Individuals have different natural talents and abilities that make them good at different things. Indeed, there are some lucky people who seem to be good at everything.

Consider this example. Matthew and Sophie try to supplement their incomes by working at weekends. They have both been to evening classes and have attended pottery and jewellery-making classes. At weekends they make pots and bracelets. Depending on how they divide their time, they can make differing combinations of these goods. Some of the possibilities are shown in Table 2.1.

The first point to notice is that Sophie is much better at both activities than Matthew. If they each devote all their time to producing pots, Matthew produces only 12 to Sophie's 18. If they each produce only bracelets, Matthew produces 12 and Sophie 36. There is another significant feature of this table. Although Sophie is better at producing both goods, the difference is much more marked in the case of bracelet production than pot production. So Sophie is relatively more proficient in bracelet production: in other words, she faces a lower opportunity cost in making bracelets. If Sophie switches from producing pots to producing bracelets, she gives up 6 pots for every 12 additional bracelets that she makes. The opportunity cost of an additional bracelet is thus 6/12 = 0.5 pots. For Matthew, there is a one-to-one trade-off between the two, so his opportunity cost of a bracelet is 1 pot.

More interesting is what happens if the same calculation is made for Matthew and pot-making. Although Sophie is absolutely better at making pots, if Matthew increases his production of pots, his opportunity cost in terms of bracelets is still 1. But for Sophie the opportunity cost of making pots in terms of bracelets is 12/6 = 2, so Matthew has the lower opportunity cost.

Why does this matter? It illustrates the potential benefits to be gained from specialisation. Suppose that both Matthew and Sophie divide their time between the two activities in such a way that Matthew produces 6 pots and 6 bracelets, and Sophie produces 6 pots and 24 bracelets. Between them, they will have produced 12 pots and 30 bracelets. However, if they each specialise in the product in which they face the

Synoptic link

The possible gains from specialisation and trade will be discussed more fully in Chapter 34 in the context of international trade.

Table 2.1 Matthew and Sophie's production

Matthew		Sophie	
Pots	Bracelets	Pots	Bracelets
12	0	18	0
9	3	12	12
6	6	6	24
3	9	3	30
0	12	0	36

Knowledge check 2.4

If Matthew were to spend all of his time producing bracelets and Sophie only produces pots, what would be the result?

lower opportunity cost, their joint production will increase. If Matthew devotes all his time to pottery, he produces 12 pots, while Sophie, focusing only on bracelets, produces 36. So between them they will have produced the same number of pots as before — but 6 extra bracelets.

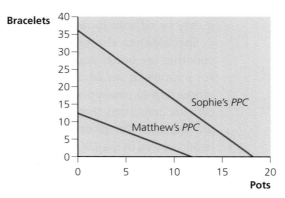

Figure 2.1 Matthew and Sophie's production possibilities

One final point before leaving Matthew and Sophie. Figure 2.1 shows their respective production possibility curves. You can check this by graphing the points in Table 2.1 and joining them up. In this case the *PPCs* are straight lines. You can see that because Sophie is better at both activities, her *PPC* lies entirely above Matthew's. The differences in opportunity cost are shown by the fact that the two *PPCs* have different slopes, as the opportunity cost element is related to the slope of the *PPC* — the rate at which one good is sacrificed for more of the other.

Although there may be many advantages that flow from specialisation, it is also important to realise that there may be a downside if individuals, firms or countries overspecialise. If Matthew spends all his time producing pots, while Sophie produces only bracelets, they may each get bored and begin to lose concentration and job satisfaction. This may be even more of a danger in the case of Adam Smith's pin production. If workers find themselves carrying out the same task day after day, the tedium may lead them to become careless and inefficient.

If a firm focuses on production of a narrow range of products and then finds that demand is falling for those products, it will face difficulties. It may therefore be advisable to maintain some diversity in the output range, in the hope that demand will not fall for all products simultaneously. Complete specialisation may not always be the best way for a firm to become successful in the long run.

Nations may also find problems if they overspecialise. For example, it could be argued that all nations should retain some agricultural activity for strategic reasons. If a nation were to be completely dependent on imported foodstuffs and then became engaged in a war, this could leave the country in a vulnerable position. Indeed, this was one of the motivations for the establishment of what became the European Union.

Specialisation and scarcity

Scarcity is at the heart of economic thinking. Resources are inherently scarce within any society, forcing choices to be made in allocating those resources between alternative uses. Specialisation and the division of labour can make a contribution towards tackling the scarcity problem by making sure that society makes the best possible use of the resources available to it.

Summary

- Adam Smith introduced the notion of division of labour, which suggests that workers can become more productive by specialising in stages of the production process.
- Specialisation enables better use of resources, so helps to address the problem of scarcity.
- Specialisation opens up the possibility of trade.
- The gains from specialisation and trade result from differences in opportunity cost.

What is a market?

Key term

market a set of arrangements that allows transactions to take place

Before going any further, it is helpful to define what is meant by a **market**. A market is simply a set of arrangements that allows transactions to take place. You will find that in economics the term is used frequently, so it is important to be absolutely clear about what it means.

A market need not be a physical location (although it could be — you might regard the local farmers' market as an example of 'a set of arrangements that allows transactions to take place'). With the growth of the internet, everyone is becoming accustomed to ways of buying and selling that do not involve direct physical contact between buyer and seller, so the notion of an abstract market should not be too alien a concept.

In relation to a particular product, a market brings together potential buyers and sellers. This will be explored in the following chapters.

Markets are very important in the process of resource allocation, with prices acting as a key signal to potential buyers and sellers. If a firm finds that it cannot sell its output at the price it has chosen, this is a signal about the way that buyers perceive the product. Price is one way that firms find out about consumers and their willingness to pay for a particular product. This will be explored more fully in Chapter 7.

Money and exchange

Key terms

barter system an economy without money so that transactions in goods and services rely on direct exchange

money as a medium of exchange the function of money that enables transactions to take place

Imagine a world without money. It is lunchtime, and you fancy a banana. In your bag you have an apple. Perhaps you can find someone with a banana who fancies an apple? But the only person with a banana available fancies an ice cream. The problem with such a **barter system** is that you need to find someone who wants what you have and who has what you want — a *double coincidence of wants*. If a whole economic system were to face this problem, undertaking transactions would be so inefficient as to be impossible. Hence the importance of **money as a medium of exchange**.

Knowledge check 2.6

Why is it important for money to be able to act as a medium of exchange?

Summary

- A market is a set of arrangements that allows transactions to take place.
- A barter system is a highly inefficient way of conducting transactions, hence the importance of money in enabling exchange to take place.
- Money plays a key role as a medium of exchange.

Case study 2.1

Singapore

Singapore

Singapore has been one of the most successful economies of the last 60 years. It is a small island state off the coast of Malaysia in Southeast Asia. In land area, it is a bit larger than the Isle of Man, but with a population of 5.6 million.

Singapore was a British colony until 1963 when it became part of the Malaysian Federation. However, it was expelled from the Federation in 1965 and became a sovereign state. At this time, the country faced major challenges. It had limited natural resources, even having to import water from Malaysia. Its main advantage was its strategic position and good harbour.

The country's political leadership was strong – indeed, it was effectively a one-party state that had the same prime minister (Lee Kuan Yew) from 1959 until 1990. The government was therefore able to influence the way in which the economy developed, focusing on rapid economic growth, support for business enterprise and promotion of exports, coupled with limitations on the democratic process. The media were subject to strong controls. Wages were under the control of the National Wages Council, designed to support the growth process. The government directed the economy through quite strong interventions.

In its early years of development, the government invested in the infrastructure needed for exports to flourish, ensuring the provision of good port facilities, and transport and communication links. The government also provided housing for the population. Foreign investment was strongly encouraged, and the country proved attractive to companies because of its low level of corruption and high security.

In 1960, Singapore's average income levels were about a quarter of those in the UK, but by the mid-2010s, average income was 27% higher than in the UK. At this time, Singapore was lauded as the sixth least corrupt nation in the world, and the third most competitive economy. In terms of the ease of doing business, the World Bank ranked Singapore at second out of 190 countries around the world.

Follow-up questions

a From the passage, identify factors that might suggest that central planning was significant in the development of Singapore's economy.

b From the passage, identify factors that might suggest that Singapore developed as a free market economy.

CHAPTER 2 QUESTIONS

A Multiple-choice questions

1 In economics, utility is:

  a The level of satisfaction that a business gains through trade

  b The level of satisfaction the government gains from taxation

  c The level of satisfaction that a consumer gains from consumption

  d The level of satisfaction that an employee gains from working

2 An economic system where resources are allocated partly thorough price signals and partly by the government is known as:

  a A market economy

  b A free economy

  c A planned economy

  d A mixed economy

3 Money acts as a medium of:

  a Exchange

  b Barter

  c Incentive

  d Enterprise

B Knowledge and understanding questions

4 Explain what is meant by an incentive. [2 marks]

5 Explain **two** differences between a planned and a market economic system. [4 marks]

6 Explain the role of the government in a market economy. [2 marks]

7 Explain, giving an example, what is meant by a barter system. [2 marks]

C Stimulus response question

8 Sahdat and Katie are both decorators. They have been asked to decorate a house, which includes both plastering and then painting all the walls in the house.

Sahdat thinks they will be able to complete the job quicker if they divide the labour so that Katie does the plastering and Sahdat does the painting.

  a Explain what is meant by the division of labour. [2 marks]

  b Evaluate the extent to which specialisation may allow Sahdat and Katie to address the problem of scarcity. [8 marks]

SECTION
1

MICROECONOMICS

Part 2
The role of markets

Chapter 3

Demand

The demand and supply model is perhaps the most famous of all pieces of economic theory — and it is also one of the most useful. It has many applications that help explain the way markets work in the real world. It is central to understanding economics. This chapter introduces the demand side of the model. Chapter 4 will introduce supply.

Learning objectives

After studying this chapter, you should be able to:
- explain the concept of ceteris paribus
- explain, with the aid of a diagram, the relationship between the price of a good or service and quantity demanded
- explain, with the aid of a diagram, the individual and market demand for a good or service
- explain, with the aid of a diagram, joint, competitive and composite demand
- explain, with the aid of a diagram, movements along the demand curve (extension or contraction)
- explain, with the aid of a diagram, shifts of the demand curve (increase or decrease)
- explain, with the aid of a diagram, consumer surplus
- explain the effects of changes in price on consumer surplus
- evaluate the impact of changes in price on consumer surplus

Demand

Key term

demand the quantity of a good or service that consumers are willing and able to buy given its price, the price of other goods, and consumers' incomes and preferences

Consider an individual consumer. Think of yourself, and a product that you consume regularly. What factors influence your **demand** for that product? Put another way, what factors influence how much of the product you choose to buy?

When thinking about the factors that influence your demand for your chosen product, common sense will probably mean you focus on a range of things. You may think about why you enjoy consuming the product. You may focus on the price of the product, and whether or not you can afford it. You may decide you have consumed a product so much that you are ready for a change, or perhaps you want to try something you've seen advertised on television, or that your friend is buying.

Whatever factors influence you, they can probably be categorised under four headings that ultimately determine your demand for a good.

First the *price of the good* is an important influence on your demand for it, and will affect the quantity you choose to buy.

There are also three non-price factors:
- Your *income* will determine how much of the good you can afford to purchase.
- The *price of other goods* may be significant.
- Almost any other factors can be listed as part of your *preferences*.

This common-sense reasoning provides the basis for the economic analysis of demand. You will find that a lot of economic analysis begins in this way, by finding a way to construct a model that is rooted in how we expect people or firms to behave.

Many different factors can influence the decision to consume a product

Individual and market demand

The discussion so far has focused on an individual consumer, and what influences his or her demand for a good or service. A similar line of argument may apply if we think in terms of the demand for a particular product — say, Xbox games. The market for Xbox games can be seen as bringing together all the potential buyers (and sellers) of the product, and market demand can be analysed in terms of the factors that influence all potential buyers of that good or service. In other words, market demand can be seen as the total quantity of a good or service that all potential buyers are willing and able to buy at any given price in a given period of time. The same four factors that influence your own individual decision to buy will also influence the total market demand for a product. In addition, the number of potential buyers in the market will clearly influence the size of total demand at any price. Notice that the market for Xbox games could be viewed as a *sub-market* of the market for entertainment products.

Joint and composite demand

The nature of demand for a product may depend upon its characteristics. For example, some products may be joint products, such as printers and print cartridges. There is no point buying a printer unless you also buy a printer cartridge, nor would you buy cartridges if you did not have a printer. These goods are demanded together as a **joint demand**. Such goods are complements. Some goods have multiple uses, so demand is seen as a **composite demand**. For example, water has multiple uses — for drinking, washing, watering the plants and so on. However, for many goods, demand is **competitive**. A good is in competition with other goods, as they are substitutes for each other.

Demand and the price of a good

Assume for the moment that the influences mentioned above, other than the price of the good, are held constant, so that the focus is only on the extent to which the price of a good influences the demand for it. This is a common assumption in economics, which is sometimes expressed by the Latin phrase **ceteris paribus**, meaning 'other things being equal'. Given the complexity of the real world, it is often helpful to focus on one thing at a time.

This ceteris paribus assumption is a powerful tool. Focusing on one influence at a time is a way of coping with the complexities of the real world and makes the analysis of economic issues much clearer than if we try to analyse everything at once. You will see many instances of it as your studies proceed.

So how is the demand for Xbox games influenced by their price? Other things being equal (ceteris paribus), you would expect the demand for Xbox games to be higher when the price is low, and lower when the price is high. In other words, you would expect an inverse relationship between the price and the quantity demanded. This is such a strong phenomenon that it is referred to as the **law of demand**.

If you were to compile a list that showed how many Xbox games would be bought at any possible price and plotted these on a diagram, this would be called the **demand curve**. Figure 3.1 shows what this might look like. As it is an inverse relationship, the demand curve slopes downwards. Notice that the demand curve need not be a straight line: its shape depends upon how consumers react at different prices.

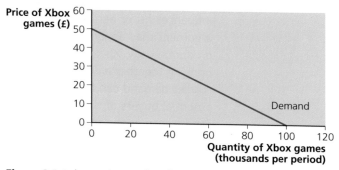

Figure 3.1 A demand curve for Xbox games

Quantitative skills 3.1

Reading a graph

An important skill is to be able to read off numerical values from a graph such as Figure 3.1. If you wanted to see what the quantity demanded would be at a particular price, you would select the price on the vertical axis, and then read off the value on the horizontal axis at that price. For example, in this figure, if price were to be set at £40, the quantity demanded would be 20,000 per period. However, if the price were only £20, the demand would be higher, at 60,000.

If you are studying maths as one of your A Level subjects, you may wonder why we draw the demand curve with price on the vertical axis and quantity on the horizontal axis, when we are saying that quantity depends upon price and not the other way round. The simple answer is that Alfred Marshall drew it this way when he became the first person to draw a demand curve in his economics textbook in 1890, and it became the norm.

You may also wonder why this is called a demand curve when it is a straight line. In fact, it need not be a straight line, but it is convenient to represent it this way. Think of it as a straight curve.

Exercise 3.1

Table 3.1 shows how the demand for trinkets varies with their price.

Table 3.1 The demand for trinkets

Price	Quantity
100	0
90	3
80	7
70	15
60	25
50	40
40	60
30	85
20	120

a Draw the demand curve.
b How many trinkets would be sold at a price of £65?
c At what price would 50 trinkets be demanded?

Extension material

The substitution effect

An analysis of why the demand curve should be downward sloping would reveal that there are two important forces at work. At a higher price, a consumer buying an Xbox game has less income left over. This is referred to as the *real income effect* of a price increase. In addition, if the price of Xbox games goes up, consumers may find other goods more attractive and choose to buy something else instead of Xbox games. This is referred to as the *substitution effect* of a price increase.

Knowledge check 3.2

What is the law of demand?

As the price of a good changes, a movement along the demand curve can be observed as consumers adjust their buying pattern in response to the price change.

Notice that the demand curve has been drawn under the ceteris paribus assumption. In other words, it was assumed that all other influences on demand (the non-price factors) were held constant in order to focus on the relationship between demand and price. There are two important implications of this procedure.

First, the price drawn on the vertical axis of a diagram such as Figure 3.1 is the *relative* price — it is the price of Xbox games under the assumption that all other prices are constant.

Second, if any of the other influences on demand changes, you would expect to see a shift of the whole demand curve. It is very important to distinguish between factors that induce a movement *along* a curve (known as an extension (or contraction) of demand), and factors that induce a shift *of* a curve (an increase or decrease in demand). This applies not only in the case of the demand curve — there are many other instances where this distinction is important.

The two panels of Figure 3.2 show this difference. In panel (a) of the figure, the demand curve has shifted to the right because of a change in one of the non-price factors that influences demand. In panel (b), the price of Xbox games falls from P_0 to P_1, inducing an extension (movement along the demand curve) as demand expands from Q_0 to Q_1.

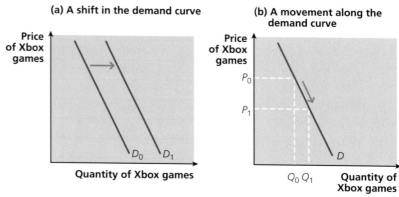

Figure 3.2 A shift in the demand curve and a movement along it

Demand and consumer incomes

The second influence on demand is consumer incomes. For a **normal good**, an increase in consumer incomes will, ceteris paribus, lead to an increase in the quantity demanded at any given price. Foreign holidays are an example of a normal good because as people's incomes rise, they tend to demand more foreign holidays at any given price.

Figure 3.3 illustrates this. D_0 here represents the initial demand curve for foreign holidays. An increase in consumers' incomes causes demand to be higher at any given price, and the demand curve shifts to the right — to D_1.

However, demand does not always respond in this way. For example, think about bus journeys. As incomes rise in a society, more people can afford to have a car, or to use taxis. This means that as incomes rise, the demand for bus journeys may tend to fall. Such goods are known as **inferior goods**.

This time an increase in consumers' incomes in Figure 3.4 causes the demand curve to shift to the left, from its initial position at D_0, to D_1 where less is demanded at any given price.

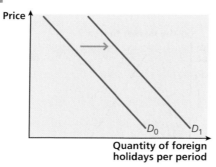

Figure 3.3 A shift in the demand curve following an increase in consumer incomes (a normal good)

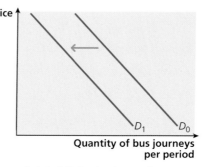

Figure 3.4 A shift in the demand curve following an increase in consumer incomes (an inferior good)

Exercise 3.2

Identify each of the following products as being either a normal good or an inferior good:
a digital camera   c potatoes   e fine wine
b magazine   d bicycle   f cheap wine

Extension material

A Giffen good

Consider the demand for a staple foodstuff such as rice or potatoes. Sir Robert Giffen pointed out that a fall in the price could mean that people would now be able to afford to enrich their diet by eating more meat. In other words, such a foodstuff could be such a strongly inferior good that the demand curve would be upward sloping. However, in spite of stories about the reaction of demand to a rise in the price of potatoes during the Great Potato Famine that occurred in Ireland in 1845–49, there have been no authenticated sightings of Giffen goods. The notion remains a theoretical curiosity.

Demand and the price of other goods

Key terms

substitutes two goods are said to be substitutes if consumers regard them as alternatives, so that the demand for one good is likely to rise if the price of the other good rises

complements two goods consumed jointly, so that an increase in the price of one good causes demand for the other good to fall

The demand for a good may respond to changes in the price of other related goods, of which there are two main types. On the one hand, two goods may be **substitutes** for each other. For example, consider two different (but similar) breakfast cereals. If there is an increase in the price of one of the cereals, consumers may switch their consumption to the other, as the two are likely to be close substitutes for each other. Not all consumers will switch, of course — some may be deeply committed to one particular brand — but some consumers are certainly likely to change over.

On the other hand, there may also be goods that are **complements** — for example, products that are consumed jointly, such as breakfast cereals and milk, or cars and petrol. Here a fall in the price of one good may lead to an increase in demand for *both* products.

Whether goods are substitutes or complements determines how the demand for one good responds to a change in the price of another. Figure 3.5 shows the demand curves (per period) for two goods that are substitutes — tea and coffee.

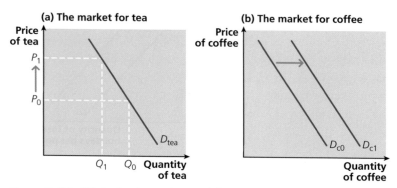

Figure 3.5 A shift in the demand curve following an increase in the price of a substitute good

If there is an increase in the price of tea from P_0 to P_1 in panel (a), more consumers will switch to coffee and the demand curve in panel (b) will shift to the right — say, from D_{c0} to D_{c1}.

For complements, the situation is the reverse: in Figure 3.6 an increase in the price of tea from P_0 to P_1 in panel (a) causes the demand curve for milk to shift leftwards, from D_{m0} to D_{m1}.

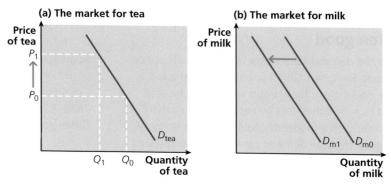

Figure 3.6 A shift in the demand curve following an increase in the price of a complementary good

Demand, consumer preferences and other influences

The discussion has shown how the demand for a good is influenced by the price of the good, the price of other goods and consumer incomes. It was stated earlier that almost everything else that determines demand for a good can be represented as 'consumer preferences'. In particular, this refers to whether you like or dislike a good. There may be many things that influence whether you like or dislike a product. In part it simply depends upon your own personal inclinations — some people like dark chocolate, others prefer milk chocolate. However, firms may try to influence your preferences through advertising or branding, and sometimes they succeed. Or you might be one of those people who get so irritated by television advertising that you compile a blacklist of products that you will never buy! Even this is an influence on your demand.

In some cases, your preferences may be swayed by other people's demand — again, this may be positive or negative. Fashions may influence demand, but some people like to buck (or lead) the trend.

You may also see a movement of the demand curve if there is a sudden surge in the popularity of a good — or, indeed, a sudden collapse in demand.

Exercise 3.3

Draw demand curves for the following situations to show how you would expect the demand curve to change (if at all). You should have price on the vertical axis and quantity on the horizontal axis. In some cases there will be a shift in the demand curve, but in others there may be an extension or contraction.

a the demand for chocolate following a campaign highlighting the dangers of obesity

b the demand for oranges following an increase in the price of apples

c the demand for oranges following a decrease in the price of oranges

d the demand for Blu-ray discs following a decrease in the price of Blu-ray players

e the demand for private transport following an increase in consumer incomes

f the demand for public transport following an increase in consumer incomes

Knowledge check 3.5

Are people likely to respond more or less strongly to a change in price as time passes?

The above discussion has covered most of the factors that influence the demand for a good. However, in some cases it is necessary to take a time element into account. Not all of the goods bought are consumed instantly. In some cases, consumption is spread over long periods of time. Indeed, there may be instances where goods are not bought for consumption at all but are seen by the buyer as an investment, perhaps for resale at a later date. In these circumstances, expectations about future price changes may be relevant. For example, people may buy works of art in the expectation that prices will rise in the future. There may also be goods whose prices are expected to fall in the future. This has been common with many high-tech products, such as the latest smartphone. Initially a newly launched product may sell at a high price, but as production levels rise, costs may fall, and prices too. People may therefore delay purchase in the expectation of future price reductions.

Summary

- The market demand for a good depends on the price of the good, consumers' incomes and preferences, the price of other goods, and the number of potential consumers.
- The demand curve shows the relationship between demand for a product and its price, ceteris paribus.
- The demand curve is downward sloping, as the relationship between demand and price is an inverse one.
- A change in price induces a movement along the demand curve, whereas a change in the other determinants of demand induces a shift in the demand curve.
- When the demand for a good rises as consumer incomes rise, that good is referred to as a normal good. When demand falls as income rises, the good is referred to as an inferior good.
- A good or service may be related to other goods by being either a substitute or a complement.
- For some products, demand may be related to expected future prices.

Consumer surplus

Think a little more carefully about what the demand curve represents. Figure 3.7 shows the demand curve for smartphones. Suppose that the price is set at P^* and quantity demanded is Q^*. P^* can be seen as the value that the last customer places on a smartphone. In other words, if the price were even slightly above P^*, there would be one consumer who would choose not to buy.

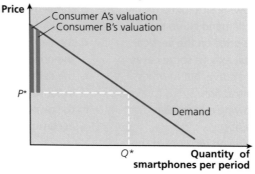

Figure 3.7 Price and benefit

To that consumer, P^* represents the benefit derived from consuming this good — it is the price that reflects the consumer's benefit from a smartphone, as it is the price that induces her to buy. In other words, it is the benefit she receives from consuming one unit of the good. The same argument could be made about any point along the demand curve, so the demand curve can be interpreted as the benefit to be derived from consuming smartphones.

In most markets, all consumers face the same prices for goods and services. This leads to an important concept in economic analysis. P^* may represent the value of smartphones to the last consumer, but what about all the other consumers who are also buying smartphones at P^*? They would all be willing to pay a higher price for a smartphone. Indeed, Consumer A in Figure 3.7 would pay a very high price indeed, and therefore values a smartphone much more highly than P^*. When Consumer A pays P^* for a smartphone, he gets a great deal, as he values the good so much more highly — as represented by the vertical green line in Figure 3.7. Consumer B also gains a surplus above her willingness to pay (the blue line).

If all these surplus values are added up, they sum to the total surplus that society gains from consuming smartphones. This is known as the **consumer surplus**, represented by the shaded triangle in Figure 3.8. It can be interpreted as the welfare that society gains from consuming the good, over and above the price that has to be paid for it.

Key term

consumer surplus the value that consumers gain from consuming a good or service over and above the price paid

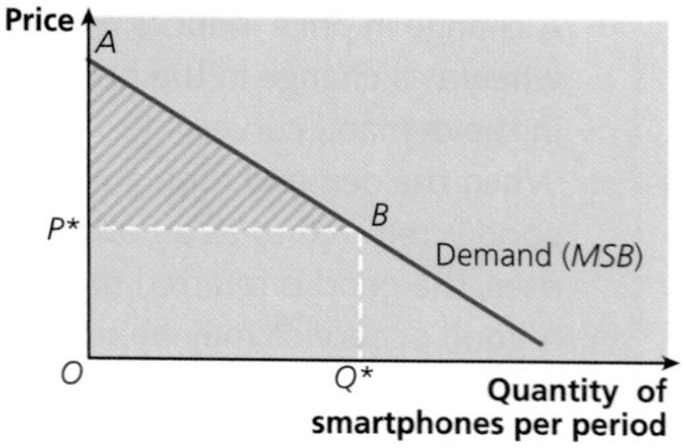

Knowledge check 3.6

Explain why consumer surplus can be interpreted as representing the welfare that society gains from consuming a good.

Figure 3.8 Consumer surplus

Interpreting areas on a diagram

In using diagrams like Figure 3.8, it is often important to be able to interpret **areas** on the graph as well as lines and positions. In this case, the area of interest is the total amount of consumer surplus.

Notice that letters are used to identify points on the diagram (in this case, the points are labelled P^*, Q^*, A, B and O). A combination of these letters then identifies the area enclosed by the points.

The area under the demand curve up to the quantity sold (Q^*) represents the total value of the good that is sold. In total, consumers spend an amount on this, which is the price multiplied by the quantity sold, namely P^* multiplied by Q^*. In Figure 3.8 this is the area of the rectangle OP^*BQ^*. The surplus is then the shaded triangle P^*AB.

Consumer surplus and price

There is a relationship between the size of consumer surplus and the price charged for a good. If the price of a good increases, this will reduce the overall size of consumer surplus, and affect the welfare that society receives from consuming the good. You can see this in Figure 3.9.

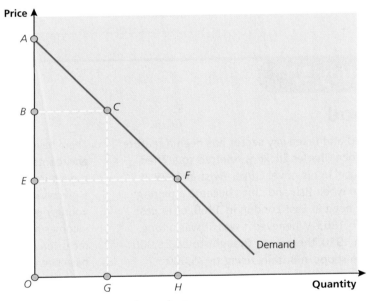

Figure 3.9 Consumer surplus and price

When the price of the good is relatively low at *OE*, quantity demanded is *OH*, consumers spend the area *OEFH*, and receive consumer surplus of *AEF*. However, if the price were to increase to *OB*, quantity demanded would fall to *OG*, spending would be the area *OBCG*, and consumer surplus would be lower than before, at *ABC*.

Suppose there is an increase in the price of cinema tickets from *OE* to *OB* in Figure 3.9. This indicates that there will be some people who will go to the cinema less frequently, and those who do go at the higher price will receive less in the way of consumer surplus than if the price had remained at *OE*. How significant is this reduction in consumer surplus (the area *BCFE*)? This will depend upon the extent of the increase in price and the shape of the demand curve, which reflects how responsive consumers are to the increase in price. This issue will be addressed further in Chapter 6.

Table 3.2 shows the price at which each of six consumers would be prepared to buy a good.

Suppose the market price is at £14.

a Which of the consumers would choose to buy the good?

b What would be Consumer A's consumer surplus at this price?

c What would be the total consumer surplus enjoyed by the consumers purchasing the good?

d What would be the total consumer surplus if the price were to increase to £16?

Table 3.2 Price at which Consumers A–F are prepared to buy a good

Consumer	Price
Consumer A	£20
Consumer B	£18
Consumer C	£16
Consumer D	£14
Consumer E	£12
Consumer F	£10

Summary

- The demand curve shows the valuation that consumers place on a good, reflecting the satisfaction they gain from consuming it.
- Consumer surplus represents the benefit that consumers gain from consuming a product, over and above the price they pay for that product.

Case study 3.1

Fast food

The fast food and takeaway sector has been a feature of the UK since Charles Dickens referred to a 'fried fish warehouse' in his novel *Oliver Twist* in 1839. It is not known when fish and chips became a pairing: it may have been in East London in 1860, or in East Lancashire in 1863. Whenever it was, it was a long time ago! In 1910, there were thought to be 25,000 fish and chip shops in Britain, rising to 35,000 in 1929.

Of course, the fast food scene has changed enormously since then, and takeaways have become a firmly entrenched part of British life. However, the number of fish and chip shops had fallen to only 10,000 by 2009, serving some 229 million fried fish takeaways. This is because other products had arrived on the scene, with 749 million burgers being served by the same year. By the mid-2010s, there were 1,249 McDonald's outlets in the UK.

There have been many changes in the market environment in recent years. The government has run a number of campaigns in an attempt to combat a perceived problem with obesity, especially among younger generations. At the same time, people's incomes have risen, albeit more slowly during the recession and slow recovery of the early 2010s. There have been social changes also, with many workers in the service industries feeling pressures on their time.

There has also been a rise in alternative sources of fast food, with pre-prepared sandwiches and wraps being readily available, and delivery service firms increasing in number.

One particular development has been the rise of fast food outlets offering a higher quality burger, such as Gourmet Burger Kitchen and Five Guys. These outlets have provided competition by producing large burgers using fresh produce and an innovative range of fillings.

Follow-up questions

a Explain how demand would be affected by government campaigns about healthy eating.

b Explain how you would expect a rise in consumer incomes to affect the demand for fast food.

c Explain how companies like McDonald's could respond to the rise of competitors such as Five Guys, and other changes to market conditions.

CHAPTER 3 QUESTIONS

A Multiple-choice questions

1 Ceteris paribus means:

  a All things are equal   **c** Nothing is equal

  b Everything is equal   **d** Other things being equal

2 The demand for a television programme is likely to increase (shift to the right) when which of the following occurs?

  a There are more television channels showing the programme

  b There is a successful advertising campaign for the television programme

  c Another popular television programme is broadcast at the same time as the television programme

  d A new season of the television programme is released on Netflix

3 When the demand for Uber increases, the demand for train travel decreases. This is an example of which kind of relationship?

  a Complementary goods   **c** Substitute goods

  b Normal goods   **d** Inferior goods

4 When there is an extension of demand there is likely to be:

  a An increase in consumer surplus and a decrease in price

  b An increase in consumer surplus and an increase in price

  c A decrease in consumer surplus and an increase in price

  d A decrease in consumer surplus and a decrease in price

B Knowledge and understanding questions

5 Explain the relationship between the price of a good and the quantity demanded.   [2 marks]

6 Explain two factors that may affect the demand for meals at a restaurant.   [4 marks]

7 Explain, with the aid of a diagram, how the demand for a car may be affected by an increase in the price of petrol.   [4 marks]

8 Explain, giving an example, what is meant by an inferior good.   [2 marks]

C Stimulus response question

9 A firm specialises in cleaning dogs. Customers bring their pets to the shop to use the wash, shampoo, hair and nail-clipping service. Many factors affect the demand for the service.

Navpreet, the owner, has conducted some market research on the relationship between the price of her service and the quantity demanded (see Table 1).

Table 1 The relationship between price and quantity

Price	Quantity demanded per week
£20	70
£25	60
£30	50
£40	40
£45	30
£50	20

  a Explain three factors that may affect the demand for Navpreet's service.   [6 marks]

  b Refer to Table 1. Draw the demand curve for Navpreet's service based on the market research.   [4 marks]

  c Refer to your answer to Question 2. Explain the impact of a decrease in price from £40 to £30 on the consumer surplus for Navpreet's services.   [4 marks]

Chapter 4

Supply

The previous chapter introduced you to the demand curve. The other key component of the demand and supply model is, of course, supply. For any market transaction, there are two parties, buyers and sellers. The question to be considered in this chapter is what determines the quantity that sellers will wish to supply to the market.

Learning objectives

After studying this chapter, you should be able to:
- explain, with the aid of a diagram, the relationship between price and quantity supplied
- explain, with the aid of a diagram, individual and market supply
- explain, with the aid of a diagram, movements along the supply curve (extension/contraction)
- explain, with the aid of a diagram, shifts of the supply curve (increase/decrease)
- explain, with the aid of a diagram, joint and competitive supply
- explain, with the aid of a diagram, producer surplus
- explain the effects of changes in price on producer surplus
- evaluate the impact of changes in price on producer surplus

The nature of supply

In discussing demand, the focus of attention was on consumers, and on their willingness to pay for goods and services. In thinking about supply, attention switches to firms (businesses), as it is firms that take decisions about how much output to supply to the market. It is important at the outset to be clear about what is meant by a 'firm'. A firm exists to organise production: firms bring together various factors of production, and organise the production process in order to produce output.

There are various forms that the organisation of a firm can take. A firm could be a *sole trader*: for example, a small business such as a newsagent where the owner and the firm have the same legal identity. Sole traders are normally run by the owner.

A firm could be in the form of a *partnership*: for example, a dental practice in which profits (and debts) are shared between the partners in the business. The owners of a partnership also share the legal identity of the business and are often involved in running the business.

Larger firms may be organised as private or public *joint stock companies*, owned by shareholders. One of the main differences between private and public limited companies is that the shares of a public limited company are traded on the stock exchange, whereas this is not the case with the private company. Companies have a separate legal identity to the owners because the shareholders do not usually run the business.

Study tip

Economists define profits as the difference between total revenue and total costs. If you are taking business studies as well as economics, you may think this definition seems familiar – but be careful, because economists define 'total costs' differently, as will be explained later.

Knowledge check 4.1

What assumption is often made by economists about the objective that underpins firms' decisions under rational decision making?

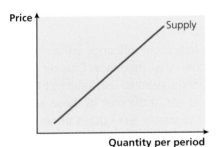

Figure 4.1 A supply curve

In order to analyse how firms decide how much of a product to supply, it is necessary to make an assumption about what it is that firms are trying to achieve. For now, we will assume that they aim to maximise profits. Later, we will see that this may not always be the case.

As discussed in Chapter 3, the demand curve shows a relationship between quantity demanded and the price of a good or service. A similar relationship between the quantity supplied by firms and the price of a good can be identified in relation to the behaviour of firms in a **competitive market** — that is, a market in which individual firms cannot influence the price of the good or service they are selling, because of competition from other firms.

Individual and market supply

As with the demand curve, there is a distinction between the supply curve of an individual firm, and the supply curve for a *market*. The individual supply curve shows the amount that an individual firm is willing and able to supply at any given price in a given period of time. The market supply curve shows the total amount of a product that firms are willing and able to supply at any given price in a given time period.

The supply curve

In such a market it can be supposed that firms will be prepared to supply more goods at a high price than at a lower one (ceteris paribus), as the higher price will bring higher profits.

The **supply curve** illustrates how much the firms in a market will supply at any given price, as shown in Figure 4.1. As firms are expected to supply more goods at a high price than at a lower price, the supply curve will be upward sloping, reflecting this positive relationship between quantity and price.

What influences supply?

We can identify six important influences on the quantity that firms will be prepared to supply to the market at any given price. They are:

- production costs
- the technology of production
- taxes and subsidies
- the prices of related goods
- expected prices
- the number of firms in the market

Synoptic link

Chapter 1 introduced the factors of production and their importance to firms. The way in which a firm's costs influence its decision making is discussed in Chapter 11.

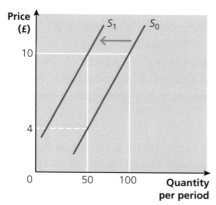

Figure 4.2 The supply curve shifts to the left if production costs increase

Costs

If firms are aiming to maximise profits, an important influence on their supply decision will be the costs of production that they face. Chapter 1 explained that in order to produce output, firms need to use inputs of the factors of production — labour, capital, land, etc. If the cost of those inputs increases, firms will in general be expected to supply less output at any given price. The effect of this is shown in Figure 4.2, where an increase in production costs induces firms to supply less output at each price. There is a decrease in supply. The curve shifts from its initial position at S_0 to a new position at S_1. For example, suppose the original price was £10 per unit. Before the increase in costs, firms would have been prepared to supply 100 units of the product to the market. An increase in costs of £6 per unit that shifted the supply curve from S_0 to S_1 would mean that, at the same price, firms would now supply only 50 units of the good. Notice that the vertical distance between S_0 and S_1 is the amount of the change in cost per unit.

Technology

If a new technology of production is introduced, which means that firms can produce more cost effectively, this could have the opposite effect, with the increase in supply shifting the supply curve to the right. For example, firms may take advantage of a new type of machinery that uses inputs more efficiently. This is shown in Figure 4.3, where improved technology induces firms to supply more output at any given price, and the supply curve shifts from its initial position at S_0 to a new position at S_1. Therefore, if firms in the initial situation were supplying 50 units with the price at £10 per unit, then a fall in costs of £6 per unit would induce firms to increase supply to 100 units (if the price remained at £10).

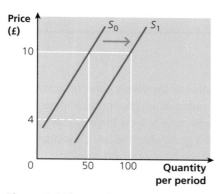

Figure 4.3 The supply curve shifts to the right if production costs fall

Synoptic link

The effect of taxes and subsidies will be discussed in more detail in Chapter 10, after we have further developed the demand and supply model.

Taxes and subsidies

Suppose the government imposes a tax on a good or service. From the firm's perspective, this is tantamount to an increase in the costs of production. This means that firms will (ceteris paribus) be prepared to supply less output at any given market price. Again, the supply curve shifts to the left. This is shown in panel (a) of Figure 4.4, which assumes a fixed per unit tax. The supply curve shifts, as firms supply less at any given market price. On the other hand, if the government pays firms a subsidy to produce a particular good, this will reduce their costs, and induce them to supply more output at any given price. The supply curve will then shift to the right, as shown in panel (b).

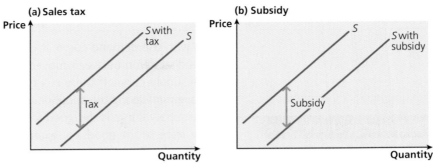

Figure 4.4 The effects of taxes and subsidies on supply

Prices of other goods

It was shown in Chapter 3 that from the consumers' perspective, two goods may be substitutes for each other, such that if the price of one good increases, consumers may be induced to switch their consumption to substitute goods. Similarly, there may be substitution on the supply side. For example, suppose that a farmer who is currently producing potatoes discovers that organic carrots are more profitable because prices have increased. The farmer may decide to switch production from potatoes to organic carrots.

A firm may face a situation in which there are alternative uses to which its factors of production may be put: in other words, it may be able to choose between producing a range of different products: a situation of **competitive supply**. A rise in the price of a good raises its profitability, and therefore may encourage a firm to switch production from other goods. This may happen even if there are high switching costs, provided the increase in price is sufficiently large.

In other circumstances, a firm may produce a range of goods jointly. Perhaps one good is a by-product of the production process of another. For example, a sheep farmer can produce both wool and meat from the sheep. An increase in the price of one of the goods may mean that the firm will produce more of both goods. This notion of **joint supply** is similar to the situation on the demand side where consumers regard two goods as complements.

Expected prices

Because production takes time, firms often take decisions about how much to supply on the basis of expected future prices. Indeed, if their product is one that can be stored, there may be times when a firm will decide to allow stocks of a product to build up in anticipation of a higher price in the future, perhaps by holding back some of its production from current sales. In some economic activities, expectations about future prices are crucial in taking supply decisions because of the length of time needed in order to increase output. For example, a building firm may see that house prices are increasing in a certain area, but cannot supply new houses immediately because they take time to build.

The number of firms in the market

As the market supply curve is the sum of the supply curves of individual firms, if more firms join the market, the market supply curve will shift. Similarly, if some firms go out of business, the market supply curve will shift to the left.

> **Key terms**
>
> **competitive supply** a situation in which a firm can use its factors of production to produce alternative products
> **joint supply** where a firm produces more than one product together

Movements along and shifts of the supply curve

As with the demand curve, it is very important to remember that there is a distinction between movements *along* the supply curve, and shifts *of* the supply curve. If there is a change in the market price, this induces a movement along the supply curve (an extension or contraction). After all, the supply curve is designed to reveal how firms will react to a change in the price of the good. For example, in Figure 4.5, if the price is initially at P_0 firms will be prepared to supply the quantity Q_0, but if the price then increases to P_1 this will induce a movement along the supply curve as firms expand the quantity supplied to Q_1.

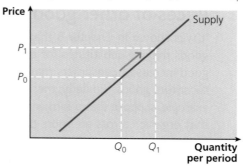

Figure 4.5 A movement along a supply curve in response to a price change

In contrast, as seen in the previous section, a change in any of the other influences on supply will induce a shift of the whole supply curve, as this affects the firms' willingness to supply at any given price.

Knowledge check 4.3

Under what conditions would there be a contraction of supply?

Knowledge check 4.4

If a producer finds that the market price of its product has increased, would this induce a contraction of supply, an extension of supply or a shift in the supply curve?

Exercise 4.2

Draw supply curves for each of the following situations to show whether there is a shift of the supply curve or a movement along it.
a The supply of accountancy services following the introduction of more efficient computer software.
b The supply of a good following an increase in taxes on sales.
c The supply of ice cream following a rise in its selling price during a hot summer.
d The supply of tennis balls after several firms in the market go bankrupt.

Study tip

As with the discussion of demand, it is important to be clear about the difference between a shift of the supply curve and a movement along it. Again, the convention is adopted to use an *extension* (or *contraction*) of supply for a movement along the supply curve, and to use an *increase* (or *decrease*) to denote a shift of the curve. It is also helpful to distinguish between those factors that affect the position of the supply curve and those that affect the position of the demand curve. Don't forget that the factors that affect the position of the supply curve are:
- production costs
- the technology of production
- taxes and subsidies
- the prices of other goods
- firms' expectations about future prices
- the number of firms in the market

Exercise 4.3

For each of the following, decide whether the demand curve or the supply curve will move, and in which direction:
a Consumers are convinced by arguments about the benefits of organic vegetables.
b A new process is developed that reduces the amount of inputs that firms need in order to produce bicycles.

Exercise 4.3 (continued)

c There is a severe frost in Brazil that affects the coffee crop.
d The government increases the rate of value added tax.
e Real incomes rise.
f The price of tea falls: what happens in the market for coffee?
g The price of sugar falls: what happens in the market for coffee?

Summary

- Firms in a competitive market can be expected to supply more output at a higher price, ceteris paribus.
- The supply curve traces out this positive relationship between price and quantity supplied.
- Changes in the costs of production, technology, taxes and subsidies, or the prices of related goods may induce shifts of the supply curve, with firms being prepared to sell more (or less) output at any given price.
- Expectations about future prices may affect current supply decisions.

Producer surplus

Key term

producer surplus the difference between the price received by firms for a good or service and the price at which they would have been prepared to supply that good or service

Knowledge check 4.5

Explain why producer surplus may be considered as the *raison d'être* of firms.

Parallel to the notion of consumer surplus is the concept of **producer surplus**. Think about the nature of the supply curve: it reveals how much output firms are prepared to supply at any given price in a competitive market. Figure 4.6 depicts a supply curve. Assume the price is at P^*, and that all units are sold at that price. P^* represents the value to firms of the last unit sold. In other words, if the price had been set slightly below P^*, the last unit would not have been supplied, as firms would not have found this profitable.

Notice that the threshold at which a firm will decide it is not profitable to supply is the point at which the price received by the firm reaches the cost to the firm of producing the last unit of the good.

The supply curve shows that, in the range of prices between point A and P^*, firms would have been willing to supply positive amounts of this good or service. So at P^*, they would gain a surplus value on all units of the good supplied below Q^*. The total area is shown in Figure 4.7 — it is the area above the supply curve and below P^*, shown as the shaded

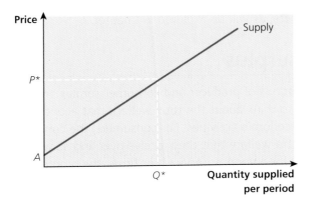

Figure 4.6 Supply and value to the firm

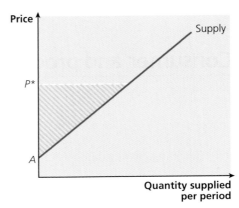

Figure 4.7 Producer surplus

Table 4.2 A firm's supply decision

Price (£)	Quantity (units)
10	1
12	2
14	3
16	4
18	5
20	6

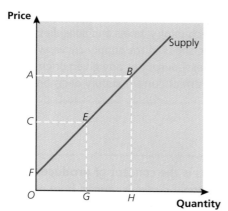

Figure 4.8 Producer surplus and price

triangle. One way of defining this producer surplus is as the surplus earned by firms over and above the minimum that would have kept them in the market. It is the *raison d'être* of firms.

Table 4.2 shows the quantity of a good that a firm would be prepared to supply at various prices. At a price of £10, the firm would only supply 1 unit of the good. However, at a price of £12, the firm would supply 2 units, but receives that price for both units of the good supplied. The firm would have been prepared to supply one of these units at £10, but receives £12, making a surplus of £2. As the price of the good rises, the firm receives more producer surplus.

The producer surplus that a firm receives is important, as it provides an incentive for firms to respond to changes in the prevailing price. Indeed, this helps to explain why the supply curve is upward sloping.

Producer surplus and price

There is a relationship between the size of producer surplus and the price charged for a good. If the price of a good increases, this will raise the overall size of producer surplus. You can see this in Figure 4.8.

When the price of the good is relatively low at *OC*, quantity supplied is *OG*, producers receive revenue of *OCEG*, and face costs of *OFEG*, and producer surplus is given by *CEF*. However, if the price were to increase to *OA*, quantity supplied would be *OH*, revenue would be the area *OABH*, and producer surplus would be higher than before, at *ABF*.

Evaluation of producer surplus

Producer surplus is the difference between the price received by firms for a good or service and the price at which they would have been prepared to supply it. It is related to profits. When the price of a good is relatively high (for example, at *OA* in Figure 4.8), the firm receives higher producer surplus than at a lower price (*OC*), by supplying more of the good to market. The shape of the supply curve shows the extent to which firms are able to expand quantity supplied in response to a price increase — and the shape of the curve also determines how much additional surplus can be made. If firms cannot readily expand supply (i.e. if the supply curve is relatively steep), the increase in quantity supplied will be smaller and the additional producer surplus will be lower.

The importance of producer surplus is that it provides an incentive for firms to adjust the quantity supplied in response to a change in the price of the good. This in turn has implications for how resources are allocated in society, as will be explored in Chapter 7.

Consumer and producer surplus

The notions of producer and consumer surplus are important when we come to think about the total welfare that economic agents receive from their economic activities. For consumers, the consumer surplus represents the extra welfare that they receive over and above what they are willing to pay for a good or service. For firms, the producer surplus represents the welfare (profit) that they receive over and above the price they are willing to accept for supplying a good or service. There is therefore a

Price

P^*

Consumer surplus

Producer surplus

Supply

Demand

Q^* Quantity per period

Figure 4.9 Consumer and producer surplus

sense in which we interpret the sum of these two surpluses as being the net welfare that society as a whole gains from the production and consumption of this good or service. It could be argued that efficient resource allocation is achieved when this is maximised.

Consumer and producer surplus can be shown on the same diagram. Figure 4.9 shows a market with price at P^* and quantity traded at Q^*. The green shaded area shows consumer surplus, while the purple shaded area represents producer surplus.

Summary

- The supply curve shows the quantity that firms would be prepared to supply at any given price.
- Producer surplus is the difference between the price received by firms for a good or service and the price at which they would have been prepared to supply that good or service.

Case study 4.1

Champagne

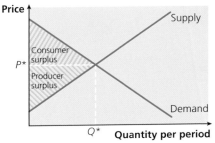

More affordable alternatives have affected the market for champagne

The market for champagne has been changing in recent years. Champagne has always commanded a premium price compared with other sparkling wines because of its reputation and status as the wine for celebrations of all kinds. Christmas is one such focus for drinking champagne, and major events such as the millennium celebrations cause blips in demand, with no party being complete without a few bottles of champagne. However, the increased availability of good-quality

alternatives to champagne at competitive prices has affected champagne producers. It has even been known for some English sparkling wines to fare well at blind tastings compared with some champagnes. Nonetheless champagne production has remained profitable, as consumer incomes have risen. Mechanisation of some parts of the production process has benefited producers.

There are strict rules governing the production of champagne. Indeed, champagne can only be called by that name if it comes from a particular designated area in France, and this has effectively limited the amount that can be produced. In early 2008, it was announced that consideration was being given to expanding the area that could be recognised as producing champagne. The proposal was accepted, and the first vines were expected to be planted in 2015, although there has been considerable resistance from existing growers. This will not affect the market for some time, as it takes time for newly planted vines to produce grapes that can be used to make wine — it is unlikely that any champagne from the expanded region will come to market before 2021.

Follow-up questions

a From the passage, identify factors that would be expected to affect the demand curve for champagne.

b From the passage, identify factors that would be expected to affect the supply curve for champagne.

CHAPTER 4 QUESTIONS

A Multiple-choice questions

1 Which of the following is unlikely to affect the supply of a soft drink?

   a The cost of the materials to produce the soft drink

   b A decrease in the price of a rival product

   c The introduction of a new machine that can produce soft drinks faster

   d An increase in value added tax (VAT)

2 An extension of supply is likely to lead to:

   a An increase in supply

   b A decrease in supply

   c An increase in quantity supplied

   d A decrease in quantity supplied

3 When there is a contraction of supply there is likely to be:

   a An increase in price and a decrease in producer surplus

   b An increase in price and an increase in producer surplus

   c A decrease in price and an increase in producer surplus

   d A decrease in price and a decrease in producer surplus

B Knowledge and understanding questions

4 Explain the relationship between the price of a good and the quantity supplied.   [2 marks]

5 Explain two factors that may cause a shift in the supply curve for bottled water.   [4 marks]

6 Dry, hot weather can cause a bad harvest of pumpkins. Explain, with the aid of a diagram, how the supply of pumpkins at Halloween may be affected by a bad harvest.   [4 marks]

7 Explain, with the aid of a diagram, what is meant by producer surplus.   [4 marks]

C Stimulus response question

8 The government imposes a tax (duty) on the sale of unleaded and diesel fuel for vehicles in the UK. The level of this taxation has increased over time.

   a Explain, with the aid of a diagram, the effect of an increase in fuel tax (duty) on the supply of fuel for vehicles in the UK.   [4 marks]

   b Apart from a decrease in fuel duty, explain two factors that could increase the supply of fuel for vehicles in the UK.   [4 marks]

Chapter 5

The interaction of markets

The previous chapters introduced the notions of demand and supply, and it is now time to bring these two curves together in order to meet the key concept of market equilibrium. The model can then be further developed to see how it provides insights into how markets operate. You will encounter demand and supply in a wide variety of contexts, and begin to glimpse some of the ways in which the model can help to explain how the economic world works.

> ### Learning objectives
> After studying this chapter, you should be able to:
> - explain, with the aid of a diagram, the interaction of demand and supply
> - explain, with the aid of a diagram, market equilibrium and disequilibrium
> - evaluate the impact of changes in demand and/or supply in one market on a related market(s)

The interaction of demand and supply and market equilibrium

Demand and supply curves begin to tell us about the behaviour of consumers and firms, but the real power of the demand and supply model arises when we bring the curves together.

Figure 5.1 shows the demand for and supply of butter. The diagram takes the demand and supply curves developed in the previous two chapters and draws them together.

Synoptic link

The demand curve was explained in Chapter 3 and the supply curve was discussed in Chapter 4.

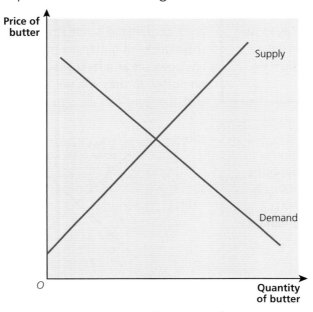

Figure 5.1 Bringing demand and supply together

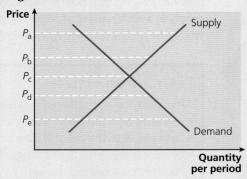

Key term

market equilibrium a situation that occurs in a market when the price is such that the quantity demanded by consumers is exactly balanced by the quantity supplied by firms

Quantitative skills 5.1

Identifying and interpreting an intersection on a diagram

You will meet many diagrams in economics where there are upward- and downward-sloping lines that intersect at some point. Such intersection points are almost always significant. In the case of demand and supply, the downward-sloping line represents demand, and the upward-sloping curve shows supply. Only at the point where the two lines meet are the decisions of consumers and firms mutually consistent. In other words, consumers are choosing to demand exactly the quantity that firms are willing and able to supply. The important question to explore is the mechanism that will lead to this equilibrium point. This in turn depends upon the incentives facing economic agents if the starting point is away from the intersection point.

Key term

excess supply a situation in which the quantity that firms are willing and able to supply exceeds the quantity that consumers wish to demand at the going price

The question of interest to us here is whether or not there can be a situation in which the quantity consumers wish to buy is the same as the quantity firms are willing to supply. Such a situation is known as the **market equilibrium**. The equilibrium can be brought about if the price is right. Think about Exercise 5.1.

Exercise 5.1

Figure 5.2 shows a demand and a supply curve and a selection of possible prices. Which price brings quantity demanded and quantity supplied together?

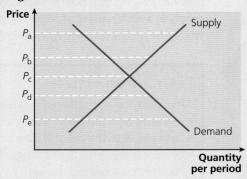

Figure 5.2 What price brings demand and supply together?

You will have seen from Exercise 5.1 that there is only one price (P_c) at which the quantity demanded is the same as the quantity supplied. This is the equilibrium price.

What if the price is not at its equilibrium value?

Figure 5.3 again shows the market for butter. You can see that P^* is the equilibrium price, at which quantity demanded and quantity supplied are equal. However, suppose that the price were to be set at a relatively high price (above P^*). At such a price, firms wish to supply lots of butter to the market. Not enough consumers want to purchase butter at such a high price, so demand is not strong. Firms now have a problem: they find that their stocks of butter are building up. What has happened is that the price has been set at a level that exceeds the value that most consumers place on butter, so they will not buy it. There is **excess supply**. The only thing that the firms can do is to reduce the price in order to clear their stocks.

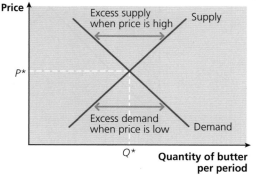

Figure 5.3 Market equilibrium

Suppose they now set their price relatively low (below P^*). Now it is the consumers who have a problem, because they would like to buy more butter at the low price than firms are willing and able to supply. There is **excess demand**. Some consumers may offer to pay more than the going price in order to obtain their butter supplies, and firms realise that they can raise the price.

When there is excess demand or excess supply, we describe the market as being in *disequilibrium*. Will this situation persist? When the price settles at P^* in Figure 5.3, there is a balance in the market between the quantity that consumers wish to demand and the quantity that firms wish to supply, namely Q^*. This is the market equilibrium. In a free market the price can be expected to converge on this equilibrium level, through movements along both demand and supply curves.

Summary
- Bringing demand and supply together, you can identify the market equilibrium.
- The equilibrium price is the unique point at which the quantity demanded by consumers is just balanced by the quantity that firms wish to supply.
- In a free market, natural forces can be expected to encourage prices to adjust to the equilibrium level.

Changes to the market equilibrium

In order to make good use of the demand and supply model, it is necessary to introduce another of the economist's key tools. You have seen the way in which a market moves towards equilibrium between demand and supply through price adjustments and movements along the demand and supply curves. Now consider what happens if there is a change in one of the factors that affects the position of demand or supply. What will then happen to the market equilibrium?

A market for dried pasta

Begin with a simple market for dried pasta, a basic staple foodstuff obtainable in any supermarket. Figure 5.4 shows the market in equilibrium. D_0 represents the demand curve in this initial situation, and S_0 is the supply curve. The market is in equilibrium with the price at P_0, and the quantity being traded is Q_0. It is equilibrium in the sense that pasta producers are supplying just the amount of pasta that consumers wish to buy at that price. This is the 'before' position. Some experiments will now be carried out with this market by disturbing the equilibrium.

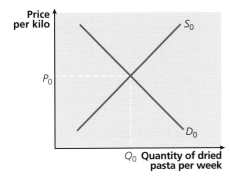

Figure 5.4 A market for dried pasta

A change in consumer preferences

Suppose that a study is published highlighting the health benefits of eating pasta, backed up with an advertising campaign. The effect of this is likely to be an increase in the demand for pasta at any given price. In other words, this change in consumer preferences will shift the demand curve to the right, as shown in Figure 5.5.

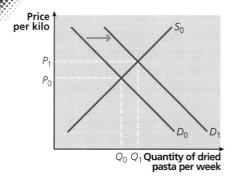

Figure 5.5 A change in consumer preferences for dried pasta

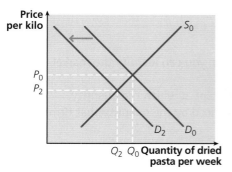

Figure 5.6 A change in the price of a substitute for dried pasta

The market now adjusts to a new equilibrium, with a new price P_1, and a new quantity traded at Q_1. In this case, both price and quantity have increased as a result of the change in preferences. There has been a movement along the supply curve (an extension of supply).

A change in the price of a substitute

A second possibility is that there is a fall in the price of fresh pasta. This is likely to be a close substitute for dried pasta, so the probable result is that some former consumers of dried pasta will switch their allegiance to the fresh variety. This time the demand curve for dried pasta moves in the opposite direction, as can be seen in Figure 5.6. Here the starting point is the original position, with market equilibrium at price P_0 and a quantity traded Q_0. After the shift in the demand curve from D_0 to D_2, the market settles again with a price of P_2 and a quantity traded of Q_2. Both price and quantity traded are now lower than in the original position.

A fall in the price of fresh pasta may result in consumers of dried pasta switching their allegiance to the fresh variety

An improvement in pasta technology

Next, suppose that a new pasta-making machine is produced, enabling dried pasta makers to produce at a lower cost than before. This technical advance reduces firms' costs, and consequently they are willing to supply more dried pasta at any given price. The starting point is the same initial position, but now it is the supply curve that shifts — to the right. This is shown in Figure 5.7.

The new market equilibrium is at price P_3, which is lower than the original equilibrium, but the quantity traded is higher at Q_3.

An increase in labour costs

Finally, suppose that pasta producers face an increase in their labour costs. Perhaps the Pasta Workers' Union has negotiated higher wages, or the pasta producers have become subject to stricter health and safety legislation, which raises their production costs. Figure 5.8 starts as usual with equilibrium at price P_0 and quantity Q_0.

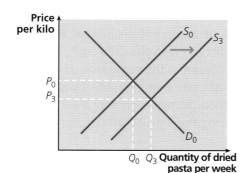

Figure 5.7 New pasta-making technology

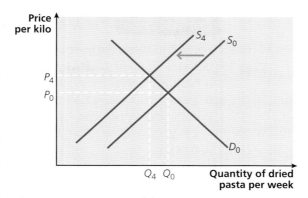

Figure 5.8 An increase in labour costs

The increase in production costs means that pasta producers are prepared to supply less dried pasta at any given price, so the supply curve shifts to the left — to S_4. This takes the market to a new equilibrium at a higher price than before (P_4), but with a lower quantity traded (Q_4).

Consumer and producer surplus

As explained in Chapter 4, the notions of producer and consumer surplus are important when we come to think about the total welfare that economic agents receive from their economic activities.

A change in the conditions of demand or supply will affect the size of consumer and producer surplus. Figure 5.9 illustrates the effect of an increase in demand: in other words, if consumers are now willing to buy more of a good at any given price. In Figure 5.9, the initial demand curve is given by D_0 and the supply curve is S. The initial equilibrium price is P_0 and the quantity traded is Q_0. In this situation, consumer surplus is the area ABP_0 and producer surplus is P_0BC. If demand shifts to D_1, equilibrium price increases to P_1 and the quantity increases to Q_1. Consumer surplus is now XYP_1 and producer surplus is P_1YC. In other words, both consumers and producers receive a higher surplus, which makes sense because consumers now value the good more highly.

Notice that a change in the price of a good or service can affect the balance between consumer and producer surplus. This in turn could be seen as a change in the distribution of surplus between consumers and producers, as well as a change in the overall level of welfare in the society.

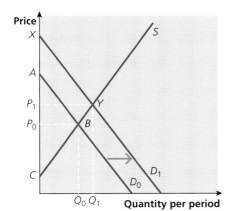

Figure 5.9 Consumer and producer surplus with an increase in demand

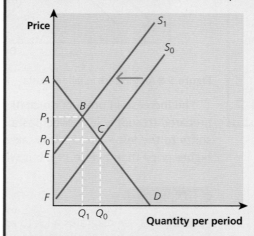
Using the demand and supply model

The demand and supply model can help in understanding how market equilibrium may be determined, and how it may change as conditions change. For example, think about the market for a commodity such as cocoa, and the way it may change over time. Cocoa is a key ingredient of chocolate, so the demand for cocoa will reflect movements in the demand for chocolate. The supply of cocoa is dependent upon the number of producers, and on the factors that affect the success of the cocoa harvest — weather conditions, the incidence of disease or parasites and so on.

Cocoa prices have been quite volatile over recent years, and the demand and supply model can help to provide an explanation. Consider Figure 5.11, which shows possible positions for the demand curve (D_x and D_y) and the supply curve (S_a, S_b and S_c).

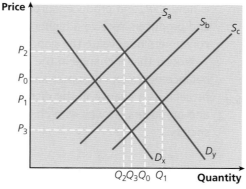

Figure 5.11 The demand and supply of cocoa

Suppose that in one period, the demand curve is D_y and supply is at S_b, which might perhaps be a year in which there is a 'normal' harvest. The equilibrium price here is P_0. Suppose that in the following period, there is an exceptional 'glut' harvest, so the supply curve shifts to S_c, but with the demand curve remaining at D_y. The price falls to a new equilibrium at P_1. If the following period brings a poor harvest, such that supply shifts to S_a, price finds a new equilibrium up at P_2. If in the following period a big harvest is accompanied by a decrease in demand (perhaps because of a recession), the market could end up with supply at S_c, demand at D_x, and an equilibrium price at P_3. You can see that the model helps to suggest possible explanations for volatility in prices in commodity markets.

The same sort of reasoning can be applied to other markets as well, whether in looking for an explanation for rising house prices, or in seeking to analyse the demand for public transport.

Related markets

Cocoa and chocolate is one example of a situation in which markets are related. In this case, the connection between the markets arises because cocoa is a key ingredient of chocolate. The potential volatility in cocoa prices has a knock-on effect on the costs faced by chocolate producers. As cocoa is less perishable than other agricultural products, it may be possible to guard against volatility by keeping reserves of cocoa in storage.

There are other situations in which a change in one market will have knock-on effects in other markets. Chapter 3 highlighted two particular ways in which markets might be interrelated – namely, when goods are either substitutes or complements.

Substitutes

Think of two goods that are substitutes for each other. For example, rice and potatoes might be seen as being substitutes for dried pasta. If the price of potatoes falls, perhaps because of a fall in the costs faced by potato growers resulting in a fall in the equilibrium price of potatoes, this could then lead to a decrease in demand for dried pasta, resulting in a lower equilibrium price and quantity.

The impact will also be felt across the markets for factors of production. There will be a decrease in demand for labour by producers of dried pasta, and a resulting reduction in wages. There is therefore a series of knock-on effects spreading across markets because they are interrelated.

How strong these effects will be depends on whether or not consumers really see these products as being close substitutes for each other. Those consumers who really love to eat pasta may not be tempted to change their eating habits just because potatoes are a bit cheaper.

Complements

If two goods are usually consumed together, they are seen to be complements. Coffee and sugar or printers and ink cartridges are possible examples of such goods. An increase in the price of a good could lead to a fall in demand for a complementary good. Again, there could be knock-on effects into factor markets if firms need to cut back on production and reduce their use of labour.

Again, it is not clear how strong such effects would be. In the case of coffee and sugar, an increase in the price of sugar may not lead to an enormous reduction in the demand for coffee, if only because sugar does not carry such a high price that it would induce a response. An increase in the price of printer ink cartridges may induce people to be more careful about how many pages they print, but the impact on the demand for printers may not be too badly affected, given that printers do not need to be replaced all that often.

The importance of scarcity

There is a more general way in which markets are interconnected, which arises because all societies face the problem of scarcity. This means that no economy can meet the combined wants of its population, and choices will need to be made about what should be produced. The economy is made up of multiple markets, and ultimately they are all connected.

Summary
- The way in which markets respond to changes in market conditions can be explored by comparing market equilibrium before and after positions.
- It is important to figure out whether the change affects demand or supply, and in which direction.
- The size and direction of the shifts of the demand and supply curves determine the overall effect on equilibrium price and quantity traded.
- Where markets are related, the effects of a change in conditions in one market may have knock-on effects elsewhere.

Exercise 5.3

For each of the following market situations, sketch a demand and supply diagram, and see what happens to the equilibrium price and quantity. Explain your answers.
a An increase in consumer incomes affects the market for bus travel.
b New regulations on environmental pollution force a firm making paint to reduce its emission of toxic fumes.
c A firm of accountants brings in new, faster computers to improve efficiency.
d An outbreak of bird flu causes consumers of chicken to buy pizza instead. (What is the effect on both markets?)

Exercise 5.4

Discuss how changes in the demand and supply of oil-based fuels could affect a related market.

Case study 5.1

A healthy diet?

The growing obsession with organic foods has led to a rise in prices

Hardly a week seems to go by without scientists or nutritionists coming up with some new finding about the healthiness of our diets. Some blueberry muffins contain more than the recommended daily intake of sugar for adults. A study alleges that real butter is more healthy than margarine. Smoked salmon from farmed fish may contain more fat than a pizza. Red wine is good for you — or is it bad for you? Dark chocolate is good for you, but is milk chocolate damaging? In March 2018, a judge in Los Angeles ruled that coffee sold in California must carry a cancer warning because the chemical acrylamide is regarded as carcinogenic. (This is a chemical created as part of the roasting process: UK and European experts say that the danger is minimal, so don't panic just yet.)

There is a growing obsession with the health and environmental benefits of organic foods. Overuse of chemical fertilisers and pesticides is seen as damaging to the environment, and potentially damaging to our health. This has resulted in a premium price for certified organic foods, notably vegetables. Wine producers in some regions have also become involved in organic (and biodynamic) production methods. However, converting to organic production and gaining authentication is a long-winded and costly process.

Follow-up questions

Suppose people become convinced of the benefits of consuming organic foods.

a Sketch a demand and supply diagram to analyse how this would affect the market for non-organic foodstuffs in the short run.

b Now use a demand and supply diagram to show how the market for certified organic foods would be affected in the short run.

c With the help of more diagrams, explain how these interdependent markets will adjust in the longer term, remembering that achieving certified organic status is slow and costly.

CHAPTER 5 QUESTIONS

A Multiple-choice questions

1 Market equilibrium will lead to:

   a Excess demand in the market

   b Excess supply in the market

   c Quantity supplied equalling quantity demanded in the market

   d Price equalling quantity supplied and demanded

2 Assume that white sliced bread is an inferior good. What is likely to happen to the market for white sliced bread when consumer incomes increase?

   a An increase in demand leading to an increase in the equilibrium quantity and price

   b An increase in demand leading to a decrease in the equilibrium quantity and price

   c A decrease in demand leading to an increase in the equilibrium quantity and price

   d A decrease in demand leading to a decrease in the equilibrium quantity and price

3 An increase in demand is likely to lead to:

   a An increase in quantity demanded and a decrease in quantity supplied

   b An increase in quantity demanded and an increase in quantity supplied

   c A decrease in quantity demanded and an increase in quantity supplied

   d A decrease in quantity demanded and a decrease in quantity supplied

B Knowledge and understanding questions

4 Draw and label a diagram showing equilibrium in a market. [3 marks]

5 Draw and label a diagram showing excess supply in a market. [3 marks]

6 Explain, with the use of a diagram, how an increase in the demand for a product may affect the equilibrium point. [4 marks]

C Stimulus response question

7 Many supermarkets sell cooked chickens. The chickens are cooked on a rotisserie in the supermarket. Each day the manager must decide how many chickens are cooked. Table 1 shows data for one supermarket's production and sales of cooked chickens over three days.

Table 1 Production and sales of cooked chicken in a supermarket

Day	Production of cooked chickens	Sales of cooked chickens	Price
Friday	100	65	£5
Saturday	100	90	£5
Sunday	100	100	£5

   a Explain, with the aid of a diagram, why there was disequilibrium for the supermarket on Friday. [4 marks]

   b Explain **two** ways in which the supermarket could avoid disequilibrium next Friday. [4 marks]

D Essay question

8 In the UK approximately 65% of households own the property they live in and 35% rent their accommodation.

Evaluate whether an increase in house prices will always lead to an increase in the demand for rented accommodation. [20 marks]

Chapter 6

Elasticity

The previous chapter explored how changes in demand and supply are reflected in a movement to a new equilibrium position. Typically, such a change in the market equilibrium entails a change in the price of the product and in the quantity traded in the market. Whether the change is reflected in price or in quantity depends upon the extent to which demand and supply are sensitive to the change in market conditions. This chapter examines this issue.

> ### Learning objectives
>
> After studying this chapter, you should be able to:
> - explain elasticity
> - explain and calculate the price elasticity of demand (*PED*)
> - explain and calculate the income elasticity of demand (*YED*)
> - explain and calculate the cross elasticity of demand (*XED*)
> - explain and calculate the price elasticity of supply (*PES*)
> - explain, with the aid of a diagram, different values of *PED*, *YED*, *XED* and *PES*
> - explain, with the aid of a diagram, the relationship between the *PED* and a firm's total revenue
> - evaluate the factors that determine the value of *PED*, *YED*, *XED* and *PES*
> - evaluate the usefulness and significance of *PED*, *YED*, *XED* and *PES*

Elasticity: the sensitivity of demand and supply

Both the demand for and the supply of a good or service can be expected to depend upon its price as well as other factors. It is often interesting to know just how sensitive demand and/or supply will be to a change in either price or one of the other determinants — for example, in predicting how market equilibrium will change in response to a change in the market environment. The sensitivity of demand or supply to a change in one of its determining factors can be measured by its **elasticity**.

> ### Key term
>
> **elasticity** a measure of the sensitivity of one variable to changes in another variable

The price elasticity of demand (PED)

Key terms

price elasticity of demand (PED) a measure of the sensitivity of quantity demanded to a change in the price of a good or service. It is measured as:

$$\frac{\text{\% change in quantity demanded}}{\text{\% change in price}}$$

elastic a term used when the price elasticity of demand is greater than 1 but less than infinity

inelastic a term used when the price elasticity of demand is less than 1 but greater than zero

The most common elasticity measure is the **price elasticity of demand (PED)**. This measures the sensitivity of the quantity demanded of a good or service to a change in its price.

The elasticity is defined as the percentage change in quantity demanded divided by the percentage change in the price.

We define the percentage change in price as $100 \times \frac{\Delta P}{P}$ (where Δ means 'change in' and P stands for 'price'). Similarly, the percentage change in quantity demanded is $100 \times \frac{\Delta Q}{Q}$.

When the demand is highly price sensitive, the percentage change in quantity demanded following a price change will be large relative to the percentage change in price. In this case, *PED* will take on a value that is smaller than −1. For example, suppose that a 2% change in price leads to a 5% change in quantity demanded — the elasticity is then −5 divided by 2 = −2.5. When the price elasticity is smaller than −1, demand is referred to as being **elastic**.

Quantitative skills 6.1

Describing elasticity

Because the *PED* is always negative, economists sometimes omit the minus sign. Strictly speaking, demand is elastic where the *PED* is smaller than −1 and inelastic if the value is between 0 and −1. Another way of expressing this is that demand is elastic when the *PED* is negative with an absolute value larger than 1, but this is quite clumsy. You may sometimes find people saying that demand is elastic when the *PED* is larger than 1. What they mean is that the *PED* is smaller than −1, that it is negative but with a numerical value greater than 1.

There are two important things to notice about this. First, because the demand curve is downward sloping, the elasticity will always be negative. This is because the changes in price and quantity are always in the opposite direction. Second, you should try to calculate the elasticity only for a relatively small change in price, as it becomes unreliable for very large changes.

When demand is not very sensitive to price, the percentage change in quantity demanded will be smaller than the original percentage change in price, and the elasticity will then be between 0 and −1. For example, if a 2% change in price leads to a 1% change in quantity demanded, then the value of the elasticity will be −1 divided by 2 = −0.5. In this case, demand is referred to as being **inelastic**.

Quantitative skills 6.2

Calculating an elasticity

Figure 6.1 shows a demand curve for pencils. When the price of a pencil is 40p, the quantity demanded will be 20. If the price falls to 35p, the quantity demanded will rise to 30. The percentage change in quantity (%ΔQD) is $100 \times \frac{10}{20} = 50$ and the percentage change in price (%ΔP) is $100 \times \frac{-5}{40} = -12.5$. So, the elasticity can be calculated as $\frac{\%\Delta QD}{\%\Delta P} = \left(\frac{50}{-12.5}\right) = -4$. At this price, demand is highly price elastic.

Quantitative skills 6.2 (continued)

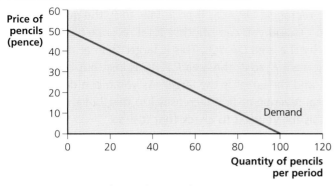

Figure 6.1 A demand curve for pencils

At a lower price, the result is quite different. Suppose that price is initially 10p, at which price the quantity demanded is 80. If the price falls to 9p, demand increases to 82. The percentage change in quantity is now $100 \times \frac{2}{80} = 2.5$, and the percentage change in price is $100 \times \frac{-1}{10} = -10$, so the elasticity is calculated as $\frac{2.5}{-10} = -0.25$, and demand is now price inelastic.

Knowledge check 6.1

Why is the *PED* always negative?

Key term

unit elastic a term used when the price elasticity of demand is equal to 1

This phenomenon is true for any straight-line demand curve: in other words, demand is price elastic at higher prices and inelastic at lower prices. At the halfway point the elasticity is exactly –1, which is referred to as being **unit elastic**.

Why should this happen? The key is to remember that elasticity is defined in terms of the percentage changes in price and quantity. So when price is relatively high, a 1p change in price is a small percentage change, and the percentage change in quantity is relatively large — because when price is relatively high, the initial quantity is relatively low. The reverse is the case when price is relatively low. Figure 6.2 shows how the elasticity of demand varies along a straight-line demand curve.

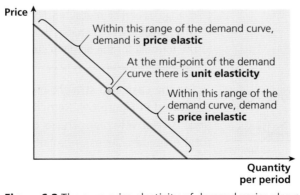

Figure 6.2 The own-price elasticity of demand varies along a straight line

The price elasticity of demand and total revenue

One reason why firms may have an interest in the price elasticity of demand is that if they are considering changing their prices, they will be eager to know the extent to which demand will be affected. For example, they may want to know how a change in price will affect their total revenue. As it happens there is a consistent relationship between the price elasticity of demand and total revenue.

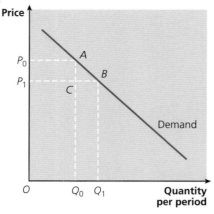

Price

P_0 ⋯⋯⋯ A

P_1 ⋯⋯⋯ B

C

Demand

O Q_0 Q_1 Quantity per period

Figure 6.3 Demand and total revenue

Total revenue is given by price multiplied by quantity. In Figure 6.3, if price is at P_0, quantity demanded is at Q_0 and total revenue is given by the area of the rectangle OP_0AQ_0. If price falls to P_1 the quantity demanded rises to Q_1, and you can see that total revenue has increased, as it is now given by the area OP_1BQ_1. This is larger than at price P_0, because in moving from P_0 to P_1 the area P_1P_0AC is lost, but the area Q_0CBQ_1 is gained, and the latter is the larger. As you move down the demand curve, total revenue at first increases like this, but then decreases — try sketching this for yourself to check that it is so.

Quantitative skills 6.3

Elasticity and total revenue

Quantitative skills 6.1 showed how to calculate the price elasticity of demand at different points along a demand curve for pencils. When the price of a pencil fell from 40 to 35, the quantity demanded rose from 20 to 30, and elasticity was calculated to be −4.

Total revenue before and after the price change can be calculated. Total revenue is equal to price multiplied by quantity, so at the original price revenue was 40 × 20 = 800. At the new lower price, total revenue was 35 × 30 = 1,050. We can therefore see that when the price elasticity of demand is elastic, a fall in price leads to a rise in revenue.

When the price of a pencil fell from 10 to 9, and quantity demanded rose from 80 to 82, demand was inelastic (−0.25). At the original price, revenue was 10 × 80 = 800, and at the lower price it was 9 × 82 = 738. This time, total revenue has fallen with a fall in price and inelastic demand.

A mathematical note: because the elasticity varies along most demand curves, we would ideally like to measure the elasticity at a particular point on the curve. When calculating using percentage changes we are measuring the elasticity along a segment of the curve (an arc), so we may sometimes get misleading results. We should therefore try to calculate for as small a change as can be measured. For those taking A Level maths, you may realise that calculus would enable us to measure elasticity at a point if we knew the formula for the demand curve.

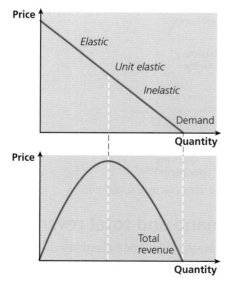

Price

Elastic

Unit elastic

Inelastic

Demand

Quantity

Price

Total revenue

Quantity

Figure 6.4 Elasticity and total revenue

For the case of a straight-line demand curve the relationship is illustrated in Figure 6.4. Remember that demand is price elastic when price is relatively high. This is the range of the demand curve in which total revenue rises as price falls. This makes sense, as in this range the quantity demanded is sensitive to a change in price and increases by more (in percentage terms) than the price falls. This implies that as you move to the right in this segment, total revenue rises. The increase in quantity sold more than compensates for the fall in price. However, when the mid-point is reached and demand becomes unit elastic, total revenue stops rising — it is at its maximum at this point. The remaining part of the curve is inelastic: that is, the increase in quantity demanded is no longer sufficient to compensate for the decrease in price, and total revenue falls. Table 6.1 summarises the situation.

Knowledge check 6.2

Suppose that a good has a *PED* of −0.3. Would you describe this as being relatively elastic or relatively inelastic?

Synoptic link

This relationship will appear again in the discussion of firm behaviour in Chapter 12.

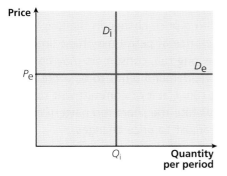

Figure 6.5 Perfectly elastic and inelastic demand

Knowledge check 6.3

What would happen to a firm's total revenue if it were to increase the price of its product when demand is elastic?

Table 6.1 Total revenue, elasticity and a price change

Price elasticity of demand	For a price increase, total revenue…	For a price decrease, total revenue…
Elastic	falls	rises
Unit elastic	does not change	does not change
Inelastic	rises	falls

So, if a firm is aware of the price elasticity of demand for its product, it can anticipate consumer response to its price changes, which may be a powerful strategic tool.

One very important point must be made here. If the price elasticity of demand varies along a straight-line demand curve, such a curve cannot be referred to as either elastic or inelastic. To do so is to confuse the elasticity with the *slope* of the demand curve. It is not only the steepness of the demand curve that determines the elasticity but also the point on the curve at which the elasticity is measured.

Perfectly elastic and perfectly inelastic demand

Two extreme cases of the price elasticity of demand should also be mentioned. Demand may sometimes be totally insensitive to price, so that the same quantity will be demanded whatever price is set for it. In such a situation, demand is said to be *perfectly inelastic*. The demand curve in this case is vertical — as in D_i in Figure 6.5. In this situation, the numerical value of the price elasticity is zero, as quantity demanded does not change in response to a change in the price of the good.

The other extreme is shown on the same figure, where D_e is a horizontal demand curve and demand is *perfectly elastic*. The numerical value of the elasticity here is infinity. Consumers demand an unlimited quantity of the good at price P_e. No firm has any incentive to lower price below this level, but if price were to rise above P_e, demand would fall to zero.

An example

A study by the Institute for Fiscal Studies for the UK found that the price elasticity of demand for wine was −1.69. This means that demand for wine is elastic. If the price of wine were to increase by 10% (ceteris paribus), there would be a fall of 16.9% in the quantity of wine demanded.

Factors that influence the price elasticity of demand

A number of important influences on the price elasticity of demand can now be identified. The most important is the availability of substitutes for the good or service under consideration. For example, think about the demand for cauliflower. Cauliflower and broccoli are often seen as being very similar, so if the price of cauliflower is high one week, people might quite readily switch to broccoli. The demand for cauliflower can be said to be price sensitive (elastic), as consumers can readily substitute an alternative product. On the other hand, if the price of all vegetables rises, demand will not change very much, as there are no substitutes for vegetables in the diet. So, goods that have close substitutes available will

Study tip

Be ready to identify the four key influences on the *PED*:

1 The availability of close substitutes for the good
2 Whether the good is perceived as a necessity
3 The proportion of income or expenditure devoted to the good
4 The time period over which elasticity is considered

tend to exhibit elastic demand, whereas the demand for goods for which there are no substitutes will tend to be more inelastic.

Associated with this is the question of whether an individual regards a good or service as a necessity or as a luxury item. If a good is a necessity, then demand for it will tend to be inelastic, whereas if a good is regarded as a luxury, consumers will tend to be more price-sensitive. This is closely related to the question of substitutes, as by labelling a good as a necessity one is essentially saying that there are no substitutes for it.

A further influence on the price elasticity of demand is the relative share of the good or service in overall expenditure. You may not notice small changes in the price of an inexpensive item that is a small part of overall expenditure, such as salt or sugar. This tends to mean that demand for that good is relatively inelastic. On the other hand, an item that figures large in the household budget will be seen very differently, and consumers will tend to be much more sensitive to price when a significant proportion of their income is involved.

Finally, the time period under consideration may be important. Consumers may respond more strongly to a price change in the long run than in the short run. An increase in the price of petrol may have limited effects in the short run. However, in the long run, consumers may buy smaller cars or switch to diesel. Therefore, demand tends to be more elastic in the long run than in the short run. Habit or commitment to a certain pattern of consumption may dictate the short-run pattern of consumption, but people do eventually adjust to price changes.

Summary

- The price elasticity of demand measures the sensitivity of the quantity of a good demanded to a change in its price.
- As there is an inverse relationship between quantity demanded and price, the price elasticity of demand is always negative.
- Where consumers are sensitive to a change in price, the percentage change in quantity demanded will exceed the percentage change in price. The elasticity of demand then takes on a value that is smaller than −1, and demand is said to be elastic.
- Where consumers are not very sensitive to a change in price, the percentage change in quantity demanded will be smaller than the percentage change in price. Elasticity of demand then takes on a value that is between zero and −1, and demand is said to be inelastic.
- When demand is elastic, a fall (rise) in price leads to a rise (fall) in total revenue.
- When demand is inelastic, a fall (rise) in price leads to a fall (rise) in total revenue.
- The size of the price elasticity of demand is influenced by the availability of substitutes for a good, whether the good is seen as a luxury or a necessity, the relative share of expenditure on the good in the consumer's budget and the time that consumers have to adjust.

Exercise 6.1

Examine Table 6.2, which shows the demand for Pedro's premium olive oil at different prices.

Table 6.2 Demand for Pedro's olive oil

Price (£)	Quantity demanded (bottles per week)
10	20
8	40
6	60
4	80
2	100

a Draw the demand curve.
b Calculate the price elasticity of demand when the price increases from £8 to £10.
c Calculate the price elasticity of demand when the price increases from £6 to £8.
d Calculate the price elasticity of demand when the price increases from £4 to £6.

The income elasticity of demand (*YED*)

Key term

income elasticity of demand (*YED*) a measure of the sensitivity of quantity demanded to a change in consumer incomes

Synoptic link

Normal and inferior goods are discussed in Chapter 3 as part of the explanation of demand.

Knowledge check 6.4

What will be the value of the *YED* if a 5% increase in consumer income leads to a 10% fall in quantity demanded?

Elasticity is a measure of the sensitivity of a variable to changes in another variable. In the same way as the price elasticity of demand is determined, an elasticity measure can be calculated for any other influence on demand or supply. **Income elasticity of demand (*YED*)** is therefore defined as:

$$YED = \frac{\% \text{ change in quantity demanded}}{\% \text{ change in consumer income}}$$

The *YED* measures the extent to which the demand for a good or service will change in response to a change in consumer incomes. The size and direction of the change in demand will depend upon how consumers perceive the good or service.

Unlike the price elasticity of demand, the income elasticity of demand may be either positive or negative. Remember the distinction between normal and inferior goods? For normal goods the quantity demanded will increase as consumer income rises, whereas for inferior goods the quantity demanded will tend to fall as income rises. So, for normal goods the *YED* will be positive, whereas for inferior goods it will be negative.

Suppose you discover that the *YED* for an economics magazine is 0.7. How do you interpret this number? If consumer incomes were to increase by 10%, the demand for the economics magazine would increase by $10 \times 0.7 = 7\%$. This example of a normal good may be helpful information for the publishers, if they know that consumer incomes are rising over time.

On the other hand, if the *YED* for coach travel is −0.3, that means that a 10% increase in consumer incomes will lead to a 3% fall in the demand for coach travel — perhaps because more people are travelling by car. In this instance, coach travel would be regarded as an inferior good.

superior good one for which the income elasticity of demand is positive, and greater than 1, such that as income rises, consumers spend proportionally more on the good

In some cases the *YED* may be very strongly positive. For example, suppose that the *YED* for digital cameras is +2. This implies that the quantity demanded of such cameras will increase by 20% for every 10% increase in incomes. An increase in income is encouraging people to devote more of their incomes to this product, which increases its share in total expenditure. Such goods are referred to as **superior goods**. Table 6.3 summarises the ranges of the *YED*.

Table 6.3 Values of the *YED*

YED value	Description
Below −1	Elastic inferior good
Between −1 and 0	Inelastic inferior good
0	No relationship between income and quantity demanded
Between 0 and 1	Inelastic normal good
Above 1	Elastic normal good — also known as a superior good

Exercise 6.2

Calculate the income elasticity of demand in each of the following circumstances. In each case, assume that consumer income rises by 5%:
a quantity demanded changes from 150 to 165
b quantity demanded changes from 80 to 78
c quantity demanded changes from 100 to 102
d quantity demanded changes from 400 to 320
e quantity demanded stays at 600

Cross elasticity of demand (*XED*)

cross elasticity of demand (*XED*) a measure of the sensitivity of quantity demanded of a good or service to a change in the price of some other good or service

Another useful measure is the **cross elasticity of demand (*XED*)**. This is helpful in revealing the interrelationships between goods. Again, this measure may be either positive or negative, depending on the relationship between the goods. It is defined as:

$$XED = \frac{\% \text{ change in quantity demanded of good X}}{\% \text{ change in price of good Y}}$$

If the *XED* is seen to be positive, it means that an increase in the price of good Y leads to an increase in the quantity demanded of good X. For example, an increase in the price of apples may lead to an increase in the demand for pears. Here apples and pears are regarded as substitutes for each other — if one becomes relatively more expensive, consumers will switch to the other. A high value for the *XED* indicates that two goods are very close substitutes. This information may be useful in helping a firm to identify its close competitors.

On the other hand, if an increase in the price of one good leads to a fall in the quantity demanded of another good, this suggests that they are likely to be complements. The *XED* in this case will be negative. An example of such a relationship would be that between coffee and sugar, which tend to be consumed together. If the *XED* were seen to be zero, this would indicate that the goods concerned were unrelated — neither substitutes nor complements.

Table 6.4 summarises the *XED* values.

Table 6.4 Values of the *XED*

XED value	Description
Below −1	Strong complement
Between −1 and 0	Weak complement
0	No relationship between the two goods
Between 0 and 1	Weak substitute
Above 1	Strong substitute

Extension material

The *XED* and the real world

Does this notion of the cross elasticity of demand have any relevance in the real world? One part of government policy that you will meet later in your study of economics is competition policy. The Competition and Markets Authority has the responsibility of safeguarding consumer interests by ensuring that firms do not exploit excessive market power. An important part of its investigations entails an evaluation of whether firms face competition in their markets. The cross elasticity of demand can reveal whether or not two products are regarded as substitutes for each other. If they are shown to be, then this implies that the firms do face competition. This is an important application of this concept, as it can affect the judgement of whether a firm is in a position to exploit its market position.

Examples

Knowledge check 6.5

If the *XED* between two goods is negative, would this suggest that the goods are substitutes or complements?

A study by the Institute for Fiscal Studies using data for the UK estimated that the cross elasticity of demand for wine with respect to a change in the price of beer was −0.60, whereas the cross elasticity with respect to the price of spirits was +0.77. These estimates are not precise and are subject to a ceteris paribus assumption, but they give us some feel for the real world. The negative cross elasticity with beer suggests that wine and beer are complements: a 10% increase in the price of beer would lead to a 6% fall in the quantity demanded of wine. In contrast, the cross elasticity of demand for wine with respect to the price of spirits is positive, suggesting that wine and spirits are substitutes. An increase in the price of spirits leads to an increase in the quantity demanded of wine.

Exercise 6.3

Calculate the cross elasticity of demand in each of the following circumstances. In each case, assume that the price of another good rises by 15%:
a quantity demanded changes from 200 to 260
b quantity demanded changes from 400 to 310
c quantity demanded changes from 500 to 560
d quantity demanded changes from 50 to 47
e quantity demanded stays at 300

Price elasticity of supply (PES)

As elasticity is a measure of sensitivity, its use need not be confined
to influences on demand, but it can also be turned to evaluating the
sensitivity of quantity *supplied* to a change in its determinants — in
particular, price.

It was argued in Chapter 4 that the supply curve is likely to be upward
sloping, so the price elasticity of supply can be expected to be positive.
In other words, an increase in the market price will induce firms to supply
more output to the market. The **price elasticity of supply (PES)** is
defined as:

$$PES = \frac{\% \text{ change in the quantity supplied}}{\% \text{ change in price}}$$

So, if the price elasticity of supply is 0.8, an increase in price of 10%
will encourage firms to supply 8% more. As with the price elasticity of
demand, if the elasticity is greater than 1, supply is referred to as being
elastic, whereas if the value is between 0 and 1, supply is considered
inelastic. *Unit elasticity* occurs when the price elasticity of supply is
exactly 1, so that a 10% increase in price induces a 10% increase in
quantity supplied.

The value of the elasticity will depend on how willing and able firms
are to increase their supply. For example, if firms are operating close to
the capacity of their existing plant and machinery, they may be unable
to respond to an increase in price, at least in the short run. So here
again, supply can be expected to be more elastic in the long run than in
the short run. Figure 6.6 illustrates this. In the short run, firms may be
able to respond to an increase in price only in a limited way, so supply
may be relatively inelastic, as shown by S_s in the figure. However, firms
can become more flexible in the long run by installing new machinery
or building new factories, so supply can then become more elastic,
moving to S_l.

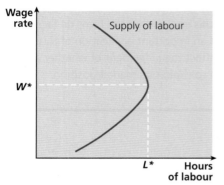

Figure 6.6 Short- and long-run supply

There are two limiting cases of supply elasticity. For some reason,
supply may be fixed such that, no matter how much price increases,
firms will not be able to supply any more. For example, it could be that
a certain amount of fish is available in a market, and however high the
price goes, no more can be obtained. Equally, if the fishermen know that
the fish they do not sell today cannot be stored for another day, they
have an incentive to sell, however low the price goes. In these cases, there
is **perfectly inelastic supply**. At the other extreme is **perfectly elastic
supply**, where firms would be prepared to supply any amount of the good
at the going price.

These two possibilities are shown in Figure 6.7. Here S_i represents a
perfectly inelastic supply curve: firms will supply Q_i whatever the price,

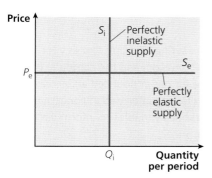

Figure 6.7 Perfectly elastic and inelastic supply

perhaps because that is the amount available for sale. Supply here is vertical. At the opposite extreme, if supply is perfectly elastic then firms are prepared to supply any amount at the price P_e, and the supply curve is given by the horizontal line S_e.

Exercise 6.4

Calculate the price elasticity of supply in each of the following circumstances. In each case, assume that the price of the good rises by 20%.
a Quantity supplied changes from 500 to 800.
b Quantity supplied changes from 200 to 220.
c Quantity supplied stays at 750.

The usefulness and significance of elasticities

Synoptic link

The way in which firms in a market may react to each other's actions is discussed in Chapter 15.

The various elasticity measures can be useful to firms and to the government as part of their decision making. For example, suppose you are responsible for choosing the price to charge for a product sold by your firm. The *PED* will be informative about how buyers of the good are likely to respond to a price change. If you know they will be sensitive to a price increase, you might hesitate about raising price because this would affect revenues.

The significance of the *PED* turns partly on the difficulty of obtaining an estimate of it. This is beyond the means of even a medium-sized firm. It may be that in some industries the market *PED* is known (although a Google search does not reveal many of these). For the firm wanting to change its price, the market elasticity may not be meaningful anyway, as much will depend upon the actions of other firms in the market.

This does not mean that firms do not have a sense of how consumers will react to a change in the price of their product, which may be helpful in setting price.

The *YED* will help to forecast changing demand if real incomes are increasing, or if the economy is heading into a recession. Knowing whether a good is normal or inferior is significant in this situation.

The *XED* helps in anticipating changes in demand if the prices of other products are changing. A firm needs to know who its competitors are when devising its own strategy, so it may be important to be aware of whether another firm's products are close substitutes, or whether they are complements. Knowing the *PES* of rival firms would be useful, but estimating a precise value is not easy.

From the government perspective, imposing an indirect tax will raise the price and lead to a fall in demand, so knowing the *PED* helps to forecast the tax revenues expected. This is explored in Chapter 10. Introducing a subsidy would reduce the selling price of a good, and knowing the *PED* allows the government to assess the impact of such a move.

It may not always be straightforward to obtain estimates of the various elasticities. However, if economic agents know about the factors that influence the elasticities and if they understand their significance, they may be able to take better decisions.

Summary

- The income elasticity of demand (*YED*) measures the sensitivity of quantity demanded to a change in consumer incomes. It serves to distinguish between normal, luxury and inferior goods.
- The cross elasticity of demand (*XED*) measures the sensitivity of the quantity demanded of one good or service to a change in the price of some other good or service. It can serve to distinguish between substitutes and complements.
- The price elasticity of supply (*PES*) measures the sensitivity of the quantity supplied to a change in the price of a good or service. The price elasticity of supply can be expected to be greater in the long run than in the short run, as firms have more flexibility to adjust their production decisions in the long run.

Case study 6.1

Rice

In 2007–08, food prices hit the headlines. There were riots on the streets of cities in many countries around the world, with protestors demonstrating against massive increases in the prices of some staple foods, especially wheat and rice.

The increases affected some countries especially severely. In much of Southeast Asia, rice is a staple commodity, forming a part of most people's daily diet. For some countries, such as the Philippines, much of the rice consumed has to be imported, so the price rises caused particular difficulties. The demonstrators wanted governments to intervene to control the prices and protect the poor.

It was reported that in some countries, poor households were coping with the price rises by changing their eating habits, by consuming less meat, or by finding other ways of cutting down. The United Nations called for worldwide action to prevent hunger and malnutrition from spreading.

Case study 6.1 (continued)

People in Southeast Asia were severely affected by the rise in the price of rice in 2007–08

Follow-up questions
a Would you expect the demand for rice to be price elastic or inelastic?
b Explain your answer to part (a), referring to the passage to provide evidence to support your explanation.
c Do you think that government intervention to control prices would be an effective answer to the problem?

Case study 6.2

Bicycles

If you had visited Shanghai in the early 1990s, one thing that would have struck you is that the roads were dominated by bicycles. Cars were relatively few in number, and in busy streets in the city centre, cars had to thread their way through the mass of bicycles.

Now, things are different. True, there are still many more bicycles on the streets than you would find in the UK but they have their own part of the road. This still causes mayhem at junctions, when cars need to turn across the cycle tracks, but things are more orderly. The number of cars has increased significantly.

Since the early 1990s, China's economy has gone through a period of rapid economic growth and transformation. As part of this process, real incomes have risen and many households have become much better off, especially in the urban areas where much of the change has been concentrated.

Case study 6.2 (continued)

Follow-up questions

a What reasons might help to explain the change in the pattern of traffic between cars and bicycles in China over the period described in the passage?

b What would you expect to be the nature of the income elasticity of demand for bicycles in China?

c What would you expect to be the nature of the income elasticity of demand for cars in China?

Case study 6.3

Fish

Imagine a remote island in the South Seas. Some of the islanders own canoes, which they use to go fishing, selling their catch on the beach when they return each day. Some islanders only go fishing occasionally, as they find it more worthwhile to spend their time on other activities. The island has no electricity, so there is no way of storing the fish that are caught — if they are not consumed on the day of the catch, they must be thrown away.

The market for fish on the island is limited by the size of the population. Fortunately for the fishermen, the islanders enjoy fish and regard it as an important part of their diet, although they also grow vegetables and raise goats and chickens. Fruit and coconuts are also abundant.

Islanders sell their catch on the beach in Fiji

Follow-up questions

a What would you expect to be the nature of the price elasticity of supply in the short run (that is, on any given day)?

b Suppose that, on one particular day, fishing conditions are so good that all fishermen return with record catches. How would this affect the price of fish?

c How might the situation in (b) affect the supply of fish on the following day?

d How would you expect the supply of fish to be affected by the invention of a new style of canoe that makes it easier to catch fish?

e How would the market be affected if this new-style canoe also enabled fish to be traded with a neighbouring island?

CHAPTER 6 QUESTIONS

A Multiple-choice questions

1 Price elasticity of demand is:

  a The responsiveness of demand to a change in price
  b The responsiveness of supply to a change in price
  c The responsiveness of quantity demanded to a change in price
  d The responsiveness of quantity supplied to a change in price

2 If a firm increases price by 10% and the sales decrease by 50% then the price elasticity of demand will be:

  a −5
  b −0.2
  c 5
  d 0.2

3 A taxi firm has estimated that the income elasticity of demand for its service is +2.5. The service would be classed as:

  a An inelastic inferior service
  b An elastic inferior service
  c An inelastic normal service
  d A superior service

4 If the price elasticity of supply for a good is +0.1 then a 20% increase in the price of a product will lead to which effect on quantity supplied?

  a An increase in quantity supplied of 2%
  b A decrease in quantity supplied of 2%
  c An increase in quantity supplied of 200%
  d A decrease in quantity supplied of 200%

B Knowledge and understanding questions

5 Calculate the price elasticity of demand if a business decreases its price from £5 to £4 and sees an increase in sales from 400 units to 500 units. [2 marks]

6 A shop has estimated the price elasticity of demand for chocolate bars to be −0.5. It currently sells 200 chocolate bars a week.

Calculate the **change** in weekly sales revenue if the firm increases the price of its products from £0.60 to £0.63 per chocolate bar. [4 marks]

7 Explain **two** factors that may affect the price elasticity of supply for a hairdresser. [4 marks]

C Stimulus response question

8 Most manufacturers of mobile phones bring out a new model each year. New phones often include new features, such as a better camera.

Most customers only purchase one mobile phone and must make a choice between the different manufacturers' products. Table 1 shows some market research data about the cross elasticity of demand for two mobile phones.

Table 1 Cross elasticity of demand for the Banana and Nova mobile phones

Sales of Banana mobile phone	Price of the Nova mobile phone
100,000	£900
80,000	£800
60,000	£700
40,000	£600

a Explain what is meant by 'cross elasticity of demand'. [2 marks]

b Calculate the estimated cross elasticity of demand for the Banana mobile phone if the price of the Nova mobile phone is reduced from £800 to £600 in a sales promotion. [2 marks]

c Nova has launched a new contract service for its mobile phone. It estimates that the cross elasticity of demand between the price of the contract and the quantity demanded of the phone is −2. Explain what this estimate may mean for Nova. [2 marks]

D Essay question

9 Holidays overseas are often considered to be a luxury purchase.

Evaluate the extent to which a fall in income will always lead to lower sales of holidays overseas. [20 marks]

Chapter 7

Prices, resource allocation and concept of the margin

Now that you are familiar with the use of the demand and supply model, it is time to take a wider view of the process of resource allocation within society. An important question is whether markets can be relied upon to guide this process, or whether there are times when markets will fail. This chapter begins to address this by examining how prices can act as market signals to guide resource allocation, and by identifying circumstances in which this process may not work effectively. In this discussion, some new tools will be needed in order to identify what constitutes an efficient allocation of resources. The chapter begins by introducing an important idea in economics — that economic agents take decisions at the margin.

> ## Learning objectives
>
> After studying this chapter, you should be able to:
> - explain the concept of the margin
> - explain total and marginal utility
> - explain diminishing marginal utility and the demand curve
> - explain and calculate marginal values
> - explain economic efficiency, both productive and allocative efficiency

The concept of the margin

Decisions, decisions...

How will you spend your evening? You have to read the chapter in your economics textbook that has been set for you, but there is a TV programme about to start that you'd quite like to watch. Will the extra benefit that you gain from watching the TV programme compensate for the cost of not reading your chapter (or having to get up early tomorrow to read it)?

A firm finds that it is falling behind on its orders. Should it take on an extra worker to enable it to catch up? Would the additional benefit that the firm would gain by keeping its customers happy compensate for the extra wage costs incurred?

One of the first economic ideas that you met at the beginning of your study of economics was the notion of *opportunity cost*. This captures the idea that when you take a decision or make a choice, you will choose on the basis of comparing the benefit you gain from a choice with the benefit from the next best alternative choice. The two examples of decisions above illustrate this notion. If you choose to watch the TV programme, you incur an opportunity cost in terms of the cost of not reading your chapter. If the firm chooses not to hire the additional worker, it incurs an opportunity cost, by keeping its customers waiting and potentially losing orders.

Synoptic link

The concept of opportunity cost was introduced in Chapter 1, and is one of the most important ideas in economics.

The marginal principle

The decisions also illustrate another important notion in economics, as in both cases the decision is taken on the basis of balancing two alternatives against each other by weighing up small changes. Economists rely heavily on the idea that firms, consumers and other economic agents can make good decisions by thinking in terms of the margin. This is known as the **marginal principle**.

You will meet this approach to decision making in a variety of situations as you study economics.

At the heart of much of economic analysis is the notion that economic agents have clear objectives, and that they take decisions that allow them to do the best they can to achieve those objectives. For example, to analyse the decisions taken by firms, it is often assumed that they set out to maximise profits. By taking decisions on the basis of small (marginal) changes, they can fine-tune their decisions and home in on the best possible position. By assuming this, economists are able to model the decisions and analyse the consequences.

Imagine you are deciding what to have for lunch. You choose a sandwich with a price of £2 because you believe that you will get at least £2 worth of benefit from it. You add on a packet of crisps with a price of £0.80, again believing you will get at least £0.80 worth of benefit from it. You see a can of drink priced at £0.90 and choose not to buy it because you don't think it will be worth it. However, the shop has a 'meal deal' offer, which means that you can have all three items for £3. Now you only need to gain £0.20 worth of benefit from the can to make it worthwhile to purchase. So, you choose to buy the meal deal. In this scenario you are using the concept of the margin to make your purchasing decision and the shop is using the concept to persuade you to buy all three.

This approach is based on the assumption that economic agents are **rational**, in the sense that they always do what they expect to bring the best possible results. By balancing the marginal benefit against the marginal cost of an action, they can achieve this. In other words, if the marginal benefit of a particular choice exceeds its marginal cost, then a rational agent would choose to proceed, but if the marginal benefit is less than marginal cost, it would be better not to proceed. The cusp decision is where marginal benefit equals marginal cost, in which situation there is no incentive to change the decision.

The marginal principle is therefore seen to be important for the construction of economic models, and important for economic decision-makers in enabling them to take rational decisions. However, it also highlights an important criticism that has been levelled at economists and at economics, and that is the assumption that economic agents behave rationally. Do firms always act to maximise profits? Do consumers never take decisions on impulse or make choices that are not in their own best interests? It is important to be aware of these issues.

Summary

- Opportunity cost is an important element in making choices.
- Decisions are often taken by considering small changes to existing behaviour.
- This approach to decision making is known as the use of the marginal principle.
- The marginal principle underpins the notion of rational decision making.
- The assumption of rationality enables economists to model the behaviour of economic agents.
- There may be circumstances in which decisions do not reflect this rational approach.

Marginal utility theory

Key terms

utility the satisfaction received from consuming a good or service

marginal utility the additional utility gained from consuming an extra unit of a good or service

Table 7.1 Utility from chocolate

Number of bars	Marginal utility (utils)	Total utility (utils)
1	30	30
2	26	56
3	21	77
4	15	92
5	8	100
6	0	100

Key term

law of diminishing marginal utility states that the more units of a good that are consumed, the lower the utility from consuming those additional units

Suppose you could measure the satisfaction that you derive from consuming a good. For example, consider the case of chocolate bars. Consuming a chocolate bar gives you a certain amount of satisfaction — which economists often refer to as **utility** in this context. Imagine that it is possible to put a numerical value on this utility, and for the sake of argument that the utility you get from consuming a chocolate bar is 30 'utils', this being the unit in which utility is measured.

Having consumed the chocolate bar, you are now offered a second, which you also consume, this time receiving 26 utils of utility. You probably get less utility from the second bar simply because you have already had some chocolate — and the more chocolate bars you eat, the less utility you are likely to get from the additional bar. Notice here that the valuation of the utility refers to the additional satisfaction that is gained from the second bar. This is therefore known as the **marginal utility** from consuming an additional chocolate bar. Indeed, there will come a time when you have eaten so much chocolate that you cannot face eating any more, as you know you would be ill. Table 7.1 shows the marginal utility that Emily gains from consuming chocolate bars.

In this example, the sixth chocolate bar gives no satisfaction to Emily, who has already had enough chocolate for the day.

The final column of the table shows the total utility that Emily gains from chocolate as she consumes more of it.

This idea that the more of a good you consume, the less additional pleasure you get from the extra unit of it is known as the **law of diminishing marginal utility**. It is a 'law' because it has been found to be universally true. If you keep consuming more of something, you get less additional satisfaction from extra units. The left-hand panel of Figure 7.1 plots the marginal utility values. The law of diminishing marginal utility ensures that the *MU* curve is downward sloping. You can see how the curve becomes steeper the more chocolate bars are consumed. In the right-hand panel, you can see the way in which total utility flattens out as more bars of chocolate are eaten.

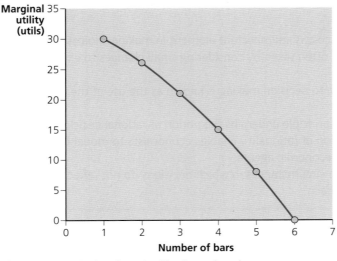
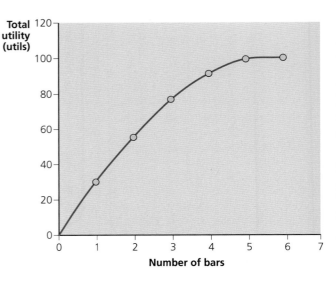

Figure 7.1 Marginal and total utility from chocolate

Knowledge check 7.3

How quickly would the marginal utility curve drop away if the product concerned was haircuts?

If it were really possible to measure satisfaction in this way, it would also be possible to calculate the total utility that Emily receives from consuming chocolate bars. For instance, if she consumes two bars, she gets 30 + 26 = 56 utils. If she has a third bar, her *total utility* will be 77 utils.

The relationship between 'total' and 'marginal' appears in many areas of economic analysis, and it is good to be clear about it. The 'marginal' value is calculated as the change in the 'total'.

Study tip

The relationship between the 'total' and the 'marginal' is not confined to this particular example of utility. It will also apply in the case of the costs faced by firms and the revenue that they receive from selling their products, and in many other contexts. It is a purely mathematical relationship, and you should watch out for it.

Marginal utility and demand

One way of interpreting the marginal utility that you receive from consuming a good is that it informs your willingness to pay for it. The higher your marginal utility, the higher the price you would be prepared to pay. So, if marginal utility were measured in terms of money, then the *MU* curve would become a person's demand curve. Consider Figure 7.2. The quantity of the good Q^* provides this individual with marginal utility of MU^*. If the price of the good were higher than MU^*, then the individual would not buy Q^* of the good, as the price exceeds his valuation. On the other hand, if price were to be set lower than MU^*, then the individual would be prepared to buy more than Q^*, as the marginal utility would be higher than the asking price. Another way of putting this is to say that the consumer will purchase the good up to the point where the price is equal to the marginal utility gained from consuming the good. Of course, a similar argument applies at each point along the *MU* curve, so this is indeed the individual's demand curve if utility could be measured in money terms.

Knowledge check 7.4

What would happen to the *MU* curve for a normal good if consumer incomes increased?

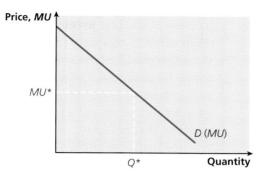

Figure 7.2 An individual's demand curve

The previous discussion of the demand curve emphasised that the curve shows the relationship between the quantity demanded of a good and its price, ceteris paribus. In other words, it focused on the relationship between demand and price holding other influences on demand constant. This argument also applies in this case. Changes in the price of other goods, in consumer incomes or in preferences would all affect the position of the *D* (*MU*) curve.

This highlights the fact that decisions about the consumption of one good are interconnected with decisions being made about other goods. If a consumer chooses to consume more of one good, that means there is less income available to be spent on other goods. Furthermore, a decision to consume more of one good will affect the consumption of complementary and substitute goods. So rather than focusing on a consumer's decisions about the demand for a single good, it is also necessary to consider the demand for a bundle of goods and services, and how a consumer can arrive at a joint decision.

Extension material

Do consumers always act rationally?

Marginal utility theory rests on the crucial assumption that consumers act rationally in taking decisions about their spending and consumption by setting out to maximise their utility. Recent advances in behavioural economics suggest that this is not always the case.

This branch of economic analysis recognises that the psychology of human decision making is more complex than the simple desire to maximise utility. People do not always focus on purely economic influences, but may act on impulse, or in response to their feelings. This can lead them to take decisions about their spending that cannot be explained only by utility maximisation. For example, they may make charitable donations or may purchase more of some goods than would be dictated by rational economic behaviour, perhaps because there were seen to be special offers available.

Increasingly, behavioural economists are using experimental situations to discover more about how people react in situations of risk and how their spending behaviour is influenced by impulse and in response to stimuli. This analysis is potentially valuable to firms: if they can understand what induces people to behave in certain ways, they may be able to influence their spending.

Discussion point
To what extent do you think charitable donations can be explained by marginal utility theory?

The allocation of resources

As Chapter 1 indicated, all societies face the fundamental economic problem of scarcity. Because there are unlimited wants but finite resources, it is necessary to take decisions on which goods and services should be produced, how they should be produced and for whom they should be produced. For an economy the size of the UK, there is therefore an immense coordination problem. Another way of looking at this is to ask how consumers can express their preferences between alternative goods so that producers can produce the best mix of goods and services. In a free market economy, prices play the key role — this is sometimes referred to as the laissez-faire approach to resource allocation.

Prices and preferences

How can consumers signal their preferences to producers? Demand and supply analysis provides the clue. Chapter 3 used the demand curve for smartphones to introduce the notion of consumer surplus, arguing that for a consumer choosing to buy a smartphone at the going price (but no higher), the price represented the willingness to pay for a smartphone. Another way of interpreting this is to say that this represents the marginal benefit that the consumer receives from a smartphone.

If we remember that the demand curve shows the willingness to pay for a smartphone at different prices, we can interpret the demand curve as showing the marginal benefit that society as a whole gains from consuming smartphones at different prices. We refer to this as the marginal social benefit (MSB) of consuming the good.

Figure 7.3 shows the demand and supply for a good for which there has been a rightward shift in the demand curve — in the figure, from D_0 to D_1. This simply means that consumers are placing a higher value on these goods — they are prepared to demand more at any given price. The result is that the market will move to a new equilibrium, with price rising from P_0 to P_1 and quantity traded from Q_0 to Q_1: there is an extension of supply (a movement along the supply curve).

Synoptic link

You can find the discussion of consumer surplus on pages 38–39.

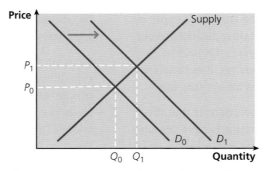

Figure 7.3 An increase in demand for a good

The shift in the demand curve is an expression of consumers' preferences; it embodies the fact that they value the good more highly now than before. The price that consumers are willing to pay represents their valuation of it.

Prices as signals and incentives

From the producers' perspective, the question is how they receive signals from consumers about their changing preferences. Price is the key. Figure 7.3 shows how an increase in demand leads to an increase in the equilibrium market price. The shift in the demand curve leads to an increase in the equilibrium price, which encourages producers to supply more of the good — there is an extension of supply. This is really saying that producers find it profitable to expand their output of the good at that higher price. The price level is therefore a signal to producers about consumer preferences.

Notice that the **price signal** works equally well when there is a *decrease* in the demand for a good or service. In Figure 7.4, for example, there has been a large fall in the demand for a good, so the demand curve has shifted to the left from D_0 to D_1 — consumers are demanding fewer of the good at any price. Producers of the good are beginning to find that they cannot sell as many at the original price, so they have to reduce their price to avoid an increase in their unsold stocks. They have less incentive to produce the good and will supply less. There is a contraction of supply and a movement along the supply curve to a lower equilibrium price at P_1, and a lower quantity traded at Q_1.

So, you can see how existing producers in a market receive signals from consumers in the form of changes in the equilibrium price, and respond to these signals by adjusting their output levels.

Firms receive signals from consumers about changing preferences but prices may also act as a rationing device if firms are unable to supply the goods that consumers want to buy. For example, suppose there is a poor coffee harvest due to bad weather conditions in Brazil. The equilibrium price will rise, and consumers will find themselves rationed.

In the long run, if firms in a market are seen to be enjoying producer surplus (that is, they are making high profits), this may attract other firms to enter the market (if they can), which would be seen as an increase in supply at the market level, so that price would fall until there was no further incentive for firms to join the market.

Summary

- If market forces are to allocate resources effectively, consumers need to be able to express their preferences for goods and services in such a way that producers can respond.
- Consumers express their preferences through prices, as prices will adjust to equilibrium levels following a change in consumer demand.
- Producers have an incentive to respond to changes in prices. In the short run this occurs through output adjustments of existing firms (movements along the supply curve), but in the long run firms will enter the market (or exit from it) until there are no further incentives for entry or exit.

Key term

price signal where the price of a good carries information to producers or consumers that guides the market towards equilibrium and assists in resource allocation

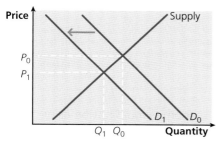

Figure 7.4 A decrease in demand

Knowledge check 7.5

What would happen to the equilibrium price if there were a good harvest, creating a glut?

Synoptic link

Chapter 13 returns to explain the long-run market equilibrium as part of the discussion of perfect competition.

Aspects of efficiency

In tackling the fundamental economic problem of scarcity, a society needs to find a way of using its limited resources as effectively as possible. In everyday language it might be natural to refer to this as a quest for *efficiency*. From an economist's point of view there are two key aspects of efficiency, both of which are important in evaluating whether markets in an economy are working effectively.

Consider these aspects in relation to the production possibility curve (*PPC*). Figure 7.5 shows a country's production possibility curve. One of the choices to be made in allocating resources in this country is between producing agricultural or manufactured goods.

Synoptic link

The production possibility curve was explained in Chapter 1.

Knowledge check 7.6

Why is it difficult to judge whether society is better of at *B* than *C* in Figure 7.5?

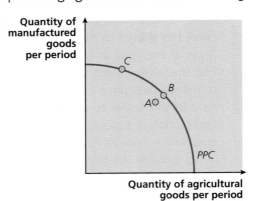

Figure 7.5 Productive efficiency

At a production point such as *A* the economy would not be using its resources fully, since by moving to a point *on* the *PPC* it would be possible to produce more of both types of good. For example, if production took place at point *B*, then more of both agricultural and manufactured goods could be produced, so that society would be better off than at *A*.

A similar claim could be made for any point along the *PPC*: it is more efficient to be at a point *on* the frontier than at some point *within* it. However, if you compare point *B* with point *C*, you will notice that the economy produces more manufactured goods at *C* than at *B* — but only at the expense of producing fewer agricultural goods.

This draws attention to the trade-off between the production of the two sorts of goods. It is difficult to judge whether society is better off at *B* or at *C* without knowing more about the preferences of consumers.

This discussion highlights the two aspects of efficiency. On the one hand, there is the question of whether or not society is operating on the *PPC*, and therefore using its resources effectively. On the other hand, there is the question of whether or not society is producing the balance of goods that consumers wish to consume. These two aspects of efficiency are known as productive efficiency and **allocative efficiency**. The term **economic efficiency** is used to describe a situation in which both productive and allocative efficiency has been achieved — in other words, a situation in which society is producing the balance of goods that consumers wish to consume at minimum cost.

Key terms

allocative efficiency achieved when society is producing the appropriate bundle of goods and services relative to consumer preferences — this occurs when price equals marginal cost

economic efficiency a situation in which both productive efficiency and allocative efficiency have been reached

Synoptic link

The costs faced by firms in the production process are explained and discussed in Chapter 11, which helps to identify points of productive efficiency.

Study tip

The idea that allocative efficiency is achieved when price is equal to marginal cost is really important, and you will come across it in many different contexts. Make sure that you understand and remember it — and are ready to use it.

Knowledge check 7.7

What are the two key aspects of efficiency?

Productive efficiency

Productive efficiency for a firm is attained when it is operating at minimum cost, choosing an appropriate combination of inputs and producing the maximum output possible from those inputs. Points on the *PPC* represent points of productive efficiency.

Allocative efficiency

Allocative efficiency is about whether an economy allocates its resources in such a way as to produce a balance of goods and services that matches consumer preferences. In a complex modern economy, it is clearly difficult to identify such an ideal result. How can an appropriate balance of goods and services be identified?

It was argued in the previous section that in the long run the market could be expected to arrive at an equilibrium price and quantity at which there was no incentive for firms either to enter the market or to exit from it.

Think about that price from the point of view of a firm. The equilibrium price is at a level where there is no further incentive to attract new firms, but no firm wishes to leave the market. In other words, no surplus is being made on that marginal unit, and the marginal firm is just breaking even on it. The price in this context would seem to be just covering the marginal cost of production (the cost of producing the last unit of output).

However, it has also been argued that from the consumers' point of view, any point along the demand curve could be regarded as the marginal benefit received from consuming a good or service.

Where is all this leading? Putting together the arguments, it would seem that market forces can carry a market to a position in which, from the firms' point of view, the price is equal to marginal cost, and from the consumers' point of view, the price is equal to marginal benefit.

This is an important result. Suppose that the marginal benefit from consuming a good were higher than the marginal cost to society of producing it. It could then be argued that society would be better off producing more of the good because, by increasing production, more could be added to benefits than to costs. Equally, if the marginal cost were above the marginal benefit from consuming a good, society would be producing too much of the good and would benefit from producing less. The best possible position is therefore where marginal benefit is equal to marginal cost — in other words, where *price is set equal to marginal cost*.

If all markets in an economy operated in this way, resources would be used so effectively that no reallocation of resources could generate an overall improvement. Allocative efficiency would be attained. The key question is whether the market mechanism will work sufficiently well to ensure that this happens — or whether it will fail. In other words, are there conditions that could arise in a market, in which price would not be set at marginal cost? This will be explored in the next two chapters.

Economic efficiency and society

If a society could reach a position of economic efficiency — that is, achieving both productive and allocative efficiency — would that always be the ideal position? After all, allocative efficiency is about producing the appropriate balance of goods and services that consumers wish to produce, and productive efficiency is about whether those goods and services are being produced at minimum cost. However, a third question remains: *for whom* are these goods and services being produced? In other words, there may also be issues surrounding *equity*.

A society could find itself in a position in which it had achieved economic efficiency, but where the resources in society were heavily concentrated in the hands of a relatively small part of the population, with other groups being excluded and living in poverty. In such a situation the authorities may see the need for resources to be redistributed in order to protect the vulnerable. It is important to remember this, as it suggests that economic efficiency is not the *only* objective of a society. Furthermore, it will be seen that there are many situations in which a free market will fail to achieve economic efficiency.

The government's role

The government's role in a totally free economy is relatively limited, but nonetheless important. A basic framework of *property rights* is essential, together with a basic legal framework. However, the state does not intervene in the production process directly. Secure property rights are significant, as this assures the incentives for the owners of capital.

Within such a system, consumers try to maximise the satisfaction (utility) they gain from consuming a range of products, and firms seek to maximise their profits by responding to consumer demand through the medium of price signals.

It is worth noting that Adam Smith also sounded a word of warning. He felt that there were too many factors that interfered with the free market system, such as over-protectionism and restrictions on trade. At the same time, he was not utterly convinced that a free market economy would be wholly effective, noting also that firms might at times collude to prevent the free operation of the market mechanism:

> People of the same trade seldom meet together, even for merriment and diversion, but the conversation ends in a conspiracy against the public, or in some contrivance to raise prices...

Source: Adam Smith, *The Wealth of Nations*, Vol. I (1796)

So there may be situations in which consumer interests need to be protected, if there is some sort of market failure that prevents the best outcome from being achieved.

Synoptic link

This goes back to Adam Smith's notion of the invisible hand, which was introduced in Chapter 1.

Synoptic link

Types of market failure will be explored in Chapters 8 and 9.

Exercise 7.2

Consider Figure 7.6, which shows a production possibility curve (*PPC*) for an economy that produces consumer goods and investment goods.

Identify each of the following (*Hint*: in some cases more than one answer is possible):

a a point of productive inefficiency
b a point of productive efficiency
c a point of allocative efficiency
d an unattainable point (*Hint*: think about what would need to happen for society to reach such a point)

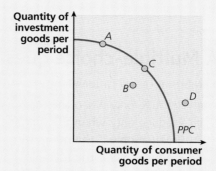

Figure 7.6 A production possibility curve

Summary

- A society needs to find a way of using its limited resources as efficiently as possible.
- Productive efficiency occurs when firms have chosen appropriate combinations of factors of production and produce the maximum output possible from those inputs.
- Allocative efficiency occurs when firms produce an appropriate bundle of goods and services, given consumer preferences.
- An individual market exhibits aspects of allocative efficiency when the marginal benefit received by society from consuming a good or service matches the marginal cost of producing it — that is, when price is equal to marginal cost.
- A society may also need to consider the distribution of resources in society, balancing equity with efficiency.

Case study 7.1

Jewellery

A local craft market is populated by a variety of stalls selling a range of items — antiques, football memorabilia, second-hand books, hand-made jewellery and other items. The same sellers are present at the market every time it opens, each with their regular place, but there are some vacant stalls. The stall holders just make enough profit to make it worth their while.

One week, the craft market is featured in the local newspaper, and an item appears on local television highlighting the quality of design and value for money of the jewellery on sale at the market. The jewellery sellers suddenly find that their stock is moving very rapidly, and

New jewellery stalls have come into the market

realise that they can increase their prices. As word gets around, some of the vacant stalls are taken up by new jewellery makers and, although the number of buyers remains high, prices drift back to their original level.

Follow-up question

Sketch a demand and supply diagram to track these changes in the market for jewellery.

A Multiple-choice questions

1 A business will rationally:

  a Produce only when the marginal cost is higher than the marginal benefit
  b Produce only when the marginal benefit is higher than the marginal cost
  c Produce only if the marginal cost is equal to the marginal benefit
  d Produce only if the marginal cost is lower than or equal to the marginal benefit

2 Which of the following statements best explains the law of diminishing marginal utility?

  a A person gains no total utility as they consume more units
  b A person gains marginal utility from every additional unit consumed
  c A person gains less total utility as they consume more units
  d A person gains less marginal utility from each additional unit consumed

3 What is the relationship between marginal utility and demand?

  a When measured in terms of money, demand and marginal utility are the same thing
  b When measured in terms of money, demand and marginal utility have an inverse relationship
  c Marginal utility is the same as the quantity demanded
  d There is no relationship between demand and marginal utility

4 Economic efficiency exists when:

  a A market is productively efficient but not allocatively efficient
  b A market is both allocatively and productively efficient
  c A market is allocatively efficient but not productively efficient
  d A market is neither productively nor allocatively efficient

5 Allocative efficiency exists when:

  a A firm produces at a minimum cost
  b A consumer pays the minimum price
  c Price equals marginal cost
  d Producers gain the maximum price

B Knowledge and understanding questions

6 Explain, using an example, the concept of the margin. [2 marks]

7 Explain what is meant by 'productive efficiency'. [2 marks]

C Stimulus response question

8 Sandy owns a buffet restaurant called The Buffet Bar. The restaurant is one that services a growing trend for unlimited food at a set price. Customers pay £13 and can then eat as much as they want within a two-hour time period.

When Sandy opened the restaurant, she was worried that customers would eat so much food that she would make a loss. However, it was clear that the marginal utility each customer gained from eating additional plates of food reduced significantly the more they ate. Table 1 illustrates this relationship.

Table 1 Marginal utility at The Buffet Bar

Number of plates of food	Total utility gained	Marginal cost per plate of food
1	6 utils	£2.50
2	12 utils	£2.50
3	17 utils	£2.50
4	20 utils	£2.50
5	21 utils	£2.50
6	15 utils	£2.50

a Refer to Table 1. Calculate the marginal utility gained by eating the fourth plate of food. [2 marks]

b Explain why the total utility may decrease when consuming the sixth plate of food. [2 marks]

c Explain, with reference to Table 1, how Sandy may have set the price per customer in her restaurant. [2 marks]

d Explain two factors that could lead Sandy to increase the price per customer in her restaurant. [4 marks]

Chapter 8

Market failure and externalities

Will markets always allocate resources effectively to meet the needs of society? Unfortunately not. There are circumstances in which markets fail, and these are the subject of this chapter and the next. If markets are to be effective in guiding the allocation of resources in society, a precondition is that market prices reflect the full costs and benefits associated with market transactions. However, there are many situations in which this is not so, and there are costs or benefits that are external to the workings of the market mechanism. This chapter examines the circumstances in which this may happen, and provides a justification for government intervention to improve the workings of the market.

> ## Learning objectives
> After studying this chapter, you should be able to:
> - explain market failure
> - explain marginal social cost, marginal external cost, marginal private cost, marginal social benefit, marginal external benefit and marginal private benefit
> - explain, with the aid of a diagram, positive and negative externalities (external benefits and external costs) in consumption and production

Market failure

Key terms

market failure a situation in which the free market equilibrium does not lead to a socially optimal allocation of resources, such that too much or too little of a good is being produced and/or consumed

marginal social benefit (MSB) the additional benefit that society gains from consuming an extra unit of a good

marginal social cost (MSC) the cost to society of producing an extra unit of a good

A key question in microeconomics is whether markets will work in such a way as to produce a good outcome for society as a whole. Market failure occurs when this is not the case. When we look at how markets do work, it turns out that there are significant situations in which markets do not produce the best outcome for society. This chapter introduces the most important reasons why such **market failure** occurs and examines one common form (externalities) in detail.

An ideal outcome for society would be where the marginal benefit that society receives from consuming each good or service matches the marginal cost of producing it. If the actual amount is larger or smaller than this, the society could be made better off. Notice that when we talk about marginal benefit and marginal cost here, it is the marginal benefit and cost to society that is relevant. We will refer to these as **marginal social benefit (MSB)** and **marginal social cost (MSC)**.

Externalities

Externalities are the main focus of this chapter, so we will explain these fully soon. In brief, if the costs that firms and consumers face and the prices to which they respond do not reflect the actual costs and benefits associated with the production and consumption of goods, then the market equilibrium will not represent the best outcome for society, even if demand seems to equal supply.

Suppose your elder sister is on a gap year before going to uni. She owns a car and is still living at home. You persuade her to give you a lift to college, although this takes her out of her way. What would she charge you for this? The journey will obviously cost her fuel, but is that the only cost? What about the wear and tear on her car? Her time? The loss of value of her car because of the increase in mileage? If she only charges you for the fuel, you will think that the journey is cheaper than it actually is and might ask her to drive you every day.

An externality exists where the economic agents do not pay all of the costs of their actions or do not take account of the benefits that may be received by third parties from their activities. These extra costs or benefits affect third parties, rather than the agents themselves.

Information failure

If markets are to perform a role in allocating resources, it is important that all relevant economic agents (buyers and sellers) have good information about market conditions, otherwise they may not be able to take rational decisions.

In order to determine their own willingness to pay, consumers must be fully aware of the benefits to be gained by consuming particular goods or services. Such benefits may not always be clear. For example, people may not fully perceive the benefits to be gained from education — or they may fail to appreciate the harmfulness of smoking tobacco.

In other market situations, economic agents on one side of the market may have different information from those on the other side: for example, sellers may have information about the goods that they are providing that buyers cannot discern. Chapter 9 explains that such information failure can lead to market failure.

Public goods

There is a category of goods known as public goods, which because of their characteristics cannot be provided by a purely free market. Street lighting is one example: there is no obvious way in which a private firm could charge all the users of street lighting for the benefits they receive from it. Such goods are also discussed in Chapter 9.

Merit and demerit goods

The government believes that some goods will be underconsumed in a free market. If people do not fully perceive the benefits to be gained from consuming a good, they will demand less than is socially desirable. In some developing countries, education may show aspects of a merit good, if parents do not fully perceive the benefits that their children could gain from it. This helps to explain low school enrolment in such countries.

There are also some goods that the government believes will be overconsumed in a free market. An obvious example is addictive recreational drugs, where consumers may misperceive the benefits from consumption. Chapter 9 examines these goods in more detail.

Synoptic link

The behaviour of firms will be discussed in Chapter 14 (which looks at monopoly), and in Chapter 15 (which looks at situations in which firms may work together in a market).

Knowledge check 8.1

Name three possible causes of market failure.

Study tip

Market failure is often used as a justification for government intervention in markets, so it is important to be aware of its various causes and to be able to recognise situations in which market failure may occur. At the heart of this is whether the free market equilibrium coincides with the socially optimum position.

Firms may exert market power

The discussion of market adjustment in the previous chapter argued that a market will evolve towards allocative efficiency when price is equal to marginal cost. However, this rested on the assumption that markets are competitive. Firms were fairly passive actors in these markets, responding perhaps rather tamely to changes in consumer preferences. The real world is not necessarily like that, and in many markets, firms have more power over their actions than has so far been suggested.

In the extreme, there are markets in which production is dominated by a single firm. For example, Google became dominant in the search engine sector, and in 2018 was fined following an investigation by the European Commission for abusing its dominant position. When a firm achieves such dominance, there is no guarantee that it will not try to exploit its position at the expense of consumers.

This is one example of how firms with a dominant position in a market may be able to restrict output and charge higher prices to consumers.

Summary

- Free markets do not always lead to the best possible allocation of resources: there may be market failure, causing the market equilibrium to diverge from the socially optimum position.
- When there are costs or benefits that are external to the price mechanism, the economy will not reach allocative efficiency.
- Markets can operate effectively only when participants in the market have full information about market conditions.
- Merit (demerit) goods are goods that the government believes are undervalued (overvalued) by consumers and as a result will be underconsumed (overconsumed) in a free market.
- Public goods have characteristics that prevent markets from supplying the appropriate quantity.
- Markets may fail when firms are able to utilise market power to disadvantage consumers.

Externalities

Key term

externality a cost or a benefit that is external to a market transaction, is therefore not reflected in market prices, and may affect third parties not involved in the transaction

'Externality' is one of those ugly words invented by economists, which means exactly what it says. It simply describes a cost or a benefit that is external to the market mechanism.

An externality will lead to a form of market failure because if the cost or benefit is not reflected in market prices, it cannot be taken into consideration by all parties to a transaction. In other words, there may be costs or benefits resulting from a transaction that are borne (or enjoyed) by some third party not directly involved in that transaction. This in turn implies that decisions will not be aligned with the best interests of society.

For example, if there is an element of costs that is not borne by producers, it is likely that 'too much' of the good will be produced. Where there are benefits that are not included, it is likely that too little will be produced. Externalities can affect either demand or supply in a market: that is to say, they may arise either in consumption or in production.

Key terms

private costs costs incurred by an individual (firm or consumer) as part of its production or other economic activities

external costs costs associated with an individual's (a firm or household's) production or other economic activities, which are borne by a third party and are not reflected in market prices

social costs the sum of private and external costs

social benefits the sum of private benefits and external benefits

private benefits the benefits received by an individual (a firm or consumer) as part of its economic activity

external benefits the benefits received by society (a firm or household) that accrues to a third party (firm or household) not engaged in that economic activity, and which are not reflected in market prices

Knowledge check 8.2

What is the difference between marginal private cost and marginal social cost?

Key term

production externality an externality that affects the production side of a market, which may be either positive or negative

Another way of expressing this is that the total cost of producing a good or service is made up of two components: the **private costs** faced by producers and the additional **external costs** that producers do not perceive. In other words, the costs to society (the **social costs**) are equal to private costs plus external costs. Similarly, **social benefits** are equal to **private benefits** that accrue to individuals plus the **external benefits** received by third parties.

In approaching this topic, begin by tackling Exercise 8.1, which offers an example of each type of externality.

Exercise 8.1

Each of the following situations describes a type of externality. Does each of these externalities arise through production or consumption?

a A factory in the centre of a town, and close to a residential district, emits toxic fumes through a chimney during its production process. Residents living nearby have to wash their clothes more frequently because of the pollution, and incur higher medical bills as a result of breathing in the fumes.

b Residents living along a main road festoon their houses with lavish Christmas lights and decorations during the month of December, helping passers-by to enjoy the festive spirit.

c A factory that produces chemicals, located on the banks of a river, installs a new water purification plant that improves the quality of water discharged into the river. A trout farm located downstream finds that its productivity increases, and that it has to spend less on filtering the water.

d Liz, a 'metal' fan, enjoys playing her music at high volume late at night, in spite of the fact that she lives in a flat with inadequate sound insulation. The neighbours prefer rock but cannot escape the metal.

Toxic fumes

Example (a) in Exercise 8.1 is a negative **production externality**. The factory emits toxic fumes. These impose costs on the residents (third parties) living nearby, who incur high washing and medical bills. The households face costs as a result of the production activities of the firm, so the firm does not face the full costs of its activity.

Toxic fumes from a factory may lead to costs for residents living nearby

So, the private costs faced by the producer are lower than the social costs: that is, the costs faced by society as a whole. The producer will take decisions based only on its private costs, ignoring the external costs it imposes on society.

Figure 8.1 illustrates this situation under the assumption that firms operate in a competitive market (i.e. there is not a monopoly). Here, D (MSB) represents the demand curve, which was characterised in Chapter 3 as representing the benefit derived from consuming a good. In other words, the demand curve represents consumers' willingness to pay for the good, and so reflects their marginal valuation of the product.

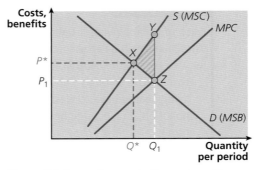

Figure 8.1 A negative production externality

Producers face marginal private costs given by the line MPC but in fact impose higher costs than this on society. Therefore, the supply curve that includes these additional costs imposed on society represents the true cost to society of producing the good. This may be regarded as being the marginal social cost S (MSC) of the firms' production.

If the market is unregulated by the government, firms will choose how much to supply on the basis of the marginal (private) cost they face, shown by MPC in Figure 8.1. The market equilibrium will therefore be at quantity traded Q_1, where firms just break even on the marginal unit sold. Price will be set at P_1.

This is not a good outcome for society, as it is clear that there is a divergence between the price in the market and the 'true' marginal cost — in other words, a divergence between marginal social benefit and marginal social cost. It is this divergence that is at the heart of the market failure. The last unit of this good sold imposes higher costs on society than the marginal benefit derived from consuming it. Too much is being produced at the market equilibrium.

In fact, the socially optimum position is at Q^*, where marginal social benefit is equal to marginal social cost. This will be reached if the price is set equal to (social) marginal cost at P^*. Less of the good will be consumed, but also less pollution will be created, and society will be better off than at Q_1.

Knowledge check 8.3

Does the presence of a negative production externality cause over-production or underconsumption?

Key term

welfare loss the social loss incurred when the market equilibrium diverges from the social optimum (where MSB = MSC), often referred to as the deadweight welfare loss

Quantitative skills 8.1

Identifying welfare loss in a diagram

The extent of the **welfare loss** that society suffers can be identified: it is shown by the shaded triangle (XYZ) in Figure 8.1. Each unit of output that is produced above Q^* imposes a cost equal to the vertical distance between MSC and MPC. The shaded area therefore represents the difference between marginal social cost and marginal benefit over the range of output between the optimum output and the free market level of output.

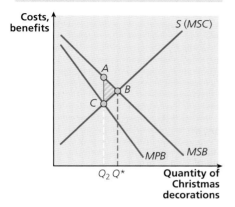

Figure 8.2 A positive consumption externality

Christmas lights

Situation (b) in Exercise 8.1 is an example of a positive **consumption externality**. Residents of this street decorate their homes in order to share the Christmas spirit with passers-by. The benefit they gain from the decorations spills over and adds to the enjoyment of others. In other words, the social benefits from the residents' decision to provide Christmas decorations go beyond the private enjoyment that they receive.

Figure 8.2 illustrates this situation. *MPB* represents the marginal private benefits gained by residents from the Christmas lights, but *MSB* represents the full marginal social benefit that the community gains, which is higher than the *MPB*. Residents will provide decorations up to the point Q_2, where their marginal private benefit is just balanced by the marginal cost of the lights. However, if the full social benefits received are taken into account, Q^* would be the optimum point: the residents do not provide enough décor for the community to reach the optimum. The shaded triangle (*ABC*) in Figure 8.2 shows the welfare loss: that is, the amount of social benefit forgone if the outcome is at Q_2 instead of Q^*. Again, there is a divergence between the free market equilibrium and the socially optimum position.

Positive and normative revisited

Situation (b) in Exercise 8.1 is a reminder of the distinction between positive and normative analysis. Economists would agree that Figure 8.2 shows the effects of a beneficial consumption externality. However, probably not everyone would agree that the lavish Christmas decorations are providing such benefits. This is where a *normative judgement* comes into play. It could equally be argued that the lavish Christmas decorations are unsightly and inappropriate, or that they constitute a distraction for drivers and are therefore likely to cause accidents. After all, not everyone enjoys the garish.

Water purification

Example (c) is a production externality that has *positive* effects. The action taken by the chemical firm to purify its waste water has beneficial effects on the trout farm, which finds that its costs have been reduced without it having taken any action itself.

Figure 8.3 shows the position facing the chemicals firm. It has relatively high marginal private costs, given by MPC. However, its actions have reduced the costs of the trout farm, so the 'social' cost of the firm's production activities is lower than its private cost. So, in this case marginal social cost, shown by MSC in the figure, is lower than marginal private cost. The firm will produce up to the point where MPC equals marginal social benefit: that is, at Q_3.

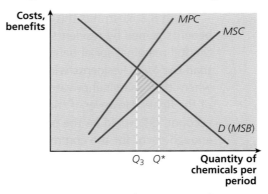

Figure 8.3 A positive production externality

In this market position, notice that the marginal benefit society receives from consuming the product is higher than the marginal social cost of producing it, so too little of the product is being consumed for society's good. Society would be better off at Q^*, where marginal social benefit is equal to marginal social cost.

Again, the shaded triangle in Figure 8.3 represents the extent of the inefficiency: it is given by the excess of marginal social benefit over marginal social cost, over the range of output between the market outcome and society's optimum position.

Rock and metal

Example (d) is a *negative* consumption externality. Liz, the metal fan, gains benefit from listening to her music at high volume, but the neighbours also hear her music and suffer as a result. Indeed, it may be that when they try to listen to rock, the metal interferes with their enjoyment. Their benefit is reduced by having to hear the metal.

Figure 8.4 illustrates this. The situation can be interpreted in terms of the benefits that accrue as a result of Liz's consumption of loud metal music. Liz gains benefit as shown by the line MPB, which represents marginal private benefit. However, the social benefit is lower than this if the vexation suffered by the neighbours is taken into account, so MSB in Figure 8.4 represents the marginal social benefits from Liz's metal.

Liz will listen to metal up to the point where her marginal private benefit is just equal to the marginal cost of playing it, at Q_4. However, the optimal position that takes the neighbours into consideration is where marginal social benefit is equal to marginal cost — at Q^*. Therefore, Liz plays too much loud metal for the good of society.

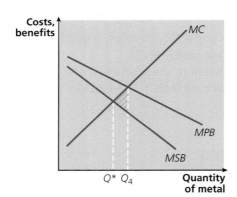

Figure 8.4 A negative consumption externality

Explain how to identify the area of welfare loss in a diagram showing the effect of a positive production externality.

Exercise 8.2

Discuss examples of some externalities that you meet in everyday situations, and classify them as affecting either production or consumption.

Study tip

Externalities are a common topic, so be ready to respond if questioned. Be very careful when drawing the diagram, especially in identifying the area representing welfare loss. If you understand *why* this area represents welfare loss, you should be able to check whether you have identified it correctly. If you are uncertain about this, look back at Quantitative skills 8.1 on page 94.

Study tip

Make sure that you understand the four varieties of externalities:
1 Negative production externality
2 Negative consumption externality
3 Positive production externality
4 Positive consumption externality
Be ready with examples of each.

Summary

- Markets can operate effectively only if all relevant costs and benefits are taken into account in decision making.
- Some costs and benefits are external to the market mechanism, and so are neglected, causing a distortion in resource allocation.
- Such external costs and benefits are known as 'externalities'.
- Externalities may occur in either production or consumption, thereby affecting either demand or supply.
- Externalities may be either positive or negative, but either way resources will not be optimally allocated if they are present.

Externalities occur in a wide variety of market situations and constitute an important source of market failure. This means that externalities may hinder the efficient allocation of scarce resources from society's perspective.

Examples of markets with externalities

Externalities and the environment

Concern for the environment has been growing in recent years, with 'green' lobbyist groups demanding attention, sometimes through demonstrations and protests. There are so many different facets to this problem that it is sometimes difficult to isolate the core issues. Externalities lie at the heart of much of the debate.

Global warming

Some of the issues are international in nature, such as the debate over global warming. The key concern here is the way in which emissions of greenhouse gases are said to be warming up the planet. Sea levels are rising and major climate change seems imminent.

One reason why this question is especially difficult to tackle is that actions taken by one country can affect other countries. Scientists argue that the problem is caused mainly by pollution created by transport and industry, especially in the richer countries of the world. However, poorer countries suffer the consequences as well, especially countries such as Bangladesh. Here, much of the land is low lying and prone to severe flooding almost every year — in some years up to three-quarters of the land area is under water at the height of the flooding.

Low-lying land in Bangladesh is prone to severe flooding

In principle, this is similar to example (a) in Exercise 8.1: it is an example of a negative production externality, in which the nations causing most of the damage face only part of the costs caused by their lifestyles and production processes. The inevitable result in an unregulated market is that too much pollution is produced.

When externalities cross international borders in this way, the problem can be tackled only through international cooperation. For example, at the Kyoto World Climate Summit held in Japan in 1997, almost every developed nation agreed to cut greenhouse gas emissions by 6% by 2010. The USA, the largest emitter of carbon dioxide, did not ratify the agreement, fearing the consequences of such a restriction for the US economy.

The Kyoto Protocol was discussed at the 2012 Doha climate change talks and it was agreed to begin a new round of negotiations. In December 2015, 196 countries adopted the Paris Agreement, a new framework designed as a coordinated effort to tackle climate change. This seemed to be a major step forward in tackling the issue, but the agreement suffered a setback in 2017, when President Trump announced that the USA would withdraw as soon as it was legal to do so. Trump argued that the deal reached had been unfair to the USA, and threatened to cost US$3 trillion in lost GDP and 6.5 million jobs. He did, however, suggest that the USA may re-join if a new deal could be reached. The withdrawal meant that the USA – the second-largest emitter of carbon dioxide — was effectively the only country in the world not to sign the agreement.

Externalities and health

Healthcare is a sector in which there is often public provision, or at least some state intervention in support of the health services. In the UK, the National Health Service is the prime provider of healthcare, but private healthcare is also available, and the use of private health insurance schemes is on the increase. Again, externalities can help to explain why there should be a need for government to intervene.

Consider the case of vaccination against a disease such as measles. Suppose an individual is considering whether or not to be vaccinated. Being vaccinated reduces the probability of that individual contracting the disease, so there are palpable potential benefits to that individual. However, these benefits must be balanced against the costs. There may be a direct charge for the vaccine, some individuals may have a phobia against needles, or they may be concerned about possible side effects. Individuals will opt to be vaccinated only if the marginal expected benefit to them is at least as large as the marginal cost.

From society's point of view, however, there are potential benefits that individuals will not take into account. After all, if they do contract measles, there is a chance of their passing it on to others. Indeed, if lots of people decide not to be vaccinated, there is the possibility of a widespread epidemic, which would be costly and damaging to many.

Figure 8.5 illustrates this point. The previous paragraph argues that the social benefits to society of having people vaccinated against measles exceed the private benefits that will be perceived by individuals, so marginal social benefits exceed marginal private benefits. Private

Knowledge check 8.6

Why might there be externality effects associated with smoking tobacco?

Synoptic link

Another aspect of healthcare provision is explored in Chapter 9.

individuals will choose to balance marginal private benefit against marginal private cost at Q_1, whereas society would prefer more people to be vaccinated at Q^*. This parallels the discussion of a positive consumption externality.

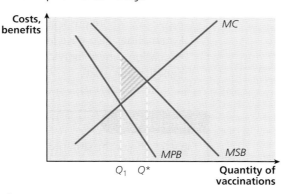

Figure 8.5 Vaccination

Externalities and education

You are reading this textbook, so it is reasonably safe to assume that you are following a course in economics. You have decided to demand education. This is yet another area in which externalities may be important.

When you decided to study A Levels (including economics), there were probably a number of factors that influenced your decision. Perhaps you intend to demand even more education in the future, by going on to study at university. Part of your decision process probably takes into account the fact that education improves your future earnings potential. Your expected lifetime earnings depend in part upon your level of qualifications. Research has shown that, on average, graduates earn more during their lifetimes than non-graduates. This is partly because there is a productivity effect: by becoming educated, you cultivate a range of skills that in later life will make you more productive, and this helps to explain why you can expect higher lifetime earnings than someone who chooses not to demand education. There is also a signalling effect, as having a degree signals to potential employers that you have the ability to cope with university study and have gained a range of skills.

What does society get out of this? Evidence suggests that, not only does education improve productivity, but a *group* of educated workers cooperating with each other become even more productive. This is an externality effect, as it depends upon interaction between educated workers — but each individual perceives only the individual benefit, and not the benefits of cooperation.

In other words, when you decide to undertake education, you do so on the basis of the expected private benefits that you hope to gain from education. However, you do not take into account the external benefits through cooperation that society will reap. So here is another example of a positive consumption externality. As with healthcare, some other aspects of education will be discussed in Chapter 9.

Knowledge check 8.7

School dropout rates tend to be high in some less developed countries. What sort of externality effect might be at work here?

Summary

- Externalities arise in many aspects of economic life.
- Environmental issues are especially prone to externality effects, as market prices do not always incorporate environmental issues, especially where property rights are not assigned.
- Externalities also arise in the areas of healthcare provision and education, where individuals do not always perceive the full social benefits that arise.

Exercise 8.3

Table 8.1 shows the situation in a market where pollution is generated by the production process.

a At what level of output would marginal social benefit be equal to marginal private cost? (*Note*: this would be the quantity of output that would be produced by firms in an unregulated competitive market.)

b By how much would marginal social cost exceed marginal private cost at this level of output?

c At what level of output would marginal social benefit be equal to marginal social cost?

d What amount of tax would induce firms to supply this quantity of output?

Table 8.1 A market with pollution

Quantity produced (thousands per week)	Marginal social benefit	Marginal private cost	Marginal social cost
10	80	5	10
20	75	10	20
30	70	20	35
40	60	32	60
50	48	48	90
60	30	75	125
70	8	110	175

Exercise 8.4

You discover that your local authority has chosen to locate a new landfill site for waste disposal close to your home. What costs and benefits for society would result? Would these differ from your private costs and benefits? Would you object?

Exercise 8.5

Each of the Figures 8.6–8.9 shows a particular type of externality.

For each figure, identify the sort of externality, and state whether the result is too much or too little output being traded in a free market.

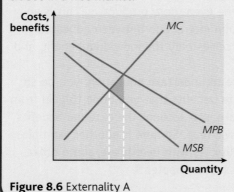

Figure 8.6 Externality A

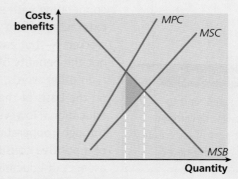

Figure 8.7 Externality B

Exercise 8.5

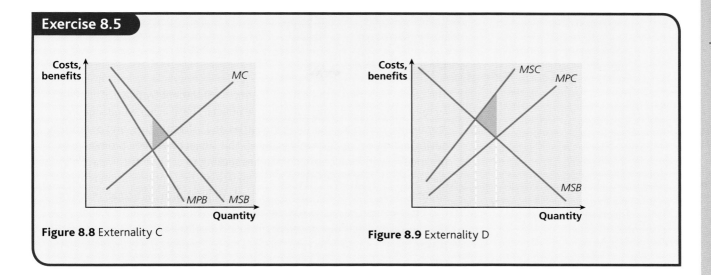

Figure 8.8 Externality C

Figure 8.9 Externality D

Case study 8.1

Healthcare: public or private?

The NHS was founded in 1948. Seventy years on, it faced crisis, with much talk in the media about long waiting lists and the NHS's failures in providing care. This revitalised the rising debate about whether healthcare should be state-provided, or whether market forces should be given a greater role. In the UK, market forces have played an increasing part in allocating resources within the public health sector, but the debate over public vs. private provision continues. So far, the proportion of health expenditure that the public sector undertakes has changed little.

What does economic analysis have to say about the matter? The justification for public provision of healthcare rests on the existence of **market failure**. There are a number of reasons why there might be some form of market failure in the provision of healthcare, whether we consider the provision of preventative or curative measures.

In the case of preventative healthcare, there may be other factors at work. Take the case of vaccination against disease. If a private competitive market provides vaccinations, an individual faces costs of the treatment, both financial and perhaps in the unpleasantness and possible risks of being vaccinated. The benefits of having been vaccinated may be perceived as relatively low if the individual sees a low probability of being infected. However, the benefits of vaccination from the point of view of society may be greater, because a widespread vaccination programme not only reduces the risk of infection for each individual but also reduces the likelihood of an epidemic.

Follow-up questions
a Explain what is meant by market failure.
b Use a diagram to explain the possible externality that may arise in relation to a vaccination programme.

Plastic oceans

The contamination of the natural marine environment by plastics has been increasing, causing a range of negative effects. These include endangering marine life, damaging maritime industries and infrastructure, and potentially having an impact on human wellbeing. This subject has been prominent in the media, with a succession of studies seeking to analyse the impact of plastics on the environment. A prime source of the contamination is litter — about 70% of litter in the oceans is made of plastic. In particular, much of this litter comprises single-use packaging, as well as rope, netting and sewage-related debris. A government report published in 2017 noted that if plastic litter continues to enter the marine environment at current rates, this will far exceed the possibility of clean-up removal.

Packaging goods has become part of our way of life, as any visit to a supermarket will demonstrate. It is cheap and convenient, and firms under pressure to keep their costs low in order to remain competitive are naturally reluctant to use more expensive but more environmentally friendly materials. This leads to a divergence between private and social costs.

Plastic pollution is crippling marine ecosystems around the globe

Follow-up questions
a Use a diagram to show the economic effect of plastic pollution on society.
b Discuss the problems in tackling this problem, given that plastic in the ocean is occurring on a global scale.

CHAPTER 8 QUESTIONS

A Multiple-choice questions

1 Which of the following would be an example of an externality?

   a A cost to a firm that is not reflected in market prices

   b A benefit to the consumer that is reflected in market prices

   c A cost to a third party not reflected in market prices

   d A benefit to a third party that is reflected in market prices

2 Which of the following would result in a positive externality?

   a $MSC = MPC$

   b $MSC > MPC$

   c $MPB < MSB$

   d $MPB = MSB$

3 A good that is likely to be overconsumed in a free market would be classed as a:

   a Merit good

   b Demerit good

   c Public good

   d Consumer good

B Knowledge and understanding questions

4 Explain two reasons why market failure may occur. [4 marks]

5 Explain, using a diagram, the effect of a negative production externality. [4 marks]

6 Explain, using a diagram, how a positive externality of consumption could lead to market failure. [4 marks]

C Stimulus response question

7 Adeel enjoys gardening and has spent a lot of money populating his garden with bright and colourful flowers and plants. He is happy to spend so much on his garden because he gains so many benefits from buying the flowers and plants.

Tina lives next door to Adeel. She can sit in her garden and see all of Adeel's plants and flowers, which she enjoys. Tina is hoping to sell her house soon and she believes that any future owner will be willing to pay more for the house because Adeel is such a good neighbour.

   a Explain, with reference to marginality, why Adeel is prepared to spend so much money on his own garden. [2 marks]

   b Explain, using a diagram, why there may be an externality involved when Tina sells her house. [4 marks]

Chapter 9

Market failure: information failure and public goods

Externalities are not the only form of market failure. There are also situations where the characteristics of a good or service can affect the effective operation of a market. This chapter explores goods with unusual economic characteristics and markets that may fail as a result of problems with information.

> ## Learning objectives
>
> After studying this chapter, you should be able to:
> - explain information failure
> - explain, with the aid of a diagram, market failure caused by information failure
> - explain asymmetric information and moral hazard
> - explain merit and demerit goods
> - evaluate consumption and production of merit goods
> - evaluate consumption and production of demerit goods
> - explain public goods, private goods and quasi-public goods
> - explain the characteristics of a public good: non-excludability, non-diminishability/non-rivalry, non-rejectability, zero marginal cost
> - explain the free-rider problem
> - evaluate the provision of public goods

Information failure

> **Key term**
>
> **asymmetric information** a situation in which some participants in a market have better information about market conditions than others

If markets are to be effective in guiding resource allocation, it is important that economic decision-makers receive full and accurate information about market conditions. Consumers need information about the prices at which they can buy and the quality of the products for sale. Producers need to be able to observe how consumers react to prices. Information is therefore of crucial significance if markets are to work. However, there are some markets in which not all traders have access to good information, or in which some traders have more or better access to it than others. This is known as a situation of **asymmetric information**, and can be a source of market failure.

Healthcare

One example of asymmetric information is in healthcare. Suppose you go to your dentist for a check-up. He tells you that you have a filling that needs to be replaced, although you have had no pain or problems with it. In this situation the seller in a market has much better information about the product than the buyer. You as the buyer have no idea whether or not the recommended treatment is needed, and without going to another dentist for a second opinion you have no way of finding out. You might think this is an unsatisfactory situation, as it seems to give a lot of power to the seller relative to the consumer. The situation is even worse where the dentist does not even publish the prices for treatment until after it has been carried out! The Office of Fair Trading criticised private dentists for exactly this sort of practice when they reported on this market. Indeed, dentists are now required by law to publish prices for treatment.

The same argument applies in the case of other areas of healthcare, where doctors have better information than their patients about the sort of treatment that is needed.

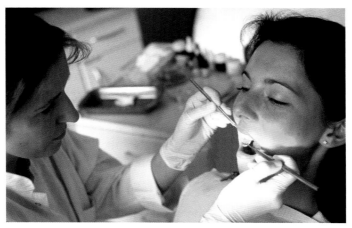

Dentists have better information than their patients about what treatments are needed

Education

The market for education is another example. Teachers or government inspectors may know more about the subjects and topics that students need to study than the students do themselves. This is partly because teachers are able to take a longer view and can see education provision from a broader perspective. Students taking economics at university may have to take a course in mathematics and statistics in their first year, and some will always complain that they have come to study economics, not maths. It is only later that they come to realise that competence in maths is crucial for the economics they will study later in their course.

How could this problem be tackled? The answer would seem to be obvious — if the problem arises from an information failure, then the answer should be to improve the information flow, in this case to students. This might be achieved by providing a convincing explanation of why the curriculum has been designed in a particular way. It may also be necessary to provide incentives for students to study particularly unpopular subjects, perhaps by making success a requirement for progression to the next stage of the course. By understanding the economic cause of a problem, it is possible to devise a strategy that should go some way towards removing the market failure.

What effect would this sort of information failure have on a market? Suppose that education provides benefits to society that are not fully understood by parents and their children. Another way of expressing this is that the perceived marginal private benefits of education are lower than the marginal social benefits that society will gain from having an educated workforce. Figure 9.1 illustrates this situation.

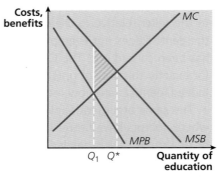

Figure 9.1 Information failure and education

In this situation, the best outcome for society would be if Q^* education was provided, this being the position in which $MSB = MC$. In a free market situation, only Q_1 would be demanded, reflecting the private perception of the value of education to individuals. You will realise that this is actually an example of a consumption externality — but it arises because private individuals (whether it be the parents or their children) do not have full information about the value of education.

Second-hand cars

One of the most famous examples of asymmetric information relates to the second-hand (or 'pre-owned', by the latest terminology) car market. This is because the first paper that drew attention to the problem of asymmetric information, by Nobel laureate George Akerlof, focused on this market.

Akerlof argued that there are two types of car. Some cars are good runners and are totally reliable, whereas some are continually breaking down and needing parts and servicing — the latter are known as 'lemons' in the USA (allegedly inspired by fruit machines, where lemons offer the lowest prize). The problem in the second-hand car market arises because the owners of cars (potential sellers) have better information about their cars than the potential buyers. In other words, when an owner decides to sell a car, he or she knows whether it is a lemon or a good-quality car — but a buyer cannot tell.

Car dealers buying second-hand cars can adopt one of two possible strategies. One is to offer a high price and buy up all the cars in the market, knowing that the lemons will be sold on at a loss but hoping for a return on the quality ones. The problem is that, if the lemons make up a large proportion of the cars in the market, this could generate overall losses for the dealers. The alternative is to offer a low price, and just buy up all the lemons to sell for scrap. In this situation, the market for good-quality used cars is effectively destroyed because owners of good-quality cars will not accept the low price — an extreme form of market failure!

Pensions

A problem faced by everyone is how they will live when they reach retirement and find that the state pension is not sufficient for them to live in the manner to which they have become accustomed. In today's

Knowledge check 9.2

Eighteen-year-olds whose parents or relatives have attended university are much more likely to take up a university place than those from families where nobody has ever attended. To what extent could the latter be a result of an information failure?

Synoptic link

The externality effects of education were discussed in Chapter 8.

Key terms

adverse selection a situation in which a person at risk is more likely to take out insurance
moral hazard a situation in which a person who has taken out insurance is prone to taking more risk

world, people are living longer and retiring with many years ahead of them. Paying part of their income into a private pension fund will supplement the state pension when they retire.

The pensions market is another market that is fraught with information problems by its very nature. A key source of information failure here arises from uncertainty and risk. Individuals face uncertainty in predicting their need for an adequate pension in their old age, which depends upon their future state of health, their longevity, and so on. There is risk involved in the sense that pension funds depend critically on movements in the stock market. There is also the fact that there is a vast array of alternative pension schemes available, many of them very complex. This makes it very difficult for individuals to know how to take a rational decision — especially when their need for a pension is many years away. If people make bad decisions about pensions, this creates problems for the future, and society may find that it needs to cope with care for the elderly, especially when improvements in health mean that more people are living longer. The regulations introduced in the UK that mean workers are automatically enrolled in a workplace pensions scheme (unless they consciously opt out) are one attempt to tackle this issue.

The insurance market

People take out insurance to cover themselves against the risk of uncertain future events. Asymmetric information can cause problems with this market in two different ways. Suppose an individual approaches an insurance company wanting health insurance. The individual knows more about his or her health and health history than the insurance company. After all, the individual knows whether they are prone to illness or if they are accident-prone. This could mean that the people most likely to take out health insurance are the ones most likely to fall ill or be involved in accidents. This is known as **adverse selection**. A second form of information failure in terms of insurance is known as **moral hazard**. An individual who has taken out insurance may be more likely to take risks, knowing that he or she is covered by insurance. For example, if someone has taken out insurance against the loss of their mobile phone, they may be less careful about leaving it around.

Summary
- Information deficiency can lead to market failure in some situations: for example, where some participants in a market have better information about some aspect(s) of the market than others.
- Examples of this include healthcare, education and second-hand cars.
- Asymmetric information can also result in problems of adverse selection and moral hazard.

Merit goods

There are some goods that the government believes will be undervalued by consumers, so that too little will be consumed in a free market. In other words, individuals do not fully perceive the benefits that they will gain from consuming such goods. These are known

Synoptic link

The distinction between normative and positive issues was discussed in Chapter 1.

as **merit goods**. This is another example of information failure, as the problem stems from people's lack of knowledge about the benefits from consuming a good or service — or, rather, from the government's belief that they lack knowledge.

One situation in which the merit good phenomenon arises is where the government is in a better position than individuals to take a long-term view of what is good for society. In particular, governments may need to take decisions on behalf of future generations as well as the present. Resources need to be used wisely in the present in order to protect the interests of tomorrow's citizens. Notice that this may require decision-makers to make normative judgements about the appropriate weighting to be given to the present as opposed to the future.

There is a strong political element involved in identifying the goods that should be regarded as merit goods: this is because of the subjective or normative judgement involved, since declaring a good to be a merit good requires the decision-maker to make a choice on behalf of the population, which may be seen as being paternalistic.

At the heart of the notion of a merit good, therefore, is the decision-maker's perception that there is a divergence between the marginal benefit that individuals perceive to arise from consuming a good, and the social benefit that actually accrues from its consumption. This is reminiscent of the arguments in Chapter 8 about consumption externalities, where a positive consumption externality arises when the marginal social benefit from consuming a good is greater than the marginal private benefit.

Milk

Pupils under 5 years old in primary education are entitled to daily free or subsidised milk under a government scheme. This replaced an earlier (more generous) scheme in which free milk was provided to all primary school pupils. This is an example of a merit good. The government saw this as a way of improving nutritional standards, when parents may not fully see the health benefits of milk. In other words, it was thought that there was a divergence between the actual benefits from consuming milk and those seen by parents.

This echoes the discussion of information failure earlier in the chapter, when education was shown as an example of how parents (or their children) might not be fully aware of its value. Figure 9.1 was used to illustrate this, and it can be used for this example as well, as it shows the situation for a merit good.

Education as a merit good

In the UK, everyone is required to attend school, at least up to age 16. Part of this requirement may be attributed to a merit good argument. It can be argued that education provides benefits to society in excess of those that are perceived by individuals. In other words, society believes that individuals will derive a benefit from education that they will not realise until after they have acquired that education. So, the government decrees that everyone must consume education up to the age of 16, whether they want to or not and whether they have the means to do so or not. This is a merit good argument. In Figure 9.1 marginal social benefit (*MSB*) was shown as being higher than marginal private benefit (*MPB*).

Therefore, society would like to provide Q^* education, where $MSB = MC$ (marginal social cost), but individuals would choose to consume only Q_1 education, where $MPB = MC$, because they do not expect the future benefits to be as high as the government does.

In this case there may be other issues affecting the market for education. Chapter 8 argued that there would also be positive externality effects if educated workers were better able to cooperate with each other. There may be a further argument that individuals may fail to demand sufficient education because of information failure: in other words, they may not perceive the full benefits that will arise from education. The situation may be aggravated if parents have the responsibility of financing their children's education, because they are taking decisions *on behalf of* their children. In the case of higher education, there is no guarantee that parents will agree with their children about the benefits of a university education — it could go either way.

In some societies it has been suggested that the merits of education are better perceived by some groups in society than others. In some less developed countries, individuals in relatively well-off households demand high levels of education, as they realise the long-run benefits that they can receive in terms of higher earnings — and, perhaps, political influence. In contrast, low-income households in remote rural areas may not see the value of education. As a result, dropout from secondary — and even primary — education tends to be high. This is clearly a merit good argument that may need to be addressed by government, perhaps by making primary education compulsory or free, or both.

Other examples of merit goods

Other examples of merit goods are museums, libraries and art galleries. These are goods that are provided or subsidised because someone somewhere thinks that communities should have more of them. Economists are wary of playing the merit good card too often, as it entails such a high normative element. It is also difficult sometimes to disentangle merit good arguments from externality effects.

Demerit goods

There is also a category of goods that governments think will be overconsumed in a free market. These are known as **demerit goods**. Obvious examples are illegal drugs and tobacco. Here the argument is that individual consumers overvalue the benefits from consuming such a good.

Exercise 9.3

Discuss whether all museums should be treated as merit goods.

Key term

demerit good a good that brings less benefit to consumers than they expect, such that too much will be consumed by individuals in a free market

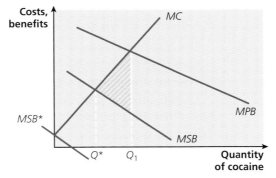

Figure 9.2 A demerit good

Figure 9.2 shows the market for a demerit good. Marginal private benefits (*MPB*) are shown as being much higher than marginal social benefits (*MSB*), so that in a free market too much of the good is consumed. Society would like to be at Q^* but ends up at Q_1. In this particular market, the government may see the marginal social benefit from consuming the good to be so low (e.g. at MSB^* in the figure) that consumption should be driven to zero.

Again, this could be interpreted as partly an information problem, in the sense that individual consumers may not perceive the dangers of consuming the good, and may overvalue it as a result. In addition, if the good is addictive, this would have the effect of making an individual's demand for the good highly inelastic in the long run. However, it is paternalistic of the government to intervene directly for this reason, although it might wish to correct other externalities — for instance, those imposed on others when addicts steal to fund their habit.

An alternative approach is to try to remove the information failure — clearly, the government has adopted this approach in seeking to educate people about the dangers of tobacco smoking.

Summary

- A merit good is one that society believes should be consumed by individuals, whether or not they have the means or the willingness to do so.
- There is a strong normative element in the identification of merit goods.
- Demerit goods are goods that society believes should not be consumed by individuals even if they wish to do so.
- In the case of merit and demerit goods, 'society' (as represented by government) believes that it has better information than consumers about these goods, and about what is good (or bad) for consumers.

Public goods

Key term

private good a good that, once consumed by one person, cannot be consumed by somebody else — such a good has excludability and is rivalrous

Most of the goods that individuals consume are **private goods**. You buy a bottle of water, you drink it, and it's gone. You may choose to share it with a friend, but you do not have to: by drinking it you can prevent anyone else from doing so. Furthermore, once it is gone, it's gone: nobody else can subsequently consume that water.

The two features that characterise a private good are that:

1 other people can be excluded from consuming it
2 once consumed by one person, it cannot be consumed by another

The first feature can be described as *excludability*, whereas the second feature might be described by saying that consumption of a private good is *rivalrous*: the act of consumption uses up the good.

Not all goods and services have these two characteristics. There are goods that, once provided, are available to all. In other words, people cannot be excluded from consuming such goods. There are other goods that do not diminish through consumption, so they are non-rivalrous in consumption. From the supplier's perspective, additional consumers can be accommodated at zero marginal cost. Goods that have the characteristics of **non-excludability** and **non-rivalry** (or non-diminishability) are known as **public goods**. When supplied to all, such goods are also **non-rejectable**: in other words, people cannot avoid consuming them.

Examples of public goods that are often cited include street lighting, a lighthouse and a nuclear deterrent. For example, once street lighting has been provided in a particular street, anyone who walks along that street at night benefits from the lighting — no one can be excluded from consuming it. So street lighting is non-exclusive. In addition, the fact that one person has walked along the street does not mean that there is less street lighting left for later walkers. So street lighting is also non-rivalrous. Furthermore, if you walk along the street at night, you cannot turn off the street lights, so it is non-rejectable. Similarly, a nuclear deterrent is provided to all, so nobody can be excluded from it, nor does one person's 'consumption' of it leave less for others. In addition, it cannot be rejected by anyone protected by it, even if they object to it in principle.

The free-rider problem

The key feature of such a market is that, once the good has been provided, there is no incentive for anyone to pay for it — so the market will fail, as no firm will have an incentive to supply the good in the first place. This is often referred to as the **free-rider problem**, as individual consumers can free-ride and avoid having to pay for the good if it is provided.

A key question is how well the market for a public good is likely to operate. In particular, will a free market reach a position where there is allocative efficiency, i.e. where price equals marginal social cost?

Think about the supply and demand curves for a public good such as street lighting. To simplify matters, suppose there are just two potential demanders of the good, a and b. Consider Figure 9.3. If it is assumed that the supply is provided in a competitive market, S represents the supply curve, reflecting the marginal cost of providing street lighting. The curves d_a and d_b represent the demand curves of the two potential demanders. For a given quantity Q_1, a would be prepared to pay P_a and b would pay P_b.

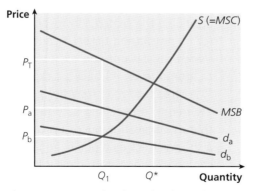

Figure 9.3 Demand and supply of a public good

If these prices are taken to be the value that each individual places on this amount of the good, then $P_a + P_b = P_T$ represents the social benefit derived from consuming Q_1 units of street lighting. Similarly, for any given quantity of street lighting, the marginal social benefit derived from consumption can be calculated as the vertical sum of the two demand curves. This is shown by the curve *MSB*. So the optimal provision of street lighting is given by $Q*$, at which point the marginal social benefit is equated with the marginal cost of supplying the good.

However, if person *a* were to agree to pay P_a for the good, person *b* could then consume Q_1 of the good free of charge, but would not be prepared to pay in order for the supply to be expanded beyond this point — as person *b*'s willingness to pay is below the marginal cost of provision beyond this point. So the social optimum at $Q*$ cannot be reached. Indeed, when there are many potential consumers, the likely outcome is that *none* of this good will be produced: why should any individual agree to pay if he or she can free-ride on others?

The free-rider problem helps to explain why these sorts of goods have typically been provided through state intervention. This begs the question of how the state can identify the optimal quantity of the good to be provided — in other words, how the government determines $Q*$. The extent to which individuals value a particular good cannot be directly observed. However, by including statements about the provision of public goods in their election manifestos, politicians can collect views about public goods provision via the medium of the ballot box. This is an indirect method, but it provides some mandate for the government to take decisions.

Note that public goods are called 'public goods' not because they are publicly provided, but because of their characteristics.

The free-rider problem makes it difficult to charge for a public good, so the private sector will be reluctant to supply such goods. In fact, pure public goods are relatively rare, but there are many goods that have some but not all of the required characteristics.

Quasi-public goods

In fact, there are many goods that are either non-rivalrous, non-excludable or non-rejectable, but not all three. One example of this is a football match. If I go to watch a premiership football match, my 'consumption' of the match does not prevent the person sitting next to me from also consuming it, so it is non-rivalrous: at least, for those attending the match. However, if I go along without my season ticket (or do not have a ticket), I can clearly be excluded from consuming the match, so it is *not* non-exclusive. It is also rejectable, as I can choose not to attend (even if I have a ticket).

A stretch of road may be considered non-exclusive, as road users are free to drive along it. However, it is not non-rivalrous, in the sense that as congestion builds up consumption is affected. This example is also imperfect as a public good because, by installing toll barriers, users can be excluded from consuming it. It may also be considered to be rejectable, as users have other route options from which to choose.

Particular problems are posed when a good is non-excludable but not non-rivalrous. These are explored in Case study 9.2.

Where goods have some features of a public good, the free market may fail to produce an ideal outcome for society. Exercise 9.4 provides some examples of goods: to what extent may each of these be considered to be non-rivalrous, non-excludable or non-rejectable?

Knowledge check 9.6

Explain the free-rider problem in the context of the provision of national defence.

Exercise 9.4

For each of the following goods, think about whether they have elements of non-rivalry, non-excludability, non-rejectability, some or neither:

a a national park

b a playground

c a theatre performance

d an apple

e a television programme

f a firework display

g police protection

h a lecture

i a Blu-ray recording of a film

j the national defence

Public goods provision

For some public goods, the failure of the free market to ensure provision may be regarded as a serious problem — for example, in such cases as street lighting or law and order. Some government intervention may be needed to make sure that a sufficient quantity of the good or service is provided. Notice that this does not necessarily mean that the government has to provide the good itself. It may be that the government will raise funds through taxation in order to ensure that street lighting is provided, but could still make use of private firms to supply the good through some sort of subcontracting arrangement. In the UK, it may be that the government delegates the responsibility for the provision of public goods to local authorities, which in turn may subcontract to private firms.

How effective will this be? The delegation of provision of a good or service to a local area may have the benefit of ensuring that decisions are taken at the local level – that is, close to those who benefit. However, local authorities face the need to provide a wide range of services, and need to set priorities between conflicting demands for limited resources. In many areas around the UK, complaints about potholes in roads suggest that local motorists do not always find the priorities set by local authorities to be to their liking.

In some other cases, it may be that changes in technology may alter the economic characteristics of a good. For example, in the case of television programmes, originally provision was entirely through the BBC, funded by the licence fee. Subsequently, ITV set up in competition, using advertising as a way of funding its supply. More recently, the advent of satellite and digital broadcasting has reduced the degree to which television programmes are non-excludable, allowing private firms to charge for transmissions.

Synoptic link

The question of the provision of public goods will be explored further in Chapter 10.

Knowledge check 9.7

Is it necessarily the case that a public good can only be provided directly by the government?

Summary

- A private good is one that, once consumed by one person, cannot be consumed by anyone else — it has characteristics of excludability and rivalry.
- A public good is non-exclusive, non-rivalrous and non-rejectable.
- Because of these characteristics, public goods tend to be underprovided by a free market.
- One reason for this is the free-rider problem, whereby an individual cannot be excluded from consuming a public good, and so has no incentive to pay for it.
- Public goods, or goods with some of the characteristics of public goods, must be provided with the assistance of the government or its agents.

Case study 9.1

Asymmetric information

Farmers often need to borrow money to farm unproductive land in Ethiopia

Joe Mpata farms a small piece of land in Ethiopia. The land is difficult to work, and unproductive. Joe would like to be able to invest in the land using better tools and fertiliser to raise productivity.

Joe approaches a bank to see if he can obtain a loan for this project. In order to take a decision on Joe's request, the bank needs information. It needs to know about the likelihood that Joe will default on the loan, either because the project may fail, or because he turns out to be unreliable. However, the bank is faced with a large number of similar requests, and finds it difficult to assess the relative merits of the projects put forward.

One problem is asymmetric information. The bank has little information on which to base its decisions. It realises that the individuals who are most likely to want to borrow could be those who are unreliable, or who want to finance risky projects. In addition, the bank is wary of lending, because without knowing more about the borrowers, it is aware that some borrowers may take more risk with their projects once they have secured a loan, which may increase the probability of default.

Most potential borrowers are unable to offer any security to the bank, as the documentation of land ownership is weak. In other words, the bank cannot accept land as collateral against the loan. As a result, the bank will only provide loans at a high rate of interest, as a way of trying to insure against default.

Follow-up questions

a Identify an example of moral hazard in the passage.
b Identify an example of adverse selection in the passage.
c How will the market be affected if reliable and low-risk potential borrowers find the interest rates being charged to be excessive?

Case study 9.2

A common problem

In mediaeval times, it was not unusual for areas of land to be designated as 'commons'. The name has persisted to today in some regions – you might think of Wimbledon Common, for example. Before enclosure from the sixteenth century, many villages had areas of common land that they could use to graze their animals free of charge. This land was therefore non-excludable for the villagers, but not non-rivalrous, as there would not be a limit on the livestock that could be put to graze. Such conditions still exist in some developing countries today.

Follow-up questions

a How would you expect a market to evolve if the good has these characteristics of being non-excludable but rivalrous?
b Give another example of where this problem could arise.

Case study 9.3

Paying for lighthouses

On the face of it, the lighthouse service seems to be a good example of a public good. In spite of the availability of accurate GPS systems that enable ships to know exactly where they are in relation to potential shipping hazards, lighthouses continue to contribute significantly to marine safety.

Once a lighthouse has been constructed and is sending out its signal, all boats and ships that pass within the range of its light can benefit from the service. Furthermore, the fact that one ship has seen the lighthouse signal does not reduce the amount of light available to the next ship. This suggests that a lighthouse is a classic example of a public good.

As with all public goods, this raises the question of how to finance the lighthouse service. Of course, it could simply be taken into public ownership, and be funded by the taxpayer. However, this could be seen to be inequitable.

A levy system has therefore been devised to pay for the lighthouse service. Ships must pay General Light Dues every time they enter or leave UK ports, and the fees collected (by Trinity House) are used to fund lighthouses, buoys and beacons around the coast. The level of the light dues is related to the size of individual ships, such that larger vessels pay a higher levy. Tugs and fishing vessels with a length below 10 metres and pleasure craft weighing less than 20 tons are exempt from the charges.

In principle, it could be argued that the existence of the Light Dues renders lighthouses excludable, as ships can be prevented from sailing if they have not paid their dues, and so could not consume the lighthouse services. However, there have been complaints from the shipping companies that small leisure craft that do not have to pay the charges make more use of the lighthouses than the larger vessels.

Nonetheless, this is one example of a charging system designed to try to overcome the free-rider problem associated with the provision of public goods.

Follow-up questions
a Explain why the second paragraph indicates that a lighthouse should be seen as a 'classic example of a public good'.
b Why would it be seen as unfair to rely on funding the lighthouse service from general taxation?
c Discuss the effectiveness of the Light Dues system as a way of overcoming the free-rider problem.

CHAPTER 9 QUESTIONS

A Multiple-choice questions

1 Which of the following is an example of moral hazard?

   a A person who takes out car insurance because the law requires it

   b A person who takes out mobile phone insurance in case they lose their phone

   c A person who takes out payment protection insurance because they know they will lose their job soon

   d A person who takes out life insurance so that they feel happy to do a bungee jump

2 Which of the following is an example of adverse selection?

   a A person who takes out car insurance because the law requires it

   b A person who takes out mobile phone insurance in case they lose their phone

   c A person who takes out payment protection insurance because they know they will lose their job soon

   d A person who takes out life insurance so that they feel happy to do a bungee jump

3 Which of the following could be classed a public good?

   a A good that is excludable and rivalrous

   b A good that is not excludable and not rivalrous

   c A good that is excludable and not rivalrous

   d A good that is not excludable and is rivalrous

4 Which of the following examples is most likely to be a quasi-public good?

   a A bottle of water

   b A public road

   c Netflix

   d A seat on an aeroplane

B Knowledge and understanding questions

5 Explain, using an example, what is meant by 'the free-rider problem'. [2 marks]

6 Explain, with the aid of a diagram, how information failure could lead to market failure. [4 marks]

7 Explain why the provision of a public good may have zero marginal cost to a business. [2 marks]

C Stimulus response question

8 If you want lights in your house, you will normally pay for the privilege. This includes the price of the light fittings, the bulbs and the electricity to power them.

However, most residential streets and many roads in the UK are lit with publicly provided lighting. Local or national government spending is used to provide most of the UK's street lighting because it is seen as a public good.

   a Explain why street lighting is seen as a public good. [4 marks]

   b Evaluate the importance of the provision of street lighting as a public good in the UK. [12 marks]

Chapter 10

Government intervention and government failure

Previous chapters have identified various ways in which markets can fail to bring about an efficient allocation of resources in a society. This chapter investigates how governments may intervene to influence markets. The chapter also explores how some well-intentioned interventions by government can sometimes produce unintended results, leading to government failure.

In this chapter, we focus on the ways in which governments may intervene to influence how markets work. Typically, such intervention takes on two forms. One possibility is to adopt a market-based policy, influencing the behaviour of producers or consumers through the market mechanism. The alternative is to influence behaviour through direct controls, such as legislation or regulation.

Synoptic link

Chapters 8 and 9 explored what is meant by market failure and hinted at some possible solutions. Here, we explore government interventions in more detail, together with some possible unintended consequences.

Learning objectives

After studying this chapter, you should be able to explain ways in which governments intervene in markets. These include through:
- taxation
- subsidies
- government expenditure
- price controls
- buffer stock systems
- public/private partnerships
- legislation
- regulation
- tradable pollution permits
- information provision
- competition policy
- explain government failure

You should also be able to:
- evaluate the effectiveness of government intervention in markets
- evaluate the causes and consequences of government failure

Government intervention in markets

As explained in previous chapters, markets fail when the price mechanism causes an inefficient allocation of resources within a society. This can occur when price is not set equal to marginal cost, or where marginal social benefit is not equal to marginal social cost. In such circumstances, it seems apparent that by improving the way in which resources are allocated, the society could become better off. In other words, market failure is often viewed as a valid reason for governments to intervene in the economy.

Most governments see it as their responsibility to try to correct some of the failures of markets to allocate resources efficiently. This has led to a wide variety of policies being devised to address issues of market failure.

Taxation

Key terms

indirect tax a tax levied on expenditure on goods or services
direct tax a tax charged directly to an individual based on a component of income

Synoptic link

The operation and impact of direct taxes are explained in Chapter 30 in the macroeconomics section of the book.

Knowledge check 10.1

Give an example of a merit good and a demerit good.

Governments need to raise funds to finance the expenditure that they undertake, and the imposition of taxes is a way of raising revenue. One way of doing this is through expenditure taxes such as value added tax (VAT), which is levied on a wide range of goods and services. Such taxes levied on goods are known as **indirect taxes**, in contrast to **direct taxes** (such as income tax), which are charged on the basis of income received by economic agents. In general, direct taxes are applied at the economy-wide level, rather than being intended to influence particular markets.

An indirect tax

Consider the effect of excise duties on such items as alcohol or tobacco. These can be seen to be intended to affect consumption of particular goods perceived to be demerit goods.

The effects of a sales tax can be seen in a demand and supply diagram. An indirect tax is paid by the seller, so it affects the supply curve for a product. Figure 10.1 illustrates a tax that is set at a constant amount per pack of cigarettes. Without the tax, the market equilibrium is at the intersection of demand and supply with a price of P_0 and a quantity traded of Q_0. The effect of the tax is to reduce the quantity that firms are prepared to supply at any given price — or, to put it another way, for any given quantity of cigarettes, firms need to receive the amount of the tax over and above the price at which they would have been prepared to supply that quantity. The effect is therefore to move the supply curve upwards by the amount of the tax, as shown in the figure. We get a new equilibrium with a higher price at P_1 and a lower quantity traded at Q_1.

How does such a tax help to address market failure? The argument here is shown in Figure 10.2. Demand (MPB) represents the marginal private benefit that consumers gain from smoking tobacco. However, the government believes that consumers underestimate the damaging effects of smoking, so that the true benefits are given by MSB (marginal social benefit). Given the marginal cost (supply) curve, in an unregulated market consumers will choose to smoke up to Q_1 tobacco. The optimum for society, however, is at Q^*.

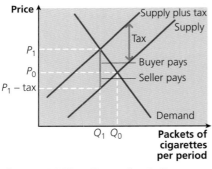

Figure 10.1 The effects of an indirect tax on cigarettes

Knowledge check 10.2

If the government removes a tax on a good, will quantity demanded of the good decrease or increase?

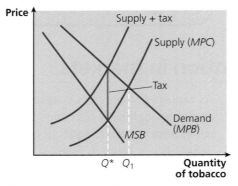

Figure 10.2 Taxing tobacco

If the government imposes a tax, shown by the red line in Figure 10.2, this effectively shifts the supply curve to the market, as seen in the figure. This raises the price in the market, so consumers are persuaded to reduce their consumption to the optimal level at Q^*. Notice that because the demand curve (MPB) is quite steep (relatively inelastic), a substantial tax is needed in order to reach Q^*. Empirical evidence suggests that the demand for tobacco is relatively inelastic — and therefore tobacco taxes have risen to comprise a large portion of the price of a packet of cigarettes.

Extension material

Who pays the tax?

An important question is: who bears the burden of the tax? If you look at Figure 10.1, you will see that the price difference between the with-tax and without-tax situations (i.e. $P_1 - P_0$) is *less* than the amount of the tax, which is the vertical distance between the with-tax and without-tax supply curves. Although the seller may be responsible for the mechanics of paying the tax, part of the tax is effectively passed on to the buyer in the form of the higher price. In Figure 10.1, the incidence of the tax falls partly upon the seller, but most of the tax is borne by the buyer.

The price elasticity of demand determines the incidence of the tax. If demand were perfectly inelastic, then the sellers would be able to pass the whole burden of the tax on to the buyers through an increase in price equal to the value of the tax, knowing that this would not affect demand. However, if demand were perfectly elastic, then the sellers would not be able to raise the price at all, so they would have to bear the entire burden of the tax.

Draw demand and supply diagrams to confirm that the statements in the previous paragraph are correct — that is, that if demand is perfectly inelastic, then the tax falls entirely on the buyers, whereas if demand is perfectly elastic, it is the sellers who have to bear the burden of the tax.

A tax on pollution

A tax can also be used to tackle a negative production externality such as pollution. Figure 10.3 illustrates the situation. Suppose that firms in the market for chemicals use a production process that emits toxic fumes, thereby imposing costs on society that the firms themselves do not face. In other words, the marginal private costs faced by these firms are less than the marginal social costs that are inflicted on society. As explained in Chapter 8, firms in this market will choose to produce up to point Q_1 and charge a price of P_1 to consumers. At this point, marginal social benefit is below the marginal cost of producing the chemicals, so it can be claimed that 'too much' of the product is being produced — that society would be better off if production were at Q^*, with a price charged at P^*.

Note that this optimum position is not characterised by *zero* pollution. In other words, from society's point of view it pays to abate pollution only up to the level where the marginal benefit of reducing pollution

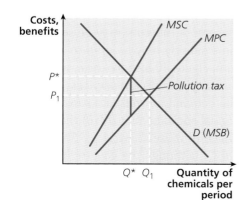

Figure 10.3 Pollution

is matched by the marginal cost of doing so. Reducing pollution to zero would be too costly.

How can society reach the optimum output of chemicals at Q^*? The **polluter pays principle** argues that polluters should face the full external costs caused by their actions. One approach would be to impose a tax on firms in line with this principle. In Figure 10.3, if firms were required to pay a tax equivalent to the vertical distance between marginal private cost (MPC) and marginal social cost (MSC), they would choose to produce at Q^*, paying a tax equal to the green line on the figure.

Knowledge check 10.4

What will be the effect if the government overestimates the size of the tax needed to discourage pollution?

A subsidy

Subsidies were mentioned in the previous chapter in the context of merit goods. They are used to encourage producers to increase their output of particular goods. Subsidies have been especially common in agriculture, which is often seen as being of strategic significance. The effect of a subsidy is to shift the supply curve down — as shown in Figure 10.4. Without the subsidy, market equilibrium is at price P_0 and the quantity traded is Q_0. With the subsidy in place, the equilibrium price falls to P_1 and the quantity traded increases to Q_1.

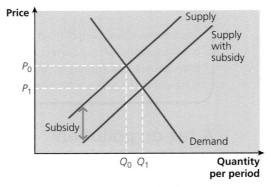

Figure 10.4 The effects of a subsidy

How does a subsidy address market failure? A museum may be seen by government as being a merit good, so a subsidy may be used to encourage more people to visit a museum. Figure 10.5 shows how such a subsidy might be used to affect the quantity of museum services provided. Demand (MPB) again shows the demand for museum services from the public, which is below the marginal social benefit (MSB) that the authorities perceive to be the true value of museum services. So, the free-market equilibrium position is at Q_1, although the government believes that Q^* is the socially optimum position. By providing a subsidy, the supply curve is shifted to the right, and consumers will choose to demand the optimum quantity at the subsidised price P_2.

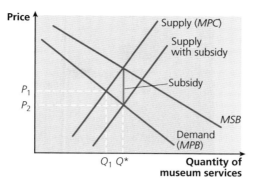

Figure 10.5 Subsidising museums

Extension material

Who receives the subsidy?

Because the price falls by less than the amount of the subsidy, the benefits of the subsidy are shared between the buyers and sellers — depending on the elasticity of demand. If the aim of the subsidy is to increase production, it is only partially successful — the degree of success also depends upon the elasticity of demand.

Summary
- Taxes and subsidies may be used to correct some forms of market failure.
- Indirect taxes may be used in the case of demerit goods.
- Subsidies can help to encourage higher demand for merit goods.

Government expenditure

Government undertakes expenditure for several reasons. This includes expenditure on the administration of government, but also to enable transfer payments to be made in order to affect the distribution of income in a society — protecting the vulnerable and addressing poverty that may exist. Some expenditures are intended to operate at the macroeconomic level, by influencing the total level of demand in the economy. What is relevant for this chapter are those parts of government expenditure that are intended to affect the operation of individual markets, for example to address market failure.

Chapter 9 discussed public goods, and argued that the free-rider problem would prevent the provision of public goods by the private sector in a free market. This does not mean that the government itself needs to provide such goods, but expenditure may be needed to encourage the private sector to provide public goods.

Earlier discussion highlighted the market failure that exists in the health and education sectors. A substantial portion of government expenditure is used to ensure the provision of healthcare and education. For example, spending on the National Health Service (NHS) amounts to approximately 7.5% of national income, with about 99% of funding coming from general taxation. The NHS accounts for about 22.5% of all UK tax revenue.

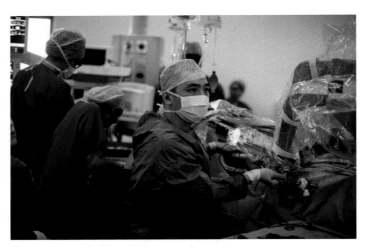
The NHS is funded largely by general taxation

The benefits from this intervention are significant. The NHS was established in 1948 to ensure that healthcare would be available to all, regardless of their wealth or income. The NHS came under pressure in the late 2010s because of growing demands for healthcare, but the principle remains — that treatment should be available to all in need of it.

Not all countries have adopted this approach. For example, healthcare in the USA relies much more heavily on private insurance. In the UK, there is also private provision that operates alongside the NHS, but this is a smaller sector.

Public–private partnerships

Knowledge check 10.7

Why is government intervention needed to ensure the supply of a public good?

Key terms

contracting out a situation in which the public sector places activities in the hands of a private firm and pays for the provision

competitive tendering a process by which the public sector calls for private firms to bid for a contract for provision of a good or service

public–private partnership an arrangement by which a government service or private business venture is funded and operated through a partnership of government and the private sector

In the case of public goods, there has to be some sort of government intervention, as a free market will not ensure the provision of these goods. Other forms of market failure (externalities or merit goods) may also require some form of intervention, even if the government does not itself provide the good or service directly. A number of ways in which the public sector can ensure provision through some sort of engagement with the private sector have been developed.

The simplest form of this is **contracting out**. Under such an arrangement, the public sector issues a contract to a private firm for the supply of some good or service. One example is waste disposal, where a local authority may issue a contract for a firm to provide the necessary waste disposal service. Competition between firms can be encouraged by a **competitive tendering** process. In other words, the contract would be announced and firms invited to put in bids specifying the quality of service they are prepared to provide, and at what price. The local authority would then be in a position to look for efficiency in choosing the most competitive bid.

More complex models of cooperation between public and private sectors have been developed, involving various kinds of **public–private partnership**. This sort of partnership is 'an arrangement by which a government service or private business venture is funded and operated through a partnership of government and the private sector' (National Audit Office). An example of this was the second Severn Bridge, which was opened in 1996 and operated by a consortium that collected tolls from all vehicles crossing into Wales. The bridge concession expired at the end of 2017 and the bridge passed into public ownership. The tolls were abolished in December 2018.

The Private Finance Initiative

The most common partnership model is the **Private Finance Initiative (PFI)**. The PFI was launched in 1992 as a way of trying to increase the involvement of the private sector in the provision of public services. This established a partnership between the public and private sectors. The public sector specifies the services that it requires, perhaps in broad terms, and then invites tenders from the private sector to design, build, finance and operate the scheme. In some cases, it may be that the project would be entirely free-standing — for example, the government may initiate a project such as a new bridge, which is then taken up by a private firm that will recover its costs entirely through user charges such as tolls. In some other cases, the project may be a joint venture between the public and private sectors. The public sector could get involved with such a venture in order to secure wider social benefits, perhaps through reductions in traffic congestion that would not be reflected in market prices, and so would not be fully taken into account by the private sector. In other cases, it may be that the private sector undertakes a project and then sells the services to the public sector, often over a period of 25 or 30 years.

The aim of the PFI is to improve the financing of public sector projects. This is partly achieved by introducing a competitive element into the tendering process, but in addition it enables the risk of a project to be shared between the public and private sectors. This was intended to enable efficiency gains to be made.

The PFI has been much debated — and much criticised because of poor quality of outputs and high cost to the taxpayer. A reformed process (PF2) was launched in December 2012, but enthusiasm for this approach has waned. The collapse of Carillon (which held a number of PFI contracts) in early 2018 fuelled the criticisms.

One effect of the PFI is to reduce the pressures on public finances by enabling greater private sector involvement in funding. However, it might be argued that this may in fact raise the cost of borrowing if the public sector would have been able to borrow on more favourable terms than commercial firms.

The introduction of a competitive element in the tendering process may be beneficial, but on the other hand it could be argued that the private sector may have less incentive than the public sector to give due attention to health and safety issues. In other words, there may be a concern that private firms will be tempted to sacrifice safety or service standards in the quest for profit. Achieving the appropriate balance between efficiency and quality of service is an inevitable problem to be faced in whatever way transport is financed and provided, for example, but it becomes a more critical issue to the extent that use of the PFI switches the focus more towards efficiency and lower costs.

Key term

Private Finance Initiative (PFI, later PF2) a funding arrangement under which the private sector designs, builds, finances and operates an asset and associated services for the public sector in return for an annual payment linked to its performance in delivering the service

---

Exercise 10.1

Discuss the advantages and disadvantages of using the PFI as a way of financing investment in projects such as a new hospital, school or student flats.

Summary
- Governments need to undertake expenditure on administration and in enabling transfer payments to the vulnerable.
- Public goods cannot be met through the free market, so governments need to intervene to ensure provision.
- Public–private partnerships have been one method of ensuring provision, but they have not always been successful.

Price controls

In some markets, governments have been seen to intervene to regulate price directly. This could be viewed as a response to market failure — for example, if it were apparent that price was not being set equal to marginal cost, so that allocative efficiency was not being achieved. In other circumstances, the government may perceive that the free market was leading to a situation in which high prices were excluding some people from the market, or where low prices were causing harm to some individuals. We will look at each in turn.

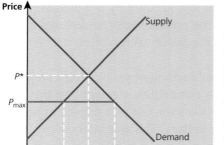

Figure 10.6 A maximum price

A maximum price

Figure 10.6 shows a market in which the equilibrium price is at P^* and quantity demanded is Q^*. Suppose that this is a good that the government thinks is beneficial for people, and it wants to encourage them to demand in greater quantity — i.e. this is a merit good. One way it could intervene would be to direct suppliers that the maximum price they could charge was P_{max}. This being so, the demand for the good would indeed be higher, at Q_d. Unfortunately, the policy may fail because suppliers will not be prepared to supply more than Q_s at this price, so the market ends up in disequilibrium. In other words, there is excess demand that cannot be met.

Rent controls: an example of a maximum price

A market in which governments have been tempted to intervene to affect prices is the housing market. House prices have escalated over the years, and a shortage of rented accommodation has arisen.

The temptation for the government is to move this market away from its equilibrium by imposing a maximum level of rent that landlords are allowed to charge their tenants.

You can use Figure 10.6 to examine the impact of this intervention. First, landlords will no longer find it profitable to supply as much rental accommodation, and so will reduce supply to Q_s. Second, at this lower rent there will be more people looking for accommodation, so that demand for rented accommodation will move to Q_d. The upshot of the rent controls, therefore, is that there is less accommodation available, and more homeless people.

It can be seen that the well-meaning rent control policy, intended to stop landlords from exploiting low-income households, merely has the effect of reducing the amount of accommodation available. This is not what was supposed to happen.

Exercise 10.2

The markets for rented and owner-occupied dwellings are likely to be interrelated, at least to some extent. Use demand and supply diagrams to examine how a rent control policy would affect the two markets in the short and long runs.

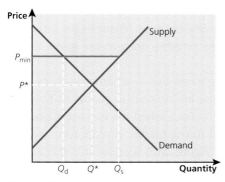

Price

P_{min}

P^*

Supply

Demand

Q_d Q^* Q_s Quantity

Figure 10.7 A minimum price

A minimum price

Figure 10.7 shows a good that the government perceives to be a demerit good so, in a free market, too much of the good is consumed. In equilibrium, the market price would be P^* and the quantity traded would be Q^*. It might be thought that one way of discouraging overconsumption of the good would be to intervene by forcing suppliers to sell at a price above the equilibrium level at, say, P_{min}. This has the desired effect, as the quantity demanded falls to Q_d. However, again we see that the market is being held in a disequilibrium position, as suppliers would be eager to sell more at the going price. There is excess supply.

Alcohol prices: an example of a minimum price

The Scottish government took the view that excessive use of alcohol was a major social concern — in other words, it viewed alcohol as a demerit good. In particular, it was perceived that low-price alcohol was encouraging behaviour that would cause health problems for individuals in the long term. It was possible for people to reach the recommended limit for alcohol consumption for only £2.50. In May 2018, a law came into effect setting a minimum price for alcohol, measured by alcoholic units. Figure 10.7 can be used to see how the market would be affected. In equilibrium, the price would be P^* and the quantity traded Q^*. Setting a minimum price at P_{min} has the desired effect of reducing demand to Q_d. On the supply side, producers would have been prepared to supply more at this price, so the market remains in disequilibrium in a situation of excess supply.

A similar situation arose in European agricultural markets when price support systems were in place. Farmers were guaranteed prices for their goods that were above the equilibrium, the main driver being a strategic one — to ensure that the sector did not run down. One result was the build-up of wine lakes and butter mountains, reflecting overproduction.

Another common example of a minimum price is where the government intervenes to impose a minimum wage, below which employers are not permitted to hire labour. This is intended to protect low-paid workers from being exploited in the labour market.

> ### Knowledge check 10.8
>
> What would be the effect of setting a minimum price that was below the equilibrium level?

Price stabilisation

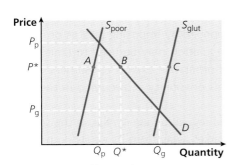

Price

P_p

P^*

P_g

S_{poor} S_{glut}

A B

C

D

Q_p Q^* Q_g Quantity

Figure 10.8 Buffer stocks

In some commodity markets, prices can exhibit volatility over time. This could arise, for example, when the supply of a good varies from period to period because of the varying state of the harvest. In such a market, the supply curve will shift to the right when the harvest is good, but shift to the left in a period when the weather is poor or where crops are affected by some disease or blight. It may also be that the demand curve tends to shift around through time, with demand for some goods reflecting fluctuations in the performance of economies. In other words, demand may shift to the left when recession bites, but to the right in times of boom and prosperity. This was discussed in Chapter 5 in relation to the market for cocoa.

Suppose that Figure 10.8 represents a market in which demand is relatively stable between periods, but in which supply varies between S_{poor} when the harvest is poor and S_{glut} when the harvest is good. The price varies between P_p and P_g. This creates a high level of uncertainty for

Key term

buffer stock a scheme intended to stabilise the price of a commodity by buying excess supply in periods when supply is high, and selling when supply is low

Exercise 10.3

Discuss why prices in some markets may be unstable from year to year and evaluate ways in which more stability might be achieved. How effective would you expect such measures to be? What would be the benefits to economic agents of having greater stability in prices?

producers, who find it difficult to form accurate expectations about the future prospects for the commodity. This means that they are less likely to invest in ways of improving productivity because of uncertain future returns. If a way could be found of stabilising the price of the good, then this could encourage producers.

A **buffer stock** is a way of attempting to do this. A scheme is set up whereby excess supply is bought up by the buffer stock in glut years to prevent the price from falling too low. In periods when the harvest is poor, stocks of the commodity are released on to the market in order to maintain the price at the agreed level. In terms of Figure 10.8, suppose that it is agreed to maintain the price at P^*. When there is a glut year, with the supply curve located at S_{glut}, there is excess supply at the agreed price of the amount BC, so this amount is bought up by the buffer stock and stored. If the supply is at S_{poor} because of a poor harvest, there is excess demand, so the buffer stock releases the quantity AB on to the market, maintaining the price.

Although this does have the effect of stabilising the price at P^*, there is a downside. If the members of the buffer stock scheme agree to maintain the price at too high a level, relative to the actual average equilibrium price over time, then it will run into difficulties. Notice in Figure 10.8 that to maintain price at P^*, the buffer stock buys up more in the glut year than it has to sell in the poor harvest year. If this pattern is repeated, then the size of stocks to be stored will rise over time. This is costly and will eventually become unsustainable.

Legislation and regulation

In some markets, the government chooses to intervene directly through legislation and regulation, rather than by influencing prices. The aim of these interventions is to influence the quantity supplied of a good or service. Legislation may be used to prevent the supply of a good, whereas regulation seeks to limit the supply without banning it altogether, or in some cases to encourage more of a good to be supplied.

Legislation can operate by declaring some goods illegal. This may also have unintended effects. Consider the situation in which action is taken to prohibit the consumption of a demerit good such as a hard drug. It can be argued that there are substantial social disbenefits arising from the consumption of hard drugs, and that addicts and potential addicts are in no position to make informed decisions about their consumption of them. One response to such a situation is to consider making the drug illegal to prevent it being sold at all.

Regulation is used to influence the demand for or supply of a good. Demand for alcohol may be affected if its sale is restricted to those aged 18 or over. In some markets, the authorities may think it important to limit the quantity of a good being supplied by imposing quotas on production and sale. For other goods, regulation may be used to limit the market power of large firms that would otherwise exploit consumers by raising price to increase their profits. This possibility is discussed in the next section under competition policy.

The economic effects of legislation and regulation are similar, in the sense that both have the effect of moving a market away from its equilibrium position. By banning a product, the effect may be to establish a black market, so that sales are hidden from the authorities but continue regardless.

Competition policy

Synoptic link

The ways in which firms may acquire (and potentially abuse) market power are discussed in Chapters 14 and 15. Competition policy is examined more fully in Chapter 14.

Competition policy is a form of regulation used to protect consumers (and, in some cases, firms) from being exploited by firms that have market power. Such market power may arise when a firm (or group of firms working together) is able to increase profits at the expense of consumers, or their suppliers. For example, firms may form a cartel (an illegal form of collusion in which firms meet to fix prices).

The Competition and Markets Authority (CMA)

Since April 2014, the conduct of the policy has been entrusted to the Competition and Markets Authority (CMA) (previously it was implemented by two agencies: the Office of Fair Trading (OFT) and the Competition Commission). The CMA investigates mergers and anticompetitive practices in markets. The expectation was that merging the OFT and the Competition Commission into a single body would simplify the implementation of competition policy in the UK, so avoiding duplication and saving costs. The CMA would also be able to operate with shorter time frames for investigations, reducing the uncertainty faced by firms that find themselves under investigation.

The main functions of the CMA are:

- investigating mergers that could potentially give rise to a substantial lessening of competition (SLC)
- assessing particular markets in which there are suspected competition problems
- antitrust enforcement by investigating possible breaches of UK or EU prohibitions against anticompetitive agreements and abuse of a dominant position
- criminal cartels — the CMA is able to bring criminal proceedings against individuals who commit the cartel offence
- consumer protection

A merger is subject to investigation by the CMA if the firms involved in the proposed merger or acquisition have a combined market share in the UK of more than 25% and if the combined assets of the firms exceed £70 million worldwide.

The CMA has a wide range of powers that it can invoke should it find that a merger is likely to result in an SLC. However, there is no presumption that the CMA will find anything wrong with a market, and the result of an investigation may be that a proposed merger raises no concerns about there being an SLC. Indeed, on a number of occasions the CMA's predecessor, the OFT, launched a consumer awareness campaign, having found that the problem with a market lay in the way consumers understood its workings, and not with the market itself.

The structure of UK policy was designed to be consistent with the stance adopted by the European Commission (EC). Brexit offers the opportunity for the UK to adopt its own independent stance, but will also bring a substantially increased workload (as the CMA only needed to pursue cases not of interest to the EC). The challenge will be to continue to coordinate action with EC investigations — and to cope with the higher workload.

Knowledge check 10.9

It has been relatively rare for the CMA to impose fines on firms for anticompetitive behaviour. Do you think this means that the policy is not working?

Summary

- The state has sometimes intervened through the direct control of prices.
- Rent controls may have the effect of reducing the amount of accommodation available.
- Regulation can be used to tackle market failure, but banning or limiting the production of a good may have unintended effects.
- Competition policy is a form of regulation used to protect consumers.

Tradable pollution permits

Earlier in the chapter the possibility of using a tax to tackle pollution was discussed. A problem with this approach is that it may be difficult to quantify the size of the tax needed to reduce pollution to a desirable level, or to identify the main culprit firms that are causing the problem. Furthermore, the costs of implementing and monitoring such a scheme are high.

Another approach is to use a tradable **pollution permit system**, under which the government issues or sells permits to firms, allowing them to pollute up to a certain limit. These permits are then tradable, so that firms that are relatively 'clean' in their production methods and do not need to use their full allocation of permits can sell their polluting rights to other firms, whose production methods produce greater levels of pollution.

> **Key term**
>
> **pollution permit system** a system for controlling pollution based on a market for permits that allows firms to pollute up to a limit

Advantages

One important advantage of such a scheme lies in the incentives for firms. Firms that pollute because of their relatively inefficient production methods will find they are at a disadvantage because they face higher costs. Rather than continuing to purchase permits, they will find that they have an incentive to produce less pollution — which, of course, is what the policy is intended to achieve. In this way, the permit system uses the market to address the externality problem — in contrast to direct regulation of environmental standards, which tries to solve pollution by overriding the market.

A second advantage is that the overall level of pollution can be controlled by this system, as the authorities control the total amount of permits that are issued. After all, the objective of the policy is to control the overall level of pollution, and a mixture of 'clean' and 'dirty' firms may produce the same amount of total emissions as uniformly 'slightly unclean' firms.

Disadvantages

However, the permit system may not be without its problems. In particular, there is the question of enforcement. For the system to be effective, sanctions must be in place for firms that pollute beyond the permitted level, and there must be an operational and cost-effective method for the authorities to check the level of emissions.

Furthermore, it may not be a straightforward exercise for the authorities to decide upon the appropriate number of permits to issue in order to produce the desired reduction in emission levels. Some alternative regulatory systems share this problem, as it is not easy to measure the extent to which marginal private and social costs diverge.

One possible criticism that is unique to a permit form of regulation is that the very different levels of pollution produced by different firms may seem inequitable — as if those firms that can afford to buy permits can pollute as much as they like. On the other hand, it might be argued that those most likely to suffer from this are the polluting firms, whose public image is likely to be tarnished if they acquire a reputation as heavy polluters. This possibility might strengthen the incentives of such firms to clean up their production. Taking the strengths and weaknesses of this approach together, it seems that on balance such a system could be effective in regulating pollution.

An example is the EU Emissions Trading System (EU ETS), which has been in operation since 2005. It now operates in 31 countries, and limits carbon emissions from more than 11,000 energy-using installations. The system works on a 'cap and trade' system. A cap is set on the total amount of greenhouse gases that can be emitted by installations that are part of the scheme, with the cap being reduced over time. Companies in the scheme receive or buy emission allowances that can then be traded with other firms. The scheme is seen as having had success in reducing emissions — by 2020 they are expected to be 21% lower compared with 2015.

Extension material

Property rights

Nobel prize winner Ronald Coase argued that the existence of property rights and transaction costs is key to understanding how markets work. In other words, the existence of a system of secure property rights is essential as an underpinning for the economy. The legal system exists in part to enforce property rights, and to provide the set of rules under which markets operate. When property rights fail, there is a failure of markets.

In this view of the world, one of the reasons underlying the existence of some externalities is that there is a failing in the system of property rights. For example, think about the situation in which a factory is emitting toxic fumes into a residential district. One way of viewing this is that the firm is interfering with local residents' clean air. If those residents could be given property rights over clean air, they could require the firm to compensate them for the costs it was inflicting. However, the problem is that, with such a wide range of people being affected to varying degrees (according to prevailing winds and how close they live to the factory), it is impossible in practical terms to use the assignment of property rights to internalise the pollution externality. This is because the problem of coordination requires high transaction costs in order for property rights to be individually enforced. Therefore, the government effectively takes over the property rights on behalf of the residents, and acts as a collective enforcer.

Ronald Coase therefore argued that externality effects could be internalised in conditions where property rights could be enforced, and where the transaction costs of doing so were not too large.

Summary

- In seeking to counter the harmful effects of externalities, governments look for ways of internalising the externality, by bringing external costs and benefits within the market mechanism.
- For example, the 'polluter pays' principle argues that the best way of dealing with a pollution externality is to force the polluter to face the full costs of its actions.
- Attempts have been made to tackle pollution through taxation or through the regulation of environmental standards.
- In some cases the allocation of property rights can be effective in curbing the effects of externalities — so long as the transaction costs of implementing it are not too high.

Information provision

Knowledge check 10.10

What is meant by the notion of asymmetric information?

Market failure can arise from information failure, especially where there is asymmetric information or where economic agents lack information or the capacity to process the information available. In such circumstances, the solution would seem to be to find a way of providing the information to remedy the situation.

One example discussed in Chapter 9 was that of second-hand cars, where car dealers may find that they cannot find buyers for good-quality cars at a fair price if potential buyers cannot distinguish quality. The solution here may be to tackle the problem at its root, by finding a way to provide information about quality. In the case of second-hand cars, AA inspection schemes or the offering of warranties may be a way of improving the flow of information about the quality of cars for sale. Buyers may then have confidence that they are not buying a lemon.

Similarly, in the case of the insurance market, the asymmetric information problem helps to explain why insurance companies try to cover themselves by insisting on comprehensive health histories of those who take out health insurance, and include exclusion clauses that entitle them to refuse to pay out if past illnesses have not been disclosed. It also helps to explain why banks may insist on collateral to back up loans.

Information problems may also be present in respect of some demerit goods. Think back to the tobacco example discussed earlier. Tobacco is seen by government as a demerit good on the grounds that smokers underestimate the damaging effects of smoking. There may also be negative externalities caused by passive smoking. At first, taxes were used to try to discourage smoking, but given the inelastic demand for tobacco, this proved ineffective. The taxes were reinforced by extensive campaigns to spread information about the damaging effects of smoking. When even this did not solve the problem, the government had to introduce regulation by prohibiting smoking in public buildings.

Evaluation of government intervention and government failure

Some roles are critical for a government to perform if a mixed economy is to function effectively. A vital role is the provision by the government of an environment in which markets can operate effectively. There must be stability in the political system if firms and consumers are to take decisions with confidence about the future. And there must be a secure system of property rights, without which markets could not be expected to work.

There may be areas of the economy where government intervention is needed for markets to work. For example, if firms are to operate effectively and to compete in international markets, they need access to public goods such as a good transport and communications infrastructure. If the government does not put sufficient resources into road maintenance, or the development of the rail network, then firms may face higher costs, and be disadvantaged relative to their international competitors. On the other hand, if the government over-invests, then there is an opportunity cost, because more resources used for infrastructure implies that fewer resources are available for private sector investment.

An example is the HS2 project, which is designed to provide a high-speed rail link between London and Birmingham, extended to Manchester and Yorkshire (Sheffield and Leeds). The first passengers to use HS2 are expected in 2026. Estimates of the cost have varied — the budget for the project in late 2017 was £55.7 billion, but some critics have claimed that it could cost £200 billion. The project has been highly contentious, raising questions about value for money as well as specifics about the route, and whether or not this is the best way of using the funds. The debate provides an example of the tension that can arise when the government seeks to invest heavily in specific projects.

The HS2 high-speed rail network has drawn protest from residents across its intended route

In addition, there are other sources of market failure that require intervention. This does not necessarily mean that governments need to substitute markets with direct action. However, it does mean that they need to be more active in markets that cannot operate effectively, while at the same time performing an enabling role to encourage markets to work well whenever this is feasible.

Such intervention entails costs. There are costs of administering, and costs of monitoring the policy to ensure that it is working as intended. Some policies have unintended effects that may not culminate in successful elimination of market failure. Indeed, in some cases government intervention may introduce new market distortions, leading to a phenomenon known as **government failure**.

It is therefore important to look out for the unintended distortionary effects that some policies can have on resource allocation in a society. In other words, there is a need to check that the marginal costs of implementing and monitoring policies do not exceed their marginal benefits.

Government intervention can only be as effective as the information on which it is based. The government faces risk and uncertainty about market conditions, and does not always have full information about the market failures that it is attempting to tackle. There is a possibility of government failure that may leave matters worse than without the interventions introduced.

> **Summary**
> - Information failure can be tackled by ensuring that economic agents have access to the information that they need.
> - Government failure can occur when well-meaning intervention by governments has unintended effects.
> - It is important for governments to intervene when markets fail to produce a good outcome for society, but it is also important that the costs of such intervention do not exceed the benefits achieved by it.

Case study 10.1

A bittersweet tax?

In his Budget in 2016, George Osborne, the then Chancellor of the Exchequer, announced a new tax intended to tackle the growing problem of childhood obesity. This soon became popularly known as the 'sugar tax', although the levy targets the producers and importers of sugary soft drinks, not all sugar and products that contain sugar. The 'Soft Drinks Industry Levy' came into effect on 6 April 2018.

The consultation document on the gov.uk website stated that:

> *This is not a tax on consumers. The government is not increasing the price of products; companies don't have to pass the charge on to their customers. If companies take the right steps to make their drinks healthier they will pay less tax, or even nothing at all.*

Source: www.gov.uk/government/news/soft-drinks-industry-levy-12-things-you-should-know

Case study 10.1 (continued)

The levy is charged at different rates according to the total sugar content, with companies having to pay 18p per litre of drink if the product contains more than 5 grams of sugar per 100 millilitres and 24p per litre if it contains more than 8 grams per millilitre. Pure fruit juices and drinks with a high milk content are exempt.

When originally announced, it was thought that revenue from the levy would be in the region of £520 million, which was intended to be used to encourage children to participate in sport. However, on the day the levy came into effect, this estimate had been reduced to £240 million.

Some firms had taken action before the introduction of the levy, by cutting the sugar content of drinks — in some cases attracting complaints from their consumers.

Several other countries have introduced similar levies. For example, in Mexico it was found that a 10% tax led to a 6% reduction in sales of sugar-sweetened drinks in 2014 (the figure for low-income households was a reduction of 9%). The Danish experience of a so-called 'fat tax' was less successful, and was repealed after just a year of operation.

The 'sugar tax' targets the producers and importers of soft drinks, rather than the consumers

Follow-up questions

a Would you expect the manufacturers of sugary drinks to absorb all of the levy, or would they pass some of the cost on to consumers? Explain your answer.

b Discuss the sort of market failure that the government was trying to tackle through the levy.

c The estimated revenue from the levy was seen as being much lower at the time of its launch than had originally been envisaged. Discuss whether this is an indication that the levy was not working.

CHAPTER 10 QUESTIONS

A Multiple-choice questions

1 The production of a product has been proven to cause a negative externality of production. Which of the following would be the most appropriate government intervention in the market?

  a   A subsidy for the product
  b   A public–private partnership with the product
  c   Competition policy
  d   A tax on the product

2 The minimum wage is an example of:

  a   Price control
  b   Government expenditure
  c   Information provision
  d   Sales tax

3 Information provision is most likely to affect:

  a   The quality of a product
  b   The demand for a product
  c   The cost of a product
  d   The production of a product

B Knowledge and understanding questions

4 Explain how legislation could be used to correct the market failure that may arise from smoking.   [2 marks]

5 Explain two ways in which the government could correct the market failure that may arise from single-use plastic pollution.   [4 marks]

6 Explain how a system of tradable pollution permits can be used to correct market failure caused by a negative externality of production.   [4 marks]

C Stimulus response question

7 On 1 May 2018, a minimum price per unit of alcohol was introduced in Scotland. Each unit of alcohol purchased must be priced at a minimum of 50p. For example, a bottle of wine containing 12 units of alcohol must be priced at a minimum of £6 per bottle.

   Similar proposals have been made for a minimum price for alcohol to be introduced in Wales and England.

  a   Explain, using a diagram, why there may be market failure in the market for alcohol.   [4 marks]
  b   Evaluate the effectiveness of a minimum price for alcohol in correcting market failure in the alcohol market.   [12 marks]

SECTION
1

MICROECONOMICS

Part 3
Business objectives

Chapter 11

Costs, economies of scale, revenue and profit

Firms need to make key decisions about production and price. Revenues and costs are an important influence on these decisions, which is why our analysis begins with exploring them. This chapter examines some of the key concepts that are needed in order to analyse the behaviour of firms, and the following chapter considers the objectives that firms may choose to pursue.

Learning objectives

After studying this chapter, you should be able to:

- explain the short and long run in terms of fixed and variable factors
- explain accounting, normal and supernormal profits
- explain, with the aid of a diagram, the law of diminishing returns
- explain, with the aid of a diagram, internal and external economies of scale
- explain, with the aid of a diagram, diseconomies of scale
- explain, with the aid of a diagram, the minimum efficient scale
- evaluate the causes of economies and diseconomies of scale
- evaluate the significance of economies and diseconomies of scale
- explain and calculate fixed, variable, total, average and marginal costs
- explain and calculate total, average and marginal revenue
- explain accounting, normal and supernormal profits
- explain and calculate profit and loss

Types of firm

Key term

firm (business) an organisation that produces output (a good or service)

The economic agents concerned with providing the supply of goods and services are **firms (businesses)**. Firms exist in order to organise production by bringing together various factors of production to supply output to market.

Internally, firms may be organised in various ways, from small businesses such as a corner shop to mega-sized multinational corporations such as Google. A key decision that all firms face concerns the scale of operations. This decision turns partly on the nature of the market that the firm is serving, but it also depends upon the technology of the sector in which it operates and the structure of costs that it faces.

Some firms may need to grow in order to compete with other large-scale businesses in global markets. There may be many reasons why firms wish to expand their operations. In some sectors, there are examples of both large and small firms. For example, in the leisure sector, your local

Google, a major multinational corporation

gymnasium may be a relatively small enterprise, but there are also some big players in the sports market, such as Chelsea FC and Sky. In the transport sector, there may be small local taxi firms, but there are also large firms such as British Airways.

Summary

- A firm is an organisation that exists to bring together factors of production in order to produce goods or services.
- Firms range, in the complexity of their organisation, from sole traders to large companies.
- Firms vary in size, from local concerns to large multinational corporations operating in global markets.

Firms and output

Synoptic link

The notion of factors of production was introduced in Chapter 1.

Key terms

short run the period in which at least one factor of production is fixed in supply

long run the period over which the firm is able to vary the inputs of all its factors of production

Firms have to make key decisions about the quantity of output that they wish to produce. This also involves taking decisions about the inputs of factors of production needed to produce this output, and the ways in which those factors are combined. An important element in taking these decisions concerns the way in which the costs of production vary with the level of output to be produced, which depends upon the prices of the factors of production and the ways in which they are combined.

This section and the next focus on the relationship between costs and the level of output produced by a firm. For simplicity, assume that the firm produces a single product using two factors of production — labour and capital.

The short run and the long run

In exploring the firm's decisions, it is important to distinguish between the **short run** and the **long run**. In the short run the firm faces limited flexibility. Varying the quantity of labour input may be relatively straightforward — a firm can increase the use of overtime, or hire more workers, fairly quickly. However, varying the amount of capital that the firm has at its disposal may take longer. For example, it takes time to commission a new piece of machinery or to build a new factory. Hence labour is often regarded as a variable factor and capital as a fixed factor. The short run is defined as the period over which the firm is free to vary the input of variable factors but not of fixed factors. In the long run, the firm is able to vary inputs of both variable and fixed factors.

The law of diminishing returns

The nature of technology in an industry will determine the way in which output varies with the quantity of inputs. However, one thing is certain. If the firm increases the amount of inputs of the variable factor (labour) while holding constant the input of the other factor (capital), it will gradually derive less additional output per unit of labour for each further increase. This is known as the **law of diminishing returns**, and is one of the few 'laws' in economics. It is a short-run concept, as it relies on the assumption that capital is fixed.

It can readily be seen why this should be the case. Suppose a firm has 10 computer programmers working in an office, using 10 computers. The 11th worker may add some extra output, as the workers may be able to 'hot-desk' and take their coffee breaks at different times. The 12th worker may also add some extra output, perhaps by keeping the printers stocked with paper. However, if the firm keeps adding programmers without increasing the number of computers, each extra worker will be adding less additional output to the office. Indeed, the 20th worker may add nothing at all, being unable to get access to a computer. In other words, as the input of a variable factor is increased, the additional output produced by each additional unit of input falls.

This can be demonstrated using a diagram that plots the amount of additional output produced as the amount of labour input is increased, holding other inputs fixed. This is known as the **marginal physical product of labour (MPP_L)**. Figure 11.1 illustrates the situation. When labour input is relatively low, the additional output produced by an extra unit of labour increases. However, beyond L^*, the additional output (MPP_L) declines as diminishing marginal returns set in. This occurs because labour input is being increased while other factors of production are fixed in supply.

Knowledge check 11.1

When considering the decisions made by firms, how do we define the 'long run'?

Key terms

law of diminishing returns a law stating that if a firm increases its inputs of one factor of production while holding inputs of the other factor(s) fixed, eventually the firm will get diminishing marginal returns from the variable factor

marginal physical product of labour (MPP_L) the additional quantity of output produced by an additional unit of labour input

Knowledge check 11.2

Why is the law of diminishing returns regarded as a short-run concept?

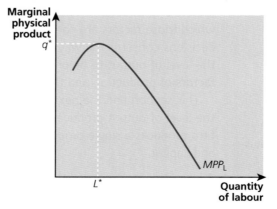

Figure 11.1 Diminishing returns and the marginal physical product of labour

Total, marginal and average costs

It is important to distinguish between total, marginal and average costs. **Total cost** is the sum of all costs that are incurred in order to produce a given level of output. Total cost will always increase as the firm increases its level of production, as this will require more inputs of factors of production, materials and so on.

Average cost is simply the cost per unit of output — it is total cost divided by the level of output produced.

Economists rely heavily on the idea that firms, consumers and other economic actors can make good decisions by thinking in terms of the margin. This is known as the marginal principle. For example, a firm may examine whether a small change in its behaviour makes matters better or worse. In this context, **marginal cost** is important. It is defined as the change in total cost associated with a small change in output. In other words, it is the additional cost incurred by the firm if it increases output by 1 unit.

Costs in the short run

Because the firm cannot vary some of its inputs in the short run, some costs may be regarded as **fixed costs** and some as **variable costs**. Total costs are the sum of fixed and variable costs:

total costs = total fixed costs + total variable costs

Variable costs include items such as the cost of raw material and other components, or the cost of labour. These are variable because more inputs are needed as the level of production increases. Fixed costs include such things as the rental on a factory or office, or the committed advertising budget. Some costs could not be recovered if the firm were to exit from the market — these are known as **sunk costs**.

A fast-food outlet may be able to expand production in the short run by hiring more staff and buying more ingredients (variable costs), but it would need to make do with its existing premises and kitchen equipment in the short run (fixed costs).

Total costs increase as the firm increases the volume of production because more of the variable input is needed to increase output. The way in which the costs will vary depends on the nature of the production process, and on whether the prices of labour or other factor inputs alter as output increases.

A common assumption made by economists is that the short-run average cost ($SATC$) curve will be U-shaped. Short-run marginal costs (SMC) mirror the MPP_L, so as diminishing returns set in at q_{dr} in Figure 11.2, marginal costs rise. The SMC cuts the $SATC$ at the minimum point of $SATC$ (at q^*), as explained in Quantitative skills box 11.1.

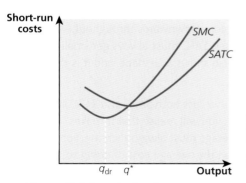

Figure 11.2 Costs in the short run

The relationship between output and costs

Table 11.1 provides an arithmetic example to illustrate the relationship between these different aspects of costs. The firm represented here faces fixed costs of £225 per week. The table shows the costs of production for up to 6,000 units of the firm's product per week. Column 3 shows total variable costs of production: you can see that these rise quite steeply as the volume of production increases. Adding fixed and variable costs gives the total costs at each output level. This is shown in column 4, which is the sum of columns 2 and 3.

Table 11.1 The short-run relationship between output and costs (in £s)

(1) Output (000 units per week)	(2) Fixed costs (STFC)	(3) Total variable costs (STVC)	(4) Total costs (2) + (3) (STC)	(5) Average total cost (4)/(1) (SATC)	(6) Marginal cost Δ(4)/Δ(1) (SMC)	(7) Average variable cost (3)/(1) (SAVC)	(8) Average fixed cost (2)/(1) (SAFC)
1	225	85	310	310		85	225
					65		
2	225	150	375	187.5		75	112.5
					60		
3	225	210	435	145		70	75
					90		
4	225	300	525	131.25		75	56.25
					175		
5	225	475	700	140		95	45
					395		
6	225	870	1,095	182.5		145	37.5

Average total cost (SATC — column 5) is calculated as total cost divided by output. To calculate marginal cost, you need to work out the additional cost of producing an extra unit of output at each output level. This is calculated as the change in costs divided by the change in output (Δ column 4 divided by Δ column 1, where Δ means 'change in').

Finally, average variable costs (SAVC, i.e. column 3/column 1) and average fixed costs (SAFC, i.e. column 2/column 1) can be calculated.

Notice that SATC initially falls as output increases, but after 4,000 units of output it begins to increase. SATC is composed of average variable and average fixed costs (SAVC and SAFC). SAFC falls continuously as output increases, because the fixed costs are being spread out across more units of output. This helps to explain why SATC initially falls. However, as diminishing marginal returns set in, average variable costs begin to increase, and this helps to explain the way that SATC varies with output.

Graphing short-run costs

Quantitative skills 11.1 showed the arithmetic relationship between the components of short-run costs. The short-run average and marginal curves based on these data are plotted in Figure 11.3. First, notice that the short-run average total cost (SATC) curve takes on a U-shape. This form is often assumed in economic analysis. SATC is the sum of average fixed and variable costs (SAFC and SAVC, respectively). Average fixed costs slope downwards throughout — this is because fixed costs do not vary with the level of output, so as output increases, SAFC must always get smaller, as the fixed costs are spread over more and more units of output. However, SAVC also shows a U-shape, and it is this that gives the U-shape to SATC.

A very important aspect of Figure 11.3 is that the short-run marginal cost (SMC) curve cuts both SAVC and SATC at their minimum points. This is always the case. If you think about this for a moment, you will realise that it makes good sense. If you are adding on something that is greater than the average, the average must always increase. For a firm, when the marginal cost of producing an additional unit of a good is higher than the average cost of doing so, the average cost must rise. If the marginal cost is the same as the average cost, then average cost will not change.

Quantitative skills 11.2 (continued)

An example can show how general this rule is. Suppose that a team newly promoted to football's premier league brings in a new striker, whose wage far exceeds that of existing players. What happens to the average wage? Of course it must increase, as the marginal wage of the new player is higher than the previous average wage. This is quite simply an arithmetic property of the average and the marginal, and always holds true.

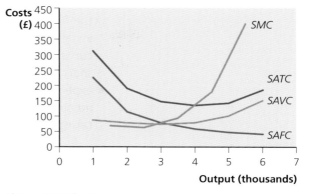

Figure 11.3 Short-run cost curves

Study tip

Remember that when you draw the average and marginal cost curves for a firm, the marginal cost curve will *always* cut average cost at the minimum point of average cost. Another way of viewing marginal cost is as the *slope* or gradient of the total cost curve.

Knowledge check 11.5

When drawing average and marginal cost curves, what is the key relationship between them?

Remember that the short-run cost curves show the relationship between the volume of production and costs under the assumption that the quantity of capital and other inputs are fixed, so that in order to change output the firm has to vary the amount of labour. The *position* of the cost curves therefore depends on the quantity of capital. In other words, there is a short-run average total cost curve for each given level of other inputs.

Exercise 11.2

In producing a good, a firm incurs fixed costs of 300. If it produces 40 units of the good, it finds that variable costs (*STVC*) amount to 140.
a Calculate *STC*, *SATC*, *SAVC* and *SAFC*.
If the firm increases output to 50 units, it now faces variable costs (*STVC*) of 200.
b Calculate *STC*, *SATC*, *SAVC*, *SAFC* and *SMC*.
When production is 60, short-run total costs (*STC*) are 660.
c Calculate short-run variable costs (*STVC*).

Costs in the long run

In the long run, a firm is able to vary capital and labour (and other factor inputs). It is therefore likely to choose the level of capital that is appropriate for the level of output it expects to produce. Figure 11.4 shows a selection of short-run average total cost curves corresponding to different expected output levels, and therefore different levels of capital. With the set of *SATC* curves in Figure 11.4, the long-run average cost curve can be seen to take on a U-shape.

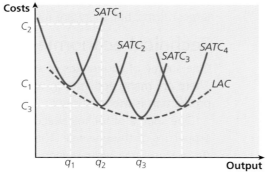

Figure 11.4 Short-run cost curves with different levels of capital input

Short-run and long-run average cost

For the firm in Figure 11.4, the choice of capital is important. Suppose the firm wants to produce the quantity of output q_1. It would choose to install the amount of capital corresponding to the short-run total cost curve $SATC_1$, and could then produce q_1 at an average cost of C_1 in the short run. However, if the firm finds that demand is more buoyant than expected, and so wants to increase output to q_2, in the short run it has no option but to increase labour input and expand output along $SATC_1$, taking cost per unit to C_2.

In the longer term, the firm will be able to adjust its capital stock and move on to $SATC_2$, reducing average cost to C_3. So, as soon as the firm moves away from the output level for which capital stock is designed, it incurs higher average cost in the short run than is possible in the long run.

In this way a long-run average cost curve can be derived to illustrate how the firm chooses to vary its capital stock for any given level of output. The dashed line in Figure 11.4 shows what such a curve would look like for the firm. The long-run average cost curve (LAC) just touches each of the short-run average cost curves, and is known as the 'envelope' of the $SATC$ curves.

Economies of scale

Key term

economies of scale occur for a firm when an increase in the scale of production leads to production at lower long-run average cost

Knowledge check 11.6

Will firms always benefit from economies of scale if they increase production?

Synoptic link

The idea of the division of labour was introduced in Chapter 2.

One of the reasons why firms find it beneficial to be large is the existence of **economies of scale**. These occur when a firm finds that it is more efficient in cost terms to produce on a larger scale.

It is not difficult to imagine industries in which economies of scale are likely to arise. For example, recall the notion of the division of labour, which you encountered earlier. When a firm expands, it reaches a certain scale of production at which it becomes worthwhile to take advantage of division of labour. Workers begin to specialise in certain stages of the production process, and their productivity increases. Because this is only possible for relatively large-scale production, this is an example of economies of scale. It is the size of the firm (in terms of its output level) that enables it to produce more efficiently — that is, at lower average cost.

Although the division of labour is one source of economies of scale, it is by no means the only source, and there are several explanations of cost benefits from producing on a large scale. Some of these are industry-specific, and so some sectors of the economy exhibit more significant economies of scale than others — it is in these activities that the larger firms tend to be found. There are no hairdressing salons in the top 10 largest firms, but there are plenty of oil companies.

Technical economies of scale

One source of economies of scale is in the technology of production. There are many activities in which the technology is such that large-scale production is more efficient.

One source of technical economies of scale arises from the physical properties of the universe. There is a physical relationship between the surface area of an object and the volume of material that it can enclose. In other words, the storage capacity of an object increases proportionately more than its surface area. A large ship can transport proportionally more than a small ship, and large barrels hold more liquid relative to the surface area of the barrel than small barrels. Hence there may be benefits in operating on a large scale.

Furthermore, some capital equipment is designed for large-scale production, and would only be viable for a firm operating at a high volume of production. Combine harvesters cannot be used in small fields, while a production line for car production would not be viable for small levels of output.

There are many economic activities in which there are high *overhead* expenditures. Such components of a firm's costs do not vary directly with the scale of production. For example, having built a factory, the cost of that factory is the same regardless of the amount of output that is produced in it. Expenditure on research and development could be seen as such an overhead, which may be viable only when a firm reaches a certain size.

Marketing

Firms need to reach their intended customers. This means that they need to devote resources to advertising in order to attract buyers. But this is not all — they also need to find out what characteristics those potential buyers are looking for in the product. This requires firms to devote part of their resources to a marketing budget.

There may be scale economies involved here, as the average spend on marketing for a large firm is likely to be less per unit sold than for a small firm. In other words, the average cost per unit of marketing may be lower for a larger firm. A large firm such as Cadbury's incurs high marketing expenditure, but because of its large volume of sales, its per unit spend is lower than some smaller-scale chocolatiers with lower sales volume. Although expenditure may increase as output increases, it will do so less than proportionately.

Management

A second source of economies of scale pertains to the management of firms. One of the key factors of production is managerial input. A certain number of managers are required to oversee the production process. As the firm expands, there is a range of volumes of output over which the management team does not need to grow as rapidly as the overall volume of the firm, as a large firm can be managed more efficiently.

All firms need to conduct certain functions such as accounting or human resource management. As a firm expands, it may be able to employ specialist staff to handle these functions, and may not need to expand those sections of the company proportionately with the growth of the business. Again, this may lead to economies of scale. For a firm operating on a small scale, it may need to buy in the expertise that it needs, for example to audit its accounts or advise on employment law. However, if its market is limited in size, or confined to a local area, this may be unavoidable, and the firm may not be looking to expand.

Finance

Large firms may have advantages in a number of other areas. For example, a large firm with a strong reputation may be able to raise finance for further expansion on more favourable terms than a small firm. In other words, a large firm may be able to persuade the bank to advance them loans at lower rates of interest than a small firm, where the risks may be seen to be greater. This, of course, reinforces the market position of the largest firms in a sector and makes it more difficult for relative newcomers to become established.

Purchasing

Once a firm has grown to the point where it is operating on a relatively large scale, it will also be purchasing its inputs in relatively large volumes. In particular, this relates to raw materials, energy and transport services. When buying in bulk in this way, firms may be able to negotiate good deals with their suppliers, and so again reduce average cost as output increases.

It may even be the case that some of the firm's suppliers will find it beneficial to locate in proximity to the firm's factory, which would reduce costs even more.

Internal and external economies of scale

The factors listed so far that may lead to economies of scale arise from the internal expansion of a firm. In other words, these **internal economies of scale** arise from the expansion of the firm. For example, as a firm grows it may find that the firm can be managed more efficiently.

However, if the firm is in an industry that is itself expanding, there may also be **external economies of scale**. Firms may benefit from the fact that they operate in an industry that is expanding.

Concentration

One example of an external economy of scale is where a firm is located close to other firms in the same industry or related activities. Such geographical concentration can mean that transport and communication links will be developed, so all firms will benefit.

Technology and skills

Some of the most successful firms of recent years have been involved in activities that require high levels of technology and skills. Web design is one example of an economic activity that has expanded rapidly. As the sector expands, a pool of skilled labour is built up that all the firms can draw upon. The very success of the sector encourages people to acquire the skills needed to enter it, colleges may begin to find it viable to provide courses and so on. Each individual firm benefits in this way from the overall expansion of the sector. The greater availability of skilled workers reduces the amount that individual firms need to spend on training.

Web design is by no means the only example of this. Formula 1 development teams, pharmaceutical companies and others similarly enjoy external economies of scale.

Economies of scope

There are various ways in which firms expand their scale of operations. Some do so within a relatively focused market, but others are multi-product firms that produce a range of different products, sometimes in quite different markets.

For example, look at Nestlé. You may immediately think of instant coffee, and indeed Nestlé produces 200 different brands of instant coffee worldwide. However, Nestlé also produces baby milk powder, mineral water, ice cream and pet food, and has diversified into hotels and restaurants.

Such conglomerate companies can benefit from *economies of scope*, whereby there may be benefits of size across a range of different products. These economies may arise because there are activities that can be shared across the product range. For example, a company may not need a finance or accounting section for each different product, nor human resource or marketing departments. Therefore, there is scope for economies to be made as the firm expands.

Exercise 11.3

Which of the following reflects a movement *along* a long-run average cost curve, and which would cause a *shift* of a long-run average cost curve?

a A firm becomes established in a market, learning the best ways of utilising its factors of production.

b A firm observes that average cost falls as it expands its scale of production.

c The larger a firm becomes, the more difficult it becomes to manage, causing average cost to rise.

d A firm operating in the financial sector installs new, faster computers, enabling its average cost to fall for any given level of service that it provides.

Diseconomies of scale

Key term

diseconomies of scale occur for a firm when an increase in the scale of production leads to higher long-run average costs

Synoptic link

The problems caused when the owners of a firm are separated from the managers who take everyday decisions are discussed in Chapter 12.

Notice that there are likely to be limits to the extent of economies of scale. At some point, **diseconomies of scale** are likely to cut in — in other words, average costs may begin to rise with an increase in output at some volume of production. There are a variety of reasons why such diseconomies may arise.

Communication

One issue that arises as a firm expands is that it becomes more difficult to communicate across the organisation. This is especially the case if the firm has to operate across a range of different locations. This makes the organisation more difficult to manage, if the central managers cannot readily communicate their needs and intentions to the workforce.

Coordination

Similarly, coordinating activity across a large firm becomes more costly and less efficient. For example, suppose that a manufacturing firm has separate factories producing components of a good, which then needs to be assembled somewhere else. Coordinating in order to establish an efficient supply chain becomes more and more difficult as the firm expands. Indeed, it is possible that some multinational corporations have divided their production activities across a number of countries in order to take advantage of local conditions or resources in different locations. This adds to the problems of coordinating the production process.

Motivation

When a firm becomes large, it comes to rely on managers to oversee everyday production activities and take day-to-day decisions. The firm's owners may find it difficult to motivate these managers to run the firm in the way that they want.

Extension material

Returns to scale

In Figure 11.5, if the firm expands its output up to q^*, long-run average cost falls. Up to q^* of output is the range over which there are economies of scale. To the right of q^*, however, long-run average cost rises as output continues to be increased, and the firm experiences diseconomies of scale. The output q^* itself is at the intermediate state of constant returns to scale.

It is important not to confuse the notion of returns to scale with the idea introduced earlier of diminishing marginal returns to a factor. The two concepts arise in different circumstances. The law of diminishing returns to a factor applies in the *short run*, when a firm increases its inputs of one factor of production while facing fixed amounts of other factors. It is therefore solely a short-run phenomenon. Diseconomies of scale (sometimes known as *decreasing returns to scale*) can occur in the *long run*, and the term refers to how output changes as a firm varies the quantities of *all* factors.

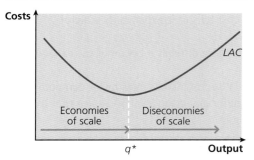

Figure 11.5 Economies and diseconomies of scale

The minimum efficient scale

Key term

minimum efficient scale the level of output at which long-run average cost stops falling as output increases

When considering long-run costs it is important to note that the point at which long-run average cost stops falling is known as the **minimum efficient scale**. This is the smallest level of output that a firm can produce at the minimum level of long-run average cost.

The long-run average cost (*LAC*) curve is often drawn as a U-shape because of the assumptions that were made about the technology of production. The underlying assumption here is that the firm faces economies of scale at relatively low levels of output, so that *LAC* slopes downwards. However, at some point decreasing returns to scale set in, and *LAC* then begins to slope upwards.

Possible shapes of the *LAC*

Will the *LAC* curve always take this shape? It turns out to be a convenient representation, but in practice the *LAC* curve can take on a variety of shapes. Figure 11.6 shows some of these. LAC_1 is the typical U-shape, which has been discussed. LAC_2 shows an example of a situation in which there are economies of scale up to a point, after which long-run average cost levels out and there is a long, flat range over which the firm faces constant returns to scale, with costs increasing at the same rate as output. LAC_3 is a bit similar, except that the constant returns to scale (flat) segment eventually runs out and diseconomies of scale set in. In LAC_4 the economies of scale continue over the whole range of output shown. This could occur in a market where the fixed costs are substantial, dominating the influence of variable costs.

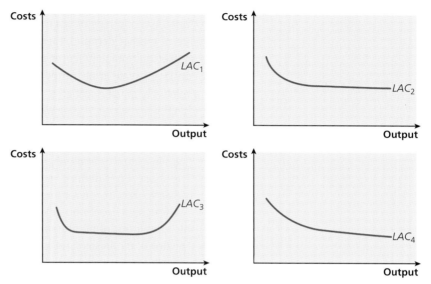

Figure 11.6 Possible shapes of the LAC curve

It transpires that the size of the minimum efficient scale relative to market demand has an important influence on the way in which a market will develop, and this has implications for the market power held by firms. This will be explored in the following chapters.

Evaluation of economies and diseconomies of scale

From a firm's perspective, the existence of economies of scale is of great importance. If the firm can produce at lower average cost by expanding its operations, there may be potential for increasing its profits — although this also depends upon the state of demand. A firm facing economies of scale therefore has an incentive to expand. Notice that such economies are more likely to be available in some activities than others, partly depending on the technology of production. Furthermore, a firm that overreaches itself and expands beyond the minimum efficient scale may find that diseconomies begin to set in.

Economies of scale are likely to be especially important for a firm that faces large fixed relative to variable costs. As the firm expands, such fixed costs are spread across more units of output, so giving rise to falling average costs. However, such fixed costs may not be present in all activities, as explained earlier. The fixed costs entailed in constructing a new rail network are enormous compared to the variable costs of carrying a few extra passengers when the network is complete. Setting up a market stall to sell craft-based products carries no such upfront expenditure.

Marketing and management economies of scale may be accessible across a wide range of sectors, as firms are able to rationalise their

Synoptic link

The influence of economies of scale on the intensity of competition will be discussed in Chapters 13–15.

management functions, but there may be limits to how large a firm grows before hitting inefficiencies and diseconomies.

The extent of economies of scale in an industry and the level of output at which diseconomies set in is also significant because it affects the operation of markets. In particular, the existence of economies of scale affects the ability of a firm to compete with other firms — and ultimately the extent of economies (or diseconomies of scale) has a major impact on the structure of the market and the number of firms that will be viable.

When diseconomies of scale set in at a low level of output relative to the size of market demand, there is likely to be scope for firms to enter the market quite readily (ceteris paribus). However, if there are substantial economies of scale, it becomes more likely that the market will be dominated by a relatively small number of firms.

Summary

- A firm may face inflexibility in the short run, with some factors being fixed in quantity and only some being variable.
- The short run is defined in this context as the period over which a firm is free to vary some factors, but not others.
- The long run is defined as the period over which the firm is able to vary the input of all of its factors of production.
- The law of diminishing returns states that if a firm increases the input of a variable factor while holding input of the fixed factor constant, eventually the firm will get diminishing marginal returns from the variable factor.
- Short-run costs can be separated into fixed, sunk and variable costs.
- There is a clear and immutable relationship between total, average and marginal costs.
- The marginal cost curve always cuts a U-shaped average cost curve at the latter's minimum point.
- Economies of scale occur when long-run average cost falls as output rises.
- The minimum efficient scale is the level of output at which long-run average cost stops falling.
- Diseconomies of scale occur when long-run average cost rises as output rises.
- The long-run average cost curve can take a variety of shapes.

Exercise 11.5

A firm faces long-run total cost conditions as shown in Table 11.2.

Table 11.2 Output and long-run costs

Output (000 units per week)	Total cost (£000)
0	0
1	32
2	48
3	82
4	140
5	228
6	352

a Calculate long-run average cost and long-run marginal cost for each level of output.

b Plot long-run average cost and long-run marginal cost curves on a graph. (*Hint*: don't forget to plot *LMC* at points that are halfway between the corresponding output levels.)

c Identify the output level at which long-run average cost is at a minimum.

d Identify the output level at which *LAC* = *LMC*.

e Within what range of output does this firm enjoy economies of scale?

f Within what range of output does the firm experience diseconomies of scale?

Revenue of firms

In Chapter 6, you saw how the total revenue received by a firm varies along the demand curve, according to the price elasticity of demand. In the same way that there is a relationship between total, average and marginal cost, there is also a relationship between **total revenue**, **average revenue** and **marginal revenue**.

Chapter 6 introduced the relationship between the demand curve and the revenues received by a firm from selling different levels of output. The relationship between total revenue and the price elasticity of demand was also explained. Indeed, ignoring indirect taxes, the price of a good is the average revenue received by the firm, and the total revenue is the price multiplied by the quantity sold.

Moving down along the demand curve, the average revenue per unit (i.e. the price) of a good falls but the quantity demanded increases. What happens to total revenue depends upon the balance between the fall in price and the increase in quantity.

You saw earlier in this chapter that there is a fixed mathematical relationship between total, average and marginal costs. The same applies to total, average and marginal revenue. Marginal revenue is the additional revenue received by the firm when it sells an additional unit of output.

When average revenue (price) falls, marginal revenue also falls, as the revenue received on the last unit is now lower. However, because all customers also experience the fall in the price, marginal revenue must fall more rapidly than average revenue. Indeed mathematically, when the demand curve is a straight line, marginal revenue always falls at twice the rate of the fall in average revenue (price).

The formulae for these are:

Total revenue = price × quantity sold

$$\text{Average revenue} = \frac{\text{total revenue}}{\text{quantity sold}}$$

$$\text{Marginal revenue} = \frac{\text{change in revenue}}{\text{change in quantity sold}}$$

Figure 11.7 reminds you of the relationship between total revenue and the price elasticity of demand (*PED*). The marginal revenue (*MR*) curve has also been added to the figure, and has a fixed relationship with the average revenue (*AR*) curve. *MR* shares the intercept point on the vertical axis (at point *A* on Figure 11.7), and has exactly twice the slope of *AR*.

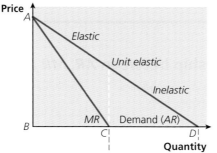
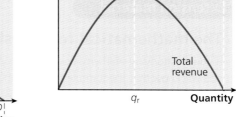

Figure 11.7 Elasticity and total revenue

The relationship between sales and revenue

Table 11.3 provides an arithmetic example to illustrate the relationship between these different aspects of revenue.

Table 11.3 The relationship between sales and revenue

(1) Quantity sold	(2) Average revenue (price, £)	(3) Total revenue (TR)	(4) Marginal revenue (MR)
0	12	0	
			10
20	10	200	
			6
40	8	320	
			2
60	6	360	
			−2
80	4	320	
			−6
100	2	200	
			−10
120	0	0	

Columns 1 and 2 describe the demand curve for this product, showing the quantities sold at each price. Column 3 calculates total revenue (TR) as column 1 multiplied by column 2. Marginal revenue is shown in column 4. This is calculated by taking the change in revenue between the points on the demand curve, expressed per unit. For example, if price goes from £10 to £8, the quantity sold increases from 20 to 40, and total revenue goes from £200 to £320, so revenue increases by £(320 − 200) = £120, which is £6 per unit sold. In the table the values for marginal revenue are shown halfway between the values in the other columns, as we are looking at the change between the successive points.

Figure 11.8 plots these values (I have not plotted all of the negative values of MR). This shows the relationship between AR and MR. The two lines (curves) share the same intercept with the y-axis, and the MR curve is exactly twice as steep as the AR line (curve). This relationship always holds.

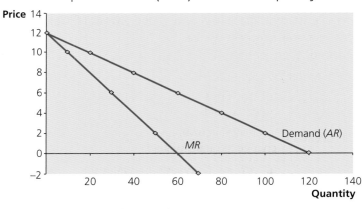

Figure 11.8 Average and marginal revenue

Notice that the MR line cuts the x-axis at the quantity 60, which is the point at which TR is at a maximum. This is also a mathematical feature of the relationship.

Extension material

The mathematical relationship between *AR*, *MR* and the *PED*

If you are studying mathematics alongside your economics, you will know that the formula for a straight line is:

$$P = a - bQ$$

This shows the inverse of the demand curve, which is what is plotted in Figure 11.8, where a and b are positive parameters.

The equation for the MR curve is then:

$$P = a - 2bQ$$

Chapter 2 also explored the way in which the price elasticity of demand (PED) varies along a linear demand curve. The formula that expresses this is:

$$MR - P(1 + (1/PED))$$

Summary

- Total revenue (*TR*) is the revenue received by a firm from selling the goods and services that it produces: it is the quantity sold multiplied by the price.
- Average revenue (*AR*) is the revenue per unit of output: *TR/Q*.
- Marginal revenue (*MR*) is the revenue received from selling an additional unit of output.
- There is a fixed (mathematical) relationship between *AR* and *MR*.
- There is a relationship between total revenue and the price elasticity of demand.

Profit and loss

Economists define profit as the difference between the total revenue received by a firm and the total costs that it incurs in production:

profit = total revenue − total cost

Total revenue here is seen in terms of the quantity of the product that is sold multiplied by the price. Total cost includes the fixed and variable costs that have already been discussed. However, one important item of costs should be highlighted before going any further.

Consider the case of a sole trader — a small local business such as a gym or a taxi firm. It seems reasonable to assume that such a firm will set out to maximise its profits. However, from the entrepreneur's perspective there is an *opportunity cost* of being in business, which may be seen in terms of the earnings that the proprietor could make in an alternative occupation. This required rate of return is regarded as a fixed cost, and is included in the total cost of production.

Small businesses, such as independent coffee shops, incur an opportunity cost from being in business

The same procedure applies to cost curves for other sorts of firm. In other words, when economists refer to costs, they include the rate of return that a firm needs to make if it is to stay in a particular market in the long run. This part of costs is known as **normal profit**. Profits made by a firm above that level are known as **supernormal profits**.

As 'opportunity cost' cannot be identified as an explicit item in the accounts, **accounting profit** differs from the economist's view of profit because of this component of costs. In other words, accounting profits are defined in terms of the explicit (observable) costs of doing business.

Notice that when total revenue is smaller than total cost, the firm makes a loss. If the total revenue equals total cost, the economist sees the firm as making normal profit, as it is covering the opportunity cost of production.

In the short run, a firm may choose to remain in a market even if it is not covering its opportunity costs, provided its revenues are covering its variable costs. Since the firm has already incurred fixed costs, if it can cover its variable costs in the short run, it will be better off remaining in business and paying off part of the fixed costs than exiting the market and losing all of its fixed costs. So, the level of average variable costs represents the **shut-down price**, below which the firm will exit from the market in the short run. In situations where firms in a market are making supernormal profits, it is likely that other firms will be attracted to enter the market. The absence or existence of supernormal profits will therefore be important in influencing the way in which a market may evolve over time.

Exercise 11.6

Table 11.4 shows how a firm's output sold and average cost vary with price.

Table 11.4 A firm's price, output and average (total) cost

Price (£)	Quantity of output sold	Average cost (£)
35	200	24
30	300	18
25	400	18
20	500	20
15	600	25

a Calculate the amount of profit made at each price.
b At what level(s) of output does the firm make supernormal profit?
c At what level(s) of output does the firm make normal profit?
d At what level(s) of output does the firm make a loss?

Case study 11.1

Economies and diseconomies of scale

In the long run, a firm faces total costs as shown in Table 11.5.

Table 11.5 Total costs for a firm

Output (units)	Total cost
100	6,000
200	8,000
300	9,000
400	10,000
500	15,000
600	24,000
700	42,000

Follow-up questions
a Calculate long-run average cost at each level of output and draw these on a graph.
b Identify the minimum efficient scale.
c Within what range of output does the firm experience economies of scale?
d Within what range of output does the firm experience diseconomies of scale?
e Discuss the factors that might give rise to an *LAC* curve with this shape.

CHAPTER 11 QUESTIONS

A Multiple-choice questions

1 Which of the following situations would be classed as 'the long run'?

   a The time period of more than one financial year
   b The time period when at least one factor of production is fixed
   c The time period when all factors of production can be varied
   d The time period when a business can make a profit

2 What best describes the law of diminishing returns?

   a The need to employ more labour as production increases
   b The increase in total costs as production increases
   c The decrease in marginal costs as production increases
   d The decrease in productivity of one factor of production as others remain fixed

3 Which of the following is **not** a type of economy of scale?

   a Developing economies of scale   c Managerial economies of scale
   b Marketing economies of scale   d Financial economies of scale

4 Which of the following is an example of a fixed cost when producing bicycles?

   a Rent of the production factory   c Wages of the production workers
   b Steel to produce the bike frame   d Rubber to produce the bike tyres

5 If a business sells each unit for £10 and has fixed costs of £7,000 a month and variable costs of £6 per unit, the profit/loss when producing 2,000 units in a month will be:

   a £20,000 per month   c £8,000 per month
   b £13,000 per month   d £1,000 per month

B Knowledge and understanding questions

6 Explain, with the aid of a diagram, how diseconomies of scale may effect a firm's operations.   [4 marks]

7 Explain, with the aid of a diagram, the minimum efficient scale.   [4 marks]

8 Explain the difference between accounting and normal profits.   [4 marks]

9 Explain what is meant by the term 'supernormal profits'.   [2 marks]

C Stimulus response question

10 Zhang owns a small shop located in a residential area of a large town. He sells grocery items such as food and laundry products.

Zhang has been given the opportunity to take over another shop in a neighbouring town. The shop would sell the same items that he already sells in his original shop.

Zhang is aware that he may gain some economies of scale from operating both shops, but he is concerned about the diseconomies of scale that he may also encounter.

   a Explain, using a diagram, how Zhang may benefit from economies of scale.   [4 marks]
   b Evaluate the possible causes of diseconomies of scale that Zhang may experience from the operation of both shops.   [8 marks]

Objectives of business

So far, we have assumed that firms act rationally, and set out to maximise their profits. This is one possible motivation for firms, and one that is readily analysed, but it is not the only possible objective. This chapter explores profit maximisation as well as alternative theories that have been put forward to explain how firms take decisions — in particular, decisions about price and output. It also begins to explore how firms take decisions about the level of output to produce and the price at which it is to be sold.

> ### Learning objectives
>
> After studying this chapter, you should be able to:
> - explain the principal–agent problem
> - explain maximisation objectives of profit, sales revenue, sales volume, growth and utility
> - explain non-maximisation objectives: profit satisficing, social welfare and corporate social responsibility
> - evaluate maximisation and non-maximisation objectives
> - evaluate the factors that influence the choice of objectives

Profit maximisation

Synoptic link

The assumption that firms would maximise profits was introduced in Chapter 7, but we now need to explore this more carefully. Profit was explained in Chapter 11.

Study tip

The $MR = MC$ rule for profit maximisation is an important one, as it applies in any market situation where a firm sets out to maximise profits, so make sure you understand and remember it.

Traditional economic analysis has tended to start from the premise that firms set out with the objective of maximising profits. How does a firm choose its output level if it wishes to maximise profits? An application of the marginal principle shows how. Suppose a firm realises that its marginal revenue is higher than its marginal cost of production. What does this mean for profits? If it were to sell an additional unit of its output, it would gain more in revenue than it would incur in additional cost, so its profits would increase. Similarly, if it found that its marginal revenue was less than marginal cost, it would be making a loss on the marginal unit of output, and profits would increase if the firm sold less. This leads to the conclusion that profits will be maximised at the level of output at which marginal revenue (MR) is equal to marginal cost (MC). Indeed, this $MR = MC$ rule is a general rule that tells a firm how to maximise profits in any market situation.

Knowledge check 12.1

If a firm were to find that it was producing at an output level at which marginal cost exceeded marginal revenue, would it be likely to increase or decrease output if it wants to maximise profits?

Figure 12.1 shows a firm operating in a market in which it has no influence over price, so it gains the same marginal revenue from the sale of each unit of output. Marginal revenue and average revenue are therefore the same. P_1, P_2 and P_3 represent three possible prices that could prevail in the market.

a For each price level, identify the output level that the firm would choose in order to maximise profits.

b For each of these output levels, compare the level of average revenue with that of average cost, and consider what this means for the firm's profits.

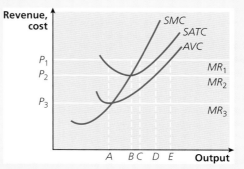

Figure 12.1 Profit maximisation in the short run

The principal–agent problem

principal–agent problem
arises from conflict between the objectives of the principals and their agents, who take decisions on their behalf

The concept of asymmetric information was first introduced in Chapter 9, which looked at the market failure caused by information failure.

The principal–agent distinction is applicable in many different contexts. In each of the following cases, identify which is the principal and which is the agent:

a the owners of a firm and the managers hired to run it

b a department store and its employees

c a department store and its customers

d an electricity supplier and consumers of electricity

e a dentist and his or her patients

The discussion so far seems reasonable when considering a relatively small owner-managed firm. In this context, profit maximisation makes good sense as the firm's motivation.

However, for many larger firms — especially public limited companies — the owners may not be involved in running the business. This gives rise to the **principal–agent problem**. In a public limited company, the shareholders delegate the day-to-day decisions concerning the operation of the firm to managers who act on their behalf. In this case the shareholders are the *principals*, and the managers are the *agents* who run things for them. In other words, there is a divorce of ownership from control. The degree of accountability of managers to the owners may be weak when the shareholders are a diverse group of individuals.

If the agents are in full sympathy with the objectives of the owners, there is no problem and the managers will take exactly the decisions that the owners would like. Problems arise when there is conflict between the aims of the owners and those of the managers. There are various motivations that managers may pursue in this situation. Shareholders (the owners) are likely to want the firm to maximise its profits, but the managers may wish to pursue other objectives — such as their own utility, for example.

The principal–agent problem arises primarily from asymmetric information. This arises because the agents have better information about the effects of their decisions than the owners (the principals), who are not involved in the day-to-day running of the business. In order to overcome this information problem, the owners must improve their monitoring of the managers' actions, or provide the managers with an incentive to take decisions that would align with the owners' objectives. For example, if the managers are offered bonuses related to profit, they will be more likely to try to maximise profits.

X-inefficiency

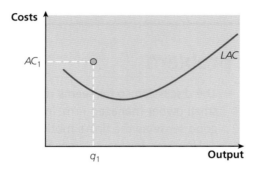

If managers are not fully accountable, they may become negligent, which may give rise to organisational slack. In other words, costs will not be minimised, as the firm is not operating as efficiently as it could. This is an example of what is called **X-inefficiency**. For example, in Figure 12.2, *LAC* represents the long-run average cost curve showing the most efficient cost positions for the firm at any output level. With X-inefficiency, a firm could end up producing output q_1 at average cost AC_1. So, in the presence of X-inefficiency the firm will be operating *above* its long-run average cost curve.

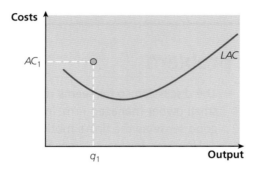

Figure 12.2 X-inefficiency

> **Key term**
>
> **X-inefficiency** occurs when a firm is not operating at minimum cost, perhaps because of organisational slack

Other maximisation objectives

Profit maximisation may not always be the motivation of firms. In other circumstances, firms or their managers may set out with other objectives in mind.

Sales revenue maximisation

The industrial economist William Baumol argued that managers might set out with the objective of maximising sales revenue. One reason is that in some firms managerial salaries are related to sales revenue rather than profits. The effects of this can be seen in Figure 12.3, which shows how total revenue (*TR*) varies as output increases. (The *TR* curve always takes this shape when the firm faces a downward-sloping straight-line demand curve.) You can see that total revenue is maximised at the peak of the *TR* curve (which is also the point at which $MR = 0$) at q_r. A revenue-maximising firm will produce more output than a profit-maximising one, and will need to charge a lower price in order to sell the extra output. This should be apparent from the fact that profits are maximised where $MR = MC$, which must be at a positive level of MR — and therefore to the left of q_r in Figure 12.3. This would be at q_π.

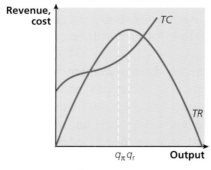

Figure 12.3 Sales revenue maximisation

Baumol pointed out that the shareholders might not be too pleased about this. The way the firm behaves then depends upon the degree of accountability that the agents (managers) have to the principals (shareholders). For example, the shareholders may have sufficient power over their agents to be able to insist on some minimum level of profits. The result may then be a compromise solution.

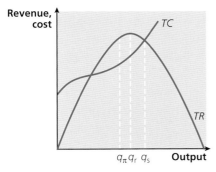

Revenue, cost

Figure 12.4 Sales volume maximisation

Sales volume maximisation

In some cases, managers may focus more on the volume of sales than on the resulting revenues. For example, a newspaper publisher may be more concerned about circulation figures than revenue. This could lead to output being set even higher, as shown in Figure 12.4. The firm would now push for higher sales up to the point where it just breaks even at q_s. This is the point at which total revenue only just covers total cost. Remember that total cost includes normal profit — the opportunity cost of the resources tied up in the firm. The firm would have to close down if it did not cover this opportunity cost.

Again, the extent to which the managers will be able to pursue this objective without endangering their positions with the shareholders depends on how accountable the managers are to the shareholders. Remember that the managers are likely to have much better information about the market conditions and the internal functioning of the firm than the shareholders, who view the firm only remotely. This may be to the managers' advantage.

Growth maximisation

A feature of the economic environment in recent years has been the increasing size of firms. Some, such as Google, Microsoft, Wal-Mart and Shell, have become giants. Why is this happening?

Firms may wish to increase their size in order to gain market power within the industry in which they are operating. A firm that can gain market share, and perhaps become dominant in the market, may be able to exercise some control over the price of its product, and thereby influence the market.

Some firms grow simply by being successful. For example, a successful marketing campaign may increase a firm's market share and provide it with a flow of profits that can be reinvested to expand the firm even more. Some firms may choose to borrow in order to finance their growth, or to issue shares (equity).

Such *organic growth* may encounter limits. A firm may find that its product market is saturated, so that it can grow further only at the expense of other firms in the market. If its competitors are able to maintain their own market shares, the firm may need to diversify its production activities by finding new markets for its existing product, or perhaps offering new products.

Instead of growing organically — that is, based on the firm's own resources — many firms choose to grow by merging with, or acquiring, other firms. The distinction here is that an *acquisition* (or takeover) may be hostile, whereas a *merger* may be the coming together of equals, with each firm committed to forming a single entity.

Growth in this way has a number of advantages: for example, it may allow some rationalisation to take place within the organisation. On the other hand, firms tend to develop their own culture, or way of doing things, and some mergers have foundered because of an incompatibility of corporate cultures.

Utility maximisation

Oliver Williamson argued that managers would set out to maximise their utility. Just as consumers gain satisfaction from consuming goods, it is argued that managers gain satisfaction in various ways. For example, they may enjoy the status of having a large team of people working for them, or they may like to have discretion over the way in which profits made by the firm are used, perhaps allowing them to have a large and well-appointed office or a prestigious company car. Again, such activity would take the firm away from its profit-maximising position, and may result in X-inefficiency.

Long-run profit maximisation

Firms may be prepared to take a long-term view of their situation. There may be times when the decision to maximise profits in the short run may damage their long-run prospects. For example, firms may undertake costly investment now in order to reap higher profits in the long term. Or firms may delay adjusting price to an increase in costs so that they maintain customer loyalty. In other words, short-run profit maximisation may not always be in the best long-run interests of the firm.

Non-maximisation objectives

Although firms may set out to take rational decisions, they may not have all the relevant information about market conditions that is needed, or might not have the capacity to analyse the information that they have. It might be that the information is costly to acquire, or costly to analyse fully. In such a situation firms do the best that they can to take good decisions, but without full information they may not achieve a fully rational outcome. This is known as a situation of **bounded rationality** — a situation in which firms try to do their best, but cannot achieve profit maximisation because they do not have enough information about market conditions, or lack the ability to interpret the market environment. Firms may therefore decide to do enough to survive, but not strive for maximisation.

Profit satisficing

Businesses may not set out to maximise anything, either consciously because they have other motivations, or as a result of the principal–agent issue. For example, it might be that managers simply prefer a quiet life, and therefore do not push for the absolute profit-maximising position, but do just enough to keep the shareholders off their backs. Herbert Simon referred to this as '**satisficing**' behaviour, where managers aim to produce satisfactory profits rather than maximum profits.

Social welfare

Not all firms aim to make profits, and enterprises such as charities are non-profit-making bodies that set out to improve social welfare, in their home economy or elsewhere in the world.

Exercise 12.3

Google 'corporate social responsibility' with the name of some large firms with which you are familiar, and check out the range of activities in which firms engage under this banner.

Key term

corporate social responsibility (CSR) actions that a firm takes in order to demonstrate its commitment to behaving in the public interest

Knowledge check 12.5

Give another example of an action taken by a firm to demonstrate a commitment to behaving responsibly.

Non-profit-making bodies clearly pursue very different objectives from firms that try to maximise profits or some other economic variable. There are many examples of such organisations that raise funds by various means to distribute to those seen to be in need.

Corporate social responsibility (CSR)

Even firms that set out to make profits may wish to develop a favourable reputation by demonstrating a commitment to acting in ways that benefit society at large, or that improve the welfare of their employees and the community in which they are located. This notion of **corporate social responsibility (CSR)** has become widespread, with firms devoting resources to promoting community programmes of various kinds and encouraging their employees to engage in volunteering activities. The motive for engaging in such activities is not necessarily humanitarian, to the extent that public demonstration of a commitment to CSR may enhance the reputation of a firm, and therefore boost its market position.

Indeed, it may now be that CSR has become a prerequisite for firms' survival. If it is perceived that failure to engage with CSR has a major impact on firms' sales, then it becomes crucial for a firm to be able to demonstrate its commitment in order to compete with its rivals. Devoting resources to CSR then becomes part of a firm's strategy to safeguard its market position.

Firms today need to demonstrate corporate social responsibility in order to survive

Choosing a firm's objective(s)

There are many factors that influence a firm's choice of objectives. In large measure, it will depend upon:

- the owners of the firm
- the managers
- the relationship between the owners and the managers
- the market environment

The owners of the firm (the shareholders) will have views of what the firm should have as a main objective. To serve their best interests, they may want the firm to maximise profits, as this provides them with an income flow. If the owners are far-sighted, they may realise that taking a long-term view may serve them best. In other words, they may be prepared to sacrifice short-run maximisation in favour of a strategy that will bring higher profits in the future.

The managers who are responsible for the day-to-day decision making may take a different view. They may prefer to keep the shareholders happy by making sufficient profit, while taking life more easily than if they are continually striving for maximisation.

The relationship between the owners (the principals) and the managers (their agents) then becomes crucial. The key issue here is the extent to which the shareholders are able to hold the managers accountable for their actions. It may be difficult to coordinate the views of multiple shareholders in order to penalise managers who diverge from the owners' prime objective — even if the shareholders were actually able to observe the behaviour of managers sufficiently closely to know whether or not they are acting against the owners' interests.

The market environment in which the firm operates is also significant in determining the choice of objectives. This is a subject for discussion in the next part of the book.

Evaluation of objectives

The discussion has revealed a range of reasons explaining why firms may depart from profit maximisation. Does this mean that it should be abandoned as an assumption?

It could be argued that some of the strategies adopted by firms may seem to diverge from profit maximisation in the short run, but may result in the maximisation of profits in the long run. For example, if all firms in a market are engaging in CSR in order to improve credibility among their customers, then it could be argued that this expenditure becomes part of operating costs, and a necessary part of maintaining the market share needed to maximise profits in the long term.

From an economic modelling perspective, being able to assume that firms maximise profits allows the economist to come to an understanding of firms' behaviour under a simple and clear assumption. This offers much more straightforward insights into this behaviour than trying to implement some of the more complex assumptions that could be made about what motivates firms' decisions. Profit maximisation then provides a benchmark for other, more complex models that enable an evaluation of how differently firms may behave under alternative assumptions. So even if it is not the case that firms always act to maximise profits, it is a useful starting point to ask how they would behave if they did maximise profits, and then explore alternative theories using profit maximisation as the benchmark against which to compare other models of behaviour.

The complexity of business organisations gives credence to the potential importance of the principal–agent problem, and the way that this highlights the discretion that managers may have in pursuing a variety of objectives. However, it could be argued that in the end the performance of businesses in delivering value to their shareholders will ultimately determine their success or failure.

Summary

- Traditional economic analysis assumes that firms set out to maximise profits, where profits are defined as the excess of total revenue over total cost.
- A firm maximises profits by choosing a level of output such that marginal revenue is equal to marginal cost.
- For many larger firms, where day-to-day control is delegated to managers, a principal–agent problem may arise if there is conflict between the objectives of the owners (principals) and those of the managers (agents).
- This may lead to satisficing behaviour and to X-inefficiency.
- William Baumol suggested that managers may set out to maximise revenue rather than profits. Others have suggested that sales volume or the growth of the firm may be the managers' objectives.

Efficiency revisited

Synoptic link

The ideas of productive and allocative efficiency were first introduced in Chapter 7.

Key terms

productive efficiency when a firm operates at minimum average cost, choosing an appropriate combination of inputs and producing the maximum output possible from those inputs

static efficiency efficiency at a particular point in time given the resources and technology available

The extent to which markets will deliver efficiency will be explored in the following chapters, but it is worth revisiting this concept to refine it a bit further.

Indeed, it has already been noted that the principal–agent problem can lead to X-inefficiency, which is one reason why the ideal combination of productive and allocative efficiency will not be achieved.

Productive and static efficiency

The notion of **productive efficiency** is closely tied to the costs firms face, particularly in relation to the average total cost of production. Productive efficiency can be seen in terms of the minimum average cost at which output can be produced, recognising that average cost is likely to vary at different scales of output. For example, in Figure 11.4 on page 141 the point q_3 may be regarded as the optimum level of output, in the sense that it minimises long-run average cost per unit of output.

From the firm's perspective, the decision process can be viewed as a three-stage procedure. First, the firm needs to decide how much output it wants to produce. Second, it chooses an appropriate combination of factors of production, given that intended scale of production. Third, it attempts to produce as much output as possible, given those inputs. Another way of expressing this is that, having chosen the intended scale of output, the firm tries to minimise its costs of production.

Notice that when the firm starts this decision process, it is likely to choose its desired output level on the basis of current or expected market conditions. However, remember the distinction between the short and the long run. Once the firm has chosen its desired scale of production, and installed the necessary capital, it is tied into that level of capital stock in the short run. If it needs to change its decision in the future, it will take time to implement the changes. In the short run, a firm may therefore be in a situation of **static efficiency**, choosing the minimum average cost, given the market conditions at that time.

Summary
- A society needs to find a way of using its limited resources as efficiently as possible.
- Productive efficiency occurs when firms have chosen appropriate combinations of factors of production, and produce the maximum output possible from those inputs.
- Productive efficiency occurs when a firm is operating at minimum long-run average cost.

Case study 12.1

Coke vs Pepsi in India

In the mid-2000s it was reported that Coca-Cola and PepsiCo were fighting to increase their sales in India. A pesticide scare in the previous year had caused sales to plummet, and the two firms were anxious to recover the situation.

The tactics they adopted were to reduce the size of the bottles for sale in order to appeal to consumers with low incomes, to cut prices, to increase the availability of the products in rural areas, and to encourage more at-home consumption in the urban areas.

It was seen that there was plenty of scope for growth in the market, as India showed one of the lowest average levels of consumption of fizzy drinks in the world, and was substantially below the Asian average. This may partly reflect the way that children have been discouraged from drinking colas by their teachers at school.

The prices being charged were rated as the world's lowest prices for cola as the two firms battled to increase their market shares. However, in consequence the firms faced reductions in their profit margins, and

continued to face competition from local producers. The logistics of supplying such a geographically large and diverse region, given the need to ensure refrigeration, added significantly to costs. Attempts were made to counter this by reducing the weight of the bottles and by making use of cheap transport in the form of bullock carts and cycle rickshaws in the rural areas.

Market analysts said that soft-drink companies should be able to improve profits, but executives remained bent on boosting volumes. The vice-president of Coca-Cola marketing in India was quoted as saying that 'any affordability strategy will put pressure on margins, but it is critical to build the market'.

The pesticide issue proved to be a long-lasting controversy, and the Kerala government filed a criminal complaint against PepsiCo over its environmental impact, although this was rejected by the Supreme Court of India in 2010. Indeed, the US Department of State named PepsiCo as one of the 12 multinationals that displayed 'the most impressive corporate social responsibility credentials in emerging markets'.

Follow-up questions
a Given the statements in the passage, do you think that Coca-Cola and PepsiCo were trying to maximise short-run profits?
b Explain your answer to (a) and comment on what the firms were trying to achieve by their strategies.
c Identify ways in which the firms were seeking to influence their costs.
d How do you think PepsiCo's record on CSR will have affected its position in the market?
e Discuss what you think the firms would want to achieve in the long run.

CHAPTER 12 QUESTIONS

A Multiple-choice questions

1 Which of the following represents the point of profit maximisation?

   a $AR = MC$
   b $MR = AC$
   c $MR = MC$
   d $AR = AC$

2 The principal–agent problem involves:

   a The divorce between ownership and control
   b Communication issues in larger organisations
   c Reduction in average costs as the scale of output increases
   d An increase in the cost of one factor of production as the other factors remain fixed

3 Which of the following describes satisficing?

   a The aim to make enough profit to satisfy the shareholders
   b The aim to sell as many units as possible
   c The aim to maximise managerial utility
   d The aim to grow as fast as possible

B Knowledge and understanding questions

4 Explain **two** maximisation objectives for a firm. [4 marks]

5 Explain **two** non-maximisation objectives for a firm. [4 marks]

6 Explain **two** factors that may influence a firm's choice of objective. [4 marks]

C Stimulus response question

7 Many firms choose to focus not just on profit maximisation but also on corporate social responsibility (CSR). This covers:

- social impact
- environmental impact
- financial impact

   a Explain what is meant by 'profit maximisation'. [2 marks]
   b Evaluate the benefits to a business of focusing on CSR. [8 marks]

D Essay question

8 'The primary objective of every company must be to maximise profit for the shareholders.' Discuss. [20 marks]

SECTION
1

MICROECONOMICS

Part 4
Market structures

Chapter 13

Market structure: perfect competition

By now you should be familiar with the notion of market failure — describing situations in which free markets may not produce the best outcome for society in terms of efficiency. One of the reasons given for this in Chapter 8 concerned a situation in which firms may be able to exert market power. It was argued that, if firms can achieve a position of market dominance, they may distort the pattern of resource allocation. It is now time to look at market structure more closely in order to evaluate the way in which markets work, and the significance of this for resource allocation. The fact that firms try to maximise profits is not in itself bad for society. However, the structure of a market has a strong influence on how well the market performs. 'Structure' here is seen in relation to a number of dimensions, but in particular to the number of firms operating in a market and the way in which they interact. This chapter considers the various forms of market structure and explains one extreme model: that of perfect competition.

Learning objectives

After studying this chapter, you should be able to:
- explain the characteristics of perfect competition
- explain, with the aid of a diagram, short-run perfect competition: supernormal profit/loss
- explain, with the aid of a diagram, long-run perfect competition: normal profits
- explain, with the aid of a diagram, the individual firm in perfect competition as a price taker
- explain, with the aid of a diagram, equilibrium price and output for a firm in perfect competition
- explain, with the aid of a diagram, allocative efficiency in short-run and long-run perfect competition
- explain, with the aid of a diagram, productive efficiency in long-run perfect competition
- evaluate the advantages and disadvantages of perfect competition

Market structure

Firms cannot take decisions without having some awareness of the market in which they are operating. In some markets, firms find themselves to be such small players that they cannot influence the price at which they sell. In others, a firm may find itself to be the only firm, which clearly gives it

market structure the market environment within which firms operate

much more discretion in devising a price and output strategy. There may also be many intermediate situations where the firm has some control over price but needs to be aware of rival firms in the market.

Economists have devised a range of models that allow such different **market structures** to be analysed. Before looking carefully at the most important types of market structure, the key characteristics of alternative market structures will be introduced. The main models are summarised in Table 13.1. In many ways, we can regard these as a spectrum of markets with different characteristics. Each form of market structure is discussed more carefully in the following chapters.

Table 13.1 A spectrum of market structures

	Perfect competition	Monopolistic competition	Oligopoly	Monopoly
Number of firms	Many	Many	Dominated by few	One
Freedom of entry	Not restricted	Not restricted	Some barriers to entry	High barriers to entry
Firm's influence over price	None	Some	Some	Price maker, subject to the demand curve
Nature of product	Homogeneous	Differentiated	Varied	No close substitutes
Examples	Cauliflowers Foreign exchange (e.g. euros)	Fast-food outlets Travel agents	Cars Mobile phones	PC operating systems Local water supply

Perfect competition

At one extreme is *perfect competition*, which is the main topic of this chapter. This is a market in which each individual firm is a *price taker*. This means that no individual firm is large enough to be able to influence the price, which is set by the market as a whole. This situation would arise where there are many firms operating in a market, producing a product that is much the same whichever firm produces it. You might think of a market for a particular sort of vegetable, for example. One cauliflower is very much like another, and it would not be possible for a particular cauliflower-grower to set a premium price for its product.

Such markets are also typified by freedom of entry and exit. In other words, it is relatively easy for new firms to enter the market, or for existing firms to leave it to produce something else. The market price in such a market will be driven down to that at which the typical firm in the market just makes enough profit to stay in business. If firms make more than this, other firms will be attracted in, and therefore supernormal profits will be competed away. If some firms in the market do not make sufficient profit to want to remain in the market, they will exit, allowing price to drift up until again the typical firm just makes enough to stay in business.

Monopoly

At the other extreme of the spectrum of market structures is *monopoly*. This is a market where there is only one firm in operation. Such a firm has some influence over price, and can choose a combination of price and output in order to maximise its profits. The monopolist is not entirely free to set any price that it wants, as it must remain aware of the demand curve for its product. Nonetheless, it has the freedom to choose a point along its demand curve.

Synoptic link

The concepts of normal and supernormal profits were explained in Chapter 11, and are crucial in understanding and evaluating the alternative models of market structure.

Synoptic link

The operation of a monopoly market is explored in Chapter 14.

Synoptic link

The market structures of monopolistic competition and oligopoly are examined in Chapter 15.

Monopolistic competition

Between the two extreme forms of market structure are many intermediate situations in which firms may have some influence over their selling price, but still have to take account of the fact that there are other firms in the market. One such market is known as *monopolistic competition*. This is a market in which there are many firms operating, each producing similar but not identical products, so that there is some scope for influencing price, perhaps because of brand loyalty. However, firms in such a market are likely to be relatively small. Such firms may find it profitable to make sure that their own product is differentiated from other goods, and may advertise in order to convince potential customers that this is the case. For example, small-scale local restaurants may offer different styles of cooking.

Oligopoly

Another intermediate form of market structure is *oligopoly*, which literally means 'few sellers'. This is a market in which there are just a few firms that dominate the market. Each firm will take decisions in close awareness of how other firms in the market may react to their actions. In some cases, the firms may try to *collude* — to work together in order to behave as if they were a monopolist — therefore making higher profits. In other cases, they may be intense rivals, which will tend to result in supernormal profits being competed away. The question of whether firms in an oligopoly collude or compete has a substantial impact on how the overall market performs in terms of resource allocation, and whether consumers will be disadvantaged as a result of the actions of the firms in the market.

Knowledge check 13.1

What form of market structure could be regarded as being at the opposite extreme of the market structure spectrum to monopoly?

Key term

barrier to entry a characteristic of a market that prevents new firms from readily joining the market

Knowledge check 13.2

Give an example of a barrier to entry that might make it difficult for new firms to enter a market.

Synoptic link

Barriers to entry are explained in more detail in Chapter 14 in the context of monopoly, where the existence of barriers to entry is a key assumption.

Barriers to entry and exit

An important influence on market structure is the existence or absence of barriers to entry and exit of firms. It has been argued that if firms in a market are able to make supernormal profits, this will act as an inducement for new firms to try to gain entry into that market in order to share in those profits. A **barrier to entry** is a characteristic of a market that prevents new firms from joining the market. The existence of such barriers is, therefore, of great importance in influencing the market structure that will evolve.

For example, if a firm holds a patent on a particular good, this means that no other firm is permitted by law to produce the product, and the patent-holding firm therefore has a monopoly. The firm may then be able to set price such as to make supernormal profits without fear of rival firms competing away those profits. On the other hand, if there are no barriers to entry in a market, and if the existing firms set price to make supernormal profits, new firms will join the market, and the increase in market supply will push price down until no supernormal profits are being made.

Firms may also face barriers to exit — a situation in which leaving a market may cause the firm to incur high costs. For example, there may be significant sunk costs that cannot be recovered if a firm leaves its market. Such costs may arise because a firm has invested in specific capital goods that cannot be used for alternative purposes, or it may have contracts with suppliers that cannot be broken.

Summary

- The decisions that firms take must be taken in the context of the market environment in which the firm operates.
- Under conditions of perfect competition, each firm must accept the market price as given but can choose how much output to produce in order to maximise profits.
- In a monopoly market, where there is only one producer, the firm can choose output and price (subject to the demand curve).
- Monopolistic competition combines some features of perfect competition, and some characteristics of monopoly. Firms have some influence over price, and will produce a differentiated product in order to maintain this influence.
- Oligopoly exists where a market is occupied by just a few firms. In some cases, these few firms may work together to maximise their joint profits. In other cases, they may seek to outmanoeuvre each other.
- An important characteristic of a market is the existence (or absence) of barriers to entry and exit.

Exercise 13.1

For each of the market situations listed below, select the form of market structure that is most likely to apply. In each case, comment on the way in which the firm's actions may be influenced by the market structure.

Forms of market structure:
1 perfect competition
2 monopoly
3 monopolistic competition
4 oligopoly

a A fairly large number of fast-food outlets in a city centre, offering various styles of cooking (Indian, Chinese, fish and chips, burgers, etc.) at broadly similar prices
b An island's only airport
c A large number of farmers selling parsnips at the same price
d A small number of large firms that between them supply most of the market for commercial vans

The model of perfect competition

Key term

perfect competition a form of market structure that produces allocative and productive efficiency in long-run equilibrium

At one end of the spectrum of market structures is **perfect competition**. This model has a special place in economic analysis, because if all its assumptions were fulfilled, and if all markets operated according to its precepts, the best allocation of resources would be ensured for society as a whole. Although it may be argued that this ideal is not often achieved, perfect competition nonetheless provides a yardstick by which all other forms of market structure can be evaluated.

Assumptions

The assumptions of the model of perfect competition are as follows:
1 Firms aim to **maximise profits**.
2 There are **many participants** (both buyers and sellers), none of which is large enough to influence price.
3 The product is **homogeneous**.
4 There are **no barriers to entry to or exit from** the market.
5 There is **perfect knowledge** of market conditions.

Profit maximisation

The first assumption is that firms act to maximise their profits. You might think this means that firms, acting in their own self-interest, are unlikely to do consumers any favours. However, it transpires that this does not interfere with the operation of the market. Indeed, it is the pursuit of self-interest by firms and consumers that ensures the market works effectively.

Many participants

This is an important assumption of the model: that there are so many buyers and so many sellers that no individual trader is able to influence the market price. The market price is therefore determined by the operation of the market.

On the sellers' side of the market, this assumption is tantamount to saying there are limited economies of scale in the industry. If the minimum efficient scale is small relative to market demand, then no firm is likely to become so large that it will gain influence in the market.

A homogeneous product

This assumption means that buyers of the good see all products in the market as being identical, and will not favour one firm's product over another. If there were brand loyalty, such that one firm was more popular than others, that firm would be able to charge a premium on its price. By ruling out this possibility the previous assumption is reinforced, and no individual seller is able to influence the selling price of the product.

No barriers to entry or exit

By this assumption, firms are able to join the market if they perceive it to be a profitable step, and they can exit from the market without hindrance. This assumption is important when it comes to considering the long-run equilibrium towards which the market will tend.

Perfect knowledge

It is assumed that all participants in the market have perfect information about trading conditions in the market. In particular, buyers always know the prices that firms are charging, and can therefore buy the good at the cheapest possible price. Firms that try to charge a price above the market price will get no takers. At the same time, traders are aware of the product quality.

Perfect competition in the short run

The firm under perfect competition

With the above assumptions, it is possible to analyse how a firm will operate in the market. An important implication of these assumptions is that no individual trader can influence the price of the product. In particular, this means that the firm is a **price taker**, and has to accept whatever price is set in the market as a whole.

As the firm is a price taker, it faces a perfectly elastic demand curve for its product, as is shown in Figure 13.1. In this figure, P_1 is the price set in the market, and the firm cannot sell at any other price. If it tries to set a price above P_1 it will sell nothing, as buyers are fully aware of the market price and will not buy at a higher price, especially as they know that there is no quality difference between the products offered by different firms in the market. What this also implies is that the firm can sell as much output as it likes at that going price — which means there is no incentive for any firm to set a price below P_1. Therefore, all firms charge the same price, P_1.

The firm's short-run supply decision

If the firm can sell as much as it likes at the market price, how does it decide how much to produce?

Chapter 12 explained that to maximise profits a firm needs to set output such that marginal revenue is equal to marginal cost. Figure 13.2 illustrates this rule by adding the short-run cost curves to the demand curve.

Remember from the previous chapter that SMC cuts the minimum points of SAVC and SATC. As the demand curve is horizontal, the firm faces constant average and marginal revenue, and will choose to produce output q_1, where $MR = MC$.

Knowledge check 13.4

What shape will the demand curve take if a firm is a price taker?

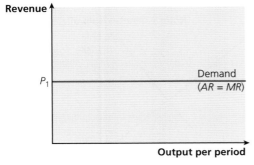

Figure 13.1 The firm's demand curve

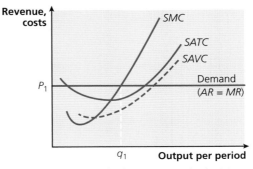

Figure 13.2 The firm's short-run supply decision

If the market price were to change, the firm would react by changing output, but always choosing to supply output at the level at which $MR = MC$. This suggests that the short-run marginal cost curve represents the firm's short-run supply curve: in other words, it shows the quantity of output that the firm would supply at any given price.

Exercise 13.2

Table 13.2 shows the costs (SAC and SMC) facing a firm under perfect competition at different levels of output.

Table 13.2 A firm's costs

Output	Short-run average cost (SAC)	Short-run marginal cost (SMC)
100	60	25
200	40	20
300	30	18
400	25	25
500	30	40
600	40	60

Remember that under perfect competition, the firm is a price taker, which means that it faces a horizontal

demand curve such that price = AR = MR. Assume that the firm maximises profit.

a If the firm faces a price of 40, how much output will the firm supply, and what will be the level of supernormal profit or loss per unit?

b If the firm faces a price of 25, how much output will the firm supply, and what will be the level of supernormal profit or loss per unit?

c If the firm faces a price of 20, how much output will the firm supply, and what will be the level of supernormal profit or loss per unit?

short-run supply (SRS) curve
for a firm operating under
perfect competition, the curve
given by its short-run marginal
cost curve above the price at
which $MC = SAVC$ — for the
industry, the horizontal sum
of the supply curves of the
individual firms

However, there is one important proviso to this statement. If the price falls below short-run average variable cost, the firm's best decision will be to exit from the market, as it will be better off just incurring its fixed costs. So the firm's **short-run supply (SRS) curve** is the SMC curve above the point where it cuts $SAVC$ (at its minimum point).

Industry equilibrium in the short run

One crucial question not yet examined is how the market price comes to be determined. To answer this, it is necessary to consider the industry as a whole. In this case there is a conventional downward-sloping demand curve, of the sort met in Chapter 3. This is formed according to the preferences of consumers in the market and is shown in Figure 13.3.

On the supply side, it has been shown that the individual firm's supply curve is its marginal cost curve above $SAVC$. If you add up the supply curves of each firm operating in the market, the result is the industry supply curve, also shown in Figure 13.3. The price will then adjust to P_1 at the intersection of demand and supply. The firms in the industry between them will supply Q_1 output, and the market will be in equilibrium.

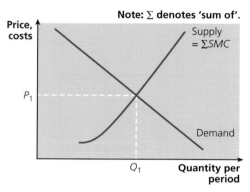

Figure 13.3 A perfectly competitive industry in short-run equilibrium

Knowledge check 13.5

Which curve represents the
individual firm's short-run supply
curve under perfect competition?

The firm in short-run equilibrium revisited

As this seems to be a well-balanced situation, with price adjusting to equate market demand and supply, the only question is why it is described as just a *short-run* equilibrium. The clue to this is to be found back with the individual firm.

Figure 13.4 returns to the position facing an individual firm in the market. As before, the firm maximises profits by accepting the price P_1 as set in the market and producing up to the point where $MR = MC$, which is at q_1. However, now the firm's average revenue (which is equal to price) is greater than its average cost (which is given by AC_1 at this level of output). The firm is therefore making supernormal profits at this price. (Remember that 'normal profits' are included in average cost.) Indeed, the amount of total supernormal profits being made is shown as the shaded area on the diagram. Notice that average revenue minus average costs equals supernormal profit per unit, so multiplying this by the quantity sold determines total supernormal profit.

This is where the assumption about freedom of entry becomes important. If firms in this market are making profits above opportunity cost, the market is generating more profits than other markets in the economy. This will prove attractive to other firms, which will seek to enter the market — and the assumption is that there are no barriers to prevent them from doing so.

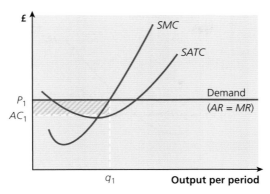

Figure 13.4 The firm in short-run equilibrium

This process of entry will continue for as long as firms are making supernormal profits. However, as more firms join the market, the *position* of the industry supply curve, which is the sum of the supply curves of an ever-larger number of individual firms, will be affected. As the industry supply curve shifts to the right, the market price will fall. At some point the price will have fallen to such an extent that firms are no longer making supernormal profits, and the market will then stabilise.

If the price were to fall even further, some firms would choose to exit from the market, and the process would go into reverse. Therefore price can be expected to stabilise such that the typical firm in the industry is just making normal profits.

Figure 13.5 shows a different situation. This firm also tries to maximise profits by setting $MC = MR$, but finds that its average cost exceeds the price. It makes losses shown by the shaded area, and in the long run will choose to leave the market. As this and other firms exit from the market, the market supply curve shifts to the left, and the equilibrium price will drift upwards until firms are again making normal profits.

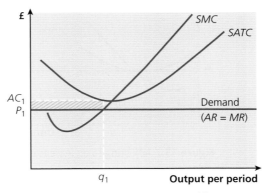

Figure 13.5 The firm in short-run equilibrium again

Perfect competition in long-run equilibrium

Figure 13.6 shows the situation for a typical firm and for the industry as a whole once long-run equilibrium has been reached and firms no longer have any incentive to enter or to exit the market. The market is in equilibrium, with demand equal to supply at the going price. The typical

Knowledge check 13.6

What is the long-run shutdown price for a firm under perfect competition?

firm sets marginal revenue equal to marginal cost to maximise profits, and just makes normal profits.

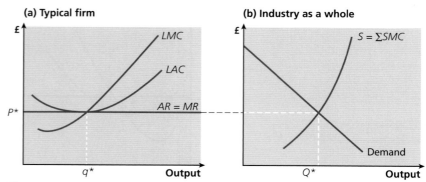

Figure 13.6 Long-run equilibrium under perfect competition for a typical firm and the industry as a whole

The long-run supply curve

Suppose there is an increase in the demand for a product. Perhaps, for some reason, everyone becomes convinced that the product is really health promoting, so demand increases at any given price. This disturbs the market equilibrium, and the question then is whether (and how) equilibrium can be restored.

Figure 13.7 reproduces the long-run equilibrium that was shown in Figure 13.6. Therefore, in the initial position market price is at P^*, the typical firm is in long-run equilibrium producing q^*, and the industry is producing Q^*. Demand was initially at D_0, but with the increased popularity of the product it has shifted to D_1. In the short run this pushes the market price up to P_1 for the industry, because as market price increases existing firms have the incentive to supply more output: that is, they move along their short-run supply curves. So in the short run a typical firm starts to produce q_1 output. The combined supply of the firms then increases to Q_1.

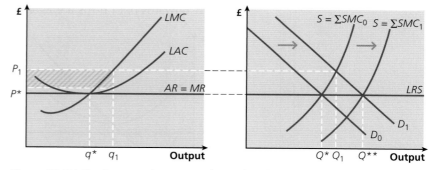

Figure 13.7 Adjusting to an increase in demand under perfect competition

However, at the higher price the firms start making supernormal profits (shown by the shaded area in Figure 13.7). Under the assumptions underpinning perfect competition, firms have perfect knowledge of market conditions, so the fact that firms in the market are making supernormal profits is known. Furthermore, there are no barriers to entry that prevent new firms joining the market. The fact that the product is homogeneous further simplifies entry. This means that in time more firms will be attracted into the market, pushing the short-run industry supply curve to the right. This process will continue until

industry long-run supply (LRS)
curve under perfect
competition, the curve that, for
the typical firm in the industry, is
horizontal at the minimum point
of the long-run average cost
curve

Knowledge check 13.7

What level of profit is made
by a firm operating under
perfect competition in long-run
equilibrium?

Study tip

These diagrams can be quite
confusing until you get used
to them, and you would be
well advised to practise both
interpreting and drawing them,
so you can be confident in using
them when you need to do so.

there is no further incentive for new firms to enter the market — which
occurs when the price has returned to P*, but with increased industry
output at Q**. In other words, the adjustment in the short run is borne
by existing firms, but the long-run equilibrium is reached through the
entry of new firms.

This suggests that the **industry long-run supply (LRS) curve** is
horizontal at the price P*, which is the minimum point of the long-run
average cost curve for the typical firm in the industry.

Strictly speaking, the LRS is perfectly flat only if all firms face equal cost
conditions, and if factor prices remain constant as the industry expands.
For example, if there is a labour shortage, industrial expansion may drive
up labour costs, causing firms to face higher costs at any output level. In
these sorts of circumstances, the LRS is slightly upward sloping.

Extension material

Different cost conditions

If firms are not identical, but face different cost conditions, then the LRS
may slope upwards. This could happen because some firms face a more
favourable environment than others. Perhaps their location confers some
advantage because they are closer to the market, or to some raw material.
This would then allow some firms to survive for longer if the market price
falls. In this case, as price falls, the least efficient firms would exit from the
market until the marginal firm just makes normal profits. Notice this also
suggests that the most efficient firms in the market are able to make some
supernormal profits even in long-run equilibrium, and it is only the marginal
firm that just breaks even.

Exercise 13.3

Starting from a diagram like Figure 13.6, track the response of a perfectly
competitive market to a decrease in market demand for a good — in other
words, explain how the market adjusts to a leftward shift of the demand curve.

Quantitative skills 13.1

Points and areas on a diagram

Figure 13.8 shows the short-run cost curves for a firm that is operating in a
perfectly competitive market. We can use a diagram like this to analyse some
key aspects of the firm's situation. Think carefully about what follows, and
make sure you understand the points and areas mentioned.

A first question is to consider at what price the firm would just make 'normal'
profits. This point would be where the price (average revenue) is just equal to
average total costs, which would be at a price OA in the figure.

If the price were indeed at OA, then we could find areas of the figure to
represent fixed and variable costs. With the price at OA the firm would produce
OQ output (where MC = MR), so, average variable costs would be given by OE,
and total variable costs would be the area OEHQ. We can then infer that total
fixed costs are the area EADH.

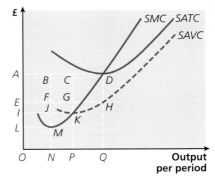

Figure 13.8 A firm operating under
short-run perfect competition

Efficiency under perfect competition

Having reviewed the characteristics of the long-run equilibrium of a perfectly competitive market, you may wonder what is so good about such a market in terms of allocative and productive efficiency.

Allocative efficiency

Synoptic link

The idea of allocative efficiency was introduced in Chapter 7, along with the notion that it will be achieved when price is equal to marginal cost.

For an individual market, allocative efficiency is achieved when price is set equal to marginal cost. In perfect competition, the process by which supernormal profits are competed away through the entry of new firms into the market ensures that price is equal to marginal cost when the market is in long-run equilibrium. So allocative efficiency is achieved. Indeed, firms set price equal to marginal cost even in the short run, so allocative efficiency is a feature of perfect competition in both the short run and the long run.

Productive efficiency

For an individual market, productive efficiency is reached when a firm operates at the minimum point of its long-run average cost curve. Under perfect competition, this is indeed a feature of the long-run equilibrium position. So productive efficiency is achieved in the long run — but not in the short run, when a firm is not necessarily operating at minimum average cost.

Evaluation of perfect competition

A criticism sometimes levelled at the model of perfect competition is that it is merely a theoretical ideal, based on a sequence of assumptions that rarely holds in the real world. Perhaps you have some sympathy with that view.

It could be argued that the model does hold for some agricultural markets. One study in the USA estimated that the price elasticity of demand for an individual farmer producing sweetcorn was −31,353, which is pretty close to perfect elasticity.

However, to argue that the model is useless because it is unrealistic is to miss a very important point. By allowing a glimpse of what the ideal market would look like, at least in terms of resource allocation, the model provides a measure against which alternative market structures can be compared. Furthermore, economic analysis can be used to investigate the effects of relaxing the assumptions of the model, which can be another valuable exercise. For example, it is possible to examine how the market is affected if firms can differentiate their products, or if traders in the market are acting with incomplete information. The impact of the internet on how markets work is also significant in this respect, as information is becoming much more accessible than ever before.

So, although there may be relatively few markets that display all the characteristics of perfect competition, that does not destroy the usefulness of the model in economic theory. It will continue to be a reference point when examining alternative models of market structure. This will become apparent as you study alternative market structures in the following chapters.

Extension material

A word of warning

Some writers, such as Nobel prize winner Friedrich von Hayek, have disputed the idea that perfect competition is the best form of market structure. Hayek argued that supernormal profits can be seen as the basis for investment by firms in new technologies, research and development (R&D) and innovation. If supernormal profits are always competed away, as happens under perfect competition, such activity will not take place. Similarly, Joseph Schumpeter argued that only in monopoly or oligopoly markets can firms afford to undertake R&D. Under this sort of argument, it is not quite so clear that perfect competition is the most desirable market structure.

Summary
- The model of perfect competition describes an extreme form of market structure. It rests on a sequence of assumptions.
- Its key characteristics include the assumption that no individual trader can influence the market price of the good or service being traded, and that there is freedom of entry and exit.
- In such circumstances each firm faces a perfectly elastic demand curve for its product, and can sell as much as it likes at the going market price: it is a price taker.
- A profit-maximising firm chooses to produce the level of output at which marginal revenue (MR) equals marginal cost (MC).
- The firm's short-run marginal cost curve, above its short-run average variable cost curve, represents its short-run supply curve.
- The industry's short-run supply curve is the horizontal summation of the supply curves of all firms in the market.
- Firms may make supernormal profits in the short run, but because there is freedom of entry these profits will be competed away in the long run by new firms joining the market.
- The long-run industry supply curve is horizontal, with price adjusting to the minimum level of the typical firm's long-run average cost curve.
- Allocative efficiency is achieved under perfect competition because price is equal to marginal cost.
- Under perfect competition in long-run equilibrium, both productive efficiency and allocative efficiency are achieved.

Competition online

One of the key assumptions of perfect competition is that all traders (buyers and sellers) have perfect knowledge of market conditions. Is this likely to happen in markets in the real world?

The internet has not always been there at our fingertips. Before it arrived on the scene, potential buyers of a good had to engage in a search process to discover what price was reasonable for a good. For example, if I needed to replace a tyre on my car, I had to work my way through the telephone directory, and phone the tyre dealers in the city until I found one that could supply the tyre I needed at the best price. Usually, I would give up after the first three or so dealers and take the best offer that was available. This meant that there was scope for individual dealers to charge a higher price than would have applied under perfect competition, so I may have ended up missing the best possible deal.

Today, if I want to discover the best price for a good I want to buy, my first step will be to go online to check availability, probably starting with Amazon, but then double-checking whether prices from stores in the city centre are comparable. Online sites therefore provide a quick way of checking market prices, and may allow potential buyers to be sure of getting a good deal.

This is not to say that all online markets are perfectly competitive: after all, Google dominates the search engine market in many countries. However, the firms that sell their goods or services through online marketing need to find ways of catching the attention of their potential clients, knowing that their rivals are doing the same.

Does this mean that prices are converging on the perfectly competitive price? Not necessarily. There are examples of goods and services whose price varies between sellers — for example, the price of onions may be different at the supermarket than at the local market.

Amazon is a first port of call for many consumers shopping online

Follow-up questions

a In the pre-internet economy, why was it possible for some dealers to charge different prices for the same product?

b Explain why the assumption that traders have perfect knowledge of market conditions is so important in the model of perfect competition.

c Given how easy it is to obtain information about the price of goods online, provide reasons why prices of goods and services may still vary between sellers.

CHAPTER 13 QUESTIONS

A Multiple-choice questions

1 If a market has many firms and a differentiated product, with few barriers to entry, which market structure is it best described as?

   a Perfect competition
   b Monopolistic competition
   c Oligopoly
   d Monopoly

2 Which of the following is not a characteristic of oligopoly?

   a Barriers to entry
   b Few firms in the market
   c Some influence over price
   d Homogeneous products

3 In the short-run perfect competition model, which of the following is not true?

   a The firm will produce at $MR = MC$
   b The firm can make supernormal profits
   c The firm will produce where $AC < AR$
   d The firm will produce at the lowest point of the AC curve

4 In the long-run perfect competition model, which of the following is true?

   a The firm will produce at $AR = AC$
   b The firm can make supernormal profits
   c The firm is a price maker
   d The firm will not be allocatively efficient

B Knowledge and understanding questions

5 Explain **two** characteristics of perfect competition. [4 marks]

6 Explain, using a diagram, the equilibrium price and output for a firm in short-run perfect competition. [4 marks]

7 Explain, using a diagram, how allocative efficiency is achieved under perfect competition in the short run. [4 marks]

C Stimulus response question

8 In a medium-sized town there are 12 barber shops that specialise in cutting and styling men's hair. The majority of these shops have a similar pricing strategy, with a basic haircut priced at £12. Most customers consider the service offered to be homogeneous.

   a Explain what is meant by the term 'homogeneous'. [2 marks]
   b Explain, using a diagram, the long-run structure of the market. [4 marks]
   c Explain one way in which a new barber shop opening in the town may be able to make supernormal profits in the short run. [2 marks]

Chapter 14

Market structure: monopoly

The previous chapter introduced the idea of market structure and explored perfect competition, which can be seen as being at one extreme of a spectrum of market structures. We now turn our attention to monopoly — said to be at the opposite extreme of the spectrum.

> ## Learning objectives
>
> After studying this chapter, you should be able to:
> - explain the characteristics of monopoly
> - explain, with the aid of a diagram, how a monopoly can make supernormal profit in both the short and long run
> - explain, with the aid of a diagram, a monopolist as a price maker
> - explain, with the aid of a diagram, equilibrium price and output for a profit-maximising monopolist
> - explain, with the aid of a diagram, productive and allocative efficiency with a profit-maximising monopolist
> - evaluate advantages and disadvantages of a monopoly
> - explain X-inefficiency
> - explain dynamic efficiency
> - explain, with the aid of a diagram, natural monopoly
> - evaluate advantages and disadvantages of a natural monopoly
> - explain, with the aid of a diagram, price discrimination by a firm with monopoly power

Assumptions of monopoly

Key term

monopoly a form of market structure in which there is only one seller of a good or service

Knowledge check 14.1

What is the significance of the assumption that there are no substitutes for the product of a monopolist for the market position of the firm?

At the opposite end of the spectrum of market structures from perfect competition is **monopoly**, which is a market with a single seller of a good. As with perfect competition, the model of monopoly rests on some key assumptions.

The assumptions of the monopoly model are as follows:
1 The firm aims to **maximise profits**.
2 There is a **single seller** of a good.
3 There are no **substitutes for the good**, either actual or potential.
4 There are **barriers** to entry into the market.

You can see that these assumptions all have their counterparts in the assumptions of perfect competition, and this is why the model can be described as being at the opposite end of the market structure spectrum.

If there is a single seller of a good, and if there are no substitutes for the good, the monopoly firm is thereby insulated from competition. Furthermore, any barriers to entry into the market will ensure that the firm can sustain its market position into the future. The assumption that there are no potential substitutes for the good reinforces the situation.

Synoptic link

Chapter 15 will explore how the market will be affected if there are potential substitutes for the good produced by a monopolist.

Barriers to entry

The existence of barriers to the entry of firms into the market is especially important in a monopoly market because these barriers enable the firm to maintain its position. Without barriers to entry, the market would soon cease to be a monopoly. Some key factors that create barriers to entry are:

- economies of scale
- high fixed costs
- cost advantages
- government regulation
- switching costs
- strategic action
- network effects

Economies of scale

Economies of scale can act as a barrier to the entry of new firms into an industry. If a monopoly firm faces significant economies of scale — for example, if the minimum efficient scale is close to the extent of market demand — then it will always be able to produce at lower cost than any potential entrant, so this will make it difficult for new firms to join the market.

High fixed costs

One situation in which a firm may face substantial economies of scale is where fixed costs are high relative to marginal costs. For example, if a potential entrant knows that it needs to invest heavily in set-up costs before being able to produce, this may deter entry.

There may be circumstances where the existing monopoly firm is able to consolidate its position by taking strategic action to affect its fixed costs to deter entry from new firms. For example, heavy investment in research and development (R&D) can make it difficult for potential entrants to become established in a market, because they need to undertake high expenditures before being able to compete with the existing firm.

Cost advantages

A monopoly firm may hold some absolute cost advantage over potential entrants. For example, the firm may have control over a key input needed for the production process. This could be control over a raw material or a supply chain. Or it might be that the firm has a locational advantage, being sited close to suppliers of a key input — or, indeed, to the market for the good.

Government regulation

In some cases, a firm may have some form of legal protection against competition. A common example of this is the patent system, whereby a firm may be protected from competition for a period following the introduction of a new innovative product. The aim of such government action is to encourage R&D and innovation in product development.

Switching costs

In some cases, the barrier to entry may arise because a firm's customers face high costs in switching to a new substitute product. Such costs may occur because a consumer has signed a contract for a fixed term, or simply because of brand loyalty. A person who is familiar with using Microsoft products may be reluctant to invest time in learning to use new systems and software.

Strategic action

Synoptic link

Such strategic action is discussed in Chapter 15.

An incumbent firm may undertake actions that create barriers to the entry of new firms. This action could be in taking out patents that the firm does not intend to use, therefore preventing new firms from setting up in a market, or it might be that the firm adopts a pricing policy that deters entry.

Network effects

Some goods or services have significant network effects. This is where people use a product because they know that there are many others who also use it. Adobe Acrobat's .pdf format is so widely used that it would be difficult for a new firm to come along with a different format for files.

The monopoly model

Key term

price maker a firm that is able to choose the selling price for its good or service, as it faces a downward-sloping demand curve

The first point to note is that a monopoly firm faces the market demand curve directly. This means that the monopolist's demand curve is downward-sloping (as explained in Chapter 3). This is different to the firm's demand curve under perfect competition, where the firm must accept the price set in the market, which means that its demand curve is horizontal. For the monopolist, the demand curve may be regarded as showing average revenue (remember that average revenue is the same as price in this context). Unlike a firm under perfect competition, therefore, the monopolist has some influence over price, and can make decisions regarding price as well as output. This is not to say that the monopolist has complete freedom to set the price, as the firm is still constrained by market demand. However, the firm is a **price maker** and can choose a location *along* the demand curve.

As with the firm under perfect competition, a monopolist aiming to maximise profits will choose to produce at the level of output at which marginal revenue (MR) equals marginal cost (MC). $MR = MC$ is always the profit-maximising level of output in whatever market structure the firm is operating. In Figure 14.1, $MR = MC$ at output Q_m. Having selected output, the monopolist then identifies the price at which that level of output can be sold by identifying the level of demand at Q_m. In Figure 14.1 this is P_m.

Chapter 6 explained the relationship between the price elasticity of demand and total revenue for a straight-line demand curve. See Figure 11.7 on page 149 for a reminder of the relevant diagram.

Notice that a monopoly will always produce in the segment of the demand curve where *MR* is positive, which implies that demand is price elastic.

This choice allows the monopolist to make supernormal profits, which can be identified as the shaded area in the figure. As before, this area is average revenue minus average cost (i.e. supernormal profit per unit) multiplied by the quantity.

It is at this point that barriers to entry become important. Other firms may see that the monopoly firm is making healthy supernormal profits, but the existence of barriers to entry will prevent those profits from being competed away, as would happen in a perfectly competitive market. With secure barriers to entry, the monopolist can continue to make supernormal profits in the long run.

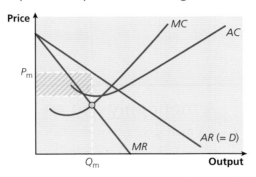

Figure 14.1 Profit maximisation and monopoly

Extension material

Does a monopoly always make supernormal profits?

A monopolist cannot be guaranteed always to make such substantial profits as are shown in Figure 14.1. The size of the profits depends upon the relative position of the market demand curve and the position of the cost curves. For example, if the cost curves in the diagram were higher, as in Figure 14.2, the monopoly would actually incur losses, as if the monopoly tries to maximise profits by choosing the output at which $MR = MC$, it will charge a price (P_m) that is below average cost (AC_m).

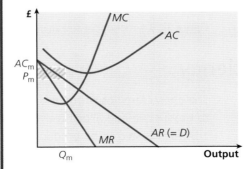

Figure 14.2 Losses made by a monopoly

Exercise 14.1

Table 14.1 shows the demand curve faced by a monopolist.

Table 14.1 Demand curve for a monopolist

Demand (000 per week)	Price (£)
0	80
1	70
2	60
3	50
4	40
5	30
6	20
7	10

a Calculate total revenue and marginal revenue for each level of demand.
b Plot the demand curve (AR) and marginal revenue on a graph.
c Plot total revenue on a separate graph.
d Identify the level of demand at which total revenue is at a maximum.
e At what level of demand is marginal revenue equal to zero?
f At what level of demand is there unit price elasticity of demand?
g If the monopolist maximises profits, will the chosen level of output be higher or lower than the revenue-maximising level?
h What does this imply for the price elasticity of demand when the monopolist maximises profits?

Knowledge check 14.2

Will a profit-maximising monopoly firm always make supernormal profits? Briefly explain your answer.

A monopoly and an increase in demand

If a monopoly experiences (or can induce) an increase in the demand for its product, it will benefit. In Figure 14.3, suppose that initially the monopoly faces the demand curve D_0. It maximises profits by setting $MR = MC$, producing Q_0 output and charging a price P_0. If the demand curve shifts to the right, notice that the MR curve will also shift, as this has a fixed relationship with the demand curve. After the increase in demand, the monopoly chooses to produce Q_1 output, where $MR = MC$, and now sets a higher price at P_1, making higher profits.

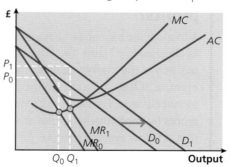

Figure 14.3 A monopoly and an increase in demand

Monopoly and efficiency

The characteristics of the monopoly market can be evaluated in relation to productive and allocative efficiency.

A firm is said to be productively efficient if it produces at the minimum point of its long-run average cost curve. It is clear from Figure 14.1 that this is extremely unlikely for a monopoly. The firm will produce at its minimum long-run average cost only if it so happens that the marginal *revenue* curve passes through this exact point — and this would happen only by coincidence.

For an individual firm, allocative efficiency is achieved when price is set equal to marginal cost. It is clear from Figure 14.1 that this will not be the case for a profit-maximising monopoly firm. The firm chooses output where MR equals MC — however, given that MR is below AR (i.e. price), price will always be set above marginal cost.

Disadvantages of monopoly

Allocative efficiency

Can we evaluate the extent to which the loss of allocative efficiency could be seen as a disadvantage of monopoly? This is best seen by comparing the monopoly market with the perfectly competitive market. To do this, the situation can be simplified by setting aside the possibility of economies of scale. This is perhaps an artificial assumption to make, but it will be relaxed later.

Suppose that there is an industry with no economies of scale, which can be operated either as a perfectly competitive market with many small firms or as a monopoly firm running a large number of small plants.

Figure 14.4 shows the market demand curve ($D = AR$), and the long-run supply curve under perfect competition (LRS). If the market is operating under perfect competition, the long-run equilibrium will produce a price of P_{pc}, and the firms in the industry will together supply Q_{pc} output. Consumer surplus is given by the area $AP_{pc}E$, which represents the surplus that consumers gain from consuming this product. In other words, it is a measure of the welfare that society receives from consuming the good.

Now suppose that the industry is taken over by a profit-maximising monopolist. The firm can close down some of the plants to vary its output over the long run, and the LRS can be regarded as the monopolist's long-run marginal cost curve. As the monopoly firm faces the market demand curve directly, it will also face the MR curve shown, so will maximise profits at quantity Q_m and charge a price P_m.

So, the effect of this change in market structure is that the profit-maximising monopolist produces less output than a perfectly competitive industry and charges a higher price.

It is also apparent that consumer surplus is now very different, as in the new situation it is limited to the area AP_mB. Looking more carefully at Figure 14.4, you can see that the loss of consumer surplus has occurred for two reasons. First, the monopoly firm is now making supernormal profits shown by the shaded area P_mBCP_{pc}. This is a redistribution of welfare from consumers to the firm, but as the monopoly is also part of society, this does not affect overall welfare. However, there is also loss to society resulting from the monopolisation of the industry. This is measured by the area of the triangle BCE. Such losses inflicted on society are often known as the *deadweight loss*.

X-inefficiency

Chapter 12 introduced the notion of X-inefficiency in the context of the principal–agent problem, the argument being that if managers of large firms were not sufficiently accountable to the firm's owners, they would not have a sufficient incentive to be as efficient as they could be. X-inefficiency could also appear in a monopoly market, if the firm

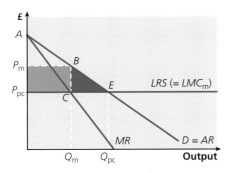

Figure 14.4 Comparing perfect competition and monopoly

Synoptic link

The concept of consumer surplus was first introduced in Chapter 3.

Knowledge check 14.3

What will be the profit situation for a monopoly that is required by the government to produce where price is equal to marginal cost?

becomes complacent about its position in the market. If the firm does not face competition (actual or potential) because of some barrier to the entry of new firms, again it could be that the incentive to be highly efficient is weak, so that X-inefficiency could creep in, and the firm may face a higher average cost curve than is optimal.

Consumer choice

If the monopoly firm is able to prevent the entry of new firms into the market, this could limit consumer choice, as new firms could be innovative in providing substitute products. There is evidence that consumers do like to have choice in a market.

Advantages of monopoly

Economies of scale

A monopoly firm may be able to take advantage of economies of scale, and so produce at lower cost than smaller firms. Even if this does not lead to productive efficiency, in the sense that the monopoly would not produce at its minimum average cost, this could still be production at lower average cost than could be achieved by a market made of many small firms. This may enable the firm to produce at lower average cost and make higher supernormal profits — and, perhaps, maintain its market position.

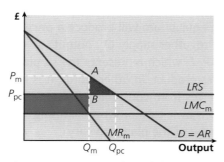

Figure 14.5 A monopoly with lower cost conditions than under perfect competition

Figure 14.5 illustrates the situation if a monopoly firm faces lower cost conditions than would apply under perfect competition. *LRS* represents the long-run supply schedule if an industry is operating under perfect competition. The perfectly competitive equilibrium would be at output level Q_{pc} with the price at P_{pc}. The monopoly alternative faces lower long-run marginal cost shown by LMC_m, so the firm produces Q_m output in order to maximise profits, and sets price at P_m.

Analysis of this situation reveals that there is a deadweight loss given by the red triangle — this reflects the allocative inefficiency of monopoly. However, there is also a gain in productive efficiency, represented by the green rectangle. This is part of monopoly profits, but under perfect competition it was part of production costs. In other words, production under the monopoly is less wasteful in its use of resources in the production process.

Is society better off under monopoly or under perfect competition? In order to evaluate the effect on total welfare, we need to balance the loss of allocative efficiency (the red triangle) against the gain in productive efficiency (the green rectangle). In Figure 14.5 it would seem that the rectangle is larger than the triangle, so society overall is better off with the monopoly. Of course, there is also the distribution of income to take into account — the area $P_m ABP_{pc}$ would be part of consumer surplus under perfect competition, but under monopoly it becomes part of the firm's profits.

Dynamic efficiency

The discussion of efficiency so far has focused on how to make the best use of existing resources, producing an appropriate mix of goods and

Knowledge check 14.4

What incentive does a monopoly firm have to sacrifice supernormal profits in order to engage in R&D?

Exercise 14.2

A rail company is awarded a franchise to operate trains on a route joining two neighbouring cities. Discuss the extent to which the company would be able to operate as a profit-maximising monopoly.

services and using factor inputs as efficiently as possible, given existing knowledge and technology. This is good as far as it goes, but it does represent a relatively static view of efficiency.

Dynamic efficiency goes one step further, recognising that the state of knowledge and technology changes over time. For example, investment in research and development today means that production can be carried out more efficiently at some future date. Furthermore, the development of new products also means that a different mix of goods and services may serve consumers better in the long term.

The notion of dynamic efficiency stemmed from the work of Joseph Schumpeter, who argued that a preoccupation with static efficiency may sacrifice opportunities for greater efficiency in the long run. In other words, there may be a trade-off between achieving efficiency today and improving efficiency tomorrow.

An example of how a monopoly firm may create dynamic efficiency is where the firm has the capacity to undertake R&D as a result of the supernormal profits it is able to earn. This is in contrast to the situation facing firms under perfect competition, which are not able to make supernormal profits in long-run equilibrium. Such R&D could not be undertaken unless the firm makes supernormal profits. However, the question of whether a monopoly firm will actually have sufficient incentive to pursue dynamic efficiency may be open to debate.

Size and global markets

Another argument that has been put forward is that allowing a firm to dominate the domestic market by expanding to its potential may enable it to compete more effectively with large foreign firms in global markets, therefore benefiting the domestic economy.

Summary

- A monopoly market is one in which there is a single seller of a good.
- The model of monopoly used in economic analysis also assumes that there are no substitutes for the goods or services produced by the monopolist, and that there are barriers to the entry of new firms.
- The monopoly firm faces the market demand curve, and is able to choose a point along that demand curve in order to maximise profits.
- Such a firm may be able to make supernormal profits and sustain them in the long run because of barriers to entry and the lack of substitutes.
- A profit-maximising monopolist does not achieve allocative efficiency and is unlikely to achieve productive efficiency either.
- A comparison of perfect competition with monopoly reveals that a profit-maximising monopoly firm operating under the same cost conditions as a perfectly competitive industry will produce less output, charge a higher price and impose a deadweight loss on society.
- Disadvantages of a monopoly are that the firm does not achieve allocative efficiency and there is a possibility of X-inefficiency and limited consumer choice.
- Advantages are that a monopoly may be able to tap into economies of scale and to use supernormal profits to engage in R&D, and therefore achieve dynamic efficiency.

How do monopolies arise?

Monopolies may arise in a market for a number of reasons. In a few instances, a monopoly is created by the authorities. For example, for 150 years the UK Post Office held a licence giving it a monopoly on delivering letters. This service was opened to some competition in the 2000s, although any company wanting to deliver packages weighing less than 350 grams and charging less than £1 could do so only by applying for a licence. The Post Office monopoly formerly covered a much wider range of services, but its coverage has been eroded over the years, and competition in delivering larger packages has been permitted for some time.

Royal Mail was privatised in October 2013, becoming a quoted company on the London Stock Exchange. The company has a 'Universal Service Obligation', under which it must continue to provide a six days a week, one price goes anywhere postal service. It delivers to 30 million addresses in the UK, and is also subject to control on prices. These obligations are subject to regulation by Ofcom.

The Royal Mail was one of the last former state-owned businesses to be privatised

The patent system offers a rather different form of protection for a firm. The patent system was designed to provide an incentive for firms to innovate through the development of new techniques and products. By prohibiting other firms from copying the product for a period of time, a firm is given a temporary monopoly.

There are markets in which firms have risen to become monopolies by their actions in the market. Such a market structure is sometimes known as a *competitive monopoly*. Firms may get into a monopoly position through effective marketing, through a process of merger and acquisition, or by establishing a new product as a widely accepted standard. For example, by the mid-2010s, Google had come to control some 90% of the search engine market in Europe.

Monopolies may also be created through mergers and acquisitions, if one firm is able to buy out its competitors or combine with them to exploit economies of scale.

A natural monopoly

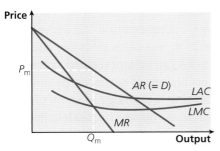

Figure 14.6 A natural monopoly

In some cases the technology of the industry may create a monopoly situation. In a market characterised by substantial economies of scale, there may not be room for more than one firm in the market. This could happen where there are substantial fixed costs of production but low marginal costs. For example, building an underground railway system in a city, a firm faces substantial expenditure in the form of fixed costs to create the network of track and stations and buy the rolling stock. However, once in operation, the marginal cost of carrying an additional passenger is very low.

Figure 14.6 illustrates this point. The firm in this market enjoys economies of scale right up to the limit of market demand. Any new entrant into the market will be operating at a lower scale, so will inevitably face higher average costs. The existing firm will always be able to price such firms out of the market. Here the economies of scale act as an effective barrier to the entry of new firms and the market is a **natural monopoly**. A profit-maximising monopoly would therefore set $MR = MC$, produce at quantity Q_m and charge a price P_m.

Such a market poses particular problems regarding allocative efficiency. Notice in the figure that marginal cost is below average cost over the entire range of output. If the firm were to charge a price equal to marginal cost, it would inevitably make a loss, so such a pricing rule would not be viable.

Nationalisation and privatisation

A number of industries that have the characteristics of a natural monopoly are utilities such as water, electricity or gas supply, the railway network and so on. In the past, a standard response to this market situation was to **nationalise** the industry (i.e. take it into state ownership), since no private sector firm would be prepared to operate at a loss, and the government would not allow firms running such natural monopolies to act as profit-maximising monopolists making supernormal profits.

However, as time went by this sort of system came to be heavily criticised. In particular, it was argued that the managers of the nationalised industries were not sufficiently accountable. The situation could be regarded as an extreme form of the principal–agent problem, in which the consumers (the principals) had very little control over the actions of the managers (their agents), a situation leading to considerable X-inefficiency and waste.

Nationalisation has been much less used in the twenty-first century, but there have been some high-profile examples. These have occurred when the government has decided to intervene to bail out failing firms. An example occurred in 2018, when the Virgin Trains East Coast franchise failed. The company was taken into public hands, to be run by the Department for Transport until 2020, when a new public–private partnership is expected to be launched.

During the period of Margaret Thatcher's Conservative government in the 1980s there was widespread **privatisation** (i.e. the transfer of nationalised industries into private ownership), one central argument being that this would force the managers to be accountable to their shareholders, which would encourage an increase in efficiency.

Key term

natural monopoly a monopoly that arises in an industry in which there are such substantial economies of scale that only one firm is viable

Knowledge check 14.5

Explain why the rail network (that is, the track) might be regarded as a natural monopoly.

Knowledge check 14.6

Why would a government not regard it as appropriate for a nationalised industry to make supernormal profits?

Key terms

nationalisation where a privately owned firm or industry is taken into public ownership
privatisation where an enterprise in public ownership is returned to private ownership

Synoptic link

Another example of nationalisation in the twenty-first century was the government intervention in taking ownership of some banks during the financial crisis of the late 2000s. This is discussed in the macroeconomics section in Chapter 39.

Knowledge check 14.7

Why would competition flourish more readily in telecommunications than in some other natural monopolies?

However, this did not remove the original problem: that these industries were natural monopolies. Therefore, wherever possible, privatisation was also accompanied by measures to encourage competition, which was seen as an even better way to ensure efficiency improvements. This proved to be more feasible in some industries than in others because of the nature of economies of scale — there is little to be gained by requiring there to be several firms in a market where the economies of scale can be reaped only by one large firm. However, the changing technology in some of the industries did allow some competition to be encouraged, especially in telecommunications.

Advantages and disadvantages of natural monopoly

The main advantage of a natural monopoly is that it is able to tap into economies of scale, and so produce at lower cost than could be achieved by having several firms, all of which produce at higher average cost.

The disadvantage of this is that it puts a lot of power into the hands of the firm operating the monopoly. If it were to choose to maximise profits, it would restrict output and raise price (as compared to a competitive market). Given that many natural monopolies supply goods and services that are seen to be essentials, this would be highly undesirable for society at large. However, forcing the firm to charge a price equal to marginal cost would entail the firm making losses, which would be unsustainable without government subsidies.

Competition policy

Synoptic link

The work of the CMA is discussed in Chapter 10.

Knowledge check 14.8

It has been relatively rare for the CMA to impose fines on firms for anticompetitive behaviour. Do you think this means that the policy is not working?

The potential welfare loss that society could experience if firms are able to exploit market power has long been recognised by governments. Competition policy is the branch of policy used to prevent firms from abusing market dominance, and to provide consumer protection. In the case of natural monopoly, regulatory bodies have been set up to monitor and influence the way in which privatised natural monopolies operate. The policy is implemented through the Competition and Markets Authority (CMA).

Under Brexit, the challenge will be to cope with the increased workload when cases currently pursued by the European Commission will come within the jurisdiction of the CMA. There will also be a need to coordinate action with the European authorities when firms operate in both EU and UK markets.

Regulation

In the case of privatised natural monopolies, regulatory bodies were set up to oversee the operation of the industries. Initially this regulation was primarily aimed to control prices, setting limits on the rate at which prices were allowed to rise, with the permitted rise set to encourage productivity improvements.

In the mid-2010s, concerns rose about the effectiveness of price regulation. It was perceived that there was too strong a focus on cost-saving rather than output delivery, and that companies were looking for static rather than dynamic efficiency. There was increasing concern about environmental issues, and the quality of output that was being produced.

The regulators Ofwat (water) and Ofgem (gas and electricity) acted to phase out the price controls, to be replaced by the RIIO ('**R**evenue using **I**ncentives to deliver **I**nnovation and **O**utputs') method. RIIO is a price control mechanism that specifies the outputs that companies are required to deliver and the revenue that they are able to earn for delivering these outputs efficiently. The aim of this change is to provide better incentives for companies to meet quality standards, rather than just focusing on costs.

Under RIIO, companies that can deliver their output targets under budget gain through the revenue generation. However, companies that fail to meet their performance targets are punished financially. Companies need to report to their regulator on an annual basis.

In the case of water supply, government strategy requires companies to provide social tariffs for customers who cannot afford to pay for water. This is also monitored as part of the performance approach.

Limits to the regulatory approach

Government intervention through direct controls has to be carefully designed to avoid introducing market distortions. This is reflected in the changing approaches over time that attempt to rectify flaws that become apparent. Asymmetric information can also come into play, when the companies have better information about the way they are operating than their regulators.

In some cases, **regulatory capture** is a further problem. This occurs when the regulator becomes so closely involved with the firm it is supposed to be regulating that it begins to champion its cause rather than imposing tough rules where they are needed.

> **Knowledge check 14.9**
>
> Explain why the presence of asymmetric information could limit the effectiveness of regulation.

> **Key term**
>
> **regulatory capture** a situation in which the regulator of an industry comes to represent the industry's interests rather than regulating it

Price discrimination

Are there any conditions in which a monopoly firm would produce the level of output that is consistent with allocative efficiency? Consider Figure 14.7. Suppose this market is operated by a monopolist that faces constant marginal cost *LMC*. What would induce the monopolist to produce at Q^*?

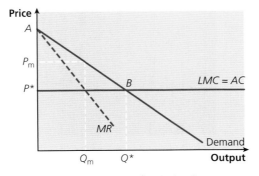

Figure 14.7 Perfect price discrimination

One of the assumptions made throughout the analysis so far is that all consumers in a market get to pay the same price for the product. This leads to the notion of consumer surplus. In Figure 14.7, if the market were operating under perfect competition and all consumers were paying the same price, consumer surplus would be given by the area $AP*B$. If the market were operated by a monopolist, also charging the same price to all buyers, then profits would be maximised where $MC = MR$: that is, at quantity Q_m and price P_m.

But suppose this assumption is now relaxed? Suppose that the monopolist is able to charge a different price to each individual consumer. A monopolist is then able to charge each consumer a price that is equal to his or her willingness to pay for the good. In other words, the demand curve effectively becomes the marginal revenue curve, as it represents the amount that the monopolist will receive for each unit of the good. It will then maximise profits at point B in Figure 14.7, where MR (i.e. AR) is equal to LMC. The difference between this situation and that under perfect competition is that the area $AP*B$ is no longer consumer surplus, but producer surplus: that is, the monopolist's profits. The monopolist has hijacked the whole of the original consumer surplus as its profits.

Key term

perfect/first-degree price discrimination situation arising in a market whereby a monopoly firm is able to charge each consumer a different price

First-degree price discrimination

From society's point of view, total welfare is the same as it is under perfect competition (but more than under monopoly without discrimination). However, now there has been a redistribution from consumers to the monopoly — and presumably to the shareholders of the firm. This situation is known as **perfect price discrimination** or **first-degree price discrimination**.

Perfect price discrimination is fairly rare in the real world, although it might be said to exist in the world of art or fashion, where customers may commission a painting, sculpture or item of designer jewellery and the price is a matter of negotiation between the buyer and supplier.

Perfect price discrimination exists in the art world

Third-degree price discrimination

There are situations in which partial price discrimination is possible. For example, students or old-age pensioners may get discounted bus fares, the young and/or old may get cheaper access to sporting events or theatres, etc. In these instances, individual consumers are paying different prices for what is in fact the same product, known as **third-degree price discrimination**.

Conditions for price discrimination

There are three conditions under which a firm may be able to price discriminate:

1 The firm must have market power.
2 The firm must have information about consumers and their willingness to pay — and there must be identifiable differences between consumers (or groups of consumers).
3 The consumers must have limited ability to resell the product.

Market power

Clearly, price discrimination is not possible in a perfectly competitive market, where no seller has the power to charge other than the going market price. So price discrimination can take place only where firms have some ability to vary the price.

Information about groups of consumers

From the firm's point of view, it needs to be able to identify different groups of consumers with different willingness to pay. What makes price discrimination profitable for firms is that different consumers display different sensitivities to price: that is, they have different price elasticities of demand.

Ability to resell

If consumers could resell the product easily, then price discrimination would not be possible, as consumers would engage in **arbitrage**. In other words, the group of consumers who qualified for the low price could buy up the product and then turn a profit by reselling to consumers in the other segment(s) of the market. This would mean that the firm would no longer be able to sell at the high price, and would no longer try to discriminate in pricing.

Price discrimination in practice

In the case of student discounts and old-age concessions, the firm can identify particular groups of consumers, and such 'products' as bus journeys or dental treatment cannot be resold. But why should a firm undertake this practice?

The simple answer is that, by undertaking price discrimination, the firm is able to increase its profits by switching sales from a market with relatively low marginal revenue to a market where it is higher. This is shown in Figure 14.8, which separates two distinct groups of consumers with differing demand curves. Thus, panel (a) shows market A and panel (b) shows market B, with the combined demand curve being shown in panel (c), which also shows the firm's marginal cost curve.

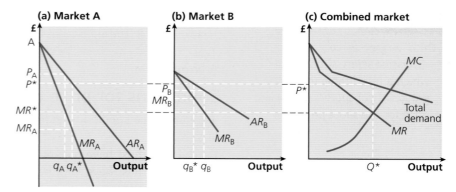

Figure 14.8 A price-discriminating monopolist

If a firm has to charge the same price to all consumers, it sets marginal revenue in the combined market equal to marginal cost, and produces Q^* output, to be sold at a price of P^*. This maximises profits when all consumers pay the same price. The firm sells q_A^* in market A, and q_B^* in market B.

However, if you look at panels (a) and (b), you will see that marginal revenue in market A is much lower (at MR_A) than that in market B (at MR_B). It is this difference in marginal revenue that opens up a profit-increasing opportunity for the firm. By taking sales away from market A and selling more in market B, the firm gains more extra revenue in B than it loses in A. This increases its profit. The optimal position for the firm is where marginal revenue is equalised in the two markets. In Figure 14.8 the firm sells q_A in market A at the higher price of P_A. In market B sales increase to q_B with price falling to P_B. Notice that in both situations the amounts sold in the two sub-markets sum to Q^*.

The consumers in market B seem to do quite well by this practice, as they can now consume more of the good. Indeed, it is possible that with no discrimination the price would be so high that they would not be able to consume the good at all.

In 2016, the CMA reported on an investigation of the energy market. One of its findings was that there was wide variation in the prices paid by domestic customers for energy, although electricity and gas are homogeneous products. Potentially, most customers could have made savings by switching suppliers, tariffs or payment methods. Indeed, average potential gains from switching were equivalent to more than 20% of customers' bills. A number of remedies were recommended to address this situation.

> **Study tip**
>
> Be ready with the three conditions that are necessary if a firm is to be able to use price discrimination:
> 1 The firm must have some market power.
> 2 The firm must be able to identify different consumers (or groups of consumers) and differences in their elasticities of demand.
> 3 There must be limited ability for consumers to resell the product.

Today, customers can make big savings when they switch energy suppliers

Exercise 14.3

In which of the following products might price discrimination be possible? Explain your answers.

a hairdressing

b peak and off-peak rail travel

c apples

d air tickets

e newspapers

f plastic surgery

g beer

Summary

- In some markets a monopolist may be able to engage in price discrimination by selling its product at different prices to different consumers or groups of consumers.
- This enables the firm to increase its profits by absorbing some or all of the consumer surplus.
- Under first-degree price discrimination, the firm is able to charge a different price to each customer and absorb all of the consumer surplus.
- The firm can practise price discrimination only where it has market power, where consumers have differing elasticities of demand for the product, and where consumers have limited ability to resell the product.

Of cabbages and rings

As a cabbage farmer, Ted must accept the price given by the market, since one cabbage is much like another.

Ted Greens has a farm on which he grows a variety of crops, including cabbages that grow well on his south field, which seems especially suited to the crop. When Ted takes his cabbage crop to market, hoping to make as much profit as possible, he finds that the price he can charge for cabbages depends on market conditions — after all, one cabbage is very much like any other. He therefore has to accept the price he can get, which is the same as that charged by his many rival producers. If he tries to set a higher price, he sells nothing, as all traders in the market have good awareness of market conditions. But as he can sell as much as he likes at the going price, there is no need to drop price below that prevailing in the market. Price tends to fluctuate from one harvest season to the next, and in some years when cabbages are plentiful, Ted finds that he barely covers his costs.

Edward de Vere owns a diamond mine — the only such mine in the country. His company cuts the stones and uses them to produce diamond rings. In selling the rings, Edward takes into account the strength of demand, choosing a price that will clear the market. He finds that by restricting the number of rings he produces, he is able to charge a higher price. By doing so he is able to increase his profits. As he controls the only source of diamonds, Edward does not have to worry about other producers entering the market, and there are no acceptable substitutes for diamonds that people are prepared to accept.

Follow-up questions

a Which of the two producers appears to operate under conditions of perfect competition, and which is a monopoly?

b Explain your answer to part (a), referring to the assumptions that underlie the two theories of market structure.

c Under what conditions would Ted Greens decide to give up growing cabbages?

d Can you think of steps that Ted Greens might take in order to improve his profits on cabbages?

e Draw a diagram to explain how Edward de Vere would react to an increase in the demand for diamond rings.

f Suppose that a foreign firm starts to import diamond rings into the country in competition with Edward de Vere. How would you expect him to react?

CHAPTER 14 QUESTIONS

A Multiple-choice questions

1 A profit-maximising and profitable monopoly that produces at $MC = MR$ will make:

   a Supernormal profit

   b Normal profit

   c Accounting profit

   d All of the above

2 Which of the following is not a characteristic of a monopoly?

   a Few barriers to entry

   b One dominant firm in the market

   c Price maker

   d A differentiated product

3 CMA stands for:

   a Competition and Microeconomics Authority

   b Company and Markets Authority

   c Competition and Markets Authority

   d Conglomerate and Markets Authority

B Knowledge and understanding questions

4 Explain **two** characteristics of a monopoly.   [4 marks]

5 Explain, using a diagram, why a monopoly may be a price maker.   [4 marks]

6 Explain what is meant by the term 'X-inefficiency'.   [2 marks]

7 Explain **two** possible advantages to an economy of a monopoly.   [4 marks]

C Stimulus response question

8 Monopolies are not always a bad thing for an economy. Sometimes the advantages outweigh the disadvantages, especially where the business can be operated without a profit motive.

Tap water is a good example of a 'natural monopoly'. To provide potable drinking water to households requires a large investment in pipes and infrastructure. A private business (in other words, not owned by the government) would have a profit motive to create this infrastructure in large populated areas because there would be a large number of potential customers. The business would be able to recoup the initial investment in a reasonable timeframe.

However, more remote or isolated households would need to be charged an exorbitant price to cover the investment costs. This could lead to an unfair distribution of water in the UK, the move away from living in anything but highly populated areas or simply no tap water supplied to these households.

In the UK, private businesses owned the tap water industry until the beginning of the twentieth century. At this point the government nationalised the industry with the aim of providing potable water, considered to be a necessity, to all households.

In 1989, the industry was privatised in England and Wales. Ten private businesses were set up together with three regulatory bodies — one to regulate and monitor the quality of water, another to regulate and monitor pollution and conservation of the waterways, and a third to regulate and monitor prices and business performance.

a   Explain what is meant by the term 'nationalised'. [2 marks]
b   Explain, using a diagram, a natural monopoly. [4 marks]
c   Evaluate the importance of setting up regulatory bodies in the privatised tap water market. [8 marks]
d   Evaluate the possible disadvantages to the UK economy of operating the tap water market as a natural nationalised monopoly. [12 marks]

D Essay question

9   Google is usually considered to be a monopoly within the UK search engine market.

Evaluate the extent to which Google demonstrates the characteristics of operating in a monopoly market. [25 marks]

Chapter 15

Monopolistic competition, oligopoly and contestable markets

Chapters 13 and 14 introduced the models of perfect competition and monopoly, and described them as being at the extreme ends of a spectrum of forms of market structure. In between those two extremes are other forms of market structure, which have some but not all of the characteristics of either perfect competition or monopoly. It is in this sense that there is a spectrum of structures. This chapter focuses on some of these intermediate forms of market structure, including a discussion of the sorts of pricing strategy that firms may adopt, and how they decide which to go for. This chapter also discusses ways in which firms may try to prevent new firms from joining a market, in terms of both pricing and non-price strategies. The theory of contestable markets completes the discussion.

Learning objectives

After studying this chapter, you should be able to:
- explain the characteristics of monopolistic competition
- explain product differentiation
- explain, with the aid of a diagram, short-run monopolistic competition, with supernormal profits or losses
- explain, with the aid of a diagram, long-run monopolistic competition, with normal profits
- explain, with the aid of a diagram, equilibrium price and output for a firm in monopolistic competition
- evaluate advantages and disadvantages of monopolistic competition
- explain characteristics of oligopoly
- explain non-price competition
- explain interdependence in the kinked demand curve model
- explain types of collusion
- explain and calculate concentration ratios
- evaluate advantages and disadvantages of oligopoly markets
- explain characteristics of a contestable market
- explain productive and allocative efficiency in a contestable market
- evaluate advantages and disadvantages of a contestable market

Monopolistic competition

If you consider the characteristics of the markets that you frequent on a regular basis, you will find that few (if any) of them display all of the characteristics associated with perfect competition. However, there may be some that show a few of these features. In particular, you will find some markets in which there appears to be intense competition among many sellers, but in which the products for sale are not identical. For example, think about restaurants. In many cities, you will find a wide range of restaurants, cafés and pubs that compete with each other for business, but do so by offering slightly different products.

The theory of **monopolistic competition** was devised by Edward Chamberlin, writing in the USA in the 1930s, and his name is often attached to the model, although Joan Robinson published her book on imperfect competition in the UK at the same time. The motivation for the analysis was to explain how markets worked when they were operating neither as monopolies nor under perfect competition.

The model describes a market in which there are many firms producing similar, but not identical, products: for example, package holidays, hairdressers and fast-food outlets. In the case of fast-food outlets, the high streets of many cities are characterised by large numbers of different types of takeaway — burgers, fish and chips, Indian, Chinese, fried chicken, and so on.

Microeconomics Part 4

Key term

monopolistic competition
a market that shares some characteristics of monopoly and some of perfect competition

Synoptic link

The models of perfect competition and monopoly were discussed in Chapters 13 and 14 as being at the opposite ends of a spectrum of market structures. The models explored in this chapter are intermediate models that fall between those extremes.

Multiple types of takeaway on the same high street are an example of monopolistic competition

Characteristics of monopolistic competition

The model of monopolistic competition shares some characteristics with perfect competition and some with monopoly. Its features are:
- a downward-sloping demand curve
- product differentiation
- freedom of entry
- many firms
- no dominant firm

A downward-sloping demand curve

As with a monopoly, a firm in monopolistic competition has some control over price. In other words it can choose the price at which it sells, rather than having to accept the market price as it would in perfect competition. A fall in price would increase the quantity demanded, so the demand curve slopes downwards. In this respect it resembles monopoly rather than perfect competition.

Product differentiation

Monopolistic competition differs from monopoly because the firm faces competition from other firms. This means that the firm needs to find ways to distinguish itself from the other firms. It does this by making its product slightly different. This allows the firms to build up brand loyalty among their regular customers, which gives them some influence over price. It is likely that firms will engage in advertising or in product design in order to maintain such brand loyalty, and heavy advertising is a common characteristic of a market operating under monopolistic competition. This strategy is known as **product differentiation**. Notice that by spending on advertising or in improving product quality and design, the firm is adding to its costs, so that the average cost curve will shift upwards.

Because other firms are producing similar goods, there are substitutes for each firm's product, which means that demand is relatively price elastic (although this does not mean that it is never inelastic). However, it is certainly not perfectly price elastic, as was the case with perfect competition. These features — that the product is not homogeneous and demand is not perfectly price elastic — represent significant differences from the model of perfect competition.

Freedom of entry

There are no (or low) barriers to entry into the market. Firms are able to join the market if they observe that existing firms are making supernormal profits. New entrants will be looking for some way to differentiate their product slightly from the others — perhaps the next fast-food restaurant will be Nepalese, or Peruvian.

This characteristic distinguishes the market from the monopoly model, as does the existence of fairly close substitutes.

Many firms

There are many firms operating in the market. For this reason, a price change by one of the firms will have negligible effects on the demand for its rivals' products.

This characteristic means that the market is also different from an oligopoly market, where there are a few firms that interact strategically with each other.

No dominant firm

Although there are many firms in the market, no individual firm is dominant. If one firm had significantly more power than others, so was able to dictate how the market operated, perhaps by setting price, then the market would work differently.

Key term

product differentiation a strategy firms adopt that marks their product as being different from their competitors'

Synoptic link

When a firm engages in advertising or product development in order to differentiate its product, it is known as non-price competition. This is also important in the context of oligopoly, and is discussed in more detail later in this chapter.

Knowledge check 15.1

Why is product differentiation an important characteristic of the model of monopolistic competition?

Synoptic link

Oligopoly models are discussed later in this chapter.

Study tip

Remember these characteristics, and why they are important in making the model of monopolistic competition distinct from both perfect competition and monopoly.

Overview

Taking these characteristics together, it can be seen that a market of monopolistic competition has some of the characteristics of perfect competition and some features of monopoly, hence its name.

Short-run equilibrium in monopolistic competition

Figure 15.1 represents short-run equilibrium under monopolistic competition. D_s is the firm's demand curve and MR_s is the corresponding marginal revenue curve. AC and MC are the average and marginal cost curves for a representative firm in the industry. If the firm is aiming to maximise profits, it will choose the level of output such that $MR_s = MC$. This occurs at output Q_s, and the firm will then choose the price that clears the market at P_s.

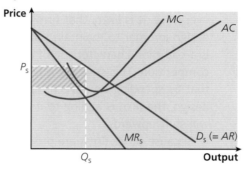

Figure 15.1 Short-run equilibrium under monopolistic competition

This closely resembles the standard monopoly diagram that was introduced in Chapter 14. As with monopoly, a firm under monopolistic competition faces a downward-sloping demand curve, as already noted. The difference is that now it is assumed that there is some freedom of entry into the market under monopolistic competition, so that Figure 15.1 represents equilibrium only in the short run. This is because the firm shown in the figure is making supernormal profits, shown by the shaded area (which is $AR - AC$ multiplied by output).

The importance of no or low barriers to entry

This is where the assumption of free entry into the market becomes important. In Figure 15.1, the supernormal profits being made by the representative firm will attract new firms into the market. The new firms will produce differentiated products, and this will affect the demand curve for the representative firm's product. In particular, the new firms will attract some customers away from this firm, so that its demand curve will tend to shift to the left. Its shape may also change, as there are now more substitutes for the original product.

Knowledge check 15.2

If a firm operating under monopolistic competition is making supernormal profits, what would you expect to happen to its demand curve?

Long-run equilibrium in monopolistic competition

This process of entry of firms will persist as long as firms in the market continue to make supernormal profits that attract new firms into the activity (or make losses, causing some firms to leave). It may be accelerated if firms are persuaded to spend money on advertising in an

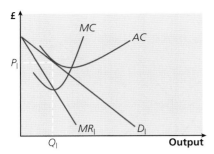

Figure 15.2 Long-run equilibrium under monopolistic competition

attempt to defend their market shares. The advertising may help to keep the demand curve downward sloping, but it will also affect the position of the average cost curve, by pushing up average cost at all levels of output.

Figure 15.2 shows the final position for the market. The typical firm is now operating in such a way that it maximises profits (by setting output such that $MR = MC$). At the same time, the average cost curve (AC) at this level of output is at a tangent to the demand curve. This means that $AC = AR$, and the firm is just making normal profit (i.e. is just covering opportunity cost). There is, therefore, no further incentive for more firms to join the market. In Figure 15.2 this occurs when output is at Q_1 and price is set at P_1.

Efficiency under monopolistic competition

One way of evaluating the market outcome under this model is to examine the consequences for productive and allocative efficiency. It is clear from Figure 15.2 that neither of these conditions will be met. For productive efficiency to be achieved, the firm would need to be operating at minimum average cost, but Figure 15.2 shows that the firm will not be at this point. Allocative efficiency requires price to be set equal to marginal cost, but a firm maximising profit under monopolistic competition will set a price higher than this, as is also shown in Figure 15.2.

Evaluation of monopolistic competition

If the typical firm in the market is not fully exploiting the possible economies of scale that exist, it could be argued that product differentiation is a disadvantage which damages society's total welfare, in the sense that product differentiation allows firms to keep their demand curves downward sloping. In other words, too many different products are being produced. However, this argument could be countered by pointing out that consumers may enjoy having more freedom of choice, which could be seen as an advantage of this type of market structure. The very fact they are prepared to pay a premium price for their chosen brand indicates they have some preference for it. For example, some people may be prepared to pay £69 to watch Chelsea FC although they could watch 90 minutes of football at AFC Wimbledon for less than £20.

Another crucial difference between monopolistic competition and perfect competition is that under monopolistic competition, firms would like to sell more of their product at the going price, whereas under perfect competition they can sell as much as they like at the going price. This is because price under monopolistic competition is set above marginal cost. The use of advertising to attract more customers and to maintain consumer perception of product differences may be considered a disadvantage of this market. It could be argued that excessive use of advertising to maintain product differentiation is wasteful, as it leads to higher average cost curves than needed. Given the higher costs, firms may need to charge higher prices. On the other hand, it may be an advantage, as the need to compete in this way may result in less X-inefficiency than under a complacent monopolist. In addition, it might be argued that with plenty of advertising, customers are better informed about the products available.

> **Knowledge check 15.3**
>
> Why are firms under monopolistic competition keen to sell more output than firms under perfect competition?

Figure 15.3 shows a firm under monopolistic competition.
a Identify the profit-maximising level of output.
b At what price would the firm sell its product?
c What supernormal profits (if any) would the firm make?
d Is this a short-run or a long-run equilibrium? Explain your answer.
e Describe the subsequent adjustment that might take place in the market (if any).
f At what level of output would productive efficiency be achieved? (Assume that *AC* represents long-run average cost for this part of the question.)

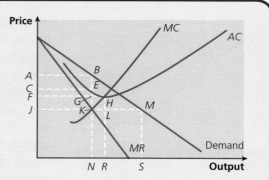

Figure 15.3 A firm under monopolistic competition

Summary

- The theory of monopolistic competition has its origins in the 1930s, when economists such as Edward Chamberlin and Joan Robinson were writing about markets that did not conform to the models of perfect competition and monopoly.
- The model describes a market in which there are many firms producing similar, but not identical, products.
- By differentiating their product from those of other firms, it is possible for firms to maintain some influence over price.
- To do this, firms engage in advertising to build brand loyalty.
- There are no barriers to entry into the market, and concentration ratios are low.
- Firms may be able to make supernormal profits in the short run.
- In response, new entrants join the market, shifting the demand curves of existing firms and affecting their shape.
- The process continues until supernormal profits have been competed away, and the typical firm has its average cost curve at a tangent to its demand curve.
- Neither productive nor allocative efficiency is achieved in long-run equilibrium.
- Consumers may benefit from the increased range of choice on offer in the market.

Oligopoly

Key term

oligopoly a market with a few dominant sellers, in which each firm must take account of the behaviour and likely behaviour of rival firms in the industry

A number of markets seem to be dominated by relatively few firms — think of commercial banking in the UK, cinemas or the newspaper industry. A market with just a few dominant sellers is known as an **oligopoly** market. An important characteristic of such markets is that when making economic decisions each firm must take account of its rivals' behaviour and reactions. The firms are therefore interdependent.

An important characteristic of oligopoly is that each firm has to act strategically, both in reacting to rival firms' decisions and in trying to anticipate their future actions and reactions. This interdependence of firms is a strong influence on their behaviour in the market, as we shall see.

The UK cinema industry is an example of an oligopoly, since it is dominated by three main firms

Unlike monopolistic competition, an oligopoly market is likely to be protected by barriers to entry, although the strength of those barriers may vary from industry to industry.

The key characteristics of an oligopoly are therefore:
- a few firms dominate the market
- there is strategic interdependence between the firms
- there are barriers to entry

There are many different ways in which a firm may take strategic decisions, and this means that there are many ways in which an oligopoly market can be modelled, depending on how the firms behave in relation to each other. This chapter reviews just a few examples.

Oligopolies may come about for many reasons, but perhaps the most significant concerns economies of scale. An oligopoly is likely to develop in a market where there are some economies of scale — economies that are not substantial enough to require a natural monopoly, but which are large enough to make it difficult for too many firms to operate at the minimum efficient scale.

Within an oligopoly market, firms may adopt rivalrous behaviour or they may choose to cooperate with each other. The two attitudes have implications for how markets operate. Cooperation will tend to take the market towards the monopoly end of the spectrum, whereas non-cooperation will take it towards the competitive end. In either scenario, it is likely that the market outcome will be somewhere between the two extremes.

Non-price competition

Key term

non-price competition a strategy whereby firms compete by advertising to encourage brand loyalty, or by quality or design, rather than on price

One feature of oligopoly is that firms may engage in **non-price competition**. Non-price competition is exactly what it says: firms do not use price to compete with rival firms, but find other ways, such as product differentiation (as used by firms in monopolistic competition). For example, they may use advertising to set apart their own products from

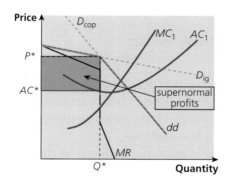

Knowledge check 15.4

Give **two** examples of ways in which firms may indulge in non-price competition.

the crowd, and encourage customers to be loyal to a brand. Alternatively, they may compete on the quality or design of their goods or services. Launching a loyalty card system can also encourage customers to stick with a particular brand. The use of clever packaging or the offering of discounts to return customers can also be effective.

Firms may favour non-price competition in an oligopoly market because there are relatively few firms in the market, so the way in which products are differentiated can be more targeted to counter the actions of rival firms. Furthermore, there may be situations in oligopoly in which firms may be reluctant to compete on price, or to become embroiled in a price war.

The kinked demand curve model

One model of oligopoly revolves around how a firm perceives its demand curve. This is called the kinked demand curve model, and was developed by Paul Sweezy in the USA in the 1930s.

The model relates to an oligopoly in which firms try to anticipate the reactions of rivals to their actions. One problem that arises is that a firm cannot readily observe its demand curve with any degree of certainty, so it must form expectations about how consumers will react to a price change.

Figure 15.4 shows how this works. Suppose the price is currently set at P^*. The firm is selling Q^* and is trying to decide whether to alter price. The problem is that there is only one point on the demand curve that can be observed: that is, when price is P^*, the firm sells Q^*.

However, the firm is aware that the degree of sensitivity to its price change will depend upon whether or not the other firms in the market will follow its lead. In other words, if its rivals ignore the firm's price change, there will be more sensitivity to this change than if they all follow suit.

Figure 15.4 shows the two extreme possibilities for the demand curve that the firm perceives it faces. If other firms *ignore* its action, D_{ig} will be the relevant demand curve, which is relatively elastic. On the other hand, if the other firms *copy* the firm's moves, D_{cop} will be the relevant demand curve.

The question then is: under what conditions will the other firms copy the price change, and when will they not? The firm may imagine that if it raises price, there is little likelihood its rivals will copy. After all, this is a non-threatening move that gives market share to the other firms. So for a price *increase*, D_{ig} is the relevant section.

On the other hand, a price reduction is likely to be seen by the rivals as a threatening move, and they are likely to copy in order to preserve their market positions. For a price *decrease*, then, D_{cop} is relevant.

Putting these together, the firm perceives that it faces a kinked demand curve (*dd*). If the firm faces cost curves MC_1 and AC_1, the shaded area shows the supernormal profit being made at the profit-maximising level of output. Notice that the marginal revenue curve has a break in it at the kink. This means that even if the firm's cost curves shift up or down, as long as the marginal cost curve cuts the marginal revenue curve where it is vertical, the firm will continue to maximise profit at Q^* output.

Figure 15.4 The kinked demand curve

Knowledge check 15.5

In the kinked demand curve model, is the price prevailing in the market likely to be volatile?

Therefore, the model predicts that if the firm perceives its demand curve to be of this shape, it has a strong incentive to do nothing, even in the face of changes in costs. However, it all depends upon the firm's perceptions. If there is a general increase in costs that affects all producers, this may affect the firm's perception of rival reaction, and so encourage it to raise price. If other firms are reading the market in the same way, they are likely to follow suit. Notice that this model does not explain how the price reaches $P*$ in the first place.

Also note that if firms are so keen to avoid competing on price, they may turn to non-price competition as a way of maintaining or increasing their market share.

The kinked demand curve model is just one way of trying to explain how firms may behave in an oligopoly, and goes some way towards explaining why firms may be keen to engage in non-price competition. However, it is not the only model to explore how firms act strategically, nor is it inevitable that firms in an oligopoly will always act competitively. They may instead perceive that it is in their best interest to work together in the market.

Collusion

Key term

cartel an agreement between firms on price and/or output with the intention of maximising their joint profits

Knowledge check 15.6

Why should cartels be made illegal?

The discussion in the previous chapter showed that a monopoly firm would maximise profits by restricting output and raising price (compared with a competitive market). If the few firms that make up an oligopoly could work together, is it possible that they could maximise their joint profits? One way in which firms can collude with each other is by forming a **cartel**.

The downside of operating a cartel is that its members may decide to cheat on the agreement, by lowering price in order to increase their market share. This is a common feature of cartels. Collusion can bring high joint profits, but there is always the temptation for each of the member firms to cheat and try to sneak some additional market share at the expense of the other firms in the cartel.

There is another downside to the formation of a cartel. In most countries around the world (with one or two exceptions, such as Hong Kong) they are illegal. For example, in the UK the operation of a cartel is illegal under the UK Competition Act, under which the Competition and Markets Authority (CMA) is empowered to fine firms up to 10% of their worldwide turnover for each year the cartel is found to have been in operation.

The operation of a cartel

You can see how a cartel might operate in Figure 15.5, which shows the situation facing a two-firm cartel (a duopoly). Panels (a) and (b) show the cost conditions for each of the firms, and panel (c) shows the whole market.

If the firms aim to maximise their joint profits, then they set $MR = MC$ at the level of the market (shown in panel (c)). This occurs at the joint level of output $Q_1 + Q_2$, with the price set at P^*. Notice that the joint marginal cost curve is the sum of the two firms' marginal cost curves.

The critical decision is how to divide the market up between the two firms. In the figure, the two firms have different cost conditions, with firm 1 operating at lower short-run average cost than firm 2. If the firms agree to set price at P^*, and each produces up to the point where marginal cost equals the level of (market) marginal

revenue at MR^*, then the market should work well. Firm 1 produces Q_1 and firm 2 produces Q_2. Joint profits are maximised, and there is a clear rule enabling the division of the market between the firms.

However, notice that firm 2 is very much the junior partner in this alliance, as it gets a much smaller market share. The temptation to cheat is obvious. If firm 2 accepts price P^*, it sees that its profits will be maximised at Q_2^*, so there is a temptation to try to steal an extra bit of market share.

Of course, the temptation is also there for firm 1, but as soon as either one of the firms begins to increase output, the market price will have to fall to maintain equilibrium, and the cartel will be broken: the market will move away from the joint profit-maximising position.

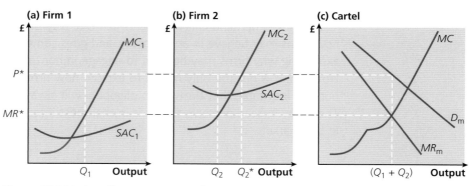

Figure 15.5 Market allocation in a two-firm cartel

Knowledge check 15.7

What factors might hinder collusion between firms?

This means that overt collusion is rare. The most famous example is not between firms but between nations, in the form of the Organisation of the Petroleum Exporting Countries (OPEC), which over a long period of time has operated a cartel to control the price of oil.

Some conditions may favour the formation of cartels — or at least, some form of collusion between firms. The most important of these is the ability of each of the firms involved to monitor the actions of the other firms, and so ensure that they are keeping to the agreement.

Other types of collusion

Although cartels are illegal, the potential gains from collusion may tempt firms to find ways of working together. In some cases, firms have joined together in rather loose strategic alliances, in which they may work together on part of their business, perhaps in undertaking joint research and development or technology swaps.

Strategic alliances

For example, in 2018 Tesco joined with Carrefour in a strategic alliance to buy products for more than 19,000 stores. This was intended to consolidate their position relative to Amazon, Aldi and Lidl. It was hoped that the alliance would result in higher sales of wine, camembert and other French products being sold in Tesco stores — and more British products being sold in Carrefour's supermarkets in France. This could also be seen as a defence against the possible repercussions of Brexit.

The airline market is another sector where strategic alliances have been important, with Star Alliance, Oneworld and SkyTeam carving up the long-haul routes between them. Such alliances offer benefits to passengers, who can get access to a wider range of destinations and business-class lounges and frequent-flier rewards, and to the airlines, which can economise on airport facilities by pooling their resources. However, the net effect is to reduce competition, and the regulators have kept a close eye on such behaviour. For example, in 2012 the European Commission launched an investigation into three members of the SkyTeam alliance to see whether they were operating against the interest of consumers.

Tacit collusion

Alternatively, firms may look for **tacit collusion**, in which the firms in a market observe each other's behaviour very closely and refrain from competing on price, even if they do not actually communicate with each other. Such collusion may emerge gradually over time in a market, as the firms become accustomed to market conditions and to each other's behaviour.

Price leadership

One way in which tacit collusion may happen is through some form of *price leadership*. If one firm is a dominant producer in a market, then it may take the lead in setting the price, with the other firms following its example. It has been suggested that the OPEC cartel operated according to this model in some periods, with Saudi Arabia acting as the dominant country.

An alternative is *barometric price leadership*, in which one firm tries out a price increase and then waits to see whether other firms follow. If they do, a new higher price has been reached without the need for overt discussions between the firms. On the other hand, if the other firms do not feel the time is right for the change, they will keep their prices steady and the first firm will drop back into line or else lose market share. The initiating firm need not be the same one in each round. It has been argued that the domestic air travel market in the USA has operated in this way on some internal routes. The practice is facilitated by the ease with which prices can be checked via computerised ticketing systems, so that each firm knows what the other firms are doing.

The frequency of anti-cartel cases brought by regulators in recent years suggests that firms continue to be tempted by the gains from collusion. The operation of a cartel is now a criminal act in the UK, as it has been in the USA for some time.

Advantages and disadvantages of an oligopoly market

When evaluating an oligopoly market in terms of the possible advantages and disadvantages, a key question is whether firms in the market collude with each other, or if they look for ways of competing with each other. The very fact that legislation has been introduced to protect consumers from market abuse by cartels and other forms of collusion between firms in an oligopoly market suggests that there is a downside to a collusive oligopoly: at least potentially. This argument is based on the way in which colluding firms may act to maximise their joint profits.

On the other hand, if firms in an oligopoly do compete intensively with each other, then consumers may benefit from seeing the price being set at a competitive level. They may also gain through having wider consumer choice.

Exercise 15.2

For each of the following markets, identify the model that would most closely describe it (e.g. perfect competition, monopoly, monopolistic competition or oligopoly):

a a large number of firms selling branded varieties of toothpaste
b a sole supplier of postal services
c a large number of farmers producing cauliflowers, sold at a common price
d a situation in which a few large banks supply most of the market for retail banking services
e a sole supplier of rail transport

Summary

- An oligopoly is a market with a few sellers, each of which takes strategic decisions based on likely rival actions and reactions.
- As there are many ways in which firms may interact, there is no single way of modelling an oligopoly market.
- One model is the kinked demand curve model, which argues that firms' perceptions of the demand curve for their products are based on their views about whether or not rival firms will react to their own actions.
- This suggests that price is likely to remain stable over a wide range of market conditions.
- If firms could join together in a cartel, they could indeed maximise their joint profits — but there would still be a temptation for firms to cheat and try to steal market share. Such action would break up the cartel, and move the market away from the joint profit-maximising position.
- However, cartels are illegal in most societies.
- Firms may therefore look for covert ways of colluding in a market: for example, through some form of price leadership.

Market concentration

As firms grow, markets may become more concentrated, especially if the growth takes place through mergers and acquisitions. With fewer firms in a market, the market may move closer to being an oligopoly, so an important question is whether such markets behave more like a competitive market or more like a monopoly.

It is helpful to have some way of gauging how close a particular market is to being a monopoly or collusive oligopoly. One way of doing this is to examine the degree of concentration in the market.

Concentration is normally measured by reference to the **concentration ratio**, which measures the market share of the largest firms in an industry. For example, the three-firm concentration ratio measures the market share of the largest three firms in the market, the five-firm concentration ratio calculates the share of the top five firms, and so on. Concentration can also be viewed in terms of employment, reflected in the proportion of workers in any industry that are employed in the largest firms.

> **Key term**
>
> ***n*-firm concentration ratio** a measure of the market share of the largest *n* firms in an industry

Quantitative skills 15.1

Calculating a concentration ratio

Consider the following example. Table 15.1 gives average circulation figures for firms that publish national newspapers in the UK (with a circulation of more than 100,000 per day). In the final column these are converted into market shares. Where one firm produces more than one newspaper, their circulations have been combined (e.g. News UK publishes both *The Sun* and *The Times*).

Table 15.1 Concentration in the UK newspaper industry, January 2018

Firm	Newspapers	Average circulation	Market share (%)
dmg media	*Daily Mail, Metro*	2,818,514	34.6
News UK	*The Sun, The Times*	1,986,152	24.4
London Evening Standard	*London Evening Standard*	888,017	10.9
Northern & Shell	*Daily Star, Daily Express*	756,719	9.3
Trinity Mirror	*Daily Mirror, Daily Record*	717,279	8.8
Telegraph Group	*Daily Telegraph*	385,346	4.7
Johnston Press	*i*	257,223	3.2
Pearson	*Financial Times*	189,579	2.3
Guardian Media Group	*The Guardian*	152,714	1.9
Total		8,151,543	100.0

The market shares are calculated by expressing the average circulation for a firm as a percentage of the total. For example, the market share of the *Financial Times* is 100 × 189,579/8,151,543 = 2.3%.

The three-firm concentration ratio is calculated as the sum of the market shares of the biggest three firms: that is, 34.6 + 24.4 + 10.9 = 69.8%.

Source: based on data from the Audit Bureau of Circulations

As stated above, concentration ratios may be calculated on the basis of either shares in output or shares in employment. Quantitative skills 15.1, the calculation was on the basis of output (daily circulation). The two measures may give different results because the largest firms in an industry may be more capital-intensive in their production methods, which means that their share of employment in an industry will be smaller than their share of output. For the purposes of examining market structure, however, it is more helpful to base the analysis of market share on output.

This might seem an intuitively simple measure, but it is *too* simple to enable an evaluation of a market. For a start, it is important to define the market appropriately. For instance, in the above example, are the *Financial Times* and *The Sun* really part of the same market?

There may be other difficulties too. Table 15.2 gives some hypothetical market shares for two markets. The five-firm concentration ratio is calculated as the sum of the market shares of the largest five firms. For markets A and B, the result is the same. In both cases the market is perceived to be highly concentrated, at 75%. However, the nature of likely interactions between the firms in these two markets is very different because the large relative size of firm 1 in market A is likely to give it substantially more market power than any of the largest five firms in market B. Nonetheless, the concentration ratio is useful for giving a first impression of how the market is likely to function.

Figure 15.6 shows the five-firm concentration ratio for a number of industrial sectors in the UK. Concentration varies from 5% in construction and 12% in printing and publishing to 71% in cement and 99% in tobacco products. In part, the difference between sectors might be expected to reflect the extent of economies of scale, and this makes sense for many of the industries shown.

Table 15.2 Market shares (% of output)

Largest firms in rank order	Market A	Market B
Firm 1	68	15
Firm 2	3	15
Firm 3	2	15
Firm 4	1	15
Firm 5	1	15

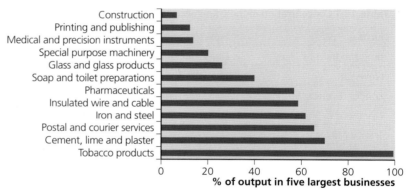

Figure 15.6 Concentration in UK industry, 2004

Source: ONS

Pricing strategies in an oligopoly

In a kinked demand curve model, firms in an oligopoly realise that a price reduction is likely to be matched by rivals, leaving all firms with lower profits but having relatively little effect on market shares. However, price wars do break out from time to time, as firms in an oligopoly try to prevent entry from new firms, or to consolidate their own position against other firms in the market.

Price wars: an example

In the early 2000s, a price war broke out in the UK tabloid newspaper market. It was initiated by the *Daily Express*, but the main protagonists were the *Daily Mirror* and *The Sun*, which joined in after a couple of weeks. The *Mirror* cut its price from 32p to 20p, and *The Sun* from 30p to 20p.

After a week at these lower prices, the editor of *The Sun* was serving champagne in the newsroom in celebration. Their reading of the situation was that the *Mirror* had not expected *The Sun* to follow the price cut. Three weeks after the *Mirror*'s price cut, it put its price back up again — followed by *The Sun*. Analysts and observers commented that the only gainers had been the readers, who had enjoyed three weeks of lower prices.

Why should firms act in this way? The *Mirror* argued that it was trying to re-brand itself, and capture new readers who would continue to read the paper even after the price returned to its normal level. This may hint at the reason for a price war — to affect the long-run equilibrium of the market. *The Sun*'s retaliation was a natural defensive response to an aggressive move.

Why initiate a price war?

In some cases a price war may be initiated as a strategy to drive a weaker competitor out of the market altogether. The motivation then is clear, especially if the initiator of the price war ends up with a monopoly or near-monopoly position in the market. It could be argued that this represents an attempt to maximise profits in the long run by establishing a monopoly position.

Price wars may also be initiated by firms wishing to break into a market. For example, the discount stores Aldi and Lidl launched low-price offers on their range of products in an attempt to compete with UK supermarkets.

Predatory pricing

Perhaps the most common context in which price wars have broken out is where an existing firm or firms have reacted to defend the market against the entry of new firms.

So-called **predatory pricing** is illegal in many countries, including in the UK and the USA. It should be noted that, in order to declare an action illegal, it is necessary to define that action very carefully — otherwise it will not be possible to prove the case in the courts. In the case of predatory pricing, the legal definition is based on economic analysis.

Remember that if a firm fails to cover average variable costs, its strategy should be to close down immediately, as it would be better off doing so. The courts have backed this theory, and state that a pricing strategy should be interpreted as being predatory if the price is set below average variable costs, as the only motive for remaining in business while making such losses must be to drive competitors out of business and achieve market dominance. This is known as the *Areeda–Turner principle* (after the case in which it was first argued in the USA).

On the face of it, consumers have much to gain from such strategies through the resulting lower prices. However, a predator that is successful in driving out the opposition is likely to recoup its losses by putting prices back up to profit-maximising levels thereafter, so the benefit to consumers is short lived.

Entry deterrence by the threat of predatory pricing

In some cases, the very threat of predatory pricing may be sufficient to deter entry by new firms, if the threat is a credible one. In other words, the

Knowledge check 15.9

Why might firms not benefit from a price war in the long run?

Key term

predatory pricing an anticompetitive strategy in which a firm sets price below average variable cost in an attempt to force a rival or rivals out of the market and achieve market dominance

Exercise 15.3

Discuss the extent to which consumers benefit from a price war.

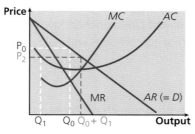

Figure 15.7 Limit pricing

existing firms need to convince potential entrants that they, the existing firms, will find it in their best interests to fight a price war, otherwise the entrants will not believe the threat. The existing firms could do this by making it known that they have surplus capacity, so that they would be able to increase output very quickly in order to drive down the price.

Whether entry will be deterred by such means may depend in part on the characteristics of the potential entrant. After all, a new firm may reckon that if the existing firm finds it worth sacrificing profits in the short run, the rewards of dominating the market must be worth fighting for. It may therefore decide to sacrifice short-term profit in order to enter the market — especially if it is diversifying from other markets and has resources at its disposal. The winner will then be the firm that can last the longest. But, clearly, this is potentially very damaging for all concerned.

Limit pricing

An associated but less extreme strategy is limit pricing. This assumes that the incumbent firm has some sort of cost advantage over potential entrants: for example, economies of scale.

Figure 15.7 shows a firm facing a downward-sloping demand curve, and so having some influence over the price of its product. If the firm is maximising profits, it is setting output at Q_0 and price at P_0. As average revenue is comfortably above average cost at this price, the firm is making healthy supernormal profits.

Suppose that the natural barriers to entry in this industry are weak. The supernormal profits will be attractive to potential entrants. Given the cost conditions, the incumbent firm is enjoying the benefit of economies of scale, although producing below the minimum efficient scale.

If a new firm joins the market, producing on a relatively small scale, say at Q_1, the impact on the market can be analysed as follows. The immediate effect is on price, as now the amount $Q_0 + Q_1$ is being produced, pushing price down to P_2. The new firm (producing Q_1) is just covering average cost, so is making normal profits and feeling justified in having joined the market. The original firm is still making supernormal profits but at a lower level than before. The entry of the new firm has competed away part of the original firm's supernormal profits.

One way in which the firm could have guarded against entry is by charging a lower price than P_0 to begin with. For example, if it had set output at $Q_0 + Q_1$ and price at P_2, then a new entrant joining the market would have pushed the price down to a level below P_2, and without the benefit of economies of scale would have made losses and exited the market. In any case, if the existing firm has been in the market for some time, it will have gone through a process of learning by doing, and therefore will have a lower average cost curve than the potential entrant. This makes it more likely that limit pricing can be used.

So, by setting a price below the profit-maximising level, the original firm is able to maintain its market position in the longer run. This could be a reason for avoiding making too high a level of supernormal profits in the short run, in order to make profits in the longer term.

Notice that such a strategy need not be carried out by a monopolist but could also occur in an oligopoly, where existing firms may jointly seek to protect their market against potential entry.

Contestable markets

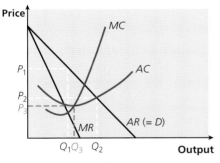

Figure 15.8 Contestability

It has been argued that in some markets, in order to prevent the entry of new firms, the existing firm would have to charge such a low price that it would be unable to reap any supernormal profits at all.

The theory of **contestable markets** was developed by William Baumol. It was in recognition of this theory that the monopoly model in Chapter 14 included the assumption that there must be no substitutes for the good, *either actual or potential*.

A contestable market is one in which new firms:
- face no barriers to entry or exit
- incur no sunk costs in entering the market
- have no competitive disadvantage compared with the incumbent firm(s)
- have access to the same technology as the incumbent(s)
- are able to enter and exit rapidly

Under these conditions, the incumbent firm cannot set a price that is higher than average cost because, as soon as it does, it will open up the possibility of **hit-and-run entry** by new firms, which can enter the market and compete away the supernormal profits.

Consider Figure 15.8, which shows a monopoly firm in a market. The argument is that, if the monopolist charges the profit-maximising price at P_1, then in a contestable market the firm will be vulnerable to hit-and-run entry — a firm could come into the market, take some of the supernormal profits, then exit again. The only way the monopolist can avoid this happening is to set price equal to average cost (for example at P_2 in Figure 15.8), so that there are no supernormal profits to act as an incentive for entry. However, if the monopoly adopted this tactic, it would still be possible for new firms to enter the market and make at least normal profit, given that by assumption there are no barriers to entry and new firms face the same technology as the incumbent firm. Of course, as soon as new firms enter the market, it ceases to be a monopoly.

The best chance a monopoly would have to prevent entry would be to make sure that the long-run average cost curve is as low as possible (no X-inefficiency), and that it does not set a price above the minimum point of the *AC* curve — for example at P_3 in Figure 15.8. However, if the firm did try to produce at this point, it would not be operating on the demand curve, so new entrants would enter the market to make normal profits. After entry, the market could end up in equilibrium with a number of firms making normal profit, the price set at P_3 and each firm producing at minimum average cost. In this situation, there would be productive and allocative efficiency. However, the theory does not set out how this position could be achieved.

For example, suppose a firm has a monopoly on a domestic air route between two destinations. An airline with surplus capacity (i.e. a spare aircraft sitting in a hangar) could enter this route and exit again without incurring sunk costs in response to profits being made by the incumbent firm. This shows how contestability may limit the ability of the incumbent firm to use its market power.

The impact of the internet on contestability

The growth of the internet has had a significant impact on the contestability of markets and hence on competitiveness. By making information more freely available, the internet has given consumers improved knowledge of market conditions and enabled them to make more informed choices. Furthermore, the growth of online sales has made it much easier for new firms to enter markets.

One good example of this is the travel industry. In 2016, UK residents made more than 70 million trips abroad, so this is a significant sector. In the past, many overseas trips, especially holidays, were arranged by high street travel agents. Although there were many retail outlets, the largest chains of travel agents were responsible for a significant market share. The internet has revolutionised this sector, with online firms competing effectively with the established firms, and individual consumers able to make their own travel arrangements much more effectively. This is an example of where increased contestability of a market has resulted in an increase in competitiveness.

Exercise 15.4

Discuss the extent to which the following markets may be considered to be contestable — or to have become more so in recent years:
a opticians
b travel agents
c financial services
d the postal service
e aircraft manufacture

Evaluation of the advantages and disadvantages of a contestable market

An advantage from society's perspective is that the price will be lower than would be set by a profit-maximising monopolist. Indeed, if the firm in Figure 15.8 sets price at P_3, new firms may effectively become price-takers, so that entry would continue until the demand at that price is satisfied. Beyond that point, the price would begin to fall, as there would be excess supply. Notice that if the market settles at P_3 with a number of firms with identical AC curves, then both allocative and productive efficiency would be achieved, as each firm would be operating at the minimum point on their average cost curve at the point at which price equals marginal cost.

There is a danger that the authorities may see this argument as meaning that no intervention is needed in contestable markets because allocative and productive efficiency would automatically be achieved. However, this assumes that the conditions for perfect contestability would be met. These are stringent. In particular the requirement that there are no sunk costs may not always be fulfilled. For example, some advertising will be needed to attract customers, which cannot be recouped. In addition, the transition to long-run equilibrium is less clear than with perfect competition, as the theory does not fully explain how new firms will join the market, nor how the final equilibrium is reached. It is also worth being aware that perfectly contestable markets are rare in the real world.

An important further point is whether the threat of entry will in fact persuade firms that they cannot set a price above average cost. Perhaps firms will risk making some profit above normal profit and then respond to entry very aggressively if and when it happens.

The internet and the growth of online sales has revolutionised the travel industry

Summary

- There are many pricing rules that a firm may choose to adopt, depending on the objectives it wishes to achieve.
- Although price wars are expected to be damaging for the firms involved, they do break out from time to time.
- This may occur when firms wish to increase their market shares, or when existing firms wish to deter the entry of new firms into the market.
- Predatory pricing is an extreme strategy that forces all firms to endure losses. It is normally invoked in an attempt to eliminate a competitor, and is illegal in many countries.
- Limit pricing occurs when a firm or firms choose to set price below the profit-maximising level in order to prevent entry. The limit price is the highest price that an existing firm can set without allowing entry.
- In contestable markets, the incumbent firm(s) may be able to make only normal profit.
- Contestability requires that there are no barriers to entry or exit and no sunk costs — and that the incumbent firm(s) have no cost advantage over hit-and-run entrants.

Case study 15.1

Competition in oligopolistic markets

An oligopolistic market is one in which firms engage in strategic competition. Strategic competition exists when the actions of one firm have an appreciable effect on its rival or rivals. Common textbook examples of oligopoly include the oil industry, motor manufacturing, soft drinks and airlines operating between particular pairs of cities. But oligopolists are not necessarily large firms. Close to the university campus in Southampton, there is a road containing several small restaurants and takeaways. They are engaged in strategic competition because if one firm were to change its prices this would have an appreciable effect on the sales and, therefore, profits of the others.

The defining characteristic of oligopoly is that the actions of one firm have an appreciable effect on its rival(s), and so when modelling such a market, it is natural to begin by assuming that each firm recognises this interdependence and takes it into account when formulating its strategy. To keep things simple, let's suppose there are just two firms in the market and each is thinking about what price to charge for its product.

One possibility is they agree to collude on a high price and split the market between them to maximise their joint profits. However, suppose that agreeing a price would be seen as a cartel, and would therefore be illegal. This means they each need to set the price without knowing what the other firm will do, and without communicating with each other.

Only if both firms set the joint profit-maximising price will they gain the best profit position. If you were running one of the firms, would you trust the other firm to set the high price? Or would you expect the other firm to set a price below the maximum to gain market share and to guard against you setting a lower price — and also to gain market share?

Let's attach some numbers to this problem. Suppose that if both firms charge a high price they each make profits of £20,000, but if they each charge a low price, each makes profits of only £5,000. On the other hand, if you charge a high price but your rival cuts its price, you will lose business and make no profits, while your rival makes £30,000. Imagine that the other firm sees the market in exactly the same way.

Follow-up questions

a In what situation would the joint profits be highest? Explain how this could be achieved.

b Do you think this outcome will be achieved? Explain your answer.

c The passage described the situation close to the campus at the University of Southampton, in which there are several restaurants operating in close proximity. Discuss whether or not they would be able to maximise their joint profits.

CHAPTER 15 QUESTIONS

A Multiple-choice questions

1 Which of the following scenarios does **not** suggest product differentiation?

   a Heinz increasing the size of its cans to be 10% bigger than any competitor

   b Lidl developing a fish counter because Tesco stores already have them

   c Pepsi developing a new flavour that is not available from any other business

   d A mobile phone company that has the exclusive rights to sell the new iPhone

2 Which of the following is **not** a characteristic of monopolistic competition?

   a Large number of firms

   b Able to make supernormal profits in the short run

   c Homogeneous products

   d Few barriers to entry and exit

3 A market has the following businesses and market shares:

- Firm A — 24% market share
- Firm B — 21% market share
- Firm C — 19% market share
- Firm D — 13% market share
- Firm E — 12% market share
- Others — 11% market share

The three-firm concentration ratio is:

   a 45%   b 64%   c 77%   d 89%

4 Which of the following is a type of collusion?

   a Perfect competition   c Barometric price leadership

   b Price differentiation   d Monopoly collusion

B Knowledge and understanding questions

5 Explain, using a diagram, short-run monopolistic competition.   **[4 marks]**

6 Explain, using a diagram, the kinked demand curve.   **[4 marks]**

C Stimulus response question

7 The UK cinema industry is dominated by three brands: Cineworld, Odeon and Vue. The three-firm concentration ratio for these firms is almost 70%.

There are many barriers to entry in the market, which is likely to be one of the reasons why the market may not be seen as highly contestable. In fact, in many geographical areas there is only one cinema.

Where there is more than one cinema in close proximity, the managers will often adjust viewing times based on the competition. Prices can also be varied to attract customers, with all-inclusive snack and drinks packages included in deals.

   a Explain what is meant by the term 'three-firm concentration ratio'.   **[2 marks]**

   b Explain **two** characteristics that mean the cinema market 'may not be seen as highly contestable'.

             [4 marks]

D Essay question

8 Evaluate the advantages and disadvantages to a business of operating in a competitive market.   **[25 marks]**

MICROECONOMICS

Part 5
The labour market

Chapter 16

The demand for labour

The economic analysis of labour markets sheds light on a range of topical issues. How are wages determined? Differences in wages between people in different occupations and with different skills can be contentious. For example, why should premiership footballers or pop stars earn such high wages compared with nurses or firefighters? This chapter begins the discussion by considering the demand for labour.

> ## Learning objectives
>
> After studying this chapter, you should be able to:
> - explain that the demand for labour is a derived demand
> - explain, with the aid of a diagram, marginal revenue product theory in relation to employment and wage determination
> - explain factors affecting the demand for labour in an industry
> - explain factors affecting the wage elasticity of demand for labour
> - explain productivity and unit labour costs

Demand for labour as a derived demand

Firms are involved in production. They organise the factors of production in order to produce output. Labour is one of the key factors of production used by firms in this process, but notice that labour is valued not for its own sake, but for the output that it produces. In other words, the fundamental reason for firms to demand labour is for the revenue that can be obtained from selling the output produced by using labour. The demand for labour is therefore a **derived demand**, and understanding this is crucial for an analysis of the labour market.

To illustrate this, consider a firm that manufactures cricket bats. The firm hires labourers to operate the machinery that is used in production. However, the firm does not hire a labourer because he or she is a nice person. The firm aims to make profit by selling the cricket bats produced, and the labourer is needed because of the labour services that he or she provides. This notion of derived demand underpins the analysis of labour markets.

It is important to be aware that although there is a tendency to talk about 'the' labour market, or about 'unemployment' in the aggregate, in reality there is not a single market for labour in the economy, but a multitude of sub-markets. This partly reflects the fact that individual workers differ from each other in terms of their characteristics and skills. There are different markets for different types of labour, such as lawyers, accountants, cleaners and bricklayers. There may also be geographic sub-markets, given that labour may be relatively immobile. An employer may perceive that it operates in a particular industry, so there may be a labour

> ### Key term
>
> derived demand where the demand for a factor of production or good derives not from the factor or good itself, but from the goods or services that it provides

> ### Study tip
>
> Be clear in your mind about this notion of a derived demand, as it underpins much of the discussion of labour markets.

> ### Knowledge check 16.1
>
> Explain why the demand for capital machinery would be seen as a derived demand.

market for an industry, or for particular skills within an industry. Indeed, a firm may find itself operating in several different sub-markets.

This interlocking pattern of labour markets is likely to evolve over time, as technology changes, bringing with it the need for different skills, and a different balance of skills.

The demand curve for labour

Consider the demand for a particular type of labour — in other words, a particular labour market. Given that the demand for labour is a derived demand, the first factor that will determine the demand for labour is the output that labour produces. Given the law of diminishing returns, which was introduced in Chapter 11, the additional output produced by labour as more labour is deployed is expected to diminish, other things remaining equal. This is because capital becomes relatively more scarce as the amount of labour increases without a corresponding increase in capital.

Important for the firm, then, is the marginal physical product of labour (MPP_L), which is the amount of additional output produced if the firm increases its labour input by 1 unit (e.g. adding 1 more person-hour), holding capital constant.

Synoptic link

The law of diminishing returns was explained in Chapter 11. The same chapter introduced the concept of the marginal physical product of labour (MPP_L). You might find it helpful to look back at this discussion, especially Figure 11.1 on page 138, which shows how the MPP_L varies with the level of output that is produced.

Key term

marginal revenue product of labour (MRP_L) the additional revenue received by a firm as it increases output by using an additional unit of labour input, i.e. the marginal physical product of labour multiplied by the marginal revenue received by the firm

Although the marginal physical product is important, what really matters to the firm is the *revenue* that it will receive from selling the additional output produced. In considering the profit-maximising amount of labour to employ, therefore, the firm needs to consider the marginal physical product multiplied by the marginal revenue received from selling the extra output, which is known as the **marginal revenue product of labour (MRP_L)**.

Employment and the wage

How does this help us to analyse the decision made by a firm about how much labour to employ?

If a firm is operating under perfect competition, then marginal revenue and price are the same and MRP_L is MPP_L multiplied by the price. However, if the firm faces a downward-sloping demand curve for its product, it has to reduce the selling price in order to sell the additional output. Marginal revenue is then lower than price, as the firm must lower the price on *all* of the output it sells, not just on the last unit sold.

Consider a firm operating under perfect competition, and setting out to maximise profits. Figure 16.1 shows the marginal revenue product curve. The question to consider is how the firm chooses how much labour input to use. This decision is based partly on knowledge of the MRP_L, but it also depends on the cost of labour.

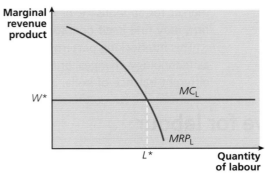

Figure 16.1 The labour input decision of a profit-maximising firm under perfect competition

The main cost of using labour is the wages paid to the workers. There may be other costs — hiring costs and so on — but these can be set aside for the moment. Assuming that the labour market is perfectly competitive, so that the firm cannot influence the market wage and can obtain as much labour as it wants at the going wage rate, the wage can be regarded as the *marginal cost of labour* (MC_L).

If the marginal revenue received by the firm from selling the extra output produced by extra labour (i.e. the MRP_L) is higher than the wage, then hiring more labour will add to profits. On the other hand, if the MRP_L is lower than the wage, then the firm is already hiring too much labour. So, it pays the firm to hire labour up to the point where the MRP_L is just equal to the wage. On Figure 16.1, if the wage is W^*, the firm is maximising profits at L^*. The MRP_L curve therefore represents the firm's demand for labour curve. This approach is known as **marginal revenue product theory** (or marginal productivity theory).

Quantitative skills 16.1

Calculating MPP_L and MRP_L

Table 16.1 shows how the total output produced by labour varies with labour input for a firm operating under perfect competition in the product market. The price of the product is £5.

Table 16.1 Output and labour input

Labour input per period	Output (goods per period)
0	0
1	7
2	15
3	22
4	27
5	29

Chapter 11 showed how marginal cost could be calculated from total cost. The same principle applies in calculating the MPP_L from the total output produced by different amounts of labour input. For example, suppose labour input is increased from 2 units to 3. The output produced by labour increases from 15 to 22, so the MPP_L is 22 − 15 = 7.

The MRP_L is then the MPP_L multiplied by the selling price of the output, which is 7 x 5 = 35. This is the additional revenue that the firm receives from selling the additional output produced by the third unit of labour employed.

Test your understanding of this in the following exercise.

Exercise 16.1

This exercise builds on Quantitative skills 16.1.

a Calculate the marginal physical product of labour (MPP_L) at each level of labour input.

b Calculate the marginal revenue product of labour (MRP_L) at each level of labour input.

c Suppose that the firm is also operating in perfect competition in the labour market, where the wage is £30. Plot the MRP_L on a graph and identify the profit-maximising level of labour input.

d Suppose that the firm faces fixed costs of £10. Calculate total revenue and total costs at each level of labour input, and check the profit-maximising level.

Extension material

Marginal revenue product theory and profit maximisation

This profit-maximising condition can be written as:

wage = marginal revenue x marginal physical product of labour

which is the same as:

$$\text{marginal revenue} = \frac{\text{wage}}{MPP_L}$$

Remember that capital input is fixed for the firm in the short run, so the wage divided by the MPP_L is the firm's cost per unit of output at the margin. This shows that the profit-maximising condition is the same as that derived for a profit-maximising firm in Chapter 12: in other words, profit is maximised where marginal revenue equals marginal cost. This is just another way of looking at the firm's decision.

Factors affecting the position of the demand for labour curve

There are a number of factors that determine the *position* of a firm's labour demand curve. First, anything that affects the marginal physical product of labour will also affect the MRP_L. For example, if a new technological advance raises the productivity of labour, it will also affect the position of the MRP_L. In Figure 16.2 you can see how the demand for labour would change if there were an increase in the marginal productivity of labour as a result of new technology. Initially demand is at MRP_{L0}, but the introduction of improved technology pushes the curve to MRP_{L1}. If the wage remains at W^*, the quantity of labour hired by the firm increases from L_0 to L_1. Similarly, in the long run, if a firm expands the size of its capital stock, this will also affect the demand for labour.

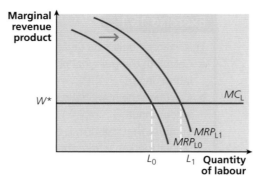

Figure 16.2 The effect of improved technology

As MRP_L is given by MPP_L multiplied by marginal revenue, any change in marginal revenue will also affect labour demand. In a perfectly competitive product market, this means that any change in the price of the product will also affect labour demand. For example, suppose there is a fall in demand for a firm's product, so that the equilibrium price falls. This will have a knock-on effect on the firm's demand for labour, as illustrated in Figure 16.3. Initially, the firm was demanding L_0 labour at the wage rate W^*, but the fall in demand for the product leads to a fall in marginal revenue product (even though the physical productivity of labour has not changed), from MRP_{L0} to MRP_{L1}. Only L_1 labour is now demanded at the wage rate W^*. This serves as a reminder that the demand for labour is a derived demand that is intimately bound up with the demand for the firm's product. This also suggests that the demand for labour will tend to increase during a boom period but fall during a recession.

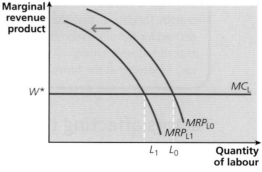

Figure 16.3 The effect of a fall in the demand for a firm's product on the demand for labour

Knowledge check 16.3

Identify three factors that influence the position of the labour demand curve.

A number of possible reasons could underlie a change in the price of a firm's product — it could reflect changes in the prices of other goods, changes in consumer incomes or changes in consumer preferences. All of these indirectly affect the demand for labour.

Summary
- The demand for labour is a derived demand, as the firm wants labour not for its own sake but for the output that it produces.
- In the short run, a firm faces diminishing returns to increases in labour input if capital is held constant.
- The marginal physical product of labour is the amount of output produced if the firm employs an additional unit of labour, keeping capital input fixed.

Summary (continued)

- The marginal revenue product of labour is the marginal physical product multiplied by marginal revenue.
- With perfect competition in the product market, marginal revenue and price are the same, but if the firm needs to reduce its price in order to sell additional units of output, then marginal revenue is smaller than price.
- A profit-maximising firm chooses labour input such that the marginal cost of labour is equal to the marginal revenue product of labour. This is equivalent to setting marginal revenue equal to marginal cost.
- The firm has a downward-sloping demand curve for labour, given by the marginal revenue product curve.
- The position of the firm's labour demand curve depends on those factors that influence the marginal physical product, such as technology and efficiency, but also on the price of the firm's product.

Wage elasticity of the demand for labour

In addition to the factors affecting the *position* of the demand for labour curve, it is also important to examine its *shape*. In particular, what factors affect the firm's elasticity of demand for labour with respect to changes in the wage rate? In other words, how sensitive is a firm's demand for labour to a change in the wage rate (the cost of labour)?

In Chapter 6 you were introduced to the influences on the price elasticity of demand, and the most important were identified as being the availability of substitutes, the relative size of expenditure on a good in the overall budget and the time period over which the elasticity is measured. In looking at the elasticity of demand for labour, similar influences can be seen to be at work.

Ease of factor substitution

One significant influence on the elasticity of demand for labour is the extent to which other factors of production, such as capital, can be substituted for labour in the production process. If capital or some other factor can be readily substituted for labour, then an increase in the wage rate (ceteris paribus) will induce the firm to reduce its demand for labour by relatively more than if there were no substitute for labour. The extent to which labour and capital are substitutable varies between economic activities, depending on the technology of production, as there may be some sectors in which it is relatively easy for labour and capital to be substituted, and others in which it is quite difficult.

In addition, capital tends to be inflexible in the short run. Therefore, if a firm faces an increase in wages, it may have little flexibility in substituting towards capital in the short run, so the demand for labour may be relatively inelastic. However, in the longer term, the firm will be able to adjust the factors of production towards a different overall balance. Therefore, the elasticity of demand for labour is likely to be higher in the long run than in the short run.

Knowledge check 16.4

Consider a firm making designer jewellery. Would you expect it to be straightforward or difficult for the firm to substitute capital for labour?

Knowledge check 16.5

Explain why the demand for labour will be more elastic in the long run than in the short run.

227

Using diagrams, explain how each of the following will affect a firm's demand for labour:

a a fall in the selling price of the firm's product
b adoption of improved working practices that improve labour productivity
c an increase in the wage (in a situation where the firm must accept the wage as market determined)
d an increase in the demand for the firm's product

The share of labour costs in total costs

The share of labour costs in the firm's total costs is important in determining the elasticity of demand for labour. In many service activities, labour is a highly significant share of total costs, so firms tend to be sensitive to changes in the cost of labour. However, in some capital-intensive manufacturing activity, labour may comprise a much smaller share of total production costs.

The price elasticity of demand for the product

These influences closely parallel the analysis of what affects the price elasticity of demand. However, as the demand for labour is a derived demand, there is an additional influence that must be taken into account: the price elasticity of demand for the product. The more price elastic is demand for the product, the more sensitive will the firm be to a change in the wage rate, as high elasticity of demand for the product limits the extent to which an increase in wage costs can be passed on to consumers in the form of higher prices.

Summary

- The elasticity of demand for labour depends upon the degree to which capital may be substituted for labour in the production process.
- The share of labour in a firm's total costs will also affect the elasticity of demand for labour.
- Labour demand will tend to be more elastic in the long run than in the short run, as the firm needs time to adjust its production process following a change in market conditions.
- As the demand for labour is a derived demand, the elasticity of labour demand will also depend on the price elasticity of demand for the firm's product.

Labour productivity and unit labour costs

Can we measure the productivity of labour? What factors affect it? And why does it matter?

Average **labour productivity** is measured simply by dividing the output produced by the amount of labour input — in other words, output produced per unit of labour. Notice that labour input here is better measured by hours worked than by the number of workers employed, because this takes into account the fact that some workers work longer hours than others — some may even work part-time only. For example, if workers in a factory between them work 500 hours in a week, and produce 2,000 units of output, then average labour productivity is $\frac{2,000}{500} = 4$. In other words, an hour of labour produces 4 units of output in this example.

The main influences on labour productivity are:

- the skills and training of the workforce
- the availability of complementary factor inputs (capital and technology)
- the organisation of the production process

Workers are not all equally productive. Some are more skilled or better trained, some have higher innate ability or talents, some are better motivated. The combination of these characteristics determines how productive the individual worker is. When workers come to work together, some are more suited to working in a team, which then influences the productivity of the overall workforce. There may indeed be externality effects such that educated workers cooperate better with each other, so raising the overall efficiency of the workforce.

Workers on the Rolls-Royce production line have high productivity because they are highly trained and work with good capital equipment

Complementary factor inputs also have a significant impact on productivity. In other words, if workers have good capital equipment with which to work, they will produce more. If technology improves, this will affect the level of productivity of labour.

The organisation of the workforce can also affect productivity. Introducing a more effective arrangement of workflows can raise productivity. For example, enabling more effective division of labour can be one way of improving the efficiency with which workers can operate.

A key reason why labour productivity is important for a firm is that it affects the ability to compete effectively with rival firms. Indeed, for a country as a whole, the relative level of productivity affects the ability to maintain international competitiveness with the nation's trading partners.

Competitiveness depends not only upon productivity but also upon labour costs. **Unit labour cost** measures the average cost of labour per unit of output. This depends upon the wage paid (and other costs associated with labour) as well as upon the productivity of labour input.

Knowledge check 16.6

What measures could be taken to improve labour productivity?

Synoptic link

International competitiveness is explained and discussed in Chapter 35.

Key term

unit labour cost the average cost of labour per unit of output

Summary
- Labour productivity is the average output per unit of labour.
- Labour productivity depends upon the skills and training of the workforce, the availability of complementary inputs and the organisation of the production process.
- Relative competitiveness also depends upon unit labour costs (the average cost of labour per unit of output).

CHAPTER 16 QUESTIONS

A Multiple-choice questions

1 Which of the following describes derived demand?

   a When two products are demanded at the same time

   b When a product is demanded for two different uses

   c When demand for a factor of production comes from the output produced by that factor, not for the factor itself

   d When demand can be switched to a competing product

2 What are unit labour costs?

   a Costs of workers divided by output

   b The average of the wage bills in a firm

   c The total cost of workers in a particular factory unit

   d The direct cost of workers

3 Which of the following could cause a shift in the demand for labour curve?

   a An increase in the supply of labour

   b A decrease in the price of labour

   c An increase in the price of the product produced by labour

   d An increase in the minimum wage

B Knowledge and understanding questions

4 Explain, using a diagram, marginal revenue product theory.   [4 marks]

5 Explain **two** factors that might affect the demand for labour in a factory.   [4 marks]

C Stimulus response question

6 The trend for younger people to go to the gym looks set to continue as the next generation enters adulthood. These young adults were all born since the year 2000.

As gyms open 24 hours a day, the need for trained professionals to work in these gyms increases. Sports therapy involves assessing sports-related injuries and devising personal treatment plans to treat those who have suffered injuries through exercise or sport.

   a Explain why the demand for sports therapy workers is a derived demand.   [2 marks]

   b Explain how marginal revenue product theory can explain the demand for sports therapy workers.

   [4 marks]

Chapter 17

The supply of labour

Attention now switches to the supply side of the labour market. What determines how much labour individuals will supply, and how does this build into the supply of labour to an industry? The concepts of economic rent and transfer earnings are also discussed: these are similar in concept to the notions of consumer and producer surplus.

> ### Learning objectives
> After studying this chapter, you should be able to:
> - explain factors affecting the supply of labour to an industry
> - explain factors affecting the wage elasticity of supply
> - explain the short-run and long-run supply of labour
> - explain, with the aid of a diagram, economic rent and transfer earnings

Labour supply

So far, labour supply has been considered only as it is perceived by a firm, and the assumption has been that the firm is in a perfectly competitive market for labour, and therefore cannot influence the 'price' of labour. Hence the firm sees the labour supply curve as being perfectly elastic, as drawn in Figure 16.1 on page 224, where labour supply was described as MC_L.

However, for an industry, the labour supply curve is unlikely to be flat. Intuitively, you might expect to see an upward-sloping labour supply curve. The reason for this is that more people tend to offer themselves for work when the wage is relatively high. This is shown in Figure 17.1.

Notice that there are different ways of looking at a labour market such as this. We can define an 'industry' in the conventional way as a particular sector, such as banking or the car industry. However, this is clearly a simplification, because banking employs a range of individual workers with different skills, as does the car industry. It may therefore be more helpful to think of the market in terms of the supply of labour to an occupation, such as accountancy, remembering that accountants may be employed in a wide range of different economic activities. One reason that this is more helpful is that it makes more sense to consider a single wage for accountants than to imagine that all workers in the car industry receive the same wage.

The effect of the wage rate on labour supply

Consider an individual worker who is deciding how many hours of labour to supply. Every choice comes with an *opportunity cost*, so if a worker chooses to take more leisure time, he or she is choosing to forgo income-earning opportunities. In other words, the wage rate can be seen as the opportunity cost of leisure. It is the income that the worker has to sacrifice in order to enjoy leisure time.

Knowledge check 17.1

Explain why the supply of labour may be perfectly elastic for a firm operating under perfect competition in the labour market.

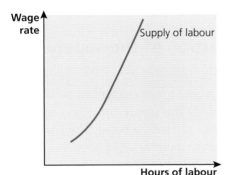

Figure 17.1 A labour supply curve for an industry

Synoptic link

The idea of income and substitution effects was introduced in an extension material box on page 33, in the context of the reaction of demand to a price change.

Now think about the likely effects of an increase in the wage rate. Such an increase raises the opportunity cost of leisure. This in turn has two effects. First, as leisure time is now more costly, so workers will tend to work longer hours and take less leisure. In other words, there is a *substitution effect*, as workers substitute work for leisure.

However, as the higher wage brings the worker a higher level of real income, a second effect comes into play, encouraging the consumption of more goods and services — including leisure, if it is assumed that leisure is a *normal good*. This is an *income effect*.

Notice that these two effects work against each other. The substitution effect encourages workers to offer more labour at a higher wage because of the effect of the change in the opportunity cost of leisure. However, the income effect encourages the worker to demand more leisure as a result of the increase in income. The net effect could go either way.

Extension material

Individual labour supply

It might be argued that at relatively low wages the substitution effect will tend to be the stronger. However, as the wage continues to rise, the income effect may gradually become stronger, so that at some wage level the worker will choose to supply less labour and will demand more leisure. The individual labour supply curve will then be backward bending, as shown in Figure 17.2, where an increase in the wage rate above $W*$ induces the individual to supply fewer hours of work in order to enjoy more leisure time.

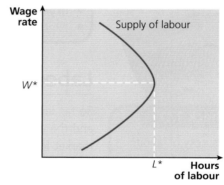

Figure 17.2 A backward-bending individual labour supply curve

Factors influencing the position of the supply curve

As with a supply curve in a market for goods, it is important to be aware of the difference between movements along the supply curve (in response to a change in the wage rate) and shifts of the supply curve. The position of the industry supply curve depends upon a number of factors:

- the wage prevailing in other industries or occupations
- the skills needed for the job and the cost and difficulty of acquiring those skills
- the number of people with the appropriate qualifications
- the non-pecuniary benefits offered by firms in the industry
- the demographic structure of the population and the availability of immigrant workers

A change in any of these factors is likely to affect the position of the supply curve, causing an increase or decrease in labour supply.

The wage in other industries or occupations

Consider the effect on the labour supply to an industry if there is a change in the wage being offered in another industry. Workers are likely to consider switching to the other industry if there is an increase in the wage on offer there. The supply curve of labour to the original industry will therefore shift to the left.

Skills and qualifications

Different industries or occupations require different skills, so the position of the supply curve will depend upon the number of individuals who have the necessary skills — and upon the cost and difficulty of acquiring those skills. Vets command high salaries, but the cost of gaining the qualifications needed to become a vet is also high, therefore limiting the number of people eligible for jobs.

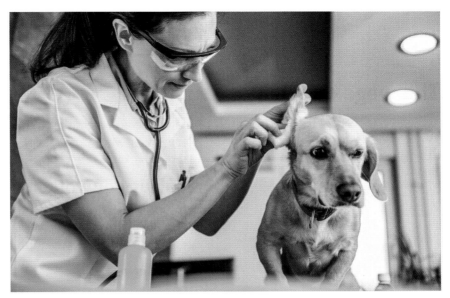

It takes 5–6 years to become a qualified vet in the UK, and many vets choose to embark on further study once qualified

Non-pecuniary benefits

Decisions about labour supply may also be influenced by job satisfaction. A worker who finds his or her work to be satisfying may be prepared to accept a lower wage than a worker who really hates every minute spent at work. Indeed, firms may provide other **non-pecuniary benefits** — in other words, firms may provide benefits that are not fully reflected in wages. These are sometimes known as *fringe benefits*. Such benefits might include a subsidised canteen or other social facilities. They could also include in-work training, pension schemes or job security. If this is the case, then in choosing one job over another, workers may not only consider the wage rate, but the overall package offered by employers. In other words, firms may be able to shift the position of their labour supply curves, as workers will be prepared to supply more labour at any given wage rate.

Knowledge check 17.2

Suppose that there is an emigration of nurses from a country, attracted by better working conditions abroad. Would this lead to an increase, decrease, extension or contraction of the supply of nurses?

Demographic factors

In the long term, the number of people in the workforce influences the supply of labour. Although this may not affect the supply curve of labour in the short run, an influx of migrant labour can do so. For example, if there is an increase in the number of migrant workers with a particular skill set, this will shift the labour supply curve to the right.

Exercise 17.1

For each of the following situations, draw a diagram to show how the supply curve of labour is affected.
a the effect on the market for engineers if there is an increase in the number of students graduating with engineering degrees
b the effect on a labour market if the wage rate increases
c the effect on the market for computer programmers if there is an increase in the wage paid to web designers
d the effect on a labour market if the qualification requirements are tightened
e the effect on labour supply to a firm that opens a new sports facility available to its workers
f an epidemic causes a decrease in the size of the working population

The wage elasticity of supply

There are several factors that may influence the elasticity of labour supply: in other words, the extent to which an increase in the wage rate in a labour market will encourage an increase in the supply of labour.

Availability of workers

Labour supply may depend upon the availability of workers. For example, if there is unemployment, there will be workers ready to take up jobs. In this case labour supply will tend to be elastic. However, if the job market is tight, supply will be relatively more inelastic.

Skills

If the workers available for work do not have the skills needed for the vacancies available, training will be needed. In this instance, labour supply is likely to be relatively inelastic.

Qualifications

In some occupations and professions, such as accountancy or nursing, specific qualifications are required, which will make labour supply relatively more inelastic. This effect will be reinforced where the profession is seen as a vocation. For example, nurses may be less sensitive to changes in the wage rate if they are committed to their jobs.

Labour immobility

If the workers who are available for work are located in areas remote from where the vacancies are appearing, this can cause problems. For example, if the available workers are living in Newcastle, but the vacancies are in London, then they may not respond to the higher wages on offer, given the costs of transport, moving house, finding new schools for their children — or even being able to find out that the jobs are available. Labour supply may therefore be relatively inelastic in the short run.

Long-run elasticity

In the long run, labour supply may be more elastic. More people may be attracted into high-paid occupations, industries or regions, even if some retraining or relocation is needed. Alternatively, firms may shift their locations to where labour is more plentiful.

Summary

- At the industry level, higher wages will encourage more people to look for jobs, so the supply curve will be upward-sloping.
- The position of the labour supply curve depends upon a range of factors.
- The wage elasticity of supply depends upon the availability of workers and their skills and qualifications.
- Labour supply is likely to be more elastic in the long run than in the short run.

Transfer earnings and economic rent

Key terms

transfer earnings the minimum payment required to keep a factor of production in its present use

economic rent a payment received by a factor of production over and above what would be needed to keep it in its present use

Many factors of production have some flexibility about them, in the sense that they can be employed in a variety of alternative uses. A worker may be able to work in different occupations and industries. For example, computers can be put to use in a wide range of activities. The decision to use a factor of production for one particular job rather than another carries an opportunity cost, which can be seen in terms of the next best alternative activity in which that factor could have been employed.

For example, consider a woman who chooses to work as a waitress because the pay is better than she could obtain as a shop assistant. By making this choice, she forgoes the opportunity to work at, say, John Lewis. The opportunity cost is seen in terms of this forgone alternative. If John Lewis were to raise its rates of pay in order to attract more staff, there would come a point where the waitress might reconsider her decision and decide to be a shop assistant after all, as the opportunity cost of being a waitress has risen.

The threshold at which this decision is taken leads to the definition of **transfer earnings**. Transfer earnings are defined in terms of the minimum payment that is required in order to keep a factor of production in its present use.

In a labour market, transfer earnings can be thought of as the minimum payment that will keep the marginal worker in his or her present occupation or sector. This payment will vary from worker to worker. Moreover, where there is a market in which all workers receive the same pay for the same job, there will be some workers who receive a wage in excess of their transfer earnings. This excess of payment to a factor over and above what is required to keep it in its present use is known as **economic rent**.

The total payments to a factor can therefore be divided between these two — part of the payment is transfer earnings, and the remainder is economic rent.

Probably the best way of explaining how a worker's earnings can be divided between transfer earnings and economic rent is through an appropriate diagram. Figure 17.3 illustrates the two concepts. Here, we

Knowledge check 17.4

An accountant is offered a job by another firm but decides to stay with her current employer, as the salary offer is only marginally higher than her present salary. Is her decision based on economic rent or on transfer earnings?

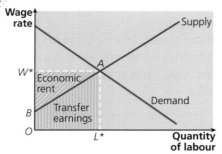

Figure 17.3 Transfer earnings and economic rent

Synoptic link

Equilibrium in the labour market is explained in Chapter 18.

Synoptic link

Producer surplus was introduced in the discussion of the supply curve (of goods and services) in Chapter 4.

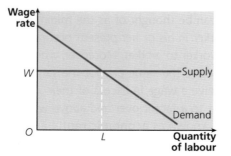

Figure 17.4 Perfectly elastic labour supply

assume that the wage rate is at W^*. In the labour market as drawn, firms' demand for labour is a downward-sloping function of the wage rate. Workers' supply of labour also depends on the wage rate, with workers being prepared to supply more labour to the labour market at higher wages. Equilibrium is the point at which demand equals supply, with wage rate W^* and quantity of labour L^*.

Think about the nature of the labour supply curve. It reveals how much labour the workers are prepared to supply at any given wage rate. At the wage rate W^*, there is a worker who is supplying labour at the margin. If the wage rate were to fall even slightly below W^*, the worker would withdraw from this labour market, perhaps to take alternative employment in another sector or occupation. In other words, the wage rate can be regarded as the transfer earnings of the marginal worker. A similar argument can be made about any point along the labour supply curve.

This means that the area under the supply curve up to the equilibrium point can be interpreted as the transfer earnings of workers in this labour market. In Figure 17.3 this is given by the area $OBAL^*$.

Total earnings are given by the wage rate multiplied by the quantity of labour supplied (here, area OW^*AL^*). Economic rent is therefore that part of total earnings that is *not* transfer earnings. In Figure 17.3 this is the triangle BW^*A. The rationale is that this area represents the total excess that workers receive by being paid a wage (W^*) that is above the minimum required to keep them employed in this market.

If you think about it, you will see that this is similar to the notion of producer surplus, which is the difference between the price received by firms for a good or service and the price at which the firms would have been prepared to supply that good or service.

The balance between transfer earnings and economic rent

What determines the balance between the two aspects of total earnings? In this connection, the elasticity of supply of labour is of critical importance.

This can be seen by studying diagrams showing varying degrees of elasticity of supply. First, consider two extreme situations. Figure 17.4 shows a labour market in which supply is perfectly elastic. This implies that there is a limitless supply of labour at the wage rate W. In this situation there is no economic rent to be gained from labour supply, and all earnings are transfer earnings. Any reduction of the wage below W will mean that all workers leave the market.

Now consider Figure 17.5. Here labour supply is perfectly inelastic. There is a fixed amount of labour being supplied to the market and, whatever the wage rate, that amount of labour remains the same. Another way of looking at this is that there is no minimum payment needed to keep labour in its present use. Now the entire earnings of the factor are made up by economic rent (i.e. the area $OWAL$).

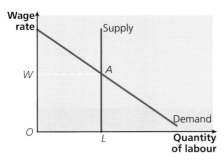

Figure 17.5 Perfectly inelastic labour supply

This illustrates how important the elasticity of labour supply is in determining the balance between transfer earnings and economic rent. The more inelastic supply is, the higher the proportion of total earnings that is made up of economic rent.

Surgeons and butchers: the importance of supply

Consider an example of differential earnings — say, surgeons and butchers. First think about the surgeons. Surgeons are in relatively inelastic supply, at least in the short run. The education required to become a surgeon is long and demanding, and is certainly essential for entry into the occupation. Furthermore, not everyone is cut out to become a surgeon, as this is a field that requires certain innate abilities and talents. This implies that the supply of surgeons is limited and does not vary a great deal with the wage rate. If this is the case, then the earnings of surgeons are largely made up of economic rent.

The situation may be reinforced by the fact that once an individual has trained as a surgeon, there may be few alternative occupations to which, if disgruntled, he or she could transfer. There is a natural limit to how many surgeons there are, *and* to their willingness to exit from the market.

How about butchers? The training programme for butchers is less arduous than for surgeons, and a wider range of people is suitable for employment in this occupation. Labour supply for butchers is therefore likely to be more elastic than for surgeons, and so economic rent will be relatively less important than in the previous case. If butchers were to receive high enough wages, more people would be attracted to the trade and wage rates would eventually fall.

In addition, there are other occupations into which butchers can transfer when they have had enough of cutting up all that meat: they might look to other sections of the catering sector, for example. This reinforces the relatively high elasticity of supply.

The importance of demand

Economic rent has been seen to be more important for surgeons than for butchers, but is this the whole story? The discussion so far has centred entirely on the supply side of the market. But demand is also important.

Indeed, it is the position of the demand curve when interacting with supply that determines the equilibrium wage rate in a labour market. It may well be that the supply of workers skilled in underwater basket weaving is strictly limited, but if there is no demand for underwater basket weavers then there is no scope for that skill to earn high economic rents. In the above example, it is the relatively strong demand for surgeons relative to their limited supply that leads to a relatively high equilibrium wage in the market.

This analysis can be applied to answer some questions that often appear about the labour market. In particular, why should the top footballers and pop stars be paid such high salaries, whereas valued professions such as nurses and firefighters are paid much less?

A footballer such as Harry Kane is valued because of the talent that he displays on the pitch, and because of his ability to bring in the crowds who want to see him play. This makes him a good revenue earner for his club, and reflects his high marginal productivity. In addition, his skills are rare — some would say unique. Harry Kane is therefore in extremely limited supply. This combination of high marginal productivity and limited supply leads to a high equilibrium wage rate.

Footballer Harry Kane — an example of high marginal productivity

For nurses and firefighters, society may value them highly in one sense — that they carry out a vital, and sometimes dangerous, occupation. However, they are not valued in the sense of displaying high marginal productivity. Furthermore, the supply is by no means as limited as in the case of top-class professional footballers. These factors taken together help to explain why there are such large differences in salaries between occupations. This is one example of how marginal productivity theory helps to explain features of the real world that non-economists often find puzzling.

Summary

- In a modern economy, there is a complex network of labour markets for workers with different skills, working in different occupations and industries.
- The total payments to a factor of production can be separated into transfer earnings and economic rent.
- Transfer earnings represent the minimum payment needed to keep a factor of production in its present use.
- Economic rent is a payment received by a factor of production over and above what would be needed to keep it in its present use.
- The balance between transfer earnings and economic rent depends critically on the elasticity of supply of a particular kind of labour.
- The position of the demand curve is also important.

CHAPTER 17 QUESTIONS

A Multiple-choice questions

1 Which of the following is not a factor affecting the supply of labour to an industry?

    a The skills needed for a job

    b The demand for the product

    c The number of people with appropriate qualifications

    d The demographic structure of the population

2 An increase in the supply of labour is likely to lead to:

    a An increase in wages and an increase in quantity

    b A decrease in wages and a decrease in quantity

    c An increase in wages and a decrease in quantity

    d A decrease in wages and an increase in quantity

B Knowledge and understanding questions

3 Explain, with the aid of a diagram, how wages are determined in a competitive market. [4 marks]

4 Explain, with the aid of a diagram, what is meant by 'economic rent'. [4 marks]

5 Explain, with the aid of a diagram, what is meant by 'transfer earnings'. [4 marks]

C Stimulus response question

6 Checkout operators are the people who 'beep' your groceries through at the supermarket. The job requires skills but these are easily learned. As internet shopping grows more popular, and with the increasing use of 'self-checkout' machines, this job is in lower demand as time progresses.

    a Explain why checkout operators are paid less than film stars. [6 marks]

    b Explain, with the aid of a diagram, how decreasing demand for checkout operators may affect the market for their labour. [4 marks]

Chapter 18

The interaction of labour markets

Having explored some of the theory of how labour markets work, this chapter explores situations in which labour markets may not operate competitively.

Learning objectives

After studying this chapter, you should be able to:

- explain, with the aid of a diagram, how wages are determined in a highly competitive market
- explain, with the aid of a diagram, the effect of changes in the demand for and supply of labour
- explain wage differentials
- explain monopsony
- evaluate the impact of a monopsonist employer on a labour market
- explain trade unions
- evaluate the impact of trade union activity on labour markets
- explain bilateral monopoly
- evaluate the impact of bilateral monopoly on a labour market
- evaluate the impact of changes in labour market flexibility and mobility of labour

Labour market equilibrium

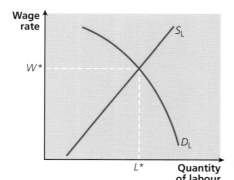

Figure 18.1 Labour market equilibrium

Bringing demand and supply curves together for an industry shows how the equilibrium wage is determined for a particular type of labour. Figure 18.1 shows a downward-sloping labour demand curve (D_L) based on marginal productivity theory, and an upward-sloping labour supply curve (S_L). Equilibrium is found at the intersection of demand and supply. If the wage is lower than W^* employers will not be able to fill all their vacancies, and will have to offer a higher wage to attract more workers. If the wage is higher than W^* there will be an excess supply of labour, and the wage will drift down until W^* is reached and equilibrium obtained.

Figure 18.2 shows how equilibrium for an individual firm relates to the competitive industry equilibrium. The right-hand panel shows equilibrium in the industry, where the wage rate is determined by the interaction of demand and supply. The equilibrium wage is W^*, and the industry demands L_I hours of work. The firm then accepts the market wage as given, so demands l_f hours of work.

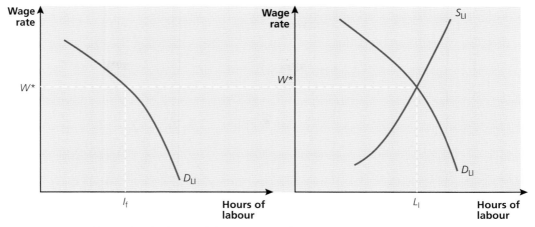

Figure 18.2 Equilibrium for the firm and the industry under perfect competition

An increase in the demand for labour

We can examine the effects of changes in market conditions. For instance, a change in the factors that determine the position of the labour demand curve will induce a movement of labour demand and an adjustment in the equilibrium wage. Suppose there is an increase in the demand for the firm's product. This will lead to a rightward shift in the demand for labour, say from D_{L0} to D_{L1} in Figure 18.3. This in turn will lead to a new market equilibrium, with the wage rising from W_0 to W_1. This leads to an extension in supply, with employment rising from L_0 to L_1.

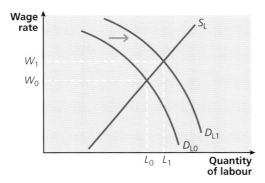

Figure 18.3 An increase in the demand for labour

This may not be the final equilibrium position, however. If the higher wages in this market now encourage workers to switch from other industries in which wages have not risen, this will lead to a longer-term shift to the right of the labour supply curve. In a free market, the shift will continue until wage differentials are no longer sufficient to encourage workers to transfer.

An increase in the supply of labour

Suppose that there is an increase in the number of trained web designers looking for work, following an expansion in the number of courses provided in colleges. How will this affect the market for web designers? Figure 18.4 illustrates. An increase in labour supply shifts the supply curve from S_{L0} to S_{L1}, with the equilibrium wage falling from W_0 to W_1 and the quantity of labour increasing from L_0 to L_1. There has been an extension of demand.

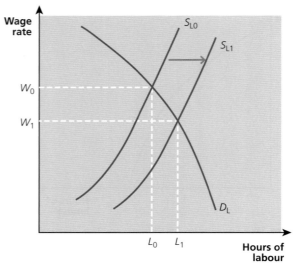

Figure 18.4 An increase in the supply of web designers

Markets for labour

Exercise 18.1

Draw a diagram to analyse the effects on labour market equilibrium if there is a fall in the selling price of a firm's product.

So far, the focus has been on the demand and supply of labour, seen sometimes through the eyes of a firm and sometimes looking at an industry labour market. As mentioned at the beginning of the chapter, it is important to remember that these are separate levels of analysis. In particular, there is no single labour market in an economy like the UK, any more than there is a single market for goods. In reality, there is a complex network of labour markets for people with different skills and for people in different occupations, and there are overlapping markets for labour corresponding to different product markets.

> ### Summary
> - Labour market equilibrium is found at the intersection of labour demand and labour supply.
> - This determines the equilibrium wage rate for an industry.
> - Changes in relative wages between sectors may induce movement of workers between industries.

Wage differentials

It is clear from looking at the real world that there exist wage differentials between individuals. Surgeons and butchers earn different amounts, as do labourers and rocket scientists. There are a number of reasons why this is the case and will always be so.

One reason, of course, is that different workers display different marginal physical products. Some may have skills resulting from innate ability and talents or from the education or training they have received. Firms will value the workers who show the skills and productivity that they require in their workforce.

Different occupations pay different wage or salary levels — which partly, of course, reflects the different marginal productivities of the occupations. We may also observe wage differentials between different locations. Wage and salary levels in London and the southeast are higher than in Northern Ireland, for example.

These differences are important, and may reflect variations in market conditions between local or regional labour markets.

More difficult to explain is why there should be wage differentials between men and women, between trade union members and non-members, or between different ethnic groups.

Discrimination

We have seen that wage differentials across different labour markets within an economy such as the UK are to be expected because of differences in marginal productivity of different workers, and differences in economic rent and transfer earnings. However, the question often arises as to whether such economic analysis can explain all of the differentials in wages that can be observed.

The Office for National Statistics reported in 2018 that the gender pay gap based on median hourly earnings for full-time employees was 9.1%, which was the lowest since 1997.

Quantitative skills 18.1

The mean and the median

The gender pay gap mentioned here is based on median hourly earnings. It is useful to be aware of what is meant by the median, which is sometimes used. You will be familiar with the notion of the *average* value of a variable. This is also known by statisticians as the *mean*. It is calculated as the sum of the values of a variable divided by the number of observations. The *median* is also a measure of central tendency, but the median is the middle observation. For example, suppose we had 5 observations on a variable, the values being 1, 3, 7, 14 and 65. The average would be (1 + 3 + 7 + 14 + 65)/5 = 18. The median would be the middle observation, which is 7. We might think that in this instance, the median is more sensible for representing the series because the mean is affected by one very high value.

The mere fact that there is inequality does not prove that there is discrimination. You have seen the way in which education and training affects earnings, so differentials between different groups of people may reflect the different educational choices made by those different groups. The gender gap may also reflect the fact that childcare responsibilities interrupt the working lives of many women. This is important in terms of training and the build-up of experience and seniority. The increasing introduction of crèche facilities by many firms is reducing the extent of this contribution to the earnings gap, but it has not eliminated it. In addition, there have been changes in social attitudes towards female education beyond the age of 16. When girls were expected to become homemakers, education beyond 16 was not highly valued, so there were generations of women who missed out on education, and consequently found themselves disadvantaged in the labour market. Although attitudes have changed, however, such effects take a long time to work their way through the system.

Summary

- In a modern economy, there is a complex network of labour markets for workers with different skills, working in different occupations and industries.
- Wage differentials arise between workers, partly from differences in marginal productivity or in labour market conditions.

Market failure in labour markets

As with product markets, there are many ways in which labour markets may fail to achieve the most desirable results for society at large. Such market failure can occur on either the demand or the supply side of the market. On the demand side, it may be that employers — as the buyers of labour — have market power that can be exploited at the expense of the workers. Alternatively, it may be that some employers act against the interests of some groups of workers relative to others through some form of discrimination in their hiring practices or wage-setting behaviour. On the supply side, there may be restrictions on the supply of some types of labour, or it may be that trade unions find themselves able to bid wages up to a level that is above the free market equilibrium.

> ### Synoptic link
>
> Market failure was first introduced in Chapter 8, as involving situations in which a market fails to bring about the most desirable outcome for society in terms of resource allocation. Remember that allocative efficiency is achieved when price is set equal to marginal cost and productive efficiency is achieved when firms produce at minimum long-run average cost.

Monopsony

> ### Key term
>
> monopsony a market in which there is a single buyer of a good, service or factor of production

> ### Synoptic link
>
> The way in which a monopoly operates was discussed in Chapter 14.

In a monopoly market, a firm with market dominance is able to restrict output, and maximise profits by setting a higher price. A similar form of market power can occur on the supply side of the market if there is a single *buyer* of a good, service or factor of production. Such a market is known as a **monopsony**.

In the discussion of the labour market so far, it has been assumed that firms in the labour market face perfect competition, and therefore must accept the market wage. However, suppose that one firm is the sole user of a particular type of labour, or is the dominant firm in a city or region, and thus is in a monopsony situation.

Such a monopsonist faces the market supply curve of labour directly, rather than simply accepting the equilibrium market wage. It views this supply curve as its average cost of labour because it shows the average wage rate that it would need to offer to obtain any given quantity of labour input.

Figure 18.5 shows a monopsonist's demand curve for labour, which is the marginal revenue product curve (MRP_L), and its supply curve of labour, seen by the firm as its average cost curve of labour (AC_L). If the market were perfectly competitive, equilibrium would be where supply equals demand, which would be with the firm using L^* labour at a wage rate W^*.

From the perspective of the monopsonist firm facing the supply curve directly, if at any point it wants to hire more labour, it has to offer a higher wage to encourage more workers to join the market — after all, that is what the AC_L curve tells it. However, the firm would then have to pay that higher wage to *all* its workers, so the *marginal cost* of hiring the extra worker is not just the wage paid to that worker, but the increased wage paid to all the other workers as well. So the marginal cost of labour curve (MC_L) can be added to the diagram.

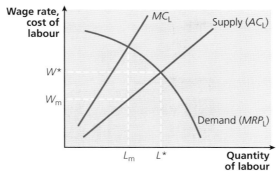

Figure 18.5 A monopsony buyer of labour

If the monopsonist firm wants to maximise profit, it will hire labour up to the point where the marginal cost of labour is equal to the marginal revenue product of labour. Therefore it will use labour up to the level L_m, which is where $MC_L = MRP_L$. In order to entice workers to supply this amount of labour, the firm need pay only the wage W_m. (Remember that AC_L is the supply curve of labour.) You can see, therefore, that a profit-maximising monopsonist will use less labour, and pay a lower wage, than a firm operating under perfect competition. This moves the market away from allocative efficiency, as the wage being paid is less than the marginal cost of labour. Firms are employing less labour than under perfect competition, and are therefore operating below the point of productive efficiency.

Evaluation of monopsony

Monopsony has an impact on the labour market in two key ways. Workers will receive lower wages than they would have under perfect competition. Furthermore, fewer workers will be employed.

The relative size of these impacts will depend upon the elasticity of demand for and supply of labour. In a market where the demand for labour is relatively wage-inelastic, the extent to which wages and employment can be forced down will be less than where demand is wage-elastic.

The elasticity of labour supply is also important. If workers can find employment elsewhere, then the supply of labour will be relatively elastic, and the monopsony employer will have less power to drive wages down. However, where workers have limited (or no) alternative employment opportunities, the monopsonist will have greater power in the market, and will be able to offer lower wages relative to the competitive outcome.

Supermarkets have been known to misuse their monopsonistic power to drive down prices for their suppliers

Exercise 18.2

Figure 18.6 shows a firm in a monopsonistic labour market.

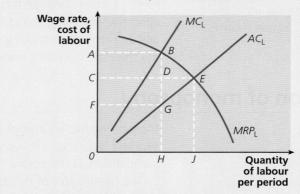

Figure 18.6 A monopsonistic labour market

a What would the wage rate be if this market were perfectly competitive, and how much labour would be employed?

b As a monopsony, what wage would the firm offer to its workers, and how much labour would it employ?

c Which area represents the employer's wage bill?

d What surplus does this generate for the firm?

Trade unions

Key term

trade union an organisation of workers that negotiates with employers on behalf of its members

Trade unions are associations of workers that negotiate with employers on pay and working conditions. Guilds of craftsmen existed in Europe in the Middle Ages, but the formation of workers' trade unions did not become legal in the UK until 1824. In the period following the Second World War, about 40% of the labour force in the UK were members of a trade union. This percentage increased during the 1970s, peaking at about 50%, but since 1980 there has been a steady decline to below 30%.

Trade unions have three major objectives:
1 wage bargaining
2 the improvement of working conditions
3 security of employment for their members

In exploring the effect of the unions on a labour market, it is important to establish whether the unions are in a position to exploit market power and interfere with the proper functioning of the labour market, and also whether they are a necessary balance to the power of employers and therefore necessary to protect workers from being exploited.

There have been some changes in the way in which trade unions have engaged in bargaining with employers, with a stronger focus on local agreements and on performance-related pay. In terms of marginal productivity theory, this emphasis on performance makes intuitive sense, as it strengthens the links between workers' productivity and their pay.

There are two ways in which a trade union may seek to affect labour market equilibrium. On the one hand, it may limit the supply of workers into an occupation or industry. On the other hand, it may negotiate successfully for higher wages for its members. It turns out that these two possible strategies have similar effects on market equilibrium.

Restricting labour supply

Figure 18.7 shows the situation facing a firm, with a demand curve for labour based on marginal productivity theory. The average going wage in the economy is given by W^*, so if the firm can obtain workers at that wage, it is prepared to employ up to L_0 labour.

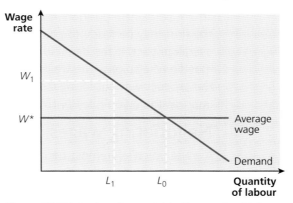

Figure 18.7 A trade union restricts the supply of labour

However, if the firm faces a trade union that is limiting the amount of labour available to just L_1, then the union will be able to push the wage up to W_1. This might happen where there is a *closed shop*: in other words, where a firm can employ only those workers who are members of the union. A closed shop allows the union to control how many workers are registered members, and therefore eligible to work in the occupation.

In this situation the union is effectively trading off higher wages for its members against a lower level of employment. The union members who are in work are better off — but those who would have been prepared to work at the lower wage of W^* either are unemployed or have to look elsewhere for jobs. If they are unemployed, this imposes a cost on society. If they are working in a second-choice occupation or industry, this may also impose a social cost, in the sense that they may not be working to their full potential.

The extent of the trade-off depends crucially on the elasticity of demand for labour, as you can see in Figure 18.8. When the demand for labour is relatively more elastic, as shown by D_{L0}, the wage paid by the firm increases to W_0, whereas with the relatively more inelastic demand for labour D_{L1} the wage increases by much more, to W_1.

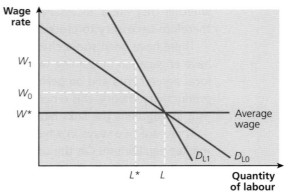

Figure 18.8 The importance of the elasticity of demand for labour

This makes good intuitive sense. The elasticity of demand is likely to be low in situations where a firm cannot readily substitute capital for labour, where labour forms a small share of total costs, and where the price elasticity of demand for the firm's product is relatively low. If the firm cannot readily substitute capital for labour, the union has a relatively strong bargaining position. If labour costs are a small part of total costs, the firm may be ready to concede a wage increase, as it will have limited overall impact. If the demand for the product is price inelastic, the firm may be able to pass the wage increase on in the form of a higher price for the product without losing large volumes of sales. Therefore, these factors improve the union's ability to negotiate a good deal with the employer.

Negotiating wages

A trade union's foremost function can be regarded as negotiating higher wages for its members. Figure 18.9 depicts this situation. In the absence of union negotiation, the equilibrium for the firm is where demand and supply intersect, so the firm hires L_e labour at a wage of W_e.

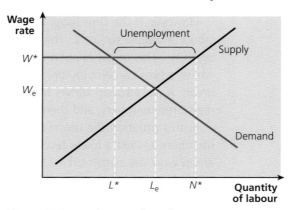

Figure 18.9 A trade union fixes the wage

If the trade union negotiates a wage of W^*, the firm cannot hire any labour below that level. The firm now employs only L^* labour at this wage. So, again, the effect is that the union negotiations result in a trade-off between the amount of labour hired and the wage rate. When the wage is at W^*, unemployment is shown on Figure 18.9 as $N^* - L^*$. Notice that there is nothing to stop the employer paying a wage that is higher than W^*, so to hire more than N^* workers, the employer would have to offer higher wages in order to attract workers into jobs.

The elasticity of demand for labour again affects the outcome, as shown in Figure 18.10. This time, with the relatively more inelastic demand curve D_{L1}, the effect on the quantity of labour employed (falls from L_e to L^{**}) is much less than when demand is relatively more elastic (falls from L_e to L^*).

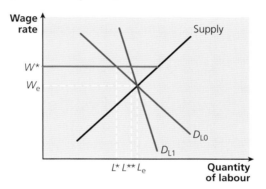

Figure 18.10 The effect of elasticity of demand for labour when the union fixes the wage

Knowledge check 18.2

Explain why trade union pressure on wages could lead to unemployment.

From the point of view of allocative efficiency, the wage is not equal to marginal cost, so trade union intervention in the market may prevent wages from acting as reliable signals to workers and firms, and therefore may lead to a sub-optimal allocation of resources.

Working conditions and job security

One possible effect of trade union involvement in a firm is that workers will have more job security: in other words, they may become less likely to lose their jobs with the union there to protect their interests.

From the firm's point of view, there may be a positive side to this. If workers feel secure in their jobs, they may be more productive, or more prepared to accept changes in working practices that enable an improvement in productivity. For this reason, it can be argued that in some situations the presence of a trade union may be beneficial in terms of a firm's efficiency. Indeed, the union may sometimes take over functions that would otherwise be part of the responsibility of the firm's human resource department.

Bilateral monopoly

It is important to notice that much of this analysis has treated the firm as being very passive in the negotiations. Suppose, however, that there is a situation, in which the monopoly trade union seller of labour faces a firm that is a monopsony buyer of labour. The resulting bilateral monopoly is illustrated in Figure 18.11. If unhindered by the trade union, the firm would offer a wage W_m and use L_m labour. However, if the union now negotiates a higher wage rate, what happens is that as the wage moves upwards from W_m, the firm will take on more labour. The market will then move back towards the perfectly competitive level (at wage W^* and quantity L^*).

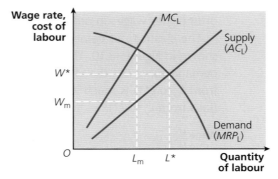

Figure 18.11 A bilateral monopoly

Evaluation of bilateral monopoly

In this situation, the market power of the two protagonists works against both of them to produce an outcome that is closer to perfect competition. It is not possible to predict where the final resting place for the market will be, but it will lie somewhere between L_m and L^*, depending upon the relative strengths and negotiating skills of the firm and the union.

Given the decline in trade union membership and the weakened power of trade unions in the UK, it may well be the case that it is the firm that has more strength in these negotiations. In any event, as has been noted, the focus of trade union activity has tended to be more upon working conditions than on wages.

Knowledge check 18.3

If the firm has the stronger hand in negotiations with a union in a bilateral monopoly situation, is the outcome likely to be towards L_m or L^*?

Summary
- A market in which there is a single buyer of a good, service or factor of production is known as a monopsony market.
- A monopsony buyer of labour will employ less labour at a lower wage than if the market is perfectly competitive.
- Trade unions exist to negotiate for their members on pay, working conditions and job security.
- If trade unions restrict labour supply, or negotiate wages that are above the market equilibrium, the net effect is a trade-off between wages and employment.
- Those who remain in work receive higher pay, but at the expense of other workers who either have become unemployed or work in second-choice occupations or industries.
- However, by improving job security, unions may (sometimes) make workers more prepared to accept changes in working practices that lead to productivity gains.
- In a bilateral monopoly situation, the monopsony power of a firm may be balanced against the monopoly power of the trade union.

Labour market flexibility

If an economy is to maintain international competitiveness of its goods and services, an essential ingredient is that the labour market is flexible.

At the microeconomic level, where a prime concern is with achieving a good allocation of resources for society, the issue is whether workers can transfer readily between activities to allow resource allocation to change through time. This requires a number of conditions to be met. Workers need to have information about what jobs are available (and, perhaps, where those jobs are available), and what skills are needed for those jobs. Employers need to be able to identify workers with the skills and talents that they need. If workers cannot find the jobs that are available, or do not have the appropriate skills to undertake those jobs, the market will not function smoothly. Similarly, if employers cannot identify the workers with the skills that they need, that too will impede the working of the market.

Arguably, the problem has become acute in recent years, with a change in the balance of jobs between skilled and unskilled workers. As the economy gears up to more hi-tech activities, and low-skill jobs are outsourced or relocated to other countries, the need for workers to acquire the right skills becomes ever more pressing.

Policies to improve the flexibility of the labour market

If it is so important for labour markets to be flexible, what steps can be taken to promote flexibility? A number of obstacles to flexibility have been identified in this chapter and the previous one. To what extent are these amenable to policy intervention?

Occupational mobility and information

The process of structural change in an economy may be impeded if the people looking for work, perhaps because they have been released from a declining sector, do not have the requisite skills for the sectors that are expanding. It is also important for unemployed workers to have good information about the jobs available.

Successive governments have been aware of this issue, and have introduced measures to provide opportunities for workers to undergo training and incentives for employers to provide it. The latest policy in this area is the apprenticeship levy, which was introduced in April 2017. This attempts to overcome the free-rider problem, and has set a target of having 3 million apprentices in place by 2020. Large employers are required to make a payment into an online service account, but can reclaim their levy payments (plus a subsidy) when they take on apprentices into approved schemes. Employers who benefit by recruiting trained workers from other firms will not be able to reclaim their levy payments. Smaller employers (with wage bills below £3 million) can claim subsidies towards the costs of taking on apprentices.

Trade union reform

As we have seen, by negotiating for a wage that is above the equilibrium level, trade unions may trade off higher wages for lower levels of

Synoptic link

The changes in the structure of employment are discussed in Chapter 28. The need to devise policies to allow the labour market to cope with this are discussed in Chapter 32.

employment. The potential disruption caused by strike action can also impede the workings of a labour market.

Tube strikes impede commuters, but they also affect the labour market

One of the most telling criticisms of trade unions has been that they have affected the degree of flexibility of the labour market. The most obvious manifestation of this is that their actions limit the entry of workers into a market.

This may happen in any firm, where existing workers have better access to information about how the firm is operating, or about forthcoming job vacancies, and so can make sure that their own positions are safeguarded against newcomers. This is sometimes known as the *insider–outsider* phenomenon. Its effect is strengthened and institutionalised by the presence of a trade union, or by professional bodies such as the Royal College of Surgeons.

This and other barriers to entry erected by a trade union can limit the effectiveness and flexibility of labour markets by making it more difficult for firms to adapt to changing market conditions.

Trade union membership has declined substantially in recent decades. This may partly reflect reforms brought in to curb the power of the unions and make it more difficult to call strike action. Also significant is that traditionally union membership has been higher in the manufacturing sector than in service sectors. The decline of manufacturing may therefore have reduced the power of the unions.

Exercise 18.3

Go online and find some recent examples of strike action that have taken place in the UK. Identify which sectors of the economy have been affected by this action and discuss whether the goal of the unions was focused on pay or on working conditions.

Extension material

Asymmetric information and the labour market

Asymmetric information can lead to market failure in labour markets.

The issue arises from the employer's perspective. When an employer is hiring new workers, a key concern is the quality of the workers applying for jobs. This is partly a question about their innate talents and abilities. It can be overcome to some extent by checking applicants' qualifications — indeed, this is why employers may insist on qualifications, even if they are not directly related to the requirements of the job.

Extension material (continued)

However, there are other differences between workers that are important. Two workers with the same qualifications may show very different productivity. Some workers are naturally hardworking and conscientious, whereas others are always taking rest breaks and getting away with as little effort as possible. At the hiring stage, the employer may not be able to distinguish between the 'workers' and the 'shirkers'.

Suppose a firm pays a wage that is the average warranted by workers and shirkers combined. As time goes by, some workers are likely to quit and go to higher-paid jobs with other firms. The employees who are most likely to leave are the more productive ones, who realise that if they are paid the average of what is right for the workers and shirkers taken together, they are being paid less than their own value. In the long run, the employer could be left with just the shirkers.

A rational response to this from the employer's perspective is to pay a wage that is higher than the average, in order to encourage the productive workers to stay with the firm. This has the additional benefit of increasing the penalty for being caught shirking (since a worker faces a greater opportunity cost of getting the sack if wages are higher). So, paying a higher-than-average wage has an additional incentive effect in that it discourages shirking.

This higher-than-average wage is known as the efficiency wage, and can be seen as a response by firms to the asymmetric information problem. One of the results in the labour market is to raise the level of involuntary unemployment, in the sense that at the higher wage there will be an increase in the number of workers who would be prepared to accept a job but are unable to find employment.

Geographic mobility

In the UK, there are significant variations in labour market conditions between regions, reflected in wage differentials. Will workers migrate from one region to another in search of higher earning opportunities? Not always.

There are a number of reasons that help to explain why workers may not be freely mobile between different parts of the country. It could be that the workers who are available are located in areas remote from where the vacancies are appearing. If the available workers are living in Leeds, but the vacancies are in London, then they may not respond to the higher wages on offer, given the costs of transport and moving house — or the difficulty of finding out that the jobs are available. There may also be social effects — people do not like to move away from their friends and relatives, or to leave the area that they know or where their favourite football team plays. Parents may not wish to disrupt their children's education.

The relatively high rate of owner-occupied housing in the UK means that workers who are owner-occupiers may need a strong inducement to move to another part of the country in search of jobs. For council house tenants, too, it may be quite difficult to relocate to a different area for employment purposes because they will have to return to the bottom of the waiting list for housing. Differences in house prices in different parts of the country add further to the problem of matching workers to jobs.

There may also be information problems, in that it may be more difficult to find out about job availability in other areas. The internet may have reduced the costs of job search to some extent, but it is still easier to find jobs in the local area, where the reputation of firms is better known to locals. Where both partners in a relationship are working, this

Knowledge check 18.4

How would you expect the immobility of labour to affect the elasticity of supply of labour?

may also make it more difficult to find jobs further afield that would suit both of them, and there is some evidence that females tend to be less mobile geographically than males.

Regional policy

There have always been differences in average incomes and in unemployment rates between the various regions of the UK. In broad terms, there are two possible responses to this — either persuade workers to move to regions where there are more jobs, or persuade the firms to move to areas where labour is plentiful. The geographic immobility of workers has already been discussed, but how about persuading firms to move to regions where labour is available?

Some measures have been taken to encourage firms to consider relocating to regions where labour is available. These have included leading by example, with some civil service functions being moved out of London.

EU funding has helped in this regard, with Scotland, Wales and Northern Ireland all qualifying for grants. Between 1999 and 2012, Regional Development Agencies (RDAs) set up by the Labour government had responsibility for promoting economic development in their regions. The RDAs were abolished as part of government efforts to reduce the budget deficit, and ceased operating in March 2012.

During the course of the 2010 Coalition Government, George Osborne, the then-Chancellor of the Exchequer, launched the concept of the Northern Powerhouse. This was a strategy designed to provide funding to revitalise cities in the north of England, devolving powers from Westminster to local people, providing funds for locally determined projects, and spending £13 billion on improving transport infrastructure.

Technology

One of the greatest fallacies perpetuated by non-economists is that technology destroys jobs. Bands of labourers known as Luddites rioted between 1811 and 1816, destroying textile machines, which they blamed for high unemployment and low wages. In the twenty-first century there is a strong lobbying group in the USA arguing that outsourcing and cheap labour in China are destroying US jobs. President Trump has reinforced this message in his tweets, and used this argument to justify the imposition of tariffs on imports of a range of products from China. The tariffs were later extended to apply to other trading partners of the USA.

In fact, new technology and an expansion in the capital stock should have beneficial effects — so long as labour markets are sufficiently flexible. Consider a market in which new technology is introduced. If firms in an industry invest in technology and expand the capital stock, this affects the marginal revenue product of labour and hence the demand for labour, as shown in Figure 18.12, where demand shifts from D_1 to D_2. In this market, the effect is to raise the wage rate from W_1 to W_2 and the employment level from L_1 to L_2.

Synoptic link

The effect of tariffs is discussed in the context of trade protectionism in Chapter 35.

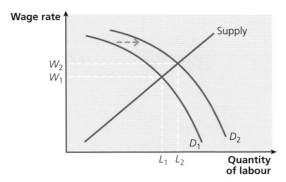

Figure 18.12 An increase in capital

However, it is important to look beyond what happens in a single market, as the argument is that it is all very well expanding employment in the technology sector — but what about the old industries that are in decline? Suppose the new industries absorb less labour than is discarded by the old declining industries? After all, if the effect of technology is to allow call centres to create jobs in India at the expense of the USA or the UK, does this not harm employment in those countries?

The counter-argument to this lies in the notion of the gains from specialisation introduced briefly in Chapter 2. This argues that countries can gain from international trade through specialising in certain activities. Setting up call centres in India frees UK workers to work in sectors in which the UK can specialise efficiently.

Do UK firms setting up call centres in India harm employment at home, or does this free up UK workers to specialise in expanding sectors?

There is one proviso, of course. It is important that the workers released from the declining sectors have (or can obtain) the skills that are needed for them to be absorbed into the expanding sectors. This recalls the question of whether the labour market is sufficiently flexible to adapt to changes in the pattern of economic activity.

Contracts and legislation

An impediment to flexibility in the labour market arises from the nature of employment contracts between employer and employees, which often specify conditions under which a worker can be released from employment. For example, contracts may specify the period of notice that a firm must give before terminating employment. This is reinforced by legislation that sets out redundancy conditions, so that firms wanting to cut jobs need to recompense workers. This may limit the ease with which firms can reduce employment in the short run, and increases the cost of doing so. This may explain why firms might not reduce their workforce when a recession affects the economy.

One way in which firms have tried to gain more flexibility in hiring and firing is through the use of part-time workers and zero-hours contracts. Part-time workers have less negotiating power with employers. Zero-hours contracts give employers even more flexibility, as employees on such contracts have no guaranteed hours at all, so actual hours worked may vary from week to week. Such contracts are naturally unpopular with workers, and there has been discussion about the extent to which they should be permitted.

Exercise 18.4

For each of the following situations, draw a demand and supply diagram for a labour market to analyse the effects on the wage rate and employment level:

a an increase in the rate of immigration of people into the country
b a reduction in the rate of Jobseeker's Allowance
c an improvement in technology that raises labour productivity
d a new health and safety regulation to safeguard workers against industrial injury
e an increase in the number of old people as a percentage of the population

Safety engineers at work on a construction site

Evaluation of labour market flexibility

It has been argued that flexibility in labour markets is important for a number of reasons. A flexible labour market enables firms to maintain their competitiveness in international markets, and helps people to find jobs more quickly. This all aids resource allocation in the economy overall.

The preceding discussion has highlighted changes that have affected flexibility in the labour markets, some the result of conscious policy and others because of the actions of firms and trade unions. Some of these have added to flexibility while others have reduced it.

For example, health and safety legislation and regulations that affect the nature of job contracts may have had the effect of reducing flexibility — and raised costs for employers. Protecting the interests and rights of workers improves the working conditions of the workforce, but may introduce less flexibility from the employers' perspective. Similarly, reforms that limit the power and influence of trade unions may improve flexibility, but at the expense of workers' rights.

The increasing use of zero-hours contracts also increases the flexibility of the labour market, but has been seen by many as a retrograde step in terms of the security of the workforce. Part-time working has grown in importance, and again may have positive and negative effects. It may have the effect of allowing some people to join the workforce who otherwise might have been excluded. On the other hand, there may be some workers who have only been able to obtain part-time employment but would have been happy to work full time.

Tighter redundancy contracts or extended maternity/paternity leave periods may benefit workers, but may be seen to reduce the flexibility of employers.

Summary
- An important factor influencing the rate of unemployment and international competitiveness is the degree of flexibility in labour markets.
- Successive governments have introduced measures to encourage workers to undertake training.
- Trade union reforms were introduced during the 1980s and have contributed to flexibility in labour markets.
- Regional policy has attempted to reduce the differentials in unemployment rates between the regions of the UK.
- Adjustment in labour markets is needed in order to cope with the changing international pattern of specialisation.

Valuing professional footballers

The football transfer market was buoyant in the summer of 2017. Among the most prominent traders were the top English Premiership clubs such as Manchester United, Liverpool and Chelsea, and big-spending European clubs such as Paris Saint-Germain. The FA Premier League has the highest revenues of any domestic football league in the world, grossing more than £4.5 billion in revenues in the 2016/17 season according to Deloitte. The top Premiership clubs also compete in the highly lucrative UEFA Champions League. The battle between TV firms for broadcasting rights is a key factor in generating these revenues.

So not surprisingly, the top English Premiership clubs are able to outbid most of their rivals to attract the best players in the world. In 2017, it was reported that the average salary of a footballer playing in the English Premier League in the 2013/14 season had reached £2.6 million per year (£50,817 per week), comfortably more than footballers playing in the top leagues in Germany, Italy and Spain. These figures suggest that a high proportion of the TV revenues goes into players' salaries — rather than into lower ticket prices.

But is there any economic justification for Paris Saint-Germain paying a transfer fee of £198 million to Barcelona for Neymar, or Juventus paying £99.2 million to Real Madrid to obtain the services of Cristiano Ronaldo?

From an economic and financial perspective, professional footballers are complex productive assets who are expected to provide a flow of services both on and off the field over the period of their employment contract. One way of valuing a professional footballer is to calculate the value of the expected flow of net benefits accruing to the holder of the asset — that is, the club. In other words, the value of a professional footballer should be related to the marginal revenue product (MRP) of the player.

Calculating the MRP of a professional footballer requires estimating the expected additional cash flows accruing to the club as a consequence of signing that player. Broadly speaking, there are two types of revenue stream that a player can generate. First, there are the revenue streams associated with the player's on-the-field contribution to team performance. Team revenues tend to be 'win-elastic'. Winning teams tend to attract more spectators, generating higher match-day revenues. Media revenues can also be win-elastic with bigger viewing audiences for the more successful teams.

Sponsorship and merchandising revenues also tend to be higher for more successful teams. But a player's value will also depend on his expected image value off-the-field. Star players can generate greater revenues by virtue of being star players irrespective of their actual impact on team performance. Glamour as well as glory makes money in professional team sports, which, when all is said and done, are part of the entertainment industry. So from an economic perspective the fundamental value of a professional footballer can be stated as:

$$MRP = (MPC \times MWR) + PIV$$

where MPC is the (expected) marginal playing contribution, MWR is the marginal win revenue and PIV is the player image value. Calculating a player's value requires an estimate of the incremental impact of the player on the team performance, an estimate of the sensitivity of the team's revenues to team performance and an estimate of the off-the-field marketing value of the player.

Follow-up questions

a Explain what is meant by the 'marginal revenue product' of a footballer.

b What is meant by the statement that team revenues tend to be 'win-elastic'?

c Explain why 'glamour as well as glory makes money'.

d To what extent does the discussion of a footballer's MRP help to explain why professional footballers command such high wages?

CHAPTER 18 QUESTIONS

A Multiple-choice questions

1 Which of the following is **not** a characteristic of a monopsony?

  a One dominant buyer of labour

  b It will hire labour up to the point where $MC_L = MRP_L$

  c It will pay higher wages than in a competitive labour market

  d It will use less labour than in a competitive labour market

2 Which of the following is a bilateral monopoly?

  a There are two dominant sellers in a market

  b There is a trade union and a monopsony employer of labour

  c There are two dominant sellers of labour

  d There is a perfectly competitive labour market

3 Emigration is:

  a The loss of labour from a country

  b The increase of labour into a country

  c The difference between labour entering and labour leaving a country

  d The return of expatriates into a country

B Knowledge and understanding questions

4 Explain, with the aid of a diagram, the impact of a monopsony on a labour market. [4 marks]

5 Explain, with the aid of a diagram, the impact of a trade union on a labour market. [4 marks]

6 Explain **two** factors that could improve the labour market flexibility in a market. [4 marks]

C Stimulus response question

7 Some media have suggested that there is a crisis in the supply of teachers to the education market. Many reasons are put forward as to why workers are not attracted into the teaching professions, such as:

- low wages relative to the qualifications needed due to a monopsony employer
- too much administration
- the need for good behaviour management skills
- larger class sizes

  a Explain what is meant by 'a monopsony employer'. [2 marks]

  b Evaluate whether low wages are likely to have the greatest impact on the supply of teachers to the market. [12 marks]

D Essay question

8 Evaluate whether government intervention is the best method of improving labour market flexibility in the UK. [25 marks]

MACROECONOMICS

Part 6
Aggregate demand and aggregate supply

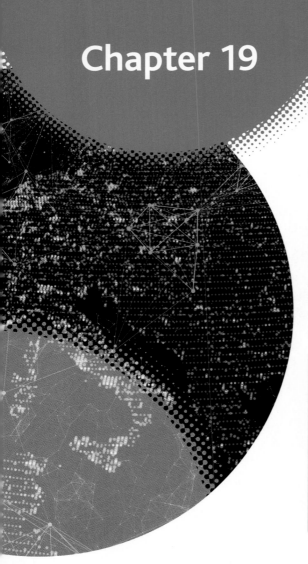

Chapter 19

The circular flow of income and aggregate demand

Section 2 deals with macroeconomics, which looks at the whole economy. The starting point is to consider the model of the circular flow of income, output and expenditure, which provides a context for measuring national income, output and expenditure. The chapter then considers the components of aggregate demand as the first step in building a model of the macroeconomy. The way in which the levels of these components are determined in practice is an important key to the operation of the economy when considered at the aggregate level.

> **Learning objectives**
>
> After studying this chapter, you should be able to:
> - explain the circular flow of income, with injections and leakages
> - explain methods of measuring national income, output and expenditure
> - explain aggregate demand and its components
> - explain, with the aid of a diagram, the relationship between aggregate demand and the price level
> - explain, with the aid of a diagram, shifts in the aggregate demand curve
> - evaluate the relationship between changes in income and consumption
> - evaluate the role of expectations

What is macroeconomics?

> **Exercise 19.1**
>
> Think about the following, and see whether you think each represents a macroeconomic or microeconomic phenomenon:
> a the overall level of prices in an economy
> b the price of ice cream
> c the overall rate of unemployment in the UK
> d the unemployment rate among catering workers in Aberdeen
> e the average wage paid to construction workers in Southampton

In microeconomics, we examine the behaviour of individual economic agents such as households, firms (businesses) and government. In contrast, macroeconomics looks at relationships in the economy as a whole. You will be familiar with some of the key concepts from reports in the media, such as unemployment, inflation or economic growth. Macroeconomists tend to refer to these as *variables*, as they vary through time. The focus is on the relationships between these macroeconomic variables. For example, we will look at the relationship between unemployment and inflation, and between total (aggregate) consumer spending and income.

In this chapter, we consider how we can think about national income (the total output of an economy in a period of time), and about the aggregate level of demand in the economy and its components.

The circular flow of income, expenditure and output

Consider a much simplified model of an economy. Assume for the moment that there are just two types of economic agent in an economy: households and firms (businesses). In other words, ignore the government and assume there is no international trade. (These agents will be brought back into the picture soon.)

In this simple world, we also assume that firms produce goods and that all the factors of production that they use (labour, capital, etc.) are supplied by households. In return for supplying factors of production households receive income, which they spend on consumer goods.

Synoptic link

The economists' approach to economic agents and factors of production was explained in Chapter 1 in the microeconomics section. This also sets out the rewards received by each factor of production.

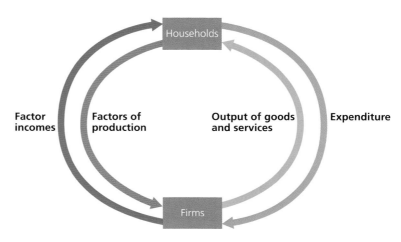

Figure 19.1 The circular flow of income, expenditure and output

Key term

circular flow of income a model of the economy that shows the movement of goods and services between households and firms and their corresponding payments in money terms, together with the supply of factors of production

This model is known as the **circular flow of income** (see Figure 19.1). The main flows in the model are as follows:

- Households supply factor services to firms, in the form of labour, land, capital and enterprise. This is represented by the red arrow in Figure 19.1.
- There is a corresponding flow of factor incomes from firms to households, including wages, salaries, rents, interest and profits. This flow is represented by the blue arrow in Figure 19.1.
- The output of goods and services produced by firms flows from firms to households in the form of consumer goods. This is the orange arrow in Figure 19.1.
- Balancing the flow of output is a flow of expenditure, as households pay for the goods they obtain from firms. This is the green arrow in Figure 19.1.

Knowledge check 19.1

What is meant by saying that this simple version of the circular flow model is a 'closed system'?

As this is a closed system, these flows must balance. This means that there are three ways in which the total amount of economic activity in this economy can be measured: by the incomes that firms pay out, by the total amount of output that is produced, or by total expenditure. Whichever method is chosen, it should give the same result.

Injections and leakages within the circular flow

An economy such as the UK's is more complicated than this, so the basic model has limited applicability from a real-world perspective. This is because it is a *closed* system, whereas in practice this is not the case, as there are **leakages** from the system and **injections** into it. These arise because of the economic activities of government and through an economy's international trade with the rest of the world.

Injections into the circular flow

There are three key injections into the circular flow:

1 government expenditure (G)
2 exports (X)
3 investment by firms (I)

The government spends money on goods and services. For example, it may spend on the provision of public goods, and has to spend in order to carry out its other governmental obligations.

Foreign residents buy goods and services produced in the home economy. From the home economy's point of view, these are exports of goods and services. Associated with exports is an inflow of expenditure from the rest of the world.

Firms also undertake expenditure when they buy capital goods, such as machinery, factory buildings or transport equipment. This is termed investment, as it involves obtaining goods that will be used in future production.

Leakages from the circular flow

On the other side of the coin, there are leakages from the circular flow, comprising:

- taxes raised by the government from households (T)
- spending on imports from the rest of the world (M)
- household savings (S)

The government raises taxes in order to finance its spending. These include direct taxes such as income tax and corporation tax, but also indirect taxes such as VAT and customs duties.

Residents in the domestic economy buy goods and services from abroad, in the form of imports. This is a leakage from the system simply because it is expenditure that is not going on home-produced goods and services. The saving activity of households also affects the circular flow, as there is a part of household income that is saved instead of being spent on goods and services.

Balance in the overall economy

The overall economy will be in balance when planned injections are equal to planned leakages. Notice that there are connections between the injections and leakages — for example, household savings may enter financial markets, and firms borrow from financial markets in order to finance their investment expenditure.

International trade also affects the circular flow. Part of the expenditure on goods and services in the economy comes from abroad in the form of exports. In addition, part of the expenditure undertaken by households is on imported goods and services.

Figure 19.2 adds leakages and injections to the circular flow diagram. The flow of expenditure is no longer just made up of household consumption expenditure on consumer goods, but is augmented by investment expenditure by firms (*I*), export expenditure from overseas (*X*) and government expenditure (*G*). These can be regarded as injections into the circular flow.

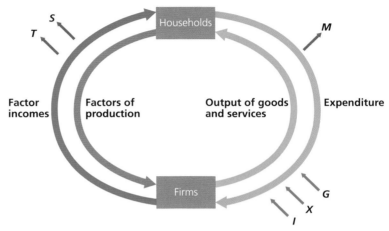

Figure 19.2 Injections and leakages in the circular flow

Notice that investment in the form of expenditure by firms on machinery, buildings and other productive resources plays an important role within the macroeconomy. By undertaking investment expenditure, firms add to the productive capacity of the economy, and so enable economic growth to take place. A change in the balance between investment and consumption activity therefore affects the long-run path of the economy.

An increase in expenditure on investment by firms may have other effects as well. In order to meet the additional demand for machinery, other firms need to expand production. This means that they need to hire extra workers — and pay them, of course. The additional workers will then spend part of their income on consumer goods, so unleashing a second round of expenditure. This phenomenon will be examined in Chapter 21.

Summary

- The circular flow of income, expenditure and output describes the relationship between these three key variables.
- The circular flow diagram needs to accommodate injections and leakages.
- The government affects the circular flow through expenditure (an injection) and taxation (a leakage).
- International trade is important because of exports (an injection) and imports (a leakage).
- The circular flow is also affected by household savings (a leakage) and by firms' investment expenditure (an injection).
- Investment affects the productive capacity of the economy in the long run, and is therefore important for economic growth.

Knowledge check 19.2

Suppose that there were to be a fall in investment expenditure by firms. How would this affect the circular flow?

Knowledge check 19.3

If people decide to save more, how will this affect the circular flow?

Measuring national income, output and expenditure

Key term

gross domestic product (GDP)
the total level of economic
activity carried out in an
economy during a given period

The circular flow model shows that there are three ways in which we can attempt to measure total economic activity in an economy — by measuring total incomes, total output produced and total expenditure. The total level of economic activity carried out in an economy during a given period is known as **gross domestic product (GDP)**.

In practice, when the Office for National Statistics (ONS) carries out the measurements, the three answers are never quite the same, as it is impossible to measure with complete accuracy. The published data for GDP are therefore calculated as the average of these three measures, each of which gives information about different aspects of a society's total resources.

The expenditure-side estimate describes how those resources are being used, so that it can be seen what proportion of society's resources is being used for consumption and what for investment etc.

The income-side estimate reports on the way in which households earn their income. In other words, it tells something about the balance between rewards to labour (e.g. wages and salaries), capital (interest), land (rents), enterprise (profits) and so on.

The output-side estimate focuses on the economic structure of the economy. One way in which countries differ is in the balance between primary production such as agriculture, secondary activity such as manufacturing, and tertiary activity such as services. Service activity has increased in importance in the UK in recent years, with financial services in particular emerging as a strong part of the UK's economic structure.

Financial services are now an important part of the UK's economic structure

Synoptic link

The importance of adjusting
for price changes to produce an
estimate of real GDP is discussed
more fully in Chapter 22.

As GDP measures the scale of economic activity in the economy, it is helpful to monitor how this changes through time. GDP is measured in money terms, so it is important to adjust the observed data to remove the effect of changing prices. The resulting measure is known as 'real GDP'. Notice that there will be other situations in which we will refer to the 'real' value of something, meaning that we have adjusted for inflation.

Knowledge check 19.4

Why would it be misleading to consider changes in GDP through time without adjusting for changing prices?

Figure 19.3 traces real GDP in the UK since 1948. In some ways this is an unhelpful way of presenting the data, as the trend component of the series is so strong. In other words, real GDP has been increasing steadily throughout the period. However, the dip that occurred in 2009 is clearly visible. There are one or two other periods in which there was a movement away from the trend, but these are relatively rare and not easy to analyse. This reflects the nature of economic variables such as GDP, where the fluctuations around trend are small relative to the trend, but can seem substantial when the economy is experiencing them.

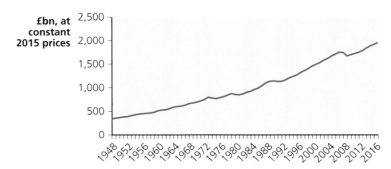

Figure 19.3 Real GDP, 1948–2017 (£bn)

Source: ONS

It is more revealing to convert these data into annual growth rates, which makes it more straightforward to identify the main periods of fluctuation, particularly periods of negative growth: that is, when the economy contracted. The rate of change of GDP is known as economic growth.

It should be noted that the measure of GDP has not been without its critics. In particular, economists have questioned whether it provides a reasonable measure of the standard of living enjoyed by the residents of a country, and whether its rate of change is therefore informative about economic growth.

Synoptic link

Economic growth and alternative measures of macroeconomic performance are discussed in Chapters 22 and 23.

Summary

- The circular flow model suggests that there are three ways in which the total level of economic activity in an economy during a period of time can be measured: by total income, by total expenditure and by total output produced.
- In principle, the three ways of measuring GDP should give the same answers, but in practice data measurements are not so accurate.
- Real GDP is a measure of the total economic activity carried out in an economy during a period by residents living on its territory, adjusted for price changes.

The components of aggregate demand

The starting point for exploring macroeconomics is to consider the components of aggregate demand. Aggregate demand simply measures the total amount that economic agents in the economy wish to spend. From the discussion of the circular flow, this includes households, firms,

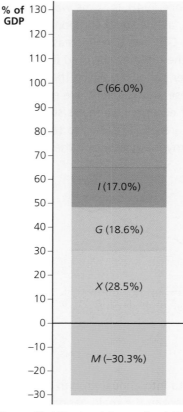

% of GDP

C (66.0%)

I (17.0%)

G (18.6%)

X (28.5%)

M (−30.3%)

Figure 19.4 The breakdown of real GDP in 2017

Note: *C* includes spending by non-profit institutions serving households, *I* includes changes in inventory holdings. The statistical discrepancy is not shown.

Source: ONS

Knowledge check 19.5

In thinking about the components of aggregate demand, which economic agent or agents undertake investment expenditure?

the government and overseas residents who buy home-produced goods and services.

The main components of aggregate demand are:

- consumption (*C*)
- investment by firms (*I*)
- government expenditure (*G*)
- net exports — that is, exports minus imports (*X – M*)

We can write this as:

$$AD = C + I + G + (X - M)$$

where *AD* denotes aggregate demand, *C* is consumption expenditure, *I* is investment, *G* is government spending, *X* is exports and *M* is imports.

Figure 19.4 shows the relative size of these components, using the expenditure-side breakdown of real GDP in the UK in 2017. Consumption (known as consumer expenditure in the ONS accounts) is by far the largest component, amounting to about 66% of real GDP in 2017. Government current expenditure accounted for 18.6%, but you should realise that this somewhat understates the importance of government in overall spending, as it excludes public spending on investment, which is treated together with private sector investment in the data. Combined public and private sector investment made up just under 17% of total GDP. This includes changes in the inventory holdings of firms. Notice that imports were rather higher than exports, indicating a negative balance of trade in goods and services.

Exercise 19.2

Suppose there is an economy in which the values in Table 19.1 apply (all measured in £ million).

Table 19.1 Values for an economy (all measured in £m)

Values	£m
Consumption	75
Profits	60
Investment	30
Government expenditure	25
Exports	50
Private saving	50
Imports	55

a Calculate the level of aggregate demand.
b Calculate the trade balance.

When in the next chapter you come to consider the conditions under which a macroeconomy will be in equilibrium, you will need to think in terms of the factors that will influence *ex ante* (planned) aggregate demand. The first step is to consider each component in turn.

The relationship between consumption and income

Consumption (consumer expenditure) is the largest single component of aggregate demand. What factors could be expected to influence the size of total spending by households? John Maynard Keynes, in his influential book *The General Theory of Employment, Interest and Money*, published in 1936, suggested that the most important determinant is **disposable income**. Disposable income here refers to the income that households have to devote to consumption and saving, taking into account payments of direct taxes and transfer payments. In other words, as real incomes rise, households will tend to spend more. However, he also pointed out that they would not spend all of an increase in income but would save some of it. Remember that this was important in the circular flow model.

Other influences on consumption

Income will not be the only influence on consumption. Consumption may also depend partly on the *wealth* of a household. Notice that income and wealth are not the same. Income accrues during a period as a reward for the supply of factor services, such as labour. Wealth, on the other hand, represents the stock of accumulated past savings. If you like, wealth can be thought of in terms of the asset holdings of households. If households experience an increase in the value of their asset holdings, this may influence their spending decisions.

Consumer expenditure theories

Later writers argued that consumption does not necessarily depend upon current income alone. For example, Milton Friedman put forward the *permanent income hypothesis*, which suggested that consumers take decisions about expenditure based on a notion of their permanent, or normal, income levels — that is, the income that they expect to receive over a 5- or 10-year time horizon. This suggests that households do not necessarily vary their consumption patterns in response to changes in income that they perceive to be only transitory. An associated theory is the Life Cycle Hypothesis, developed by Franco Modigliani, who suggested that households smooth their expenditure over their lifetimes, on the basis of their expected lifetime incomes. So, people tend to borrow in their youth against future income, then in middle age, when earning more strongly, they pay off their debts and save in preparation to fund their expenditure in retirement. Consumer expenditure therefore varies by much less than income, and is based on expected lifetime earnings rather than on current income.

If part of household spending is financed by borrowing, the rate of interest may be significant in influencing the total amount of consumption. An increase in the rate of interest that raises the cost of borrowing may deter expenditure. In macroeconomics, the **rate of interest** is an important variable. In the present context, if a household or firm wants to borrow in order to finance expenditure, the rate of interest is the cost of borrowing, because it would need to be repaid on the loan. It is also the reward for lending.

Synoptic link

The importance of the rate of interest will be explained in more detail in later chapters, especially Chapters 31 and 37.

At the same time it may encourage saving, as the return on saving is higher when the interest rate is higher. The rate of interest may also have an indirect effect on expenditure through its effect on the value of asset holdings. In addition, households may be influenced in their decisions by their expectations about future inflation. Notice that some of these effects may not be instantaneous: that is, consumption may adjust to changes in its determinants only after a time lag.

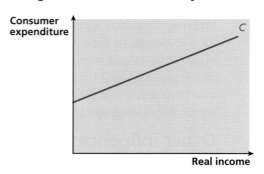

Figure 19.5 The consumption function

Key term

consumption function the relationship between consumer expenditure and disposable income — its position depends upon the other factors that affect how much households spend on consumer expenditure

This **consumption function** can be portrayed as a relationship between consumer expenditure and income. This is shown in Figure 19.5, which focuses on the relationship between consumer expenditure and household income, ceteris paribus: in other words, in drawing the relationship between consumer expenditure and income, it is assumed that the other determinants, such as wealth and the interest rate, remain constant. A change in any of these other influences will affect the *position* of the line.

Evaluation of the consumption function

In practice, it is not expected that the empirical relationship between consumption and income will reveal an exact straight line, if only because over a long time period there will be changes in the other influences on consumption, such as interest rates and expected inflation. Figure 19.6 shows that the hypothesis is not totally implausible, as indicated by the fact that most of the scatter points are quite close to the fitted line. However, there are some points that diverge from the pattern towards the end of the period, suggesting that the relationship was affected by the recession that followed the financial crisis of the late 2000s.

Knowledge check 19.6

How will the consumption function be affected if households become pessimistic about the future, and decide to save more?

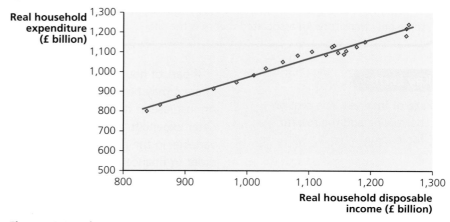

Figure 19.6 Real consumption and disposable income in the UK, 1997–2017

Source: based on data from ONS

Although income may not be the only determinant of consumption, there is a clear relationship. An increase in real disposable income will lead to an increase in consumption, although if households save part of the additional income, the increase in consumption will be lower than the increase in income. The significance of this will be explored in Chapter 21.

Investment

The rate of interest is also likely to be influential in affecting firms' decisions about investment spending. Again, this is because the interest rate represents the cost of borrowing. So, if firms need to borrow in order to undertake **investment**, they may be discouraged from spending on investment goods when the rate of interest is relatively high.

Investment leads to an increase in the productive capacity of the economy, by increasing the stock of capital available for production. This capital stock comprises plant and machinery, vehicles and other transport equipment, and buildings, including new dwellings, which provide a supply of housing services over a long period.

Although important, the rate of interest is not likely to be the only factor that determines how much investment firms choose to undertake. First, not all investment has to be funded from borrowing — firms may be able to use past profits for this purpose. However, if firms choose to do this, they face an opportunity cost. In other words, profits can be used to buy financial assets that will provide a rate of return dependent on the rate of interest. The rate of interest is therefore still important, as it represents the opportunity cost of an investment project.

In considering an investment project, firms will need to form expectations about the future stream of earnings that will flow from the investment. Their expectations about the future state of the economy (and of the demand for their products) will therefore be an important influence on current investment. This is one reason why it is argued that inflation is damaging for an economy, as a high rate of inflation increases uncertainty about the future and may dampen firms' expectations about future demand, thereby discouraging investment.

Figure 19.7 shows the relationship between investment and the rate of interest. The investment demand function I_{D0} is downward sloping because investment is relatively low when the rate of interest is relatively high. An improvement in business confidence for the future would result in more investment being undertaken at any given interest rate, so the investment function would move from I_{D0} to I_{D1}.

Key term

investment in the circular flow, expenditure undertaken by firms to add to the capital stock

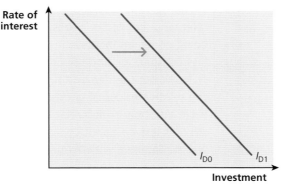

Figure 19.7 Investment and the rate of interest

Synoptic link

The speed with which expectations adjust can also affect the ability of the economy to reach equilibrium, as we will see in Chapter 20.

Synoptic link

The way in which government expenditure can be seen as part of policy will be explored in the discussion of fiscal policy in Chapter 30.

The importance of expectations

Both consumption and investment expenditures are affected by the expectations formed by households and firms respectively. This influences the state of aggregate demand. If economic agents have pessimistic views about the future course of the economy, this can result in aggregate demand being lower than it otherwise would have been. Households may decide that they need to save more (and therefore spend less) to provide security for the future. Firms may decide not to undertake investment if they do not expect demand to be buoyant in the future.

These expectations can be self-fulfilling, as if demand is lower than it could be, then firms find they were justified in not investing, and the economy could enter a downward spiral. Of course, the reverse may happen — if everyone is optimistic about the future course of the economy, then demand may increase, firms will invest, and the productive capacity of the economy will increase.

Government expenditure

By and large, you might expect government expenditure to be decided by different criteria from those influencing private sector expenditures. Indeed, some aspects of government expenditure might be regarded as part of macroeconomic policy. Some other aspects of government expenditure may vary automatically with variations in the overall level of economic activity over time. For example, unemployment benefit payments are likely to increase during recessionary periods.

From the point of view of investigating macroeconomic equilibrium, however, government expenditure can be regarded as mainly *autonomous*: that is, independent of the variables in the model that will be constructed in this chapter.

Net exports

Finally, there are the factors that may influence the level of exports and imports. Most imports into the UK are normal goods, so as real incomes rise over time, there will be an increase in demand for imported goods. However, the demand for exports will depend upon changes in income in the UK's trade partners. If there is slow economic growth in the countries that are customers for the UK's exports, then this will have an impact on aggregate demand in the UK. The global recession that set in during the late 2000s had a noticeable effect on world trade.

Another factor that will affect both exports and imports is the exchange rate between sterling and other currencies. This affects the relative prices of UK goods and those produced overseas. Other things being equal, an increase in the sterling exchange rate makes UK exports less competitive and imports into the UK more competitive.

However, the demand for exports and imports will also depend upon the relative prices of goods produced in the UK and the rest of the world. If UK inflation is high relative to elsewhere, this will tend to make UK exports less competitive and imports more competitive. In 2018, a trade war threatened, with President Trump raising tariffs against some imports from China, later also extended to EU countries. This brought retaliatory action from China and the EU. The tariffs on goods from China were doubled again in May 2019, bringing retaliation in kind from China.

President Trump signs a 2017 memorandum on addressing China's practices related to intellectual property, leading to an eventual trade war between the two countries the following year

Synoptic link

The importance of the exchange rate is examined in Chapter 27. Protectionist policies are discussed more fully in Chapter 36 following the explanation of why countries engage in international trade.

The demand for imports into the UK will depend partly upon the level of domestic aggregate income, and the demand for UK exports will depend partly upon the level of incomes in the rest of the world. Therefore, a recession in the EU will affect the demand for UK exports.

The aggregate demand curve

Key term

aggregate demand (AD) curve the relationship between the level of aggregate demand and the overall price level — it shows planned expenditure at any given possible overall price level

Study tip

It is important to remember this difference between the aggregate demand curve and the microeconomic demand curve for a product. In the macroeconomic context, always label the vertical axis as 'Price level', as a reminder. The horizontal axis represents real GDP.

Having explored how the components of aggregate demand are determined, the next step is to look at the aggregate demand (AD) curve, which shows the relationship between aggregate demand and the overall price level. Formally, this curve shows the total amount of goods and services demanded in an economy at any given overall level of prices.

It is important to realise that this is a very different sort of demand curve from the microeconomic demand curves that were introduced in Chapter 3, where the focus was on an individual product and its relationship with its own price. Here the relationship is between the *total* demand for goods and services and the overall price level. So, aggregate demand is made up of all the components discussed above, and price is an average of all prices of goods and services in the economy.

Figure 19.8 shows an aggregate demand curve. The key question is why it slopes downwards. To answer this, it is necessary to determine the likely influence of the price level on the various components of aggregate demand that have been discussed in this chapter, as prices have not been mentioned explicitly (except for how expectations about inflation might influence consumer spending). First, however, the discussion needs to be cast in terms of the price *level*.

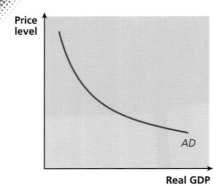

Figure 19.8 An aggregate demand curve

When the overall level of prices is relatively low, the purchasing power of income is relatively high. In other words, low overall prices can be thought of as indicating relatively high real income. Furthermore, when prices are low, this raises the real value of households' wealth. For example, suppose a household holds a financial asset such as a bond with a fixed money value of £100. The relative (real) value of that asset is higher when the overall price level is relatively low. From the above discussion, this suggests that, ceteris paribus, a low overall price level means relatively high consumption. Conversely, an increase in the average price level reduces purchasing power, so reducing the quantity of real output demanded: this is the **wealth effect**.

A second argument relates to interest rates. When prices are relatively high, people are more likely to need to borrow in order to finance their spending, which will drive up interest rates, which in turn will discourage consumption and investment and therefore lead to lower aggregate demand.

A third argument concerns exports and imports. It has been argued that, ceteris paribus, when UK prices are relatively low compared with the rest of the world, this will increase the competitiveness of UK goods, leading to an increase in foreign demand for UK exports, and a fall in the demand for imports into the UK as people switch to buying UK goods and services.

All of these arguments support the idea that the aggregate demand curve should be downward sloping. In other words, when the overall price level is relatively low, aggregate demand will be relatively high, and when prices are relatively high, aggregate demand will be relatively low.

Other factors discussed above will affect the *position* of the AD curve. For example, Figure 19.9 shows how the aggregate demand curve shifts from AD_0 to AD_1 following an increase in government expenditure.

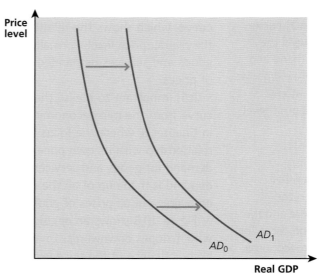

Figure 19.9 A shift in aggregate demand

Knowledge check 19.7

What factors would induce a shift of the aggregate demand curve, and what would induce a movement along it?

It is very important to be aware of the distinction between a movement along and a shift of the aggregate demand curve. A change in the overall price level induces a movement along the *AD* curve, but a change in any of the components of aggregate demand will result in a shift of the *AD* curve. For example, an increase in government expenditure would lead to a rightward shift of the *AD* curve. The effects of this on the macroeconomy will be analysed after we have explored the aggregate supply curve.

Summary
- Aggregate demand is the total demand in an economy, made up of consumer expenditure, investment, government spending and net exports.
- Consumer expenditure is the largest of these components and is determined by income and other influences, such as interest rates, wealth and expectations about the future.
- Investment leads to increases in the capital stock and is influenced by interest rates, past profits and expectations about future demand.
- Government expenditure may be regarded as largely autonomous.
- Trade in goods and services (exports and imports) is determined by the competitiveness of domestic goods and services compared with the rest of the world, which in turn is determined by relative inflation rates and the exchange rate. Imports are also affected by domestic income, and exports are affected by incomes in the rest of the world.
- The aggregate demand curve shows the relationship between aggregate demand and the overall price level.

Exercise 19.3

State whether each of the following statements about aggregate demand and/or the aggregate demand curve is true or false.
a The aggregate demand curve shows the relationship between the level of aggregate demand and the overall price level in an economy.
b The aggregate demand curve shows planned expenditure in an economy at any given possible overall price level.
c As the aggregate price level falls, the demand for goods and services in the economy rises and more of each good or service will be demanded.
d Government expenditure is regarded as autonomous, and affects the shape of the aggregate demand curve.
e The way in which consumption and investment respond to changes in the interest rate affects the shape of the aggregate demand curve.
f Investment expenditure by firms is the largest component of aggregate demand in an economy.

Investment and the financial crisis

Investment in capital goods includes expenditure by firms on plant and machinery, buildings and transport equipment. In other words, this is expenditure on produced resources that will be used in future production of goods and services. Firms also need to spend on depreciation to replace old capital goods. Government also contributes to investment, in particular by expenditure on infrastructure that contributes to the smooth running of the economy. This means that investment is very important for the economy, as it contributes to economic growth by providing the capital resources needed to increase the productive capacity of the economy.

The amount of investment expenditure that firms undertake depends upon many factors. For firms to remain viable they need to make profits, and investment is one way of improving their profit prospects. Indeed, in a competitive market environment, a firm may need to invest just to keep up with competitors by remaining cost-effective in its production methods.

Investment expenditure now is intended to bring benefits in the future, although the costs come in the present.

For example, investment in a new factory must be paid for in the present, although the benefits will not accrue until some future period. (The same reasoning applies to government expenditure on a high-speed train link or a tunnel under Stonehenge, which will only bring benefits in the future.) Firms' expectations about their future prospects will therefore figure heavily in their decision making.

Another key factor to take into account is how firms will finance their spending in the period before the investment begins to provide a return. Firms may be able to finance investment expenditure from their existing resources, such as past profits. Otherwise, they may need to borrow now against the future returns.

Figure 19.10 shows investment in the UK as a percentage of GDP from 2005 to 2017. (Note that 'gross fixed capital formation' is the term used by the ONS to describe 'investment' in the national accounts.) This covers the period of the global financial crisis of the late 2000s and its aftermath.

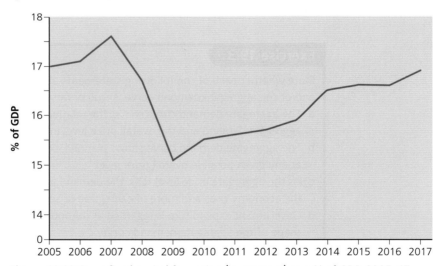

Figure 19.10 Gross fixed capital formation (investment) as a % of GDP, 2005–17

Follow-up questions

a What factors could explain the percentage of GDP devoted to investment in the 2005–17 period shown in Figure 19.10?

b From 2009 onwards, interest rates were at an all-time low. How would this be expected to affect firms' willingness to undertake investment?

CHAPTER 19 QUESTIONS

A Multiple-choice questions

1 Which of the following is **not** a leakage form the circular flow of income?

   a Savings

   b Taxation

   c Imports

   d Exports

2 The components of aggregate demand are:

   a $C + I + G + (X - M)$

   b $C + I + G + (X + M)$

   c $C + I + G + (M - X)$

   d $C + I + G + (M + X)$

3 Which of the following is most likely to shift the *AD* curve to the right?

   a A decrease in government spending

   b A decrease in investment

   c A decrease in savings

   d A decrease in exports

B Knowledge and understanding questions

4 Explain what is meant by the term 'GDP'.   [2 marks]

5 Explain, with the aid of a diagram, the relationship between *AD* and the price level.   [4 marks]

6 Explain **two** factors that could cause the *AD* curve to shift to the left.   [4 marks]

C Stimulus response question

7 In 2008, most major world economies suffered from a series of factors that decreased consumer incomes. In the UK this led to a slowdown and eventual fall in GDP.

   a Explain how a decrease in consumer income may lead to a fall in GDP.   [4 marks]

   b Evaluate whether a decrease in consumer income will always lead to a fall in GDP.   [12 marks]

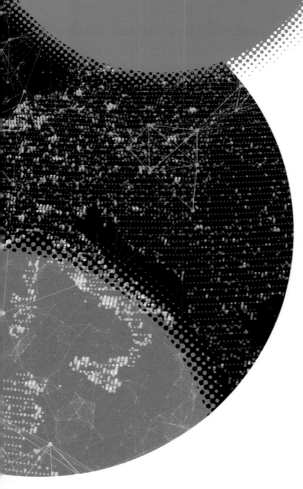

Aggregate supply and the interaction of aggregate demand and supply

Having seen what is meant by aggregate demand, it is now time to investigate aggregate supply and the factors that influence it. This chapter also explores the notion of macroeconomic equilibrium. As in microeconomics, this relates to the process by which balance can be achieved between the opposing forces of demand and supply. However, there are some important differences in these concepts when applied at the macroeconomic level.

Learning objectives

After studying this chapter, you should be able to:
- explain aggregate supply
- explain, with the aid of a diagram, the relationship between aggregate supply and price level in the short run and long run
- explain, with the aid of a diagram, shifts in the aggregate supply curve in the short run and long run
- explain, with the aid of a diagram, Keynesian and neoclassical approaches to aggregate supply
- explain assumptions underlying the aggregate demand and aggregate supply models
- explain equilibrium in the macroeconomy
- evaluate effects of changes in aggregate demand and aggregate supply on macroeconomic indicators

Aggregate supply

The previous chapter discussed the notion of aggregate demand and introduced the aggregate demand curve. In order to analyse the overall macroeconomic equilibrium, it is necessary to derive a second relationship: that between aggregate supply and the price level.

Aggregate supply covers the output of all sorts of goods and services that are produced within an economy during a period of time. However, it is not simply a question of adding up all the individual supply curves from individual markets. Within an individual market, an increase in price may induce higher supply of a good because firms will switch from other markets in search of higher profits. What we now need to be looking for is a relationship between the *overall* price level and the total amount supplied, which is quite different given the interrelated nature of markets at the microeconomic level.

The total quantity of output supplied in an economy in a period of time depends upon the quantities of inputs of factors of production employed: that is, the total amounts of labour, capital and other factors used. The ability of firms to vary output in the short run will be influenced by the degree of flexibility the firms have in varying inputs. It is therefore important to distinguish between short-run and long-run aggregate supply.

Short-run aggregate supply

Figure 20.1 Aggregate supply in the short run

Key term

short-run aggregate supply (SRAS) curve a curve showing how much output firms would be prepared to supply in the short run at any given overall price level

Synoptic link

The decisions that firms take to maximise profits, and the concept of diminishing returns, are discussed in the microeconomics component, in Chapter 11.

Knowledge check 20.1

Explain why the *SRAS* curve is upward-sloping.

Knowledge check 20.2

What would induce a movement up along the *SRAS* curve?

In the short run, firms may have relatively little flexibility to vary their inputs. Money wages are likely to be fixed, and firms will not be able to expand the amount of capital needed in the production process. Furthermore, raw materials may be in short supply, and firms may find that hiring additional workers brings less additional output than is obtained from existing workers because of the lack of additional machinery. However, at a higher price level firms will want to produce more in order to increase their profits. This suggests that in the short run, aggregate supply may be upward sloping, as shown in Figure 20.1, where *SRAS* represents **short-run aggregate supply**.

Underlying the aggregate supply curve are the decisions taken by firms about production levels at any given price. Firms are assumed to choose how much output to produce in order to maximise profits. In the short run, firms must take as given:

- the state of technology and the effectiveness with which factors are used
- the total supply of factors of production

The state of technology and the total supply of factors of production change only gradually through time, which is why the short-run aggregate supply curve is important: it shows how firms act in that short run.

On the other hand, input prices can change more rapidly — for example, wage rates can change, as can the prices of some inputs such as oil or other raw materials. These changes in input prices affect the costs faced by firms, and can affect the position of the *SRAS* curve.

The cost of inputs

There are several factors that could influence costs in the short run. For example, suppose there is a change in the cost of raw materials. If a key raw material becomes more limited in supply, perhaps because reserves are exhausted, then the prices of inputs will tend to rise, so raising firms' costs of production. They may then choose to supply less output at any given product price — and the aggregate supply curve will shift to the left.

The price of oil has been subject to significant variations over time. Oil is a key input for many firms, and an increase in the price of oil affects the cost of energy and transport. It also affects the economy in many other ways, as oil is a key input in the production of many fertilisers used in the agricultural sector. The price of oil may therefore have a significant impact on the position of aggregate supply in the short run by affecting the costs faced by firms.

An increase in the price of oil can affect energy, transport and the agricultural sector

Knowledge check 20.3

How would a fall in labour costs affect the *SRAS* curve?

Synoptic link

The significance of the exchange rate and the way in which it is determined is explained in Chapter 27.

Another key input for firms is labour, so an increase in labour costs will also affect the position of the short-run aggregate supply curve.

The exchange rate

Where firms rely on imported inputs of raw materials, energy or component parts used in production, a change in the exchange rate could affect aggregate supply by affecting the domestic price of imported inputs, and in turn affecting the costs faced by firms. This could be favourable, of course, depending on the direction in which the exchange rate changes. It could be that the exchange rate rises (appreciates), so reducing the domestic price of imports. Firms may then be prepared to supply more output at any given price.

The exchange rate can change in the short run for a variety of different reasons, so firms may face some quite sudden changes in their costs. One way that firms can guard against this is through the nature of the contracts drawn up with their foreign suppliers, if future prices can be specified in a way that hedges against possible exchange rate fluctuations.

Government intervention

There are some forms of government intervention that can affect firms' costs in the short run. An increase in regulation that forced firms to spend more on health and safety measures would raise costs. An increase in the rate of corporation tax would have similar effects.

Shifts in the short-run aggregate supply curve

If any of the factors assumed to influence aggregate supply in the short run change, then the aggregate supply curve will shift. The costs facing firms are the main cause of shifts in the *SRAS* curve.

For example, given that aggregate supply arises from the use of inputs of factors of production, one important influence is the price of factor inputs. Other factors that influence the costs faced by firms will also be important, as mentioned above.

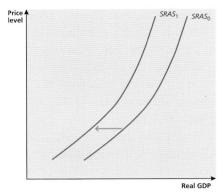

Price level

SRAS₁ SRAS₀

Real GDP

Figure 20.2 A shift in the *SRAS* curve

Figure 20.2 shows how the short-run aggregate supply curve will respond if the government introduces measures that require firms to spend more on health and safety. The increase in costs means that firms will be prepared to supply less output at any given price, so the *SRAS* curve shifts to the left.

Exercise 20.1

For each of the following, state whether the short-run aggregate supply curve would shift to the left or to the right:
a the discovery of a new source of a raw material, reducing its price
b an increase in the exchange rate
c an increase in wage rates
d a fall in the price of oil

Summary

- In the short run, firms aiming to maximise profits will be prepared to supply more output at higher prices.
- There is therefore an upward-sloping relationship between real output and the price level.
- Changes in factor prices may lead to a shift in the position of the short-run aggregate supply curve.

Long-run aggregate supply

The discussion so far has focused on short-run aggregate supply. However, it is also important to consider how aggregate supply can be viewed in the longer term. This is an area where different groups of economists have held different views.

Key terms

neoclassical economists economists who argued that markets would allow the economy to adjust to equilibrium

Monetarist School group of economists who argued that the economy would always converge on an equilibrium level of output

natural rate of output the long-run equilibrium level of output that corresponds to full employment

Extension material

Views of aggregate supply

Early economic thinkers (the so-called 'classical' economists such as Adam Smith) argued that prices would adjust to ensure that resources were efficiently allocated in society. As economic theory developed, this idea was adopted by **neoclassical economists**, who argued that the government should adopt a *laissez faire* approach to the economy — in other words, the market could be left alone to find its way to equilibrium. Keynes disputed this approach, and it is this disagreement that sparked off a debate about the shape of the long-run aggregate supply curve.

An influential school of macroeconomists, known as the **Monetarist School**, argued along neoclassical lines that the economy would always converge on an equilibrium level of output that they referred to as the **natural rate of output**.

The debate developed during the 1970s, and is significant because of the implications for the conduct and effectiveness of policy options. Indeed the monetarists had a major impact on the policies adopted by Margaret Thatcher in the UK and Ronald Reagan in the USA in the 1980s.

Some economists argued, along neoclassical lines, that the economy would always find its way to overall equilibrium, which corresponds to a situation in which the economy is at full employment. Full employment is a situation in which the economy is making full use of its factors of production, and is therefore producing at the full capacity level of output — the maximum that the economy could produce.

If the economy does quickly move to such an equilibrium, then the long-run relationship between aggregate supply and the price level would be vertical, shown as *LRAS* in Figure 20.3. Here Y_{FE} is the so-called natural rate of output: that is, the full employment level of aggregate output. In other words, aggregate supply is not sensitive to the price level, because the economy always readjusts rapidly back to full employment.

An opposing school of thought (often known as the **Keynesian School**) held that the macroeconomy was not sufficiently flexible to enable continuous full employment. They argued that the economy could settle at an equilibrium position below full employment, at least in the medium term. In particular, inflexibilities in labour markets would prevent adjustment. For example, if firms had pessimistic expectations about aggregate demand, and thus reduced their supply of output, this would lead to lower incomes because of the workers being laid off. This would then mean that aggregate demand was indeed deficient, so firms' pessimism was self-fulfilling.

These sorts of argument led to a belief that there would be a range of output over which aggregate supply would be upward sloping. Figure 20.4 illustrates such an aggregate supply curve, in which Y_{FE} represents full employment; however, when the economy is operating below this level of output, aggregate supply is somewhat sensitive to the price level, becoming steeper as full employment is approached.

Table 20.1 summarises both views.

Key term

Keynesian School a group of economists who believed that the macroeconomy could settle at an equilibrium that was below full employment

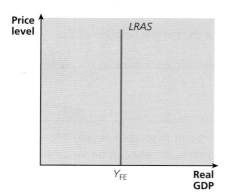

Figure 20.3 Aggregate supply in the long run (the neoclassical view)

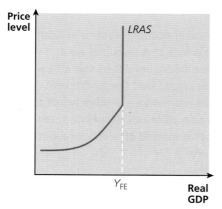

Figure 20.4 Aggregate supply in the long run (the 'Keynesian' view)

Table 20.1 Summary of neoclassical and Keynesian views

Neoclassical view	Keynesian view
LRAS is vertical at the full employment level.	*LRAS* is upward-sloping for a range of output below full employment.
The economy converges rapidly to full employment.	The economy could settle at a level of output below full employment.
Policy intervention is not needed because the economy adjusts rapidly.	Policy intervention may be needed to move towards full employment.
Aggregate supply is not sensitive to the price level.	Aggregate supply is sensitive to the price level when the economy is below full employment.

Knowledge check 20.4

Which group of economists would argue that the long-run aggregate supply (*LRAS*) curve is vertical?

Shifts in the long-run aggregate supply curve

The position of the long-run supply curve depends upon:

- the quantity of factor inputs available
- the effectiveness with which factor inputs are used

The quantity of factor inputs

As far as labour input is concerned, an increase in the size of the workforce will affect the position of aggregate supply. In practice, the size of the labour force tends to change relatively slowly unless substantial international migration is taking place: for example, the expansion of membership of the EU in May 2004 led to significant migration into the UK.

An increase in the quantity of capital will also have this effect, by increasing the capacity of the economy to produce. However, such an increase requires firms to have undertaken investment activity. In other words, the balance of spending between consumption and investment may affect the position of the aggregate supply curve in future periods.

Demographic changes and migration can also affect the size of the workforce in the long run. The UK and many other advanced economies have been characterised by an ageing population in recent years. As more people live longer into retirement, the working population falls as a proportion of the total, and the *LRAS* curve may shift to the left. One response to this pattern has been the changes to the retirement age. Until 2011, the default retirement age in the UK was 65 years, but this was abolished so that those who wished to continue to work beyond 65 could do so. In many developing countries in sub-Saharan Africa, the HIV/AIDS epidemic was especially devastating to people of working age, so reduced the size and effectiveness of the labour force. In-migration can also affect the size of the workforce.

The effectiveness with which factor inputs are used

The effectiveness with which inputs are utilised is another important influence on the position of the aggregate supply curve. Advances in technology are one route through which inputs can be more effectively utilised. New machinery can improve the efficiency with which other inputs are used, and the development of new materials can also have an impact. Such developments can reduce firms' costs and increase the amount of aggregate output that can be produced, leading to a shift in the long-run aggregate supply curve. This is shown in Figure 20.5, where aggregate supply (under Keynesian assumptions) was originally at $LRAS_0$. Technological change that improves efficiency in the use of capital and other inputs means that firms are prepared to supply more output at any given overall price level, so the aggregate supply curve shifts to $LRAS_1$. Under neoclassical assumptions, the *LRAS* curve would be vertical, initially at Y_{FE0}, shifting to Y_{FE1}.

Synoptic link

The effects of demographic changes and migration are analysed in Chapter 18, which deals with interactions in labour markets.

Figure 20.5 A shift in long-run aggregate supply

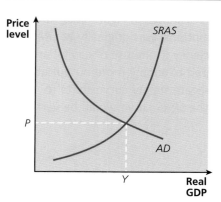

Labour as a factor of production can also become more effective and productive, and can be seen as a form of human capital. Improvements to education and the provision of skills training can improve the productivity of labour, again leading to a rightward shift of long-run aggregate supply. Training and education may be especially important for an economy that is undergoing structural change, so that workers need to be prepared to move between occupations. Government encouragement or provision of such training can improve the flexibility of the labour market and affect aggregate supply.

Exercise 20.2

For each of the following, identify whether the change described will affect short-run or long-run aggregate supply, and whether the result is a leftward or rightward shift:

a a fall in the exchange rate that affects the price of imported inputs
b an increase in the rate of immigration
c an increase in the price of oil
d a reduction in corporation tax
e the introduction of new super-computers

Summary

- It is useful to distinguish between neoclassical and Keynesian views about the shape of the long-run aggregate supply curve.
- Neoclassical economists have argued that the economy always converges rapidly on equilibrium at the natural rate of output, implying that policies affecting aggregate demand have an impact only on prices, leaving real output unaffected. The aggregate supply curve in this world is vertical.
- The Keynesian view is that the economy may settle at an equilibrium that is below full employment, and that there is a range over which the aggregate supply curve slopes upwards.
- The position of the long-run aggregate supply curve depends upon the quantity of inputs available, and on the efficiency with which they are utilised.

Macroeconomic equilibrium in the short run

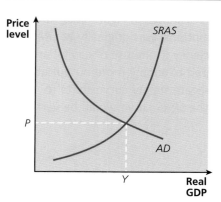

Figure 20.6 Macroeconomic equilibrium

Bringing aggregate demand and aggregate supply together, the overall equilibrium position for the macroeconomy can be identified. In Figure 20.6, with aggregate supply given by *SRAS* and aggregate demand by *AD*, equilibrium is reached at the real GDP level *Y*, with the price level at *P*.

This is an equilibrium, in the sense that if nothing changes then firms and households will have no reason to alter their behaviour in the next period. At the price *P*, aggregate supply is matched by aggregate demand.

Can it be guaranteed that the equilibrium will occur at the full employment level of real GDP? For example, suppose that in Figure 20.7 the output level Y_{FE} corresponds to the full employment level of

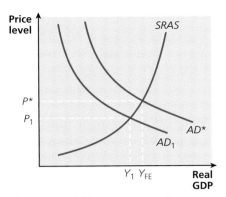

Figure 20.7 Will macroeconomic equilibrium be at full employment?

output — that is, the level of output that represents productive capacity when all factors of production are fully employed. If aggregate demand is at AD^*, the macroeconomic equilibrium is at this full employment output Y_{FE}. However, if the aggregate demand curve is located at AD_1 the equilibrium will occur at Y_1, which is below the full employment level, so there is surplus capacity in the economy.

It may be possible to produce more than Y_{FE} in the short run, but only on a temporary basis, perhaps by the use of overtime. In other words, in the short run it is possible that the $SRAS$ curve could move to a position with equilibrium to the right of Y_{FE}, but this would be unsustainable in the long run, so the $SRAS$ curve would move back to the left.

Macroeconomic equilibrium in the long run

In the long run, the equilibrium level of real output cannot be higher than Y_{FE} and can only be below Y_{FE} under Keynesian assumptions. Figure 20.8 shows the long-run equilibrium. Under Keynesian assumptions, the equilibrium could settle with real output at Y_K and price level P_K. Under neoclassical assumptions, the $LRAS$ curve would be vertical at Y_{FE}, so the price level would be at P_n. Indeed, if the AD curve were to intersect the $LRAS$ curve anywhere in the vertical segment, the equilibrium level of real output would be Y_{FE}, even under Keynesian assumptions.

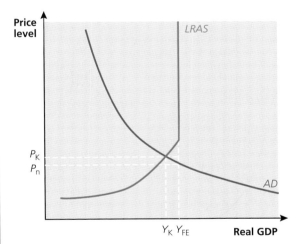

Figure 20.8 Long-run macroeconomic equilibrium

Changes to macroeconomic equilibrium

Having identified macroeconomic equilibrium, it is possible to examine how this will change in response to changes in the macroeconomic environment.

An increase in aggregate demand

The position of the aggregate demand curve depends on the components of aggregate demand: consumption, investment, government spending and net exports. Factors that affect these components will affect aggregate demand.

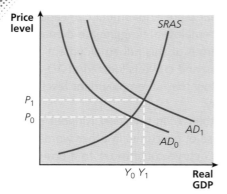

Figure 20.9 A shift in aggregate demand in the short run

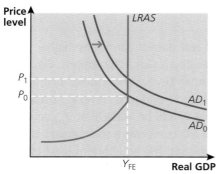

Figure 20.10 A shift in aggregate demand in the long run

Consider Figure 20.9, which shows the short-run position. Suppose that the economy begins in equilibrium with aggregate demand at AD_0. The equilibrium level of real GDP is Y_0, and the price level is at P_0. An increase in government expenditure will affect the position of the aggregate demand curve, shifting it to AD_1. The economy will move to a new equilibrium position, with a higher output level Y_1 and a higher price level P_1.

Figure 20.10 shows the long-run equilibrium. If aggregate demand increases from AD_0 to AD_1, the new equilibrium will be at the intersection of AD and $LRAS$. In this instance, the increase in aggregate demand has no effect on real GDP, but results in a higher equilibrium price level. Only if the economy begins below Y_{FE} would an increase in aggregate demand affect real output — and it would still be accompanied by an increase in the equilibrium price level. Indeed, with a neoclassical (vertical) $LRAS$ curve, this would always be the case.

How can the short-run and long-run situations be reconciled? Figure 20.11(a) demonstrates this, using a neoclassical $LRAS$ curve. The economy begins with real output at its full employment level Y_{FE} and the price level at P_0. There is an increase in aggregate demand from AD_0 to AD_1. Firms respond by increasing output, and there is a movement along the short-run aggregate supply curve $SRAS_0$. Real output has increased to Y_1 and the price level has risen to P_1. As the economy begins to adjust, firms find that their costs rise because of rising raw material prices and wage costs. This means that there is a shift of the short-run aggregate supply curve from $SRAS_0$ to $SRAS_1$. Real output has returned to the full employment level, but the economy is left with a higher equilibrium price level at P_2.

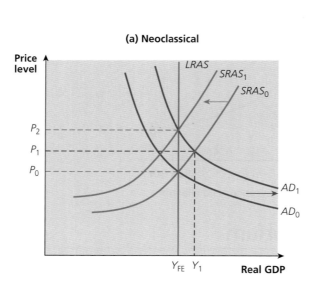

(a) Neoclassical

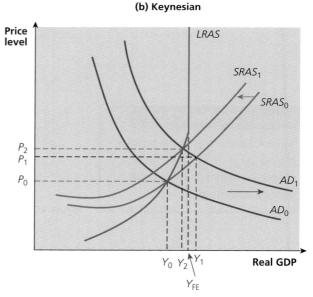

(b) Keynesian

Figure 20.11 Adjustment following an increase in aggregate demand

With a Keynesian AD curve, the impact depends upon the starting position. If the original equilibrium is in the vertical part of the $LRAS$ curve, then the discussion is the same as for the neoclassical version. However, Figure 20.11(b) shows what happens if the initial equilibrium is in the upward-sloping section of the $LRAS$ curve, with real GDP at Y_0 and the price level at P_0. The increase in aggregate demand takes the equilibrium to Y_1 in the short run, with price rising to P_1. Real GDP is above the full employment level, so again the *SRAS* curve will shift back to $SRAS_1$. The final position is with price level P_2 and real GDP at Y_2. The price level has increased by less than in the neoclassical case, and real GDP has moved closer to full employment.

This adjustment process would work in reverse if there were an initial fall in aggregate demand. There would be an initial movement along the *SRAS* curve, with equilibrium real output and price level falling. However, at this point, the neoclassical and Keynesian versions of the subsequent adjustment would differ. Under neoclassical assumptions, the economy would adjust rapidly, and the economy would return to full employment. However, under Keynesian assumptions, the economy could settle in a new equilibrium position with real output and price level both being lower. This situation could persist, and leave the economy below full employment.

The effect of a supply shock in the short run

The *AD/AS* model can also be used to analyse the effects of an external shock that affects aggregate supply. For example, suppose there is an increase in oil prices arising from a disruption to supplies in the Middle East. This raises firms' costs, and leads to a reduction in aggregate supply. Again, we can examine the likely effects on equilibrium.

Figure 20.12 analyses the short-run situation. The economy begins in equilibrium with output at Y_0 and the overall level of prices at P_0. The increase in oil prices causes a movement of the aggregate supply curve from $SRAS_0$ to $SRAS_1$, with aggregate demand unchanged at *AD*. After the economy returns to equilibrium, the new output level has fallen to Y_1 and the overall price level has increased to P_1.

At the time of the first oil price crisis back in 1973–74, the UK government of the day tried to maintain the previous level of real output by stimulating aggregate demand. This had the effect of pushing up the price level, but did not have any noticeable effect on real output. In the long run, the impact of a supply shock would depend upon whether the shock was a temporary or a permanent change. If this change turns out to be permanent, there could be a shift in long-run aggregate supply.

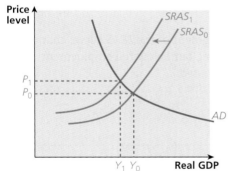

Figure 20.12 A supply shock in the short run

Shifts of and movements along the *AD* and *AS* curves

As in many other circumstances, it is important to be aware of the distinction between shifts *of* the *AD* and *AS* curves, and movements *along* them. Typically, if a shock affects the position of one of the curves, it will lead to a movement *along* the other. For example, if the *AS* curve shifts as a result of a supply shock, the response is a movement *along* the *AD* curve, and vice versa. Thus, in trying to analyse the effects of a shock, the first step is to think about whether the shock affects *AD* or *AS*, and the second is to analyse whether the shock is positive or negative: that is, which way the relevant curve will shift. The move towards a new equilibrium can then be investigated.

For each of the following, decide whether the change affects aggregate demand or (long-run) aggregate supply, and draw a diagram to illustrate the effects on equilibrium real output and overall price level using a Keynesian *LRAS* curve. Undertake this exercise first for a starting position in the vertical part of the *LRAS* curve, and then for an initial position further to the left, where *LRAS* is upward-sloping:

a a technological advance that improves the efficiency of capital

b a financial crisis in Asia that reduces the demand for UK exports

c an improvement in firms' expectations about future demand, such that investment expenditure increases

d the introduction of new health and safety legislation that causes an increase in firms' costs

For each of these changes, indicate whether the result is a shift of or a movement along the *AD* and *LRAS* curves.

Summary

- Macroeconomic equilibrium occurs at the intersection of *AD* and *SRAS* in the short run, and at the intersection of *AD* and *LRAS* in the long run.
- It is possible to analyse the effects of changes in the factors that influence aggregate demand and aggregate supply.
- Changes in the components of aggregate demand shift the aggregate demand curve. This causes a movement along the short-run aggregate supply curve.
- In the long run, within the vertical segment of the *LRAS* curve, changes in *AD* affect only the overall price level, but below full employment both price and real output will be affected.

AD/AS model and macroeconomic indicators

Synoptic link

The key macroeconomic indicators will be explained more fully in Chapters 22 to 27, and the performance of the UK economy is discussed in Chapter 28.

Changes in aggregate demand and aggregate supply can affect the key macroeconomic indicators used to monitor the performance of an economy. These key indicators are associated with the targets of macroeconomic policy, and include:

- stability in prices
- full employment
- economic growth
- stability on the balance of payments
- a balanced government budget
- a fair distribution of income
- safeguarding the environment

For the moment, the focus will be on the first three of these objectives.

Stability in prices

The *AD/AS* model explains how the equilibrium overall price level for an economy is reached. It also explains how an increase in aggregate demand when the economy is at full employment will result in a higher equilibrium price level, but with no change in the level of real output. If aggregate demand continues to increase, then the price level will continue to rise, and the result is inflation.

Full employment

When the macroeconomy is in equilibrium at a given level of real output, there is an implied level of employment — and hence a level of unemployment. The position of the *AD/AS* equilibrium therefore determines whether the economy is at full employment. With a neoclassical vertical *LRAS* curve, the economy always returns rapidly to full employment. However, with a Keynesian interpretation of the *AD/AS* model it is possible for the macroeconomy to settle in equilibrium below the full employment level. In this situation, a shift in aggregate demand is needed to take the economy back towards full employment.

Economic growth

Long-run economic growth can be seen as a shift to the right of the long-run aggregate supply curve. This may be caused by an increase in the quantity of factors of production available in the economy, or an improvement in the efficiency with which they are utilised. Short-run economic growth in the *AD/AS* model may be a short-run response to an increase in aggregate demand, which may not be sustainable if it takes the economy temporarily beyond the full employment level. Alternatively, it may be a situation in which the macroeconomy is returning to equilibrium having been positioned below full employment.

Summary
- In using the *AD/AS* model to analyse policy options, it is useful to distinguish between neoclassical and Keynesian views about the shape of the aggregate supply curve.
- Neoclassical economists have argued that the economy always converges rapidly on equilibrium at the natural rate of output, implying that policies affecting aggregate demand have an impact only on prices, leaving real output unaffected. The long-run aggregate supply curve in this world is vertical.
- The Keynesian view is that the economy may settle at an equilibrium that is below full employment, and that there is a range over which the long-run aggregate supply curve slopes upwards.

The importance of expectations

Land previously used to grow food crops is increasingly being used to grow biofuel crops

In mid-2008, the UK economy was seen to be in a state of crisis. Economic growth had slowed (although it was still positive, so technically the economy had not yet entered into recession). Inflation had been affected by a number of world events. China's economy was continuing to expand at an unprecedented rate, and was having an impact on world prices by its strong demand for oil, foodstuffs and other commodities. The growth in demand for biofuels was fuelling a rise in the prices of some key food items, including rice and wheat. This was partly because land previously used to grow food was being turned over to grow crops to be made into biofuels. These effects were beginning to take their toll on the UK economy. Surveys of business confidence showed that firms were expecting a recession, and house prices were falling.

Follow-up questions

a Identify factors described above that would be expected to affect aggregate demand and/or aggregate supply. Draw diagrams to illustrate the effects of these on macroeconomic equilibrium.

b The Brexit process will affect the UK economy in many ways. How do you think these effects can be portrayed in the *AD/AS* framework?

CHAPTER 20 QUESTIONS

A Multiple-choice questions

1 Which of the following is **not** likely to lead to an increase in AS?

   a Increased government spending on a new road network
   b Increased foreign investment
   c Increased spending on imports
   d Increased education levels in society

2 The neoclassical approach to long-run aggregate supply suggests:

   a An increase in AD will not lead to an increase in real GDP
   b An increase in AD will lead to an increase in GDP
   c An increase in LRAS will lead to a contraction of AD
   d A decrease in LRAS will not lead to a contraction of AD

3 The Keynesian approach to long-run aggregate supply suggests:

   a An increase in AD will lead to an increase in GDP
   b An increase in AD will not lead to an increase in GDP
   c An increase in AD will lead to an increase in the price level
   d It is impossible to state

B Knowledge and understanding questions

4 Explain what is meant by the term 'macroeconomic equilibrium'. [2 marks]

5 Explain, with the aid of a diagram, the effects of an increase in SRAS on macroeconomic equilibrium in the short run. [4 marks]

6 Explain two factors that could cause the LRAS curve to shift to the right. [4 marks]

C Stimulus response question

7 HS2 is a government-led project that aims to link London with many cities in the north of England. The construction of this high-speed rail network is due to be completed over the next 15 years. The project is likely to cost over £50 billion, although some estimates say it could cost up to £200 billion.

   a Explain how the building of HS2 might affect AD in the economy. [4 marks]
   b Explain how HS2 might affect LRAS in the economy. [4 marks]

Chapter 21

The multiplier and the accelerator

Chapter 20 showed how aggregate demand and aggregate supply combine to produce equilibrium in real GDP and the price level. The focus was on alternative views about aggregate supply. We now explore additional ideas about the factors that influence changes in aggregate demand, beginning with the national income multiplier that arose from the writings of Keynes in his General Theory. We also introduce the idea of the accelerator, which may reinforce the multiplier effect.

Learning objectives

After studying this chapter, you should be able to:

- explain, with the aid of a diagram, the national income multiplier
- explain and calculate average and marginal propensities to consume, save and withdraw
- explain factors that determine the size of the national income multiplier
- explain and calculate the size of the national income multiplier
- explain, with the aid of a diagram, the impact of the national income multiplier on aggregate demand
- explain, with the aid of a diagram, the accelerator
- explain, with the aid of a diagram, the impact of the accelerator on aggregate supply
- explain, with the aid of a diagram, output gaps in the context of the aggregate demand and supply model and a production possibility curve (*PPC*)
- evaluate the causes and consequences of an output gap

The multiplier

Key term

multiplier the ratio of a change in equilibrium real income to the autonomous change that brought it about

In his General Theory, Keynes pointed out that there may be **multiplier** effects in response to certain types of expenditure. Suppose that the government increases its expenditure by £1 billion, perhaps by increasing its road-building programme. The effect of this is to generate incomes for households — for example, those of the contractors hired to build the road. Those contractors then spend part of the additional income (and save part of it). By spending part of the extra money earned, an additional income stream is generated for shopkeepers and café owners, who in turn spend part of *their* additional income, and so on. Therefore, the original increase in government spending sparks off further income generation and spending, causing the multiplier effect. In effect, equilibrium output may change by more than the original increase in expenditure.

Notice that it is the act of spending that allows these multiplier effects to be perpetuated. However, if the households who receive additional income do not spend some of that income, the effects are diluted. In other words, injections into the circular flow can initiate multiplier effects, but leakages determine the size of the effect.

The size of this multiplier effect depends upon how much of the additional income is:

- saved by households
- spent on imported goods
- returned to the government in the form of direct taxes

These items constitute leakages from the system, in the sense that they detract from the multiplier effect. For example, if households save a high proportion of their additional income, this clearly reduces the multiplier effect, as the next round of spending will be that much lower. This seems to go against the traditional view that saving is good for the economy.

The average and marginal propensities to consume

Synoptic link

Keynes's ideas about the consumption function, in which the most important influence on consumption is disposable income, were explained in Chapter 19. The importance of the margin is explained in Chapter 7.

Key terms

average propensity to consume the proportion of income that households devote to consumer expenditure
marginal propensity to consume (mpc) the proportion of additional income devoted to consumer expenditure
marginal propensity to save (mps) the proportion of additional income that is saved by households

Synoptic link

The circular flow model was introduced in Chapter 19.

In order to calculate the size of the multiplier effect, some additional ideas and definitions are needed, building on Keynes's ideas about consumption.

Keynes defined the **average propensity to consume** as the ratio of consumer expenditure to income, and the **marginal propensity to consume (mpc)** as the proportion of an increase in disposable income that households would devote to consumer expenditure. The **marginal propensity to save (mps)** is the proportion of additional income that is saved by households.

Study tip

A 'propensity' to do something is a tendency. In the present context, economic agents are said to have a propensity (tendency) to use any additional (marginal) income in a number of ways — to consume, to save, to spend on imports, to tax, and so on.

Quantitative skills 21.1

Calculating the average and marginal propensities to consume

Suppose that in an economy, household consumption (C) is £80 and disposable income (Y) is £100. The average propensity to consume is calculated as $C/Y = 80/100 = 0.8$. If disposable income increases to 110 and consumption rises to 87, we can calculate the marginal propensity to consume as the proportion of the increase in income that is devoted to consumption. We need to divide the change in consumption by the change in income. In other words, it is $(87 − 80)/(110 − 100) = 0.7$.

The important element in considering the multiplier is the role played by injections and leakages, which appeared in the circular flow model. The multiplier effects that Keynes discussed are triggered by injections into the circular flow, whereas the size of the multiplier effects is determined by the leakages.

marginal propensity to import
(*mpm*) the proportion of
additional income that is spent
on imports of goods and services
marginal propensity to tax
(*mpt*) the proportion of
additional income that is taxed
marginal propensity to
withdraw (*mpw*) the
proportion of additional income
that is withdrawn from the
circular flow — the sum of the
marginal propensities to save,
import and tax

Knowledge check 21.1

How will the multiplier be affected
if there is an increase in the
marginal propensity to consume?

Exercise 21.1

Calculate the multiplier if
households save 20% of any
additional income that they
receive and spend 10% on
imports. Assume that the marginal
tax rate is 10%. Check how the
multiplier changes if the marginal
tax rate increases to 20%.

The leakages from the circular flow are savings, imports and taxes. In
the same way that the marginal propensity to consume is defined as the
proportion of additional income devoted to consumer expenditure, the
marginal propensity to import (*mpm*) is the proportion of additional
income that is spent on imported goods and services, and the **marginal
propensity to tax (*mpt*)** is the proportion of additional income that
is taxed.

In calculating the size of the multiplier, it is the total size of the
leakages that is important, and we define the **marginal propensity
to withdraw (*mpw*)** as the proportion of additional income that is
withdrawn from the circular flow — the sum of the marginal propensities
to save, import and tax.

In summary:

$$mpw = mps + mpt + mpm$$

$$mpc = 1 - mpw$$

The injections into the circular flow come in the form of government
expenditure, investment and exports. The fact that injections can have a
multiplied effect on equilibrium output and income seems to make the
government potentially very powerful, as by increasing its expenditure it
can have a multiplied effect on the economy's output and income.

Quantitative skills 21.2

Calculating the multiplier

A numerical value for the multiplier can be calculated with reference to the
withdrawals from the circular flow. Suppose that the *mps* is 0.25, the *mpm*
is 0.1 and the *mpt* is 0.15. The *mpw* is then 0.25 + 0.1 + 0.15 = 0.5. The
multiplier formula is 1 divided by the marginal propensity to withdraw
(1/*mpw*). If the *mpw* is 0.5, then the value of the multiplier is 2, so for every
£100 million injection into the circular flow, there will be a £200 million
increase in equilibrium output.

It is worth noting that the size of the leakages may depend in part
upon whether or not firms are able to increase output. If domestic supply
is inflexible, and therefore unable to meet an increase in demand, more of
the increase in income will spill over into purchasing imports, and this will
dilute the multiplier effect.

Exercise 21.2

Identify each of the following as an injection or a leakage, and state whether
it increases or decreases the impact of the multiplier:
a saving by households
b expenditure by central government
c spending by UK residents on imported goods and services
d expenditure by firms on investment
e spending by overseas residents on UK goods and services
f income tax payments

In terms of the *AD/AS* diagram, the existence of the multiplier means
that if there is an increase in an injection (e.g. investment or government

spending), the *AD* curve moves further to the right than it otherwise would have done, because of the multiplier effects. Figure 21.1 shows this. The initial increase in spending takes aggregate demand from AD_0 to AD_1, but subsequently, the multiplier effect pushes aggregate demand further to the right, to AD_2.

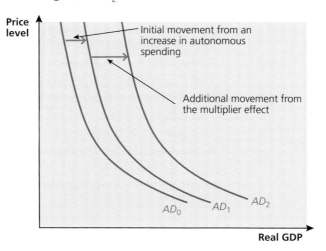

Figure 21.1 The effect of the multiplier on aggregate demand

The multiplier and macroeconomic equilibrium

It is important to be aware that the multiplier affects the extent to which the *AD* curve shifts when there is an increase in autonomous expenditure, but this does not mean that there will necessarily be a long-lasting effect on macroeconomic equilibrium. If you look back at Figure 20.10 on page 286, you can see that an increase in aggregate demand when the initial equilibrium is in the vertical part of the long-run aggregate supply curve does not affect the equilibrium level of real GDP, but merely leads to an increase in the price level. The multiplier may affect the extent of the rightward shift of *AD*, but this will only be translated into a higher price level when the economy returns to equilibrium.

If the initial equilibrium was in the upward-sloping part of a Keynesian *AD* curve, then the multiplier would carry the economy closer to the full employment level of real GDP, but even this effect would be diluted somewhat by an increase in the equilibrium price level.

Summary

- An increase in autonomous spending (an injection into the circular flow) may give rise to a magnified impact on aggregate demand through a multiplier effect.
- The marginal propensity to consume is the proportion of additional income that households devote to consumer spending.
- The marginal propensity to withdraw depends upon the marginal propensities to save, import and tax.
- The size of the multiplier depends upon the marginal propensity to withdraw.
- The multiplier effect is diluted in the long run as the economy moves to equilibrium.

The accelerator

Key term

accelerator a theory by which the level of investment depends upon the change in real output

Knowledge check 21.3

How will the accelerator work if firms expect there to be a fall in demand for their products?

Synoptic link

Such cyclical fluctuations in output are a common feature of many economies, and give rise to what is known as the economic cycle, which is discussed in Chapter 22.

The idea of the multiplier is based on the induced effects of expenditure that spread the initial effects of an increase in spending. A similar notion is that of the **accelerator**. The notion of the accelerator arises from one of the driving forces behind firms' investment. Some investment is needed for depreciation (i.e. replacement for old or outdated equipment and to allow for wear and tear). However, most investment is needed for when firms wish to expand capacity. If there is an increase in demand for a firm's product (or if a firm expects there to be an increase in demand), it may need to expand capacity in order to meet the increased demand. This suggests that one of the determinants of the level of investment is a change in expected demand. Notice that it is the *change* in demand that is important, rather than the level, and it is this that leads to the notion of the accelerator. In other words, if a firm sees a significant expansion in demand for its product, this can initiate the accelerator if the firm expects this change to signal more increases in the future.

Suppose that the economy is below full employment and begins to recover. As the recovery begins, demand begins to increase, and firms undertake investment in order to expand capacity. In other words, the accelerator effect cuts in, as firms observe the change in demand and need more capital to meet expected future demand. However, as the economy approaches full capacity, the growth rate slows down — and hence investment falls, as it reacts to the change in output. This occurs because the accelerator goes into reverse.

The multiplier and accelerator interact with each other. If there is an increase in output following an increase in aggregate demand, the accelerator induces an increase in investment. The increase in investment then has a multiplier effect that induces an additional increase in demand. In this way, the multiplier and accelerator reinforce each other. The downside to this is that the same thing happens when output slows, as this leads to a fall in investment, which has negative multiplier effects. This interaction between the multiplier and the accelerator can result in cyclical fluctuations in the level of output.

The accelerator and aggregate supply

There is an extra twist to the accelerator effect. As firms increase investment expenditure, the productive capacity of the economy increases. This means that there is an increase in the full employment level of real GDP. In other words, the long-run aggregate supply curve shifts to the right.

Figure 21.2 shows how this process works. Assume a neoclassical long-run aggregate supply curve, which initially is at $LRAS_0$. The economy starts in equilibrium with real GDP at Y_{FE}. The equilibrium price level is P_0. Firms anticipate an increase in demand, and undertake investment in order to increase capacity, so there is an increase in aggregate demand, from AD_0 to AD_1. In the short run, there is an extension of aggregate supply, and a movement along the $SRAS$ curve to real GDP at Y_1 and price level P_1. However, the long-run effect of the increase in investment is to lead to an increase in long-run aggregate supply, so the $LRAS$ curve shifts to the right. In Figure 21.2, the shift results in a new equilibrium level of full employment real GDP at Y_1, (but notice that the new level could be to the right or left of this position).

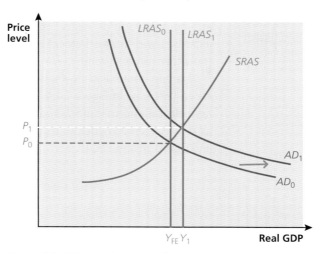

Figure 21.2 The accelerator and macroeconomic equilibrium

If the economy settles at the new full employment level of real GDP, firms may cease to expect further increases in demand and reduce their investment expenditure, which would then put the accelerator process into reverse.

Summary
- The accelerator arises when firms increase investment because they expect demand to increase.
- The accelerator effect reinforces the multiplier when firms respond to a change in real GDP.
- The increase in investment affects aggregate supply in the long run by expanding the productive capacity of the economy.
- The interaction between the accelerator and the multiplier can give rise to fluctuations in equilibrium real GDP.

An output gap

Key term

output gap the difference between the actual level of real GDP and the full employment level

We have seen that the macroeconomy may be subject to external shocks that may take it away from its equilibrium position, so at any point in time real GDP may deviate from the full employment level, either above or below. The difference between actual GDP and the full employment level is known as the **output gap**.

At any point in time, real GDP can be above or below the full employment level, so the output gap can be positive or negative. When real GDP is above the full employment level (as it can be before it readjusts), the output gap is positive. If real GDP is below the full employment level, the output gap is negative.

The output gap can be identified through an *AD/AS* diagram, as in Figure 21.3. The figure shows a Keynesian *LRAS* curve, with the *AD* curve

Synoptic link

The way in which real GDP may fluctuate through time around an underlying trend is known as the economic cycle, and is discussed in Chapter 22.

initially located in such a position that the equilibrium level of output is at Y_1, which is below the full employment rate (at Y_{FE}). The output gap is the difference between the actual and potential levels of real GDP (i.e. $Y_1 - Y_{FE}$). In this instance, the output gap is negative. If you look back at Figure 20.11(a) on page 286, you can see that when aggregate demand increases with a neoclassical *LRAS* curve, there is a positive output gap in the short run, given by $Y_1 - Y_{FE}$.

The gap could also be shown in relation to the production possibility curve (*PPC*), as in Figure 21.4. The figure shows a country's *PPC* between agricultural and manufactured goods. If it is producing at a point such as *A*, it is operating below its potential capacity output (which would be any point on the *PPC*).

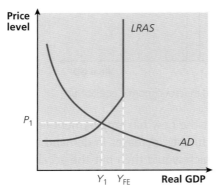

Figure 21.3 The output gap in the *AD/AS* model

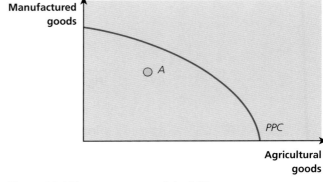

Figure 21.4 The output gap and the *PPC*

Causes and consequences of an output gap

Knowledge check 21.4

How would a positive output gap be shown on a *PPC* diagram?

A positive output gap may occur if there is an increase in aggregate demand when the economy is already at full employment, perhaps because of an increase in government expenditure or export demand. In the short run, GDP can rise above the full employment rate, with a movement up along the short-run aggregate supply curve, possibly reinforced by multiplier effects. Firms will be prepared to supply more output in the short run in response to the increase in demand, by using factor inputs more intensively. However, this will be unsustainable in the longer run, as prices begin to rise and firms face higher input costs. The consequence is therefore that there will be upward pressure on the price level, but little if any effect on real GDP in the long term.

A negative output gap arises when real GDP falls below the full employment level. This could occur if there is a negative external shock to aggregate demand, for example if there is a global slowdown that results in a fall in the demand for exports, or if the government decides to cut back on expenditure. The consequences of this depend on whether the decrease in aggregate demand is permanent or temporary, and whether the economy faces a neoclassical or a Keynesian long-run aggregate supply curve.

The consequences of a negative output gap are potentially more significant under Keynesian assumptions about aggregate supply, as compared with the neoclassical view. If, under neoclassical assumptions, the long-run aggregate supply curve is vertical, then the economy will return to equilibrium, although how rapidly is open to debate.

Evaluation of the output gap

Fluctuations in aggregate demand can give rise to an output gap, which may be positive or negative. Under neoclassical assumptions, the economy returns rapidly to its full-employment equilibrium. This suggests that an output gap would only be evident in the short run. Such fluctuations do arise, sometimes on a regular cycle, as is explained in Chapter 22.

Any of the components of aggregate demand (*AD*) can be the source of an increase in *AD*. For example, it could be that the government increases its expenditure because it believes that unemployment is higher than it should be, or perhaps firms have high expectations for the future and decide to increase their investment spending.

If the economy is subjected to an increase in *AD* when it is at full employment, then real GDP can move beyond the full employment level, but only during the adjustment period. This may have beneficial effects on real GDP in the short run, but the question is whether those short-run gains are sufficient to offset the long-run increase in the price level that is a consequence of the increase in *AD*. If the increase is repeated in subsequent periods, the consequences will be more severe, as this will result in demand-pull inflation.

The causes and consequences of a decrease in *AD* are of especial importance for the economy. Again, any of the components of aggregate demand can be a source of a decrease in *AD*. For example, if firms form pessimistic expectations about the future demand for their products, they may decide to reduce their investment spending. There are many factors that could give rise to such a change, such as the uncertainty during the Brexit negotiations, or the trade war initiated by President Trump.

The consequences of such a fall in *AD* depend crucially on whether the economy is facing a neoclassical or a Keynesian long-run aggregate supply (*LRAS*) curve. Neoclassical economists would argue that there are forces in the economy that would carry the economy back to full employment — possibly quite rapidly. However, with a Keynesian *LRAS*, the economy could settle at an equilibrium that is below full employment. This will occur if the intersection with *AD* comes in the upward-sloping segment of the Keynesian *LRAS* curve. The resulting negative output gap could then persist, with consequences for long-lasting high unemployment.

The impact of a decrease in *AD* depends crucially on whether the change is temporary or permanent, and on the shape of the *LRAS* curve and the speed with which the economy is able to adjust back to long-run equilibrium.

Synoptic link

Inflation is where prices increase year-on-year. Demand-pull inflation and its consequences are explained in Chapter 25.

Exercise 21.3

Suppose an economy that is already experiencing a negative output gap experiences a fall in the demand for exports.
a Using Keynesian assumptions about *LRAS*, use a diagram to show how the equilibrium will be affected.
b How will your discussion differ if the *LRAS* follows neoclassical assumptions?

Summary
- An output gap arises when real GDP is above or below the full employment level.
- The output gap can be positive (when real GDP is above the full employment level), or negative (when real GDP is below full employment).
- Under Keynesian assumptions about long-run aggregate supply, a negative output gap may persist.

CHAPTER 21 QUESTIONS

A Multiple-choice questions

1 If households have an income of £5,000 and consumption is £3,500, what is the average propensity to consume?

   a 0.8   **b** 0.7   **c** 1.43   **d** 1.7

2 The accelerator effect is based on increases and decreases in which component of *AD*?

   a Consumption   **c** Government spending

   b Exports   **d** Investment

3 If real GDP is below the full employment level then this is said to be a:

   a Negative output gap   **c** Recession

   b Positive output gap   **d** Slump

B Knowledge and understanding questions

4 Explain what is meant by the 'national income multiplier'.   [2 marks]

5 Explain, with the aid of a diagram, the effect of the accelerator on aggregate demand.   [4 marks]

6 Explain, with the aid of a diagram, what is meant by a positive output gap.   [4 marks]

C Stimulus response question

7 After the credit crunch, the UK experienced a negative output gap. Although remaining negative, this output gap has been shrinking as the UK economy has experienced economic growth.

   a Explain one possible reason why the UK economy may have experienced a negative output gap after the credit crunch.   [2 marks]

   b Evaluate the possible consequences for the UK economy of a negative output gap.   [8 marks]

SECTION
2

MACROECONOMICS

Part 7
Economic policy objectives

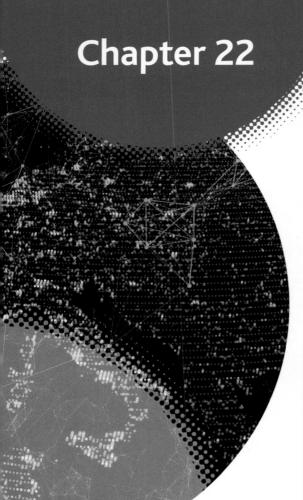

Chapter 22

Economic growth

One of society's prime responsibilities is to provide a reasonable standard of living for its citizens and to promote their well-being. Hence one of the major objectives for economic policy in the long run is to enable improvements in well-being, and in order to do this it is first necessary to expand the resources available within society. A key element in this process is to achieve economic growth, which is the subject of this chapter. However, there may be more to well-being than just growth, and the chapter also explores some of the limitations of a strategy that aims to maximise GDP growth. In reality, GDP tends to fluctuate over time around an underlying trend. This is known as the economic cycle, and is discussed towards the end of the chapter.

> ## Learning objectives
> After studying this chapter, you should be able to:
> - explain economic growth
> - explain the policy objective of economic growth
> - explain real and nominal gross domestic product (GDP) and changes in GDP over time
> - explain, with the aid of a diagram, short-run and long-run economic growth
> - explain and calculate economic growth rates
> - explain and calculate GDP per capita
> - explain the different stages of the economic cycle
> - evaluate the causes and consequences of economic growth in the short run and the long run

What is economic growth?

Macroeconomics Part 7

Key terms

long-run economic growth the expansion of the productive capacity of an economy

short-run economic growth an increase in actual GDP

Economic growth is one of the most carefully monitored indicators of the performance of an economy. Whenever the latest growth figures are issued by the Office for National Statistics (ONS), or forecasts are published by the Treasury or other bodies, the Press pick up on it and offer their pronouncements about whether the economy is doing better or worse than expected. But what do we mean by 'economic growth'? From an economist's perspective, there are two key ways of looking at economic growth.

Long-run economic growth can be thought of as an expansion of the productive capacity of an economy. If you like, it is an expansion of the potential output of the economy.

Short-run economic growth is where aggregate output increases in the short run in response to an increase in aggregate demand or an improvement in utilisation of the factors of production — for example, when unemployment falls. This is measured in terms of the rate of change of gross domestic product (GDP).

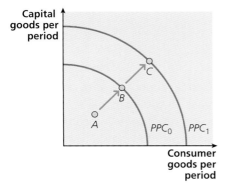

Figure 22.1 Short- and long-run economic growth

Chapter 1 discussed economic growth in terms of the production possibility curve (*PPC*). In Figure 1.4 on page 13, long-run economic growth was characterised as an outward movement of the production possibility curve from PPC_0 to PPC_1. In other words, economic growth enables a society to produce more goods and services in any given period as a result of an expansion in its resources. Short-run economic growth takes place when an economy moves towards the *PPC* from a point *within* it. Remember that if the economy is operating inside its *PPC*, it is failing to use all of its factors of production effectively, so a move towards the *PPC* is possible when employment rises and output increases as a result.

Notice that when economists measure economic growth using the rate of change of GDP as an indicator, they are not necessarily measuring long-run economic growth. The actual rate of GDP growth may reflect the increased utilisation of factors of production, which is not the same as an increase in potential GDP.

In Figure 22.1, a movement from *A* to *B* represents a move to the *PPC*. This is an increase in actual output resulting from using up surplus capacity in the economy, and represents short-run (actual) economic growth — notice that moving from *A* to *B* does not entail an increase in productive capacity. On the other hand, a movement of the *PPC* itself, enabling the move from *B* to *C*, represents long-run economic growth. When economists observe a change in GDP, they cannot easily distinguish between the two sorts of effect, especially if the economy is subject to an economic cycle — in other words, if the economy is not always operating at full capacity. Long-run economic growth can also be seen in terms of the underlying trend rate of growth of real GDP.

Long-run economic growth can also be shown in the *AD/AS* model as an increase in long-run aggregate supply. For example, in Figure 22.2, there has been such an increase, with a shift from $LRAS_0$ to $LRAS_1$. The full employment level of real GDP increases from Y_{FE0} to Y_{FE1}, reflecting the expansion of the productive capacity of the economy. Associated with this shift, the price level falls from P_0 to P_1 and there is an extension in aggregate demand.

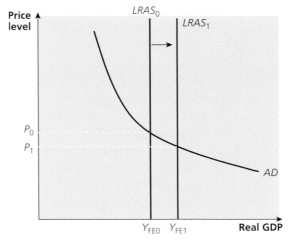

Figure 22.2 An increase in long-run aggregate supply

Knowledge check 22.1

If there is an increase in the full-employment level of real GDP, would this be classified as short-run or long-run economic growth?

Exercise 22.1

Which of the following represent long-run economic growth, and which may just entail a move to the *PPC* (i.e. short-run economic growth)?

a an increase in the rate of change of potential output

b a fall in the unemployment rate

c improved work practices that increase labour productivity

d an increase in the proportion of the population joining the labour force

e an increase in the utilisation of capital

f a rightward shift in the *LRAS* curve

The policy objective of economic growth

Expanding the availability of resources in an economy enables the standard of living in the country to increase. In the industrial economies, populations have come to expect steady improvements in incomes and resources. The economy's performance in terms of expansion of resources is a key indicator of success in macroeconomic policy, which explains why the media and politicians monitor it so closely.

Therefore for any society, economic growth is likely to be seen as a fundamental objective — perhaps even the most important one, as it could be argued that other policy objectives are subsidiary to the growth target. In other words, the control of inflation and the maintenance of full employment are seen as important short-run objectives, because their achievement facilitates long-run economic growth.

Synoptic link

These other key objectives of macroeconomic policy are discussed in Chapters 23–26.

The importance of data

Study tip

Although data are important in economics, notice that it is *not* necessary to learn lots of detailed facts and statistics about the UK economy. However, it is of course important to be familiar with recent events and general trends in the performance of the economy.

To monitor the performance of the economy, it is crucial to be able to observe how the economy is functioning, and for this you need data. Economics, especially macroeconomics, is mainly a non-experimental discipline. It is not possible to conduct experiments to see how the economy reacts to various stimuli in order to learn how it works. Instead, it is necessary to observe the economy, and to come to a judgement about whether or not its performance is satisfactory, and whether the evidence supports macroeconomic theories about how the economy works.

Most of the economic statistics used by economists are collected and published by various government agencies. Such data in the UK are published mainly by the Office for National Statistics (ONS). Data on other countries are published by the International Monetary Fund (IMF), the World Bank and the United Nations, as well as national sources. There is little alternative to relying on such sources because the accurate collection of data is an expensive and time-consuming business.

Care needs to be taken in the interpretation of economic data. It is important to be aware of how the data are compiled, and the extent to which they are indicators of what economists are trying to measure. It is also important to remember that the economic environment is ever changing, and that single causes can rarely be ascribed to the economic events that are observed. This is because the ceteris paribus condition that underlies so much economic analysis is rarely fulfilled in reality. In other words, you cannot rely on 'other things remaining constant' when using data about the real world.

It is also important to realise that even the ONS cannot observe with absolute accuracy. Indeed, some data take so long to be assembled that early estimates are provisional in nature and subject to later revision as more information becomes available. Data used in international comparisons must be treated with even greater caution.

Real and nominal measurements

The measurement of economic variables poses many dilemmas for statisticians. Not least is the fundamental problem of what to use as units of measurement. Suppose economists wish to measure the total output produced in an economy during successive years. In the first place, they cannot use volume measures. They may be able to count how many computers, cars, tins of paint and cauliflowers the economy produces — but how do they add all these different items together to produce a total?

An obvious solution is to use the money values. Given prices for all the items, it is possible to calculate the money values of all these goods and so produce a measurement of the total output produced in an economy during a year in terms of pounds sterling. However, this is just the beginning of the problem because, in order to monitor changes in total output between two years, it is important to be aware that not only do the volumes of goods produced change but so too do their prices. In effect, this means that, if pounds sterling are used as the unit of measurement, the unit of measurement will change from one year to the next as prices change.

This is a problem that is not faced by most of the physical sciences. After all, the length of a metre does not alter from one year to the next, so if the length of something is being measured, the unit is fixed. Economists, however, have to make allowance for changing prices when measuring in pounds sterling.

Measurements made using prices that are current at the time a transaction takes place are known as measurements of **nominal values**. When prices are rising, these nominal measurements will always overstate the extent to which an economic variable is growing through time. Clearly, to analyse performance, economists will be more interested in **'real' values** — that is, the quantities produced after having removed the effects of price changes. One way in which these real measures can be obtained is by taking the volumes produced in each year and valuing these quantities at the prices that prevailed in some base year. This then enables allowance to be made for the changes in prices that take place, permitting a focus on the real values. These can be thought of as being measured at *constant prices*.

For example, suppose that last year you bought a tub of ice cream for £3, but that prices have risen, so that this year you had to pay £3.30 for the same tub. Your volume of consumption of the item has not changed, but your spending has increased. If you were to use the value of your

Synoptic link

Index numbers are explained in Chapter 25, which sets out how a price index is used to represent the general level of prices in an economy.

Key terms

real GDP GDP at constant prices, taking account of changing prices through time

nominal GDP GDP at current prices, taking no account of changing prices through time

Study tip

It is really important to remember that economic growth is not measured by the level of GDP but by the percentage rate of change of real GDP.

spending to measure changes in consumption through time, it would be misleading, as you know that your *real* consumption has not changed at all (so is still £3), although its *nominal* value has increased to £3.30.

Quantitative skills 22.1

Converting nominal measurements to real

It is worth being aware that the ratio of the current (nominal) value of a variable to its constant price (real) value (multiplied by 100) is a price index. For example:

$$100 \times \frac{\text{nominal GDP}}{\text{real GDP}} \quad \text{is a price index}$$

So, if we know GDP at current prices and we know the relevant price index, we can calculate the real value of GDP.

For example, in 2017, GDP for the UK in current prices was estimated to be £2.038 billion, and the underlying price index was 104 (based on 2015 = 100). The real value of GDP can therefore be calculated as

$$100 \times \frac{2.038}{104} = \text{£1.960 billion}$$

The same principle applies to other economic variables that change through time. For example, we need to distinguish between **real GDP** and **nominal GDP**. Economic growth in a given period is therefore measured by the percentage rate of change of real GDP.

Quantitative skills 22.2

Calculating a percentage change

In macroeconomics it is often important to be able to calculate the percentage change in a variable. For example, it may be that there is interest in knowing how rapidly prices are changing, or in calculating the rate of economic growth. In the earlier example, the price of a tub of ice cream was supposed to have increased from £3 to £3.30. To calculate the percentage change in the price, calculate the change in price (3.30 − 3 = 0.30) and express that as a percentage of the original value. In other words, the percentage change is:

$$100 \times (3.30 - 3) \div 3 = 10\%$$

Notice that the change in the variable is always expressed as a percentage of the initial value, not the final value.

Knowledge check 22.4

If a country's real GDP was £120 billion and the underlying price index was 105, what would be the value of nominal GDP?

Summary

- Economic growth is important as it allows improvements in the standard of living of a country's citizens over time.
- Economic growth is primarily monitored through changes in GDP.
- There is a distinction between real GDP (GDP measured at constant prices) and nominal GDP (which does not take changing prices into account).
- The percentage change in real GDP measures economic growth in a given period.
- As economists cannot easily conduct experiments in order to test economic theory, they rely on the use of economic data: that is, observations of the world around them.
- Data measured in money terms need to be handled carefully, as prices change over time, thereby affecting the units in which many economic variables are measured.

GDP and growth

Table 22.1 provides data on real GDP for the period 2005–17. Calculate the growth rate of GDP for each year from 2005/06 to 2016/17. In which year was growth at its highest and in which year was it at its lowest?

Table 22.1 Real GDP in the UK, 2005–17 (£bn)

Year	Real GDP
2005	1,676
2006	1,717
2007	1,758
2008	1,749
2009	1,676
2010	1,704
2011	1,729
2012	1,755
2013	1,791
2014	1,845
2015	1,889
2016	1,925
2017	1,960

Key term

gross national income (GNI) GDP plus net income from abroad

GDP is a way of measuring the total output of an economy over a period of time, and its rate of change is used as a measure of economic growth. Although real GDP can provide an indicator of the quantity of resources available to citizens of a country in a given period, as an assessment of the standard of living it has its critics.

GDP focuses on the domestic economy. However, it is also important to recognise that residents of the economy also receive some income from abroad — and some income earned in the domestic economy is sent abroad. **Gross national income (GNI)** takes into account these income flows between countries, and for some purposes is a more helpful measure — indeed, this is the standard measure used by the World Bank to compare average incomes across countries. This measure was formerly known as gross national product (GNP).

Figure 19.3 on page 267 shows real GDP since 1948. You can see that during this period, real GDP grew in almost every year but that there are some years where it dipped. In particular, notice how real GDP fell after 2007 before rising again.

It is important to note that this shows the *level* of real GDP, so to calculate growth it is necessary to compute the annual rate of change. This is done in Figure 22.3, which shows the annual growth rate of real GDP in the UK since 1960. You can see that it is quite difficult to determine the underlying trend because the year-to-year movements are so volatile. Figure 22.4 takes 5-yearly average growth rates over the same period, with the horizontal red line showing the underlying trend rate of growth. Again, you can see that the recession of the late 2000s was well out of line with previous experience.

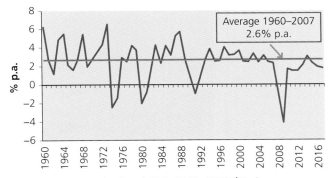

Figure 22.3 Growth of real GDP, 1960–2017 (% change over previous year)

Source: ONS

Study tip

GDP measures the output produced in an economy in a period of time, whereas GNI measures the income available within the economy. GDP is used when monitoring output produced, but GNI is more helpful when we want to measure the standard of living.

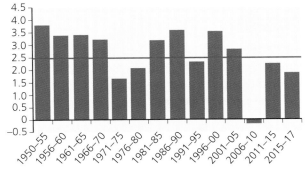

Figure 22.4 Average annual growth rates in the UK since 1950

Source: calculated from ONS data

The data for GDP are also provided on a quarterly (i.e. four times per year) basis. Like many other macroeconomic variables, the level of real GDP tends to fluctuate with the seasons of the year. For example, GDP tends to be higher in the Christmas quarter (from October to December), but then fall in the following period. These regular fluctuations also occur for things like inflation and unemployment, and can distract from the overall pattern through time. For this reason, a process of **seasonal adjustment** is undertaken. This smoothens out these regular fluctuations throughout the year. Figure 22.5 illustrates real GDP using quarterly data from 2012 to 2017. You can see how the seasonally adjusted series focuses on the underlying trend, removing the distractions of the seasonal variations.

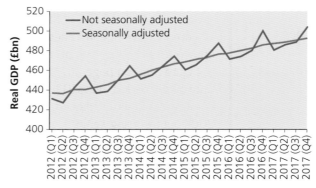

Figure 22.5 Real GDP in the UK with and without seasonal adjustment, 2012–17

GDP tends to be higher during the busy Christmas shopping period

Quantitative skills 22.3

Calculating GDP per capita

Suppose you want to compare living standards in China and Malaysia. To make a comparison meaningful, it would not make sense to look only at GDP or GNI. You need to adjust for the size of population. In other words, you need to calculate an average level of resources per person.

In 2016, GDP in China was US$11,199,145 million, whereas in Malaysia it was US$296,359 million. However, China's population was 1,379 million, compared with Malaysia's 31 million. It is more meaningful to compare average GDP per person (which is known as **GDP per capita**). For China this was US$11,199,145/1,379 = US$8,121. For Malaysia, GDP per capita was US$9,560.

Causes of economic growth

Short-run economic growth

Economic growth is possible in the short run if the economy is operating below full employment, so that utilisation of factors of production can be increased. This would be represented by a movement to the *PPC* from a position within it.

Such short-run growth could be initiated by an increase in aggregate demand, which could be the result of an increase in its components (consumption, government expenditure, net exports or investment), or by tax cuts. The move could also be the result of an increase in short-run aggregate supply.

Notice that of these changes, only investment (perhaps encouraged by lower interest rates) affects long-run aggregate supply. If the economy begins at full employment, the increase in aggregate demand only enables short-run (actual) economic growth. In the longer term, the economy returns to the full employment level (see the explanation of Figure 20.11 on page 286 to see how this would work).

Long-run economic growth

At a basic level, production arises from the use of factors of production — capital, labour, enterprise and so on. Capacity output is reached when all factors of production are fully and efficiently utilised. From this perspective, long-run economic growth can come either from an increase in the quantity of the factors of production, or from an improvement in their efficiency or productivity.

Knowledge check 22.5

Name the two key ways in which productive capacity can increase.

Capital

Capital is a critical factor in the production process. Therefore, an increase in capital input is one source of economic growth. In order for capital to accumulate and increase the capacity of the economy to produce, investment is needed.

In the national accounts, the closest measurement that economists have to investment is 'gross fixed capital formation'. This covers net additions to the capital stock, but it also includes depreciation. However, it is the net addition to capital stock that generates an increase in productive capacity, enabling long-run economic growth.

Technology

The contribution of capital to growth is reinforced by technological progress, as the productivity of new capital is greater than that of old capital that is being phased out. For example, the speed and power of computers has increased enormously over recent years, which has had a great impact on productivity. Effectively, this means that technology is increasing the contribution that investment can make towards enlarging capacity output in an economy. Innovation can also be important, through the invention of new forms of capital and new ways of using existing capital, both of which can contribute to economic growth.

Synoptic link

Externalities (including those that affect human capital) are discussed in Chapter 8. Merit goods are explained in Chapter 9.

Efficiency

Productivity is a measure of the efficiency of a factor of production. For example, **labour productivity** measures output per worker, or output per hour worked. The latter is the more helpful measure, as total output is affected by the number of hours worked, which does vary somewhat across countries. **Capital productivity** measures output per unit of capital. **Total factor productivity** refers to the average productivity of all factors, measured as the total output divided by the total amount of inputs used.

An increase in productivity raises aggregate supply and the potential capacity output of an economy, and so contributes to economic growth.

Labour

Capital has sometimes been seen as the main driver of growth, but labour too has a key contribution to make. There is little point in installing a lot of high-tech equipment unless there is the skilled labour to operate it.

There is relatively little scope for increasing the size of the labour force in a country, except through international migration. The quality of labour input is more amenable to policy action. Education and training can improve the productivity of workers, and can be regarded as a form of investment in **human capital**.

Education and healthcare may have associated externalities. In particular, individuals may not perceive the full social benefits associated with education, training and certain kinds of healthcare, and therefore may choose to invest less in these forms of human capital than is desirable from the perspective of society as a whole. Another such externality is the impact of human capital formation on economic growth as a justification for viewing education and healthcare as merit goods. For many developing countries, the provision of healthcare and improved nutrition can be seen as additional forms of investment in human capital, since such investment can lead to future improvements in productivity.

Summary
- Economic growth can stem from an increase in the inputs of factors of production, or from an improvement in their productivity, i.e. the efficiency with which factors of production are utilised.
- Investment contributes to growth by increasing the capital stock of an economy, although some investment is to compensate for depreciation.
- The contribution of capital is reinforced by the effects of technological progress.
- Labour is another critical factor of production that can contribute to economic growth: for instance, education and training can improve labour productivity. This is a form of human capital formation.

The economic cycle

Historically, the performance of economies has tended to fluctuate over time in a cyclical fashion. This is known as the **economic cycle**. It is illustrated in Figure 22.6. The economic cycle describes the way in which

GDP fluctuates through time around an upward trend. At any point in time, GDP may be below or above its trend (full employment) value, the difference being known as the output gap. This is defined as the actual level of output minus the potential level. If the economy is in recession, with actual GDP below the full employment GDP, then the gap is negative. If actual GDP is above the trend level, the gap is positive.

Consider an economy at point A on Figure 22.6. At this stage in the cycle, the economy is entering a period of recession, in which GDP is falling. This continues until point B, the trough of the cycle, at which point GDP stops falling and begins to grow again. At point C, the economy is showing growth in actual GDP, but GDP is still below its trend value — only at point D does the economy hit the trend. In other words, between points A and D, the output gap is negative. Beyond point D the economy moves into a boom period (as at point E), where the level of GDP is above its trend value and the output gap is positive. At point F the cycle reaches its peak and stops increasing — beyond this point actual GDP again begins to fall, and then the story repeats. Notice that in practice the economy is regarded as being in **recession** when GDP falls in two successive quarters.

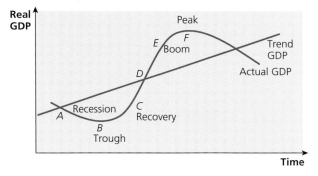

Figure 22.6 The economic cycle

This process reinforces the important distinction between growth in the short run, and growth in the long run. As already explained, the term *long-run economic growth* is used to refer to the process by which there is an increase in the trend, or potential, rate of growth of GDP: in other words, when there is an increase in long-run aggregate supply — an increase in the productive capacity of the economy. Indeed, this is the process by which GDP is able to follow an upward trend over time as productive capacity increases. However, there are also short-run changes in the actual level of GDP: for example, between points B and C on Figure 22.6, there will be an observed increase in real GDP. This is *short-run economic growth*, and is not to be confused with the changing capacity of the economy through time. This short-run economic growth can occur (for example) because unemployed factors of production are being drawn into use when the economy is recovering or in boom.

From a policy perspective, it is important to know at what stage the economy is located. When the output gap is negative, and the level of output is below trend, then it may be tempting for policy-makers to try to 'fill the gap' by stimulating aggregate demand. However, this would be dangerous when the output gap is positive, as the main effect would be on the price level. This will be explained more carefully later.

Figure 22.3 on page 307 shows the rate of change of (actual) real GDP each year since 1960. Also marked on the graph is the long-run average rate of growth, which was about 2.6% p.a. between 1960 and 2007 (just before the onset of the financial crisis and subsequent recession). This shows that the rate of growth of actual real GDP has been relatively volatile over this period — sometimes showing substantial variation from one year to the next, the most extreme example being when the annual growth rate fell from +6.5% in 1973 to −2.5% in 1974. This graph suggests that the economic cycle is not very regular, and certainly the growth rate appears to become more stable towards the end of the period shown.

One classic example of a cycle occurred from 1984 to 1993, as shown in Figure 22.7 — here the output gap was positive from 1985 to 1988, then became negative as the economy went into recession.

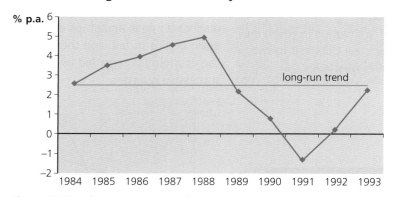

Figure 22.7 A classic economic cycle

Source: ONS

In mid-2008, the chancellor of the exchequer took the unprecedented step of stating publicly that the UK was heading for its biggest recession since the Second World War. Figure 22.8 shows quarterly data for the period 2003 to 2008, showing the information that was available to the chancellor when he made this claim. He proved to be correct.

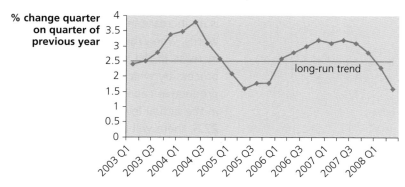

Figure 22.8 The UK economy heading for recession?

Figure 22.9 shows actual GDP (in levels terms) since 1960, together with the trend that would have been followed on the basis of the average growth rate between 1960 and 2007 (the year before recession set in). Although the two series do not diverge by very much for most of the period, you can see the way in which the actual path of real GDP fluctuates around the trend, especially in the middle part of the period.

Knowledge check 22.7

Looking at the path of GDP after 2008 in Figure 22.9, would you say that the economy has returned to its previous trend growth rate?

Also very apparent in the figure is the recession that started in 2008, when GDP dipped significantly below its trend value.

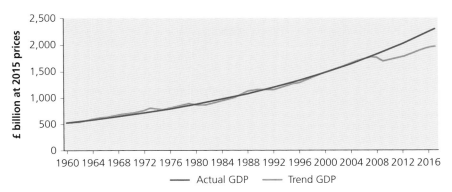

Figure 22.9 Actual and trend real GDP

Figure 22.10 shows the growth rates of GDP per capita in selected countries from 1971 to 2016. Although the graph looks a little congested, it is useful because it shows that there are some periods when fluctuations occur simultaneously across countries. For example, look at what happened in 1974/75, when all countries shown were negatively affected by the oil price shock of 1973/74. Notice that all countries enjoyed a more stable period of growth between about 1984 and 1990. So there may be periods in which there are common cycles across countries. On the other hand, there are also exceptions to this — for example, Japan's negative growth in 1998 and 1999, which was not shared by the other countries in the graph. The recession of the late 2000s clearly affected all of these economies, sending growth strongly negative in 2008 and 2009.

It is important to be aware that if countries do follow common patterns — at least in some periods — then this implies that domestic economic policy may not be the only influence on an economy's performance.

Summary

- Many economies display fluctuations around an underlying trend rate of growth, known as the economic cycle.
- Short-run economic growth occurs at some points in the economic cycle when the economy is in recovery or boom.
- A situation in which real GDP falls for two consecutive quarters is known as a recession.
- In some periods, recession affects several countries simultaneously.

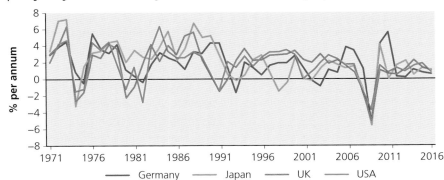

Figure 22.10 Growth of real GDP per capita in selected OECD countries, 1971–2016

Source: World Bank

The consequences of economic growth

The importance of economic growth has been brought into sharp focus through the crisis of the late 2000s, the effects of which are still being felt in many countries. After a period of relative stability during the 2000s, the onset of financial crisis initiated not only a slowdown in the growth of GDP but a period in which GDP was falling. The concerns raised by this period highlight the serious consequences when economic growth does not occur.

Figure 22.11 shows how such a recession affected the UK in late 2008, with GDP growth being negative for six consecutive quarters. The UK was not the only economy affected by this, and many advanced countries followed a similar pattern — indeed, countries like Greece were more severely hit in this period. The consequences of such a recession are significant. If output is falling, and firms are reducing their production, it is likely that they are laying off workers, so that unemployment rises. This then leads to falling incomes, which reduce aggregate demand and may lead to further drops in output, prolonging the recession. You can see from Figure 22.11 that the recovery from recession has been sluggish.

Study tip

Remember that it is *negative* growth that defines a recession: in Figure 22.11 the *growth rate* of GDP fell in 2011, but it did not become negative, so this would not count as a recession.

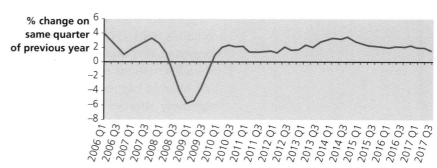

Figure 22.11 Economic growth in the UK since 2006

Source: ONS

The benefits and costs of economic growth

Economic growth in the long run entails an expansion of productive capacity, which in turn expands the resources available within the country. This means that standards of living can improve, together with levels of healthcare provision and educational opportunities. This is the fundamental benefit of economic growth, allowing the country's population to enjoy better living conditions and hopefully improving people's morale.

Growth can also mean higher employment, or improved employment opportunities and working conditions. People may also benefit from an improved environment and from advancing technology. From the government's perspective, tax revenues may increase, allowing higher expenditure that further adds to the improvements in living standards.

Economic growth also brings costs, perhaps most obviously in terms of pollution and degradation of the environment. In designing long-term policy for economic growth, governments need to be aware of the need to maintain a good balance between enabling resources to increase and safeguarding the environment. Pollution reduces the quality of life, so pursuing economic growth without regard to this may be damaging. This means that it is important to consider the long-term effects of economic growth — it may even be important to consider the effects not only on today's generation of citizens but also on future generations.

Although economic growth may expand the resources available, there is no guarantee that these will be evenly distributed among the population. If growth leads to higher concentration of income and wealth in a relatively small proportion of people, then inequality may increase. This may lead to increasing tension and even to civil conflict.

Exercise 22.3

Discuss with your fellow students the various benefits and costs associated with economic growth, and evaluate their relative importance.

Summary

- Economic growth remains important for all countries, at whatever stage of development.
- Recession represents an interruption to the economic growth process, and recovery may be slow.
- There may be costs attached to economic growth, particularly in respect of the environment.

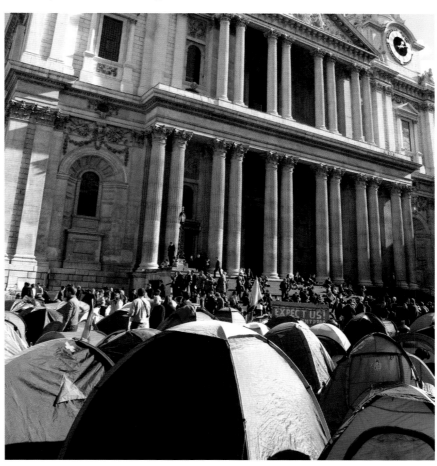

Tents surround St Paul's Cathedral during the Occupy London protests of 2011/12

Extension material

The environment as a factor of production

One way of viewing the environment is as a factor of production that needs to be used effectively, just like any other factor of production. In other words, each country has a stock of *environmental* capital that needs to be utilised in the best possible way.

However, if environmental capital is to be used appropriately, it must be given an appropriate value and this can be problematic. If property rights are not firmly established — as they are not in many less developed countries — it is difficult to enforce legislation to protect the environment. Furthermore, if the environment (as a factor of production) is under-priced, then firms will use 'too much' of it.

There are externality effects at work here too, in the sense that the loss of biodiversity is a global loss, and not just something affecting the local economy. In some cases there have been international externality effects of a more direct kind, such as when forest fires in Indonesia caused the airport in Singapore to close down because of the resulting smoke haze.

Case study 22.1

China's economic growth

Heavy smog in Beijing, China

Since China adopted market reforms in the late 1970s, its economy has enjoyed a period of rapid economic growth that is unprecedented by historical standards. One of the characteristics of this period of rapid growth has been the gradual move towards allowing market forces to operate after a long period of central planning. This would be expected to have benefits for the economy in terms of the efficiency of resource allocation.

Although China's success in achieving such rapid economic progress has been much admired, it has also been much criticised, for a number of reasons.

One source of criticism centres on the environmental damage that results from a rapid rate of economic growth. A key ingredient of the growth process — especially in terms of industrialisation — is an expansion in energy supplies. Factories cannot operate without reliable electricity and other energy sources. Proposals to double China's production of hydroelectric power caused concerns about the effects of new dams on river levels in downstream countries in Southeast Asia and in India.

Air pollution has become a severe problem, with heavy smog levels in Beijing and other cities. The problem is not confined within China's boundaries, and neighbours Japan and South Korea have suffered from pollution spreading from China into their territories.

Booming car ownership raises further concerns: one prediction is that the number of cars in China had reached 173 million by 2015 (from just 4 million in 2000). This number continues to rise rapidly, and China is the largest car producer in the world. The effect of this on the demand for oil has already been reflected in higher world prices — China is already the world's second biggest oil importer (behind the USA). China is also the world's biggest producer of coal, which accounts for some 80% of the country's energy use.

All of this means that China has now overtaken the USA as the largest emitter of carbon dioxide. It seems unlikely that environmental damage on this sort of scale is sustainable from a global perspective.

Follow-up questions
a Explain why a move towards a market-based system would be expected to 'have benefits for the economy in terms of the efficiency of resource allocation'.
b Discuss how the cross-border externalities caused by pollution could be tackled.
c Discuss whether China should seek to restrain the growing car ownership that is a by-product of rapid economic growth, which has led to rising real incomes.

CHAPTER 22 QUESTIONS

A Multiple-choice questions

1 If a country has a population of 0.5 million and a GDP of £56 billion, what is the GDP per capita?

   a £11,200,000

   b £1,120,000

   c £112,000

   d £11,200

2 A recession is defined as:

   a Two quarters of negative economic growth

   b Two months of negative economic growth

   c A fall in GDP

   d A fall in national income

3 Long-run economic growth can be shown using:

   a A shift to the right of *AD*

   b A shift to the left of *AD*

   c A shift to the right of *LRAS*

   d A shift to the left of *LRAS*

B Knowledge and understanding questions

4 Explain, with the aid of a diagram, the difference between short-run and long-run economic growth. [4 marks]

5 Explain **two** stages of the economic cycle. [4 marks]

6 Explain what is meant by 'nominal economic growth'. [4 marks]

C Stimulus response question

7 Throughout the 2000s, China saw strong economic growth. The Chinese government is seeking to continue this growth at a rate of over 6%, but the economy appears to have been slowing down since 2015.

Some of the drivers for economic growth included a large population of working age, massive amounts of investment and a high level of productivity.

   a Explain one possible reason why the Chinese government has a policy of economic growth. [2 marks]

   b Evaluate the possible consequences for China's economy of a slowing of economic growth. [12 marks]

D Essay question

8 Evaluate the main causes of economic growth in the UK economy. [20 marks]

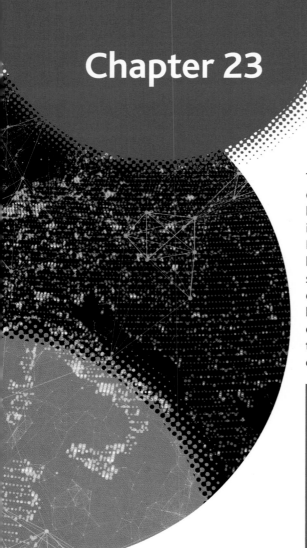

Chapter 23

Development

This chapter explores the relationship between economic growth and economic development, and looks at ways in which economic and human development can be recognised. The focus here is on alternative indicators of development, such as GDP or GNI per capita and the Human Development Index. Countries in different parts of the world have followed different paths to development, with varying degrees of success. Differences partly reflect the different characteristics of each country. Less developed countries do seem to share some characteristics, but each country also faces its own configuration of problems and opportunities. This chapter explores some of the common characteristics that less developed countries display but also examines some of the key differences between them.

> ## Learning objectives
>
> After studying this chapter, you should be able to:
> - explain the structure of an economy in terms of primary, secondary and tertiary sectors
> - explain the policy objective of sustainable development
> - evaluate the relationship between economic growth and sustainable development
> - evaluate the usefulness of macroeconomic indicators such as GDP, the Human Development Index and other alternative social and cultural indicators

Defining development

Key term

development a process by which real per capita incomes are increased and the inhabitants of a country are able to benefit from improved living conditions, i.e. lower poverty and enhanced standards of education, health, nutrition and other essentials of life

The first step is to define what is meant by '**development**'. You might think that it is about economic growth — if a society can expand its productive capacity, surely that is development? But development means much more than this. Economic growth may well be a necessary ingredient, since development cannot take place without an expansion of the resources available in a society. However, it is not a sufficient ingredient because those additional resources must be used wisely, and the growth that results must be the 'right' sort of growth.

Wrapped up with development are issues concerning the alleviation of poverty — no country can be considered 'developed' if a substantial portion of its population is living in absolute poverty. Development also requires structural change, and possibly changes in institutions and, in some cases, cultural and political attitudes.

Synoptic link

Issues concerned with poverty are discussed in Chapter 29.

The structure of economic activity

Chapter 23 Development

Key terms

primary sector the sector in which production uses natural resources, including the extraction of raw materials and the growing of crops

secondary sector the sector involving the production of manufactured goods

tertiary sector the sector involving production of services — may include the quaternary sector, which is production based on information technology and information products

Knowledge check 23.1

Would investment banking be classified as primary, secondary or tertiary activity?

An important characteristic of an economy is the way in which economic activity is made up of different sectors. This can be envisaged in terms of a division into **primary**, **secondary** and **tertiary** production activities. The primary sector involves the extraction of raw materials and the growing of crops. It includes agriculture, the extraction of minerals (and oil), forestry, fishing and so on. The secondary sector is where these raw materials or crops are processed or transformed into goods. It includes various forms of manufacturing activity, ranging from the processing of food to the manufacture of motor vehicles or computer equipment. The tertiary sector is concerned with the provision of services. It includes transport and communication, hairdressing, financial services and so on. A subset of tertiary activity involves intellectual services. This is sometimes known as the quaternary sector and includes hi-tech industry, information technology, some forms of scientific research and other 'information products'.

Dependence on the primary sector

Figure 23.1 contrasts the structure of economic activity in two very different economies — Ethiopia and the UK. These data do not exactly correspond to the primary, secondary and tertiary divisions, as 'Other industry' includes mining, construction, electricity, water and gas. Nonetheless, the contrast is striking. In the UK, the agricultural sector has dwindled almost to nothing, and services have become the dominant form of activity, although industry still accounts for almost 20% of GDP. In Ethiopia, manufacturing activity takes up 4% of GDP. Agriculture, on the other hand, contributes 37% of GDP.

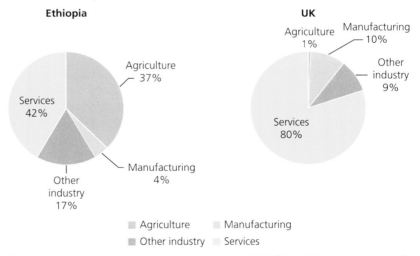

Figure 23.1 The structure of economic activity, 2016 (% of GDP by value added)

Source: based on data from World Development Indicators

Study tip

When comparing GDP or GNI across countries, it is important to take account of differences in the size of population by looking at the average per person. Such measures are known as GDP per capita, which is simply GDP divided by population.

Many less developed countries (LDCs) have an economic structure that is strongly biased towards agriculture. Figure 23.2 shows the percentage of GDP coming from the agricultural sector in a range of countries (measured in terms of value added). The countries are ranked in descending order of GDP per capita.

In interpreting these data, it is important to be aware that labour productivity tends to be lower in agriculture than in other sectors.

The data therefore understate the importance of agriculture in the structure of the economy, as the percentage of the labour force engaged in agriculture is higher than the agricultural share of output. This is further reinforced by the importance of unrecorded agricultural production in the subsistence sector. In other words, if farmers produce food for their own consumption, this will not be included in the measurement of GDP.

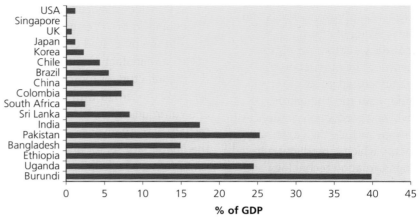

Figure 23.2 Agriculture value added as % of GDP, 2016

Source: based on data from World Development Indicators

Knowledge check 23.2

Consider a good where output is highly dependent on weather conditions, which vary from year to year. Will the resulting volatility in price be greater or lower if the demand for the good is relatively price-inelastic?

The high importance of agriculture can affect LDCs in a number of ways. Agriculture tends to display lower productivity than other sectors, and there is less scope for exploiting increasing returns to scale than in manufacturing activity. High dependence on agriculture therefore tends to be correlated with low income per head. In addition, primary producers tend to face difficulties in international markets, with volatility in commodity prices and a long-run tendency for agricultural prices to fall relative to prices of manufactured goods.

Summary
- Economic activity can be classified into primary, secondary and tertiary production activities.
- Primary activity centres on agriculture and mineral extraction, secondary activity focuses mainly on manufacturing activity, tertiary activity is concerned with the provision of services.
- Many LDCs have an economic structure that is biased towards the primary sector.
- Agriculture is often characterised by low productivity.

Which are the less developed countries?

There is no single definitive list of countries that are regarded as being the LDCs, and it is important to be aware that this term is used to refer to a wide range of countries with differing characteristics. Although a high dependence on agriculture is common to many LDCs, this is by no means the only defining characteristic.

In broad terms, the countries regarded as LDCs are concentrated in four major regions: sub-Saharan Africa, Latin America, South Asia and Southeast Asia. This excludes some countries in the 'less developed' range, but relatively few. For some purposes it may be necessary to treat China separately, rather than including it as part of Southeast Asia, partly because of its sheer size, and partly because it has followed a rather different development path.

Farmers in Vietnam, an LDC, harvest sedge to weave sedge mats

Indicators of development

GNI per capita

The first step is to be able to measure 'development'. A first step is to compare average income levels across countries, by using GDP per capita (or GNI per capita), as suggested in the previous chapter. GNI per capita is the standard measure used by the World Bank to compare income levels across countries, so that will be our starting point.

Figure 23.3 provides data on GNI per capita for a selection of countries from each of the four major regions in 2016. These countries will be used as examples throughout this discussion. Because of the diversity of countries in each of the regions, such a selection must be treated with a little caution. Singapore, South Korea and China have been chosen to represent East Asia and the Pacific, in order to highlight three countries that have achieved rapid economic growth over a sustained period.

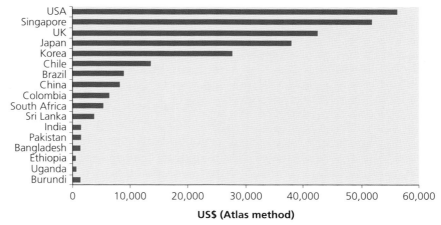

Figure 23.3 GNI per capita, 2016 (US$)

The extreme differences that exist around the globe are immediately apparent from the data. However, in trying to interpret these data, a number of issues need to be borne in mind, as the comparison is not as straightforward as it looks.

Exchange rate problems

The data presented in Figure 23.3 are expressed in terms of US dollars, using the Atlas method (which the World Bank uses to classify countries by income). This allows economists to compare average incomes using a common unit of measurement. At the same time, however, it may create some problems.

It is important to compare average income levels in order to evaluate the standard of living, and compare standards across countries. In other words, the aim is to assess people's command over resources in different societies, and to be able to compare the purchasing power of income in different countries.

GNI is calculated initially in terms of local currencies, and subsequently converted into US dollars using official exchange rates. Will this provide information about the relative local purchasing power of incomes? Not necessarily.

One reason for this is that official exchange rates are sometimes affected by government intervention. Indeed, in many of the LDCs, exchange rates are pegged to an international currency — usually the US dollar. In these circumstances, exchange rates are more likely to reflect the government's policy and actions than the relative purchasing power of incomes in the country under scrutiny. For example, a government may choose to maintain an overvalued currency in order to try to maximise the earnings from its exports. In the case of China, the government has been tempted into the opposite situation, maintaining an undervalued currency in order to maximise export volume.

Where exchange rates are free to find their own equilibrium level, they are likely to be influenced strongly by the price of internationally traded goods, which is likely to be a very different combination of goods than that typically consumed by residents in these countries. Again, it can be argued that official exchange rates may not be a good reflection of the relative purchasing power of incomes across countries.

The UN International Comparison Project has been working on this problem for many years. It now produces an alternative set of international estimates of GNI based on *purchasing power parity* (PPP) exchange rates, which are designed to reflect the relative purchasing power of incomes in different societies more accurately. Figure 23.4 shows estimates for GNI per capita using the same set of countries that were used in the previous figure.

You may notice that the gap between the low-income and high-income countries seems a bit less marked when PPP dollars (PPP$) are used as the unit of measurement. In other words, the estimates based on US dollars exaggerate the gap in living standards between rich and poor countries. This is a general feature of these measurements — that measurements in US dollars tend to understate real incomes for low-income countries and overstate them for high-income countries compared with PPP$ data.

Knowledge check 23.3

Give reasons why official exchange rates may not be ideal for comparing purchasing power across countries.

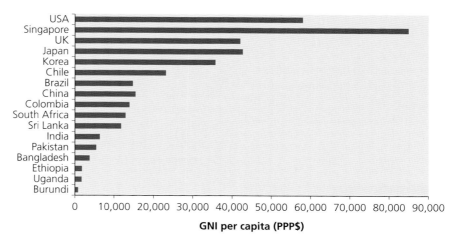

Figure 23.4 GNI per capita, 2016 (PPP$)

Source: based on data from World Development Indicators

Put another way, people in the lower-income countries have a stronger command over goods and services than is suggested by US-dollar comparisons of GNI per capita. You will also see that in some cases, using PPP$ alters the rankings of the countries — for example, compare Singapore with the USA in Figures 23.3 and 23.4.

Figure 23.5 shows the relative size of GNI per capita in PPP$ for the regional groupings of countries around the world in 2016. The gap in income levels between the LDCs and the Organisation for Economic Co-operation and Development (OECD) countries shows very clearly in the graph. Equally, the gap between the countries of sub-Saharan Africa and South Asia, on the one hand, and those in East Asia and Latin America, on the other, is apparent.

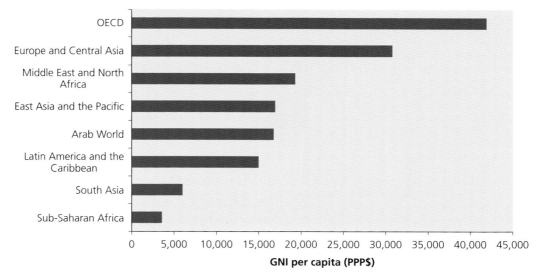

Figure 23.5 GNI per capita, regional groupings 2016 (PPP$)

Source: based on data from World Development Indicators

The informal sector and the accuracy of data

Even when measured in PPP$, GNI (or GDP) has limitations as a measure of living standards. One limitation that is especially important

Knowledge check 23.4

Give some examples of aspects of the standard of living that are not captured in the measurement of GNI or GDP.

Synoptic link

The question of inequality in income distribution is discussed in Chapter 29.

when considering low-income countries is that in many LDCs there is considerable *informal economic activity*, which may not be captured by a measure like GNI, based on monetary transactions. Such activity includes subsistence agriculture, which remains important in many countries, especially in sub-Saharan Africa. In other words, GNI may not capture production that is directly used for consumption. Remember that GNI is measured by adding up the total transactions that take place in an economy. In the case of barter or production for consumption, there are no transactions to be measured, so they will not be captured in GNI.

Income distribution

Another important limitation of GNI per capita (or GDP per capita) as a measure of living standards is that it is an *average* measure, and so does not reveal information about how income is distributed among groups in society.

Based on the latest data from World Development Indicators, the poorest 10% of households in South Africa received less than 1% of total income, whereas the richest 10% received 51%. In Belarus, on the other hand, the poorest 10% received 4% of income and the richest 10% received 23%. These are extreme examples of the degree of inequality in the distribution of income within countries.

Tembisa, Johannesburg — where rich meets poor

Social indicators

A further question that arises is whether GNI or GDP can be regarded as a reasonable indicator of a country's *standard of living*. GNI (or GDP) provides an indicator of the total resources available within an economy in a given period, calculated from data about total output, total incomes or total expenditure. This focus on summing the transactions that take place in an economy over a period can be seen as a rather narrow view of what constitutes a country's standard of living. After all, it may be argued that the quality of people's lives depends on more things than simply the material resources that are available.

For one thing, people need to have knowledge if they are to make good use of the resources that are available. Two societies with similar income levels may nonetheless provide very different quality of life for their inhabitants, depending on the education levels of the population. Furthermore, if people are to benefit from consuming or using the available resources, they need a reasonable lifespan coupled with good health. So, good standards of health are also crucial to a good quality of life.

It is important to remember that different societies tend to set different priorities for the pursuit of growth and the promotion of education and health. Some countries have higher levels of health and education than other countries with similar levels of GNI per capita. This needs to be taken into account when judging relative living standards by comparing GNI per capita. For a given level of real GNI per capita, there may be substantial differences in living standards between a country that places a high priority on providing education and healthcare, and one that devotes resources to military expenditure. In the longer term, there may also be significant differences between a society that spends its resources on present consumption, and one that engages in investment in order to increase consumption in the future.

A reasonable environment in which to live may be seen as another important factor in one's quality of life. There are some environmental issues that can distort the GDP measure of resources. Suppose there is an environmental disaster — perhaps an oil tanker breaks up close to a beautiful beach. This reduces the overall quality of life by degrading the landscape and preventing enjoyment of the beach. However, it does not have a negative effect on GNI — on the contrary, the money spent on clearing up the damage actually adds to GNI, so that the net effect of an environmental disaster may be to *increase* the measured level of GNI!

Exercise 23.1

Table 23.1 presents some indicators for two countries, A and B. Discuss the extent to which GNI per capita (here measured in PPP$) provides a good indication of relative living standards in the two countries.

Table 23.1 Relative living standards

	Country A	Country B
GNI per capita (PPP$)	11,578	11,445
Life expectancy (in years at birth)	56.1	75.2
Adult literacy rate (%)	93.0	98.0
Infant mortality rate (per 1,000 live births)	33.3	5.7
% of population living on less than $1.90 per person per day	13.77	0.21

Discuss what other indicators might be useful in this evaluation.

Key term

Human Development Index (HDI) a composite indicator of the level of a country's development, varying between 0 and 1

The Human Development Index

To deal with the criticism that GNI per capita fails to take account of other dimensions of the quality of life, in 1990 the United Nations Development Programme (UNDP) devised an alternative indicator, known as the **Human Development Index (HDI)**. This was designed to provide a broader measure of the stage of development that a country had reached. It has since become a widely used indicator.

Figure 23.6 Components of the Human Development Index

Knowledge check 23.5

In Ethiopia in 2017, mean years of schooling were 2.6 whereas expected years of schooling were 8.4. What does this imply for changes in the education system?

The basis for the HDI is that there are three key aspects of human development: resources, knowledge of how to make good use of those resources, and a reasonable life span in which to make use of those resources (see Figure 23.6). The three components are measured by, respectively, GNI per capita in PPP$, indicators of education (mean years of schooling and expected years of schooling) and life expectancy. The measurements are then combined to produce a composite index ranging between 0 and 1, with higher values reflecting higher human development.

GNI per capita (in PPP$) represents resources in this set-up, and is intended to reflect the extent to which people have command over resources. The education indicators pick up two rather different aspects of this important component of human development. *Mean* years of education can be seen as a way of reflecting educational attainment, as it measures the average number of years of schooling that were received by people aged 25 and above in their lifetime. It therefore tells us something about the extent to which there has been past investment in education. *Expected* years of schooling, on the other hand, reveals something about the current state of education in an economy. That is, it identifies the number of years of schooling that a child of school entrance age can expect to receive, given current patterns of enrolment and access to education. Life expectancy is the natural indicator of expected lifespan, and is also closely related to the general level of health of people in the country.

Values of the HDI for 2016 are charted in Figure 23.7 for the selected countries. You can see that the gap between low and high human development is less marked than when GDP or GNI per capita is used. Notice that the countries in the graph are still ranked by GNI per capita (from Figure 23.3). Therefore, the somewhat jagged appearance of Figure 23.7 is informative. For example, compare Sri Lanka and South Africa. Sri Lanka had significantly lower GNI per capita in Figure 23.3, but outperforms South Africa in terms of the HDI. This suggests that the GNI per capita measure may understate the standard of living achieved in Sri Lanka, which may have performed relatively well in terms of education and health indicators. Similarly, Uganda seems to have done well compared with other countries with similar GNI per capita levels.

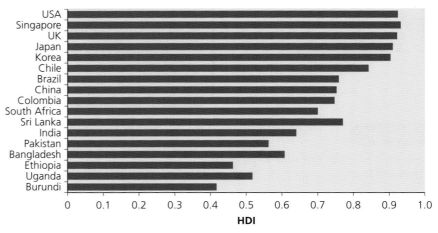

Figure 23.7 The Human Development Index, 2016

Source: *Human Development Report*

Figures 23.8 and 23.9 show the levels of two of the measures that enter into the HDI: life expectancy and mean years of schooling. It would seem that life expectancy is partly responsible for the low ranking of South Africa in the HDI, as its level of life expectancy is out of kilter with its average income level. Comparing Uganda with Ethiopia and Burundi, you can see that there was little difference in terms of life expectancy, but a more significant difference in mean years of schooling. These data therefore give us some idea of the diversity between countries that was mentioned earlier.

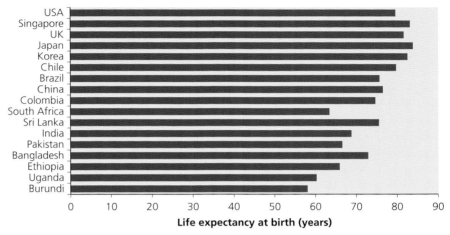

Figure 23.8 Life expectancy at birth

Source: *Human Development Report*

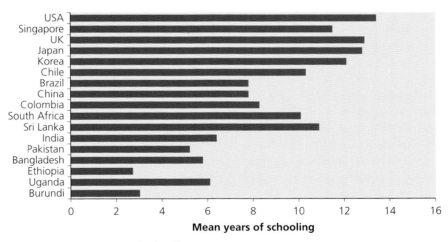

Figure 23.9 Mean years of schooling

Source: *Human Development Report*

> ### Knowledge check 23.6
>
> Looking at Figures 23.8 and 23.9, did Ethiopia perform relatively better on knowledge or health provision?

In part, this diversity reflects differing priorities that governments have given to different aspects of development. Countries such as Brazil have aimed primarily at achieving economic growth, while those such as Sri Lanka have given greater priority to promoting education and healthcare.

There is a view that growth should be the prime objective for development, since by expanding the resources available the benefits can begin to trickle down through the population. An opposing view claims that by providing first for basic needs, more rapid economic growth can be facilitated. The problem in some cases is that growth has not resulted in the trickle-down effect, and inequality remains. It may be significant that countries such as Brazil and South Africa, where the GNI per capita ranking is high relative to the HDI ranking, are countries in which there remain high levels of inequality in the distribution of income.

The HDI may be preferred to GNI per capita as a measure of development on the grounds that it reflects the key dimensions of development as opposed to growth. However, it will always be difficult to reduce a complex concept such as development to a single statistic. The diverse characteristics of LDCs demand the use of a range of alternative measures in order to identify the configuration of circumstances and problems facing a particular country.

Other indicators of development

The HDI is a useful composite indicator that is more informative about relative living standards across countries. Its components have been carefully chosen using the most reliable data about overall resourcing (GNI per capita in PPP$) and well-chosen data about health and education. However, it still neglects some important dimensions of development. The UNDP has recognised this, and has produced a number of other indicators designed to complement the HDI, notably in respect of inequality, gender and poverty.

The Inequality-adjusted HDI (IHDI)

Data relating to inequality in the three components of the HDI (health, education and income) are used to adjust the HDI to try to estimate the extent to which potential human development is lower because of inequalities. For example, earlier in the chapter it was noted that there was relatively high inequality in South Africa. In terms of the IHDI, the conclusion drawn is that the loss in potential human development due to inequality in South Africa amounts to 34.7%.

Gender inequality

The situation of women in many countries has been a major concern. Women tend to receive less education, are exposed to greater health risks, and receive lower incomes. The UNDP has produced two ways of exploring gender inequality across countries. One approach is simply to calculate the HDI separately for females and males. In more developed countries, female life expectancy is often significantly higher than for males, so the difference in HDI levels between females and males is not great, even where females face lower GNI per capita. Indeed, there are some countries (e.g. Estonia) where females have a higher HDI than males. Elsewhere the picture is very different: for example, in Pakistan, female HDI is more than 25% lower than for males. A second measure focuses on the key gender issues of health, empowerment and the labour force.

Characteristics of LDCs

There are many other indicators that can be used to capture the varied characteristics of LDCs that may contribute to their progress in achieving development. For example, the pattern of economic activity may be important, as heavy dependence on low productivity agriculture may hinder economic growth. Access to good infrastructure can be captured by data on access to electricity, sanitation or clean water. Transport and communications are also vital for development, so access to the internet or mobile phones, or the quality of roads, are all important indicators that can provide clues to the problems faced by particular countries.

Exercise 23.3

Table 23.2 presents data for three countries on a range of indicators, using data from the World Bank. Can you identify which of these countries is likely to have the lowest and highest GNI per capita (PPP$)?

Table 23.2 Indicators of development

Indicator	Country A	Country B	Country C
Life expectancy at birth (years)	65.5	62.2	48.9
Expected years of schooling	10.3	11.1	11.4
FDI inflow (% of GDP)	5.3	2.3	0.8
Mobile cellular subscriptions (per 100 people)	41.8	81.3	76.4
Unemployment (% of total labour force)	2.1	11.0	25.3
HIV/AIDS prevalence (% of population aged 15–49)	0.6	5.4	27.2
Infant mortality (aged under 5 per 1,000 births)	49.6	49.4	60.7
Agriculture valued added (% of GDP)	24.4	35.6	9.9

Extension material

Happiness and well-being

The justification given for wanting economic growth is that it expands choice for people and provides the resources needed to enable them to enjoy an enhanced quality of life. Increasing attention is being given to whether economic growth can actually deliver this. To put it another way, does higher income bring more happiness?

Richard Easterlin drew attention to a paradox. He argued that, although happiness and income appear to be correlated at a point in time, happiness does not appear to increase as income increases through time. In other words, rapid economic growth does not seem to bring with it an increase in happiness.

Figure 23.10 shows an overall life satisfaction index produced by the UN. This is based on surveys carried out by Gallup in countries around the world. The index is based on a 10-point scale, with 10 indicating the most satisfied. It is intended to capture people's perceptions of how satisfied they are with their life.

Perhaps the first attempt to shift the focus towards happiness rather than material prosperity was when Bhutan's ruler announced in 1972 that he was committed to improving 'gross national happiness', based on Buddhist spiritual values rather than measuring output. The ideas have gradually begun to catch on, and there have been attempts to refine the analysis and measurement of happiness.

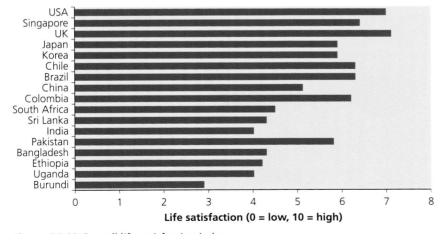

Figure 23.10 Overall life satisfaction index

Source: *Human Development Report*

Summary

- Less developed countries (LDCs) are largely located in four major regions: sub-Saharan Africa, Latin America, South Asia and Southeast Asia.
- These regions have shown contrasting patterns of growth and development.
- GDP (or GNI) is a widely used measure of the total amount of economic activity in an economy over a period of time.
- Average GNI per person neglects the important issue of income distribution.
- GNI may also neglect some important aspects of the quality of life.
- The Human Development Index (HDI) recognises that human development depends upon resources, knowledge and health, and therefore combines indicators of these key aspects.
- Different countries have different characteristics, and face different configurations of problems and opportunities.

Sustainable development

Key term

sustainable development
'development that meets the needs of the present without compromising the ability of future generations to meet their own needs' (Brundtland Commission, 1987)

Synoptic link

Externality effects are discussed in Chapter 8.

Living standards in the advanced economies have progressed almost beyond imagining in recent decades, and now many developing countries are aspiring to follow the same route — and some of them are succeeding. Can this process go on forever?

There are clear externality effects of economic growth in relation to the environment. As economic growth gets under way, there are environmental side effects. Pollution and the threat of climate change have cast doubt on whether it is possible to achieve **sustainable development**. The most helpful definition of this was produced by the Brundtland Commission in 1987.

Functions of the environment

One way of thinking about the environment is that it can be seen as a factor of production, as it provides inputs into the production process in the form of natural resources. However, the environment is more complex than being simply a provider of inputs for the production process. Figure 23.11 identifies three crucial functions of the environment in today's world.

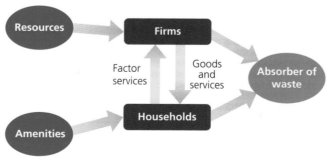

Figure 23.11 Three functions of the environment

Resources

One important function of the environment is to supply resources that are required in the production process. Firms need energy as an input to production, in the form of oil, natural gas, electricity, etc. Notice that electricity can be generated by a range of processes, using either renewable methods from wind farms or non-renewable methods based on coal or oil.

Amenities

The environment also supplies amenities to households. People get utility from visiting a pleasant clean beach, walking in the woods or playing in the park. Enjoying clean air and living in a pleasant location contributes to people's quality of life. The provision of amenities is therefore an important function that the environment fulfils.

Absorber of waste

Perhaps less often noticed is the third function that the environment provides, as an absorber of waste. Firms and households generate waste, which somehow has to be absorbed. The environment is crucial in the process of waste disposal.

Sustainability?

Figure 23.11 illustrates the situation. The environment provides inputs for firms in the form of natural resources and inputs for households in the form of amenities. Both firms and households generate waste.

A key issue to be explored is whether this process is sustainable in the long run. In other words, does the environment have the capacity to support the three functions indefinitely? To what extent can the environment continue to supply the natural resources that firms need as inputs? To what extent can the amenities provided by the environment be conserved for the future? Does the absorption of waste cause damage to the environment that will affect its capacity to continue to provide resources and amenities in the future? These questions are some of the most important facing the global economy.

Another way of viewing sustainable development is to say that the stock of environmental capital should not decline over time. In other words, generations in the future should inherit a stock of resources that enables them to enjoy at least as high a quality of life as that enjoyed by today's generation.

Sustainable development and economic growth

Although the advanced countries are now taking action to reduce environmental damage and conserve resources for the future, many commentators have argued that this is too little, too late. However, a dilemma arises in the context of the developing countries that have been the subject of much of this chapter. The poverty and poor living conditions that characterise so many countries, especially in sub-Saharan Africa, cannot be tackled without economic growth. But can this growth take place in a sustainable way?

331

Figure 23.12 shows one aspect of this situation. China has been one of the great success stories of recent decades, achieving rapid economic growth and reducing poverty levels. India has also been growing at a rapid rate. In Figure 23.12 you can see one of the side effects of this success, with China having become the largest emitter of carbon dioxide into the atmosphere in a period when emissions in the EU and the USA have been stabilising.

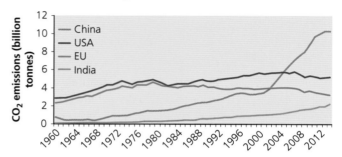

Figure 23.12 Carbon dioxide emissions

The link between economic growth and environmental degradation is a clear one. In the case of China, there are several aspects to notice. During the process of industrialisation, it is crucial to ensure that energy supplies keep pace with demand, as factories cannot operate effectively without reliable electricity and other energy sources. China has become the world's second biggest oil importer (behind the USA), and is the world's largest producer of coal, which is not the cleanest of energy technologies. China has recognised the problem, and has been making attempts to reduce its dependence on coal.

China is not a unique example, but it is the world's largest country in population terms, and has experienced economic growth at an unprecedented rate in recent decades. The underlying point here is that it is all very well finding ways of pushing the long-run aggregate supply curve to the right, but this is not necessarily the best strategy for long-run sustainable development.

For economic growth to be sustainable, these environmental effects must be taken into account, or there is a real danger the improved standard of living that flows from the growth process will be obtained only at the expense of the quality of life of future generations. This may require growth to be slowed in the short run in order to devote resources to the development of renewable and cleaner energy sources. However, it is politically and morally difficult to impose this on newly emerging societies in which there is widespread poverty, especially when the richer nations of the world continue to enjoy high standards of living while causing pollution of their own.

Sustainable development is not all about the environment. In 2015 the UN member states adopted the 2030 Agenda for Sustainable Development, which recognises that:

ending poverty and other deprivations must go hand-in-hand with strategies that improve health and education, reduce inequality, and spur economic growth — all while tackling climate change and working to preserve our oceans and forests.

Source: https://sustainabledevelopment.un.org/sdgs

Summary

- Economic growth has externality effects on the environment.
- Sustainable development would allow meeting the needs of the current generation without compromising the ability of future generations to meet their own needs.
- The environment fulfils three key functions, providing resources and amenities, but also acting as an absorber of waste.
- A key question is whether the environment has the capacity to continue to support all three functions in the long term.

Case study 23.1

Wildlife tourism

Tanzania's rich wildlife attracts tourists from all over the world

Tanzania is among the lowest-income countries in the world, with GNI per capita of US$900 in 2016. It is located in sub-Saharan Africa, and relies heavily on agriculture for employment, income and export earnings. In 2015, agriculture made up 68% of employment and 31% of GDP by value added. A total of 58% of its merchandise exports consisted of agricultural goods. Could Tanzania benefit from tourism?

In its favour, Tanzania has a rich wildlife and the potential to offer safari holidays, so there are resources that could attract foreign visitors. But can promoting tourism be achieved without doing damage to the environment and to biodiversity?

The internet has raised awareness of the variety of wildlife around the globe — it is easy to learn about animals and their habitats, which can then encourage people to want to visit and see the animals in their natural surroundings. At the same time, rising real incomes fuel the demand for tourism, and many active retirees have the income and the leisure time available to travel.

However, habitats are shrinking, affecting the supply side of the tourism market. Some destinations have become overcrowded. Indeed, it is said that to visit the Masai Mara in Kenya is to find tourists looking at other tourists, rather than at wildlife.

The challenge is, therefore, to reconcile the need for protecting nature with the need to stimulate economic growth and development.

Another key objective of encouraging tourism in a country like Tanzania is to ensure that local communities benefit, and are not alienated by visitations by rich tourists. If local communities are to benefit, they need to be involved in projects and to understand the need to manage local ecosystems.

An example in Tanzania is the Ruaha Carnivore Project, launched in 2009 in association with Oxford University. This is based in the Ruaha National Park, which is home to significant populations of lions, cheetahs and African wild dogs. It is also home to local people who do not always see the value of cohabiting with carnivores that are prone to attacking their livestock. The project has therefore needed to work closely with local communities to reduce human–carnivore conflict.

In 2015, international tourism accounted for 23.8% of Tanzania's total exports.

Follow-up questions

a Discuss why promoting wildlife tourism could damage the environment and biodiversity.
b Why might the expansion of tourism impose costs on local communities?
c What benefits might there be for local communities if tourism increases?
d Would Tanzania be better off industrialising rather than promoting international tourism?

CHAPTER 23 QUESTIONS

A Multiple-choice questions

1 If a business specialises in fishing then it would be classed as operating in which economic sector?

   a Primary

   b Secondary

   c Tertiary

   d Quarternary

2 The HDI does not contain which of the following measurements?

   a GDP per capita

   b GNI per capita

   c Indicators of education

   d Life expectancy

B Knowledge and understanding questions

3 Explain what is meant by the term 'sustainable development'. [2 marks]

4 Explain **two** reasons why GDP may not be a good measure of development. [4 marks]

5 Explain the relationship between economic growth and sustainable development. [3 marks]

D Essay question

6 Evaluate the usefulness of the HDI as a measure of development. [25 marks]

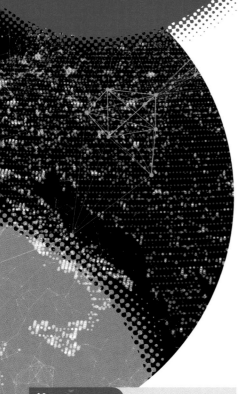

Chapter 24

Employment

Full employment is a key macroeconomic objective. The existence of high unemployment suggests that the economy is not operating at full capacity, but some kinds of unemployment will always be present in a dynamic economy. This chapter explores the nature of employment and unemployment, and examines some of the problems in measuring unemployment as well as setting out the causes and consequences of this important indicator.

Learning objectives

After studying this chapter, you should be able to:
- explain employment and unemployment
- explain the policy objective of full employment
- explain the Labour Force Survey and claimant count measures of unemployment
- evaluate the causes and consequences of unemployment
- evaluate the effects of full employment

Employment and the UK workforce

In 2017, there were 42.4 million people living in the UK aged between the ages of 16 and 64. These people are considered to be of working age, although 65 is no longer seen as the normal retirement age. Figure 24.1 shows how they were distributed between three key economic categories: the employed, the unemployed and the economically inactive. Those **in employment** in this context include both those who are employed by firms or other organisations (such as government) and also the self-employed. The **economically inactive** include students, and those who have retired, are sick or are looking after family members. Also included are **discouraged workers** — people who have failed to find work and have given up looking. In other words, the economically inactive category includes all those people in the age range who are not considered to be active in the **workforce**. The **unemployed** are those who are in the workforce but who are without jobs (a more precise definition will be provided soon).

The number of those employed is an important indicator, given that they contribute to the production process in their role as the factor of production 'labour'. Figure 24.2 shows the number of employees in each year since 1971. You can see that the total number employed has increased substantially over this period, from 25.7 million in 1984 to nearly 34 million in 2017. It is also interesting to note that, although the number employed fell in 2009 as recession began to bite, it recovered quite quickly, with employment in 2017 being slightly higher than it had been in 2008. You can also see that the number of part-time workers increased proportionately more, from 4.4 million (17.2% of the total) in 1984 to 7 million (20.6%) in 2017.

Key terms

in employment (employed) people who are either working for firms or other organisations, or self-employed

economically inactive those people of working age who are not looking for work, for a variety of reasons

discouraged workers people who have been unable to find employment and who are no longer looking for work

workforce people who are economically active — either in employment or unemployed

unemployed people who are economically active but not in employment

Knowledge check 24.1

Would the unemployed be classified as being economically active or inactive?

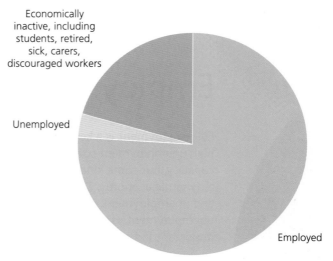

Figure 24.1 The structure of the UK population aged between 16 and 64 years, 2017

Source: ONS

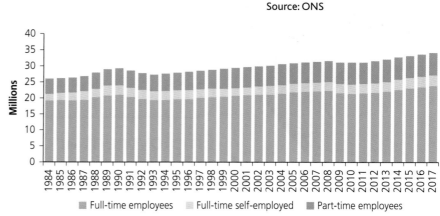

Figure 24.2 Employees in the UK, 1984–2017

Source: based on data from ONS

Full employment as a policy objective

Key term

full employment a situation where people who are economically active in the workforce and are willing and able to work (at going wage rates) are able to find employment

Full employment is seen as one of the core macroeconomic policy objectives. Having large numbers of people without jobs means that the economy is not making the best use of its labour resources, and is therefore sacrificing potential output that could be produced. It is also undesirable from the perspective of the individuals who find themselves unemployed.

Synoptic link

The notion of a full employment level of real GDP was introduced in Chapter 20 in the context of the *AD/AS* model. The full employment level of real GDP corresponds to a situation in which the economy is operating at its full capacity level, utilising its resources (including workers) effectively.

However, does this mean that everyone should have a job or be self-employed? Setting aside those who are economically inactive, there will always be some unemployment in a society, if only because there will be some people between jobs, or engaging in job search. Furthermore, if the economy were to be operating very close to full capacity, this would be likely to put upward pressure on wages and therefore prices. In other words, there may be a conflict between achieving full employment and maintaining the stability of prices.

So full employment does not mean that unemployment will be zero. But it is difficult to specify a particular percentage that would constitute full employment. This may vary in different periods, and in different countries, partly reflecting the degree of flexibility in the labour market.

Measuring unemployment

The measurement of unemployment in the UK has also been contentious over the years, and the standard definition used to monitor performance has altered several times, especially during the 1980s, when a number of rationalisations were introduced.

Historically, unemployment was measured by the number of people registered as unemployed and claiming unemployment benefit (Jobseeker's Allowance (JSA)). This measure of employment is known as the **claimant count of unemployment**. People claiming JSA must declare that they are out of work, and capable of, available for and actively seeking work, during the week in which their claim is made.

The claimant count of unemployment has now been superseded by the ILO unemployment rate as a measure of unemployment

One of the problems with the claimant count is that although people claiming JSA must declare that they are available for work, it nonetheless includes some people who are claiming benefit but are not actually available or prepared for work. It also excludes some people who would like to work, and who are looking for work, but who are not eligible for unemployment benefit, such as women returning to the labour force after childbirth. The transition to Universal Credit caused some problems, as there were some individuals who previously would have claimed JSA who were now on Universal Credit, but were not always identified as

Key terms

claimant count of unemployment the number of people claiming JSA each month

ILO unemployment rate (*Labour Force Survey* **unemployment**) measure of the percentage of the workforce who are without jobs, but are available for work, willing to work and looking for work

being out of work. The ONS stresses that the claimant count is not a measure of unemployment, although it 'can provide a useful indication of how unemployment is likely to vary between areas and over time' (ONS, 2017).

Because of these problems, the claimant count has been superseded for official purposes by the so-called **ILO unemployment rate**, a measure based on the UK *Labour Force Survey*. This identifies the number of people available for work, and seeking work, but without a job. This definition corresponds to that used by the International Labour Organisation (ILO), and is closer to what economists would like unemployment to measure. It defines as being unemployed those people who are:

– without a job, want a job, have actively sought work in the last four weeks and are available to start work in the next two weeks; or

– out of work, have found a job and are waiting to start it in the next two weeks

Source: Labour Market Statistics

Exercise 24.1

In Greece in late 2017, there were 6,885 people aged between 15 and 64. Of these, 3,706 were employed and 2,193 were economically inactive.
Calculate the number of people in this age bracket who were unemployed and the percentage unemployment rate.

Quantitative skills 24.1

Calculating the percentage rate of unemployment

When calculating the percentage rate of unemployment, the key question concerns the portion of the active workforce who are unemployed at any point in time. This is calculated by expressing the number of unemployed as a percentage of the active workforce (i.e. employed plus unemployed). At the end of 2017 it was estimated that there were 31.054 million people in employment and 1.338 people unemployed. The percentage rate was therefore: $100 \times 1.338 \div (31.054 + 1.338) = 4.13\%$.

Figure 24.3 shows the ILO unemployment rate since 1971, expressed as a percentage of the workforce. The surge in unemployment in the early 1980s stands out on the graph, when the percentage of the workforce registered as unemployed more than doubled in a relatively short period. Although this seemed to be coming under control towards the end of the 1980s, unemployment rose again in the early 1990s before a steady decline into the new millennium, rising again in the financial crisis and recession of the late 2000s and tailing off towards the end of the 2010s.

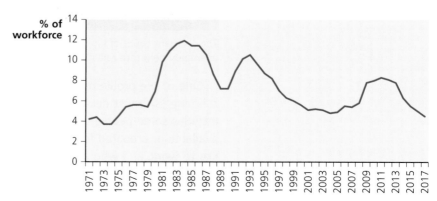

Figure 24.3 ILO unemployment rate, 1971–2017

Problems of measurement

It is important to be aware of the difficulties in measuring unemployment accurately. The claimant count is unreliable because it only captures those people who are eligible for JSA, so it excludes some people who might be validly recognised as being unemployed. For example, it excludes people returning to the workforce after raising children or for other reasons of absence. It also excludes those who are on government training schemes and a range of other categories of people. The ILO unemployment data are based on sample evidence, and extrapolated up to give the picture for the UK as a whole. The sample cannot be guaranteed to be fully representative. From the perspective of economic analysis, it would also be helpful to know how many people are unemployed in the sense of not being able to find employment at their desired wage, but this is not covered in the definition.

Measuring unemployment in developing countries becomes even more difficult. If there is no social security system, unemployed workers have no incentive to register as being unemployed. Furthermore, there may be people who cannot find jobs for which they are qualified, and who take jobs in second-choice occupations. This is a form of *underemployment*: for example, where qualified lawyers or doctors find themselves working as taxi drivers. In the UK context, underemployment could take the form of workers being unable to work for as many hours as they would like.

Causes of unemployment

frictional unemployment
unemployment associated with job search: that is, people who are between jobs

structural unemployment
unemployment that arises because of changes in the pattern of economic activity within an economy

Frictional unemployment

There will always be some unemployment in a dynamic economy. At any point in time, there will be workers transferring between jobs. Indeed, this needs to happen if the pattern of production is to keep up with changing patterns of consumer demand and relative opportunity cost. In other words, in a typical period of time there will be some sectors of an economy that are expanding and others that are in decline. It is crucial that workers are able to transfer from those activities in decline to those that are booming. Accordingly, there will be some unemployment while this transfer takes place, and this is known as **frictional unemployment**.

Structural unemployment

In some cases, this transfer of workers between sectors may be quite difficult to accomplish. For example, coal mining may be on the decline in an economy, but international banking may be booming. It is clearly unreasonable to expect coal miners to turn themselves into international bankers overnight. In this sort of situation there may be some longer-term unemployment while workers retrain for new occupations and new sectors of activity. Indeed, there may be workers who find themselves redundant at a relatively late stage in their career and for whom the retraining is not worthwhile, or who cannot find firms that are prepared to train them for a relatively short pay-back time. Such unemployment is known as **structural unemployment**. It arises because of the mismatch between the skills of workers leaving contracting sectors and the skills required by expanding sectors in the economy.

Structural unemployment may be reinforced when unemployed workers find that they do not have the skills required to adapt to changing

Key terms

cyclical unemployment
unemployment that arises during the downturn of the economic cycle, such as a recession

demand-deficient unemployment unemployment that arises because of a deficiency of aggregate demand in the economy, so that the equilibrium level of output is below full employment

seasonal unemployment
unemployment that arises in seasons of the year when demand is relatively low

technology (technological unemployment), or if the available jobs are in a different location (geographical unemployment).

Cyclical unemployment

Unemployment could also arise in a period of recession, when the demand for workers is low. This is sometimes referred to as **cyclical unemployment**.

Demand-deficient unemployment

In addition, there may be periods when the economy is in equilibrium below full employment because of a deficiency in aggregate demand, which is known as **demand-deficient unemployment**. A solution to this might be to boost aggregate demand, but not all economists believe that this is appropriate, as will be discussed later.

Seasonal unemployment

There may also be times of the year when the demand for labour varies because of seasonal effects: for example, the tourist sector experiences quiet periods during the winter. This may give rise to **seasonal unemployment**.

Wage inflexibility

A further reason for unemployment concerns the level of wages. Figure 24.4 shows a labour market in which a free market equilibrium would have wage W^* and quantity of labour L^*. If for some reason wages were set at W_0, there would be disequilibrium between labour supply (at L_s) and labour demand (at L_d). Expressing this in a different way, here is a situation in which there are more workers seeking employment at the going wage (L_s) than there are firms prepared to hire at that wage (L_d). The difference is unemployment.

Knowledge check 24.3

In Figure 24.3 you can see how unemployment was affected in the recession that followed the financial crisis. What sort of unemployment was this?

Synoptic link

The operation of labour markets is discussed in Chapters 16–18 as part of the microeconomics component.

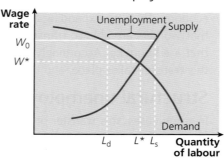

Figure 24.4 Unemployment in a labour market

There are a number of reasons why this situation might arise. Trade unions may have been able to use their power and influence to raise wages above the equilibrium level, thereby ensuring higher wages for their members who remain in employment but denying jobs to others. Alternatively, it could be argued that real wages will be inflexible downwards. So, a supply shock that reduced firms' demand for labour could leave wages above the equilibrium, and they may adjust downwards only slowly. This argument that unemployment could be caused by **real wage inflexibility** was advanced by economists in the Keynesian school as a reason why unemployment might be persistent.

Key term

real wage inflexibility an argument that if real wages do not adjust downwards the result would be persistent unemployment

voluntary unemployment
situation arising when an
individual chooses not to accept
a job at the going wage rate
involuntary unemployment
situation arising when an
individual who would like
to accept a job at the going
wage rate is unable to find
employment

Voluntary unemployment

Finally, if unemployment benefits are set at a relatively high level compared with wages in low-paid occupations, some people may choose not to work, thereby creating some **voluntary unemployment**. From the point of view of those individuals, they are making a rational choice on the basis of the options open to them. From society's point of view, however, there needs to be a balance between providing appropriate social protection for those unable to obtain jobs and trying to make the best use of available resources for the benefit of society as a whole.

Exercise 24.2

Classify each of the following types of unemployment as arising from frictional, structural, demand-deficient or other causes, and decide whether they are voluntary or involuntary:

a unemployment arising from a decline of the manufacturing sector and the expansion of financial services
b a worker leaving one job to search for a better one
c unemployment that occurs in the trough of the economic cycle
d unemployment that arises because the real wage rate is held above the labour market equilibrium
e unemployment of workers in the tourist sector during the winter months
d unemployment arising from slow adjustment to a fall in aggregate demand
e unemployment arising because workers find that low-paid jobs are paying less than can be obtained in unemployment benefit

Migration and unemployment

A contentious issue in recent years has been the question of migration, and the effect of an inflow of migrants on the domestic labour market. From the point of view of economic analysis, this issue turns on the characteristics of immigrant workers, especially in relation to skills. If immigrant workers have skills that are complementary to those of native workers, then an inflow of migrants can have beneficial effects on the domestic economy, by raising national income, resulting in an increase in the demand for workers. The situation is different where migrants are substitutes for domestic workers, such that the result may be a decrease in the equilibrium wage, and an increase in unemployment among native workers.

Consequences of unemployment

Perhaps the most obvious consequence of unemployment is the costs it imposes on prospective workers, in the sense that **involuntary unemployment** carries a cost to each such individual in terms of forgone earnings and the need to rely on social security support. At the same time, the inability to find work and to contribute to the family budget may impose a cost in terms of personal worth and dignity.

From society's perspective, if the economy is operating below full capacity, then it is operating within the *PPC*, and therefore is not making the best possible use of society's resources. In other words, if those unemployed workers were in employment, society would be producing more aggregate output, and the economy would be operating more efficiently overall.

When unemployment is high, the government will find that it raises less tax revenue in the form of income tax, but will face high expenditure in the form of social security payments. Firms will be unable to sell as much output as previously, so will make lower profits. In addition, when unemployment is rising and aggregate demand is falling, there will be negative multiplier effects, so other workers will suffer, either by becoming unemployed, or by being able to work fewer hours.

Long-term unemployment has potentially important social effects. Workers who are unemployed for a long period will become dispirited and deskilled, and therefore find it increasingly difficult to get back into the workforce. A by-product of this may be an increase in crime and vandalism, imposing costs on other members of society.

Frictional unemployment, on the other hand, may have beneficial effects. Workers who are able to find better jobs will lead to an improvement in the overall efficiency of production, and could potentially improve allocative efficiency, by moving to sectors for which demand is buoyant.

Summary

- The population of working age is made up of the employed, the unemployed and the economically inactive.
- Full employment is an objective of macroeconomic policy, as unemployment is costly to those who are unemployed and to society as a whole.
- Unemployment is measured in two ways. The claimant count is based on the number of people claiming JSA. The ILO measure is based on a sample of the population through the Labour Force Survey.
- Unemployment arises for a variety of reasons, and there will always be some unemployment in the economy, even when the economy is in equilibrium.

Exercise 24.3

Visit the website of the ONS (at www.ons.gov.uk/) and find out the latest data for unemployment. Has the performance of the economy in respect of this variable improved or deteriorated in the last year?

The effects of full employment

On the face of it, achieving full employment seems a no-brainer as a policy objective. Why would you not want to be using the economy's resources to the full? Full employment means not only that the economy is operating efficiently but that society is avoiding the negative consequences that can flow from high unemployment.

A common misconception is that full employment means unemployment should be zero. This chapter has argued that this is not going to happen, as there will always be some unemployment present in the economy, if only frictional unemployment as people change jobs in a dynamic economy.

Another view of full employment is that it occurs when there is no cyclical or demand-deficient unemployment. This corresponds to the full employment level of real GDP as used in the *AS/AD* model. However, if you look back at Figure 20.10 on page 286, you can see that if there

Knowledge check 24.4

Suppose that the economy is operating below full employment. How would you show this in relation to the economy's *PPC*?

Synoptic link

The potential problems caused by persistent price increases (i.e. inflation) are discussed in Chapter 25. The relationship (trade-off) between unemployment and inflation is analysed in Chapter 33.

is an increase in aggregate demand when the economy begins at the full employment level of real GDP, the result is an increase in the price level but no change in real GDP. In other words, when the economy is operating at full employment, it may be vulnerable in the face of an increase in aggregate demand because of the potential effect on prices.

In the light of the possible pressure on prices, some economists have argued that full employment should be regarded as the level of unemployment at which there is no tendency for inflation to accelerate.

It is also worth being aware that the measured level of employment and unemployment may not be a true representation of whether the economy is at capacity. There may be people who are employed, but who would like to work more or differently. For example, some part-time workers might prefer a full-time job, while some people may find themselves in second-choice occupations, in which they are less productive than they could be. However, notice that in late 2018, 85.8% of part-time workers indicated that they did not want a full-time job. There may also be discouraged workers, who are not registered as being economically active, so do not appear in the unemployment figures.

The definition of full employment is therefore rather imprecise. These arguments may suggest that we cannot be exactly sure whether or not the economy is at full employment. However, it remains an important objective of policy, given the negative consequences of having high unemployment.

Summary
- There will always be some unemployment in an economy, so full employment does not imply zero unemployment.
- If full employment is regarded as a situation with no cyclical or demand-deficient unemployment, then an increase in aggregate demand would put upward pressure on the price level.
- Some economists have argued that full employment should be regarded as the level of unemployment that does not lead to an acceleration in the inflation rate.
- Although full employment is difficult to measure precisely, it remains an important objective of macroeconomic policy.

The cost of unemployment

By setting full employment as a key objective of macroeconomic policy, there is an underlying presumption that unemployment is a bad thing. But what are the costs associated with unemployment?

From society's point of view there are some obvious costs. If people are unemployed, they are not contributing to society's output, so there is an opportunity cost in relation to the work that unemployed individuals could have been providing. High unemployment may create a feeling of low morale, and therefore affect firms' expectations of future demand for their products. If this is so, they may decide to invest less in expanding capacity, which would then affect the rate of economic growth.

There may also be social impact arising from a high rate of unemployment, as some commentators have pointed to the effect of unemployment on crime or social disorder.

On the other hand, if unemployment is low, this could put pressure on prices, potentially resulting in inflation.

It should also be remembered that it is important the economy responds to changes in the economic environment. At any point in time, there are likely to be some activities that are in decline, and others that are expanding. This is the nature of a dynamic economy. The labour market therefore needs to be sufficiently flexible to allow workers to transfer from declining to expanding sectors — even if this requires retraining and a period of unemployment.

There is also the issue of the costs incurred by the individuals who are unemployed. They may face not only loss of income and descent into relative poverty, but also a loss of dignity and the ability to contribute to society.

In considering this, it is important to distinguish between short- and long-run unemployment and between voluntary and involuntary unemployment. Individuals may choose to be unemployed (i.e. be part of voluntary unemployment) for various reasons. It could be that they simply want to find a better job than the one they have, or to join an expanding sector where they can be better paid. Of course, there may also be those who view the available social security benefits as being adequate for their needs, enabling them to enjoy more leisure.

Involuntary unemployment may be of more concern, as it involves people who would like to work but cannot find suitable employment. Even this may not be of major concern if the period for which they are unemployed is relatively short. Of most concern are those who are long-term involuntarily unemployed.

Follow-up questions

a Evaluate the consequences of unemployment from the point of view of society as a whole.

b Discuss the extent to which society should be concerned about the situation facing individuals who are unemployed.

CHAPTER 24 QUESTIONS

A Multiple-choice questions

1 If a person chooses not to work, or look for employment, they are classified as:
   a Unemployed
   b Employed
   c Economically inactive
   d Economically active

2 Which of the following is a reason for the use of the ILO unemployment rate as opposed to the claimant count?
   a It includes everyone who is claiming Jobseeker's Allowance
   b It is a survey of every household in the UK
   c It excludes people who are not eligible for unemployment benefit
   d It includes people who are actively seeking work but not eligible for unemployment benefit

3 If a worker has been made redundant because a machine has replaced the job role they performed, this would be classed as which type of unemployment?
   a Cyclical
   b Structural
   c Seasonal
   d Demand-deficient

B Knowledge and understanding questions

4 Explain what is meant by the term 'unemployment'. [2 marks]

5 Explain **two** reasons why a government might pursue a policy objective of full employment. [4 marks]

6 Explain **two** possible causes of unemployment. [4 marks]

C Stimulus response question

7 Unemployment in Australia has been falling in recent years. It hit its lowest rate in 2018 for over 6 years, and this level now meets the Reserve Bank's (the central bank of Australia's) definition of full employment.
   a Explain what is meant by the term 'full employment'. [2 marks]
   b Evaluate the possible effects of full employment on the Australian economy. [12 marks]

D Essay question

8 Evaluate the main causes of unemployment in the UK economy. [20 marks]

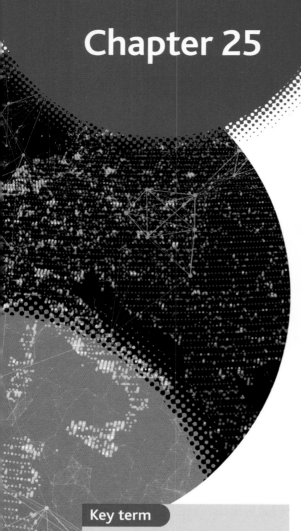

Inflation

Inflation is one of the key indicators of macroeconomic performance, and its control has been a primary objective of governments. This chapter explores what is meant by inflation, how it is calculated and why it is so important.

Learning objectives

After studying this chapter, you should be able to:

- explain inflation, deflation, disinflation and hyperinflation
- explain the policy objective of low and stable inflation
- explain how inflation is measured using the consumer price index (CPI) and the retail price index (RPI)
- explain and calculate the rate of inflation using index numbers
- evaluate the causes and consequences of inflation and deflation

Inflation

Inflation is an increase in the overall level of prices in an economy. It may not be immediately apparent as to why this matters, but clearly it has mattered to governments, as successive governments for the past 40 years and more have adopted policies intended to ensure that there is low and stable inflation.

Although economic growth may be seen as the most fundamental objective of macroeconomic policy, attention has often been more focused on the control of inflation. This is because it is feared that if inflation is high and volatile, this will deter firms from undertaking investment and therefore hinder economic growth. Firms base their investment plans on their expectations of the future. If inflation is high and volatile, it becomes more difficult for firms to form reliable expectations about the future, or to be sure of the likely return on their investment expenditure. To put it another way, it is believed that a stable macroeconomic environment is crucial if there is to be economic growth.

If the control of inflation is to be a policy objective, then some way of monitoring it is needed. The first step is therefore to measure the average level of prices in the economy. Inflation can then be calculated as the percentage rate of change of prices over time.

Key term

inflation the rate of change of the average price level: for example, the percentage annual rate of change of the consumer price index

Study tip

If you are writing an essay, be careful not to claim that inflation is a policy objective of the government — it is low and stable inflation that is the objective!

Index numbers

In setting out to measure the general level of prices in an economy, there is no obvious way of producing a meaningful 'average' price. The solution is to use **index numbers**, which is a form of ratio that compares the value of a variable with some base point.

index number a way of comparing the value of a variable with a base observation such as a location or past period (e.g. the retail price index measures the average level of prices relative to a past year, known as a base period)

For example, suppose the price of a 250-gram pack of butter last year was 1.20p, and this year it is 1.80p. How can the price between the two periods be compared? One way of doing it is to calculate the percentage change using the formula introduced earlier: $100 \times (1.80 - 1.20) \div 1.20 = 50\%$.

Quantitative skills 25.1

Creating an index number

Another way of showing how prices have changed is to calculate an index number. In the above example, the current value of the index could be calculated as the current value divided by the base value, multiplied by 100. In other words, this would be $100 \times 1.80 \div 1.20 = 150$. The resulting number gives the current value relative to the base value.

This turns out to be a useful way of expressing a range of economic variables where you want to show the value relative to a base period. Index numbers can also be used to compare between regions or to compare variables measured in different units — anything where you want to compare with some base level.

Knowledge check 25.1

If a bundle of goods costs 4% higher in year 2 than in year 1, what would be the value of an index for year 2 based on year 1 = 100?

This technique is used to show the average level of prices at different points in time. For such a general price index, one procedure is to define a typical basket of commodities that reflects the spending pattern of a representative household. The cost of that bundle can be calculated in a base year, and then in subsequent years. The cost in the base year is set to equal 100, and in subsequent years the index is measured relative to that base date, thereby reflecting the change in prices since then. For example, if in the second year the weighted average increase in prices were 2.5%, then the index in year 2 would take on the value 102.5 (based on year 1 = 100). Such a general index of prices could be seen as an index of the *cost of living* for the representative household, as it would give the level of prices faced by the average household relative to the base year.

Exercise 25.1

Table 25.1 contains data on oil and petrol prices.

Table 25.1 Prices of oil and petrol

Date	Oil price ($ per barrel)	Average petrol price, South East region (£ per litre)	Average supermarket petrol price (£ per litre)
March 2015	61.2	1.118	1.099
March 2016	39.5	1.031	1.003
March 2017	51.4	1.204	1.116
March 2018	65.5	1.206	1.168

Source: the AA

a Construct index numbers based on March 2015 = 100 and compare the movements in the price of petrol in the South East region with the price of oil during this period.

b Construct index numbers to compare petrol prices in the South East with the average supermarket price for each of the periods.

The consumer price index and inflation

The most important general price index in the UK is the **consumer price index (CPI)**, which the government has used to set its inflation target since the beginning of 2004. This index is based on the prices of a bundle of goods and services measured at different points in time. A total of 180,000 individual price quotes on more than 700 different products are collected by the ONS each month, through visits to shops, and using the telephone and internet. Data on spending from *Household Final Monetary Consumption Expenditure* are used to compile the weights for the items included in the index. These weights are updated each year, as changes in the consumption patterns of households need to be accommodated if the index is to remain representative.

The index was much criticised because it excluded housing costs of owner-occupiers and council tax, and a new index was launched in March 2013 to remedy this. This index is known as **CPIH** and its rate of change became the ONS's headline measure of inflation in March 2017. Notice that CPIH covers the costs associated with owning, maintaining and living in one's own home, based on estimating a rental equivalent, but this does not include mortgage interest payments.

It is important to remember that the CPI or CPIH provides a measurement of the *level* of prices in the economy. This is not inflation: inflation is the *rate of change* of prices, and the percentage change in the CPI provides one estimate of the inflation rate.

Notice that the CPI sets out to measure the way that inflation affects the 'average' or representative family, but individual households whose consumption pattern differs from the norm may experience inflation in different ways — for example, pensioners may have different patterns of consumption and may experience inflation in a different way.

Exercise 25.2

Table 25.2 provides data on consumer prices for the UK, USA and Brazil.

Table 25.2 Consumer prices

	Consumer price index (2011 = 100)		
	UK	USA	Brazil
2006	89.4	94.4	82.9
2007	91.5	95.1	85.9
2008	94.8	96.7	90.8
2009	96.8	98.4	95.2
2010	100.0	100.0	100.0
2011	104.5	103.2	106.6
2012	107.4	105.3	112.4
2013	110.2	106.8	119.4
2014	111.8	108.6	126.9
2015	111.8	108.6	138.4
2016	112.6	110.1	150.5

Source: data from IMF

a Calculate the annual inflation rates for each of the countries from 2007 to 2016.

b Plot these three inflation series on a graph against time.

c By what percentage did prices increase in each country over the whole period — that is, between 2006 and 2016?

d Which economy do you judge to have experienced most stability in the inflation rate?

Alternative measurements of inflation

The traditional measure of inflation in the UK for many years was the **retail price index (RPI)**, which was first calculated (under another name) in the early twentieth century to evaluate the extent to which workers were affected by price changes during the First World War. This was later replaced by RPIX, which is the RPI excluding mortgage interest payments.

The CPI replaced RPIX partly because it is believed to be a more appropriate indicator for evaluating policy effectiveness. In addition, it has the advantage of being calculated using the same methodology as is used in other countries within the EU, so that it is more useful than the RPIX for making international comparisons of inflation.

The CPI and RPI are based on the same source of data, although there are some significant differences in the coverage and the detail of the calculation. Both measures set out to calculate the overall price level at different points in time. Each is based on calculating the overall cost of a representative basket of goods and services at different points in time relative to a base period. Both are produced from the same raw data but use different formulae to produce the index. The result of these calculations is an index that shows how the general level of prices has changed relative to the base year. The rate of inflation is then calculated as the percentage rate of change of the price index, whether it be the CPI, CPIH or RPI.

A typical basket of goods may cost considerably more after a few years' inflation

Differences between the CPI and RPI

The CPI, CPIH and RPI differ for a number of reasons, partly because of differences in the content of the basket of goods and services that are included, and partly in terms of the population of people who are covered by the index. For example, in calculating the weights, the RPI excludes pensioner households and the highest-income households, whereas the CPI does not. There are also some other differences in the ways that the calculations are carried out. RPIX removes mortgage interest payments from the RPI.

Figure 25.1 shows data for the rates of change of the CPI, RPI and CPIH since 2007. These rates have been calculated on a monthly basis, computing the percentage rate of change of each index relative to the value 12 months previously. Notice that by calculating the inflation rate with reference to the index 12 months previously, seasonal variations are smoothed out — this is an alternative approach to the seasonal adjustment process outlined in Chapter 22.

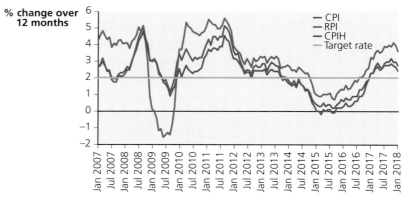

Figure 25.1 Alternative inflation measures in the UK, 2007–18

Source: based on data from ONS

A noticeable characteristic of Figure 25.1 is that for much of the period the CPI and CPIH have shown a lower rate of change than the RPI (except in 2009). In part this reflects the way in which the prices are combined, but it also reflects the fact that different items and households are covered. Since its introduction, the CPIH has stayed quite close to the CPI.

Until the end of 2003, the government's target for inflation was set at 2.5% per annum in the RPIX. After that date, the target for the CPI was set at 2% per annum. Since 1997, the Bank of England has had the responsibility of ensuring that inflation remains within one percentage point of this target. You can see from Figure 25.1 that inflation accelerated (on all three measures) during 2008, partly because of rising food prices in world markets, before plummeting in the global financial crisis that hit in late 2009. Notice how RPI inflation actually went negative at this time. This partly reflected the fact that interest rates were at an all-time low, which affected mortgage interest payments, causing RPI to fall for a period. Inflation then accelerated again, remaining above the target rate until 2015.

Deflation

The recession that began to affect many advanced countries in the late 2000s raised the possibility that the overall level of prices in an economy might fall. This situation of negative inflation is known as **deflation**. Figure 25.1 showed that the UK experienced falling prices according to the RPI for a period. This is not to be confused with **disinflation**, which refers to a period in which inflation falls relative to the previous period, in other words a period in which inflation decelerates.

Deflation is sometimes perceived to be bad for the economy on the grounds that economic agents will see this as a sign that the economy

Key terms

deflation a fall in the average level of prices (negative inflation)

disinflation a fall in the rate of inflation

Knowledge check 25.4

If the rate of change of prices decelerates but remains positive, would this be described as deflation or disinflation?

Study tip

Be careful not to confuse falling prices (deflation) with falling inflation. Falling inflation just means that prices are rising less quickly than before.

Exercise 25.3

Table 25.3 shows annual inflation in the UK between 2007 and 2011, as measured by changes in the RPI.

Table 25.3 RPI inflation in the UK, 2007–11

	RPI inflation
2007	4.3
2008	4.0
2009	−0.5
2010	4.6
2011	5.2

Identify the years in which there was inflation, deflation and disinflation.

Key term

hyperinflation a situation in which inflation reaches extreme or excessive rates

is in terminal decline. Indeed, if people expect prices to continue to fall, they may postpone purchases in the expectation of being able to buy at a lower price in the future. This would then mean a fall in demand in the economy, perpetuating the recession. However, central banks have ways of intervening to prevent deflation being long-lived, and it is not clear that consumers would actually act in the way described. It is worth noting that since records of the RPI began in the UK in 1948, there has been only one year in which deflation occurred.

Hyperinflation

When inflation gets completely out of control, a situation of **hyperinflation** may arise. When inflation is running at an extreme or excessive rate, the associated costs can also be extreme.

Hyperinflation has been rare in developed countries in recent years, although many Latin American economies were prone to hyperinflation for a period in the 1980s, and some of the transition economies also went through very high inflation periods as they began to introduce market reforms — one example of this was the Ukraine, where inflation reached 10,000% per year in the early 1990s. Another example is the African country of Zimbabwe, where *The Economist* in April 2013 claimed that inflation had reached 230,000,000% in 2008.

Summary
- Inflation is the rate of change of the general level of prices in an economy.
- Index numbers are helpful in comparing the value of a variable with a base date or unit, and are used to arrive at a measure of the average level of prices in an economy.
- In December 2003 the government adopted the consumer price index (CPI) as its preferred measure of the price level, and inflation is monitored through the rate of change of CPI.
- A version of the CPI known as CPIH is now the ONS's headline measure of inflation — this includes housing costs of owner-occupiers and council tax.

Causes of inflation

Inflation occurs when there is a rise in the general price level. However, it is important to distinguish between a one-off increase in the price level and a sustained rise over a long period of time.

Cost-push inflation

Suppose there is a one-off permanent rise in the price of oil. Such an increase means that firms face higher production costs, because oil is a key input. Therefore, this is one reason why prices may begin to increase. In the *AD/AS* model, this would be seen as a decrease in short-run aggregate supply. In Figure 20.12 on page 287, aggregate supply moves from $SRAS_0$ to $SRAS_1$ and the price level rises from P_0 to P_1. Notice that real GDP falls from Y_0 to Y_1.

In this way, inflation may be initiated by an increase in the costs faced by firms. This is referred to as **cost-push inflation**, as the increase in the overall level of prices is cost-driven. However, the *AD/AS* diagram only shows that there would be a one-off increase in the price level, which is not the same as saying there would be persistent inflation.

Demand-pull inflation

An alternative explanation for a rise in the general price level could come from the demand side, where an increase in aggregate demand leads to a rise in prices, especially if the economy is close to its full capacity. An increase in the price level emanating from the demand side of the macroeconomy is referred to as **demand-pull inflation**.

An increase in aggregate demand can arise from an increase in any of the components of aggregate demand, or from a cut in taxes. In terms of the *AD/AS* model, an increase in expenditure by consumers, firms or government would cause a rightward shift in *AD*, as would an increase in exports or a decrease in taxes. This is shown in Figure 25.2, with a shift from AD_0 to AD_1 and an increase in the price level from P_0 to P_1. In this case, real GDP remains at Y_{FE}. However, the *AD/AS* diagram again shows that there would be a one-off increase in the price level, which is not the same as saying there would be persistent inflation.

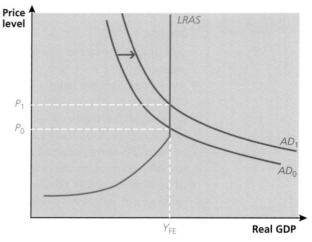

Figure 25.2 An increase in aggregate demand

Why should there be persistent inflation?

Why should there be *persistent* increases in prices over time? The *AD/AS* model shows that there may be one-off movements in either aggregate demand or aggregate supply that may lead to one-off changes in the overall price level, but unless the movements continue in subsequent periods there is no reason to suppose that inflation will continue. One explanation is provided by changes in the supply of money circulating in an economy.

Persistent inflation can take place only when the **money stock** grows more rapidly than real output. This can be shown in terms of aggregate demand and aggregate supply. If the money supply increases, firms and households in the economy find they have excess cash balances: that is, for a given price level they have more purchasing power than they expected to have. Their impulse will therefore be to increase their spending, which will cause the aggregate demand (*AD*) curve to move to the right. They will probably also save some of the excess, which will tend to result in lower interest rates — which will then reinforce the increase in aggregate demand. However, as the *AD* curve moves to the right, the equilibrium price level will rise, returning the economy to the full employment equilibrium.

If the money supply continues to increase, the process repeats itself, with prices then rising persistently. One danger of this is that people will get so accustomed to the process that they speed up their spending decisions, which simply accelerates the whole process.

To summarise, the analysis suggests that, although a price rise can be triggered on either the supply side or the demand side of the macroeconomy, persistent inflation can arise only through persistent excessive growth in the money stock.

Synoptic link

The role of money and its relationship with inflation is discussed more fully in Chapter 38.

Consequences of inflation

A crucial question is why it matters if an economy experiences inflation.

Uncertainty and investment

If firms cannot confidently predict the rate of change of prices, the increase in uncertainty may be damaging, and they may become reluctant to undertake the investment that would expand the economy's productive capacity.

Resource allocation

Furthermore, as Chapter 7 emphasised, prices are very important in allocating resources in a market economy. Inflation may consequently inhibit the ability of prices to act as reliable signals in this process, leading to a wastage of resources and lost business opportunities.

Effects on income distribution

As inflation accelerates, there could be an increase in inequality in the distribution of income, because some groups in society are less able to protect themselves against rising prices. In particular, pensioners and others on fixed incomes find the value of their incomes (and savings) are diluted by rising prices.

Effect on wages

Another consequence of high inflation is that workers negotiate for higher wages to compensate for the increase in prices. This further increases the costs faced by firms, which may reinforce the inflationary process.

Menu and shoe-leather costs

When inflation is very high and volatile, firms have to keep amending their price lists, which raises the costs of undertaking transactions. These costs are often known as the *menu costs* of inflation — however, these should not be expected to be significant unless inflation really is very high. A second cost of very high inflation is that it discourages people from holding money because, at the very high nominal interest rates that occur when inflation is high, the opportunity cost of holding money becomes great. People therefore try to keep their money in interest-bearing accounts for as long as possible, even if it means making frequent trips to the bank — for which reason these are known as the *shoe-leather costs* of inflation.

This reluctance to use money for transactions may inhibit the effectiveness of markets. For example, there was a period in the early 1980s when inflation in Argentina was so high that some city parking fines had to be paid in litres of petrol rather than in cash. Markets will not work effectively when people do not use money and the economy begins to slip back towards a barter economy. The situation may be worsened if taxes or pensions are not properly indexed so that they do not keep up with inflation.

Inflation as a policy objective

Although the menu costs and shoe-leather costs become important only at quite high rates of inflation, the potential negative consequences of inflation have elevated the control of inflation to one of the central planks of UK government macroeconomic policy. However, it should be noticed that the target for inflation has not been set at zero. During the period when the inflation target was set in terms of RPIX, the inflation target was 2.5%. From 2004 the target for CPI inflation was 2%.

The reasoning here is twofold. One argument is that it has to be accepted that measured inflation will overstate actual inflation, partly because it is so difficult to take account of quality changes in products such as smartphones, where it is impossible to distinguish accurately between a price change and a quality change. Second, wages and prices tend to be sticky in a downward direction: in other words, firms may be reluctant to lower prices and wages. A modest rate of inflation (e.g. 2%) therefore allows relative prices to change more readily, with prices rising by more in some sectors than in others. This may help price signals to be more effective in guiding resource allocation.

Study tip

The key costs of inflation are:
- uncertainty reduces incentives for investment
- prices fail to be reliable signals for resource allocation
- redistribution of income away from those on fixed incomes
- menu costs
- shoe-leather costs
- reluctance to use money for transactions

Exercise 25.4

Suppose that next year inflation in the UK economy suddenly takes off, reaching 15% per annum — in other words, prices rise by 15% — but so do incomes. Discuss how this would affect your daily life. Why would it be damaging for the economy in the future?

Inflation in the UK and throughout the world

Given that the UK has not experienced extreme inflation, and has indeed enjoyed relatively low inflation in recent years, you may wonder why these consequences of inflation are perceived to be so damaging that policy is dedicated towards controlling it. Looking at the history of inflation in the UK and at experiences around the world may help to explain why governments worry so much about it.

Figure 25.3 shows a time path for the rate of change in price levels in the UK since 1949. RPI has been used for this purpose, as the CPI was introduced only in 1997, so there is no consistent long-run series for it. The figure provides the backdrop to understanding the way the UK economy evolved during this period. Apart from the period of the Korean War, which generated inflation in 1951–52, the 1950s and early 1960s were typified by a low rate of inflation, with some rapid acceleration becoming apparent in the early 1970s.

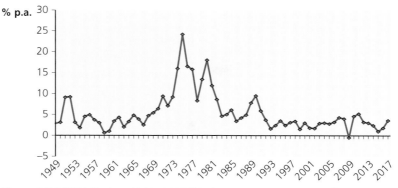

Figure 25.3 RPI inflation, 1949–2017 (% change over previous year)

Source: ONS

The instability of the 1970s was due to a combination of factors. Oil prices rose dramatically in 1973–74 and again in 1979–80, which certainly contributed to rising prices, not only in the UK but worldwide. However, inflation was further fuelled by the abandonment of the fixed exchange rate system, under which sterling had been tied to the US dollar until 1972. Under a fixed exchange rate system, the government must dedicate the use of monetary policy to maintaining the value of the currency.

However, the transition to a floating exchange rate system freed up monetary policy in a way that was perhaps not fully understood by the government of the day. As you can see in Figure 25.3, prices were allowed to rise rapidly — by nearly 25% in 1974–75. The diagram also shows how inflation was gradually reined in during the 1980s, and underlines the relative stability that has now been achieved, with inflation keeping well within the target range set by the government until the late 2000s, as noted above.

Figure 25.4 shows something of the extent to which the UK's experience is typical of the pattern of inflation worldwide. You can see from this how inflation in the advanced countries followed a similar general pattern in the early 1970s, with a period of gradual control after 1980. However, you can also see that the emerging and developing economies in the world experienced inflation at a much higher average rate after 1974 because they proved to be less able to bring prices under control after the oil price shocks. Much of this reflects events in Latin America, which suffered especially high rates of inflation in the 1980s and 1990s. This instability in the macroeconomic environment has almost certainly hindered development in the countries affected, and makes it important to understand how inflation is generated and how to curb it.

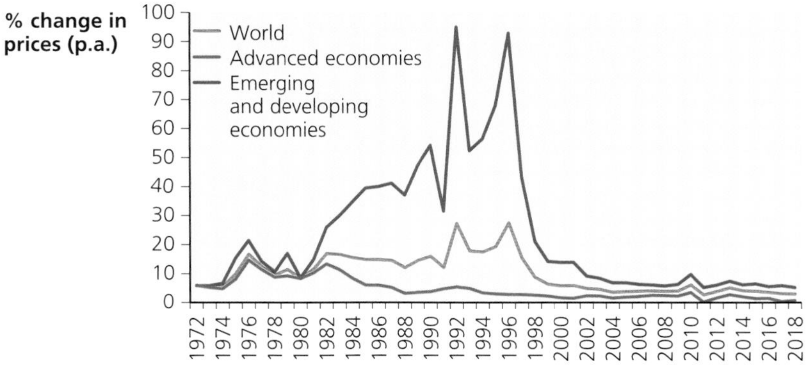

Synoptic link

The relationship between monetary policy and the exchange rate is discussed in Chapters 27 and 31.

Knowledge check 25.7

Why would rising oil prices lead to an increase in other prices?

Figure 25.4 World inflation since 1972 (% change in the CPI)

Summary

- The control of inflation has been the major focus of macroeconomic policy in the UK since about 1976.
- Low inflation reduces uncertainty, and may encourage investment by firms.
- Inflation can be initiated on either the supply side of an economy or the demand side.
- When inflation reaches an extreme rate it is known as hyperinflation.
- High inflation imposes costs on society and reduces the effectiveness with which markets can work.
- Deflation is negative inflation, and may need corrective action by the central bank to avoid perpetuating a recession.
- Disinflation occurs when the rate of inflation falls, but without necessarily becoming negative.

Case study 25.1

The UK economy in mid-2008

Figures 25.5 and 25.6 respectively show monthly inflation and unemployment in the UK between the beginning of 2004 and March 2008. Imagine that you are the chancellor of the exchequer considering the state of the economy.

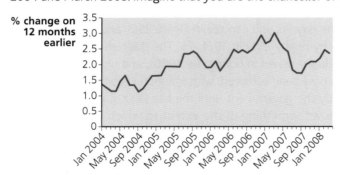

Figure 25.5 Inflation in the UK, 2004–08

Source: based on data from ONS

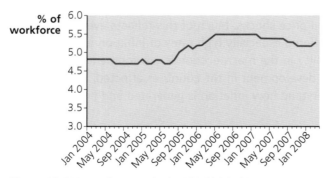

Figure 25.6 Unemployment in the UK, 2004–08

Source: based on data from ONS

Follow-up question

Discuss whether these two indicators give cause for concern about the performance of the economy. What other information would you need in order to come to a judgement?

After you have thought about this, look back at Figures 25.1 and 24.3 to see what happened next.

CHAPTER 25 QUESTIONS

A Multiple-choice questions

1 When the rate of inflation falls, this is called:

   a Deflation

   b Disinflation

   c Hyperinflation

   d Reinflation

2 Which of the following is a difference between the RPI and CPI measures of inflation?

   a The RPI does not include mortgage payments whereas the CPI does include mortgage payments

   b The RPI includes pensioners whereas the CPI does not include pensioners

   c The RPI uses a different basket of goods to the CPI

   d The RPI is reported as an index number whereas the CPI is not reported as an index number

3 If the CPI had a value of 105 in 2017 and 110 in 2018, then inflation increased by:

   a 5%

   b 4.76%

   c 4.55%

   d 4%

B Knowledge and understanding questions

4 Explain what is meant by the term 'inflation'. [2 marks]

5 Explain **two** reasons why a government might pursue a policy objective of low and stable inflation. [4 marks]

6 Explain **two** possible causes of inflation in an economy. [4 marks]

C Stimulus response question

7 In 2015, the UK economy came close to experiencing a period of sustained deflation. The main drivers of this deflationary period were falling fuel prices, a strong pound pushing the price of imported goods down and reduced university tuition fees.

   a Explain what is meant by the term 'deflation'. [2 marks]

   b Evaluate the possible consequences of deflation in the UK economy. [12 marks]

Chapter 26

The balance of payments

The UK economy is an open economy — in other words, it engages in international trade, exporting and importing goods and services. This chapter analyses these transactions and explores ways in which the domestic economy can be influenced by the international environment. The transactions are itemised in the balance of payments, which has significance for the performance of the economy.

Learning objectives

After studying this chapter, you should be able to:
- explain the balance of payments
- explain the components of the current account: trade in goods, trade in services, primary and secondary income
- explain the policy objective of a sustainable balance of payments position
- explain imbalances on the balance of payments
- explain and calculate balances on the different components of the balance of payments
- evaluate the causes and consequences of imbalances on the balance of payments

The balance of payments

Macroeconomics Part 7

Key term

balance of payments a set of accounts showing the transactions conducted between residents of a country and the rest of the world

Knowledge check 26.1

Explain why the balance of payments must always balance overall.

The **balance of payments** is a set of accounts that monitors the transactions that take place between UK residents and the rest of the world.

For an individual household it is important to monitor incomings and outgoings, as items purchased must be paid for in some way — either by using income or savings, or by borrowing. In a similar way, a country has to pay for goods, services or assets that are bought from other countries. The balance of payments accounts enable the analysis of such international transactions.

As with the household, transactions can be categorised as either incoming or outgoing items. For example, if a car made in the UK is exported (i.e. purchased by a non-resident of the UK), this is an 'incoming' item, as the payment for the car is a credit to the UK. On the other hand, the purchase of French cheese (an import) is a debit item.

Similarly, all other transactions entered into the balance of payments accounts can be identified as credit or debit items, depending upon the direction of the payment. In other words, when money flows into the country as the result of a transaction, that is a credit. If money flows out, it is a debit. As all items have to be paid for in some way, the overall balance of payments when everything is added together must be zero. However, individual components can be positive or negative.

It is important to be able to monitor these transactions because of the increasing interconnectedness of economies through the process of international trade — a process known as *globalisation*. This is the way in which economies have become more and more interconnected as a result of rapid changes in the technology of communications and transport, and with increasing deregulation of markets. The UK's decision to reduce its dependence upon the EU through Brexit goes against this trend, and a success from this will depend on being able to develop new links with economies elsewhere in the world.

In line with international standards, the accounts that make up the balance of payments are divided into three categories. The **current account** identifies transactions in goods and services, together with income payments and international transfers. Income payments here include the earnings of UK nationals from employment abroad and payments of investment income (known as primary income). Transfers (secondary income) are mainly transactions between governments — for example, between the UK government and EU institutions — which have made up the largest component during the UK's membership of the EU. Flows of bilateral aid and social security payments abroad are also included here.

The **financial account** measures transactions in financial assets, including investment flows and central government transactions in foreign exchange reserves.

The **capital account** is relatively small. It contains capital transfers, the largest item of which is associated with migrants. When a person changes status from a non-resident to a resident of the UK, any assets owned by that person are transferred to being UK-owned.

Figure 26.1 shows the relative size of the main accounts since 1980. Notice that these data are in current prices, so no account has been taken of changing prices during the period. This has the effect of compressing the apparent magnitude of the variables in the early part of the period (when prices were relatively low) and exaggerating the size towards the end of the period. Expressing these nominal values as a percentage of nominal GDP (as in Figure 26.2 for a longer period) provides a less misleading picture.

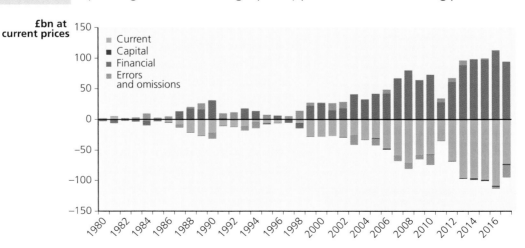

Figure 26.1 The UK balance of payments, 1980–2017

Source: based on data from ONS

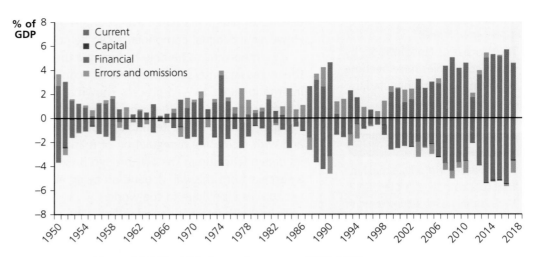

Figure 26.2 The UK balance of payments, 1950–2017

Source: calculated from ONS data

Knowledge check 26.3

Why is it helpful to express the variables in Figure 26.2 as a percentage of GDP?

As the total balance of payments must always be zero, the surplus (positive) components must always exactly match the deficit (negative) items. However, both graphs indicate that the magnitudes of the three major accounts vary through time.

The current account

Commentators often focus on the current account. Three main items appear on this account:

- trade in goods and services
- primary income
- secondary income (transfers)

Trade in goods and services

The balance of trade in goods and services is simply the balance between UK exports and imports of such goods and services. If UK residents buy German cars, this is an import and counts as a negative entry on the current account. On the other hand, if a German resident buys a British car, this is an export and constitutes a positive entry. Notice that not all of the trade carried on involves physical goods, and the trade in services is also important, especially for an economy like the UK.

The process of trading with other countries creates important connections across national borders. After all, UK exports become the imports of its trading partners. In principle, this suggests that overall the sum of all countries' trade balances should be zero. In practice, this will not be the case — if only because of data inaccuracies and mis-recordings. However, it is important to realise that the demand for UK exports depends in part upon economic conditions in its trading partners.

Synoptic link

Net exports comprise an important part of aggregate demand, as discussed in Chapter 19. Trade policies and negotiations are discussed in Chapter 36.

Quantitative skills 26.1

Calculate the balance of an item in the balance of payments accounts

In 2017, exports of goods were estimated as £342.5 billion and imports were £478.1 billion. The balance of trade in goods was therefore total exports minus imports: that is, 342.5 − 478.1 = −£135.6 billion.

Primary income

Primary income is the second important item in the current account. In addition to employment income from abroad, this comprises earnings accruing to domestic citizens on past investment abroad (less income earned by overseas residents who own assets in the UK). The largest item in this part of the account is earnings from direct investment, although there is also an element of portfolio investment — earnings from holdings of bonds and other securities.

Secondary income

Secondary income is made up of current transfers. These include taxes and social contributions received from non-resident workers and businesses, remittances, bilateral aid flows and military grants. However, the largest item is transfers with EU institutions, which showed a deficit of £9.4 billion in 2016.

The financial account

The financial account shows transactions associated with changes in the ownership of the UK's foreign financial assets and liabilities. There are four categories of these transactions:

1 foreign direct investment
2 portfolio investment
3 transactions in other financial assets
4 reserve assets

> **Knowledge check 26.4**
>
> Would an increase in the income from portfolio investment be an item on the current, financial or capital account?

> **Synoptic link**
>
> Financial instruments created through securitisation are discussed in Chapter 38, which examines the financial sector. Exchange rate systems are explored in Chapter 27.

An important part of the financial account is where UK investors undertake investment overseas, and where overseas investors purchase assets in the UK. It is important to remember that although the net flows of such foreign direct investment are part of the financial account, the income received in future years appears in the current account.

Portfolio investment relates to equities and securities. However, other types of financial assets have become increasingly important, including various forms of financial derivatives such as options and financial futures. These make up the third category registered in the financial account.

The final category concerns reserve assets such as gold and foreign exchange held by the Bank of England. These were important when the country was operating a fixed exchange rate system, but transactions are infrequent in a system of floating exchange rates.

The capital account

The capital account is relatively small. The largest item relates to the flows of capital associated with migration. If someone migrates to the UK, that person's status changes from being a non-resident to being a resident. His or her property then becomes part of the UK's assets and a transaction has to be entered in the balance of payments accounts. There are also some items relating to various EU transactions. The balance on this account is very small compared to the other components, and has never been greater than 0.1% of GDP.

Allocate each of the following items to the current, financial or capital account and calculate the balances for each account. Check that (together with errors and omissions) the total is zero. All data refer to 2015, at current prices in £ billion.

a Trade in goods	−118.6
b Net direct investment	−76.1
c Investment income	−42.8
d Current transfers	−22.8
e Transactions in reserve assets	−21.1
f Trade in services	+86.3
g Capital transfers	−2.0
h Compensation of employees	−0.1
i Total net portfolio investment	+139.0
j Other transactions in financial assets	+103.1
k Errors and omissions	+9.2

Causes and consequences of imbalances

As already mentioned, the overall balance of payments (combining the credit and debit items from all three accounts) must always be zero because outgoings must be equal to incomings — in other words, everything must be paid for. However, this does not mean that each of the three accounts will always balance, and imbalances can arise for a number of reasons. Notice that the focus here will be on the current and financial accounts, given that the capital account is so small.

The current account

The current account has been in deficit every year since 1984. There are several possible causes of a deficit on the current account of the balance of payments.

- Changes in the structure of economic activity affect the pattern of trade in goods and services.
- The competitiveness of domestic production relative to other countries is important. If productivity at home is weak, or if domestic firms are producing poor quality products, then the demand for exports will be relatively low.
- If inflation in the home country is high relative to elsewhere, this will again discourage exports and encourage imports. With high inflation, rising labour costs can fuel this process.
- Rapid economic growth can draw in imports and contribute to a current account deficit.

Figure 26.3 shows the components of the current account. You can see that overall it is the trade in goods and in services that has the strongest impact on the current account balance, with the overall balance on the current account (CBAL) tracking the trade in goods quite closely in the 1990s. However, more recently the trade in goods has moved further into deficit, reinforced by a higher deficit in primary income. This has been partially offset by a gradual increase in the surplus on trade in services.

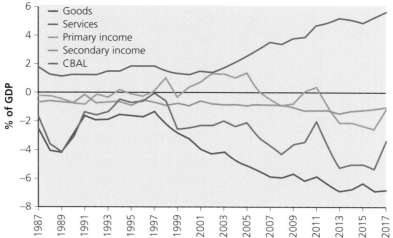

Figure 26.3 The composition of the current account since 1987 (balances)

Source: calculated from ONS data

Knowledge check 26.5

Looking at Figure 26.3, which item contributed most clearly to the smaller current account deficit in 2011?

This pattern is not new. Trade in goods has traditionally shown a deficit for the UK — it has shown a surplus in only 6 years since 1950. On the other hand, trade in services has recorded a surplus in every year since 1966. This imbalance partly reflects changes in the pattern of economic activity in the UK, with manufacturing in decline and services expanding. Exports of cars and consumer goods have typically shown a significant deficit, whereas services such as insurance and financial services have been in surplus.

Manufacturing and exports of cars are on the decline in the UK

This and the other causes outlined above are all concerned with the relative competitiveness of goods produced domestically compared with those produced abroad. If a country loses international competitiveness, then net exports are likely to fall, so reducing aggregate demand and potentially resulting in an increase in unemployment. To some extent, these effects can be mitigated through exchange rate movements.

There is an important consequence that arises if persistent deficits are being sustained over long periods of time. A deficit on the current account

Synoptic link

International competitiveness is discussed in Chapter 35, and exchange rates in Chapter 27.

must be balanced by a surplus on the financial and capital accounts if the overall balance of payments is to be zero. In the short run, it may be possible to finance the trade deficit by selling UK financial assets to foreigners or by borrowing from overseas. However, this might not be regarded as desirable in the longer term, if it affects the overall ownership pattern of British assets. For this reason, the current account cannot be viewed in isolation from the rest of the balance of payments.

The financial account

The trend towards globalisation means that both inward and outward investment increased substantially during the 1990s, although there was a dip after 2000. However, Figure 26.2 shows that the financial account has been in strong surplus in the early part of the twenty-first century, although it dipped during the financial crisis of the late 2000s.

The surplus on the financial account is in part forced by the deficit on the current account. If an economy runs a current account deficit, it can do so only by running a surplus on the financial account. Effectively, what is happening is that, in order to fund the current account deficit, the UK is selling assets to foreign investors and borrowing abroad.

An important question is whether global trade imbalances like this are sustainable in the long run. Selling assets or borrowing abroad has future implications for the current account, as there will be outflows of investment income and debt repayments in the future following today's financial surplus. It also has implications for interest rate policy. If the authorities were to hold interest rates high relative to the rest of the world, this would tend to attract inflows of investment, again with future implications for the current account.

Figure 26.4 shows the time path of foreign direct investment in the UK since 1987, again expressed as a percentage of GDP. You can see that the flows in and out of the UK since the late 1990s have been quite volatile. This arises partly because the flows tend to be dominated by large-scale mergers and acquisitions, which cause sudden changes in the size of the flow. For example, when SABMiller (a company with headquarters in the UK) was taken over by Anheuser-Busch in 2016, this generated a positive item on the financial account, but the profits subsequently generated by the company flow out of the UK, and constitute a negative item on the current account.

Knowledge check 26.6

If there is an increase in inward foreign direct investment in the present, how will the current account of the balance of payments be affected in the future?

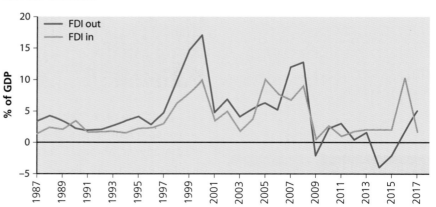

Figure 26.4 Foreign direct investment in the UK

Source: based on data from ONS

The overall balance of payments

Overall, the balance of payments must be maintained at zero, but imbalances on the current and financial accounts can be important.

The overall balance on the current account partly reflects changes in the pattern of economic activity, with manufacturing in decline and services expanding. This partly reflects changes in the international competitiveness of UK goods and services. Within the current account, the deficit in the trade in goods is partly offset by the surplus in services, but overall the current account shows a persistent deficit.

This deficit needs to be balanced by a surplus on the financial account, implying the sale of UK assets abroad. This then has long-term consequences for the current account, because of the outflow of income that is part of the current account, a consequence that may be of concern in the long term. However, changes in the exchange rate have an important impact on the relative competitiveness of UK goods and services. This is discussed in the next chapter.

Summary

- The balance of payments is a set of accounts that contains details of the transactions that take place between the residents of an economy and the rest of the world.
- The accounts are divided into three sections: the current, financial and capital accounts.
- The current account identifies transactions in goods and services, together with income payments and international transfers.
- The financial account measures transactions in financial assets, including investment flows and central government transactions in foreign reserves.
- The capital account, which is relatively small, contains capital transfers.
- The overall balance of payments must always be zero.
- The current account has been in persistent deficit since 1984, reflecting a deficit in trade in goods that is partly offset by a surplus in invisible trade.
- The financial account has been in strong surplus — as is required to balance the current account deficit.

Case study 26.1

The UK balance of trade

Figure 26.5 shows the UK's balance of trade in goods since 1990, measured in current prices. The picture is startling, showing a steady increase in the deficit since 1997, following a period of relative stability.

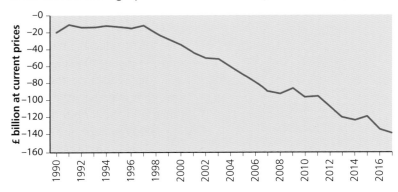

Figure 26.5 The UK balance of trade in goods since 1990

Source: ONS

There are several possible causes underpinning this picture. One relates to the production of North Sea oil and gas, which peaked in the late 1990s, and has declined steadily since then. Secondly, the structure of economic activity has been changing, such that the trade balance in services has increased steadily, which partly offsets the decline in the goods trade balance.

Overall, the negative trade balance has contributed to the overall deficit on the current account of the balance of payments, which has meant that the overall balance of payments has only been maintained by surpluses on the financial account.

Follow-up questions

a Explain why the fact that the trade balance as shown in Figure 26.5 is measured in current prices could affect the interpretation of the data.
b Explain why the changing structure of the economy may have affected the trade deficit.
c Evaluate the consequences of an increasing deficit in the trade balance for the balance of payments.

CHAPTER 26 QUESTIONS

A Multiple-choice questions

1 Which of the following is not a component of the current account?

   a Trade in goods

   b Trade in services

   c Transfers of ownership of fixed assets

   d Secondary income

2 Which of the following is true?

   a The balance of payments does not include services

   b The balance of payments only reflects trade with the EU

   c The balance of payments monitors transactions between the UK and the rest of the world

   d The balance of payments only includes the current account

3 When a UK business sells a product abroad this is known as:

   a An import

   b An export

   c A surplus

   d A deficit

B Knowledge and understanding questions

4 Explain what is meant by the term 'primary income'. [2 marks]

5 Explain **two** reasons why a government might pursue a policy objective of a sustainable balance of payments position. [4 marks]

6 Explain **two** possible causes of an imbalance on the balance of payments. [4 marks]

C Stimulus response question

7 The UK has shown a deficit in trade in goods every year since 1986. However, the trade in services has shown a surplus every year since 1966.

   a Explain what is meant by a deficit in trade in goods. [2 marks]

   b Evaluate the possible consequences for the UK economy of the balance of payments position. [12 marks]

Chapter 27

Exchange rates

Exchange rates play an important role in the macroeconomy. The rate at which one country's currency exchanges for that of another influences the competitiveness of domestic firms in international markets, and is inextricably linked with the state of the balance of payments. The way in which the exchange rate is determined has wide-reaching effects on the conduct and effectiveness of macroeconomic policy. This chapter investigates why the exchange rate is so important, and how the various systems for determining its value work.

Learning objectives

After studying this chapter, you should be able to:
- explain and calculate exchange rates
- explain, with the aid of a diagram, the determination of exchange rates in fixed and floating exchange rate systems
- evaluate the causes and consequences of exchange rate changes
- evaluate the advantages and disadvantages of different exchange rate systems

The exchange rate

Closely associated with the balance of payments is the **exchange rate** — the price of one currency in terms of another. The exchange rate is important because it influences the prices that domestic consumers must pay for imported goods, services and assets, and also the price that foreigners pay for UK goods, services and assets. A foreign exchange transaction is needed whenever trade takes place. If, as a UK resident, you buy goods from abroad, you need to purchase foreign exchange — say, euros — and you have to supply pounds in order to buy euros. Similarly, if a French tourist in the UK buys UK goods or services, the transaction needs to be carried out in pounds, so there is a demand for pounds. For example, suppose that the exchange rate between pounds sterling and the euro is 1.1 (€ per £). If you go on holiday to Spain and take £50 with you for spending money, you would get 50 × 1.1 = 55 euros.

The foreign exchange market is shown in Figure 27.1. The demand for pounds arises from overseas residents (e.g. in the USA or the euro area) wanting to purchase UK goods, services or assets, whereas the supply of pounds emanates from domestic residents wanting to purchase overseas goods, services or assets. The balance of payments accounts itemise these transactions, which entail the demand for and supply of pounds. Notice that the demand for currency is a *derived demand* — therefore pounds are demanded when people holding dollars or other currencies want to buy British. Similarly, pounds are supplied when people holding sterling want to buy foreign goods, services or assets.

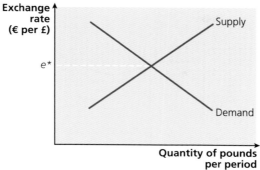

Figure 27.1 The market for pounds sterling

The demand curve is downward sloping because when the €/£ rate is low, UK goods, services and assets are relatively cheap in terms of euros, so demand is relatively high. When the €/£ rate is relatively high, Europeans receive fewer pounds for their euros, so the demand will be relatively low.

The supply curve of pounds is upward sloping. When the €/£ rate is relatively high, the supply of pounds will be relatively strong, as UK residents will get plenty of euros for their pounds and so will demand European goods, services and assets, supplying pounds in order to buy the foreign exchange needed for the transactions. When the €/£ rate is low, European goods, services and assets will be relatively expensive for UK residents, so fewer pounds will be supplied.

The market is in equilibrium at e*, where the demand for pounds is just matched by the supply of pounds. This position has a direct connection with the balance of payments. If the demand for pounds exactly matches the supply of pounds, this implies that there is a balance between the demand from Europeans for UK goods, services and assets and the demand by UK residents for European goods, services and assets. In other words, the balance of payments is in overall balance.

The demand for UK exports in world markets depends upon a number of factors. In some ways, it is similar to the demand for a good. In general, the demand for a good depends on its price, on the prices of other goods, and on consumer incomes and preferences. In a similar way, you can think of the demand for UK exports as depending on the price of UK goods, the price of other countries' goods, incomes in the rest of the world and foreigners' preferences for UK goods over those produced elsewhere. However, in the case of international transactions the exchange rate is also relevant, as this determines the purchasing power of foreigners' incomes in the UK. Similarly, the demand for imports into the UK depends upon the relative prices of domestic and foreign goods, incomes in the UK, preferences for foreign and domestically produced goods and the exchange rate. These factors come together to determine the balance of demand for exports and imports.

The exchange rate plays a key role in influencing the levels of both imports and exports. Figure 27.2 shows the time path of the US$/£ exchange rate since 1997. It seems to have remained fairly steady during this period, although there was a fall in the exchange rate at the time of the financial crisis, and another following the Brexit vote.

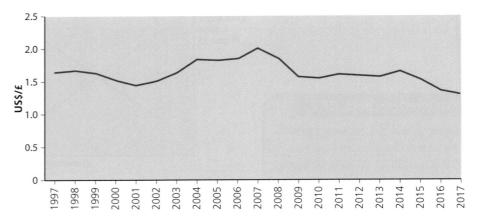

Figure 27.2 The nominal exchange rate, US$/£ since 1997

Source: Bank of England

Exercise 27.1

Visit the Bank of England website at **www.bankofengland.co.uk/ statistics/exchange-rates**.
Has the sterling rate against the dollar risen or fallen since the 2017? What does this imply?
How has the rate against the euro moved recently?

The exchange rate has been likened to the price of a good, and is therefore subject to demand and supply. This being so, is the exchange rate always determined by the free interaction of demand and supply? And why does it matter? The rest of this chapter explores these important issues.

Summary

- The foreign exchange market can be seen as operating according to the laws of demand and supply.
- The demand for pounds arises when non-residents want to buy UK goods, services or assets.
- The supply of pounds arises when UK residents wish to buy foreign goods, services or assets.
- When the exchange rate is at its equilibrium level, this automatically ensures that the overall balance of payments is zero.

A fixed exchange rate system

Key term

fixed exchange rate system a system in which the government of a country agrees to fix the value of its currency in terms of that of another country

One way in which the level of the exchange rate is set is where the authorities agree to manage the exchange rate — by fixing the value of their currency relative to that of another country, they operate a **fixed exchange rate system**.

During the Bretton Woods conference at the end of the Second World War, it was agreed to establish such a system, under which countries would commit to maintaining the price of their currencies in terms of the US dollar. This system remained in place until the early 1970s. For example, from 1950 until 1967 the sterling exchange rate was set at $2.80, and the British government was committed to making sure that it stayed at this rate. This system became known as the Dollar Standard.

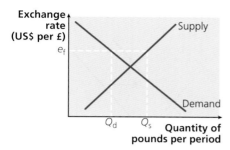

Figure 27.3 Maintaining a fixed exchange rate

Occasional changes in exchange rates were permitted after consultation, if a currency was seen to be substantially out of line — as happened for the UK in 1967.

Figure 27.3 illustrates how this works. Suppose the authorities announce that the exchange rate will be set at e_f. Given that this level is set independently by the government, it cannot be guaranteed to correspond to the market equilibrium, and in Figure 27.3 it is set above the equilibrium level. At this exchange rate the supply of pounds exceeds the demand for pounds. This can be interpreted in terms of the overall balance of payments. If there is an excess supply of pounds, the implication is that UK residents are trying to buy more American goods, services and assets than Americans are trying to buy British: in other words, there is an overall deficit on the balance of payments.

In a free market, you would expect the exchange rate to adjust until the demand and supply of pounds came back into equilibrium. However, with the authorities committed to maintaining the exchange rate at e_f, such adjustment cannot take place. However, the UK owes the USA for the excess goods, services and assets that its residents have purchased, so the authorities then have to sell **foreign exchange reserves** in order to make the books balance.

In terms of Figure 27.3, Q_d represents the demand for pounds at e_f and Q_s represents the supply. The difference represents the amount of foreign exchange reserves that the authorities have to sell to preserve the balance of payments. Such transactions are incorporated into the financial account of the balance of payments.

Notice that the *position* of the demand and supply curves depends on factors other than the exchange rate that can affect the demand for British and American goods, services and assets in the respective countries. It is likely that, through time, these will shift in position. For example, if the preference of Americans for British goods changes through time, this will affect the demand for pounds.

Consider Figure 27.4. For simplicity, suppose that the supply curve remains fixed but demand shifts. Let e_f be the value of the exchange rate that the UK monetary authorities have undertaken to maintain. With the demand for pounds at D_0 in panel (a), the chosen exchange rate corresponds to the market equilibrium, and no action by the authorities is needed. If Americans develop a liking for British TV programmes, the demand for pounds increases to D_1. With the exchange rate at e_f there is a shortage of pounds, and to prevent the exchange rate from appreciating to e_1, the monetary authorities in the UK need to supply additional pounds in return for US dollars. The supply of pounds increases to S_1 to maintain the fixed exchange rate. Conversely, if the demand for pounds falls from D_0 to D_2 in panel (b), because Americans want to buy fewer goods from the UK, there would be an excess supply of pounds, and the British monetary authorities would need to use foreign exchange reserves to buy up the surplus pounds in order to maintain the exchange rate, and the supply curve would shift to S_2 as the excess money supply is withdrawn from circulation.

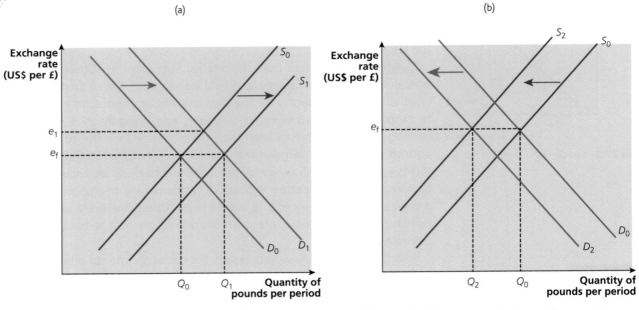

Figure 27.4 Maintaining a fixed exchange rate: (a) an increase in demand for pounds; (b) a decrease in demand for pounds

Key terms

devaluation process whereby a government reduces the price of its currency relative to an agreed rate in terms of foreign currency

revaluation process whereby a government raises the price of domestic currency in terms of foreign currency

Synoptic link

The operation of monetary policy is discussed in Chapter 31.

In the long term, the system will operate successfully for the country so long as the chosen exchange rate is close to the average equilibrium value over time, so that the central bank is neither running down its foreign exchange reserves nor accumulating them.

A country that tries to hold its currency away from equilibrium indefinitely will find this problematic in the long run, as it will cause a persistent trade imbalance. A persistent disequilibrium may need to be addressed by realigning the value of the currency, either by reducing the price of its currency (a **devaluation**) to tackle persistent current account deficits, or by raising the price of the currency (a **revaluation**) to deal with persistent surpluses.

During the Dollar Standard period, the British economy went through what became known as a 'stop–go' cycle of growth. Whenever the government tried to stimulate economic growth, the effect was to suck in imports, as the marginal propensity to import was high. The effect of this was to generate a deficit on the current account of the balance of payments, which then had to be financed by selling foreign exchange reserves.

This process has two effects. First of all, in selling foreign exchange reserves, domestic money supply increases, which then puts upward pressure on prices, threatening inflation. In addition, the Bank of England had finite foreign exchange reserves, and could not allow them to be run down indefinitely. This meant that the government had to rein in the economy and reduce money supply, thereby slowing the rate of growth again — hence the label 'stop–go'.

The Bretton Woods Dollar Standard broke down in the early 1970s. Part of the reason for this was that such a system depends critically on the stability of the base currency (i.e. the US dollar). During the 1960s the USA's need to finance the Vietnam War meant that the supply of dollar currency began to expand, one result of which was accelerating inflation in the countries that were fixing their currency in terms of the US dollar. It then became increasingly difficult to sustain exchange rates at fixed levels. The UK withdrew from the Dollar Standard in June 1972.

The USA's need to finance the Vietnam War resulted in accelerating inflation in the countries that were fixing their currency to the US dollar

Summary

- After the Bretton Woods conference at the end of the Second World War, the Dollar Standard was established, under which countries agreed to maintain the values of their currencies in terms of US dollars.
- In order to achieve this, the monetary authorities engaged in foreign currency transactions to ensure that the exchange rate was maintained at the agreed level, accumulating foreign exchange reserves to accommodate a balance of payments surplus and running down the reserves to fund a deficit.
- Occasional realignments were permitted, such as the devaluation of sterling in 1967.
- Under a fixed exchange rate system, monetary policy can be used only to achieve the exchange rate target.
- The Bretton Woods system broke down in the early 1970s.

Exercise 27.2

A firm wants to purchase a machine tool that is obtainable in the UK for a price of £125,000, or from a US supplier for $300,000. Suppose that the exchange rate is fixed at £1 = $3.

a What is the sterling price of the machine tool if the firm chooses to buy in the USA?

b From which supplier would the firm be likely to purchase?

c Suppose that, between ordering the machine tool and its delivery, the UK government announces a devaluation of sterling, so that when the time comes for the firm to pay up, the exchange rate is £1 = $2. What is the sterling price of the machine tool bought from the USA?

d Comment on how the competitiveness of British goods has been affected.

e Discuss the effects that the devaluation is likely to have on the economy as a whole.

Floating exchange rates

Under a **floating exchange rate system**, the value of the currency is allowed to find its own way to equilibrium. In some ways, this seems a much simpler way to operate, but it turns out that there are some complications, which are discussed below.

Suppose there is a decrease in demand for UK-produced goods. This means that the demand for sterling shifts to the left, as in Figure 27.5, as fewer pounds are needed to support a lower level of transactions. In a floating exchange rate system, the authorities do not intervene to support the value of the currency, so the equilibrium exchange rate falls (depreciates), from e_0 to e_1. Equilibrium is restored in the foreign exchange market, and the overall balance of payments is also maintained.

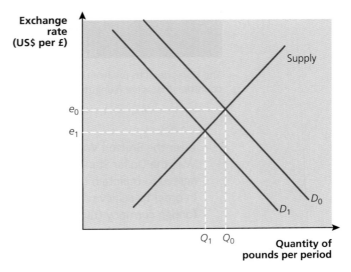

Figure 27.5 The exchange rate in a floating exchange rate system

This means that in this sort of system, the overall balance of payments is automatically assured, and the monetary authorities do not need to intervene to make sure it happens. In practice, however, governments have tended to be wary of leaving the exchange rate entirely to market forces, and there have been occasional periods in which intervention has been used to affect the market rate.

Causes of changes in the exchange rate

A fixed exchange rate system

When a fixed exchange rate system is in operation, changes in the exchange rate are rare by the very nature of the system. The authorities maintain the rate at the agreed level, and changes only occur when the authorities realise that the agreed rate is causing persistent problems by being a long way from the equilibrium value.

A floating exchange rate system

If the foreign exchange market is left free to find its own way to equilibrium, there are several reasons for the exchange rate to change.

The key factors that determine the exchange rate in a floating rate system are:

- relative inflation rates
- the trade balance
- net investment in the UK
- speculation
- relative interest rates and monetary policy

Relative inflation rates

Exchange rate equilibrium also implies a zero overall balance of payments. If the exchange rate always adjusts to the level that ensures this, it might be argued that the long-run state of the economy is one in which the competitiveness of domestic firms remains constant over time. In other words, you would expect the exchange rate to adjust through time to offset any differences in inflation rates between countries.

Extension material

The purchasing power parity theory

The purchasing power parity theory of exchange rates argues that this is exactly what should be expected in the long run if there are differences in inflation rates between countries. The nominal exchange rate should adjust in such a way as to offset changes in relative prices between countries.

The trade balance

The exchange rate in a free market is determined by the demand and supply for the currency. This means that changes in the balance between exports and imports can affect the exchange rate. An increase in the demand for exports implies an increase in the demand for sterling, so would lead to an appreciation of the currency (ceteris paribus).

Net investment in the UK

An increase in foreign direct investment would have similar effects. If the UK becomes an attractive prospect for foreign investors, this could also lead to an appreciation — or at least upward pressure on the exchange rate.

Speculation

In the short run the exchange rate may diverge from its long-run equilibrium. An important influence on the exchange rate in the short run is speculation. So far, the discussion of the exchange rate has stressed mainly the current account of the balance of payments. However, the financial account is also significant, especially since regulation of the movement of financial capital was liberalised. Some of these capital movements are associated with foreign direct investment, but sometimes there are also substantial movements of what has come to be known as **hot money**: that is, stocks of funds that are moved around the globe from country to country in search of the best return. The size of the stocks of hot money is enormous, and can significantly affect exchange

Key term

hot money stocks of funds that are moved around the world from country to country in search of the best return

375

rates in the short run. Changes in the domestic real interest rate can have a significant effect on these flows.

Such movements can influence the exchange rate in the short run. The returns to be gained from such capital flows depend on the relative interest rate in the country targeted, and on the expected exchange rate in the future, which in turn may depend on expectations about inflation.

Suppose you are an investor holding assets denominated in US dollars, and the UK interest rate is 2% higher than that in the USA. You may be tempted to shift the funds into the UK in order to take advantage of the higher interest rate. However, if you believe that the exchange rate is above its long-run equilibrium, and therefore is likely to fall, this will affect your expected return on holding a British asset. Indeed, if investors holding British assets expect the exchange rate to fall, they are likely to shift their funds out of the country as soon as possible — which may then have the effect of pushing down the exchange rate. In other words, this may be a self-fulfilling prophecy. However, speculators may also react to news in an unpredictable way, so not all speculative capital movements act to influence the exchange rate towards its long-run equilibrium value.

Interest rates and monetary policy

Financial flows into or out of the UK may be induced by the relative level of interest rates. If UK interest rates are high relative to elsewhere, this may attract an inflow of financial capital, so putting upward pressure on the interest rate and leading to an appreciation. The significance of this is that changes in the stance of monetary policy will have an effect on the exchange rate under a floating exchange rate system. These become an important part of the operation of monetary policy. Indeed, the decision of the monetary authorities in setting interest rates may be partly influenced by movements in the exchange rate.

Summary

- Under a floating exchange rate system, the value of a currency is allowed to find its own way to equilibrium without government intervention.
- This means that an overall balance of payments of zero is automatically achieved.
- The purchasing power parity theory argues that the exchange rate will adjust in the long run to maintain international competitiveness, by offsetting differences in inflation rates between countries.
- In the short run, the exchange rate may diverge from this long-run level, particularly because of speculation.
- The exchange rate is therefore influenced by relative interest rates and expected inflation, as well as by news about the economic environment.

Knowledge check 27.4

Give an example of how the sterling exchange rate has been affected by a news item.

Synoptic link

The influence of the exchange rate in the context of monetary policy is discussed in Chapter 31.

Evaluation of different exchange rate systems

In evaluating whether a fixed or a floating regime is to be preferred, there are many factors to be taken into account. This section will consider three consequences that flow from adopting either a fixed or a floating exchange rate system. First, it is important to examine the extent to which the respective systems can accommodate and adjust to external shocks that push the economy out of equilibrium. Second, it is important to consider the stability of each of the systems. Finally, there is the question of which system best encourages governments to adopt sound macroeconomic policies.

Adjustment to shocks

Every economy has to cope with external shocks that occur for reasons outside the control of the country. A key question in evaluating exchange rate systems is whether there is an effective mechanism that allows the economy to return to equilibrium after an external shock.

Under a floating exchange rate system, much of the burden of adjustment is taken up by changes in the exchange rate. For example, if an economy finds itself experiencing faster inflation than other countries, perhaps because those other countries have introduced policies to reduce inflation, then the exchange rate will adjust automatically to restore competitiveness.

However, if the country is operating a fixed exchange rate system, the authorities are committed to maintaining the exchange rate, and this has to take precedence. Therefore, the only way to restore competitiveness is by deflating the economy in order to bring inflation into line with other countries. This is likely to bring with it a transitional cost in terms of higher unemployment and slower economic growth. In other words, the burden of adjustment is on the real economy, rather than on allowing the exchange rate to adjust.

The Bretton Woods system operated for more than 20 years in a period in which many economies enjoyed steady economic growth. However, in the UK the system brought about a stop–go cycle, in which the need to maintain the exchange rate hampered economic growth, because of the tendency for growth to lead to an increase in imports and therefore to a current account deficit. The increasing differences between inflation rates in different countries led to the final collapse of the system, suggesting that it was unable to cope with such variation.

Furthermore, a flexible exchange rate system allows the authorities to utilise monetary policy in order to stabilise the economy — remember that under a fixed exchange rate system, monetary policy has to be devoted to the exchange rate target.

Stability

When it comes to stability, a fixed exchange rate system has much to commend it. After all, if firms know that the government is committed to maintaining the exchange rate at a given level, they can agree future contracts with some confidence. Under a floating exchange rate system, trading takes place in an environment in which the future exchange rate has to be predicted. If the exchange rate moves adversely, firms then face potential losses from trading. This foreign exchange risk is reduced under a fixed rate regime.

> **Knowledge check 27.5**
>
> Why would differences in inflation rates between countries create problems with operating a fixed exchange rate system?

377

Evaluation of the consequences of exchange rate changes

As has been outlined, exchange rate changes have some far-reaching consequences.

Under a flexible exchange rate system, the exchange rate adjusts to maintain international competitiveness in the long run. However, it also responds to external events and to financial movements induced by speculators. Such changes are not under the control of the authorities, but yet can have an impact on the real economy through the effect on prices of imports and exports.

The exchange rate may also be affected by policies introduced by the monetary authorities to address other policy targets. Suppose that two countries have been experiencing rapid inflation, and one of them decides to tackle the problem. It raises interest rates to dampen domestic aggregate demand, which leads to an **appreciation** of its currency. For the other country, the effect is a **depreciation** of the currency. (If one currency appreciates, the other must depreciate.) The other country therefore finds that its competitive position has improved, and it faces inflationary pressure in the short run. It may then also choose to tackle inflation, which in turn will affect the other country. These spillover effects could be minimised if the countries were to harmonise their policy action, but this is not always straightforward to achieve.

Critics of the flexible exchange rate system argue that it is too flexible for its own good. If governments know that the exchange rate will always adjust to maintain international competitiveness, they may have no incentive to behave responsibly in designing macroeconomic policy. They may be tempted to adopt an inflationary domestic policy, secure in the knowledge that the exchange rate will bear the burden of adjustment. In other words, a flexible exchange rate system does not impose financial discipline on individual countries. In this situation, changes in the exchange rate can result in inflationary pressure.

Under a fixed exchange rate system, changes in the exchange rate are few and far between. However, if the exchange rate is held away from its equilibrium level for a long time, speculation may begin to reinforce the pressure for a devaluation (or revaluation), and the economy may take some time to adjust when the change is eventually made.

Key terms

appreciation a rise in the exchange rate within a floating exchange rate system
depreciation a fall in the exchange rate within a floating exchange rate system

Study tip

Make sure that you can distinguish between a depreciation and a devaluation, and between an appreciation and a revaluation.

Exercise 27.3

Critically evaluate the following statements, and discuss whether you regard fixed or floating exchange rates as the better system.
a A flexible exchange rate regime is better able to cope with external shocks.
b A fixed exchange rate system provides a more stable trading environment and minimises risk.
c Floating exchange rates enable individual countries to follow independent policies.

Summary

- There are strengths and weaknesses with both fixed and floating exchange rate systems. A floating exchange rate system is more robust in enabling economies to adjust following external shocks, but it can lead to volatility and so discourage international trade.
- The move towards a fixed exchange rate system within the EU was partly in recognition that international trade is encouraged by stability in trading arrangements.
- Under a floating exchange rate system, much of the burden of adjustment to external shocks is borne by changes in the exchange rate, rather than by variations in the level of economic activity, which may be affected more under a fixed exchange rate system.
- A fixed exchange rate system offers stability, in the sense that firms know the future value of the currency, whereas under a floating rate regime there is more volatility.
- A fixed exchange rate system imposes discipline upon governments, and may facilitate international policy harmonisation.

Case study 27.1

Balancing the balance of payments

There are many ways in which the overall balance of the balance of payments can be achieved — which sometimes becomes controversial. An example of this was the way that China's exchange rate policy in the early 2000s facilitated its rapid economic growth but left a legacy of distrust between China and other countries (especially the USA).

One way in which the balance of payments is made to balance is through allowing the exchange rate to respond to the relative levels of supply and demand in the foreign exchange market. In other words, if the exchange rate is free to find its market level, it will tend to move to equalise the demand and supply of currency.

However, the balance of payments depends not only on trade in goods and services but also on transactions in financial assets. The demand for a country's financial assets depends not only on the exchange rate but also on the relative rate of interest in different countries. If UK interest rates are high compared with those elsewhere in the world, there will tend to be an inflow of financial capital. The resulting financial surplus will tend to cause the exchange rate to appreciate. This in turn affects the competitiveness of domestic goods and services, so the net result may be that the financial account surplus will be offset by a deficit on the current account.

Some countries have chosen to treat the balance of payments in a different way, by fixing the exchange rate in terms of some other currency, such as the US dollar. What this means is that any surplus or deficit on current or financial accounts must be offset by the purchase or sale of reserve assets (that is, financial assets denominated in terms of US dollars) in order to maintain the price of the currency.

The choice between fixing the exchange rate and allowing it to find its market value has a major effect on the structure of the balance of payments. This is illustrated in Figure 27.6, which shows the structure of the balance of payments for the USA and China in 2003.

In the USA, where the exchange rate is allowed to find its own market value, the accounts revealed a substantial current account deficit in 2003 (amounting to nearly 5% of GDP), balanced by a financial account surplus. In contrast, China showed surpluses on both the current and the financial account, balanced by substantial transactions in reserve assets, showing that the Chinese authorities had been artificially holding the value of their currency away from its equilibrium value.

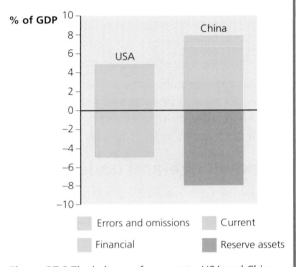

Figure 27.6 The balance of payments, USA and China, 2003

Source: IMF

Why should they want to do this? One reason is that it allowed China to maintain rapid growth in exports, by keeping its goods highly competitive in international markets, while at the same time attracting flows of inward foreign direct investment. In order to do this, it had to purchase US dollar-denominated assets — such as US Treasury Bills. In turn, this allowed the USA to maintain its current account deficit, funded partly by the sale of Treasury Bills.

A by-product of this strategy is that interest rates in the USA were lower than they would otherwise have been. This may have contributed to the financial crisis that followed.

Follow-up questions

a Discuss this strategy from the perspective of China. What are both the benefits and the risks of pursuing it?

b Now view the strategy from the USA's viewpoint. Why would the USA want to persuade China to revalue its currency?

c Why might China's strategy have contributed to the financial crisis?

d Comment on how the strategy adopted by China may have had consequences in terms of a legacy in its relationship with the USA.

CHAPTER 27 QUESTIONS

A Multiple-choice questions

1 Which of the following scenarios shows the pound appreciating?

   a £1 was worth $1.20 and is now worth $1.15

   b $1 was worth £0.90 and is now worth £1

   c £1 was worth $0.90 and is now worth $1.05

   d $1 was worth £1.30 and is still worth £1.30

2 If the value of a currency is left to market forces, then it is said to be:

   a A floating exchange rate system

   b A fixed exchange rate system

   c A pegged exchange rate system

   d A variable exchange rate system

3 If a currency depreciates then it is likely to have which of the following effects on an economy?

   a An increase in imports and an increase in exports

   b A decrease in imports and a decrease in exports

   c An increase in imports and a decrease in exports

   d A decrease in imports and an increase in exports

B Knowledge and understanding questions

4 Explain what is meant by the term 'exchange rate'. [2 marks]

5 Explain, with the aid of a diagram, how the price of a currency is determined in a floating exchange rate system. [4 marks]

6 Explain **two** possible advantages to a country of using a floating exchange rate system. [4 marks]

C Stimulus response question

7 In 2000, Denmark had a referendum to decide if the country should adopt the euro. The majority of the country voted against adoption and, to this day, Denmark still uses the krone.

The krone uses a fixed exchange rate system. It is pegged (fixed) to the value of the euro.

Denmark shares a border with Germany, which uses the euro, and Sweden, which does not. Both Germany and Sweden are important trading partners of Denmark, together with the UK.

   a Explain what is meant by a 'fixed exchange rate system'. [2 marks]

   b Evaluate the possible advantages and disadvantages to Denmark of pegging the value of the krone to the euro. [12 marks]

D Essay question

8 The value of the pound depreciated significantly after the referendum vote to leave the EU on 26 June 2016.

Evaluate the likely consequences to the UK economy of a depreciation of the pound. [20 marks]

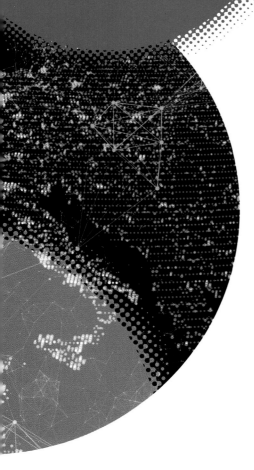

Chapter 28

Trends in macroeconomic indicators

The previous chapters have introduced the key macroeconomic variables that are important for the macroeconomy. This chapter focuses attention on the performance of the UK economy over the past 20 years and evaluates its current performance with that of other developed, emerging and developing economies.

Learning objectives

After studying this chapter, you should be able to:

- explain key trends in the UK macroeconomic performance in the last 20 years
- evaluate the current performance of the UK economy compared with other developed economies, emerging and developing economies

Trends in the UK's macroeconomic performance

How well is the UK economy performing in terms of the most important macroeconomic indicators? There have been significant developments in the economy in the past 20 years in real GDP, economic growth, employment, inflation, the balance of payments and productivity. The discussion here focuses on the period since 1997, highlighting the key features of each of these variables. Of particular significance in this period was the financial crisis that affected the economy (and that of other developed economies) in the late 2000s. The decision to leave the European Union, decided by the referendum of 2016, is also likely to affect the performance of the economy for the years to come.

In the late 1990s and early 2000s, the UK economy had enjoyed a period of relative stability, and the prospects for the global economy looked promising. However, the financial crisis that began in 2008 had a major impact on the UK economy, as will be apparent in the following discussion. It was triggered in the financial sector, when the banking sector got into difficulties. The effects spread, pushing the economy into a recession from which recovery was slow.

Real GDP and economic growth

Arguably real GDP and economic growth are the most significant macroeconomic variables when it comes to assessing the performance of an economy, as real GDP represents the resources available to the citizens

Synoptic link

The policy response to the financial crisis will be explored in Chapter 31, and the causes of the crisis will be outlined in Chapter 39.

Synoptic link

The concepts of real GDP and economic growth were introduced in Chapter 22.

of an economy in a given period, and economic growth shows how real GDP is changing through time.

Figure 28.1 shows the time path of real GDP since 1997. Also shown in the figure is the underlying trend of real GDP, calculated over the period from 1997 to 2007 (before the financial crisis set in). Notice how real GDP fell in 2008 and 2009 before beginning to recover from 2010 onwards.

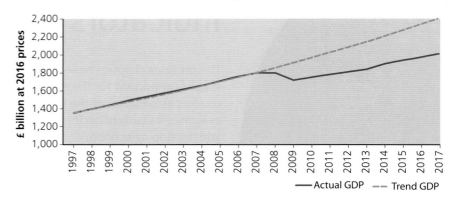

Figure 28.1 Real GDP in the UK since 1997

Source: calculated from ONS data

From 2009 onwards, the line representing actual real GDP is less steep than the trend line, suggesting that real GDP was growing less rapidly than it would have been if the previous trend value had continued. This is also clear in Figure 28.2, which shows the annual rate of change of real GDP.

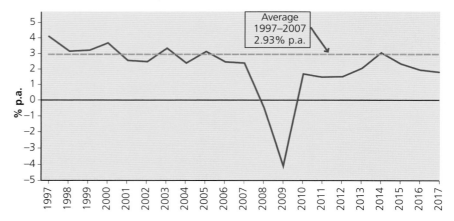

Figure 28.2 Growth of real GDP since 1997 (% change over previous year)

Source: calculated from ONS data

The severity of the recession in 2008 and 2009 is clearly evident in this figure, which shows the growth of real GDP at well below trend. Indeed, the recovery has not been able to match the previous experience. Between 1997 and 2007, the average growth rate of the UK economy was 2.93% per annum. Between 2009 and 2017, the average was only 1.96% per annum. In 2017, real GDP was approximately 15% below what it would have been if the recession had not happened and if real GDP had continued to grow at the previous trend rate.

Employment and unemployment

There have been appreciable changes in the level and structure of employment in the UK since 1997. This can be seen in Figure 28.3.

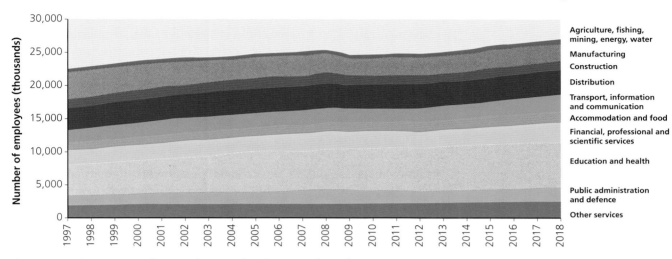

Figure 28.3 The structure of UK employment (April–June each year)

Source: based on data from ONS

Synoptic link

Employment (and unemployment) were discussed in Chapter 24.

Quantitative skills 28.1

Area graphs

Figure 28.3 is an example of an 'area graph', in which the values for each individual sector are stacked up on top of each other. Therefore the height of the total area shows the total employment in each year, and the coloured segments show the relative size of the individual sectors. This sort of graph is useful when we want to look at how the shares of individual sectors change over time.

The total level of employment dipped at the time of the recession in 2008–09, but less markedly than the dip in real GDP. In the recession, real GDP fell by 4.5% between 2007 and 2009, but total employment fell by only 1.5%. This may have partly been because some employers were holding on to their workers even as output was falling, perhaps expecting the recession to be short-lived. After all, rehiring costs can be high, so employers may prefer to wait before reducing their workforce. In 2018, total employment was 20% higher than it had been in 1997.

The figure also shows that the structure of employment changed during this period. For example, employment in the manufacturing sector constituted 18% of the total in 1997, but this had declined to less than 10% by 2018. Indeed, the recession had a greater impact on the manufacturing sector than on most other activities, with the sector employing more than half a million fewer workers in 2009 compared with 2007. In the same period, employment in education and health increased by more than 300,000.

This decline of manufacturing activity was a continuation of a longstanding trend. In 1978, manufacturing activity had been responsible for about 27% of employee jobs. This process was known

Knowledge check 28.1

Identify the sector that has the largest share of employment throughout the period. Which sector has the smallest share?

as deindustrialisation, and was balanced by an expansion of the service sector, which by 2017 was responsible for about 83% of total employment in the UK.

You should not be too surprised at such changes in the pattern of activity over time. In part they may reflect changes in the pattern of consumer demand as incomes have increased. As real incomes rise, the demand for some goods increases more rapidly than for others. For luxury goods, which have an income elasticity of demand greater than 1, the proportion of income spent on them increases as income itself increases. It is worth noting that the demand for many leisure items is likely to be income elastic. So, for example, as real incomes rise, it would be expected that the demand for capital goods associated with leisure activity, such as digital cameras and iPads, would rise more than proportionately with income. At the same time, the demand for some other goods and services may slacken. If the market economy is working effectively in encouraging the production of those goods and services that people wish to buy, then the structure of economic activity should also change, with some sectors expanding and others contracting.

Patterns of international trade have also changed over time, especially in the context of closer European integration, which may have affected the pattern of specialisation between countries. For example, as China has become a source of competitively priced manufactured goods, economies like the UK have been able to focus on the sorts of service sector activity at which they excel.

The flip side of employment is unemployment, which tends to attract more attention in the news. Figure 28.4 shows the number of unemployed in the UK (on the *Labour Force Survey* measure) in each year since 1997. It is important to monitor unemployment when judging the performance of an economy because it imposes costs both on those who are unemployed and also on society as a whole. If there is widespread unemployment, the nation is not producing as much output as it could.

Synoptic link

Patterns of international trade and trade policies are discussed in Chapters 35 and 36.

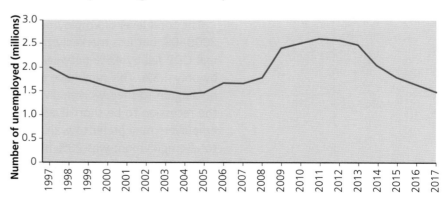

Figure 28.4 Number of unemployed (millions)

Source: data from *Labour Force Survey*

Again, the impact of the recession can be seen clearly in the figure, although unemployment did not begin to rise significantly until 2009, in which year it rose by more than 600,000. However, unemployment fell steadily after 2013, and by mid-2018 it was at its lowest point since the mid-1970s, despite the recession and the uncertainty over Brexit, which might have been expected to result in higher unemployment, especially given the slow recovery in economic growth.

Inflation

The control of inflation has been seen as a key policy objective, and is another important indicator of the economy's performance. The incoming Labour government in 1997 introduced inflation targeting, delegating responsibility for keeping inflation within a target range to the Bank of England. Since 2004, the target has been centred on 2% per annum increase in the CPI. Figure 28.5 shows inflation since 1997 on a quarterly basis, using the CPI measure.

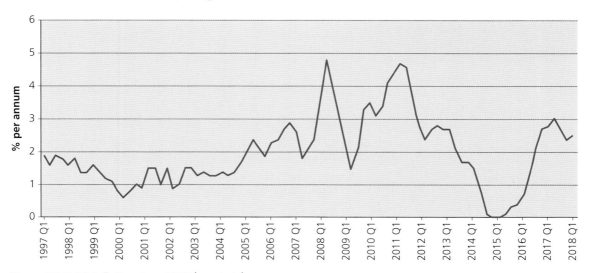

Figure 28.5 CPI inflation since 1997 (quarterly)

Source: based on data from ONS

Synoptic link

The significance of inflation is discussed in Chapter 25, along with an explanation of how it is measured. The policy measures used to control inflation are discussed in Chapter 31.

The figure shows that inflation was relatively stable in the early part of the period. However, there was a sudden acceleration in 2008, with inflation reaching 4.8% in the third quarter of that year. This was partly due to a global rise in food prices. However, the onset of recession was reflected in a (short-lived) disinflation in 2009, followed by another period of accelerating inflation in the early 2010s before plunging almost to zero in 2015. Inflation then returned to a more normal state in 2017–18.

Although the period from 2008 looks to have been an unstable one in terms of the behaviour of CPI inflation, this reflected the events and uncertainties of the times. We will see later in the chapter that this was not untypical of the pattern witnessed in other developed economies.

The balance of payments

When monitoring the performance of the economy, the balance of payments must be considered. Figure 28.6 shows the balance in the current account of the balance of payments since 1997, expressed as a percentage of GDP.

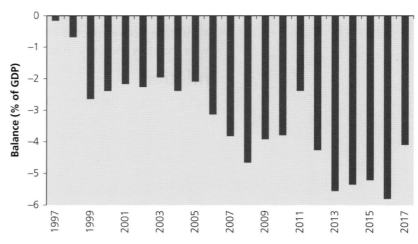

Figure 28.6 The current account of the UK balance of payments

Source: based on data from ONS

Synoptic link

The balance of payments is explained in Chapter 26, which also explores the causes and consequences of imbalances on the balance of payments.

Knowledge check 28.2

What would be the impact of a sustained surplus on the financial account of the current account of the balance of payments?

You can see from the figure that the current account was in deficit for the entire period since 1997. This is not unusual for the UK, as the last time that the current account was in surplus was back in 1983. More notable is that the size of the deficit relative to GDP has been at its highest towards the end of the period. Indeed, the deficit in 2016 was at a record level in the period since the Second World War.

The significance of this is that the overall balance of payments must be zero, so a deficit on the current account must be offset by a surplus elsewhere in the accounts. In other words, there must be a surplus on the financial account. Such a surplus is primarily achieved by the sale of UK financial assets abroad, which may not be sustainable in the longer term.

International competitiveness

In analysing the UK's position with its trading partners, the relative competitiveness of UK goods and services is an important issue. The UK has persistently shown a deficit on the current account over a long period of time, but especially in the 2000s. Does that imply that UK goods are uncompetitive in international markets?

One important factor that affects the UK's competitive position is the relative costs of production in different countries, which influence the prices that firms can charge. In particular, if UK firms face higher unit labour costs than their trading partners, this puts them at a disadvantage in terms of costs. This reflects different levels of productivity across countries. Remember that productivity is a measure of productive efficiency: for example, labour productivity is output per unit of labour input. Different countries show appreciable differences in efficiency by this measure.

Figure 28.7 shows output per hour worked in the UK expressed as an index based on the first quarter of 1997 = 100. You can see that productivity on this measure increased steadily until 2008 (again, the time of the recession), but seems to have stagnated since then.

Synoptic link

The notion of productivity was introduced in Chapter 22, where it was noted that increasing productivity is a source of economic growth.

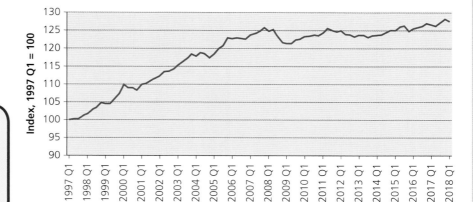

Figure 28.7 Output per hour worked in the UK (index, 1997 Q1 = 100)

Source: based on data from ONS

Exercise 28.1

Visit the website of the Office for National Statistics at www.ons.gov.uk/ to see how the UK economy is developing. Can you detect the impact of the Brexit outcome on the economy?

The performance of the UK economy compared with other economies

Study tip

Notice that you are expected to be familiar with trends in the UK economy, but should you be asked to compare the UK with some other economy, the necessary information would be provided, so you do not need to learn lots of facts about other countries.

Having explored the performance of the UK economy over the past 20 years, it is also important to set this performance in an international context. The UK is an open economy, trading with other countries, and its performance relative to its trading partners is relevant.

Real GDP and economic growth

Figure 28.8 compares GNI per capita in 2016 with selected European countries. It shows that the UK has a similar level of average income per head to that of Germany, and a slightly higher level than that of France and the EU as a whole. However, compared with countries in Scandinavia, such as Norway and Sweden, the UK enjoys lower GNI per capita.

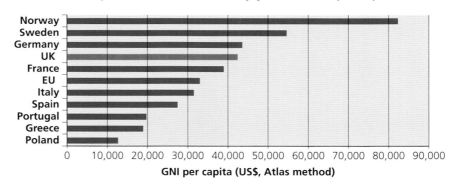

Figure 28.8 GNI per capita, 2016 (US$)

Source: based on data from World Bank

Synoptic link

The concept of GDP per capita is explained in Chapter 19. GNI per capita explained in Chapter 22.

This performance might be regarded as being satisfactory, but it is also important to examine economic growth, and whether the UK is maintaining its relative international position or falling behind. This is pertinent given the experience of the recession that has been outlined earlier in the chapter. Figure 28.9 shows economic growth in a selection of European countries since 1997, based on the annual growth of real GDP.

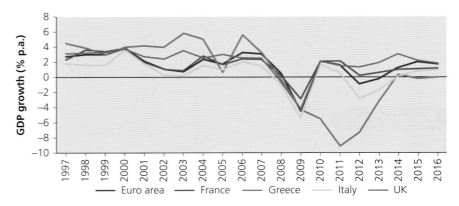

Figure 28.9 Economic growth in selected countries

Source: based on data from World Bank

Immediately apparent from the figure is that the UK was not alone in suffering from recession in the late 2000s, as all of the countries display a marked dip in growth at that time. What is also apparent is the deep recession and very slow recovery experienced by Greece, which had still not recovered by 2016. However, the UK seems to have performed relatively well compared with the other European countries shown in the figure, especially compared with France and Italy.

The UK and emerging economies

In the early 2000s, a group of countries were identified as experiencing rapid economic growth and closing the gap on the developed economies. These emerging economies became known as the BRIC countries, based on their initials (**B**razil, **R**ussia, **I**ndia and **C**hina). These economies were originally just a set of countries identified as having some characteristics in common. However, they began forming a political group and having summit meetings, and in 2011 they invited South Africa to join them. At this point in time, the BRICS accounted for about 18% of world GDP and 15% of world trade, and contained about 40% of the world's population. If economic growth continues at current rates, the group will gain increasing economic and political influence relative to the G7.

The BRICS countries

Figure 28.10 compares economic growth in the original four BRIC countries with that of the UK since 1997. The consistency and rapidity of growth during the 2000s reveals why these countries were singled out for attention, although Brazil was perhaps rather less successful in terms of its growth rates. The UK's performance looks modest by comparison.

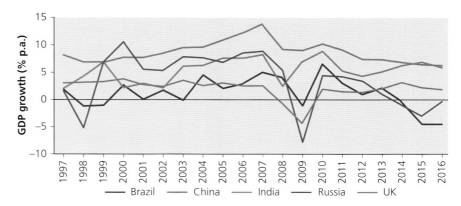

Figure 28.10 Economic growth in the original BRICs and the UK

Source: based on data from World Bank

What makes the performance of the BRICs more startling is the size of their economies, both in population and in the size of GDP. The achievements of the economies of China and India are especially impressive, in each case starting from a relatively low base — and for these two economies, the growth seemed relatively robust in the face of the global recession. China's economy in particular has shown little sign of slowing down. However, the factors underlying the growth performance were different in each case, as these economies are all at very different stages in terms of average incomes, and display different characteristics, both politically and economically.

It is also interesting to compare the UK's experience of the recession with that of the BRICs. Brazil and Russia were clearly affected by the recession, but China and India seem to have weathered this period more effectively, maintaining positive growth throughout.

The UK and developing countries

Chapter 23 discussed development and the situation facing developing countries. If you look back at Figure 23.4 on page 323, you will realise that the gulf in living standards between the UK and countries in sub-Saharan Africa is substantial. This makes it difficult to undertake a meaningful comparison of living standards. However, we can compare economic growth, which should give an indication of whether or not the gap between developing countries and developed countries like the UK is narrowing. Figure 28.11 shows economic growth in different regions of the world, including the UK, since 1997.

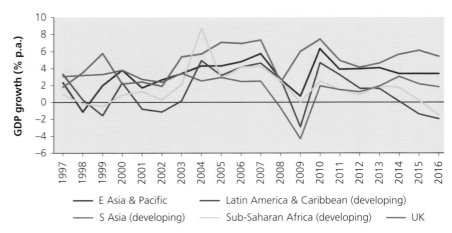

Figure 28.11 Economic growth in developing countries, E Asia and the Pacific, and the UK

Source: based on data from World Bank

This shows a mixed pattern, with the regions showing diverse patterns of growth during this period. However, there is no evidence from these data that the developing countries are making significant progress in terms of narrowing the gap in living standards. For example, developing countries in sub-Saharan Africa have performed relatively well since 1997, and seem to have experienced occasional spurts in growth and a less pronounced dip at the time of the recession. However, given the extent of the gap in income levels, this will not have had much impact on differences in living standards. This is a major challenge for the future.

Unemployment

Figure 28.12 shows the percentage unemployment rate in 2016 for a range of European countries including the UK.

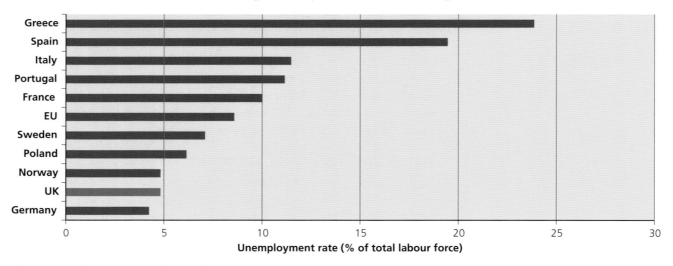

Figure 28.12 Unemployment (%), 2016

Source: based on data from World Bank

Of the countries shown, the UK has the second-lowest rate of unemployment, so on this measure the performance has been good. The high rate of unemployment in Greece reflects the long-lasting recession that the country has experienced. The strong performance of Germany reflects the strength of that economy.

Inflation

As explained earlier in the chapter, the control of inflation has been a high priority for successive governments. Figure 28.13 shows inflation in the UK since 1997 compared with some other European countries.

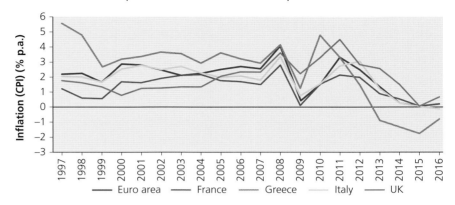

Figure 28.13 Inflation in selected countries

Source: based on data from World Bank

You can see that the UK experienced relatively low and stable inflation in the first part of this period compared with the other countries shown. All saw an acceleration in 2008 and a sharp drop in 2009. Since then, inflation in the UK has been a bit higher than elsewhere, but not substantially so. When it comes to discussing macroeconomic policy it will be important to remain aware that external shocks can affect countries simultaneously. There are occasions on which the media are quick to criticise governments for poor management of the economy when the cause of problems may be external, and affecting many countries together.

> **Knowledge check 28.3**
>
> Identify years in which the Greek economy experienced deflation.

The balance of payments

As discussed earlier, the current account of the UK balance of payments has been in persistent deficit for many years. Figure 28.14 shows that the UK is not typical of the other countries with which we have been comparing it.

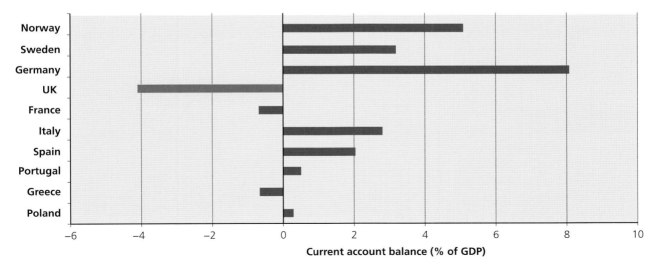

Figure 28.14 The balance of payments current account balance, 2017

Source: based on data from World Bank

Of the countries shown, only the UK has a substantial deficit: indeed, among the others only France and Greece do not show a surplus, and their deficits are much smaller relative to GDP. Does this matter? In Chapter 26, it was pointed out that a deficit on the current account has to be covered by a surplus elsewhere, and that this could have consequences for the longer term. However, Chapter 27 noted that the effects of a current account deficit could be offset (at least to some extent) by movements in the exchange rate.

Productivity

Figure 28.15 shows output per hour in industry in a selection of European countries, expressed as an index based on the UK = 100. This indicates that the UK is only moderately successful in terms of its labour productivity when compared with some other European countries. This could suggest that low productivity is contributing to the poor performance of the economy in relation to the current account of the balance of payments.

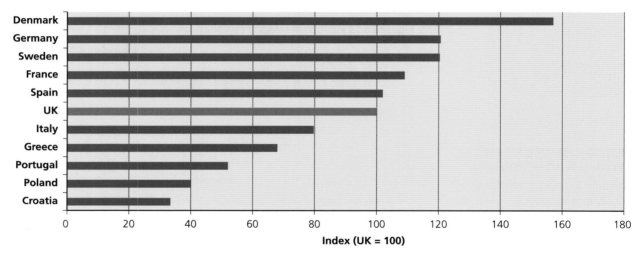

Figure 28.15 Output per hour in industry (index, UK = 100), 2014

Source: calculated from ONS, Eurostat data

Knowledge check 28.4

What does it mean if the index of labour productivity for Norway based on the UK = 100 is 331.9?

Exercise 28.2

Visit the World Bank's World Development Indicators website at http://databank.worldbank.org/data/source/world-development-indicators and compare the UK's performance with another country (or countries) of your choice to evaluate how well the economy is faring.

Figure 28.16 compares the UK performance with other European countries in relation to the changes in total factor productivity through time. This shows that the UK has followed a very similar pattern to other developed countries since 2005.

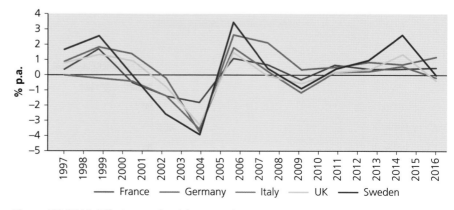

Figure 28.16 Multifactor productivity growth

Source: OECD

Summary

- The period since 1997 has seen significant developments in the UK's performance on the key macroeconomic indicators.
- In particular, the recession of the late 2000s affected all relevant variables, particularly by interrupting the process of economic growth.
- There were significant changes in the structure of employment with the continued decline of manufacturing activity.
- Inflation was stable until the recession of the late 2000s.
- The current account of the balance of payments was in continual deficit throughout the period.
- Other developed countries experienced a similar pattern — except in terms of the current account of the balance of payments.
- Some emerging economies enjoyed rapid economic growth, and some were able to avoid the worst impact of the recession.
- Developing countries experienced some economic growth, but much more is needed if they are to close the gap on the developed economies.

Case study 28.1

The UK's productivity puzzle

Productivity is crucial for any economy for a number of reasons. For one thing, relative productivity levels across countries influence the international competitiveness of an economy's output. If the products that a country seeks to export are lacking in quality and/or design, and if they are inefficiently produced, then it will always be difficult to compete abroad. For another thing, it is increases in productivity through time that allow living standards to increase. If productivity is stagnant, workers will not see their earnings increasing over time.

Figure 28.17 shows the time path of output per worker since the first quarter of 2000. The 'actual' series is an index based on 2000 Q1 = 100. The 'trend' series is based on calculating the average rate of change between 2000 Q1 and 2008 Q2, then extrapolating this forward to the first quarter of 2018. In other words, the trend shows how productivity would have changed had it continued to increase at its previous average rate. This shows the extent to which productivity has stagnated since the onset of recession in 2008.

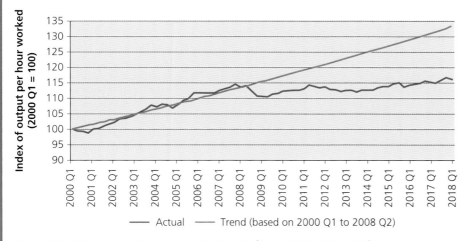

Figure 28.17 Output per hour worked in the UK (index, 2000 Q1 = 100)

Source: calculated from ONS data

This is not a new story. The UK has attracted criticism for its poor productivity performance for many years. The consensus often appears to be that the UK's performance on this key variable has been dismal, and that the UK is near the foot of the productivity league table.

The way in which the recession affected productivity (which continued to stagnate afterwards) was shared by many of the UK's trading partners, but this is little consolation if the UK is really at the bottom of the league table. In fact, this is not completely true, as the UK's relative international position is middle-of-the-table rather than bottom. However, the UK does lag behind key trading partners such as France, Germany and Denmark (see Figure 28.15).

The impact of globalisation should be positive for productivity, as the increasing interconnectedness of economies should make it easier for technology transfer to take place. Furthermore, the mobility of labour within the EU should have allowed the spread of good working practices and human capital. These effects should bring productivity levels closer across countries.

So what can the UK do about its position? The economy performs well in some areas, in particular in terms of new start-up companies and investment in research and development. However, Andy Haldane (Chief Economist at the Bank of England) argues that one of the key factors that the UK is not getting right is the dissemination of new techniques. In other words, the UK does well in terms of having some world-class companies at the cutting edge of technology and efficiency, but also has a long tail of companies that have been slow to come up to speed.

This would suggest that encouraging the dissemination of best practice techniques, and investment in human capital, is what is needed if the UK is to close the productivity gap.

Follow-up questions

a What are the links between productivity and international competitiveness?

b If firms decided to hold on to workers during a recession instead of making them redundant, how would this affect the productivity measures?

c If globalisation facilitates convergence of productivity levels across countries, how would the UK be likely to perform following Brexit?

d Why would investment in human capital be beneficial for productivity growth?

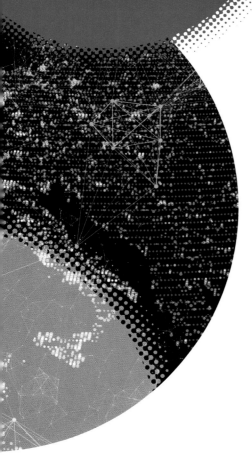

Chapter 29

Income distribution and welfare

This chapter explores an important aspect of macroeconomic performance: namely, the way that income and wealth are distributed in an economy. Part of macroeconomic policy is concerned with the redistribution of resources in order to reduce inequality between groups in society. In order to evaluate the effectiveness of such policies, it is important to be able to measure and monitor changes in inequality through time and to compare the degree of inequality across countries. The chapter will also explore the related issue of poverty and how to measure it.

> ## Learning objectives
> After studying this chapter, you should be able to:
> - explain income and wealth, distribution and inequality
> - explain the policy objective of a more even distribution of income
> - explain, with the aid of a diagram, the distribution of income using a Lorenz curve
> - explain inequality data: Gini coefficients and relevant quartiles
> - explain absolute and relative poverty
> - evaluate the causes and consequences of poverty and inequality

Income and wealth

Key terms

income the flow of wages, salaries and earnings from other sources in a period
wealth the stock of accumulated assets

It is important to be aware of the distinction between **income** and **wealth**. Income is the *flow* of wages and earnings from other sources in a period, whereas wealth is the *stock* of accumulated assets. An example of such assets would be where an individual owns property. If an individual saves part of his or her income, this accumulates as wealth. However, wealth may also come from other sources — in particular, from legacies. Ownership of wealth can also generate a flow of income in the form of interest and dividend payments.

Knowledge check 29.1

Give an example of wealth held by a household.

Synoptic link

The distinction between income and wealth was introduced in Chapter 19 during the discussion of consumption.

The distribution of income and wealth and inequality

The **income distribution** describes how national income is distributed among the population. You will be aware that not everyone receives the

Key terms

income distribution the way in which national income is distributed among the population of a country

wealth distribution the way in which the nation's wealth is distributed among the population of a country

Synoptic link

The reasons for wage differentials are discussed in the context of labour markets in Chapter 17.

Synoptic link

The use of taxes to affect the distribution of income is explained in Chapter 30 as part of the discussion of fiscal policy.

same income, so there is some inequality in the income distribution. The same applies for the **wealth distribution** — indeed wealth tends to be more unevenly distributed than income, so there is inequality in the distribution of wealth. There are differences between countries in the extent of such inequality in income and wealth.

There are reasons based in microeconomic analysis for expecting there to be differences in income and wealth between individuals and groups in society. For example, there may be differences between the productivity of individual workers that give rise to wage differentials. Differences in wealth may arise from legacies, so that some individuals begin life with a stock of wealth inherited from relatives.

These differences in income and wealth mean that there will always be some inequality in any society, in the sense that some individuals and groups will have greater command over resources than others. In other words, resources will not be equally distributed across society.

The policy objective of a more even distribution of income

Inequality in the distribution of income and wealth may be significant in society if it becomes excessive, or if there are households and individuals who become vulnerable because of low income and/or wealth. A sense of social justice suggests that the vulnerable groups in society should be protected and assured of a reasonable level of welfare.

In the UK, the government affects the distribution of income through the use of taxation and transfer payments that help to provide some social security for vulnerable groups. Taxation and government spending cannot be treated in isolation from other policies being implemented at the macroeconomic level.

Inequality in income and wealth is an issue at the macroeconomic level partly because there may be a link between the degree of inequality in society and the rate of economic growth.

The distribution of income may become especially significant for some less developed countries (LDCs), where the need to address concerns about extreme poverty and provide for the basic needs of society may have a high priority. One of the problems with this is that there may be a Catch-22 situation, in which economic growth is impeded by the existence of extreme poverty, but extreme poverty cannot be tackled until economic growth has taken place. The government then faces a difficult dilemma: should the focus of policy be on alleviating poverty in order to enable economic growth, or should it be to promote economic growth in order to have the resources to tackle poverty?

Inequality is not only of concern to LDCs. In the advanced countries, there is still unrest that arises from the existence of inequality between groups, or between regions within a country. Dealing with this by redistributing resources may have an opportunity cost in diverting resources from other priorities. Furthermore, taxing the rich heavily in order to divert resources to the poor may affect the incentives for high-paid workers.

These are some of the issues to be addressed in relation to this topic. However, the first step is to explore ways in which the distribution of income (and wealth) can be described and monitored.

Measuring inequality in society

An important limitation of GDP (or GNI) per capita as a measure of living standards is that it is an average measure, and so does not reveal information about how income is distributed among groups in society. Inequality is present in all societies, and always will be. However, the degree of inequality varies from one country to another. Before exploring the causes of inequality, and the policies that might be used to influence how income and wealth are distributed within society, it is necessary to be able to characterise and measure inequality. This is important in order to be able to judge relative standards of living in different countries or different periods.

One way of presenting data on this topic is to rank households in order of their incomes, and then calculate the share of total household income that goes to the poorest 10%, the poorest 20% and so on.

Quantitative skills 29.1

Deciles, quintiles and quartiles

When the groups are divided into tenths in this way, they are referred to as deciles. So, the poorest 10% is the first decile, the next 10% is the second decile, and so on. Similarly, the poorest 20% is the first quintile. The poorest 25% is the first quartile. This is useful in trying to explore the pattern of the distribution of income because it quantifies the difference between income going to low-income and high-income households.

Note: for purposes of the A Level you only need to know about quartiles.

According to the World Bank, the top decile (richest 10%) of households in Brazil receives 55.8 times higher income than the lowest decile (poorest 10%). In Belarus, on the other hand, the ratio is only 5.5. These are extreme examples of the degree of inequality in the distribution of income within countries.

Table 29.1 presents some data for three developed countries. Notice that the unit of measurement is normally the household rather than the individual, on the presumption that members of a household tend to share their resources — a millionaire's life-partner may not earn any income, but he or she is not usually poor.

Table 29.1 Distribution of income in the UK, the USA and Norway, by quintiles (%)

	UK, 2012	USA, 2013	Norway, 2012
First decile	2.9	1.7	3.6
First quintile	7.5	5.1	9.3
Second quintile	12.3	10.3	14.4
Third quintile	17.0	15.4	18.1
Fourth quintile	23.1	22.7	22.9
Top quintile	40.1	46.4	35.3
Top decile	24.7	30.2	20.9
Ratio top quintile: first quintile	5.3	9.1	3.8

Source: World Development Indicators

It can be seen that in the UK, households in the top quintile receive 5.3 times more income than those in the poorest quintile. On the basis

Knowledge check 29.2

Calculate the decile ratio for each of the countries in Table 29.1. Do these give the same ranking as for the quintile ratios in the table?

Key term

Lorenz curve a graphical way of depicting the distribution of income within a country

of these data, inequality in the UK is lower than that in the USA but higher than that in Norway.

The Lorenz curve

The structure of this information is quite different from the sorts of data that economists normally encounter, and it would be helpful to find an appropriate type of diagram to allow the data to be presented visually. The usual types of graph are not well suited to presenting such data, but there is a method of presenting the data visually via the **Lorenz curve**. Several examples of Lorenz curves are shown in Figure 29.1.

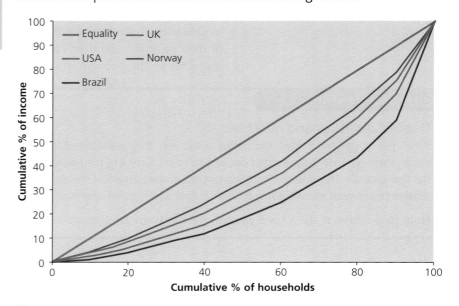

Figure 29.1 Lorenz curves

Source: World Development Indicators

Lorenz curves are constructed as follows. The curves for the UK, USA and Norway are based on the data in Table 29.1. The first step is to convert the numbers in the table into *cumulative* percentages. In other words (using the UK as an example), the data show that the poorest 20% receive 7.5% of total household income, the poorest 40% receive 7.5% + 12.3% = 19.8%, the poorest 60% receive 19.8% + 17.0% = 36.8%, and so on. It is these cumulative percentages that are plotted to produce the Lorenz curve, as in Figure 29.1. (The figure also plots the lowest and highest deciles.)

Suppose that income were perfectly equally distributed between households. In other words, suppose the poorest 10% of households received exactly 10% of income, the poorest 20% received 20%, and so on. The Lorenz curve would then be a straight line going diagonally across the figure.

To interpret the country curves, the closer a country's Lorenz curve is to the diagonal equality line, the more equal is the distribution. You can see from the figure that Norway comes closest to the equality line, bearing out the earlier conclusion that income is more equally distributed in that country. The UK and the US curves are closer together, but there seems to be slightly more inequality in the USA, as its Lorenz curve is further from the equality line. Brazil has also been included on the figure, as an example of a society in which there is substantial inequality.

Knowledge check 29.3

Explain why Figure 29.1 suggests that income inequality is more pronounced in Brazil than in the USA.

Exercise 29.1

Use the data provided in Table 29.2 to calculate the ratios of top decile income to bottom decile income, and of top quintile income to bottom quintile income. Then draw Lorenz curves for the two countries, and compare the inequalities shown for Belarus and South Africa with each other and with the countries already discussed.

Table 29.2 Income distribution in Belarus and South Africa

	Percentage share of income or consumption	
	South Africa	**Belarus**
Lowest decile	0.9	3.9
Lowest quintile	2.5	9.3
Second quintile	4.7	14.0
Third quintile	8.0	17.7
Fourth quintile	15.9	22.4
Highest quintile	68.9	36.7
Highest decile	51.3	22.6

Source: World Development Indicators

The Gini coefficient

Key term

Gini coefficient a measure of the degree of inequality in a society

The Lorenz curve is fine for comparing income distribution in just a few countries. However, it would also be helpful to have an index that could summarise the relationship in a numerical way. The **Gini coefficient** does just this. It is a way of trying to quantify the equality of income distribution in a country, and is obtained by calculating the ratio of the area between the equality line and the country's Lorenz curve (area A in Figure 29.2) to the whole area under the equality line (area $A + B$ in Figure 29.2).

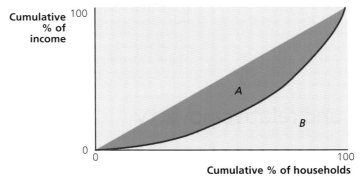

Figure 29.2 The Gini coefficient and the Lorenz curve

Table 29.3 The Gini coefficient

Country	Gini coefficient
USA	41.1
UK	32.6
Norway	25.9
Brazil	51.5
Belarus	27.2
South Africa	63.4

Source: World Development Indicators

In published data, the Gini coefficient is expressed as a percentage (i.e. multiplied by 100). The closer the Gini coefficient is to 100, the further the Lorenz curve is from equality, and the more unequal is the income distribution. The Gini coefficient values for the countries in Figure 29.1 (and Table 29.2) are shown in Table 29.3.

The Gini coefficient can be used to see how the overall income distribution has changed over time. This is shown in Figure 29.3.

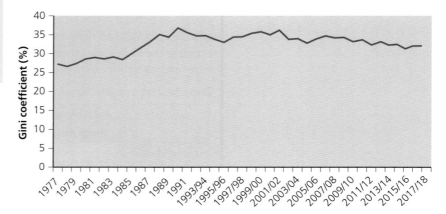

Figure 29.3 Gini coefficient for disposable income in the UK, 1977–2017/18

The figure shows that income inequality worsened slightly during the 1980s but has remained fairly steady since then.

Finally, it is worth noting that in the UK, wealth is more unequally distributed than income.

Summary

- Microeconomic analysis identifies a number of reasons why different individuals and groups in society may receive differential pay.
- At the macroeconomic level, income distribution is important partly because fiscal policy is a key tool in redistributing income and wealth.
- The degree of inequality may also affect economic growth and social stability.
- One indicator of inequality is the ratio of the top to the lowest decile (or quartile) of households in the income distribution.
- The Lorenz curve offers a graphical way of portraying the distribution of income.
- These data can be quantified in the form of the Gini coefficient.

Absolute and relative poverty

All societies are characterised by some inequality — and some poverty. Although the two are related, they are not the same. Indeed, poverty might be regarded as one aspect of inequality.

If there is a wide gap between the richest and poorest households, it is important to evaluate just how poor those poorest households are, and whether they should be regarded as being 'in poverty'. This requires a definition of poverty.

One approach is to define a basket of goods and services that is regarded as being the minimum required to support human life. Households that are seen to have income that falls short of allowing them to purchase that basic bundle of goods would be regarded as being in **absolute poverty**.

A common way of measuring the poverty rate in a country is to estimate the percentage of the population living below a poverty line, known as a **headcount ratio**. The poverty line in this context is an estimate of the income needed to ensure basic human survival. People living below this level are perceived to be in absolute poverty. To enable international comparisons of poverty levels, the World Bank has defined an **International Poverty Line**. This is based on 2011 PPP prices, and from October 2015 it was set at PPP$1.90. The line has to be reset every few years in line with changing prices over time. The World Bank estimated that around 700 million people worldwide were living beneath this level in 2015. Some individual countries set their own national poverty line to reflect local conditions.

Locals line up at a food station in Krisrooa, Kenya, during the famine of 2016–17

Progress has been made to reduce the number of people living in absolute poverty on this definition, except in sub-Saharan Africa, where the number continues to rise. However, there was concern that poverty remained a problem, with people living on incomes that were not significantly higher than the International Poverty Line. In October 2018, the World Bank launched additional poverty lines to reflect typical national poverty lines in lower- and upper-middle income countries. It was estimated that in 2015, over a quarter of the world's population were surviving on less than $2.20 per day, and almost a half on less than $5.50 per day.

Figure 29.4 shows the percentage headcount ratio for a range of countries. Notice that countries in the figure are ranked from top to bottom in ascending order of GNI per capita in PPP$.

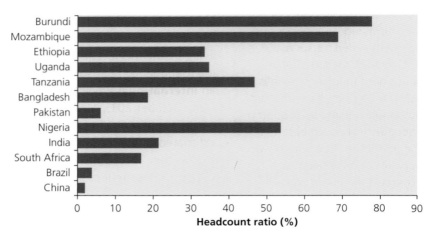

Figure 29.4 Percentage of population living below the International Poverty Line in selected countries

Source: World Development Indicators

Quantitative skills 29.2

More about interpreting graphs

When you are faced with a graph such as that in Figure 29.4, where the countries are ranked in order of another variable, you can learn about the relationships between variables from observing the pattern of the bars. In this case, we have the headcount ratio shown for a number of countries that are ranked in order of GNI per capita. If there had been a perfect correlation between relative poverty levels and GNI per capita, then the pattern of the bars would be smooth. However, this is not the case. Bangladesh and Pakistan show relatively low headcount ratios relative to some countries with a higher GNI per capita, such as Nigeria.

Knowledge check 29.5

Calculate the median income level for the UK in 2015.

Key term

persistent poverty where a household is currently in relative income poverty and has also been in this state in at least 2 of the preceding 3 years

For a country like the UK, this absolute poverty line is not helpful, as so few people fall below it. Therefore poverty is defined in *relative* terms. If a household has insufficient income for its members to participate in the normal social life of the country, it is said to be in **relative poverty**. This too is defined in terms of a threshold poverty line, set at 60% of the median adjusted household disposable income. (The median is the income of the middle-ranked household.)

In Europe (including the UK), estimates of poverty are based on a regular survey of households conducted in EU member states and some other selected countries. In 2015, the UK's threshold for poverty was set at £12,567. Households with income below this are described as being in relative income poverty (or being 'at risk of poverty') — households that experience this in the current year and at least two of the three preceding years are said to be in **persistent poverty**.

Figure 29.5 presents some data for a range of European countries in 2015. The proportion of people below the relative poverty line varies substantially across these countries, from 9.6% in Iceland to 25.4% in Romania. The UK shows relative income poverty that is below, but close to, the EU average, and persistent poverty that is well below the average. Indeed, the UK's persistent poverty rate was the fifth-lowest among the EU member states.

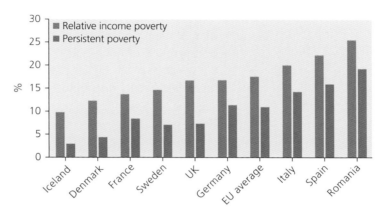

Figure 29.5 Relative and persistent poverty in 2015, selected countries

Source: ONS

The percentage falling below the poverty line is not a totally reliable measure, as it is also important to know *how far* below the poverty line households are falling. Therefore the income gap (the distance between household income and the poverty line) is useful to measure the intensity of poverty as well as its incidence.

Exercise 29.2

Imagine that you are the Minister for Poverty Alleviation in a country in which the (absolute) poverty line is set at $500. Of the people living below the poverty line, you know that there are two distinct groups, each made up of 50 individuals. The people in group 1 have an income of $450, whereas those in group 2 have only $250. Suppose that your budget for poverty alleviation is $2,500.

a Your prime concern is with the most needy: how would you use your budget?

b Suppose instead that your prime minister instructs you to reduce the percentage of people living below the poverty line: do you adopt the same strategy for using the funds?

c How helpful is the poverty line as a strategic target of policy action?

Causes of inequality and poverty

Inequality arises through a variety of factors, some relating to the operation of the labour market, some reflecting patterns in wealth (through the ownership of assets), and some arising from the actions of governments.

The distribution of wealth

Perhaps the most obvious way in which inequality in wealth and the ownership of assets influences inequality and its changes through time is through inheritance. Wealth that accumulates in a family over time and is then passed down to succeeding generations constitutes a source of inequality that does not arise from the current state of the economy or the operations of markets.

During 2012–14 people in the highest decile were estimated to own 45% of identified wealth in the UK, and were 5.2 times wealthier than the bottom 50% of households. The Gini index for total wealth in 2014 was 63, which is much higher than that for income, indicating that wealth is much less evenly distributed than income.

A wealthy residential street in Kensington, London

Notice that, although wealth and income are not the same thing, inequality in wealth can *lead to* inequality in income, as wealth (the ownership of assets) creates an income flow — from interest, rents and profits — which then feeds back into a household's income stream.

A significant change in the pattern of ownership of assets in recent decades has been the increase in home ownership and the rise in house prices. For those who continue to rent their homes, and in particular for those who rent council dwellings, this is a significant source of rising inequality.

For developing countries, there is also considerable inequality in the distribution of ownership of assets. Financial markets in developing countries are much less well developed than in developed countries, and many people, especially in the rural areas, do not have access to the formal financial institutions. This inevitably means a concentration in the ownership of financial assets. Furthermore, the ownership of land is highly concentrated in some countries. This is notably the case in much of Latin America, and has contributed to the relatively high levels of inequality that have characterised that region. The situation is further complicated

Knowledge check 29.6

In a period of rising house prices, is the main impact on income or on wealth inequality?

by the fact that property rights are weak in many developing countries, so that even if a household has farmed a piece of land for generations, it may not be able to demonstrate ownership rights over that land. Such inequality in the ownership of assets leads also to inequality in income distribution.

Labour market explanations

As explained in Chapter 17, there are several ways in which the labour market is expected to give rise to inequalities in earnings. Inequality could arise from demand and supply conditions in labour markets, which respond to changes in the pattern of consumer demand for goods and services, and changes in international comparative advantage between countries. Furthermore, differences in the balance between economic rent and transfer earnings in different occupations and economic sectors reinforce income inequalities.

However, a by-product of changes in the structure of the economy may be rising inequality between certain groups in society. For example, if there is a change in the structure of employment away from unskilled jobs towards occupations that require a higher level of skills and qualifications, then this could lead to an increase in inequality, with those workers who lack the skills to adapt to changing labour market conditions being disadvantaged by the changes taking place. In other words, if the premium that employers are prepared to pay in order to hire skilled or well-qualified workers rises as a result of changing technology in the workplace, then those without those skills are likely to suffer.

The decline in the power of the trade unions may have contributed to the situation, as low-paid workers may find that their unions are less likely to be able to offer employment protection. It has been argued that this is a *good* thing if it increases the flexibility of the labour market. However, again a balance is needed between worker protection and having free and flexible markets.

The difference in earnings between female and male workers has also been highlighted. In the UK, female workers on average earn 16.8% lower wages than males (based on the male median wage). This is a smaller gap than in the USA, where females receive wages 18.1% below males. However, this is a much greater gap than in some other countries such as Italy (5.6%) and Denmark (5.8%). Research by the Institute for Fiscal Studies showed that the wage gap in the UK has fallen for female workers whose highest educational attainment was at GCSE level, but has remained more or less constant for women with A Levels or degree-level qualifications since the 1990s. Some of the earnings differences between men and women can be explained by the fact that when women have to take time out from working to look after children, they lose human capital by missing out on work experience. However, such market explanations may not suffice to explain all the differences in earnings that are observed.

Demographic change

A feature of many developed countries in recent years has been a change in the age structure of the population. Improved medical drugs and treatments have meant that people are living longer, and this has

Knowledge check 29.7

Does the existence of a persistent wage gap between male and female workers necessarily mean that there is discrimination in the workplace?

combined with low fertility rates to bring about an increase in the proportion of the population who are in the older age groups. This has put pressure on the provision of pensions, and increased the vulnerability of this group in society. State pensions have been funded primarily by the contributions of those in work, but if the number of people of working age falls as a proportion of the whole population, then this funding stream comes under pressure.

Government intervention

There are a number of ways in which government intervention influences the distribution of income in a society, although not all of these interventions are expressly intended to do so. Most prominent is the range of transfer payments and taxation that has been implemented. Another example is minimum wage legislation, which was also intended to protect the poor. Overall, these measures have a large effect on income distribution.

Consequences of poverty and inequality

It could be argued that some inequality is inevitable within a free market, capitalist society. Indeed, it could be argued that without some inequality, capitalism could not operate, as it is the pursuit of gain that provides firms with the incentive to maximise profits, workers with the incentive to provide labour effort, and consumers with the incentive to maximise their utility. It is the combination of these efforts by economic agents that leads to good resource allocation, through the working of Adam Smith's 'invisible hand'. In a world in which every individual was guaranteed the same income as everyone else, there would be no incentive for anyone to strive to do better. However, few would argue for this. More important is that there should be equality of opportunity.

The consequences of high levels of poverty are severe. People living in absolute poverty are likely to face inadequate nutrition, poor health and little access to education. They can then be trapped in a vicious cycle: without good health and education they cannot obtain earning opportunities, and cannot escape from poverty. From society's point of view, this means that the country's potential labour force is not being fully utilised, which hinders economic growth.

The real dilemma for society concerns how much inequality and poverty can be tolerated. The balance between protecting the vulnerable and providing opportunities and incentives for social and economic improvement is difficult to resolve. This reflects the fact that different people take different viewpoints on the matter so that a consensus is hard to achieve. When we consider the global inequity in the distribution of resources, the dilemma is even greater. With absolute poverty continuing to increase in sub-Saharan Africa, do the developed nations have a responsibility to assist? Or do problems in the domestic economy take a higher priority?

The impact of economic growth on inequality

Weak institutions and poor governance in developing countries mean that measures such as taxation and transfers to influence the distribution of income are largely untried or ineffective. The economist and Nobel laureate Simon Kuznets argued that there is expected to be a relationship between the degree of inequality in the income distribution and the level of development that a country has achieved. He claimed that in the early stages of economic development, income is fairly equally distributed, with everyone living at a relatively low income level. However, as development begins to take off, there will be some individuals at the forefront of enterprise and development, and their incomes will rise more rapidly. So in this middle phase the income distribution will tend to worsen. At a later stage of development, society will eventually be able to afford to redistribute income to protect the poor, and all will begin to share in the benefits of development.

This can be portrayed as the relationship between the Gini coefficient and the level of development. The thrust of the Kuznets hypothesis is that this should reveal an inverted U-shaped relationship, as shown in Figure 29.6. The empirical evidence in support of the relationship is not strong, although there is some support for the idea that it does hold in some regions of the world.

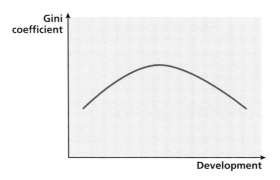

Figure 29.6 The Kuznets curve

Extension material

Weaknesses in the Kuznets hypothesis

One reason why the empirical support for the Kuznets hypothesis is rather weak is that the relationship may not show up clearly in cross-section data — in other words, when the evidence is based on looking at how the relationship varies across countries at a single point in time. Looking at how the relationship changes through time for individual countries (known as *time-series data*) might be more revealing, but unfortunately, data on inequality are expensive to compile and are not collected on a regular basis.

It is also worth noting that there are substantial regional variations in the degree of inequality. Latin America has been known for wide inequality between groups in society, whereas eastern Europe has shown much lower levels of inequality, partly because inequality was low across the Soviet bloc. This may also conceal the underlying Kuznets relationship.

Exercise 29.3

The UK government is committed to devoting 0.7% of GDP to providing Overseas Development Assistance to developing countries in order to help reduce global inequality. Discuss the merits and demerits of maintaining this commitment in the face of increasing difficulties in the domestic economy.

Summary

- Some degree of inequality in income and wealth is present in every society.
- Absolute poverty measures whether individuals or households have sufficient resources to maintain a reasonable life.
- Relative poverty measures whether individuals or households are able to participate in the life of the country in which they live: this is calculated as 60% of median adjusted household disposable income.
- Inequality arises from a range of factors.
- The distribution of wealth is strongly influenced by the pattern of inheritance, but in recent years changing patterns of home ownership, coupled with rises in house prices, have also been significant.
- The natural operation of labour markets gives rise to some inequality in income.
- Government action influences the pattern of income distribution, with the net effect being a reduction in inequality.
- Society faces a dilemma in agreeing how much inequality is acceptable, and how to influence it without damaging incentives.

Case study 29.1

Inequality and economic growth

If you visit Rio de Janeiro, you may be surprised to see high metal fences in front of many of the luxurious multi-storey buildings along the lovely beaches of Copacabana. However, it is not really surprising, given that Rio has one of the highest crime rates in Brazil, exacerbated by the high level of income inequality. It is not uncommon to find a substantial gap between the rich and the poor in many societies. Inequality exists in both developing and developed countries. For example, Nobel laureate Paul Krugman has noted that the 13,000 richest families in the USA have almost as much income as the 20 million poorest households — those 13,000 families have incomes 300 times that of average families. Therefore, it is important to examine the effects of such income inequality, not only on the crime rate and social behaviour but also on the economy.

Level of income inequality

The level of income inequality depends primarily on the distribution of assets and wages as well as on government policy. First, an important factor is the distribution of productive assets such as land. If land ownership is concentrated among a few owners, which is typical of many agriculture-dominated developing economies, then income inequality tends to be high in such countries. In addition, if the ownership of minerals and natural resources is concentrated among the elite, then countries well endowed with natural resources — especially mineral resources such as oil, diamonds, copper, and so on — tend also to have higher asset and income inequality than other types of economy. Another factor that explains variations across countries is the rural–urban inequality within developing countries, which is the result of urban bias.

Overall, income inequality depends to a large extent on earnings inequality, as in many countries earnings account for 60–70% of total income. In some countries, rising wage inequality has often been ascribed to technological change. New technologies generate a demand for skills. This favours higher-skilled workers over lower-skilled ones and leads to increasing wage differentials between skilled and unskilled workers. In addition, education tends to play an important role in reducing income inequality.

So, if some groups in a society do not have access to education, this leads to higher earnings inequality and therefore higher income inequality. Therefore, earnings inequality is clearly an important contributor to the increases in overall income inequality witnessed in many countries recently.

Case study 29.1 (continued)

Economic performance and output

But how does inequality influence economic performance and output? More unequal societies tend to develop larger groups of people who are excluded from opportunities that others enjoy. Poor people may not have the same chances in life as richer people, and may therefore never quite realise their full productive potential. This may be because they do not get as good an education as those afforded by richer families, or because they can't get loans to start up a business as easily, or because they can't afford the insurance they would require to undertake some risky — but productive — venture. An income distribution with lots of poor people, or unequally distributed opportunities, would under-utilise its aggregate productive potential to a greater degree than a distribution with relatively fewer poor people, or one where opportunities were more equitably distributed. Both theory and empirical evidence suggest that these incomplete realisations of economic potential are not of concern only to those who care about equity *per se*. They also affect aggregate economic potential, and therefore aggregate output and its rate of growth.

The impact on growth may also be negative when the gap between the rich and the poor widens excessively. For instance, rural economies with very high land concentration in a few hands and landlessness for the majority face very high shirking and supervision costs. For these reasons, these economies tend to be less efficient (e.g. to have lower yields per hectare) than more equitable agrarian systems, even when accounting for the economies of scale in marketing, processing and shipping that benefit larger farms.

Political instability and social problems

Finally, high levels of income inequality can also create political instability and social problems and very negatively affect growth over both the short and long term. There is increasing evidence of a strong relation between inequality and the crime rate. Income differences between households create *psychological stress* for the relatively poor that may explain higher morbidity, mortality and violence rates. Social tensions, in turn, erode the security of property rights, augment the threat of expropriation, drive away domestic and foreign investment, and increase the cost of business security and contract enforcement.

Follow-up questions

a Identify the key causes of inequality in a society.

b Explain and evaluate how inequality in wealth can cause inequality in income.

c Explain why political instability may be a consequence of inequality.

d In your own words, outline the main ways in which inequality may have an impact on economic growth.

CHAPTER 29 QUESTIONS

A Multiple-choice questions

1 Which of the following is a way of measuring inequality in society?

   a The demand curve
   b The Human Development Index
   c The Gini coefficient
   d The retail price index

2 Relative poverty can be defined as:

   a Household income is below 70% of median adjusted household income
   b Household income is below 60% of median adjusted household income
   c Household income is below 50% of median adjusted household income
   d Household income is below 40% of median adjusted household income

3 Which of the following Gini coefficients shows the most equal distribution of income?

   a 65.2
   b 56.7
   c 56.2
   d 43.1

B Knowledge and understanding questions

4 Explain the difference between income and wealth. [2 marks]

5 Explain **two** reasons why a government might pursue a policy objective of a more even distribution of income. [4 marks]

6 Explain **two** possible causes of inequality in an economy. [4 marks]

D Essay question

7 Evaluate the most significant consequences of poverty in an economy. [25 marks]

SECTION
2

MACROECONOMICS

Part 8
Implementing policy

Chapter 30

Fiscal policy

This chapter is the first of three that explore the main policy instruments that the authorities can use in seeking to control the performance of the UK economy, and evaluate the extent to which such methods of control are likely to be effective. This chapter examines fiscal policy, which has always been an important part of the government's armoury of instruments. The way that the government carries out its expenditure and taxation policies has important impacts on performance. Monetary policy is explored in Chapter 31. Chapter 32 explains policies that are intended to affect the supply side of the economy.

> ## Learning objectives
>
> After studying this chapter, you should be able to:
> - explain, with the aid of a diagram, the government budget
> - explain, with the aid of a diagram, current and capital government expenditure
> - explain, with the aid of a diagram, a budget surplus, deficit and balanced budget
> - explain, with the aid of a diagram, cyclical and structural budget positions
> - explain, with the aid of a diagram, national and government debt
> - explain, with the aid of a diagram, discretionary fiscal policy and automatic stabilisers
> - explain, with the aid of a diagram, crowding out
> - explain, with the aid of a diagram, direct, indirect, progressive, proportional and regressive taxation
> - explain, with the aid of a diagram, the Laffer curve
> - explain and calculate average and marginal tax rates
> - evaluate the effectiveness of using fiscal policy to achieve the government's macroeconomic objectives

What is fiscal policy?

> **Key term**
>
> fiscal policy decisions made by the government on its expenditure, taxation and borrowing

Fiscal policy covers a range of policy measures that affect government expenditures and revenues. As the government has discretion over the amount of expenditure that it undertakes and the amount of revenue that it chooses to raise from taxation, these can be manipulated in order to influence its policy objectives.

Fiscal policy may be used to correct for market failure. For example, taxes may be used to counter the impact of externalities, and government expenditure may be used to ensure the adequate provision of public goods. At the macroeconomic level, fiscal policy can be used to influence the level of aggregate demand, and to influence the distribution of income.

The government budget

Key terms

government budget the balance between government receipts and outlays

government current expenditure spending by the government on goods and services

transfer payments occur when the government provides benefits (in cash or in kind) to poor households

government capital expenditure spending by government on capital projects

Fiscal policy can be used to affect the level of aggregate demand in the economy, under the influence of Keynesian thinking. The overall balance between government receipts and outlays comprises the **government budget**. Receipts come mainly from taxation, while outlays cover the range of expenditures undertaken by government. The government's plans for expenditure and taxation are set out in the annual Budget statement presented to Parliament (also known as the Annual Financial Statement).

Government expenditure

Government undertakes spending on a wide range of goods and services. **Government current expenditure** is spending on goods and services for immediate use. This includes **transfer payments** such as social security payments, but also covers expenditure on the wages of civil servants and on the NHS and education, which takes a significant portion of the budget. **Government capital expenditure** is spending that is investment for the future benefit of the economy. This covers expenditure on infrastructure projects such as Crossrail and HS2. Such projects are intended to facilitate economic growth.

Education takes a significant portion of the government current expenditure budget

Knowledge check 30.1

How would spending on building a tunnel under Stonehenge be classified?

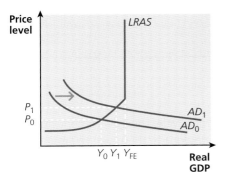

Figure 30.1 Fiscal policy and aggregate demand

The level of government expenditure can influence the level of aggregate demand. In Figure 30.1, macroeconomic equilibrium is initially at the intersection of aggregate supply (*LRAS*) and the initial aggregate demand curve (AD_0), so that real output is at Y_0, which is below the full employment level of output at Y_{FE}. As government expenditure is one of the components

Synoptic link

The *AD/AS* model was introduced in Chapters 19 and 20. Notice that Figure 30.1 assumes a Keynesian aggregate supply curve. The significance of this is explored later in this chapter.

Knowledge check 30.2

Give an example of a fiscal measure that would increase aggregate demand.

Synoptic link

The multiplier was introduced in Chapter 21.

of aggregate demand, an increase in such expenditure moves the aggregate demand curve from AD_0 to AD_1. In response, the economy moves to a new equilibrium, in which the overall price level has risen to P_1 but real output has moved to Y_1, which is closer to the full employment level Y_{FE}.

In this scenario, government expenditure is treated as an injection into the circular flow, and it will be reinforced by the multiplier effect. In Figure 30.1, an increase in government expenditure is effective in raising the level of real output in the economy, although some of the increase is dissipated in the form of an increase in the overall level of prices. Notice that, if the multiplier is relatively low, the reinforcement of fiscal policy through this route will also be relatively weak. Remember that the strength of the multiplier effect depends on the size of withdrawals from the circular flow. For example, if consumers have a high propensity to import, this will weaken the impact of the multiplier.

Knowledge check 30.3

Explain why the multiplier effect is weakened if the marginal propensity to import is relatively high.

The overall government budget position

Key terms

government budget deficit
a situation in which government expenditure exceeds government revenue

government budget surplus
a situation in which government expenditure is less than government revenue

government balanced budget
a situation in which government expenditure equals government revenue

Although the focus of the discussion so far has been on government expenditure, fiscal policy also refers to taxation. In fact, the key issue in considering fiscal policy is the balance between government expenditure and government revenue, as it is this balance that affects the position of aggregate demand directly.

When total government expenditure exceeds revenues, there is a **government budget deficit**, whereas if revenues exceed expenditure, there is a **government budget surplus**. In the event that revenues were to equal expenditure, there would be a **balanced budget**. This is rarely achieved in any single year, but for sustainability, having a balanced budget may be seen as a long-term objective for the government.

An increase in the government budget deficit (or a decrease in the government budget surplus) moves the aggregate demand curve to the right. The budget deficit may arise either from an increase in expenditure or from a decrease in taxation, although the two have some differential effects.

Knowledge check 30.4

If government expenditure is greater than revenue from taxation, will there be a budget deficit or budget surplus?

Cyclical and structural deficits

Key term

cyclical deficit a government budget deficit that occurs during the downturn of the business cycle, but disappears in the upturn

As the economy goes through an economic cycle, the government budget deficit will tend to fluctuate. During the downturn, there will be an increase in the deficit, as spending on benefits will rise, and tax revenues will fall. In other words, there will be a cyclical element to the size of the deficit. Such a **cyclical deficit** will fade away as the economy returns to its trend.

structural deficit a government budget deficit that persists even when the economy is at full employment

A situation in which the budget remains in deficit even with the economy at full employment is known as a **structural deficit**. This would need to be addressed, as it would not be sustainable in the long run, because it would need to be financed in some way. If the government needs to borrow in order to finance the budget, this will need to be repaid at some time in the future, and interest paid on it in the interim.

The national debt and government borrowing

Key term

national debt the total amount of government debt, based on accumulated previous deficits and surpluses

If the government spends more than it raises in revenue, the resulting deficit has to be financed in some way. The government budget deficit is known as the *public sector net cash requirement* (PSNCR). Part of the PSNCR is covered by borrowing, and the government closely monitors its *net borrowing*. Over time, such borrowing leads to *net debt*, which is the accumulation of past borrowing, known as the **national debt**. The Labour government that was in power from 1997 to 2010 aimed to keep this below 40% — and was successful in achieving this until the financial crisis hit.

A major argument in favour of controlling the level of public sector net debt arose from a concern for the long-run effects of policy on spending and borrowing. It was argued that sustainable economic growth has to take into account the needs of future generations. It can be argued that future generations should not have to meet the cost of the consumption of the present population.

Knowledge check 30.5

Explain why a structural deficit would be unsustainable if it were not addressed.

While public sector debt was stable at less than 40% of GDP, it was not seen as being of major concern. However, the financial crisis of the late 2000s led to a refocusing of macroeconomic policy. Figure 30.2 shows the impact of the crisis on this policy target. The crisis was initially seen in the banking system. In the UK, it began with the failure of Northern Rock in 2008, followed by problems in other commercial banks. The bailout of these banks which was needed to safeguard the financial system led to the enormous increase in public sector net debt evident in Figure 30.2. The government's stake in bailed-out banks has been gradually reduced, as the banks involved were in the process of being returned to the private sector. However, the legacy of the crisis is evident, as public sector debt remains at more than 80% of GDP, and the need to bring down the level of debt has coloured policy design.

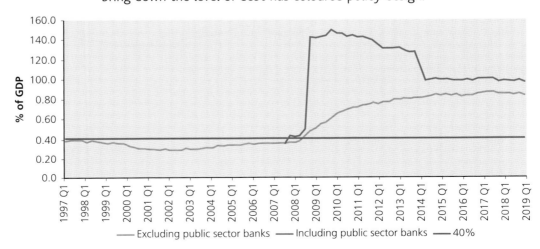

Figure 30.2 Public sector net debt (% of GDP)

Source: ONS

The overall size of the budget deficit may limit the government's actions in terms of fiscal policy. In addition, the overall pattern of revenue and expenditure has a strong effect on the overall balance of activity in the economy. A neutral government budget can be attained either with high expenditure and high revenues, or with relatively low expenditure and revenues. Such decisions affect the overall size of the public sector relative to the private sector. Over the years, different governments in the UK have taken different decisions on this issue — and different countries throughout the world have certainly adopted different approaches.

In part, such issues are determined through the ballot box. In the run-up to an election, each political party presents its overall plans for taxation and spending, and typically they adopt different positions as to the overall balance. It is then up to those voting to give a mandate to whichever party offers a package that most closely resembles their preferences.

Extension material

Voting based on fiscal policy

Notice that there is a limit to how effective this process can be. The policies adopted by a government during its term of office cover a wide range of different issues, and individual voters may approve of some but not others — but they only get to vote once every 5 years or so, and then only on the whole package of measures. When the election comes round, the debates may be dominated by issues that happen to be contentious at the time, rather than the overall ideology of the parties. Furthermore, if the election turns out to be indecisive, so that the result is a coalition across parties with differing manifestos, the resulting policies may turn out to be a mixture. Another pertinent issue is whether or not voters will be fooled by being offered (or given) tax cuts just before an election, as they may know that the reality will be different in the long term.

Figure 30.3 shows the time path of government current expenditure as a share of GDP since 1975. There are minor fluctuations around a downward trend, especially during the 1980s, when many public sector enterprises were transferred into private ownership. However, it has been fairly constant since the mid-1990s. Notice that this does not give the full picture, as public sector investment is not taken into account in these data.

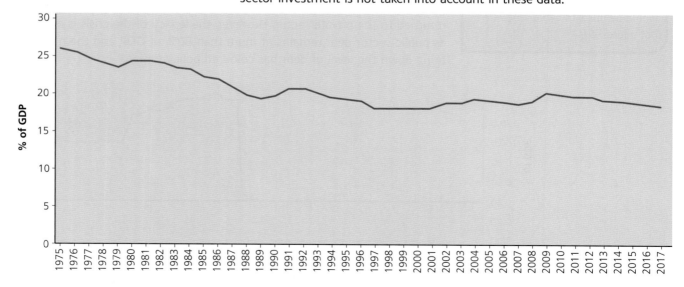

Figure 30.3 Government final consumption, 1950–2017

Source: based on data from ONS

Macroeconomics Part 8

Figure 30.4 provides an international perspective, showing the share of combined current and capital expenditure by governments in a range of countries. This reveals something of a contrast between, on the one hand, Ireland, Korea and Switzerland, and on the other hand, many other European countries, where governments have been more active in the economy. In part this reflects the greater role that government plays in some countries in providing services such as education and healthcare, whereas in other countries the private sector takes a greater role, often through the insurance market.

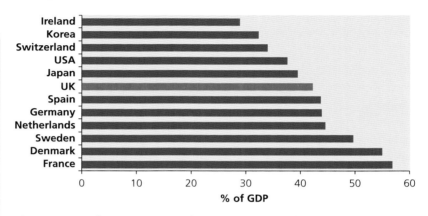

Figure 30.4 Total government spending as a percentage of GDP, selected countries, 2015

Source: OECD

Discretionary fiscal policy and automatic stabilisers

It is important to distinguish between discretionary and automatic changes in government expenditure. Some items of government expenditure and receipts vary automatically with the economic cycle. They are known as **automatic stabilisers**. For example, if the economy enters a period of recession, government expenditure will rise because of the increased payments of unemployment and other social security benefits, and revenues will fall because fewer people are paying income tax, and because receipts from VAT are falling. This helps to offset the recession without any active intervention from the government.

The effect of the automatic stabilisers can be seen in Figure 30.5. Suppose the economy begins at full employment with long-run supply given by $LRAS$ and with aggregate demand at AD_0. Equilibrium real GDP would be at Y_{FE} and the overall price level at P_0. If there is a decrease in aggregate demand to AD_1, equilibrium real GDP falls to Y_1 and the overall price level falls to P_1. The fall in real GDP is accompanied by a fall in employment (a rise in unemployment), so the government finds that its expenditure rises with more people claiming benefits. Furthermore, with fewer people in employment, tax revenues fall, because people are earning less and spending less. The effect is that the fall in aggregate demand is automatically partially offset by the increase in the government budget deficit. In Figure 30.5, this is represented by the shift of aggregate demand to AD_2, so real GDP will be at Y_2. The fall in real GDP is partially offset by the effect of the automatic stabilisers, without the government having taken any conscious measures.

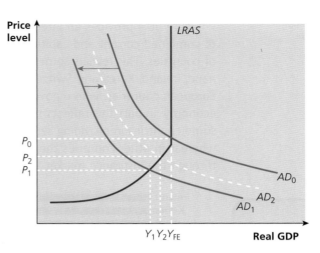

Figure 30.5 The effect of automatic stabilisers

Knowledge check 30.6

Give examples of how automatic stabilisers could affect the economy when it is in the boom phase of the economic cycle.

Key term

discretionary fiscal policy a situation in which the government uses its discretion to intervene in the economy in an attempt to stabilise it

Also important is the question of whether the government can or should make use of **discretionary fiscal policy** in a deliberate attempt to influence the course of the economy. The key issue is whether or not the economy has spare capacity, because attempts to stimulate an economy that is already at full employment will merely push up the price level.

There are many examples of how excessive government spending can create problems for the economy. Such problems arose in a number of Latin American economies during the 1980s. In Brazil, a range of policies was brought to bear in an attempt to reduce inflation, including direct controls on prices. However, with no serious attempt to control the fiscal deficit, inflation continually got out of control, reaching almost 3,000% in 1990. Only when the deficit was reduced did it become possible to bring inflation down to a more reasonable level. More recently, the collapse of Zimbabwe's economy was accompanied by inflation at such a high level that the printing presses could not keep up with the need for banknotes.

Fiscal policy and the *AD/AS* model

It is important to understand how fiscal policy can be analysed using the *AD/AS* model. As already noted, the overall balance between government receipts and outlays affects the position of the aggregate demand curve, which is reinforced by multiplier effects. An increase in the government budget deficit has the effect of shifting the aggregate demand curve to the right.

Figure 30.6 shows that shifting the aggregate demand curve in this way affects only the overall price level in the economy when the aggregate supply curve is vertical — and remember that the neoclassical argument is that it would always be vertical. Hence a key issue for a government considering the use of fiscal policy is knowing whether there is spare capacity in the economy, because otherwise an expansion in aggregate demand from increased government spending will push up prices, but leave real output unchanged.

Exercise 30.2

Use *AD/AS* analysis to consider the effect of an expansionary fiscal policy on the equilibrium level of real output and the overall price level. Undertake this exercise with different initial positions along the neoclassical long-run aggregate supply curve, first analysing an economy that begins at full employment and then one in which aggregate demand creates an equilibrium that is below full employment. Discuss the differences in your results.

Key terms

crowding out process by which an increase in government expenditure 'crowds out' private sector activity by raising the cost of borrowing

crowding in process by which a decrease in government expenditure 'crowds in' private sector activity by lowering the cost of borrowing

Knowledge check 30.7

How will a fall in government expenditure affect the private sector if the government reduces its borrowing?

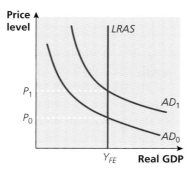

Figure 30.6 Demand-side policy with a neoclassical *LRAS* curve

Under the multiplier, any increase in injections leads to a multiplied increase in equilibrium output. The size of these induced effects will depend upon the marginal propensity to withdraw.

In terms of the *AD/AS* diagram, the existence of the multiplier means that if there is an increase in government expenditure, the *AD* curve moves further to the right than it otherwise would have done, because of the multiplier effects. However, this does not mean that equilibrium income will increase by the full multiplier amount. Looking more closely at what is happening, you can see that there are some forces at work that are acting to weaken the multiplier effect of an increase in government expenditure.

One way in which this happens is through interest rates. If the government finances its deficit through borrowing, a side effect is to put upward pressure on interest rates, which then may cause private sector spending — by households on consumption and by firms on investment — to decline, as the cost of borrowing has been increased. This process is known as the **crowding out** of private sector activity by the public sector. It limits the extent to which a government budget deficit can shift the aggregate demand curve, especially if the public sector activity is less productive than the private sector activity that it replaces. In principle, there could also be a **crowding in** effect if the government runs a surplus and therefore puts downward pressure on interest rates.

Summary

● Fiscal policy is the use of government expenditures and revenues to influence the economy.
● The government budget is the overall balance between its outgoings and its incomings.
● The budget is in deficit when expenditures exceed receipts, but it may also be in surplus or in balance.
● The budget varies with the economic cycle as expenditures increase and revenues decline during periods of recession.
● A structural deficit occurs when the government faces a budget deficit even when the economy is at full employment.
● Government borrowing to finance a deficit accumulates into the national debt.
● The effects of cyclical movements in the budget deficit act as automatic stabilisers, but the government may also intervene by using discretionary fiscal policy in an attempt to stabilise the economy.
● Discretionary fiscal policy can be destabilising.
● The shape of the long-run aggregate supply curve is an important influence on the impact of fiscal policy.

Direct and indirect taxes

Fiscal policy, and taxation in particular, has not only been used to influence aggregate demand or to establish a balance between the public and private sectors of an economy. In addition, taxation remains an important weapon against some forms of market failure, and it also influences the distribution of income. In this context, the choice of using direct or indirect taxes is important.

Direct taxes

In the UK the main direct taxes are income tax, corporation tax (paid by firms on profits), capital gains tax (paid by individuals who sell assets at a profit), inheritance tax and petroleum revenue tax (paid by firms operating in the North Sea). There is also the council tax, collected by local authorities and National Insurance Contributions (NIC).

Direct taxes (taxes on incomes) tend to be **progressive**. In other words, higher income groups pay tax at a higher rate. With a tax such as income tax, its progressive nature is reflected in the way the tax rate increases as an individual moves into a higher income range. In other words, the **marginal tax rate** increases as income increases. The progressive nature of the tax ensures that it does indeed help to reduce inequality in income distribution.

Figure 30.7 shows average direct tax rates for households by quintile group in 2015/16. Notice that the figure shows *average* rather than *marginal* tax rates. When average rates are rising, marginal tax rates are higher than the average. Exercise 30.3 illustrates this.

Knowledge check 30.8

Looking at Figure 30.7, would you say that employees' NIC payments are progressive or regressive?

Exercise 30.3

Table 30.1 shows the amount of tax paid by an individual as income increases. Calculate the average and marginal tax rates at each of the income levels. (*Remember the definition of the marginal tax rate provided above.*)

Table 30.1 Tax paid as income increases

Income	Tax paid
£1,000	£100
£2,000	£300
£3,000	£600
£4,000	£1,000

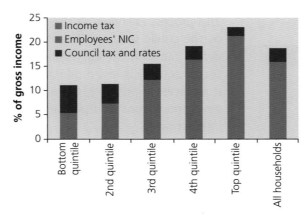

Figure 30.7 Average direct taxes by quintile households, 2015/16

Source: ONS

Figure 30.7 shows how income tax is progressive, as the average tax rate increases from 3.8% in the bottom quintile to 16.5% in the top quintile. However, it also shows that council tax is certainly not progressive, as it takes a higher percentage from the bottom quintile than from the top.

Indirect taxes

Indirect taxes are taxes that are paid on items of expenditure, rather than on income. Examples of indirect taxes are value added tax (VAT), which is charged on most goods and services sold in the UK, tobacco taxes, excise duties on alcohol and oil duties. These specific taxes are levied per unit sold. When demand is price inelastic, producers are able to pass much of an increase in the tax rate on to consumers, whereas if demand is price elastic they have to absorb most of the increase as part of their costs.

The effect of indirect taxes can sometimes be **regressive**: in other words, indirect taxes may impinge more heavily on lower-income households.

Why should some of these taxes be regressive? Take the tobacco tax. In the first place, the number of smokers is higher among lower-income groups than among the relatively rich — research has shown that only about 10% of people in professional groups now smoke compared with nearly 40% of those in unskilled manual groups. Second, expenditure on tobacco tends to take a lower proportion of income of the rich compared with that of the poor, even for those in the former group who do smoke. So, the tobacco tax falls more heavily on lower-income groups than on the better-off. It is estimated that for households in the bottom quintile of the income distribution in 2015/16, indirect taxes accounted for 27.0% of their disposable income, compared with 14.4% for households in the top quintile. The largest share of indirect tax was VAT, which accounted for 11.4% of disposable income of households in the bottom quintile, compared with 7.1% for the top quintile.

Notice that a tax that is simply **proportional** to income would be neither regressive nor progressive, but would be charged at the same percentage rate to all taxpayers.

The Laffer curve

An important rationale for fiscal policy is the need to raise revenue in order to finance the government's expenditure. But does an increase in tax rates necessarily lead to a rise in tax revenue? Arthur Laffer argued that the answer to this was 'no'. He pointed out that changes in tax rates have two effects on tax revenue. The arithmetic says that an increase in tax rates will increase the tax revenue. However, there is also an economic effect. As tax rates rise, incentive effects come into play, tending to work against the arithmetic effect, as people have less incentive to supply effort at the higher tax rates. The relationship can be captured in the so-called *Laffer curve*, an inverted U-shaped relationship between the tax rate and the amount of revenue raised, as shown in Figure 30.8.

At low rates of tax, revenue increases, but beyond t^*, the revenue begins to fall. If an economy has been operating with a tax rate above t^*, then a *reduction* in the tax rate would actually *increase* the revenue raised by the tax. It is worth noting that Laffer himself pointed out that he had not invented the concept, as it can be found in the writings of Keynes, not to mention Ibn Khaldun, a fourteenth-century Muslim philosopher.

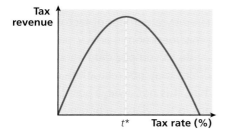

Figure 30.8 The Laffer curve

Influencing income distribution

The balance between regressive and progressive taxes is important if the government wishes to influence the distribution of income in order to reduce inequality. Progressive taxes such as income tax have a direct impact on the distribution of income. In addition, government expenditure on benefits constitutes a transfer of resources from the rich to the poor.

In the UK, there are two forms of benefit that households can receive to help equalise the income distribution. First, there are various types of cash benefit, such as Income Support, Child Benefit, Incapacity Benefit and Working Tax Credit. These are designed to protect families whose income in certain circumstances would otherwise be very low. These are being replaced by Universal Credit. Second, there are benefits in kind, such as health and education. These accrue to individual households depending on the number of members of the household and their age and gender. Of these, the cash benefits are far more important in influencing the distribution of income. For the lowest quintile such benefits make up about three-fifths of growth in income. They are also significant for the second quintile.

Achieving a balance of taxation between direct and indirect taxes is an important aspect of the government's redistributive policy. A switch in the balance from direct to indirect taxes will tend to increase inequality.

Summary

- Direct taxes are taxes levied directly on incomes.
- Direct taxes tend to be progressive, falling more heavily on those on higher incomes.
- The Laffer curve indicates that raising the rate of a tax does not necessarily result in an increase in tax revenue.
- Indirect taxes are levied on expenditures, and can be regressive because of people's spending patterns.
- Taxes and transfer payments can be used to affect the distribution of income.

The effectiveness of fiscal policy

The implementation of fiscal policy is hindered by a number of factors. The government faces uncertainty in designing macroeconomic policy, partly because of the availability of data. It takes time to compile data about the current state of the economy, so the authorities may not realise the extent to which intervention is required. Furthermore, it is not always possible to anticipate problems that might arise, perhaps in the global economy rather than domestically. In any case, fiscal policy does not affect the economy instantly — for example, changes in tax rates cannot be introduced straight away. The effects of any policy change then take time to affect how economic agents behave. All of this means that by the time fiscal policy takes effect, the original reason for using it may have gone away.

Even without these timing issues, the impact of fiscal policy may be diluted if the government needs to borrow in order to stimulate aggregate demand, because this may cause an increase in interest rates and lead to crowding out. So, how effective is fiscal policy in achieving the government's macroeconomic objectives?

Economic growth

Both economic analysis and the UK experience support the view that fiscal policy should not be used as an active stabilisation device. If the authorities were to intervene by increasing government expenditure to shift aggregate demand during a period when economic growth was slow, this could damage the economy. Some of the increase in aggregate demand would be dissipated in higher domestic prices and higher imports.

However, this does not mean that there is no role for fiscal policy in a modern economy. The balance that is achieved between the private and public sectors can have an important influence on the overall level of economic activity, and upon economic growth, so the importance of designing an appropriate fiscal policy should not be underestimated.

Stability in prices

Can fiscal policy be used to tackle inflation? Where the economy suffers from demand-pull inflation, a reduction in government expenditure may help to reduce inflationary pressure. This could be effective if the economy is at full employment with a neoclassical *LRAS* curve, where a change in aggregate demand affects the price level but has no effect on real GDP. However, if the economy is below full employment under Keynesian assumptions, a reduction in aggregate demand may result in lower real GDP and higher unemployment.

Politically, using fiscal policy to tackle inflation may be unpopular, as a decrease in government expenditure may be seen as heralding a period of austerity.

Full employment

It may be tempting for the government to use fiscal policy in times of unemployment, increasing aggregate demand to encourage higher employment. Under neoclassical assumptions, this would be counterproductive, as the economy would be expected to return to full employment equilibrium without intervention. Indeed, the dangers of discretionary fiscal policy have been discussed earlier in the chapter.

A balanced government budget

In the aftermath of the financial crisis, fiscal policy was used to try to counteract the recession that was affecting the economy. However, this is not a policy that could be used in the long run, because of the effect on the national debt. The government was intent on reducing the size of the national debt to a sustainable level, but was also faced with pressure from many government departments to increase funding. There were funding shortages in the NHS and the education sector, among others. The need to safeguard the environment adds further pressure on government expenditure. The dilemma of how to fund much-needed expenditure without leaving high levels of debt for future generations is a continuing issue.

A fair distribution of income

Another key role for fiscal policy is in affecting the distribution of income within society. Taxes and transfers can have a large effect on income distribution. This in turn may have effects on the economy by affecting the incentives that people face in choosing their labour supply.

Notice that fiscal policy (in the form of taxes and subsidies) is also used in the context of microeconomics to address issues of market failure. This is discussed in Chapter 10.

Achieving a balance of taxation between direct and indirect taxes is an important aspect of the government's redistributive policy. A switch in the balance from direct to indirect taxes will tend to increase inequality in a society. The incentive effects must also be kept in mind. High marginal tax rates on income can have a disincentive effect; if people know that a large proportion of any additional work they undertake will be taxed away, they may be discouraged from providing more work. In other words, cutting income tax can encourage work effort by reducing marginal tax rates. This is yet another reminder of the need for a balanced policy — one that recognises that, while some income redistribution is needed to protect the vulnerable, disincentive effects may arise if the better-off are over-taxed.

Summary

- Discretionary use of fiscal policy to affect aggregate demand may not have the desired effects.
- An increase in aggregate demand may affect prices more than real output.
- The effects of an increase in aggregate demand on real output may be uncertain because of the difficulty in forecasting its timing and impact.
- Taxes may be used to address issues of market failure.
- Taxes can also affect the distribution of income, but policy-makers need to be aware of the importance of maintaining good incentives.

Case study 30.1

The HS2 project and the macroeconomy

The quality of a nation's infrastructure provides important support for business. If a country's transport and communication system is inefficient, firms will find it difficult to compete with foreign firms. However, in 2010 the Organisation for Economic Cooperation and Development (OECD) ranked Britain as only 33rd in the world for the quality of its infrastructure.

One project undertaken by the UK government was HS2, designed to provide a new high-speed rail link between London and Birmingham, to be extended in two directions: to northwest England (Manchester) and Yorkshire (Sheffield and Leeds). This would be the largest infrastructure construction project in Europe.

The project involves large-scale expenditure in the short run; in 2013, the total cost was estimated at £42.6 billion at 2011 prices, but the estimate has since been revised upwards, and the budget was stated as £55.7 billion in late 2017. However, some critics of the project suggest that the final cost could be as much as £200 billion. The first passengers are expected to travel on HS2 in 2026. Costs include the capital costs of purchasing land and constructing railway lines, stations, depots and rolling stock. There would be some multiplier effects of these expenditures while the project is being undertaken. When completed, the project will ease existing capacity constraints and allow more rapid travel between London and the destinations in the north. It is claimed that for each £1 spent on the project, the UK will receive £2.30 in benefits.

Follow-up questions

a Use an *AD/AS* diagram to analyse the short-run effects of this project.

b With reference to another *AD/AS* diagram, discuss the expected long-run impact of the HS2 project on the macroeconomy.

CHAPTER 30 QUESTIONS

A Multiple-choice questions

1 Which of the following would not be classed as government expenditure?

  a Disability benefit payments
  b NHS wage payments
  c National Insurance payments
  d Jobseeker's Allowance payments

2 If government revenue exceeds government expenditure, then this would be classed as a budget:

  a Surplus
  b Deficit
  c Balance
  d Differential

3 Which of the following best describes automatic stabilisers?

  a Changes to government revenue and expenditure that happen without direct intervention
  b Changes to government revenue and expenditure that require direct intervention
  c Keeping the budget so that revenue always automatically meets expenditure
  d Allowing government revenue and expenditure to adjust to the economic cycle without direct intervention

B Knowledge and understanding questions

4 Explain what is meant by 'discretionary fiscal policy'. [2 marks]

5 Explain, with the aid of a diagram, the relationship between the taxation rate and the amount of government revenue raised through taxation. [4 marks]

6 Explain, with the aid of a diagram, the likely effect on an economy of an increase in taxation. [4 marks]

C Stimulus response question

7 One of the most important elements of UK government fiscal policy is Budget day, when the chancellor of the exchequer outlines the government's fiscal policy for the future.

In October 2018, the chancellor outlined the following policies:

- Expenditure for public services will grow above inflation until 2023.
- Fuel duty (taxation) was frozen for the ninth year in a row.
- A new tax on large digital firms' revenue would be issued from April 2020.

  a Explain, using an example, what is meant by 'expenditure for public services'. [2 marks]
  b Evaluate the likely effects of the fiscal policies outlined in the data. [12 marks]

D Essay question

8 Evaluate the effectiveness of fiscal policy in achieving the government macroeconomic objective of economic growth. [20 marks]

Chapter 31

Monetary policy

The previous chapter discussed fiscal policy — the use of government spending and taxation to influence the economy. The second way in which the authorities attempt to steer the economy is using monetary policy. This entails the use of interest rates and the supply of money to influence the path of the economy. This is the focus of this chapter.

Learning objectives

After studying this chapter, you should be able to:
● explain, with the aid of a diagram, changes in money supply
● explain, with the aid of a diagram, changes in interest rates
● explain, with the aid of a diagram, inflation rate targets
● explain, with the aid of a diagram, quantitative easing
● explain, with the aid of a diagram, the influence of exchange rates
● evaluate the effectiveness of using monetary policy to achieve the government's macroeconomic objectives

The tools of monetary policy

Monetary policy involves the manipulation of monetary variables in order to influence aggregate demand in the economy, with the intention of meeting the government's macroeconomic objectives. The key tools are money supply and the interest rate, but the exchange rate also has an important impact.

Money supply

The **money supply** is the quantity of money that is in circulation in the economy. In a modern economy, money performs four important functions. First, it is a medium of exchange. In other words, money is what is used when people undertake transactions — for example, when you buy a sandwich or a burger for lunch. Second, money is a store of value: people (or firms) may choose to hold money in order to undertake transactions in the future. If this were not the case, there would be no reason for people to accept money in exchange for goods or services. Money is also a unit of account: it is a way of setting prices so that the value of different goods and services can be compared. Finally, money is a standard of deferred payment. Firms signing contracts for future transactions need to be able to set prices for those transactions.

Key terms

monetary policy decisions made by the government regarding monetary variables such as money supply and interest rates
money supply the quantity of money that is in circulation in the economy

Synoptic link

You can find more discussion about the topics of money supply and interest rates in Chapter 37.

Firms and households choose to hold some money. They may do this in order to undertake transactions, or as a precaution against the possible need to undertake transactions at short notice. In other words, there is a *demand for money*. However, in choosing to hold money they incur an opportunity cost, in the sense that they forgo the possibility of earning interest by purchasing some form of financial asset.

This means that the interest rate can be regarded as the opportunity cost of holding money — put another way, it is the price of holding money. At high rates of interest, people can be expected to choose to hold less money, as the opportunity cost of holding money is high. *MD* in Figure 31.1 represents a money demand curve. It is downward sloping.

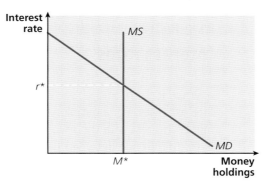

Figure 31.1 The demand for money

> ### Knowledge check 31.1
> Explain why the interest rate can be regarded as the opportunity cost of holding money.

Suppose the government wants to set the money supply (*MS*) at *M** in Figure 31.1. This can be achieved in two ways. If the government controls the supply of money at *M**, equilibrium will be achieved only if the interest rate is allowed to adjust to *r**. An alternative way of reaching the same point is to set the interest rate at *r** and then allow the money supply to adjust to *M**. The government can do one or the other — but it cannot set money supply at *M** and hold the interest rate at any value other than *r** without causing disequilibrium. In other words, it is not possible to control both money supply and interest rates simultaneously and independently.

Figure 31.2 shows what would happen if the authorities were to engineer an increase in money supply. The rightward shift in money supply from MS_0 to MS_1 results in a new equilibrium with the interest rate having fallen from r_0 to r_1.

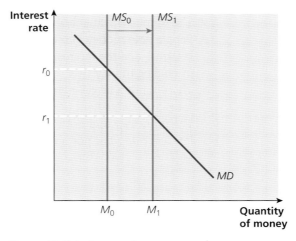

Figure 31.2 An increase in money supply

A problem with attempting to control the money supply directly is that the complexity of the modern financial system makes it quite difficult to pin down a precise definition or measurement of money. There is a wide range of financial assets with different characteristics, some of which can be accessed quickly if the owner needs to undertake transactions.

Furthermore, the lending behaviour of the commercial banks can influence money supply, as by increasing their lending, banks can create credit. This makes it more difficult for the central bank to exert control over money supply.

If the central bank cannot control the amount of money supply with any precision, then this becomes an unreliable policy instrument, as the effects cannot be predicted. For this reason, the use of money supply as an instrument was replaced by a focus on using the interest rate.

Interest rates

Although the previous section talked about 'the interest rate', this is a simplification. In the real-world economy, there are many different interest rates. For example, if you borrow from a bank, you will pay a higher interest rate than would be paid to you on your savings. Indeed, it is this difference between the rates for savers and borrowers that enables the banks to make a profit.

Similarly, interest rates on financial assets differ depending on the nature of the asset. In part, these differences reflect different degrees of risk associated with the assets. A risky asset pays a higher interest rate than a relatively safe asset. A long-term asset tends to pay a higher interest rate than a short-term asset, although the differences have been quite small in the early part of the twenty-first century. This will be discussed further in Chapter 37.

Changing the interest rate will affect the state of equilibrium in the money market, but why does this matter? If we want to explore how changing the interest rate will influence the economy, we need to examine the way in which changes in the interest rate (or in money supply) would have an impact on aggregate demand.

Summary

- Monetary policy entails the manipulation of monetary variables in order to influence aggregate demand in the economy.
- The prime instrument of monetary policy is the interest rate.
- People hold money in order to undertake transactions (among other reasons), and the interest rate can be regarded as the opportunity cost of holding money.
- There is not a single interest rate in the economy, but a variety of rates associated with the wide range of financial assets available.
- The monetary authorities can control either the money supply or interest rates, but not both independently.

How does monetary policy work?

Key terms

central bank the banker to the government, performing a range of functions, which may include issue of coins and banknotes, acting as banker to commercial banks and regulating the financial system

Bank of England the UK's central bank

transmission mechanism of monetary policy the channel by which monetary policy affects aggregate demand

Synoptic link

The role of the central bank (and the Bank of England in particular) is discussed in Chapter 39.

Knowledge check 31.2

Explain why investment may be sensitive to the rate of interest.

All developed and most developing countries have a **central bank**, fulfilling a range of roles, including being banker to the government. The central bank may also be responsible for the issue of coins and banknotes, for acting as banker to commercial banks and for regulating the financial system. In the UK, this role is taken by the **Bank of England**.

In evaluating the tools of monetary policy, it is important to understand the route by which a change in a monetary variable can have an effect on the real economy. In other words, how does a change in money supply, or the interest rate, affect the level of equilibrium output in the economy?

The monetary transmission mechanism

In drawing this analysis together, an important issue concerns the relationship between the rate of interest and the level of aggregate demand. This is critical for the conduct of monetary policy, because the interest rate has been seen as the prime instrument of monetary policy in recent years — and monetary policy is seen as the prime instrument of macroeconomic policy. By setting the interest rate, monetary policy is intended to affect aggregate demand through the so-called **transmission mechanism of monetary policy**.

At a higher interest rate, firms undertake less investment expenditure because fewer projects are worthwhile. In addition, a higher interest rate may encourage higher saving, which also means that households undertake less consumption expenditure. This may then reinforce the impact on investment because if firms perceive consumption to be falling, this will affect their expectations about future demand, and further dampen their desire to undertake investment. These factors lower the level of aggregate demand, shifting the AD curve to the left.

This can be seen by looking at Figure 31.3. The initial equilibrium is with real output at Y_0, the price level at P_0 and the rate of interest at r_0. An increase in the rate of interest to r_1 will need to be balanced by a decrease in money supply to maintain money market equilibrium. However, more significant is the effect on investment, which is shown in the middle panel of the figure. The increase in the rate of interest leads to a fall in investment from I_0 to I_1. This will cause the aggregate demand curve to move from AD_0 to AD_1, resulting in a lower overall price level P_1 and a lower real output level at Y_1. The lower level of real output arises because the $LRAS$ curve was drawn under Keynesian assumptions with an upward-sloping segment.

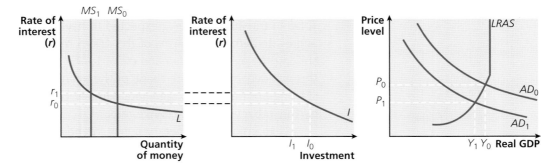

Figure 31.3 The interest rate and aggregate demand

Notice that this may not be the end of the story. If one of the effects of the higher interest rate is to discourage investment, this will also have long-term consequences. Investment allows the productive capacity of the economy to increase, leading to a rightward drift in the *LRAS* curve. With lower investment, this process will go into reverse, leaving the economy with lower productive capacity than it otherwise would have had.

The *AD/AS* graph is drawn in terms of the overall price level. However, in a dynamic context, high interest rates may be needed in order to maintain control of inflation. A reduction in interest rates would, of course, have the reverse effect.

In creating a stable macroeconomic environment, the ultimate aim of monetary policy is not simply to keep inflation low, but to improve the confidence of decision-makers, and thereby encourage firms to invest in order to generate an increase in production capacity. This will stimulate economic growth and create an opportunity to improve living standards.

The influence of exchange rates

In considering the transmission of monetary policy, it is also important to consider the exchange rate — that is, the rate at which one currency exchanges against another.

This is because the exchange rate, the interest rate and the money supply are all intimately related. If UK interest rates are high relative to elsewhere in the world, they will attract overseas investors, increasing the demand for pounds. This will tend to lead to an appreciation in the exchange rate — which in turn will reduce the competitiveness of UK goods and services, reducing the foreign demand for UK exports and encouraging UK residents to reduce their demand for domestic goods and buy imports instead.

Under a fixed exchange rate regime, the monetary authorities are committed to maintaining the exchange rate at a particular level, so could not allow an appreciation to take place. In this situation, monetary policy is powerless to influence the real economy, as it must be devoted to maintaining the exchange rate. Under a floating exchange rate system, monetary policy is freed from this role, but even so it must be used in such a way that the current account deficit of the balance of payments does not become unsustainable in the long run.

Monetary policy in practice

The monetary transmission mechanism explains the way in which a change in the interest rate affects aggregate demand in the economy. A fall in the interest rate is expected to have an expansionary effect on aggregate demand. In terms of the *AD/AS* model, this has the effect of shifting the aggregate demand curve to the right. The effectiveness of this will depend upon the shape of the aggregate supply curve and the starting position of the aggregate demand curve. This would be reinforced by the impact on the exchange rate.

An expansionary monetary policy intended to stimulate aggregate demand would be damaging if the economy were close to (or at) full employment, as the main impact would be on the overall price level rather than real output. This suggests that monetary policy should also not be used to stimulate aggregate demand. However, monetary policy can still play an important role in managing the economy. This arises through its influence on the price level and hence the rate of change of prices — that is, inflation.

Inflation targeting

Soon after the general election of 1997, the UK introduced inflation targeting. This approach to monetary policy gives independence to the central bank to set interest rates in order to meet an inflation target set by the government. The idea of this was to boost the credibility of government policy, by establishing a firm commitment to controlling inflation, as the control of money supply would now be out of the government's control. It cannot expand money supply to boost aggregate demand in order to create a temporary boom that might bolster its popularity in the lead-up to an election.

Monetary policy in the UK therefore became the responsibility of the Bank of England. The Bank's Monetary Policy Committee (MPC) meets each month to decide whether or not the interest rate needs to be altered. If the rate of inflation threatens to accelerate beyond the target rate, the Bank of England can intervene by raising interest rates, thereby having a dampening effect on aggregate demand and reducing the inflationary pressure. In reaching its decisions, the MPC takes a long-term view, projecting inflation ahead over the next 2 years. In the case of the British approach to this policy, the target range is *symmetric*: in other words, the MPC is required to take action (or explain itself) if the inflation rate falls below the target range as well as if it rises above it. In contrast, the European Central Bank faces an *asymmetric target*, being only required to act when the inflation rate rises above the target range, but without a lower range.

Operationally, the MPC sets the interest rate, which it pays on commercial bank reserves. This is known as bank rate. The commercial banks tend to use this rate as their own base rate, from which they calculate the rates of interest that they charge to their borrowers. If the MPC changes bank rate, the commercial banks soon adjust the rates they charge to borrowers. These will vary according to the riskiness of the loans — for example, credit cards are charged at a higher rate than mortgages — but all the rates are geared to the base rate set by the commercial banks, and hence indirectly to bank rate set by the Bank of England.

However, decisions to change the rate of interest are not taken solely in the light of expected inflation. In its deliberations about the interest rate, the MPC takes a wide variety of factors into account, including developments in:

- financial markets
- the international economy
- money and credit
- demand and output
- the labour market
- costs and prices (e.g. changes in oil prices)

A good example was in 2008, when the UK and other countries were struggling to cope with the financial crisis (the 'credit crunch'). At this time, inflation was accelerating, and had reached a rate that was more than one percentage point above the target. This being so, it might have been expected that the Bank of England would raise interest rates in order to stem aggregate demand and bring inflation back into line with the target. However, this would have been damaging in other ways, pushing the economy further into recession. With house prices falling, an increase in interest rates could also have damaged this sector. It was also thought that there were other pressures affecting the world economy that would in any case mean that the rate of inflation was likely to slow down of its own accord. In the event, inflation accelerated way beyond its target range, but the MPC refrained from raising bank rate because of fears that the recession would become even deeper, or that the economy would recover more slowly.

Multiple houses for rent on a residential UK street — a sign of testing economic times?

It is also important to remember that the transmission mechanism has a third channel in addition to the effects of the change in interest rate on consumption and investment. This third channel arises through the exchange rate, so that monetary policy cannot be considered in isolation from exchange rate policy. The (interest) transmission mechanism of monetary policy is summarised in Figure 31.4.

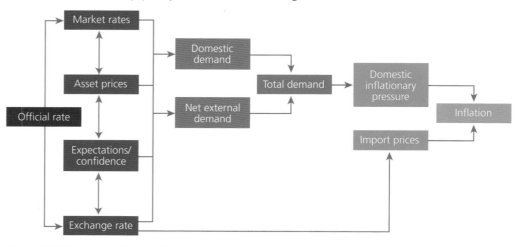

Figure 31.4 The transmission of monetary policy

Source: Bank of England

Evaluation of monetary policy

The prime objective of monetary policy is to control inflation, creating a stable macroeconomic environment in which firms will be encouraged to invest, so that economic growth will be achieved. Monetary policy is able to influence economic growth, but mainly by this indirect route. Similarly, by creating a stable macroeconomic environment, monetary policy creates the conditions in which economic agents can form reliable expectations about the future course of the economy, which allows a smooth adjustment to equilibrium.

The close relationship between monetary policy and the exchange rate means that the central bank must be aware of the possible impact of its decisions on the balance of payments. Raising the interest rate relative to other countries is likely to attract foreign investors, creating a surplus on the financial account, and putting upward pressure on the exchange rate. The end result is likely to be a deficit on the current account to balance the surplus on the financial account. Care must be taken to ensure that this is sustainable in the long run.

Monetary policy was used to try to stimulate aggregate demand in the recession that followed the financial crisis in an attempt to stabilise the economic cycle and to keep unemployment under control. However, this was a short-term measure, rather than an attempt to influence the long-run growth path. Other objectives of macroeconomic policy such as a fair distribution of income or a balanced government budget are tackled through fiscal measures. In other words, the effectiveness of monetary policy should be judged through its ability to meet the inflation target.

For a decade after the responsibility for monetary policy was delegated to the Bank of England, monetary policy was seen to be highly effective in enabling the achievement of the inflation target. You can see this in Figure 31.5. Inflation stayed within the required one percentage point of its target, moving outside that range in only one month between January 2004 and April 2008. However, matters then took a turn for the worse with the onset of the financial crisis and the ensuing recession, and inflation accelerated beyond its limit before coming back into range.

In looking at the relationship between interest rates and inflation, it is useful to be aware that there are long time lags between initiating a change in the interest rate and the final impact on the inflation rate. The Bank of England has noted that it can take about 2 years before the full effect on inflation has worked through the system. Decisions about the interest rate therefore need to be based on the forecast of inflation between 2 and 3 years ahead.

The need to combat recession led to bank rate being reduced to 0.5% in March 2009. This situation creates problems for monetary policy, as having reached such a

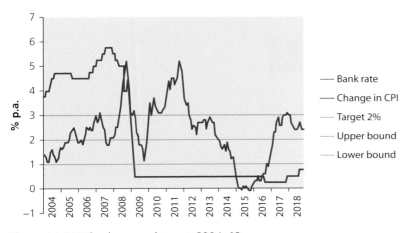

Figure 31.5 UK bank rate and target, 2004–18

Sources: ONS, Bank of England

low level for bank rate, it is no longer possible to reduce the interest rate much further — it would not be possible for bank rate to be negative. Keynes had pointed to the danger that such a situation would arise, referring to this as the **liquidity trap**. He argued that in a deep recession, monetary policy would become ineffective in affecting aggregate demand. Interest rates could fall no further, and any increase in money supply would be absorbed by an increase in the cash holdings of firms and individuals, as they would not buy financial assets with such a low return.

Quantitative easing

The Bank of England announced that it would start to inject money directly into the economy, effectively switching the instrument of monetary policy away from the interest rate and towards the quantity of money. This would be achieved by a process known as **quantitative easing**, by which the Bank purchases assets such as government and corporate bonds, so releasing additional money into the system through the banks and other financial institutions from which it buys the assets. The hope was that this would allow banks to increase their lending, and therefore combat the threat of deflation — and perhaps help to speed recovery. This suggests that the Bank did not believe that the economy was in a liquidity trap, so that an increase in money supply could still affect aggregate demand.

So, how does quantitative easing work? The starting point is that the Bank of England uses electronically created money to buy high-quality financial assets, with the stated aim of improving the flow of credit in the economy, so allowing firms to obtain finance for investment. Figure 31.6 shows the transmission mechanism from asset purchases to bank lending.

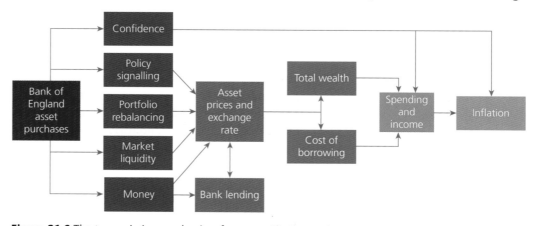

Figure 31.6 The transmission mechanism from quantitative easing

Source: Bank of England

The initial impact of asset purchases is intended to give economic agents confidence that action is being undertaken and to provide clear signals of policy intent. This will also encourage a rebalancing of portfolios, provide market liquidity and increase the supply of money.

The improvement in confidence will affect asset prices and the exchange rate, as well as spending and income in the economy. This could also affect inflation, but this was considered less important than the recession that was building — indeed inflation was decelerating anyway. These other effects of the asset purchases will work together to reinforce the impact on asset prices and the exchange rate, with the increase in money supply operating through the impact on bank lending. The adjustment in asset prices and the exchange rate will also affect total wealth and the cost of borrowing, in turn affecting spending and income.

In this way, monetary policy can be used to mitigate the effects of recession, even with bank rate at its lowest point. The key part of this is the provision of credit to allow the economy to function more effectively.

It is important to be aware that the UK was certainly not alone in facing this combination of circumstances. A number of countries had also enjoyed relative stability for several years, followed by a more turbulent period. This in itself suggests that the conduct of monetary policy cannot claim full responsibility for the period of calm, nor perhaps be entirely blamed for the subsequent problems.

The UK's recovery from recession was slow, and the time-path of real GDP remained stubbornly below trend. You can see in Figure 31.5 that inflation fell below the target range in 2015 and 2016, even turning negative in some months. In August 2016, the MPC agreed to cut bank rate to 0.25% in an attempt to bring inflation back towards the target — and in recognition of the weakening prospects for growth following the EU referendum result. Inflation began to move back into the target range, and in late 2017 the MPC brought bank rate back up to 0.5% as inflation hit the top of its target range. Bank rate was increased further to 0.75% in August 2018.

It is also important to realise that for monetary policy to be and remain effective, it must be viewed in combination with other policies being implemented at the same time — in particular, there needs to be coordination with fiscal policy.

Exercise 31.2

Visit the Bank of England website to find out when was the most recent change in bank rate: www.bankofengland.co.uk/monetary-policy/the-interest-rate-bank-rate. What effect would this be expected to have?

Evaluation of demand-side policies

Both fiscal and monetary policy operate through the demand side of the economy, affecting the position of the *AD* curve in order to influence the path of the economy.

Whether intervention is needed in response to an external shock depends upon if the economy adjusts rapidly back to equilibrium at the natural rate, or whether the adjustment process is long and persistent.

The financial crisis represented one of the greatest external shocks to hit developed economies since the Second World War. So how effective were demand-side policies in responding to the crisis?

In both the UK and the USA, a combination of fiscal and monetary policy measures were introduced.

In terms of fiscal policy, governments on both sides of the Atlantic launched fiscal stimulus packages in the form of increased expenditure. In the UK, the government also introduced changes to direct taxes and implemented a temporary reduction in the rate of VAT. The strength of this approach is that the measures take effect quite quickly, and help to safeguard employment. However, the downside is that running a budget deficit in this way adds to public sector net debt, as the expenditures need to be financed.

435

Exercise 31.3

Discuss why rules-based fiscal or monetary policy may help to reinforce the effectiveness of policy measures.

Monetary policy was also used in an attempt to stimulate aggregate demand, through cuts in interest rates and quantitative easing. The need to bail out failing banks further added to public sector debt.

The message from *AD/AS* analysis is that stimulating aggregate demand is not a solution to long-run economic growth, except insofar as it entails investment expenditure that adds to a nation's productive capacity. Although the measures taken through demand-side policy during the financial crisis may have cushioned the impact, in the long run it is by supply-side policies that economic growth can be restored. These are discussed in the next chapter.

Summary

- Money supply does not provide a reliable control mechanism, so the prime instrument of monetary policy is the interest rate.
- The transmission mechanism from the interest rate to aggregate demand works through investment and consumption, and indirectly via the exchange rate.
- The Bank of England's Monetary Policy Committee has the responsibility for setting the interest rate at such a level as to achieve the government's inflation target, taking account of the general domestic and international economic environment.
- Monetary policy cannot focus solely on meeting the inflation target, but must also operate with an awareness of other developments in the macroeconomy.
- With the advent of the financial crisis in the late 2000s, a new approach was needed.
- Quantitative easing was introduced to help manage an economy in recession.
- It is also important that monetary policy is coordinated with other policy measures being implemented that affect the macroeconomy.

Case study 31.1

The Monetary Policy Committee

The Monetary Policy Committee of the Bank of England (MPC) takes responsibility for meeting the government's inflation target, using bank rate as its main instrument. By setting bank rate, the Bank is able to influence other interest rates in the economy and therefore influence aggregate demand.

There have been periods in which the Bank has allowed inflation to move outside its target range. In such circumstances, the Governor is required to write a letter to justify the decision not to change bank rate. However, there have also been periods when bank rate has been at such a low level that it has not been possible to reduce it any further.

Follow-up questions

a Explain how changing bank rate influences aggregate demand.

b In deciding to allow inflation to move beyond its target range, what factors might the MPC take into consideration?

c How was the MPC able to continue to influence aggregate demand in the economy when bank rate was at its all-time low?

d Evaluate the effectiveness of recent decisions taken by the MPC in achieving the government's macroeconomic objectives in the light of the conditions facing the economy.

In tackling these questions, you may find it helpful to visit the Bank of England website to see the factors that influenced recent decisions by the MPC – whether it has chosen to change bank rate or to leave it unchanged: **www.bankofengland.co.uk/monetary-policy**. In particular, look at the most recent inflation report.

CHAPTER 31 QUESTIONS

A Multiple-choice questions

1 If interest rates are increased then which of the following effects would be most likely?

   a An increase in savings and an increase in borrowing

   b A decrease in savings and a decrease in borrowing

   c An increase in savings and a decrease in borrowing

   d A decrease in savings and an increase in borrowing

2 Monetary policy is used to affect:

   a Short-run aggregate supply

   b Long-run aggregate supply

   c Aggregate demand

   d Demand

B Knowledge and understanding questions

3 Explain what is meant by 'quantitative easing'. [2 marks]

4 Explain, with the aid of a diagram, how changes in the interest rate can be used to affect inflation in an economy. [4 marks]

5 Explain the relationship between interest rates and exchange rates. [4 marks]

C Stimulus response question

6 The Bank of England is tasked with controlling inflation using monetary policy. Despite very low levels of interest rates since 2009, the Monetary Policy Committee (MPC) raised interest rates from 0.25% to 0.5% in 2017 and again from 0.5% to 0.75% in 2018.

   a Explain two likely effects on the UK economy of increasing interest rates. [2 marks]

   b Evaluate the effectiveness of the MPC's decision to increase interest rates in order to achieve the government's objective of low and stable inflation. [12 marks]

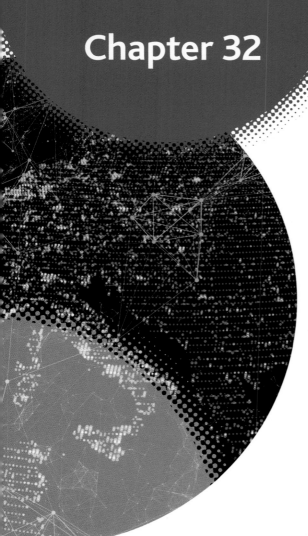

Chapter 32

Supply-side policy

Fiscal and monetary policy, discussed in the previous two chapters, have been mainly aimed at affecting aggregate demand. In this chapter, we look at policies aimed at affecting long-run aggregate supply, known as supply-side policies.

Learning objectives

After studying this chapter, you should be able to:
- explain, with the use of diagrams, privatisation and deregulation
- explain, with the use of diagrams, improved labour market flexibility
- explain, with the use of diagrams, reforms of the tax and benefit system
- explain, with the use of diagrams, investment in infrastructure, education, training, research and development
- explain, with the use of diagrams, subsidies
- explain, with the use of diagrams, competition policy
- explain, with the use of diagrams, immigration control
- evaluate the effectiveness of using supply-side policy measures to achieve the government's macroeconomic objectives

Policies affecting aggregate supply

Demand-side policies have been aimed primarily at stabilising the macroeconomy in the relatively short run, but with the hope of affecting aggregate supply in the long run, by influencing firms' and households' confidence in the future path of the economy. However, there are also policies that can be used to influence the long-run aggregate supply curve directly. These **supply-side policies** can take two forms. The neoclassical economists recommend **market-based policies**, based on freeing up markets, providing improved incentives for enterprise and initiative. Others advocate **interventionist policies** by which the authorities should intervene directly in ways that stimulate aggregate supply.

Supply-side policies are directed at affecting long-run aggregate supply, and are therefore important for the macroeconomic objective of economic growth. These policies are much less concerned with other objectives of the government. Supply-side policies focus on affecting the determinants of aggregate supply in order to shift the *LRAS* curve to the right.

The factors that influence the position of long-run aggregate supply were discussed in Chapter 20. Recall that the position of the long-run supply curve depends upon:
- the quantity of factor inputs available
- the effectiveness with which factor inputs are used

A key component of economic growth is investment. This is one of the components of aggregate demand, so an increase in investment shifts the *AD* curve. However, investment also allows an increase in the productive capacity of the economy, which then affects the position of the *LRAS* curve. It is this aspect of investment that is important in the context of supply-side policy measures.

Many of the supply-side policy measures examined in this chapter have already been discussed in the microeconomics section, but we are now exploring the extent to which these microeconomic policies have an impact on the macroeconomy, as they influence the position of the *LRAS* curve.

Market-based policies

There are several policies that have been advocated to allow markets to work more effectively. The underlying argument here is that too much government intervention can hamper firms in achieving productive efficiency. Such policies are favoured in the neoclassical approach.

Privatisation and deregulation

In the past, some industries were taken into public ownership in the belief that this would protect consumers from being exploited. However, it was later realised that this was leading to inefficiency, because incentives and accountability for managers of these publicly owned enterprises were inadequate. Such enterprises have been sold back into the private sector through a process known as privatisation. This was intended to stimulate aggregate supply by improving efficiency, as managers became accountable to their shareholders, rather than to some government body or their customers. Similarly, there are situations in which industries have been over-regulated, and again, deregulation has been put forward as a supply-side policy on the grounds that regulation can tie the hands of a firm's managers and provide weak incentives to achieve efficiency.

Neoclassical economists argue that if markets are free to operate without too much interference from government, there will be an improvement in productive efficiency, so that firms will be able to supply more output at any given price. This will have the effect of shifting the long-run aggregate supply curve (*LRAS*) to the right, as shown in Figure 22.2 on page 303, where the *LRAS* curve shifts from $LRAS_0$ to $LRAS_1$, with full employment real GDP increasing from Y_{FE0} to Y_{FE1}. The price level falls from P_0 to P_1.

Improved labour market flexibility

An important supply-side approach is to find ways of improving the flexibility of the labour market. Where labour markets are flexible, the structure of economic activity can more readily be adjusted to changing patterns of global demand. If declining low-productivity sectors can give way to more dynamic activities where productivity is higher, then productive efficiency improves, and this will lead to a rightward shift in the long-run aggregate supply curve.

One possibility is to limit the power of the trade unions, whose actions can sometimes lead to inflexibility, either through resistance to new working practices that could improve productivity or by pushing up wages so that the level of employment is reduced. It has also been argued that abolishing the minimum wage would improve flexibility. However, this must be balanced against the need to protect low-paid workers.

Maintaining the flexibility of markets is one way in which the macroeconomic stability promoted by disciplined fiscal and monetary policy can improve aggregate supply. Macroeconomic stability enables price signals to work more effectively, as producers are better able to observe changes in relative prices. This can promote allocative efficiency. The net effect of all this is again to shift the *LRAS* curve to the right.

Reforms of the tax and benefit system

Incentive effects are important in economic analysis. In this context, questions have been raised about the extent to which the tax system provides appropriate incentives to supply work effort.

There are dangers in having a taxation system that is too progressive. Most people accept that income tax should be progressive — that is, that those on relatively high incomes should pay a higher rate of tax than those on low incomes — as a way of redistributing income within society and preventing inequality from becoming extreme. However, there may come a point at which marginal tax rates are so high that a large proportion of additional income is taxed away, reducing incentives for individuals to supply additional effort or labour. This could also have an effect on aggregate supply. Again, however, it is important to balance these incentive effects against the distortion caused by having too much inequality in society.

An important influence on labour supply, particularly for low-income workers, is the level of unemployment benefit. If unemployment benefit is provided at too high a level, it may inhibit labour force participation, in that some workers may opt to live on unemployment benefit rather than take up low-skilled (and low-paid) employment. In such a situation, a reduction in unemployment benefit may induce an increase in labour supply, which again will move the aggregate supply curve to the right.

Such a policy needs to be balanced against the need to provide protection for those who are unable to find employment. It is also important that unemployment benefit is not reduced to such a level that workers are unwilling to leave their jobs to search for better ones, as this may inhibit the flexibility of the labour market.

Exercise 32.1

Use diagrams to examine the effect of an increase in *LRAS* under neoclassical assumptions, and under Keynesian assumptions where the initial equilibrium is in the upward-sloping section of the *LRAS*. Discuss the results.

Synoptic link

Labour markets and their operation are discussed in Chapters 16–18.

Interventionist policies

Synoptic link

The various forms of market failure are explained in Chapters 8 and 9.

Markets do not always operate effectively, as there are forms of market failure that can prevent an optimal allocation of resources from being reached. Interventionist supply-side policies aim to address these issues of market failure, and may complement the market-based policies.

Education and training

An important interventionist supply-side policy takes the form of encouraging workers (and potential workers) to undertake education and training to improve their productivity and raise their human capital.

This takes place partly through education in schools and colleges in preparation for work. It is important, therefore, that the curriculum is designed to provide key skills that will be useful in the workplace. However, this does not mean that all education has to be geared directly to providing skills. For example, problem-solving and analytical skills can be developed through the study of a wide range of disciplines.

Adult education is also important. When the structure of the economy is changing, retraining must be made available to enable workers to move easily between sectors and occupations. This is crucial if structural unemployment is not to become a major problem. For any society, education and skills are necessary to enable workers to switch into new activities in response to structural changes in the economy. For example, workers displaced from manufacturing industry are likely to need retraining if they are to find jobs in the service sector. Workers released from agriculture in a less developed country will need training before they can become productive members of the industrial workforce.

Knowledge check 32.2

Explain what is meant by human capital.

Apprentices learn bricklaying at a UK college

The market may not deliver the training that is necessary, as firms will not invest in training workers unless they can be sure that they will not be poached by competitors once they have completed their training. The government may therefore need to provide incentives. One particular concern has been the number of young people aged between 16 and 18

Knowledge check 32.3

Why might the government need to intervene to encourage firms to train their workers?

Synoptic link

The need to ensure adequate provision of public goods is discussed in Chapter 9 during the analysis of market failure. The provision of infrastructure is discussed in Chapter 10.

Exercise 32.2

Discuss the relative merits of government spending on improving the country's road network as compared to increasing spending on the NHS.

who are not in education, employment or training (known as NEETs). At the end of 2016 it was estimated that 6% of 16–18-year-olds were in this category. The Department for Education has piloted a number of initiatives to tackle this problem.

This sort of intervention by government can improve the flexibility of the labour market, by enabling workers to move more readily between jobs — or even occupations. Education and training also have a direct impact on the productivity of workers, which can improve productive efficiency.

Again, the impact of such measures is to result in a rightward shift in the long-run aggregate supply curve, as was shown in Figure 22.2 on page 303.

Infrastructure

An important area of government expenditure relates to the provision of infrastructure. Firms need there to be efficient transport and communication networks, and other types of infrastructure that enable markets to operate effectively. The public goods aspects of infrastructure mean that the free market mechanism will not adequately provide for them, so government intervention is needed.

The objective of investing in infrastructure is to improve future productive efficiency, which again should have the effect of shifting long-run aggregate supply to the right. However, a word of caution is needed. Government undertakes expenditure for a wide variety of reasons. This means that it is important to set priorities in the allocation of funds. We will return to this later in the chapter, but for the moment consider Exercise 32.2.

Subsidies

One of the hindrances to structural change in the economy has been that declining sectors of activity have not always been located in the same regions as the expanding sectors, making it difficult for displaced workers to gain employment in the newly growing industries. In England, this led to a North–South divide, with industries in the North in decline, and the growth areas being in the South.

This phenomenon is not unique to the UK economy, and across Europe there are substantial differences in unemployment rates. One way in which this can be tackled is through the use of subsidies. For example, firms that agree to set up their operations in disadvantaged regions could be offered incentives in the form of investment subsidies. The UK has operated such subsidies in the past, and the European Commission has also provided assistance to regions with high unemployment rates. Indeed, regions such as Wales in the UK benefited from such subsidies.

By giving subsidies in this way, the hope is to influence aggregate supply. However, it must be remembered that funding for the subsidies need to be financed somehow, and the danger is that by providing subsidies to encourage investment in some areas, there will be less investment elsewhere.

Information gaps are a form of market failure. One area in which this may be a problem is in the labour market, where workers may not have adequate information about job opportunities in other regions of the economy. By providing information about job vacancies, the authorities may be able to encourage mobility of workers, therefore improving the way in which the labour market operates. Subsidies for key workers in regions where housing and transport costs are high may also be a useful interventionist strategy to encourage labour mobility.

Research and development

One of the most important influences on economic growth, as set out in Chapter 22, is technological change. As technology improves over time, production becomes potentially more efficient. One way of achieving technological progress is through research and development (R&D). In spite of its universities and research institutes, the UK has not devoted as much funding to R&D as some other advanced countries. You can see something of this in Figure 32.1, which shows the percentage of GDP devoted to R&D in a range of countries.

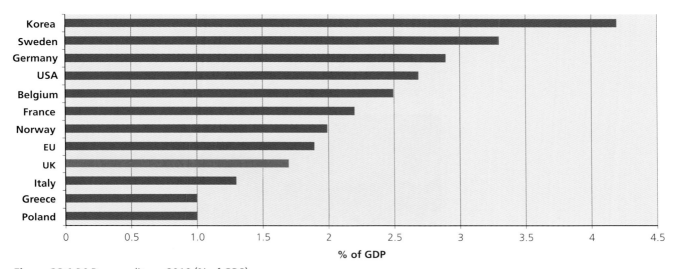

Figure 32.1 R&D expenditure, 2016 (% of GDP)

Source: based on data from OECD

This may be an area in which the UK could do more, perhaps through direct government funding, or by tax relief on R&D expenditure. However, again it may be important to bear in mind the opportunity cost of supporting R&D relative to other areas of government spending.

Competition policy

A recurrent theme in many policy statements from governments and international organisations like the World Bank and the IMF has been the importance of promoting competition. There are several reasons why this might be important in influencing aggregate supply. One possibility is that a monopoly firm in a market may be able to use its market power to maximise profits by restricting output and raising price. If such a firm is forced to confront competition from other firms, it may have to temper its use of that market power, and reduce price in order to sell more output and protect its market share.

The intensity of competition may also affect firms' willingness to improve productivity. It is possible that in some markets the lack of competition will produce complacency, depriving firms of the incentive to operate at maximum efficiency. Policies that promote competition may therefore lead to improvements in both allocative and productive efficiency.

Synoptic link

Competition policy is discussed in Chapter 14.

Competition policy aims to promote competition by monitoring the actions of firms in order to protect consumers from the abuse of monopoly power.

Immigration control

A highly contentious issue has been that of the control of immigration, which has aroused some emotional debate. In considering the topic, it is important to focus on the economic arguments.

The discussion of economic growth in Chapter 22 focused on factors that affect the position of the aggregate supply curve. It argued that an increase in capacity output can come either from an increase in the quantity of the factors of production, or from an improvement in their efficiency or productivity. A tightening of immigration control would mean that the workforce would be smaller than it otherwise may have been, suggesting that the aggregate supply curve would shift to the left.

Those who argue that the UK should accept fewer immigrants assume that migrant workers will become unemployed and be a burden to taxpayers, or that they will take the jobs of native workers, and thus increase the level of unemployment.

Fruit pickers work in the vineyard at Chapel Down Wines in Kent, UK

Translating this into economic terms, this reflects an assumption that migrant workers will be substitutes for native workers. Figure 32.2 illustrates the situation. Labour supply increases from S_{L0} to S_{L1}, employment increases to L_1 but the wage rate falls to W_1.

If migrants have different skills than native workers, then the situation is rather different. If the migrants have higher productivity than native workers, there will be an increase in the demand for labour, and a resulting increase in both employment and the wage rate. Furthermore, the multiplier effect from the incomes of the migrant workers will mean that there is also an increase in the demand for unskilled workers, so there will be a positive impact on unskilled native workers. Indeed, if the migrant workers share their knowledge and skills with other native workers, their productivity will also increase.

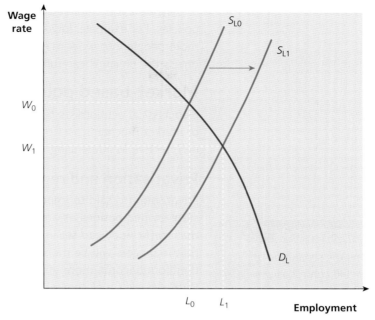

Figure 32.2 An increase in the workforce when immigrants are substitutes for native workers

What is the connection with supply-side policy? The argument seems to suggest that there could be positive supply-side effects from encouraging immigration of skilled workers. If Brexit leads to a fall in such immigration, the net impact could be negative.

Summary
- Supply-side policies aim to influence long-run aggregate supply.
- Some policies are market-based, aiming to allow markets to operate more freely, reflecting neoclassical ideas.
- Market-based policies include privatisation and deregulation, improving the flexibility of the labour market and reforming the tax and benefit system.
- Other policies are more interventionist, intended to address market failures.
- Interventionist policies include education and training, investment in infrastructure and R&D, subsidies, competition policy and immigration control.

Evaluation of supply-side policies

In general, the strengths of supply-side policies are that they are targeted on specific problems that can inhibit economic growth by limiting the productive capacity of the economy. Supply-side policies can be important in shifting aggregate supply and enabling an increase in the productive capacity of the economy. However, it is also important to remember that these are policies for the long term, and many of them take time to become effective. For each of the policies discussed, there may be problems in identifying the magnitude of the effects that can be anticipated.

A weakness is the need for careful balancing of the effects of some policies. For example, lowering unemployment benefits to encourage more people into work may cause suffering for those unable to work, unless the policy is carefully designed.

Market-based policies

Neoclassical economists tend to favour policies that are based on the use of market mechanisms. Critics argue that market forces may not always be effective in influencing the supply side of the economy.

Privatisation and regulation

Privatisation is said to improve efficiency mainly because managers of state-owned businesses are not held accountable for their actions, so that inefficiency can set in. If such enterprises are privatised, it is argued that managers will be more accountable to their shareholders, and may therefore become more efficient. However, will this happen in practice? With separation of control from ownership with multiple shareholders, the principal–agent problem may emerge, such that managers may still find themselves able to pursue their own objectives.

In some cases, privatisation has failed to deliver. For example, in 2018 the franchise to run the East Coast main railway line was terminated and train operations were brought into public ownership.

Deregulation is said to improve efficiency by freeing firms from unnecessary restrictions on their behaviour. Whether this will be the case depends upon the nature of the regulation that was in place, and on whether it was excessive. Critics might argue that freedom from regulation gives a firm the freedom to exert its market power, which would not necessarily lead to an increase in aggregate supply.

Improving labour market flexibility

The key argument in favour of improving the flexibility of labour markets is that it allows the economy to respond more rapidly to changes in global demand conditions. This enables aggregate supply to increase because firms are better able to provide the goods and services that people at home and abroad want to buy. For example, if the power of trade unions is limited, workers may be more free to accept jobs that are available, and employers will be able to offer jobs at the equilibrium wage rather than having the level of employment restricted by union rules. This may indeed have a positive impact on aggregate supply, which would be seen as favourable, as long as employers do not abuse their new freedom.

There is also an important question to consider, which is whether market forces will be sufficient to ensure flexibility without some additional measures. For example, it might be argued that some interventionist policies may also be required to ensure full flexibility, perhaps by provision of the education and training needed for workers to be ready for new jobs and occupations.

Reforming taxes and benefits

This aspect of policy is aimed at improving incentives, by making sure that high tax rates for the well-paid do not discourage the supply of

Knowledge check 32.5

Explain why the separation of ownership and control allows managers to pursue their own objectives.

Synoptic link

The principal–agent problem is discussed in Chapter 12.

effort, and by making sure that the levels of benefits are not set so high that workers will not accept low-paid jobs.

The success of this approach depends crucially on getting an appropriate balance. At the top end of the income distribution, the question is one of maintaining incentives to work while still enabling a fair redistribution of income from rich to poor. In terms of benefits, the issue is balancing the need to protect the vulnerable against encouraging individuals to accept jobs and therefore contribute to aggregate supply.

Interventionist policies

There are two key issues when it comes to evaluating interventionist measures. One is the awareness that in most cases, such policies are effective only in the long term. For example, influencing aggregate supply through improving the education system is a long-run policy, and even the provision of retraining for displaced workers may not be achievable in the short run. However, this is a crucial part of supply-side policy, which complements the market-based approach and enhances the flexibility of labour markets. The need for such intervention is to correct for the market failure that is present. The improvement of infrastructure is another policy that may only have long-term effects. However, this is also necessary because of the need to deal with market failure.

The second key issue is the question of opportunity cost that was mentioned earlier. Balance is also needed here, providing appropriate investment for the future, but maintaining essential services for the present generation.

In the case of R&D expenditure, there is an additional complication. Competition policy may be used to prevent firms from gaining market dominance and being able to make high profits, but it may be that only large firms can make enough profit to be able to undertake R&D. Again, there is the question of balance.

Exercise 32.3

For each of the following policies, identify whether it is an example of fiscal, monetary and/or supply-side policy. Discuss how each policy affects either aggregate demand or aggregate supply (or both), and examine its effects on equilibrium real output and the overall price level:

a an increase in government expenditure
b a decrease in the rate of unemployment benefit
c a fall in the rate of interest
d legislation limiting the power of trade unions
e encouragement for more students to attend university
f provision of retraining in the form of adult education
g a reduction in the highest rate of income tax
h measures to break up a concentrated market
i an increase in bank rate

Summary

- There has been some debate about the effectiveness of market-based policies, and the magnitude of their impact has been questioned.
- Improving incentives through reforming taxes and benefits needs to maintain a balance between improving incentives and protecting vulnerable groups in society.
- Some market-based policies may need to be supported by interventionist actions, for example in providing education and training.
- Interventionist policies are often effective mainly in the long run, and a balance needs to be reached between laying the foundations for future improvements in aggregate supply and meeting the needs of the present generation.

Case study 32.1

Macroeconomic policy instruments

Governments in a modern economy have three main types of policy instrument for affecting the macroeconomy — monetary policy, fiscal policy and supply-side policy. Monetary policy is dedicated to ensuring the stability of the economy by influencing aggregate demand. Fiscal policy is used to maintain balance in the economy between public and private sectors and between present and future generations of citizens. Supply-side policies are dedicated to affecting the productive capacity of the economy, operating primarily through microeconomic incentives.

Follow-up question
Explain these distinctions between the types of policy instrument. Discuss the roles of each type of policy in meeting the government's macroeconomic objectives.

CHAPTER 32 QUESTIONS

A Multiple-choice questions

1 Which of the following is not likely to be classed as a supply-side policy?

   a Privatisation of the NHS

   b Making taxation more progressive

   c Encouraging more competition in markets

   d Government spending on benefits

2 Which of the following is most likely to increase long-run aggregate supply?

   a More controls on immigration

   b A reduction in labour market flexibility

   c A fall in the size of the average family

   d Deregulation of a large industry

B Knowledge and understanding questions

3 Explain what is meant by 'supply-side policies'. [2 marks]

4 Explain, with the aid of a diagram, how an increased government focus on education can affect the macroeconomy. [4 marks]

5 Explain, with the aid of a diagram, how privatisation may affect aggregate supply in an economy. [4 marks]

D Essay question

6 Evaluate the effectiveness of supply-side policies in achieving economic growth. [20 marks]

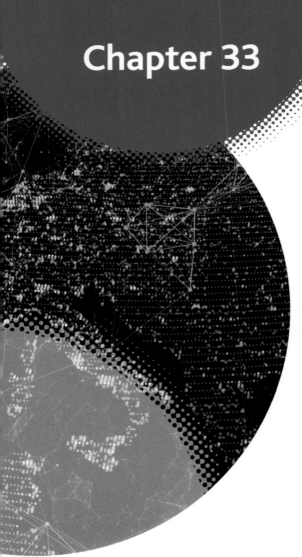

Chapter 33

The Phillips curve and policy conflicts

The macroeconomy is characterised by trade-offs between variables and conflicts between policy objectives. In this chapter we explore one of the most famous trade-offs. This is captured by the Phillips curve, which concerns the relationship between unemployment and inflation. We also examine the conflicts that can arise between macroeconomic policy objectives.

> **Learning objectives**
> After studying this chapter, you should be able to:
> * explain the natural rate of unemployment and the non-accelerating inflation rate of unemployment (NAIRU)
> * explain, with the aid of a diagram, the short-run and long-run Phillips curves
> * evaluate the usefulness of the Phillips curve for macroeconomic policy-makers
> * evaluate conflicts and trade-offs between policy objectives

Trade-offs and conflicts

A **trade-off** exists when a gain in one item must be accompanied by a loss in some other item. For example, if you have limited funds to spend, you may find that you can only buy more pizza by buying less ice cream. In other words, you must trade off more pizza for less ice cream. This is clearly closely allied to the notion of opportunity cost that you encountered early on in your study of economics. Trade-offs occur in macroeconomics when an improvement in one variable can only be obtained with a deterioration in some other variable.

Conflicts can arise between policy objectives when such trade-offs exist. For example, it may be that economic growth can only be maximised at the cost of damaging the environment. These conflicts will be explored later in the chapter.

The Phillips curve

The *AD/AS* model is helpful in analysing equilibrium in the macroeconomy. It identifies the equilibrium price level and the level of real output given the position of the aggregate demand and supply curves. However, in reality the macroeconomy is in a continual state of change. Economic growth takes place as the economy progresses through time, and the normal situation is one of inflation, rather than a static price level.

A first step towards looking at the macroeconomy in a more dynamic setting is to examine the **Phillips curve**, which is based upon a relationship between unemployment and the rate of inflation. This is named after an economist from New Zealand, Bill Phillips, who in 1958 claimed that he had found an 'empirical regularity' that had existed for almost a century and that traced out a relationship between the rate of unemployment and the rate of change of money wages. He claimed that this relationship had remained stable for a period of almost a hundred years. This was rapidly generalised into a relationship between unemployment and inflation (by arguing that firms pass on increased wages in the form of higher prices).

Figure 33.1 shows what became known as the Phillips curve. Although Phillips began with data, he also came up with an explanation of why such a relationship should exist. At the heart of his argument was the idea that when the demand for labour is high, firms will be prepared to bid up wages in order to attract labour. To the extent that higher wages are then passed on in the form of higher prices, this would imply a relationship between unemployment and inflation: when unemployment is low, inflation will tend to be higher, and vice versa.

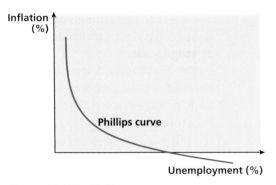

Figure 33.1 The Phillips curve

From a policy perspective, this suggests a trade-off between unemployment and inflation. If the Phillips curve relationship holds, attempts to reduce the rate of unemployment are likely to raise inflation. On the other hand, a reduction in inflation is likely to result in higher unemployment. This suggests that it might be difficult to maintain full employment and low inflation at the same time. For example, Figure 33.2 shows a Phillips curve that is drawn such that to achieve an unemployment rate of 5%, inflation would need to rise to almost 15% per annum. This would not be acceptable today, when people have become accustomed to much lower inflation rates. Furthermore, to bring inflation down to zero would require an unemployment rate of 15%. Having said that, as recently as 1990 the UK economy was experiencing inflation of nearly 10% and unemployment of 7%, which is not far from this example.

Nonetheless, the Phillips curve trade-off offers a tempting prospect to policy-makers. For example, if an election is imminent, it should be possible to reduce unemployment by allowing a bit more inflation, thereby creating a feel-good factor. After the election, the process can

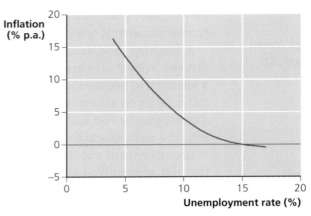

Figure 33.2 The Phillips curve unemployment/inflation trade-off

be reversed. This suggests that there could be a political economic cycle induced by governments seeking re-election. In other words, politicians, who see that in the short run an electorate is concerned more about unemployment than inflation, could exploit the conflict between policy objectives.

The 1970s provided something of a setback to this theory, when suddenly the UK economy started to experience both high unemployment and high inflation simultaneously, suggesting that the Phillips curve had disappeared. This combination of stagnation and inflation became known as **stagflation**.

One possibility is that the Phillips curve had not in fact disappeared, but had moved. Suppose that wage bargaining takes place on the basis of *expectations* about future rises in retail prices. As inflation becomes embedded in an economy, and people come to expect it to continue, those expectations will be built into wage negotiations. Another way of viewing this is that expectations about price inflation will influence the *position* of the Phillips curve. If this is the case, then the relationship shown in Figure 33.1 should be seen as the short-run Phillips curve.

Figure 33.3 shows some empirical data for the UK to explore whether there is evidence of the Phillips curve trade-off. The scatter of points joined by the red line plots inflation and unemployment between 1986 and 1995, showing a negative relationship between these variables. The green scatter shows data for the later period 2006 to 2017. This does not connect well with the earlier trade-off, and appears to show a much flatter relationship (especially if we ignore the 2009 observation, which was an abnormal year in which inflation went negative). The relationship also seems to have shifted to the left, with unemployment being appreciably lower. This could be interpreted as a shift of the curve as well as a flattening. Indeed, with the Bank of England ensuring that inflation remains in its target range, we might expect the Phillips curve to be flatter even when unemployment fluctuates.

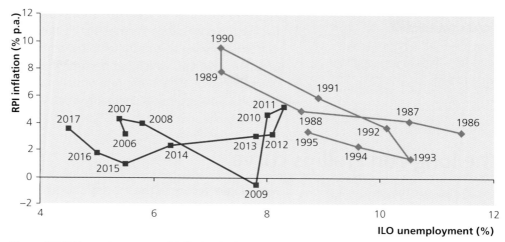

Figure 33.3 Unemployment and inflation in the UK, 1986–95 and 2006–17

Source: based on data from ONS

Exercise 33.1

Table 33.1 shows data on unemployment and inflation for three European countries.

Table 33.1 Unemployment (U) and inflation (ΔP) in France, Germany and Italy

Year	France		Germany		Italy	
	U (%)	ΔP (% p.a.)	U (%)	ΔP (% p.a.)	U (%)	ΔP (% p.a.)
2006	8.8	1.9	10.1	1.8	6.8	2.2
2007	8.0	1.6	8.9	2.3	6.1	2.0
2008	7.4	3.2	7.4	2.8	6.7	3.5
2009	9.1	0.1	7.6	0.2	7.7	0.8
2010	9.3	1.7	7.0	1.1	8.4	1.6
2011	9.2	2.3	5.8	2.5	8.4	2.9
2012	9.8	2.2	5.4	2.1	10.7	3.3
2013	10.3	1.0	5.2	1.6	12.1	1.2
2014	10.3	0.6	5.0	0.8	12.7	0.2
2015	10.4	0.1	4.6	0.1	11.9	0.1
2016	10.1	0.3	4.1	0.4	11.7	−0.1
2017	9.4	1.2	3.5	1.7	11.2	1.3

Source: data from Eurostat

For each of the countries, plot a scatter diagram similar to Figure 33.3, labelling each point and joining successive observations with a line. Discuss any patterns that emerge from the graph, and comment on any differences between the countries.

The natural rate of unemployment

In discussing the *AD/AS* model, it was argued that there was a full employment level of real GDP, sometimes known as the natural rate of output. Under neoclassical assumptions, the economy would always adjust to this level of real GDP, so that the long-run aggregate supply (*LRAS*) curve would be vertical at this full employment level.

Corresponding to this full employment level of real GDP is a rate of unemployment, which has become known as the natural rate of unemployment. This is the rate of unemployment in which there is only frictional and structural unemployment, as real wages will have adjusted to the equilibrium level.

The long-run Phillips curve

How do we reconcile the moving short-run Phillips curve with the natural rate of unemployment? Figure 33.4 shows how this might work. $SRPC_0$ represents the initial Phillips curve. Suppose we start with the economy at the *natural rate of unemployment* U_{nat}. If the economy is at point *A*, with inflation at π_0 and unemployment at U_{nat}, the economy is in equilibrium. If the government then tries to exploit the Phillips curve by allowing inflation to rise to π_1, the economy moves in the short run to point *B*. However, as people realise that inflation is now higher, they adjust their expectations. This eventually begins to affect wage negotiations — the Phillips curve then moves to $SRPC_1$, and unemployment returns to the natural rate. The economy settles at *C* and is again in equilibrium, but now with higher inflation than before, and the same initial rate of unemployment. For this reason, the natural rate of unemployment is sometimes known as the **non-accelerating inflation rate of unemployment (NAIRU)**. The **long-run Phillips curve (*LRPC*)** is vertical at the natural rate of unemployment.

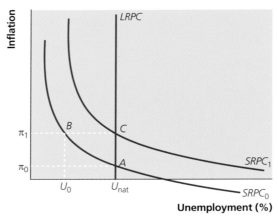

Figure 33.4 The long-run Phillips curve

The problem that arises with this is of how to get back to the original position with a lower inflation rate. This can happen only if people's expectations adjust so that lower inflation is expected. This means that the economy has to move down along $SRPC_1$, pushing up unemployment in order to reduce inflation. Then, once expectations adjust, the Phillips curve will move back again until the natural rate of unemployment is restored. If this takes a long time, the cost in terms of unemployment will be high.

Adaptive expectations

Notice that an important assumption here is that economic agents base their behaviour on expectations about the future course of the economy. But how do they form these expectations?

One possibility is that expectations are formed based on the past performance of the economy. Economic agents observe the economy in one period, and then adapt to that when forming expectations about the future. This is known as *adaptive expectations*. Their expectations are shaped by the past.

The neoclassical economists rejected this view, arguing that economic agents would always take decisions

on the basis of all the information available. In other words, they would not simply assume that the economy would behave consistently with past experience. Instead they would use all of the information available, understanding how the economy operates and avoiding systematic errors. For example, they would have as good an information set as the government and would therefore be able to predict how the government would react to changes in the economy. This theory is known as *rational expectations*, and helps to explain how it is that the economy will reach its equilibrium so rapidly.

The Phillips curve and macroeconomic policy

How important is the Phillips curve for the design of macroeconomic policy? When policy-makers first came across the trade-off between unemployment and inflation, it became tempting to exploit the trade-off for electoral purposes. It seemed possible to expand the economy in the run-up to an election, getting unemployment to fall and creating a feel-good factor, while allowing inflation to creep up, ready to be brought back down after the election. This is clearly not helpful for the economy in the long run.

The disappearance of the Phillips curve in the 1970s put a damper on this approach, and it became apparent that the cost of bringing inflation back under control was high.

Some commentators argued that the Phillips curve (even if it did exist) could not be used for short-term political expediency because, once economic agents realised what the government was doing, they would factor it into their expectations formation process, and would therefore discount the government's attempts to manipulate the economy. If the neoclassical economists were correct, trying to affect the natural rate was doomed to failure.

This parallels the discussion of discretionary fiscal policy, which has been criticised on the grounds that trying to manipulate aggregate demand would be futile because the economy would always return to its equilibrium. Under neoclassical assumptions, this adjustment would be rapid.

Summary
- The Phillips curve claims a trade-off relationship between unemployment and inflation, although the appearance of stagflation in the 1970s cast doubt on the hypothesis.
- The position of the Phillips curve may be seen to depend on people's expectations about future inflation, so that in the long run the Phillips curve may be vertical at the natural rate of unemployment (or the non-accelerating inflation rate of unemployment, the NAIRU).

Conflicts and trade-offs between policy objectives

With the range of policy instruments available to the authorities, it is important to investigate whether they will be mutually compatible, or whether conflict could arise between them.

Notice that the key objectives of macroeconomic policy are:

- economic growth
- full employment
- low inflation
- stability in the balance of payments
- an acceptable distribution of income
- a balanced government budget
- protection of the environment

There are many possible hindrances to achieving all of these objectives simultaneously because of possible conflicts between them.

Unemployment and inflation

The chapter so far has discussed the Phillips curve, which identified a relationship between unemployment and inflation. If the Phillips curve relationship holds, attempts to reduce the rate of unemployment are likely to raise inflation. On the other hand, a reduction in inflation is likely to result in higher unemployment. This suggests that it might be difficult to maintain full employment and low inflation at the same time. Indeed, attempting to achieve economic growth when the economy is already at full employment could lead to inflation.

This is an example of where policy-makers need to be aware of the trade-off between these objectives when designing the mix of macroeconomic policy, and be aware of the dangers of trying to exploit the trade-off.

This trade-off between unemployment and inflation is by no means the only example.

Economic growth and the current account of the balance of payments

In some circumstances, conflict can arise between achieving economic growth and attaining equilibrium on the current account of the balance of payments. An increase in economic growth resulting in higher real incomes could lead to an increase in imports of goods and services, if UK residents spend a high proportion of their additional income abroad. This was seen as a major problem during the fixed exchange rate era of the 1950s and 1960s, when any deficit on the current account had to be met by running down foreign exchange reserves. This led to a 'stop–go' cycle of macroeconomic policy, where every time growth began to accelerate, the current account went into deficit, and policy then had to be adjusted to slow down the growth rate to deal with the deficit.

Although this may be less of an issue under a floating exchange rate system, too rapid a rate of economic growth may increase the demand for imports, such that the current account deficit has to be balanced by a surplus on the financial account.

Synoptic link

The importance of the balance of payments was discussed in Chapter 26, and exchange rates in Chapter 27.

Knowledge check 33.3

Explain why the current account of the balance of payments might act as a constraint on economic growth when the government is committed to supporting the exchange rate.

Economic growth and inflation

A possible conflict may arise between economic growth and stability in prices, if an inappropriate strategy is adopted. Previous chapters have argued that the key to achieving economic growth is supply-side policies that can lead to a rightward shift in the long-run aggregate supply (*LRAS*) curve. If the authorities try to encourage economic growth by using demand-side policies, the result may be upward pressure on the price level, which could lead to inflation if the policy continues in operation.

You should by now be familiar with the way in which an increase in aggregate demand when the economy is at full employment has no effect on real GDP in the long run, but merely pushes up the equilibrium price level. For example, look back at Figure 25.2 on page 352, which shows the effect of an increase in *AD*.

Fiscal and monetary policy

It was seen earlier that fiscal policy may have implications for the interest rate. If the government increases its expenditure, perhaps with the intention of improving infrastructure or subsidising education and training, one side effect could be to require higher borrowing and push up interest rates. This could in turn lead to an inflow of hot money, affecting the exchange rate and the competitiveness of domestic goods in international markets. This suggests that there may be circumstances in which fiscal and monetary policy come into conflict, given that interest rates are a key part of the transmission of monetary policy. Consequently, a way must be found of coordinating fiscal and monetary policy. This is naturally difficult to do, given the way that the Bank of England acts independently of the government in conducting monetary policy in order to meet the inflation target.

Over-enthusiastic use of discretionary fiscal policy can also interfere with the objective of maintaining a stable government budget position, and create problems for the economy in the future.

Designing the policy mix

Conflict may also arise because of trade-offs that exist between other policy objectives. Too rapid a rate of economic growth may put upwards pressure on prices, leading to inflation. Inflation may cause problems with international competitiveness, and therefore have an impact on the balance of payments. However, reducing demand in order to control inflation may lead to unemployment. Rapid economic growth may also increase inequality within a society, if only a minority of people enjoy the benefits — and growth may also cause damage to the environment.

The existence of these trade-offs makes it important to be able to design a policy mix that can resolve the conflicts, or at least reduce their consequences.

In the context of the aggregate demand/aggregate supply model, it is clear that demand- and supply-side policies are aimed at achieving rather different objectives.

The primary rationale for monetary and fiscal policies is to stabilise the macroeconomy. In this, fiscal policy has come to take on a subsidiary role, supporting monetary policy. This was not always the case, and there have been periods in which fiscal policy has been used much more actively to try to stimulate the economy. The fact that fiscal policy has not always been well implemented does not mean that such policies cannot be valuable tools — but it does warn against misuse.

In the UK, the use of monetary policy with the support of fiscal policy seemed to be working reasonably effectively until the onset of the financial crisis in late 2008. Furthermore, it seemed to be operating in such a way as to complement the supply-side policies. When a stable macroeconomic environment is created, microeconomic markets are able to operate effectively and investment is encouraged, thereby leading to a boost in aggregate supply. Supply-side policies aim to influence aggregate supply directly, either raising the supply of factor inputs or improving productivity and efficiency. However, the UK operates within the global economy, and the financial crisis brought with it a period of recession from which the economy was slow to recover.

The design and conduct of economic policy may therefore be seen as an elaborate balancing act. Differing policy objectives need to be prioritised, as in many cases there may be conflict between them. Choices have to be made about the balance to be achieved between fiscal, monetary and supply-side policies.

The consensus view in the early part of the twenty-first century was that fiscal policy should be used to achieve the desired balance between the public and private sectors. Monetary policy should be devoted to meeting the government's inflation target in order to create a stable macroeconomic environment. This would then encourage growth and enable improvements in the standard of living. Problems arose when fiscal policy was forced into action in order to protect the financial system, resulting in an escalation of public debt.

In the long run, supply-side policies are perhaps the most important, as these contribute to raising efficiency and increasing the productive capacity of the economy. The keynote in policy design lies in enabling markets to operate as effectively as possible.

Summary
- The Phillips curve suggests that there could be a trade-off between unemployment and inflation, so a policy to reduce unemployment may have a long-run impact on inflation.
- The pursuit of economic growth can cause problems for the balance of payments.
- Rapid economic growth may also have negative environmental effects.
- The use of fiscal policy through government expenditure can have an impact on interest rates and come into conflict with monetary policy.
- Discretionary fiscal policy has implications for maintaining a stable government budget.
- The design of macroeconomic policy is an elaborate balancing act.

Case study 33.1

Macroeconomic policy conflicts

Suppose that you are a policy-maker in a country and consider some of the issues involved in designing macroeconomic policy.

Policy-makers must consider all demands on the economy, such as military spending, when delivering an economic policy package

Suppose that the central bank has been given the task of achieving the inflation target, so is intent on achieving low inflation within the target range. The minister responsible for employment issues insists that a high priority must be given to reaching full employment. The trade secretary is concerned about the deficit on the current account of the balance of payments. The green lobby insists that more resources need to be devoted to protecting the environment. The health minister demands more funding for the health service, and the defence secretary points out the need to reinforce military spending. As if this wasn't enough, there is also pressure to reduce income inequality in the country. You are also keen to promote economic growth in order to improve the standard of living for your citizens. The Office for Budget Responsibility is insistent that the level of public sector net debt needs to be reduced.

Follow-up questions

a To what extent are these competing policy objectives valid and mutually consistent?

b Is it possible to create a policy package to achieve all of these demands simultaneously?

CHAPTER 33 QUESTIONS

A Multiple-choice questions

1 NAIRU stands for:

    a Non-accelerating interest rate of unemployment

    b Non-accelerating inflation rate of unemployment

    c Non-accelerating investment rate of unemployment

    d Non-accelerating income rate of unemployment

2 The Phillips curve shows the relationship between which of the following?

    a Unemployment and the rate of interest

    b Unemployment and the rate of government spending

    c Unemployment and the rate of taxation

    d Unemployment and the rate of inflation

B Knowledge and understanding questions

3 Explain what is meant by the 'natural rate of unemployment'. [2 marks]

4 Explain, with the aid of a diagram, the relationship between unemployment and inflation in the short run. [4 marks]

C Stimulus response question

5 Governments often find conflicts between the objectives that they are trying to achieve.

In the 1980s there was strong economic growth in the UK economy, accompanied by high levels of inflation. This inflation level came down significantly in 1991 when a period of negative economic growth was experienced.

This is not always the case, though, and after an economic recovery, the UK economy again encountered strong economic growth between 1993 and 2007. However, this time the level of inflation was under control and within government targets.

    a Apart from economic growth and low and stable inflation, identify **two** macroeconomic objectives of government. [2 marks]

    b Evaluate whether there is always a conflict between the macroeconomic objectives of government for economic growth and low and stable inflation. [12 marks]

D Essay question

6 Evaluate the usefulness of the Phillips curve for macroeconomic policy-makers. [25 marks]

SECTION 2

MACROECONOMICS

Part 9
The global context

Chapter 34

International trade

The world economy is becoming increasingly integrated, and it is no longer possible to think of any single economy in isolation. The UK economy is no exception. It relies on international trade, engaging in exporting and importing activity, and many UK firms are increasingly active in global markets. This situation has created opportunities for UK firms to expand and become global players, and for UK consumers to have access to a wider range of goods and services. However, there is also a downside: global shocks, whether caused by increases in oil prices, financial crises or the emergence of China as a world economic force, can reverberate throughout economies in all parts of the world.

> ### Learning objectives
> After studying this chapter, you should be able to:
> - explain international trade
> - explain patterns of international trade over time
> - evaluate the advantages and disadvantages of international trade to developed, emerging and developing countries

Trade between nations

Countries all around the world engage in international trade. This is partly for obvious reasons: for example, the UK is not a sensible place to grow bananas on a commercial scale, but people living in the UK like to eat bananas. International trade enables individuals to consume goods that cannot be easily produced domestically. It makes sense for bananas to be produced in countries where the conditions are good for doing so.

Trade between nations is not new, as it has taken place from earliest times. However, as transport and communications developed, and the Industrial Revolution brought opportunities for manufacturing goods, the scope for trade increased dramatically. The volume of world trade expanded in the period after the Second World War, in particular as countries became more interconnected. Later in this chapter, you will see that this has not benefited all countries equally.

Synoptic link

The gains that can be achieved through international trade (and some of the issues that arise) are explained more fully in Chapter 35.

Openness to international trade

The extent to which different countries engage in international trade varies enormously, as can be seen in Figure 34.1, which shows total trade (exports plus imports) as a percentage of GDP. In some cases, the extent of dependence on trade reflects the availability of natural resources in a country, but it may also reflect political attitudes towards trade.

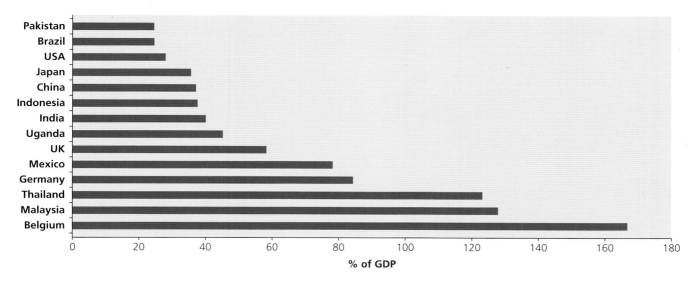

Figure 34.1 Trade as a percentage of GDP, 2016

Source: data from World Bank

The USA has a large and diverse economy, with a wealth of natural resources, and does not depend heavily on trade. Brazil, India and Pakistan have a similarly low level of dependence, but this partly reflects a conscious policy over many years to limit the extent to which their economies have to rely on external trade. At the other extreme, countries such as Malaysia and Thailand have followed policies that promote exports, believing that this will allow more rapid economic growth. China was closed to international trade for a long period but is now increasingly relying on exporting in order to stimulate economic growth.

You may be curious as to how it is possible for a country to display a ratio of trade to GDP that is greater than 100%. The reason is that exports include re-exports, i.e. goods that are imported, perhaps as components for other goods, and then exported again. In other words, there is some double-counting going on here.

The pattern of global trade

Moves towards closer integration between countries have strongly affected the pattern of world trade. For example, European integration has made Western Europe a major player in world trade. Something of this can be seen in Figure 34.2(a), which shows the destination of world merchandise exports in 2017 (i.e. the percentage of the world's exports *imported* by each region). You can see that almost 40% of the world's exports head for Western Europe and 14% to North America. Asia has also become an important part of the world trade scene, with China expanding its trading at an unprecedented rate in recent years.

Figure 34.2(b) shows the origin of world merchandise imports (i.e. the percentage of the world's imports *exported* by each region). Given the size of its population, Africa contributes very little to world trade.

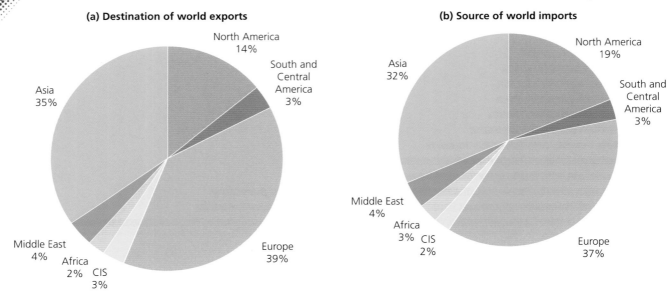

(a) Destination of world exports

North America 14%
South and Central America 3%
Europe 39%
CIS 3%
Africa 2%
Middle East 4%
Asia 35%

(b) Source of world imports

North America 19%
South and Central America 3%
Europe 37%
CIS 2%
Africa 3%
Middle East 4%
Asia 32%

Figure 34.2 Destination and source of world exports and imports, 2017

Note: CIS — the Commonwealth of Independent States, including associate and former member states

Source: World Trade Organization

Exercise 34.1

Next time you go shopping, make a list of the goods you see on offer that have been imported from elsewhere in the world. See if you can detect any patterns in the sorts of goods that come from different parts of the world.

Table 34.1 shows the size of trade flows between regions. The rows of the table show the exports from each of the regions to each other region, while the columns show the pattern of imports from each region. The numbers on the 'diagonal' of the table (in bold type) show the trade flows *within* regions. One notable feature of the table is the high involvement of Europe in world trade, accounting for 38.0% of imports and 37.7% of the exports. Of course, this includes substantial flows within Europe. In contrast, Africa shows very little involvement in world trade, in spite of the fact that, in population terms, it is far larger.

Indeed, trade flows between the developed countries — and with the more advanced developing countries — have tended to dominate world trade, with the flows between developing countries being relatively minor. This is not surprising, given that by definition the richer countries have greater purchasing power. However, the degree of openness to trade of economies around the world also varies as a result of conscious policy decisions. Some countries, especially in East Asia, have adopted very open policies towards trade, promoting exports in order to achieve export-led growth. In contrast, countries such as India and a number of Latin American countries have been much more reluctant to become dependent on international trade, and have adopted a more closed attitude towards trade.

The global pattern of trade has changed over time. The expansion of the EU and the Single European Market has altered the pattern of trade, with member countries more likely to trade with each other because of the falling transactions costs when markets are deregulated. The rapid growth of China and India as active trading nations has also had an impact on the direction of trade flows.

Table 34.1 Intra- and interregional merchandise trade, 2016 (US$bn)

Origin	North America	South and Central America	Europe	CIS	Africa	Middle East	Asia	World
North America	**1,105**	156	356	10	26	72	462	2,187
South and Central America	119	**115**	89	6	14	15	146	506
Europe	529	93	**4,106**	133	173	200	654	5,888
CIS	17	3	207	**77**	15	15	83	417
Africa	28	8	133	2	**68**	17	82	338
Middle East	56	5	99	4	24	**86**	314	588
Asia	1,028	138	847	87	160	238	**2,745**	5,243
World	2,884	517	5,837	319	481	643	4,487	**15,167**

Note: CIS — the Commonwealth of Independent States

Knowledge check 34.1

Why do you think that the share of intraregional trade (that is, trade within a region) is much higher for Europe than for North America?

Exercise 34.2

a Using the data provided in Table 34.1, calculate the share of each region in world exports and imports. Think about the factors that might influence the contrasting performance of the EU and Africa. Also, for each region calculate the share of exports and imports that are within the region and comment on any significant differences that you find.

b Are there any aspects of the pattern of world trade that took you by surprise? Can you find reasons for these?

Quantitative skills 34.1

Using percentages

In Table 34.1, origin countries are shown in the rows and destination countries in the columns. For example, to identify the exports from (say) Europe to Asia, you need to look in the Europe row and the Asia column, which is $654 billion. The world column shows total exports from each of the row regions, so the total of Europe exports is $5,888 billion. The share of Europe's exports going to Asia is therefore $100 \times 654/5{,}888 = 11.1\%$. In similar fashion, the share of Europe's imports coming from Asia is $100 \times 847/5{,}837 = 14.5\%$. Make sure you understand why this is the case.

The data discussed so far have focused on trade in goods. However, trade in commercial services has also become significant. Table 34.2 shows the leading exporters and importers of merchandise and commercial services in 2017.

Table 34.2 Leading countries in exports and imports of goods and services

Merchandise				Commercial services			
Exports		Imports		Exports		Imports	
Country	*% of world*	*Country*	*% of world*	*Country*	*% of world*	*Country*	*% of world*
China	12.8	USA	13.4	USA	14.4	USA	10.2
USA	8.7	China	10.2	UK	6.6	China	9.1
Germany	8.2	Germany	6.5	Germany	5.7	Germany	6.3
Japan	3.9	Japan	3.7	France	4.7	France	4.7
Netherlands	3.7	UK	3.6	China	4.3	Netherlands	4.2

Note: The UK ranked 10th in exports of merchandise and 6th in imports of commercial services.

Source: World Trade Organization

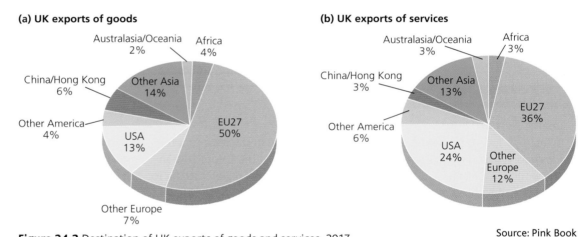
Changes in the employment structure of the economy were noted in Chapter 28.

China's prominence as an exporter and importer is worth noting, as this reflects a period of rapid economic growth from a lowly start. This is discussed later in the chapter.

From the UK perspective, the importance of exports of commercial services is clear from the table, the UK being the second-largest exporter of services, but only the tenth-largest exporter of goods. This reflects the changes in the structure of the economy that have taken place in recent decades.

The pattern of UK trade

Figures 34.3(a) and (b) show the destination of UK exports of goods and services to major regional groupings in the world. The most striking feature of these charts is the extent to which the UK relies on Europe and the USA for about 70% of its exports. Figures 34.4(a) and (b) reveal a similar pattern for the UK's imports of goods and services. Notice also that imports of goods from China (including Hong Kong) have become significant — and comprise a much larger share in imports than in exports.

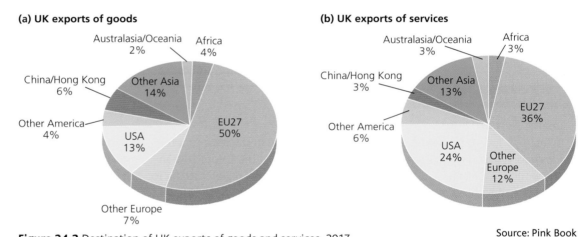

(a) UK exports of goods

Australasia/Oceania 2%
Africa 4%
China/Hong Kong 6%
Other Asia 14%
Other America 4%
EU27 50%
USA 13%
Other Europe 7%

(b) UK exports of services

Australasia/Oceania 3%
Africa 3%
China/Hong Kong 3%
Other Asia 13%
Other America 6%
EU27 36%
USA 24%
Other Europe 12%

Figure 34.3 Destination of UK exports of goods and services, 2017

Source: Pink Book

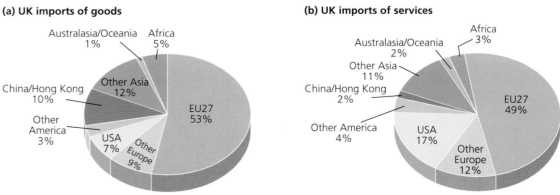

(a) UK imports of goods

Australasia/Oceania 1%
Africa 5%
China/Hong Kong 10%
Other Asia 12%
Other America 3%
USA 7%
Other Europe 9%
EU27 53%

(b) UK imports of services

Africa 3%
Australasia/Oceania 2%
Other Asia 11%
China/Hong Kong 2%
Other America 4%
USA 17%
EU27 49%
Other Europe 12%

Figure 34.4 Source of UK imports of goods and services, 2017

Source: Pink Book

The proportion of UK trade (both exports and imports) that is with Europe has undergone substantial change over recent decades. In 1960, when the Commonwealth was still thriving and the UK was ambivalent about the idea of European integration, about 30% of UK exports went to other European countries (23% of exports of goods in 1960). Figure 34.5 shows how this changed with the UK as a member of the EU. By 1990 exports to the EU had reached more than 60% of the UK's total exports.

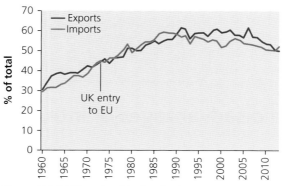

Figure 34.5 UK trade with the EU since 1960

Source: data from OECD

Figure 34.6 shows UK trade with the EU with goods and services separated, since 2000. In 2000, the EU was receiving about 60% of the UK's exports of goods, and more than half of the UK's imports of both goods and services were coming from the EU. This declined somewhat after then, but in 2017, 49% of UK exports were still going to the EU, and 55% of its goods imports were coming from the EU.

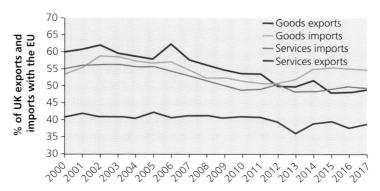

Figure 34.6 UK trade with the EU since 2000

Source: based on data from ONS

A substantial share of exports of goods from the UK consists of manufactured goods, especially road vehicles together with machinery and equipment of various types, and pharmaceuticals. Many of these commodities are also imported in large volumes. In part, this reflects the way in which commodity groups are defined. For example, there are many different types of road vehicle and pharmaceutical product, and specialisation may mean that firms in particular countries focus on particular types of vehicle or drug. By specialising in this way, they may be able to tap economies of scale that would otherwise not be

Knowledge check 34.2

Explain why a country might both export and import the same sort of products.

available within the domestic market. Exports of services are also a large and increasing share of UK exports, particularly financial services and insurance.

Summary

- All countries engage in international trade to some degree.
- Some countries are more open to trade than others.
- Trade has increased with the closer integration of economies.
- Trade flows between developed countries have dominated, with the flows between developing countries being relatively minor.
- The UK has come to rely heavily on trade with the EU, with trade in services becoming increasingly important.

Advantages and disadvantages of international trade

International trade has become important to all countries. It brings with it some significant advantages and disadvantages.

Developed countries

The advantages of international trade for developed countries are clear. Trade gives developed countries access to raw materials — natural resources that they do not have within their own boundaries. This was especially important in the early years of economic growth, when countries such as the UK were able to obtain key raw materials needed by the newly growing manufacturing sector. This may be less important in today's world, but it remains significant.

International trade allows a widening of consumer choice, giving access to a wide range of commodities that could not readily be produced in the domestic market. In return, trade gives developed countries access to a wider market for their output.

Firms that operate in global markets may also be able to gain technical knowledge that enables an increase in productive efficiency. Building networks of suppliers and collaborators can be valuable in the long run.

There are also disadvantages. Perhaps the most significant of these is that when countries become more closely integrated, they may become more susceptible to external shocks. An example was during the period of financial crisis in the late 2000s, when crisis spread rapidly between countries.

Emerging economies

In many ways, emerging economies such as the BRICS (**B**razil, **R**ussia, **I**ndia, **C**hina, **S**outh Africa) built their success on international trade. In earlier generations, the so-called 'tiger' economies (Hong Kong, Singapore, Taiwan and South Korea) also benefited greatly from economic growth that was fuelled by exports.

For economies trying to make the transition from less developed to developed, engaging with international trade is crucial. Without a large market for their products it is difficult to exploit economies of scale in production. Furthermore, international markets can provide capital goods and technical expertise that are important for an economy wanting to develop a manufacturing base.

Synoptic link

There is further discussion of the impact of globalisation (the process by which economies have become more closely integrated) in Chapter 35.

Synoptic link

The BRICS economies were introduced in Chapter 28.

The tiger economies went through a process of economic growth at a time when word trade was expanding rapidly, and when many of the advanced economies were moving into new economic activities — high value-added production and service sectors. This left a gap in the market that the tigers were able to fill.

In the case of China, the economy had been little exposed to international trade from the time of the revolution in 1949. With reforms introduced in 1979, China began to experience an unprecedented period of economic growth. At the beginning of this process, China's GDP per capita was below that of countries such as Bangladesh or Sierra Leone. By 2016, GDP per capita in China was some 15 times higher than in Sierra Leone.

Much of this success was built on expanding exports, taking advantage of China's large supply of relatively low-cost labour to expand its manufacturing base.

Such heavy dependence on exports could create vulnerability. If there is a slowdown in world trade, such as happened in the financial crisis of the late 2000s, this could spread not only among the advanced economies but also to the emerging economies.

If you look back at Figure 28.10 on page 389, you can see that China was less affected by the recession than might have been expected, although there does seem to have been something of a slowdown in the aftermath. Russia and Brazil did not escape so easily, and suffered a dip in their progress.

If you look back at Figure 28.10 on page 389

Developing countries

It might be expected that developing countries would have the most to gain from international trade, but they seem to have benefited least.

For many developing countries, the size of the home market is relatively small. People are living on low incomes, so have limited spending power. Firms are therefore unable to grow to the size needed to exploit economies of scale. By gaining access to foreign markets, they might be able to overcome this.

Furthermore, developing countries lack the expertise to build capital goods or to take advantage of technical advances. Again, international trade could give access to machinery and technical expertise that could allow the development of industries. It would seem that developing countries could therefore gain much from engaging in international trade. Indeed, the World Bank and the IMF have encouraged developing countries to become more open to international trade.

Developing countries have not been able to tap into the potential gains from trade for a number of reasons. Their economies tend to be dominated by primary production, whether it be agriculture or mineral production. Agriculture in particular tends to be a low productivity activity, and prices of primary products are notoriously volatile and liable to fall over time relative to the prices of manufactured goods.

People in developing countries lack the skills needed for modern production, and firms that do try to enter world markets often find that they face more powerful and experienced foreign producers that will be able to compete strongly with any new entrants.

All of this means that developing countries find it difficult to gain entry to overseas markets.

Knowledge check 34.3

Did India suffer from the financial crisis more or less severely than the UK?

Knowledge check 34.4

Why might volatility in primary products cause problems for developing countries?

Summary

- Access to world markets allows countries to access goods and services that they may not be able to produce efficiently in the home economy.
- Industries can purchase the raw materials needed for production.
- Consumers gain a wider range of products for consumption.
- Increasing integration of economies across the world improves access, but also creates potential vulnerability in the face of external shocks.
- Developed countries have gained through trade but did find that the recession of the late 2000s spread rapidly.
- Emerging economies gained substantially from being able to enjoy periods of export-led growth.
- Developing countries have gained the least from international trade, lacking the resources to take full advantage of the opportunities and being over-dependent on primary production.

Case study 34.1

Trade: who benefits?

The UK imports a great many products, from Audi cars to Hollywood blockbusters, from other European countries and overseas. At the same time, companies based in the UK, from Vauxhall to the BBC, sell their products to customers abroad.

As the Nobel prize-winning economist Paul Krugman argued in an interview to the BBC, international trade matters, as it helps firms to specialise and produce in large quantities. At the same time, it expands everyone's choice. Indeed, if you walk down the cookie aisle in a UK supermarket you will see that it has cookies from Denmark, Britain and the United States, as people enjoy variety. This, of course, applies to both exports and imports: the BBC exports the *Dr Who* series to Europe and the USA, while BBC4 has taken to showing Scandinavian and other European subtitled crime drama. Cadbury exports chocolate to the USA and Germany, while British supermarkets import Milka from Germany and Belgian Godiva chocolate.

International trade in goods is an important and integral part of any economy. As well as material goods, firms may trade in services such as banking and consultancy, invest directly in other companies abroad or contract a foreign company to produce a specific good exclusively for them.

British supermarkets import chocolate from other countries, such as Hershey's from the US

Many world markets are dominated by large firms with strong market power that find it profitable to operate on a global scale, producing and selling in many different countries. The appearance of China as a world power has shifted the balance of international trade to a surprising degree, but for many developing countries, trade has failed to deliver potential gains.

Follow-up question
Discuss the extent to which different countries have gained from international trade. Have you detected ways in which Brexit has affected the UK's position in relation to international trade?

CHAPTER 34 QUESTIONS

B Knowledge and understanding questions

1 Explain what is meant by 'international trade'. [2 marks]

2 Explain **two** possible disadvantages to a developing country of international trade. [4 marks]

3 Explain **two** possible advantages to a developing country of international trade. [4 marks]

C Stimulus response question

4 In 2018, the USA imposed tariffs on imported steel. A tariff is a tax that aims to reduce the number of goods being imported, and it can be used to protect a country's domestic production.

In response to the US tariffs on imported steel, many countries have retaliated by imposing tariffs on the import of some American-produced goods.

Evaluate the possible disadvantages to the US economy of international trade. [12 marks]

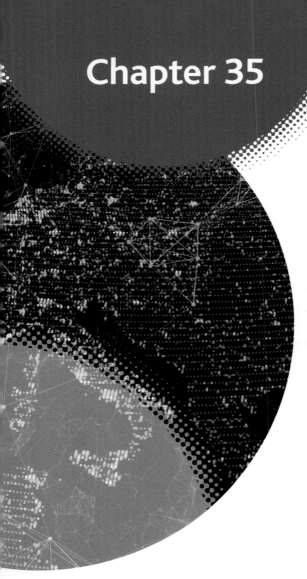

Chapter 35

Globalisation

Economies around the world have become increasingly interconnected as technology in transport and communications has been revolutionised and markets have been deregulated. This process of closer integration of the world economy is known as globalisation, which is the topic of this chapter.

Learning objectives

After studying this chapter, you should be able to:
- explain globalisation
- explain international competitiveness
- explain absolute and comparative advantage
- explain and calculate the terms of trade
- explain the Marshall–Lerner condition and J-curve
- evaluate comparative advantage as an explanation of international trade patterns
- evaluate the causes and consequences of globalisation for developed, emerging and developing countries
- evaluate the impact of the performance of emerging economies on other economies

Globalisation

Key term

globalisation a process by which the world's economies are becoming more closely integrated

The term 'globalisation' has been much used in recent years, including by the protest groups that have demonstrated against it. It is therefore important to be clear about what the term means before seeking to evaluate its strengths and weaknesses.

Ann Krueger, the first deputy managing director of the International Monetary Fund (IMF), defined globalisation as 'a phenomenon by which economic agents in any given part of the world are much more affected by events elsewhere in the world'. Joseph Stiglitz, the Nobel laureate and former chief economist at the World Bank, defined it as follows:

> Fundamentally, [globalization] is the closer integration of countries and peoples of the world which has been brought about by the enormous reduction of costs of transportation and communication, and the breaking down of artificial barriers to the flows of goods, services, capital, knowledge, and (to a lesser extent) people across borders.

Source: J. Stiglitz, *Globalization and its Discontents* (Penguin, 2004)

On this basis, globalisation is crucially about the closer integration of the world's economies. Critics have focused partly on the environmental effects of rapid global economic growth, and partly on the opportunities that powerful nations and large corporations have for exploiting the weak.

Causes of globalisation

The quotation from the book by Joseph Stiglitz not only defines what is meant by globalisation, but also offers reasons for its occurrence.

Transportation and communication costs

One of the contributory factors to the spread of globalisation was undoubtedly the rapid advances in the technology of transportation and communications.

Improvements in transportation enabled firms to fragment their production process to take advantage of varying cost conditions in different parts of the world. For example, it is possible to site labour-intensive parts of a production process in areas of the world where labour is relatively plentiful, and therefore relatively cheap.

Furthermore, communications technology developed rapidly with the growth of the internet and e-commerce, enabling firms to compete more easily in global markets. The importance of email and other forms of communication such as video-conferencing and Skype should not be underestimated. It is now taken for granted that there can be instant communication across the globe. This has made it very much easier for firms to communicate within their organisations and with other firms, and has certainly fuelled the closer integration of firms and economies. The emergence of a global media presence enables the rapid sharing of information and ideas, keeping consumers well informed about new products coming to the market.

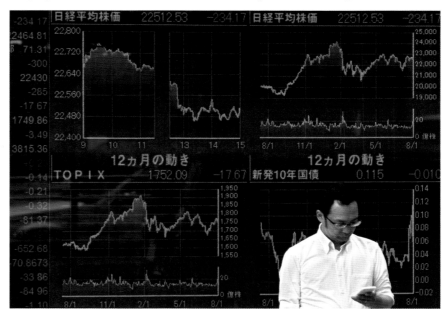

Globalisation and advances in technology have enabled firms to compete more easily in global markets

Knowledge check 35.1

The internet allows knowledge to be shared across national boundaries. How would you expect this to facilitate globalisation?

These technological changes augmented existing economies of scale and scope, enabling firms to grow. In the countries in which they operate, the sheer size of some multinational corporations gives them political as well as economic power.

Reduction of trade barriers

A second factor that has contributed to globalisation was the successive reductions in trade barriers during the period since the Second World War,

Key terms

General Agreement on Tariffs and Trade (GATT) the precursor of the WTO, which organised a series of 'rounds' of tariff reductions

World Trade Organization (WTO) a multilateral body now responsible for overseeing the conduct of international trade

Synoptic link

The role of the WTO in promoting freer trade is discussed in Chapter 36. Free trade areas and customs unions are also explained in Chapter 36, as are the launch of Brexit and the 'America First' stance of President Trump, which seem to buck this trend.

Synoptic link

The effects of migration on labour markets were discussed in Chapter 32 in the context of supply-side policies.

first under the auspices of the **General Agreement on Tariffs and Trade (GATT)**, and later under the **World Trade Organization (WTO)**, which replaced it.

In addition to these trade-liberalising measures, there has been a trend towards the establishment of free trade areas and customs unions in various parts of the world, with the EU being just one example.

By facilitating the process of international trade, such developments have encouraged firms to become more active in trade, and so have added to the impetus towards globalisation.

Deregulation of financial markets

Hand in hand with these developments, there were moves towards removing restrictions on the movement of financial capital between countries, thereby making it much easier for firms to operate globally. This has been reinforced by developments in technology that enable financial transactions to be undertaken more quickly and efficiently.

This whole process has led to changes in the pattern of trade between countries — for example, as the UK became more closely integrated with the rest of Europe, there has been an increase in the share of UK trade that is with the rest of Europe, although the USA also remains a significant trading partner.

Migration

In Europe, the formation of the Single European Market enabled freer movement of people within Europe. The effects of this were reinforced by the ending of the Cold War, which affected global labour supply.

> ### Summary
> - Globalisation is a process by which the world's economies have become more closely integrated.
> - Causes of globalisation include advances in transport and communication, reduction of trade barriers and deregulation of financial markets.

International competitiveness

The relative competitiveness of UK goods and services is an important issue in the context of the balance of payments. If the UK persistently shows a deficit on the current account, does that imply that UK goods are uncompetitive in international markets?

There are several factors that affect international competitiveness, some of which have been discussed in earlier chapters. The rise of globalisation makes this especially important. A key issue surrounds the prices at which UK goods and services can be sold abroad, which depends upon the exchange rate and relative inflation rates.

Figure 27.2 on page 370 showed the sterling–dollar exchange rate. The relatively flat pattern through time suggests that the competitiveness of UK products remained fairly constant over the period shown. In other words,

The balance of payments is explained in Chapter 26 and the exchange rate in Chapter 27. Both are relevant when it comes to a discussion of international competitiveness. Chapter 28 explains the relevance of productivity levels in influencing how efficient UK producers are compared with foreign competitors.

Americans wanting to buy UK goods got more or less the same amount of pounds for their dollars in 2017 as in 1997, other things being equal.

However, some care is needed, because other things do not remain equal. In particular, remember that the competitiveness of UK goods in the US market depends not only on the exchange rate but also on movements in the prices of goods over time, so this needs to be taken into account, If the prices of UK goods have risen more rapidly than prices in the USA, this will have partly offset the downward movement in the exchange rate.

Figure 35.1 shows the exchange rate again (for a longer period this time). You can now see that the exchange rate fell substantially from its peak in the early 1970s. However, the figure also shows the ratio of UK/US consumer prices (plotted using the right-hand scale). This reveals that between 1971 and 1977, UK prices rose much more steeply than those in the USA and continued to rise relative to the USA until the 1990s. Therefore, the early decline in the exchange rate was offset by the movement in relative prices. Similarly, UK prices rose relative to those in the USA as the exchange rate fell in the mid-2010s.

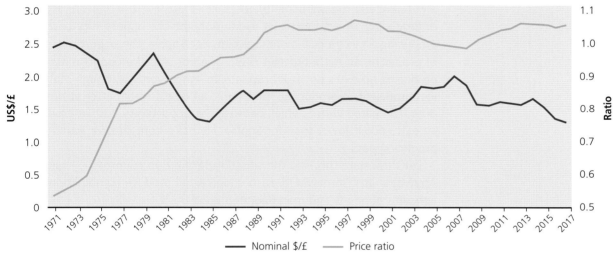

Figure 35.1 The exchange rate, US$/£, and the ratio of UK/US prices since 1971

Source: based on data from Bank of England, IMF, OECD

Summary
- The relative competitiveness of UK goods affects the balance of payments position.
- This is especially important in the context of globalisation.
- An important influence is the price at which UK goods and services sell in overseas markets, which in turn depends upon the exchange rate and on relative inflation rates.

Absolute and comparative advantage

Chapter 34 discussed the pattern of international trade, and the way that countries tend to specialise in producing and trading particular goods and services that seem well suited to their situation. The notion

Synoptic link

You can find Matthew and Sophie's story in Chapter 2 on page 23.

of comparative advantage appeared in the writing of David Ricardo in the early nineteenth century, and this theory helps to explain patterns of trade.

The idea is related to that of specialisation, which was explained in Chapter 2 using an example that involved Matthew and Sophie, who produced pots and bracelets by working at weekends.

The first two columns of Table 35.1 shows how many pots and bracelets each of them could make in a given time.

Table 35.1 Matthew and Sophie's output

	Number of pots	Number of bracelets	Opportunity cost of a bracelet	Opportunity cost of a pot
Matthew	12	12	1 pot	1 bracelet
Sophie	18	36	0.5 pots	2 bracelets

Sophie is better than Matthew at producing both pots and bracelets: she has an absolute advantage in producing both goods. However, there is a difference in the opportunity costs. For Matthew, the opportunity cost of producing an extra bracelet is one pot, and the opportunity cost of producing an extra pot is one bracelet. For Sophie, the opportunity cost of producing an extra bracelet is 0.5 of a pot, and the opportunity cost of producing an extra pot is 2 bracelets. In other words, although Matthew is less proficient at producing both items, he is relatively better at producing pots (compared with Sophie), because the opportunity cost of producing an extra pot is lower than for Sophie. He has a comparative advantage in producing pots.

Let's translate this into the situation facing two countries — call them Anywhere and Somewhere. Each country can produce combinations of agricultural goods and manufactured goods.

Suppose that there are differences between the countries in the efficiency with which they use their factors of production. For example, it may be that Anywhere can produce manufactured goods using fewer resources than Somewhere. Anywhere would then be said to have an **absolute advantage** in the production of manufactured goods as compared with Somewhere. It could be the case that Anywhere has an absolute advantage in the production of both manufactured and agricultural goods as compared with Somewhere. However, this does not mean that trade could not be beneficial. This turns on the *relative* efficiency with which the two countries produce the two types of goods. If Somewhere is relatively more efficient at producing agricultural goods than manufactured goods, then it has a **comparative advantage** in producing agricultural goods, by producing them at lower opportunity cost.

Consider the example of Anywhere and Somewhere from the previous paragraph. Assume (for simplicity) that the two countries are of similar size in output terms, although Somewhere uses more resources in production than Anywhere because of the absolute advantage held by Anywhere. Their respective *PPCs* are shown in Figure 35.2.

Key terms

absolute advantage a country's ability to produce a good using fewer resources than another country

comparative advantage a country's ability to produce a good *relatively* more efficiently (i.e. at lower opportunity cost) than another country

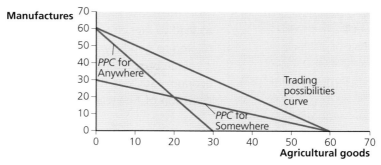

Figure 35.2 Trading possibilities for Anywhere and Somewhere

The pattern of comparative advantage held by the two countries is reflected in the different slopes of the countries' *PPCs*. In the absence of trade, each country is constrained to consume along its *PPC*. For example, if Somewhere wants to consume 20 units of manufactures, it can consume a maximum of 20 units of agricultural goods.

However, suppose that each country were to specialise in producing the product in which it has a comparative advantage. Anywhere could produce 60 units of manufactures and Somewhere could produce 60 units of agricultural goods. If each country were to specialise completely in this way, and if trade were to take place on a one-to-one basis (i.e. if one unit of manufactures is exchanged for one unit of agricultural goods), it can be seen that this would expand the consumption possibilities for both countries. The **trading possibilities curve** in Figure 35.2 shows the potential consumption points for each country in this situation.

For example, if Somewhere still wishes to consume 20 units of manufactures, it could now produce 60 units of agricultural goods, and exchange 20 units of them for 20 units of manufactures. It would then have its 20 units of manufactures, but have more agricultural goods than without trade. In this particular exchange, Anywhere would now have 40 units of manufactures and 20 units of agricultural goods, and would also be better off than without trade.

The **law of comparative advantage** states that overall output can be increased if countries specialise in producing the goods in which they have a comparative advantage.

Key terms

trading possibilities curve shows the consumption possibilities under conditions of free trade

law of comparative advantage a theory arguing that there may be gains from trade arising when countries specialise in the production of goods or services in which they have a comparative advantage

Exercise 35.1

Figure 35.3 shows production possibility curves for two countries, each of which produces both coats and scooters. The countries are called Here and There.

a Suppose that Here produces 200 scooters and There produces 100: how many coats are produced in each country?

b Now suppose that 300 scooters and 200 coats are produced by Here, and that There produces only coats. What has happened to total production of coats and scooters?

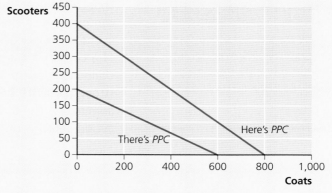

Figure 35.3 Coats and scooters

In the above examples and exercises, specialisation and trade are seen to lead to higher overall production of goods. Although the examples are related to goods, you should be equally aware that services too might be a source of specialisation and trade. This is potentially important for an economy such as the UK's, where there is a comparative advantage in the provision of financial services.

The terms of trade

One of the key factors that determines who gains from international trade is the **terms of trade**, defined simply as the ratio of export prices to import prices.

Suppose that both export and import prices are rising through time, but import prices are rising more rapidly than export prices. This means that the ratio of export to import prices will fall — which in turn means that a country must export a greater volume of its goods in order to acquire the same volume of imports.

Quantitative skills 35.1

Calculating and interpreting the terms of trade

Export and import prices are expressed as index numbers, based on a particular year. Suppose we want to know how the terms of trade have changed in 2018 relative to 2000. This can be done using the data in Table 35.2, which shows price indexes for exports and imports based on 2000 = 100.

The terms of trade represent the relative price change over the period, so for 2018 we calculate the ratio of the price of exports to the price of imports. This is normally expressed as a percentage (i.e. as an index number), so the calculation is 100 x 131.5/128.6 = 102.3. The terms of trade increased by 2.3% between 2000 and 2018. This indicates that the same volume of exports will purchase a greater volume of imports in 2018 than in 2000.

Table 35.2 Price indexes for exports and imports (2000 = 100)

Date	Price index of exports	Price index of imports
2000	100.0	100.0
2018	131.5	128.6

A fall in the terms of trade indicates that the same volume of exports will purchase a smaller volume of imports than before. A downward movement in the terms of trade is therefore unfavourable for an economy. Figure 35.4 shows the terms of trade for selected countries since 2000. You can see from this that different countries can experience changes in the terms of trade in very different ways in the same period of time. This depends strongly on the pattern of a country's exports and imports. For the countries shown, Uganda's exports are dominated by coffee, so coffee prices have a strong influence on the terms of trade. For Zambia, it is copper that dominates. The terms of trade for the UK varied very little over this period, relative to Zambia or Sierra Leone.

Macroeconomics Part 9

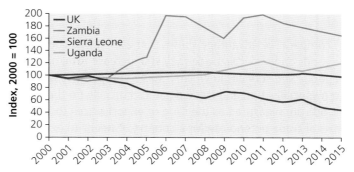

Figure 35.4 The terms of trade in selected countries, 2000–15 (2000 = 100)

Source: World Development Indicators

The terms of trade are calculated purely with respect to prices and take no account of changing volumes of trade. In other words, a deterioration in the terms of trade does not necessarily mean that an economy is worse off, so long as the volume of trade is increasing sufficiently rapidly.

Extension material

The net barter terms of trade

The terms of trade described in the text are known more formally as the *net barter* terms of trade. As noted, the net barter terms of trade relate solely to the relative prices of exports and imports, so do not take into account changes in the volume of exports and imports. The *income* terms of trade take the volume of trade into account, being defined as the value of a country's exports divided by the price of imports. In other words, this measures the purchasing power of a country's exports in terms of the price of its imports. It is possible for all countries to experience an increase in the income terms of trade simultaneously.

In recent years, concerns have been raised about the effect of changes in the terms of trade for less developed countries (LDCs). One problem faced by LDCs that export primary products is that they are each too small as individual exporters to be able to influence the world prices of their products. They must accept the prices that are set in world commodity markets.

Exercise 35.2

In 2015, the terms of trade index for the United Arab Emirates was 192.6 (based on 2000 = 100). For Sierra Leone it was 44.1, and for Bolivia it was 99.7. Explain what is implied by these statistics for each country.

Extension material

The terms of trade and developing countries

Movements in the terms of trade have been especially important for developing countries, which tend to rely on exporting primary products. Problems have arisen in both the short run and the long run. In the short run, primary product prices have tended to be highly volatile. Developing countries are typically too small in the market to be able to influence prices, so have experienced volatility in export revenues.

In the long run, there has been a tendency for non-fuel primary product prices to fall relative to prices of manufactured goods, so that many developing countries have experienced a long-term deterioration in the terms of trade, reducing the value of their exports.

Summary

- The theory of comparative advantage shows that even if one country has an absolute advantage in the production of goods and services, trade may still increase total output if each country specialises in the production of goods and services in which it has a comparative advantage.
- Who gains from specialisation and trade depends crucially on the prices at which exchange takes place.
- The terms of trade are measured as the ratio of export prices to import prices.
- When the terms of trade deteriorate for a country, it needs to export a greater volume of goods to be able to maintain the same volume of imports.

The J-curve effect and Marshall–Lerner condition

Synoptic link

The operation of a fixed exchange rate system and the effects of devaluation are discussed in Chapter 27.

Under a fixed exchange rate system, it may be tempting to use devaluation to improve competitiveness. At a lower value of the pound, you would expect an increase in the demand for exports and a fall in the demand for imports, ceteris paribus.

However, this does not necessarily mean that there will be an immediate improvement in the current account. One reason for this concerns the elasticity of supply of exports and import substitutes. If domestic producers do not have spare capacity, or if there are time lags before production for export can be increased, then exports will not expand quickly in the short run, and so the impact of this action on exports will be limited. Furthermore, similar arguments apply to producers of goods that are potential substitutes for imported products, which reinforces the sluggishness of adjustment. In the short run, therefore, it may be that the current account will worsen rather than improve, in spite of the change in the competitiveness of domestic firms.

This is known as the **J-curve effect**, and is shown in Figure 35.5. Time is measured on the horizontal axis, and the current account is initially in deficit. A devaluation at time *A* initially pushes the current account further into deficit because of the inelasticity of domestic supply. Only after time *B*, when domestic firms have had time to expand their output to meet the demand for exports, does the current account move into surplus.

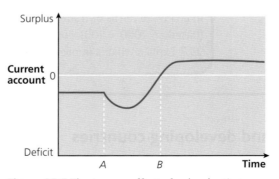

Figure 35.5 The J-curve effect of a devaluation

A second consideration relates to the elasticity of demand for exports and imports. Again, if competitiveness improves but demand does not respond strongly, there may be a negative impact on the current account. If the demand for exports is price inelastic, a fall in price will lead to a

Key terms

J-curve effect a situation following a devaluation, in which the current account deficit moves further into deficit before improving

Marshall–Lerner condition the condition that devaluation will have a positive effect on the current account only if the sum of the elasticities of demand for exports and imports is negative and numerically greater than 1

fall in revenue. There is reason to expect that the demand for exports is relatively inelastic in the short run. In many cases, exports may be supplied under contracts that cannot be immediately renegotiated. Furthermore, people and firms may wait to see whether the devaluation is permanent or temporary, and so not revise their spending plans in the short run.

The **Marshall–Lerner condition** states that devaluation will have a positive effect on the current account only if the sum of the elasticities of demand for exports and imports is negative and numerically greater than 1. If there is a devaluation, there will be a quantity effect and a price effect. At the new exchange rate, the quantity effect on the trade balance will be positive because exports tend to increase and imports to decrease. However, there is also a negative price effect, because export prices in terms of foreign currency have fallen and import prices in domestic currency have risen. The trade balance (measured in revenue terms) will improve only if the quantity effect fully offsets the price effect — in other words, if the Marshall–Lerner condition holds true.

Comparative advantage and the pattern of international trade

The law of comparative advantage helps to explain the pattern of international trade. Indeed, globalisation may be seen as a process that enables countries to enhance the way in which their comparative advantage can be exploited. In some cases, it may enable some countries to develop new specialisations, and so alter the pattern of their comparative advantage.

From the point of view of economic analysis, it would seem likely that this process of globalisation, and the increasing use of comparative advantage, would be welcomed by countries around the world. However, it seems that this is not a universal view. Countries often seem reluctant to open their economies fully to international trade, and have tended to intervene to try to protect their domestic producers from what is perceived as excessive and possibly unfair competition from foreign firms.

In the light of these twin problems, it is perhaps no surprise that many LDCs see themselves as trapped by their pattern of comparative advantage, rather than being in a position to exploit it. They have therefore been reluctant to continue in such a state of dependency on primary products, but the process of diversification into a wide range of products has been difficult to achieve.

A potential change in this pattern was seen in 2007 and 2008, with food prices rising rapidly. These included the prices of some staple commodities such as maize and rice. The net effect of this on LDCs was mixed. Countries in a position to export these commodities benefited from the rise in prices — that is, an increase in their terms of trade. However, there are many LDCs that need to import these staple commodities and for them the terms of trade deteriorated. These trends were interrupted by the onset of recession in many developed countries in 2008.

The degree to which a country or region engages in trade depends upon several factors. One important influence is the extent to which a country has the resources needed to trade — in other words, whether

Synoptic link

The ways in which countries can try to protect themselves from foreign competition are explained in Chapter 36.

Knowledge check 35.4

Give examples of products that might be suitable for developing countries seeking to diversify away from primary products.

it can produce the sorts of goods that other countries wish to buy. However, it also depends upon the policy stance adopted by a country. Some countries have been very open to international trade. For example, a number of countries in Southeast Asia built success in economic growth on the basis of promoting exports. In contrast, there are countries such as India that in the past were less eager to trade, and introduced policies that hindered their engagement with trade.

Extension material

Heckscher–Ohlin

Two Swedish economists, Eli Heckscher and Bertil Ohlin, argued that a country's comparative advantage would depend crucially on its relative endowments of factors of production. They argued that the optimal techniques for producing different commodities varied. Some commodities are most efficiently produced using labour-intensive techniques, whereas others could be more efficiently produced using relatively capital-intensive methods. This then suggests that if a country has abundant labour but scarce capital, its natural comparative advantage would lie in the production of goods that require little capital but lots of labour. In contrast, a country with access to capital but facing a labour shortage would tend to have a comparative advantage in capital-intensive goods or services.

Summary

- Globalisation may be seen as a process that enables countries to make the best use of their comparative advantage.
- Some countries have nonetheless been reluctant to be open to international trade.
- Some developing countries are trapped by their comparative advantage in the production of primary goods.

Consequences of globalisation

The causes of globalisation were discussed earlier in the chapter, but what of the consequences? Globalisation has had significant effects on countries, governments, producers, consumers, workers and the environment. Not all of these effects have been positive. At the heart of the globalisation process has been the increased interdependence of economies, which has had profound effects.

Standards of living

By enabling increased specialisation and trade, globalisation has allowed economic growth to take place. This has enabled an increase in standards of living for people in many countries.

In developed countries, globalisation has allowed more consumer choice, as a wider range of products has become accessible. The emerging economies have benefited by being able to enjoy economic growth in supplying the demands of consumers in the developed countries. Developing countries have not always benefited as strongly, partly because of low incomes that mean many products remain out of reach. There is also the danger that inappropriate products and lifestyles may spread at the expense of local cultures.

McDonald's restaurants are becoming a common sight in LDCs, such as this restaurant in Morocco

Structural change

Increased specialisation comes with a transitional cost. Countries have had to adjust to new patterns of economic activity. For example, many developed countries have seen their economies go through a transition in which traditional sectors such as manufacturing have declined in the face of competition from LDCs. This process is known as deindustrialisation. The service sectors have expanded, but workers displaced from manufacturing occupations do not always find it easy to retrain for service sector jobs. Some producers have been unable to compete with lower-cost producers from elsewhere in the world, but others have flourished as service activity has expanded. In theory, there should be long-term benefits from making this transition, but sometimes the short-term costs are more evident.

The emerging economies have again benefited by being able to move into areas of economic activity vacated by the developed countries. This has helped to fuel their rapid and persistent economic growth. Developing countries are beginning to benefit also, but many lack the resources and skills to be able to compete with the developed and emerging economies.

Foreign direct investment

An important aspect of globalisation has been the spread of **foreign direct investment (FDI)** by **multinational corporations (MNCs)**. These are companies whose production activities are carried out in more than one country. The UN Conference on Trade and Development has identified three main reasons for FDI:

1 market seeking
2 resource seeking
3 efficiency seeking

First, some MNCs may engage in FDI because they want to sell their products within a particular market, and find it preferable to produce within the market rather than elsewhere: such FDI is *market seeking*. Second, MNCs may undertake investment in a country in order to take advantage of some key resource. This might be a natural resource such as oil or natural gas, or a labour force with certain skills, or simply cheap unskilled labour: such FDI is *resource seeking*. Third, MNCs may simply review their options globally, and decide that they can produce most efficiently in a particular location. This might entail locating just part of their production chain in a certain country. Such FDI is *efficiency seeking*.

Developed and emerging economies have benefited from FDI, partly because most began life in those economies, so the profits tend to flow to them. The spread of technology through the actions of MNCs has been beneficial to developed countries, and to the emerging economies that have been able to use the enterprise and physical capital now located in their countries. For example, the opening up of China to foreign investment proved a magnet for MNCs wanting to gain access to this large and growing market.

For developing countries, FDI can have positive and negative effects. On the positive side, it is hoped that FDI will bring potential gains in employment, tax revenue, capital and technology, with consequent beneficial impact on economic growth. This may be seen as especially important for countries that especially lack capital and technology or the ability to raise tax revenue. However, there is a downside, as these potential benefits may not always be as strong as had been hoped. In particular, if profits are repatriated to shareholders elsewhere in the world, the long-term impact of FDI may be diluted, rather than feeding back into economic growth. For LDCs, the tax concessions negotiated by foreign transnational firms may reduce the benefits, and the technology may not be appropriate, or not disseminated.

Knowledge check 35.5

Suppose an MNC brings investment into a developing country. How would you expect this to affect employment in the host country?

Interdependence of economies

One of the issues concerning a more closely integrated global economy is the question of how robust the global economy will be to shocks. In other words, globalisation may be fine when the world economy is booming, as all nations may be able to share in the success. But if the global economy goes into recession, will all nations suffer the consequences? There are a number of situations that might cause the global economy to take a downturn, which then affects countries and their governments around the world.

Oil prices

Oil prices seem to provide one possible threat. Historically, sudden changes in oil prices have caused widespread disruption: for example, in 1973–74 and in 1979–80. Arguably, national economies in the twenty-first century are less vulnerable to changes in the price of oil than they were in 1973. However, volatility in the price of such a key commodity is significant.

The price of oil is significant because of its importance to so many businesses as an energy source, so fluctuations in its price can have knock-on effects across the global economy. Higher oil prices have highlighted awareness of environmental issues, and stimulated the search for new sources of energy.

Financial crises

Given the increasing integration of financial markets, a further concern is whether globalisation increases the chances that a financial crisis will spread rapidly between countries, rather than being contained within a country or region.

An example of the dangers of close interdependence began to unfold in 2007–08, when the financial crisis began to bite, and commercial banks in several countries found themselves in financial crisis. This followed a period in which relatively low interest rates had allowed a bubble of borrowing. When house prices began to slide, many banks in several countries found that they had overextended themselves, and had to cut back on lending, in some cases threatening their viability. This affected a number of countries simultaneously, and there was a danger that the financial crisis would affect the real economy, leading to a recession. This was a recession that would affect countries all around the globe because of the new interconnectedness of economies. It became apparent that no single country could tackle the problem alone, as measures taken to support the banks in one economy had rapid knock-on effects elsewhere. Once this was realised, coordinated action was taken, and in October 2008 the central banks of several countries reduced their bank rates together. This was followed by action aiming to salvage the situation and avoid a full-blooded recession.

By early 2009, the UK economy was officially in recession, bank rate had been driven down to an unprecedented 0.5%, and the Bank of England was introducing quantitative easing to try to stimulate the economy. One of the problems was that the commercial banks had become reluctant to lend, so firms that wanted to invest were finding it difficult to obtain funds. Attempts were made to coordinate the efforts of governments of key countries around the world — for example, at the G20 Summit held in London in April 2009. As time went by and the recession deepened, a number of countries in the Eurozone faced crises with the level of public debt. This affected Ireland, Greece and Portugal in particular, all of which needed bailouts.

Synoptic link

The financial crisis will be discussed further in Chapters 38 and 39.

Some emerging economies, notably India and China, were able to continue to enjoy economic growth through the period of the crisis, although subsequently, they too experienced something of a slowdown.

The experience of developing countries was mixed, some of them continuing to grow through the period.

The environment

Critics of globalisation have pointed to the impact that the increase in trade associated with globalisation may be having on the environment, especially in the context of climate change and global warming. This is bound up with the notion of **sustainable development**, which refers to the effect that economic growth and increased trade may have on future generations.

> ### Exercise 35.3
>
> Evaluate the consequences (positive and negative) of globalisation for developed, emerging and developing economies. You might do this as a group activity with your fellow students, having three groups each looking at one type of economy. You can then compare results.

Locals sift through rubbish on the banks of the polluted Adyar River, in Chennai, India

Summary

- An increase in specialisation and trade arising because of globalisation can increase consumer choice.
- Specialisation may require structural change, which brings transitional costs.
- Closer integration raises the risk of contagion, allowing shocks to spread between countries.
- Oil prices have been volatile, and threaten to destabilise economies.
- Financial crises may spread more rapidly under globalisation.
- Globalisation may have negative environmental consequences.

The impact of the emerging economies

Industrialisation and economic growth began in Britain and other countries in Western Europe and North America, and by the 1960s there was a divide between those countries that had gone through the development and growth process and those that had not. Since the 1960s, relatively few countries have managed to bridge the gap in living standards.

There was a group of countries that became known as the newly industrialised countries (NICs) that made the transition. These included some countries in Southeast Asia, such as Singapore, South Korea, Taiwan and Hong Kong, and some Latin American countries, although the latter group fell foul of hyperinflation, which interrupted their progress.

More recently, some other countries have accelerated in terms of economic growth and human development: namely, the emerging economies. This group has included the so-called BRICS countries, and a less-defined group including Thailand, Malaysia and Turkey, among others.

The success of these countries has had a significant impact on the performance of other countries. The initial impact of the NICs was mainly positive. They were producing goods that the developed countries had been accustomed to produce. However, the expansion of service sector activity and hi-tech products meant that the NICs were filling a gap left by the developed countries.

The rise of China as an economic superpower produced rather different responses, and the developed countries began to see a possible threat to their dominance.

China and the USA

In the early to mid-2000s, the global economy was faced with two seemingly distinct but related phenomena: the rapid growth of the Chinese economy, and the deficit on the US current account of the balance of payments. The US current account deficit arose partly from the heavy public expenditure programme of the Bush administration. However, the deficit grew to unprecedented levels partly through the actions of China and other East Asian economies that had chosen to peg their currencies to the US dollar. Effectively, this meant that those economies were buying US government securities as a way of maintaining their currencies against the dollar, thereby keeping US interest rates relatively low and allowing the American public to borrow to finance high consumer spending.

Who gained from this situation? The USA was able to spend, and China was able to sell, fuelling its rapid rate of economic growth. In due course, China agreed to allow its currency to adjust towards its true equilibrium — albeit rather slowly.

The events left a legacy of distrust between the USA and China. In 2018, President Trump imposed heavy tariffs on imports from China, initially on goods such as solar panels and washing machines, later on steel and aluminium. Further tariffs were announced as the year went by, not only affecting China but other countries as well. There were also threats that Trump tariffs would be imposed on imported cars from Europe. China retaliated by imposing its own tariffs on goods from the USA. Such a trade war would have a major impact on world trade.

Knowledge check 35.6

If a country keeps the exchange rate away from its equilibrium by accumulating reserves in the form of foreign assets, will this keep the exchange rate above or below its equilibrium?

Synoptic link

The impact of tariffs is discussed in Chapter 36.

Exercise 35.4

Find out how this trade war between the USA and China has developed since 2018. Discuss the effects it is having on world trade.

Summary

- The initial impact of emerging economies was positive, as they filled gaps left when developed economies restructured towards services and high value-added manufacturing.
- As China began to transform into a superpower, its rapid economic growth was perceived to be a threat, especially in the USA.

Case study 35.1

FDI and developing countries

One of the main problems that faces many developing countries is that they lack physical capital, which means that they must continue to rely on primary production to provide employment and export revenues. One possible solution to this could be to attract foreign direct investment from MNCs in order to provide a stimulus for economic growth.

From the perspective of developing countries, this could be an attractive path to development and economic growth. MNCs could bring much-needed capital and technology, managerial skills and knowledge of how to operate in international markets. They could provide employment for local workers and tax revenue for the government. As growth begins to take off, this would provide savings to enable further investment, therefore feeding the growth process.

In spite of these potential advantages, there have been many criticisms of MNC presence in developing countries. MNCs are large enough to have substantial economic and political power when they locate in a developing country, and the size of possible benefits may depend upon the objectives that the MNC has in choosing where to locate.

Follow-up question
Discuss the potential consequences for a developing country seeking to attract foreign direct investment. Why might these fail to deliver expected benefits?

CHAPTER 35 QUESTIONS

A Multiple-choice questions

1 If a country has a comparative advantage in the production of pasta then:
   a   It can produce pasta using less resources than any other country
   b   It can produce pasta at a lower cost than any other country
   c   It can produce pasta relatively more efficiently than another country
   d   It can produce pasta that is better quality than another country

2 Which of the following is **not** a reason for increased globalisation?
   a   A reduction in trade barriers
   b   More competition from global brands
   c   Fewer tariffs
   d   More global transportation networks

3 A country's terms of trade have decreased from 100 to 98. Which of the following statements is true?
   a   The same volume of exports will purchase a greater volume of imports
   b   The same volume of exports will purchase a lower volume of imports
   c   The same volume of exports will purchase the same volume of imports
   d   The same volume of exports will purchase twice as many imports

B Knowledge and understanding questions

4 Explain what is meant by the 'Marshall–Lerner condition'.   [2 marks]

5 Explain **two** ways in which globalisation has increased international trade.   [4 marks]

6 Explain, using the theory of comparative advantage, how international trade can benefit
   an economy.   [4 marks]

C Stimulus response question

7 Togo (Togolese Republic) is a West African country that is ranked as one of the poorest in the world.
   Like many developing countries, much of Togo's economy is based on agriculture, and it mainly exports
   primary sector products.

   Togo has had a negative trade balance since 2014.

   a   Explain what is meant by 'primary sector'.   [2 marks]
   b   Explain what is meant by 'a negative trade balance'.   [2 marks]
   c   Evaluate the likely consequences of globalisation for the Togo economy.   [8 marks]

D Essay question

8 Evaluate the extent to which comparative advantage explains international trade patterns.   [25 marks]

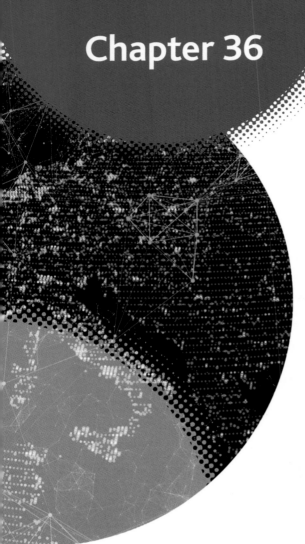

Chapter 36

Trade policies and negotiations

For much of the period since the Second World War, there have been moves towards closer economic integration through free trade areas, customs unions and deeper forms of integration. The previous chapter discussed globalisation, and the factors that enabled countries to become more interconnected. However, during the 2010s there has been a backlash against this. The UK voted to leave the EU, and the USA raised tariffs, provoking a reaction from China in particular. This chapter looks at measures that countries can use to protect their domestic economies. It also explains the various ways in which countries may choose to work together through economic integration. Overseeing international trade (and encouraging freer trade) is the World Trade Organization. Its role is also evaluated.

Learning objectives

After studying this chapter, you should be able to:

- explain protectionism
- explain economic integration through free trade areas, customs unions, monetary union and economic union
- evaluate the advantages and disadvantages of protectionism and free trade
- explain, with the aid of a diagram, the impact of tariffs and quotas on trade creation and trade diversion
- evaluate the role of the World Trade Organization in promoting free trade

Protectionism

Synoptic link

Comparative advantage is explained in Chapter 35.

Comparative advantage is just one of many reasons for countries to engage in international trade. Trade enables consumers in a country to have access to products that could not be produced at home, and enables producers to have access to new markets and resources. In some cases it allows producers to take advantage of economies of scale that would not be possible if they had to rely only on selling to the domestic market. From the country's perspective, export-led growth may be possible, and there are countries such as China and other countries in Southeast Asia that have benefited from this. It is also possible that exposure to competition from foreign firms provides a good incentive for domestic firms to become more efficient, raising the quality of their goods or the efficiency with which they are produced. Consumers may then gain from a wider variety of available products, improved quality and lower prices.

In spite of these potential gains from trade, countries have often
seemed reluctant to open their economies fully to international trade,
and have tended to intervene in various ways to protect their domestic
producers: a process known as **protectionism**.

Forms of protectionism

When recession began to threaten in 2008, there was strong lobbying in
several countries, including the USA, in favour of introducing protectionist
measures. Indeed, in the lead-up to the G20 Summit in April 2009, the
World Bank reported that the 17 members of that group had taken a total
of 47 trade-restricting steps in the previous months. However, the drive
towards globalisation had created a more integrated global economy, in
which many firms relied on a global supply chain. With the production
process fragmented between different parts of the world, the dangers
of protectionism become more severe, and the possibilities of rapid
contagion from a crisis become acute.

Tariffs

Key term

tariff a tax imposed on imported
goods

A policy instrument commonly used in the past to give protection to
domestic producers is a **tariff**. Tariff rates in the developed countries have
been considerably reduced in the period since the Second World War, but
tariffs are nonetheless still in place.

Figure 36.1 shows how a tariff is expected to operate. D represents the
domestic demand for a commodity, and S_{dom} shows how much domestic
producers are prepared to supply at any given price. The price at which
the good can be imported from world markets is given by P_w. If dealing
with a global market, it is reasonable to assume that the supply at the
world price is perfectly elastic. So, in the absence of a tariff, domestic
demand is given by D_0, of which S_0 is supplied within the domestic
economy and the remainder $(D_0 - S_0)$ is imported. If the government
wishes to protect this industry within the domestic economy, it needs
to find a way of restricting imports and encouraging home producers to
expand their capacity.

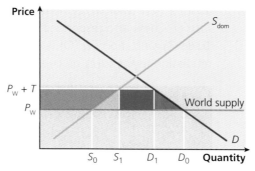

Figure 36.1 The effects of a tariff

When a tariff is imposed, the domestic price rises to $P_w + T$, where T
is the amount of the tariff. This has two key effects. One is to reduce
the demand for the good from D_0 to D_1. The second is to encourage
domestic producers to expand their output of this good from S_0 to S_1. As
a consequence, imports fall substantially (to $D_1 - S_1$). On the face of it,
the policy has achieved its objective. Furthermore, the government has
been able to raise some tax revenue (given by the green rectangle).

However, not all the effects of the tariff are favourable for the economy. Consumers are certainly worse off, as they have to pay a higher price for the good; they therefore consume less, and there is a loss of consumer surplus. Some of what was formerly consumer surplus has been redistributed to others in society. The government has gained the tariff revenue, as mentioned. In addition, producers gain some additional producer surplus, shown by the dark-blue area. There is also a deadweight loss to society, represented by the red and pale-blue triangles. In other words, society is worse off overall as a result of the imposition of the tariff.

Effectively, the government is subsidising inefficient local producers, and forcing domestic consumers to pay a price that is above that of similar goods imported from abroad.

Some would try to defend this policy on the grounds that it allows the country to protect an industry, therefore saving jobs that would otherwise be lost. However, this goes against the theory of comparative advantage, and forces society to incur the deadweight loss. In the longer term it may delay structural change. For an economy to develop new specialisations and new sources of comparative advantage, there needs to be a transitional process in which old industries contract and new ones emerge. Although this process may be painful, it is necessary in the long run if the economy is to remain competitive. Furthermore, the protection that firms enjoy which allows them to reap economic rents from the tariff may foster complacency and an inward-looking attitude. This is likely to lead to X-inefficiency, and an inability to compete in the global market.

Even worse is the situation that develops where nations respond to tariffs raised by competitors by putting up tariffs of their own. This has the effect of further reducing the trade between countries, and everyone ends up worse off, as the gains from trade are sacrificed. President Trump's decision to extend the tariffs on steel to Canada, the EU and Mexico in 2018 brought an immediate response from those countries, threatening a trade war that would leave all involved worse off as a result. President Trump decided to reduce the steel tariffs against Canada and Mexico in May 2019, opening the possibility of renewing discussions about a new trade agreement. When tariffs against China were raised further, China also responded with tariffs of its own. Although the World Trade Organization (WTO) is committed to reducing tariffs over time, retaliation in the form of 'countervailing duties' is permitted.

A steel plant: President Trump's decision to reduce the tariffs on steel against Canada and Mexico brought hope of a new trade agreement

Quotas and non-tariff barriers

An alternative policy that a country may adopt is to limit the imports of a commodity to a given volume. For example, a country may come to an agreement with another country that only a certain quantity of imports will be accepted by the importing country. Such arrangements are known as **quotas** (or as voluntary export restraints (VERs)).

Figure 36.2 illustrates the effects of a quota. D represents the domestic demand for this commodity, and S_{dom} is the quantity that domestic producers are prepared to supply at any given price. Suppose that, without any agreement, producers from country A would be prepared to supply any amount of the product at a price P_a. If the product is sold at this price, D_0 represents domestic demand, of which S_0 is supplied by domestic producers and the remainder $(D_0 - S_0)$ is imported from country A.

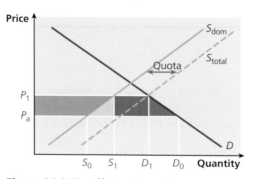

Figure 36.2 The effects of a quota

When a quota is imposed, total supply is now given by S_{total}, which is domestic supply plus the quota of imports allowed into the economy from country A. The market equilibrium price rises to P_1 and demand falls to D_1, of which S_1 is supplied by domestic producers and the remainder is the agreed quota of imports.

Figure 36.2 shows who gains and who loses by this policy. Domestic producers gain by being able to sell at the higher price, so (as in the case of the tariff) they receive additional surplus given by the dark-blue area. Furthermore, the producers exporting from country A also gain, receiving the green rectangle (which, in the case of the tariff, was tax revenue received by the government). As in the case of the tariff, the two triangles (red and pale blue) represent the loss of welfare suffered by the importing country.

Such an arrangement effectively subsidises the foreign producers by allowing them to charge a higher price than they would have been prepared to accept. Furthermore, although domestic producers are encouraged to produce more, the protection offered to them is likely to lead to X-inefficiency and weak attitudes towards competition.

There have been many examples of such agreements, especially in the textile industry. For example, the USA and China had long-standing agreements on quotas for a range of textile products. Ninety-one such quotas expired at the end of 2004 as part of China's accession to the WTO. As you might expect, this led to extensive lobbying by producers in the USA, especially during the run-up to the 2004 presidential election. Trade unions in the USA supported the producers, arguing that 350,000 jobs had been lost since the expiry of earlier quota agreements in 2002. In the case of three of these earlier agreements, some restraint had been reinstated for bras, dressing gowns and knitted fabrics. Producers in other countries, such as Sri Lanka, Bangladesh, Nepal, Indonesia, Morocco, Tunisia and Turkey, were lobbying for the quotas to remain, regarding China as a major potential competitor. However, for the USA at least, it can be argued that the removal of the quotas would allow domestic consumers to benefit from lower prices, and would allow US textile workers to be released for employment in higher-productivity sectors, where the USA maintains a competitive advantage.

Extension material

A production subsidy

Another way in which a country may attempt to restrict trade is by subsidising domestic producers to enable them to compete more effectively with imports. Figure 36.3 illustrates a possible scenario.

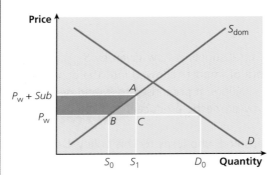

Figure 36.3 The effects of a production subsidy

This shows domestic demand and supply for a product that can be imported at the world price P_w. Without intervention, demand is D_0, of which S_0 is supplied by domestic producers, with the remainder being imported.

Assume that the country is too small a producer to affect the world price. If the government decides to pay a subsidy of an amount Sub to domestic producers, this affects the supply curve such that it is horizontal up to S_1 in Figure 36.3. This encourages domestic firms to increase production up to S_1, but unlike the case of the tariff, domestic consumers are still able to buy the good at the world price, so there is not the same impact on consumer surplus. Imports are $D_0 - S_1$, so this measure has reduced the country's dependence on imported goods.

Producers gain from this, receiving the additional producer surplus given by the dark-blue shaded area. However, this needs to be covered by the government, as does the area ABC in the figure, which represents the production inefficiency that was a deadweight loss in the case of the tariff.

The total cost to the government of providing the subsidy is therefore the sum of the dark- and light-blue areas. The downside of this approach is that these funds need to be raised from elsewhere in the economy, so distorting the allocation of resources in other markets. Although consumers are better off in respect of this product with the subsidy than with a tariff, as taxpayers they may pay the price in other ways. Furthermore, it is not clear that subsidising domestic production in this way provides any better incentives for efficiency than the tariff approach. If governments wish to encourage firms to become more efficient in order to compete, a better approach might be to subsidise education and training or research and development to improve production techniques, and so tackle the problem more directly. Of course, this would depend upon what was causing the inefficiency in the first place.

At the WTO ministerial summit in Nairobi in 2015, it was agreed that developed country members would eliminate all export subsidies immediately, and that developing country members would eliminate them by the end of 2018.

Key term

non-tariff barrier (NTB) an obstacle to free trade other than a tariff (e.g. quality standards imposed on imported products)

There are other ways in which trade can be hampered, one example being the use of what are known as **non-tariff barriers (NTBs)**. These often comprise rules and regulations that control the standard of products that can be sold in a country. It is difficult to quantify the importance of such measures, but the frequency with which disputes arise at the WTO suggests that they have had significant effects on trade.

Knowledge check 36.3

Explain how trade would be affected if a country insisted that all imports of a particular product had to be imported through a single understaffed office.

Exercise 36.1

Figure 36.1 showed the effects of a tariff.

If a country decides to remove the tariff, identify the effects on:

a consumers of the good

b producers of the good

c the government

Advantages and disadvantages of protectionism

The debate on whether countries should engage in protectionism or allow free trade has a long history, and still does not seem to have been resolved, given the USA's decision to raise tariffs in 2018 — and the impulse of other countries to respond in kind. Some of the arguments that have been advanced by politicians in favour of protectionism have little grounding in economic analysis.

There may be political reasons for wanting to protect domestic industries. For example, there may be strategic arguments that a country should always maintain an agricultural sector so as not to be over-dependent on imported foodstuffs, as this could be disastrous in the event of war. Such arguments were used in setting up the Common Agricultural Policy in Europe. President Trump's arguments for imposing a levy on steel imports in 2018 similarly claimed that the USA's steel industry was suffering from unfair competition, which was a threat to national security.

Key terms

sunset industry an industry in decline that needs protection for its displaced workers

infant industry an industry that needs protection from international competition in the short run so it can learn to become competitive

Some have also argued that domestic industries should be protected because of the impact of high unemployment among workers displaced from declining sectors — so-called **sunset industries**. This is really an argument about the period of transition to more open trade, as it could also be noted that workers released from those declining sectors could, in time, be redeployed in sectors that are more efficient in comparative advantage terms.

A common line of argument is about the need to protect so-called **infant industries**. This may be especially important in the context of less developed countries (LDCs) wanting to develop their manufacturing sectors. The argument is that protecting a domestic industry from international competition will allow the new activities to become familiar with the market so that in the longer term they will be able to compete. A problem with both infant and sunset industries is that once protection is put in place, it is difficult to remove. The infants may never grow up and declining sectors may never expire completely.

Knowledge check 36.4

Why might over-protection of an infant industry be ineffective in allowing the industry to compete in global markets?

The impact of protectionism

Protectionist policies have a number of effects on economic agents in a country. These effects differ according to which policy is in operation, but are most clearly illustrated with reference to the imposition of a tariff, which is the most common form of protectionist policy.

Consumers

In general, consumers are likely to be worse off as a result of protectionist measures. In the case of a tariff, consumer surplus is lower after a tariff, as consumers must pay a higher price for the good, and will consume less.

Producers

Producers in the domestic economy will gain from protection, as they will receive higher producer surplus (at the expense of consumers). However, their incentives to produce efficiently will be low, so in the long run they may never become able to compete effectively in world markets. The infant industry benefits are rarely delivered.

Governments

When a government imposes a tariff, it gains by the revenue that it raises. This may be valuable for the government of a developing country that faces problems with raising revenue through other forms of taxation because of the lack of an administrative structure. The balance of payments will be affected, as imports will fall after the imposition of a tariff. Whether domestic production will actually rise to compensate will depend upon the elasticity of supply. If home producers are unable to respond by increasing production, then the benefits from the tariff will be lower.

Living standards

For society as a whole, the imposition of a tariff carries a deadweight welfare loss, so overall well-being is lower with a tariff in place.

Equality

Protectionist measures entail a redistribution of resources, from consumers to producers, so there may be an increase in inequality in the society.

Free trade

David Ricardo's theory of comparative advantage, developed in the early nineteenth century, formed the basis of the arguments for free trade, and still has some resonance today. This suggests that it is possible for countries to gain from trade by specialising in the production of goods in which they have a comparative advantage.

The core idea of free trade is that international trade should be carried out without restrictions in the form of such measures as tariffs, quotas or non-tariff barriers. This has been debated since the nineteenth century, with the proponents of free trade winning the argument until times of recession, which tended to bring out the protectionist arguments.

The free trade argument was widely accepted in the period after the Second World War, and there was a move towards dismantling the structure of tariffs that had been put in place. Successive rounds of tariff reductions were agreed, overseen by the General Agreement on Tariffs and Trade (GATT), which was the precursor of the WTO (discussed later in this chapter).

In the twenty-first century, protectionism again came back into fashion, following the recession that followed the financial crisis. Indeed, the idea of free trade is not without its critics, such as economist Ha-Joon Chang.

One line of criticism is historically based. In the Industrial Revolution, Britain led the world in the development of manufacturing industry. Was this based on the principles of free trade? It can be argued that Britain's success was built on being able to import raw materials from its colonies, but although Britain was keen to import these materials under free trade conditions, it was also ready to restrict the ability of other nations to follow in its footsteps. For example, India was subjected to heavy tariffs on its textile workshops, forcing it to become a source of raw cotton rather than textiles. This protected the Lancashire textile mills.

The South Korean economy went through a period of rapid economic growth from the 1960s. Again, this was facilitated by high subsidies for firms and tariff barriers. There are other examples of the way in which industries have been protected to allow rapid economic growth to take place, often at the expense of potential competing nations.

A second line of argument notes that Ricardo's analysis rested on the assumption that capital and other factors of production were immobile, providing support for local specialisation. When factors of production are more mobile — as in today's world — this argument becomes less compelling.

Where there is imbalance of economic power between trading partners, the gains from trade may not be evenly spread between the countries involved. In particular, developing countries have gained less from trade than many developed countries, partly because of actions taken by the developed countries.

There may be strategic reasons for not becoming over-dependent on imports of key goods. Countries may wish to nurture new forms of economic activities and believe that such new industries need some protection from foreign competitors until they have become better able to hold their own.

A busy seaport, where imported goods are delivered by the container load

In the case of the Trump tariffs, there was a move away from free trade because it was perceived that domestic industries were being subject to unfair competition from foreign producers (in particular from China). The retaliation from trading partners reduces the gains made from imposing tariffs, and the danger is that all countries involved will be made worse off.

This is why the debate about free trade continues. The potential economic gains seem clear from the economic theory, but those gains may not always arise, and there may be political considerations to be taken into account.

Summary

- There has often been a tendency for governments to intervene to inhibit trade by the use of protectionist measures.
- Such measures include tariffs, quotas and the imposition of regulations.
- The use of such measures entails the sacrifice of potential gains from trade, but there may be circumstances in which countries feel justified in using them.
- The validity of some of these arguments is open to debate.
- The debate on free trade versus protectionism continues, with potential economic gains from free trade needing to be balanced against political and strategic considerations.

Economic integration

Key terms

trading bloc where a group of countries in a region agree to cooperate in international trade through some sort of free trade area or other form of association

free trade area a group of countries that agree to remove tariffs, quotas and other restrictions on trade between the member countries, but have no agreement on a common barrier against non-members

The possibility of implementing totally free trade on a global scale is unlikely to be realised, but an important influence on the pattern of world trade has been the establishment of **trading blocs** in different parts of the world. These are intended to encourage freer trade among groups of nations, normally on a regional basis, in order to tap the potential gains from trade.

Regional trade integration can take a variety of forms, representing differing degrees of closeness. By reducing the barriers to trade, specialisation can be encouraged, and there should be potential gains from the process. In practice, there may be other economic and political forces at work that affect the nature of the gains, and the extent to which integration will be possible — and beneficial.

Free trade areas

One level of integration is the formation of a so-called **free trade area**. Before the UK joined the European Economic Community in 1973, it was part of the European Free Trade Area (EFTA), together with other countries in Europe that had not joined the Community. The original countries were Austria, Denmark, Norway, Portugal, Sweden, Switzerland and the UK. Finland, Iceland and Liechtenstein joined later, but some EFTA members left in order to join the EU, leaving just Iceland, Liechtenstein, Norway and Switzerland as members of EFTA in the early years of the twenty-first century.

The notion of a free trade area is that countries within the area agree to remove internal tariff and quota restrictions on trade between them, while still allowing member countries to impose their own pattern of tariffs and quotas on non-members. The lack of a common external tariff wall may cause problems within the member countries. If one country has lower tariffs than the rest, the natural tendency will be for imports into the area to be channelled through that country, with goods then being resold to other member countries. This may distort the pattern of trade and cause unnecessary transaction costs associated with trading activity. It is worth noting that free trade areas are normally concerned with enabling free trade in goods and do not cover the movement of labour.

In spite of these problems, a free trade area does allow member countries to increase their degree of specialisation, and may bring gains. EFTA is not the only example of such an arrangement. In Southeast Asia, the Association of South-East Asian Nations (ASEAN) began to create a free trade area in 1993. This involved six nations (Brunei, Indonesia, Malaysia, the Philippines, Singapore and Thailand). The group was later expanded to include Cambodia, Laos, Myanmar and Vietnam. Progress towards eliminating tariffs in this group has been relatively slow, but intense competition from the rapidly growing Chinese economy provides a strong motivation for accelerating the process. ASEAN has the aim of establishing a free trade area by the year 2020.

Another major trading group operating a free trade area is the North American Free Trade Association (NAFTA), which covers the USA, Canada and Mexico. The agreement was signed in 1992 and launched in 1994, and has led to an expansion of trade between those countries. NAFTA came under political pressure under the Trump presidency, and renegotiation of the treaty led to a rebranding of the agreement as the United States–Mexico–Canada Agreement (USMCA). This was agreed in October 2018, but still required Congress ratification. The new agreement has included changes intended to make trading between the partners fairer. Negotiations stalled when President Trump raised tariffs on steel and aluminium being imported into the USA from Canada and Mexico. Talks began again when these tariffs were lifted in 2019.

Customs unions

A **customs union** is one notch up from a free trade area, in the sense that in addition to eliminating tariffs and quotas between the member nations, a common external tariff wall is set up against non-member nations. Again, the prime reason for establishing a customs union is to encourage trade between the member nations. Notice that a customs union does not need the member countries to have a common currency.

Advantages and disadvantages of customs unions

There are some disadvantages of customs unions. The transactions costs involved in administering the union cannot be ignored, and where there are traditional rivalries between nations, there may be political sensitivities to overcome. This may impede the free working of the union, especially if some member nations are more committed to the union than others, or if some countries have close ties with non-member states.

Knowledge check 36.5

In 2017, Canada accounted for about 77% of the USA's imports of steel, and Mexico accounted for a further 9%. What would you expect to be the result of the USA imposing a 25% tariff on imported steel?

Key term

customs union a group of countries that agree to remove restrictions on trade between the member countries, and set a common set of restrictions (including tariffs) against non-member states

Knowledge check 36.6

What is the key difference between a customs union and a free trade area?

It is also possible that a geographical concentration of economic activity will emerge over time within the union. This may result where firms want to locate near the centre of the area in order to minimise transportation costs. Alternatively, it may be that all firms will want to locate near the richest part of the market. Over time, this could mean that firms tend to concentrate in certain geographical areas, while the countries that are more remote, or which have smaller populations or lower average incomes, become peripheral to the centre of activity. In other words, over time, there may be growing inequality between regions within the union.

These disadvantages must be balanced against the benefits. For example, it may be that it is the smaller countries in the union that have the most to gain from tapping economies of scale that would not be accessible to them if they were confined to selling only within their domestic markets.

In addition to these internal economies of scale, there may be external economies of scale that emerge over time as the transport and communications infrastructure within the union improves. Furthermore, opening up domestic markets to more intense competition may induce efficiency gains, as firms will only be able to survive in the face of international competition by adopting best practice techniques and technologies. Indeed, another advantage of a customs union is that technology may be disseminated among firms operating within the union.

Common markets

It may be that the countries within a customs union wish to move to closer integration, by extending the degree of cooperation between the member nations. A **common market** adds to the features of a customs union by harmonising some aspects of the economic environment between them. In a pure common market, this would entail adopting common tax rates across the member states, and a common framework for the laws and regulations that provide the environment for production, employment and trade. A common market would also allow for the free movement of factors of production between the member nations, especially in terms of labour and capital (land is less mobile by its nature!). Given the importance of the public sector in a modern economy, a common market would also set common procurement policies across member governments, so that individual governments do not favour their own domestic firms when purchasing goods and services. The Single European Market has encompassed most of these features, although tax rates have not been harmonised across the countries that are included.

Economic and monetary union

An alternative form of integration is where countries choose to share a common currency, but without the degree of cooperation that is involved with a free trade area or common market. Such an arrangement is known as a **monetary union** or a *currency union*. Full **economic and monetary union** combines the common market arrangements with a shared currency (or permanently fixed exchange rates between the member

Key terms

common market a set of trading arrangements in which a group of countries remove barriers to trade among them, including adopting a common set of barriers against external trade and allowing free movement of factors of production

monetary union a situation in which countries adopt a common currency

economic and monetary union a set of trading arrangements the same as for a common market, but in addition having a common currency (or permanently fixed exchange rates between the member countries) and a common monetary policy

countries). This requires member states to follow a common monetary policy, and it is also seen as desirable to harmonise other aspects of macroeconomic policy across the union.

The adoption of permanently fixed exchange rates is a contentious aspect of proposals for economic and monetary union, as governments are no longer able to use monetary policy for internal domestic purposes. This is all very well if all countries in the union are following a similar economic cycle, but if one country becomes poorly synchronised with the others, there may be major problems.

For example, it could be that the union as a whole is enjoying a boom, and setting interest rates accordingly. For an individual member country suffering a recession, this could mean deepening and prolonging the recession, as it would not be possible to relax interest rates in order to allow aggregate demand to recover.

A successful economic and monetary union therefore requires careful policy coordination across the member nations. Notice that economic and monetary union involves fixed exchange rates between the member countries, but does not necessarily entail the adoption of a common currency, although this may follow at some stage.

Structural change

A feature that all of these forms of integration have in common is that they involve the removal of barriers to trade among member countries. It is important to be aware that not all parties will see this as a good thing. In order to benefit from increased specialisation and trade, countries need to allow the pattern of their production to change. The benefits to the expanding sectors are apparent, but it is also the case that industries that formerly enjoyed protection from competition will become exposed to competition, and will need to decline in order to allow resources to be transferred into the expanding sectors. This can be a painful process for firms that need to close down, or move into new markets, and for workers who may need to undergo retraining before they are ready for employment in the newly expanding parts of the economy.

An especially contentious area of debate in the UK concerns the structural change that has taken place in recent decades, in which manufacturing activity has declined and financial services have expanded. This seems to reflect the changing pattern of the UK's comparative advantage, in which banking, finance and insurance have become a major strength of the economy, whereas the manufacturing sector has found it more difficult to compete with the host of new entrants into this market from elsewhere in the world.

Trade creation and trade diversion

Such increased trade within a trading bloc is beneficial when there is **trade creation**. This is where the formation of the customs union allows countries to specialise more, and therefore to exploit their comparative advantage. The larger market for the goods means that more economies of scale may be available, and the lower prices that result generate additional trade between the member nations. These lower prices arise partly from the exploitation of comparative advantage, but also from the

---

Synoptic link

The interaction between the exchange rate system and monetary policy is discussed in Chapter 31.

Knowledge check 36.7

Why must member states under economic and monetary union follow a common monetary policy?

Exercise 36.2

Look back at Figure 28.3 on page 383, which shows how the structure of employee jobs in the UK changed between 1997 and 2018. Discuss whether the process of deindustrialisation that has taken place will benefit the economy in the long run.

Key term

trade creation the replacement of more expensive domestic production or imports with cheaper output from a partner within the trading bloc

removal of tariffs between the member nations. A country joining the bloc is able to replace more expensive domestic production or imports with cheaper output from a partner within the bloc.

Figure 36.4 illustrates the effects of trade creation. It shows the demand and supply of a good in a certain country that joins a customs union. Before joining the union, the price of the good is T, which includes a tariff element. Domestic demand is D_0, of which S_0 comes from domestic producers, and the remainder is imported. When the country joins the customs union, the tariff is removed and the domestic price falls to P. Consumers benefit from additional consumer surplus, given by the area $PTBG$. However, notice that not all of this is pure gain to the country. The area $PTAC$ was formerly part of producer surplus, so there has been a redistribution from domestic firms to consumers. $ABFE$ was formerly tariff revenue collected by the government, so this represents effectively a redistribution from government to consumers. The area ACE is a net gain for the country, as this represents resources that were previously used up in the production of the good, but which can now be used for other purposes. The area BFG also represents a welfare gain to the country.

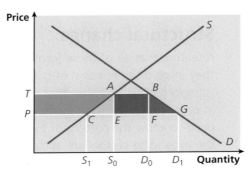

Figure 36.4 The effects of trade creation

However, it is also important to be aware that becoming a member of a customs union may alter the pattern of trading relationships. A country that is part of a customs union will be more inclined to trade with other members of the union because of the agreement between them, and because of the absence of internal tariffs. However, given the common external tariff, it is quite possible that members of the union are not the most efficient producers on the global stage. So there may be a situation of **trade diversion**. This occurs where a member country of a customs union imports goods from other members *instead* of from more efficient producers elsewhere in the world. This may mean that there is no net increase in trade, but simply a diversion from an external source to a new source within the union. In this situation, there are not necessarily the same gains from trade to be made.

Figure 36.5 helps to show the effects of trade diversion. Here, D represents the demand curve for a commodity that is initially imported from a country outside the customs union. It is assumed that the supply of the good from the non-member is perfectly elastic, as shown by S_n. However, the importing country imposes a tariff of the amount T, so the quantity imported is given by Q_n, and the price charged is $P_n + T$.

Key term

trade diversion the replacement of cheaper imported goods by goods from a less efficient trading partner within a bloc

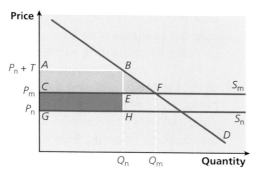

Figure 36.5 The effects of trade diversion

After the importing country joins the customs union, the tariff is removed, but the good is now imported from a less efficient producer within the union. The supply from this member country is assumed to be elastic at S_m, so the new price is P_m and the quantity is Q_m.

In examining the welfare effects, there are two issues to consider. First, notice that consumer surplus has increased by the area *ABFC*. However, this is not pure gain to the economy because, in the original position, the government was collecting tariff revenue of the amount *ABHG*. In other words, the increase in consumer surplus comes partly as a pure gain (the triangle *BFE*), but partly at the expense of the government (*ABEC*). This is not all, because the area *CEHG* was also formerly part of tariff revenue, but now is a payment by domestic consumers to producers in the other (member) country. This means that whether the country is better or worse off depends upon the relative size of the areas *BFE* (which is a gain) and *CEHG* (which is a loss).

Evaluation of tariffs and quotas

The UK relies heavily on trade with the EU. Figure 34.5 on page 467 shows the percentage of UK exports and imports with countries in the EU, with data going back to 1960. Between 1960 and 1973 (when the UK became a member of the EU), exports and imports rose from about 30% of the total to about 45%. After entry, trade with the EU expanded further. By the 1990s, exports to the EU comprised around 60% of the UK's exports, and imports slightly lower. It is therefore difficult to consider the UK in isolation from its European trading partners.

By joining the EU, the UK was able to benefit from trade creation, by increasing its trade with other countries in the union. It may also have run the danger of some trade diversion, by severing its trade links with its former trading partners. As the EU expanded, the opportunities for trade creation increased, especially when newly joining countries displayed a different pattern of comparative advantage to the existing members.

In any decision to join a customs union there is a need to balance the opportunity to benefit from trade creation against the dangers of trade diversion. A key question concerns the relative pattern of comparative advantage among the members of the customs union and the trading partners outside of it. In other words, does joining the customs union offer rich opportunities because of the nature of the other member

> **Knowledge check 36.8**
>
> Suppose that when a country becomes part of a trading bloc, it finds that it can replace goods that it previously imported with lower-priced goods produced within the bloc. Is this trade creation or trade diversion?

countries, so that trade creation becomes highly likely? Or do the member countries offer a more limited range of trading opportunities compared with existing partners outside of the union?

The USA under President Trump has taken a different attitude towards trade and tariffs, initiating a trade war against China. The driving force behind this has been the desire to insulate American industry against perceived unfair competition from China. The response from China led to an escalation of tariffs, from which consumers in the USA stand to lose the most.

The UK and Brexit

In the referendum vote of 23 June 2016, the British electorate voted to leave the EU. For the vast majority of economists, this came as a shock, as it seemed to fly in the face of economic arguments regarding the benefits gained from trade and closer integration of economies. While the rest of the world (apart from the USA) was globalising and moving towards closer interrelationships between countries, here was the UK seemingly moving in the opposite direction.

Those in favour of leaving the EU argued that membership of the Single Market imposed too many restrictions on the UK and prevented the formation of trade agreements with other countries. In other words, the UK could be better off leaving the EU (even if this meant facing tariffs on exports to Europe), as this then enables freer trade with other trading partners. With the UK outside the EU, the benefits previously gained through past trade creation will be diluted, so to succeed outside the union the UK government needs to find new options for trading with non-EU countries.

In the event, the vote was not based solely on economic principles. Political considerations and unease over a perceived growing inequality and immigration influenced voting behaviour. A further concern was sovereignty, and whether the UK should have fewer ties to European regulations.

The economic future of the UK economy depends upon the results of negotiations on the terms of exit, and on whether the UK is able to reach trade deals with countries outside the EU. Whatever the outcome, almost all economists agree that the long-term consequence of leaving the EU is negative. Some estimates suggested that even with a 'soft' Brexit, in which the UK remains in the Single Market (like Norway), UK households may be some 1.3% worse off. A harder Brexit under which the UK trades with the EU under WTO rules may leave households some 2.7% worse off. Research at the Centre for Economic Performance points out that if the likely effect on productivity and foreign direct investment is taken into account, then the long-run impact may be between 6.3% and 9.5%.

There are strong arguments to suggest there are potential gains from specialisation and trade. The challenge for the UK post-Brexit is to find a way of preserving and creating trading relationships that allow the country to continue to gain from international trade.

Exercise 36.3

Review recent progress with the Brexit process. How has the UK economy responded to changes in the global environment?

A harder Brexit could leave households around 2.7% worse off

Summary
- Economic integration can take a variety of forms, of differing degrees of closeness.
- A free trade area is where a group of countries agree to remove restrictions on trade between them, but without having a common external tariff.
- A customs union is a free trade area with an agreed common set of restrictions on trade with non-members.
- A common market is a customs union in which the member countries also agree to harmonise their policies in a number of key respects.
- Economic and monetary union entails fixed exchange rates between member countries, but not necessarily agreement to adopt a common currency.
- Closer economic integration can entail trade creation, in which member countries benefit from increased trade and specialisation.
- However, there may also be trade diversion, in which countries divert their trading activity from external trade partners to countries within the trading bloc.
- Trade diversion does not always bring gains, as the producers within the bloc are not necessarily more efficient than external producers.

The role of the World Trade Organization

The WTO (and its precursor the General Agreement on Tariffs and Trade (GATT)) have championed freer trade, and encouraged the removal of tariff barriers. Initially, Bretton Woods set up the GATT with a brief to oversee international trade. This entailed encouraging countries to reduce tariffs, but the GATT also provided a forum for trade negotiations and for settling disputes between countries. The GATT was replaced by the WTO in 1995. Between them, these organisations have presided over a significant reduction in the barriers to trade between countries — not only tariffs, but other forms of protection too.

The WTO also monitors the establishment and operations of trading blocs, and performs an important role in arbitrating in the case of disputes between countries that arise in relation to the conditions under which trade takes place.

The economic arguments in favour of allowing freer trade are strong, in the sense that there are potential gains to be made from countries specialising in the production of goods and services in which they have a comparative advantage. Globalisation facilitates and accelerates this process. And yet, there have sometimes been violent protests against globalisation, directed in particular at the WTO, whose meeting at Seattle in 1999 ended in chaos following demonstrations in the streets.

Tension has always been present during moves towards freer trade. Even if the economic arguments appear to be compelling, nations are cautious about opening up to free trade. In particular, there has been concern about jobs in the domestic economy. This is partly because there are transitional costs involved in liberalising trade, as some economic activities must contract to allow others to expand. Vested interests can then lead to lobbying and political pressure, as was apparent in the USA in the early part of the twenty-first century. There is also the question of whether globalisation will allow recession to spread more quickly between countries.

In many ways, the WTO gets caught in the middle. It has responsibility for encouraging moves towards free trade, and therefore comes under pressure from nations that want to keep some degree of protection because they are unwilling to undergo the transitional costs of structural change. The WTO therefore has the unpalatable job of protecting countries from themselves, enforcing short-term costs in the interests of long-term gains.

In 2000, new talks started covering agriculture and services. The fourth WTO Ministerial Conference in Doha in November 2001 incorporated these discussions into a broader work programme, the Doha Development Agenda. The WTO website indicates that this agenda includes work on non-agricultural tariffs, trade and environment, WTO rules such as anti-dumping and subsidies, investment, competition policy, trade facilitation, transparency in government procurement, intellectual property, and a range of issues raised by developing countries.

Progress on the Doha agenda has been far from smooth. This is partly because agriculture is an especially contentious area, with the USA, the EU and Japan having large-scale policies in place to support their agricultural sectors. In the case of the EU's Single Market, some moves have been made towards reforming the Common Agricultural Policy, but progress has not been as rapid as developing countries would like — remembering that agriculture is especially important for many of the LDCs. Reluctance on the part of the rich nations to provide concessions in these key areas, combined with determination on the part of LDCs to make genuine progress, results in a seeming deadlock.

The so-called 'Bali package' of measures was agreed in 2013, amid great optimism among ministers. This was followed by the 'Nairobi package' in December 2015, but the crucial issues surrounding agriculture remained, and President Trump's adversarial attitude towards the WTO before and after his election may have implications for the organisation's future.

The anti-globalisation protests are based on rather different arguments. One concern is that economic growth can proceed only at some cost to the environment. It has been argued that by fragmenting the production process, the cost to the environment is high. This is partly because the need to transport goods around the world uses up valuable resources. It is also argued that nations have an incentive to lower their environmental standards in order to attract multinational corporations by enabling low-cost production. This is not so much an argument against globalisation as an argument that an international agency is required to monitor global environmental standards.

It has also been suggested that it is the rich countries of the world that stand to gain most from increasing global trade, as they have the market power to ensure trading conditions work in their favour. Again, the WTO may have a role here in monitoring the conditions under which trade takes place. At the end of the day, trade allows an overall increase in global production and more choice for consumers. The challenge is to ensure that these gains are equitably distributed, and that the environment can be conserved.

Summary

- The World Trade Organization (WTO) has a responsibility to promote trade by pursuing reductions in tariffs and other barriers to trade, and also discharges a role in dispute settlement between nations.
- The transitional costs for individual economies in terms of the need for structural change have encouraged politicians to turn to protectionist measures.
- Critics of globalisation and the WTO have pointed to the environmental costs of rapid global economic growth and the expansion of trade, and have argued that it is rich countries and multinational corporations that gain the most, rather than less developed countries.

The European Union

The European Union (EU) is one of the most prominent examples of regional trade integration, and has progressed further than most in evolving towards economic and monetary integration. The UK joined the EU in 1973, but remained outside the euro area when it was established. The combined population of the EU28 member states in 2016 was more than 510 million, compared with 323 million in the USA.

From the moment of formation of the European Economic Community (EEC) in 1957, the member countries began working towards the creation of a single market in which there would be free movement of goods, services, people and capital. In other words, the idea was to create a *common market* in which there would be no barriers to trade. The EEC was a *customs union* in which internal tariffs and non-tariff barriers were to be removed and a common tariff was to be set against the rest of the world.

A package of measures that came into effect in January 1993 created the Single European Market (SEM). The key measures were the removal (or reduction) of border controls and the winding down of non-tariff barriers to trade within the EU. In this way, physical, technical and fiscal barriers were removed.

Tariff barriers between EU countries had been abolished, but a range of non-tariff barriers had built up over the years as countries sought to protect domestic employment. It was expected that the removal of these obstacles to trade, combined with the removal of border controls, would reduce the transactions costs of trade within the EU. However, it is not easy to quantify these gains.

As trade increases, firms will find that they are operating in a larger market. This should allow them to exploit more fully the economies of large-scale production. From society's point of view, this should lead to a more efficient use of resources, as long as the resulting trade creation effects are stronger than any trade diversion that may take place.

Firms find that they face more intense competition within that larger market from firms in other parts of the EU. This then brings up the same arguments that are used to justify privatisation — that intensified competition will cause firms or their managers to seek more efficient production techniques, perhaps through the elimination of X-inefficiencies. This again is beneficial for society as a whole.

The establishment of the SEM was seen by some as an end in itself, but others regarded it as a step towards full monetary integration, in which all member states would adopt a single currency, thereby reducing the transaction costs of international trade even more.

In the event, 12 countries (Austria, Belgium, Finland, France, Germany, Greece, Ireland, Italy, Luxembourg, the Netherlands, Portugal and Spain) formed the single currency (euro) area, which came into operation on 1 January 2002. Slovenia joined the Eurozone in 2007, followed by Cyprus and Malta in 2008, Slovakia in 2009, Estonia in 2011 and Latvia in 2014.

The operation of the euro area has not been trouble-free. A key issue is the inability to adopt independent macroeconomic policies when there is a common interest rate across the members. This caused some difficulty during the financial crisis, when the divergence between (for example) Germany and Greece became all too apparent.

Follow-up questions

a Identify the benefits that were expected to flow from the establishment of the EU.
b Explain why the adoption of the euro meant that member countries could not pursue an independent monetary policy. What problems could this cause?
c Explain how trade creation and trade diversion could affect the operation of the EU.

Case study 36.2

Tariff retaliation

Tariffs on international imports attempt to protect the employment levels within a country

Tariffs are the most common form of protectionist measure. In 2018, the USA was concerned about the effect that international trade was having on employment levels, and launched a series of tariff increases on a range of goods. This case study explores the possible implications of this situation.

Table 36.1 shows the gains that two countries could make under different tariff rates. The gains for Country A are shown in red and those for Country B are shown in blue.

To read the table, take the example of Country A first of all. If Country B imposes no tariff, then Country A receives 100 if it also imposes no tariff, but if Country B imposes a high tariff, Country A would only gain 30 if B imposes a high tariff.

Table 36.1 Tariffs

		Country B					
		No tariff		Medium tariff		High tariff	
Country A	No tariff	100	100	50	125	30	80
	Medium tariff	125	50	70	70	20	90
	High tariff	80	30	90	20	40	40

Follow-up questions

a Which combination of tariff levels would maximise the joint gains of the two countries?
b Which combination of tariff levels would represent the worst joint outcome for the two countries?
c Suppose that Country B imposes no tariff. What level of tariff would maximise the gain for Country A?
d If Country A goes ahead and imposes the tariff that would maximise its gain, what level of tariff would maximise the gain for Country B?
e If Country B imposes this level of tariff, what is Country A's best strategy?
f Discuss whether this situation is likely to apply in the event of a tariff war between the USA and its trading partners.

CHAPTER 36 QUESTIONS

A Multiple-choice questions

1 Which of the following would not be classed as protectionism?

   a   Introducing a tariff
   b   Introducing a quota
   c   Introducing a customs union
   d   Introducing a non-tariff barrier

2 A customs union would involve:

   a   The free movement of labour
   b   Tariffs between member countries
   c   A common currency
   d   A common external tariff

3 Trade creation involves:

   a   The replacement of more expensive domestic production or imports with cheaper goods produced by trading partners within the trading bloc
   b   The protection of a domestic market
   c   The replacement of cheaper imported goods with more expensive goods
   d   The creation of a common fiscal policy

B Knowledge and understanding questions

4 Explain what is meant by the term 'free trade area'. [2 marks]

5 Explain trade creation, with the aid of a diagram. [4 marks]

6 Explain, with the aid of a diagram, how a tariff could lead to trade diversion. [4 marks]

7 Explain **two** benefits to a country of increased protectionism. [6 marks]

C Stimulus response question

8 Albania (officially the Republic of Albania) lies in southeastern Europe. The country has sought membership of the EU economic union for many years — it applied for EU membership in 2009 and was granted 'candidate' status in 2014. The process is long and involves meeting many political, economic and social criteria before membership is granted.

   a   Explain what is meant by 'economic union'. [2 marks]
   b   Evaluate the potential advantages to Albania of membership of the EU economic union. [12 marks]

D Essay question

9 Evaluate the role of the WTO in promoting freer world trade. [25 marks]

SECTION
2

MACROECONOMICS

Part 10
The financial sector

Chapter 37

Money and interest rates

This chapter explores the role of money in the economy. It has often been argued that the quantity of money in the economy — and its rate of growth — are crucial in influencing the rate of inflation, and hence the overall performance of the economy. However, it has also been noted that money stock is difficult to define, measure, monitor and control. This chapter explains why this is the case, setting out the various sources of money and credit creation in a modern economy. It also discusses the main theories that seek to explain the importance of money in the macroeconomy. Finally, it outlines the way in which interest rates are determined.

Learning objectives

After studying this chapter, you should be able to:
- explain the functions and characteristics of money
- explain narrow and broad money in terms of liquidity
- explain the creation and supply of money
- explain the relationship between the money supply and the price level
- explain the Fisher equation of exchange
- explain, with the help of a diagram, the determination of interest rates

Money in the modern economy

Money plays an important role in the modern economy. However, Chapter 31 noted that the monetary authorities find it difficult to measure and monitor the amount of money in the economy, let alone try to control it directly. Why should this be? Part of the explanation is that there are many sources of money in a modern, open economy. In other words, it is not simply a question of measuring, monitoring and controlling the quantity of banknotes and coins in circulation.

Chapter 2 explained how money is important as a **medium of exchange**, enabling transactions to be undertaken efficiently. In order to fulfil this role, money must be something that is acceptable to both buyers and sellers. Nobody would accept money in payment for goods or services if they did not trust that they could proceed to use money for further transactions. Money must therefore also act as a **store of value**: it must be possible to use it for future transactions. This quality of money means that it can be used as one way of storing wealth for future purchases. Money also allows the value of goods, services and other assets to be compared — it provides a **unit of account**. In this sense, prices of goods reflect the value that society places on them, and must be expressed in money terms.

A further role for money is that it acts as a **standard of deferred payment**. For example, a firm may wish to agree a contract for the future

Key terms

money as a medium of exchange the function of money that enables transactions to take place

money as a store of value the function of money that enables it to be used for future transactions

money as a unit of account the function of money that allows the value of goods, services and other assets to be compared

money as a standard of deferred payment the function of money that allows contracts for payment at a future date to be agreed

delivery of a good, or may wish to hire a worker to be paid at the end of the month. Such contracts are typically agreed in terms of a money value.

All of these *functions of money* are important to the smooth operation of markets, and are crucial if prices are to fulfil their role in allocating resources within society.

To summarise, money performs four key roles, as:

1 a medium of exchange
2 a store of value
3 a unit of account
4 a standard of deferred payment

In order to fulfil these functions, money needs to have certain characteristics:

- *portability*: money must be easy to carry
- *divisibility*: money needs to be readily divided into small parts in order to undertake transactions
- *acceptability*: money must be generally acceptable if it is to act as a medium of exchange
- *scarcity*: money cannot be in unlimited supply, nor should it be able to be counterfeited
- *durability*: money needs to be able to withstand wear and tear in use
- *stability in value*: the value of money must remain reasonably stable over time if money is to act as a store of value

Many commodities have acted as money at various times in various circumstances. For example, cigarettes acted as money in prisoner of war camps during the Second World War. In parts of West Africa, slaves were used as money in historical periods — slaves were portable but were neither divisible nor durable.

Money supply

Synoptic link

Money supply was also discussed in Chapter 31 in the context of monetary policy.

The money supply is the quantity of money that is in circulation in the economy. The central bank is responsible for issuing notes and coins, which clearly have the key characteristics of money. However, there are

The Bank of England is responsible for issuing notes and coins in the UK

other financial assets that come very close to meeting the requirements to be regarded as 'money'. The quantity of money in the economy has an important influence on the overall price level (and its rate of change), as will be explained later in the chapter. This makes it important for the central bank to be able to measure and monitor the size of money supply.

It may be possible to measure and monitor the quantity of legal money such as cash and banknotes, but other assets that also fulfil the functions of money, such as bank deposits and other financial assets, are less straightforward to observe. This helps to explain why it is difficult to measure and monitor the amount of money in the economy. These other assets have varying degrees of **liquidity**. Liquidity refers to the ease with which an asset can be converted into a form in which it can be used to undertake a transaction.

Cash and banknotes are the most liquid assets, as they can be used for transactions directly. Current (chequing) accounts are almost as liquid, but although savings accounts in banks may also be quite quickly converted to cash, there may be a time delay or a cost involved. Shares or government bonds are much less liquid, as it takes time to convert them into cash. Nonetheless, they are examples of several types of assets that can be regarded as being near-money. The central bank can control the quantities of some of these assets, but not all.

Narrow and broad money

One traditional way of measuring the money stock was from the *monetary base*, which comprised all notes and coins in circulation. Together with the commercial banks' deposits at the Bank of England, this was known as **narrow money**, or **M0**. This was intended to measure the amount of money held for transactions purposes. However, with the increased use of electronic means of payment, M0 has become less meaningful as a measure, and the Bank of England stopped issuing data for M0 in 2005.

There are many assets that are 'near-money' that are highly liquid and can readily be converted into cash for transactions. **Broad money**, or **M4**, is a measure of the money stock that includes M0 together with sterling wholesale and retail deposits with monetary financial institutions such as banks. In other words, it includes all bank deposits that can be used for transactions, even though some of these deposits may require a period of notice for withdrawal. However, M4 is held not only for transactions purposes but also partly as a store of wealth.

Credit creation

Another complication for the monetary authorities is that the operations of commercial banks can influence the quantity of money. Banks accept deposits from their customers, and issue loans. The way in which they undertake lending has an impact on the quantity of money.

The credit creation multiplier

Think first of all about the way in which the money supply is created. This is not simply a question of controlling the amount of notes and coins the central bank issues. With so many different assets that act as near-money in a modern economy, the real picture is more complicated. The actions of the commercial banks also have implications for the size of money supply.

One of the reasons why it is difficult for a central bank to control the supply of money is the way that the commercial banks are able to create credit. Consider the way that commercial banks operate. They accept deposits from customers, and supply them with banking services. However, they also provide loans — and this is how they make profits.

Suppose that the government undertakes a piece of expenditure and finances it by issuing money. The firms receiving the payment from the government are likely to bank the money they receive, so bank deposits increase. From the perspective of the commercial banks, they know it is unlikely that all their customers will want to withdraw their money simultaneously, so they will lend out some of the additional deposits to borrowers, who are likely to undertake expenditure on goods or services. As their expenditures work their way back into the banking system, the commercial banks will find they can lend out even more, and so the process continues. In other words, an increase in the amount of money in the economy has a multiplied effect on the amount of credit the banks create. This process is known as the **credit multiplier**.

Consider an arithmetic example illustrated in Figure 37.1. Suppose that the commercial banks always act such as to hold 10% of their assets in liquid form — that is, as cash in the tills. If an extra £100 is lodged as deposits, the commercial banks will add £10 to the cash in tills, and lend out the remaining £90. When that £90 finds its way back into the hands of the bank, it will keep £9 as cash, and lend out the remaining £81. And so on. The process will stop when the bank is back to a cash ratio of 10%. The original extra £100 will have been converted into £100 in cash, and £900 in loans!

Figure 37.1 Credit creation

The value of the multiplier is given by 1 divided by the cash ratio that the commercial banks decide to hold. The smaller is this ratio, the larger is the credit multiplier. If the commercial banks want to hold only 5% of their assets in the form of cash, then the credit multiplier will be 1/0.05 = 20.

The significance of this relationship is that changes in the supply of cash have a multiplied impact on the amount of credit in the economy. This makes monetary control through money supply a highly imprecise business, especially if the central bank does not know exactly what the commercial banks' desired liquidity ratio is. In the past, one way that the monetary authorities tried to control money supply was to impose requirements on the proportion of assets that banks held in liquid form. However, this is also imprecise, as banks need not hold exactly the proportion required, in order to give themselves some leeway in the short run. This method of control was abandoned long ago, although the commercial banks are required to keep a small portion of their assets as cash at the Bank of England. This is purely for operational reasons.

Summary

- Money plays an important role in the macroeconomy, fulfilling functions as a medium of exchange, a store of value and a standard of deferred payment.
- There are several different sorts of assets that have the necessary characteristics to achieve these functions.
- Money supply is difficult to measure or control because money can be generated from a range of sources.
- Commercial banks can influence money supply through their lending policy via the credit multiplier.

Money and inflation

Why should the quantity of money or credit in circulation be so important? The classical economists argued that there was a close relationship between money supply and the price level, and that prices can only increase persistently if money supply itself increases persistently, or if money supply persistently grows more rapidly than real output.

The Fisher equation of exchange

The overall price level comes to be determined through the mechanism of the quantity theory of money in classical thinking. To explain this requires a new concept, that of the **velocity of circulation (V)**. If the money supply is defined as the quantity of money (notes and coins) in circulation in the economy, the velocity of circulation is defined as the speed with which that money supply changes hands. It is defined as the volume of transactions divided by the money supply.

In practice, the volume of transactions is seen as being represented by nominal income, which is the level of real income (Y) multiplied by the average price level (P). If V is the velocity of circulation, and M is the size of the money supply, then the following equation holds:

$$V = PY/M$$

Key terms

velocity of circulation (V) the rate at which money changes hands, the volume of transactions divided by money supply

Fisher equation of exchange specifies the relationship between money supply (M), the velocity of circulation (V), the price level (P) and real income (Y), namely $MV = PY$

Notice that this is just a definition, sometimes known as the **Fisher equation of exchange**, after the American economist Irving Fisher. Multiplying both sides of the equation by M gives:

$$MV = PY$$

Knowledge check 37.3

In a particular year, nominal income in an economy is £3,600 million and money supply is £720 million. What is the velocity of circulation?

Exercise 37.1

In the equation $MV = PY$, define each of the terms and explain the assumptions that a classical economist would make about each of them. To what extent would you accept these assumptions as describing a modern economy?

In a classical world, the velocity of circulation (V) would be constant — or at least would be stable over time. Furthermore, real output would always tend rapidly towards the natural rate. These assumptions together with the $MV = PY$ equation provide us with a direct link between money (M) and the overall price level (P). This relationship suggests that prices can only increase persistently if money supply itself increases persistently, and that money (and prices) have no effect on real output.

To summarise, the analysis suggests that although a price rise can be triggered on either the supply side or the demand side of the macroeconomy, persistent inflation can arise only through persistent excessive growth in the money stock, which can be seen in terms of persistent movements of the aggregate demand curve.

How can we interpret this in terms of aggregate demand and aggregate supply? If the money supply increases, then firms and households in the economy find they have excess cash balances — that is, for the given price level they have stronger purchasing power than they had anticipated. Their impulse will therefore be to increase spending, which will cause the aggregate demand curve to move to the right. They will probably also save some of the excess, which will tend to result in lower interest rates — which then reinforces the increase in aggregate demand. However, as the AD curve moves to the right, the equilibrium price level will rise, and return the economy to equilibrium.

Figure 37.2 illustrates this in the case of a neoclassical long-run aggregate supply — recall that the AS curve would be vertical at the full employment level under neoclassical assumptions. If aggregate demand begins at AD_0, and then shifts to AD_1, the figure shows that price increases from P_0 to P_1, but real output remains unchanged at Y_{FE}.

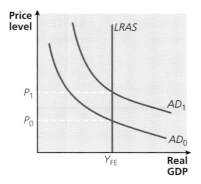

Figure 37.2 A monetary expansion

If money supply continues to increase, the process repeats itself, with price then rising persistently. One danger of this is that people get so accustomed to the process that they speed up their spending decisions, and this accelerates the whole process. Inflation could then accelerate out of control.

To summarise, the analysis suggests that persistent inflation can only arise through persistent excessive growth in the money stock, which can be seen in terms of persistent movements of the aggregate demand curve.

Quantitative skills 37.2

Real and nominal interest rates

It is worth being aware that when there is inflation in an economy, there is an important distinction between nominal and real interest rates. The stated rate of return on a financial asset represents the nominal return. For example, if you invest £100 now at an annual fixed rate of 5%, you expect to receive £105 in a year's time. However, if inflation has been proceeding at 2% per annum over that year, the value of your investment has been eroded by that 2% increase in prices. The *real rate of interest* is therefore the net return after allowing for inflation. This can be approximated as the difference between the nominal rate and the inflation rate. In the above example, the real rate of interest would be 5 − 2 = 3%.

Knowledge check 37.4

If inflation was 40.9% and the (nominal) interest rate was 31.2%, what would be the real interest rate?

Exercise 37.2

Sketch an *AD/AS* diagram with a Keynesian shape for aggregate supply. Discuss the extent to which this produces different results from those outlined above when there is an increase in money supply.

Extension material

Evaluation of the Fisher equation

How significant is the quantity theory relationship in understanding the operation of the macroeconomy?

Remember that the equation of exchange is a definition, and only becomes a theory if some assumptions are made. The strength of the theory therefore rests on the validity of those assumptions — namely, that the velocity of circulation is constant and that real output would always tend to the natural rate. This goes back to the debate between the neoclassical and Keynesian schools. The former argued that the economy would always return to equilibrium rapidly. The stability of the velocity of circulation is closely related to the stability of the demand for money relationship, and the

monetarists thought this would be stable — if it existed at all. The Keynesians, on the other hand, did not believe that the economy would always return to equilibrium, and thought that the demand for money (and hence the velocity of circulation) could be quite volatile. Under these assumptions, the direct relationship between money and the price level would be broken.

Either way, the difficulty of identifying money supply makes it difficult to explore the real-world relationship between money and prices. The rapidity of technological progress in financial markets has complicated things even more.

Summary

- The quantity theory suggests that there is a direct relationship between money and the overall price level.
- Persistent inflation can only occur if money supply persistently grows more rapidly than real incomes.
- The validity of the quantity theory relationship depends upon the validity of the underpinning assumptions.

The determination of interest rates

Chapter 31 introduced the idea that the equilibrium interest rate could be seen as being determined by the intersection of the demand for and the supply of money and that the interest rate can be interpreted as the opportunity cost of holding money.

The demand for money

There are three key motives for holding money: the transactions demand, the precautionary demand and the speculative demand. Between them they determine the demand for money.

The transactions demand for money

The first motive for holding money is clear — people and firms will hold money in order to undertake transactions. This is related to the need to use money when buying goods and services, and is closely associated with the functions of money as a medium of exchange and a unit of account. The demand for money for this purpose will mainly be determined by the level of income, because it is the level of income that will determine how many transactions people and firms will wish to undertake. The rate of interest (the opportunity cost of holding money) may be less important than income in this instance.

The precautionary demand for money

People and firms may also hold money for precautionary reasons. They may wish to have liquid assets available in order to guard against a sudden need to cover an emergency payment, or to take advantage of a spending opportunity at some point in the future. The opportunity cost of holding money may come into play here, as if the return on financial assets is high, people may be less inclined to hold money in a relatively liquid form.

The speculative demand for money

The rate of interest may affect the demand for money through another route. If share (or bond) prices are low (and the rate of interest paid is therefore high), then the opportunity cost of holding money is high, and people and firms will tend to hold shares. On the other hand, when the interest rate is low, and share prices are high, people will be more likely to hold money. This effect will be especially strong when people and firms see share prices as being unreasonably high, so that they expect them to fall. In this case, they may speculate by selling bonds in order to hold money, in anticipation of taking advantage of future expected falls in the price of bonds.

Liquidity preference

If the interest rate may be regarded as being the opportunity cost of holding money, it can be argued that economic agents, whether households or firms, will display a demand for money, arising from the functions that money fulfils in a modern economy. This theory of **liquidity preference**, as it is known, was noted by Keynes in his *General Theory*. Figure 31.1 (see page 427) illustrates what is implied for the money market. It is expected that the demand for money will be lower when the rate of interest rate is relatively high, as the opportunity cost of holding money is high. People will be more reluctant to forgo the rate of return that has to be sacrificed by holding money. When the rate of interest is relatively low, this will be less of a concern, so the demand for money will be relatively high. This suggests that the money demand curve (*MD*) will be downward sloping. If money supply is fixed at *M** in Figure 31.1, then the money market will be in equilibrium at the rate of interest *r**.

The existence of this relationship means that the monetary authorities have to be aware of the need to maintain (or allow) equilibrium in the money market. Interest rates and money supply cannot be fixed independently. This is a clear constraint on the use of monetary policy.

An important question is the extent to which the demand for money is stable. If money demand were to be volatile, moving around from one time period to the next, then it would be virtually impossible for the monetary authorities to have any precise control over the market. The situation is further complicated by the way that interest rates influence behaviour. The degree to which the demand for money is sensitive to the rate of interest will also be important. This will be reflected in the shape of the *MD* curve. Notice that because the level of income is also important in determining money demand, this will affect the *position* of the *MD* curve in the diagram. An increase in income will lead to a rightward shift in money demand, as people and firms will require larger money holdings when incomes are higher.

The market for loanable funds

Although the rate of interest can be interpreted as being the opportunity cost of holding money, this is not the only way of viewing it. From a firm's point of view, it may be seen as the cost of borrowing. For example, suppose that a firm is considering undertaking an investment project. The rate of interest represents the cost of borrowing the funds needed in order to finance the investment. The higher the rate of interest is, the less will investment projects be seen as being profitable. If the firm is intending to finance its investment from past profits, the interest rate is still pertinent, as it then represents the return that the firm could obtain by purchasing a financial asset instead of undertaking the investment. Either way, the rate of interest is important in the decision-making process.

The rate of interest is also important to households, to whom it may represent the return on saving. Households may be encouraged to save more if the return on their saving is relatively high, whereas when the rate of interest is low, the incentive to save is correspondingly low. Within the circular flow of income, expenditure and output, it is the flow of saving from households that enables firms to obtain the funds needed for their investment expenditure. It is now apparent that the rate of interest may play an important role in bringing together these flows.

The **market for loanable funds** is shown in Figure 37.3. The investment schedule is shown as downward sloping, because firms will find more investment projects to be worthwhile when the rate of interest rate is low. The savings schedule is shown to be upward sloping because a higher rate of interest is expected to encourage households to supply more saving. In other words, the supply of loanable funds will be higher when the rate of interest rate is relatively high.

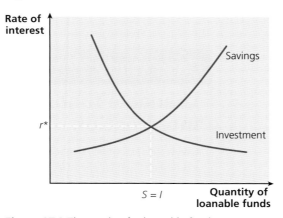

Figure 37.3 The market for loanable funds

Keynes believed that this could lead to instability in financial markets. He argued that investment and saving would be relatively insensitive to the rate of interest, such that the schedules in Figure 37.3 would be relatively steep. Investment would depend more crucially on firms' expectations about the future demand for their products, which could be volatile, moving the investment schedule around and so leading to instability in the rate of interest. Keynes therefore came to the conclusion that governments should manage aggregate demand in order to stabilise the economy.

The interest rate and the central bank

The discussion in this section has described how interest rates are determined in a way that allows the money market to be in equilibrium. In practice, the situation is complicated by the way that the central bank uses the interest rate as a way of influencing aggregate demand and stabilising the economy.

By setting bank rate, the central bank influences other interest rates on the range of financial assets, as the commercial banks take a lead from changes in bank rate. During the financial crisis, the Bank of England also influenced money supply through its use of quantitative easing.

Summary

- People and firms within the economy choose to hold money for certain purposes.
- The demand for money reflects transactions, precautionary and speculative motivations.
- The rate of interest can be regarded as the opportunity cost of holding money.
- Keynes developed liquidity preference theory, showing how the demand for money would be related to the rate of interest.
- It has been argued that both investment and saving depend upon the rate of interest.
- The rate of interest is important in determining equilibrium of saving and investment within the market for loanable funds.

Case study 37.1

Loanable funds and government intervention

Given the lack of physical capital in many developing countries, governments have been keen to encourage higher rates of investment. Given that investment depends partly upon the cost of borrowing, one policy that has been used is to hold interest rates below their equilibrium so that firms can borrow at attractive rates and so undertake investment.

Follow-up question

Use a diagram showing equilibrium in the market for loanable funds (as was illustrated in Figure 37.3). Discuss how the market would be affected by the policy described. Do you think that such a policy would be effective?

CHAPTER 37 QUESTIONS

A Multiple-choice questions

1 Which of the following is not a function of money?

   a A medium of exchange

   b A store of value

   c A flow of wealth

   d A standard of deferred payment

2 To fulfil its function, money must be:

   a Scarce

   b Unacceptable

   c Indivisible

   d Unstable

3 The Fisher equation of exchange states:

   a Prices multiplied by income equals money multiplied by credit

   b Prices multiplied by income equals credit multiplied by velocity

   c Prices multiplied by income equals money multiplied by velocity

   d Prices multiplied by income equals investment multiplied by credit

B Revision questions

4 Explain the relationship between money supply and the price level. [2 marks]

5 Explain the difference between narrow and broad money. [2 marks]

6 Explain, with the aid of a diagram, how interest rates may be determined using the theory of liquidity preference. [6 marks]

7 Explain, with the aid of a diagram, how interest rates may be determined using the theory of loanable funds. [6 marks]

C Stimulus response question

8 Is money changing? When was the last time you worried about having some coins and notes in your pocket before you left the house? Many more people are turning away from traditional forms of payment and using contactless payment, even for small purchases. If you drive up to a McDonald's window, you are likely to see many cars ahead of you paying not with cash but with a simple tap of their card, smartphone or smartwatch.

It has been reported that in 2018, UK shops saw more contactless payments than any other type of 'in-store' payment, and this is only likely to increase in the future.

   a Explain how contactless payment systems demonstrate **two** of the characteristics of money. [4 marks]

   b Explain how contactless payment may **not** demonstrate **two** of the characteristics of money. [4 marks]

Chapter 38

The financial sector

The financial sector has been seen as a crucial part of the macroeconomy, especially since the financial crisis of the late 2000s. For developing and emerging economies, the need to be able to raise finance for investment and for development projects is paramount. The lack of a fully functioning stock market or extensive networks of branch banks acts as a constraint on the development process, especially in rural areas where many households face a struggle for survival. This chapter explores the importance of savings and investment for economic growth and human development, and how access to finance can be accomplished.

> ## Learning objectives
>
> After studying this chapter, you should be able to:
> - explain the role of the financial sector
> - explain the role of savings and investment in promoting economic development
> - explain the Harrod–Domar model
> - explain microfinance
> - evaluate the role of the financial sector in promoting economic development

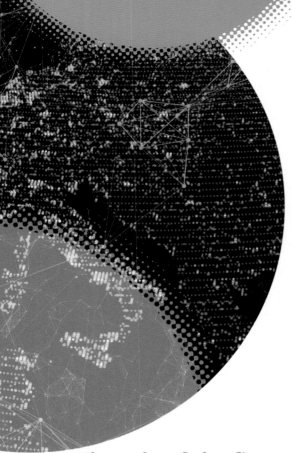

The role of the financial sector

The financial sector provides the environment in which economic activity takes place, which entails a number of key roles.

> ### Knowledge check 38.1
>
> Why is investment so important for the economy?

Facilitating saving

Individuals need to undertake saving, and businesses and individuals need to be able to borrow. It is through financial markets that savings can be mobilised for investment.

Individuals (and firms) wish to save for various reasons. It may be that a household needs to accumulate funds for future spending. This may partly depend upon where an individual is in the life cycle. When young, there may be a need to save in order to have a deposit on a house. Savings may also be needed to support people in retirement. The financial sector offers opportunities for people to earn a return through saving, and so have funds for later purposes. At current rates of interest, the returns may not provide a strong incentive for this.

Facilitating borrowing

The other side of the coin is that firms – and households – wish to borrow. Financial markets therefore provide opportunities to obtain loans.

Synoptic link

A simple version of the circular flow model was introduced in Chapter 19.

Synoptic link

Barter as a means of undertaking transactions was discussed in Chapter 2 — it is not a practicable way of allowing an economy to operate. Hyperinflation and the costs of inflation were discussed in Chapter 25.

This was seen in the circular flow model, where the savings behaviour of households enables firms to borrow in order to finance their investment.

Again, the rate of interest is important, as this represents the cost of borrowing. Firms will borrow for investment as long as the rate of return on the investment exceeds the cost of borrowing. Households will borrow in order to undertake expenditures, but will also need to be aware of the cost of borrowing.

Facilitating the exchange of goods and services

On a practical level, financial markets need to facilitate the transactions that take place with the exchange of goods and services. The importance of this can be seen by observing behaviour in countries that have experienced hyperinflation. When inflation reaches very high levels, people begin to try to avoid using money for transactions. Firms have to keep changing their prices, and people go frequently to the bank rather than keeping cash in their pockets. The transactions costs of this behaviour are high, and underline the importance of having stable financial systems in order to facilitate transactions.

Knowledge check 38.2

What is the term used by economists to describe the situation in which individuals visit the bank frequently in order to minimise their cash holdings?

Forward markets

Financial markets that operate in the modern economy also enable transactions to be conducted on the basis of contracts for future delivery — these are known as *forward* or *futures markets*. These are especially important in relation to transactions in certain commodities and in foreign exchange. Such arrangements are a way in which economic agents can reduce the riskiness of transactions.

An example is a where a manufacturing enterprise needs to buy commodities as inputs to its production process. Given the volatility of some commodity prices, there is uncertainty about the prices that will hold in future periods. Futures markets can help by allowing firms to contract forward to buy the commodities they know they will need at a future period at an agreed price at that agreed future date.

Commonly used futures markets include commodities such as oil, grain or precious metals — or foreign exchange. An airline may buy fuel forward. Firms that rely on imported inputs may use the futures market for foreign currency that they know they will need for future transactions.

Knowledge check 38.3

Why might commodity prices be volatile?

The market for equities

The market for equities is also an important part of the modern financial system, by which firms can obtain funds through the stock market for their investment plans. The whole business of insurance and pension funds is based on the existence of stock markets. This allows investors to buy a stake in businesses that they see as offering the potential for future profits.

The New York Stock Exchange, the world's largest stock trading platform

The financial sector in emerging and developing countries

Developing countries face particular problems in relation to the financial sector. Formal financial institutions are less well equipped to provide financial services. Stock markets may not exist, or may not function effectively. The provision of banking services to rural areas is fraught with difficulties. The banks are not readily able to assess the credit-worthiness of potential borrowers. There is a situation of asymmetric information here, as the borrowers have much better information about the riskiness of proposed projects than the banks can obtain, so are likely to be charged high interest rates. Property rights may be weak, so that borrowers cannot provide collateral that the banks would accept. This forces borrowers into the informal market, where local moneylenders have monopoly power and can charge exorbitant rates of interest.

Summary

- Financial institutions provide the key link between borrowers and lenders, facilitating saving and borrowing.
- The exchange of goods and services is an important role for the financial system.
- At times, it is useful for economic agents to agree transactions to be undertaken at a future date, so the existence of forward markets is a role for the financial system.
- The market for equities is also an important part of a modern financial system.
- Financial markets in developing countries may not be able to fulfil the key roles needed for development.

Saving and investment

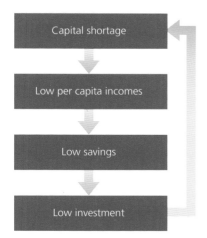

Figure 38.1 A low-level equilibrium trap

> **Knowledge check 38.4**
>
> Explain why a shortage of capital means low per capita income.

> **Key term**
>
> **Harrod–Domar model** a model of economic growth that emphasises the importance of savings and investment

For developing and emerging economies, a high priority is to enable economic growth to take place. Resources are needed to tackle poverty and provide the physical and social infrastructure required for human development. One way of viewing economic growth is as a shift in aggregate supply. This suggests that the focus must be on investment, which is necessary to enable an increase in productive capacity. If investment is to take place, then saving is also necessary in order to provide the finance for investment.

Furthermore, a country in which there are high levels of poverty, and in which many households face low income-earning opportunities, needs to devote much of its resources to consumption. The question for developing countries is, therefore, how to overcome this problem in order to kick-start a process of economic growth.

Figure 38.1 illustrates the problem. A shortage of capital means low per capita income, which means low savings, which in turn means low investment, limited capital, and hence low per capita incomes. In this way a country can get trapped in a *low-level equilibrium* situation.

For both developed and developing countries, the potential productive capacity of the economy depends fundamentally on two things: the quantity of factors of production available within the economy, and the efficiency with which they are utilised. By increasing the quantity and/or quality of the factors of production and their productivity, the aggregate supply curve can be shifted to the right.

For the developing countries, the problem is magnified because of lack of resources. In many cases, human capital is low, and there are limited resources to devote to education, training and improving health. Capital tends to be scarce, and the flows of foreign direct investment (FDI) — especially to the poorest countries — are relatively low. Markets do not operate effectively to allocate resources efficiently. There are therefore many obstacles to be overcome in seeking to promote growth and development. So, how can savings be mobilised to enable investment?

The Harrod–Domar model

This idea is supported by the **Harrod–Domar model** of economic growth, which first appeared in separate articles by Roy Harrod in the UK and Evsey Domar in the USA in 1939. This model was to become significant in influencing developing countries' attitudes towards the process of economic growth. It was developed in an attempt to determine how equilibrium could be achieved in a growing economy.

The basic finding of the model was that an economy can remain in equilibrium through time only if it grows at a particular rate. This unique stable growth path depends on the savings ratio and the productivity of capital. Any deviation from this path will cause the economy to become unstable. This finding emphasised the importance of savings in the process of economic growth, and led to the conclusion that a country seeking economic growth must first increase its flow of savings.

Figure 38.2 illustrates the process that leads to growth in a Harrod–Domar world. Savings are crucial in enabling investment to be undertaken — always remembering that some investment will have to be used

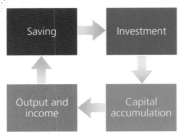

Figure 38.2 The Harrod–Domar process of economic development

Study tip

This is quite a useful schematic diagram describing the process of economic growth, as long as you remember all the ways in which it may fail to work smoothly.

Key terms

foreign exchange gap a situation in which a developing country is unable to import the goods that it needs for development because of a shortage of foreign exchange

capital flight a situation in which savings generated in a developing country are invested abroad

to replace existing capital that has worn out. Investment then enables capital to accumulate and technology to be improved. The accumulation of capital leads to an increase in output and incomes, which leads to a further flow of savings, and the cycle begins again. This figure highlights a number of problems that may prevent the Harrod–Domar process from being effective for developing countries.

Generating a flow of savings in a developing country may be problematic. When incomes are low, households may have to devote most of their resources to consumption, and so there may be a lack of savings.

Even if a flow of savings can be generated, it is then important to transform the savings into investment. This is the process by which the sacrifice of current consumption leads to an increase in productive capacity in the future. However, in many developing countries financial markets are undeveloped, so it is much more difficult for funds to be recycled into investment.

A further prerequisite for savings to be converted into investment is that there must be entrepreneurs with the ability to identify investment possibilities, the skill to carry them through and the willingness to bear the risk. Such entrepreneurs are in limited supply in many developing countries.

For investment to be productive in terms of raising output and incomes in the economy, it is crucial for firms to have access to physical capital, which will raise production capacity. Given their limited capability of producing capital goods, many developing countries have to rely on capital imported from the more developed countries. This may be beneficial in terms of upgrading home technology, but such equipment can be imported only if the country has access to the foreign currency to pay for it. One of the most pressing problems for many countries is that they face a **foreign exchange gap** — in other words, they find it difficult to earn sufficient foreign exchange with which to obtain imports of capital and other inputs, required in order to allow manufacturing activity to expand. In order to do this, physical capital is needed, together with key inputs to the production process. Indeed, many developing countries need to import food and medical supplies in order to develop their human capital. Human capital, in the form of skilled, healthy and well-trained workers, is as important as physical capital if investment is to be productive. A shortage of foreign exchange may therefore make it difficult for the country to accumulate capital.

Another problem in mobilising savings generated domestically is that potential investors may perceive that they can get a higher return by investing in foreign companies abroad rather than domestically. This process is known as **capital flight**. It may be reinforced if the country has encouraged FDI by multinational corporations (MNCs). These companies may attract funds from domestic investors. Furthermore, the capital flight may often be augmented when MNCs repatriate their profits to overseas shareholders.

In principle, it might be thought that today's developing and emerging economies have an advantage over the countries that developed in earlier periods. In particular, they can learn from earlier mistakes, and import technology that has already been developed, rather than having to develop it anew. This suggests that a *convergence* process should be going on, whereby countries are able to adopt technology that has already been produced, and thereby grow more rapidly and begin to close the gap with the more developed countries.

However, by and large this has not been happening for those countries that remain under-developed, and a lack of human capital has been suggested as one of the key reasons for the failure. This underlines the importance of education in laying the foundations for economic growth as well as contributing directly to the quality of life.

Harrod–Domar and external resources

Figure 38.3 extends the earlier schematic presentation of the process underlying the Harrod–Domar model of economic growth. This has been amended to underline the importance of access to technology and human capital.

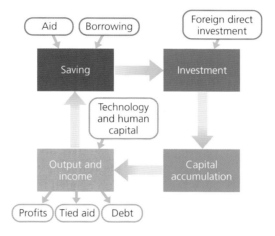

Figure 38.3 The Harrod–Domar process of economic development augmented

Can a developing country supplement its domestic savings with a flow of funds from abroad? Figure 38.3 identifies three possible injections into the Harrod–Domar process. First, it might be possible to attract flows of overseas assistance from higher-income countries. Second, perhaps the amount of investment could be augmented directly by persuading MNCs to engage in FDI. Third, the developing country might be able to borrow on international capital markets to finance its domestic investment.

It is worth noting that each of these ways of attracting external resources has a downside associated with it. As far as overseas assistance is concerned, in the past such flows have been seen by some donor countries as part of trade policy, and have brought less benefit to developing countries than had been hoped. In the case of the MNCs, there is a tendency for the profits to be repatriated out of the country, rather than recycled into the economy. Finally, international borrowing has to be repaid at some future date, and many developing countries have found themselves burdened by debt that they can ill afford to repay. This became a major problem to the extent that the World Bank launched the Heavily Indebted Poor Countries (HIPC) Initiative to tackle unsustainable debt through debt forgiveness. Debt levels became more manageable during the 2000s.

Knowledge check 38.5

Under what conditions could international borrowing be successful in raising economic growth in a developing country?

Exercise 38.1

Discuss the extent to which developing countries can gain from international flows of financial capital.

Summary

- Although development is a broader concept than economic growth, growth is a key ingredient of development.
- The Harrod–Domar model of economic growth highlights the importance of savings, and of transforming savings into productive investment.
- However, where markets are underdeveloped, this transformation may be impeded.
- Human capital is also a critical ingredient of economic growth.
- If resources cannot be generated within the domestic economy, a country may need to have recourse to external sources of funding.

Microfinance

For many developing countries, a particular problem has been the provision of finance for small (but important) projects in rural areas. Where a large portion of the population live in the rural areas, the difficulty of raising funds for investment has been an impediment to improving agricultural productivity — in spite of the significance of this sector in many developing countries.

There are elements of market failure in rural credit markets. In particular, there is an information failure. In the absence of branch banking, people in the rural areas do not have access to the formal financial sector. The commercial banks based in the urban areas do not have the information needed to be able to assess loan applications for rural projects. Furthermore, property rights are not secure, so it may be difficult to provide collateral against loans, when ownership of land cannot be proved.

This means that many people in the rural areas are forced to depend upon informal markets for credit, borrowing from local moneylenders or merchants at high, sometimes punitive, interest rates. The rates of interest in the informal sector tend to be much higher than are available in the formal sector, partly because of the risk premium, with it being difficult to assess the probability of default. In addition, local moneylenders may have monopoly power, as people in a village may not be able to access other sources of finance.

Attempts have been made to remedy this situation through **microfinance** schemes. This approach was pioneered by the Grameen Bank, which was founded in Bangladesh in 1976. The bank made small-scale loans to groups of women who otherwise would have had no access to credit, and each group was made corporately responsible for paying back the loan. The scheme has claimed great success, both in terms of the constructive use of the funds in getting small-scale projects off the ground and in terms of high pay-back rates.

Key term

microfinance schemes that provide finance for small-scale projects in developing countries

The Grameen Bank

Workers at a garment factory in Dhaka, Bangladesh

In 1974, a severe famine afflicted Bangladesh, and a flood of starving people converged on the capital city, Dhaka. Muhammad Yunus was an economics professor at Chittagong University. He tells how he was struck by the extreme contrast between the neat and abstract economic theories that he was teaching, and the plight of those surviving in bare poverty, or suffering and dying in the famine.

He also tells how he decided to study the problem at first hand, taking his students on field trips into villages near to the campus. On one of these visits they interviewed a woman who was struggling to earn a living by making bamboo stools. For each stool that she made, she had to borrow the equivalent of 15p for the raw materials. Once she had paid back the loan, at interest rates of up to 10% per week, her profit margin was just 1p. The woman was never able to escape from her situation because she was trapped by the need to borrow, and the need to pay back at such punitive rates of interest. Her story was by no means unique, and Yunus was keen to find a way of enabling women like her to have access to credit on conditions that would allow them to escape from poverty. He began experimenting by lending out some of his own money to groups in need.

Muhammad Yunus launched the Grameen Bank experiment in 1976. The idea was to provide credit for small-scale income-generating activities. Loans would be provided without the need for collateral, with borrowers being required to form themselves into groups of five with joint responsibility for the repayments. The acceptance of this joint responsibility and the lack of collateral helped to minimise the transaction costs of making and monitoring the loans.

On any criteria, the project proved an enormous success. The repayment record has been impressive, although the Grameen Bank charges interest rates close to those in the formal commercial sector, which are much lower than those of the informal moneylenders. Since the initial launch of the bank, lending has been channelled primarily to women borrowers, who are seen to invest more carefully and to repay more reliably — and to be most in need.

After 20 years of operation, more than $2.4 billion had been loaned by Grameen Bank, including more than 2 million loans for milch cows, nearly 100,000 for rickshaws, 57,000 for sewing machines and many more for processing, agriculture, trading, shop keeping, peddling and other activities. By mid-2015, $17.3 billion had been disbursed, and by the end of 2017, Grameen had 8.93 million borrowers, 97% of whom were women. The Bank covered more than 97% of villages in Bangladesh.

As for the impact of Grameen loans in economic terms, the loans are seen to have generated new employment, to have reduced the number of days workers are inactive, and to have raised income, food consumption and living conditions of Grameen Bank members — not to mention their social impact on the lives of millions of women.

Muhammad Yunus and the Grameen Bank were awarded the Nobel peace prize in 2006.

Exercise 38.2

Identify ways in which market failure has caused problems in the provision of small-scale credit for projects in developing countries.

How successful has the microfinance movement been? The Grameen Bank has provided finance to many people in many parts of the world. Attempts to replicate the Grameen model have also had some success, but in many cases have struggled to be sustainable in funding terms, needing support from governments or non-governmental organisations (NGOs). It has been argued that some banks operating on the Grameen model have had to rely on substantial subsidies to remain viable.

Summary

- The provision of credit in developing countries is problematic, especially in rural areas.
- This is partly due to forms of market failure.
- In the absence of access to formal credit arrangements, the informal market operates, charging high interest rates relative to the formal sector.
- Microfinance is one way in which attempts have been made to provide credit for small projects in developing countries.
- The Grameen Bank in Bangladesh pioneered such methods, using group-lending schemes focusing on women.

Evaluation of the financial sector in development

The Harrod–Domar approach suggests that saving and investment are crucial ingredients for a strategy to promote economic growth and human development. If funds cannot be raised domestically, then an injection of funds from abroad will be necessary, in the form of FDI, overseas assistance or borrowing on international financial markets.

Whichever approach is adopted, the financial sector is vital as a way of channelling the resources to where they are needed. This needs to be accomplished in a way that addresses areas of market failure. Rural credit markets may need specific attention, but funds also need to be provided for improvements in physical and social infrastructure that will then enable markets to operate effectively. In other words, funds are needed for physical infrastructure such as road and communication links, market facilities and so on. In addition, it is important to be able to invest in human capital, by providing education and healthcare and ensuring adequate nutrition for the population.

All this is challenging for developing countries with limited resources. Where the financial sector has been able to work effectively, countries have been able to show progress on many fronts. This has been evident in the emerging economies. The economies that entered a period of rapid growth in the 1960s found ways of mobilising funds. For example, both Korea and Singapore laid the foundations for rapid growth by finding ways of encouraging saving, the funds from which were then channelled into productive investment and infrastructure. More recently, China's success in mobilising FDI has been one of the key factors in enabling growth.

In sub-Saharan Africa, economic growth has been more elusive. Financial markets have not developed to the same extent as in East Asia, nor have stock markets flourished. Such funds as have been generated — for example, through overseas assistance or international borrowing — have not always been used effectively.

However, there are some encouraging signs for countries in sub-Saharan Africa. Some countries were able to maintain some momentum of growth through the period of global recession, and have made progress in alleviating poverty (although there is still a long way to go).

Some progress has also been made in the financial sector, from what may be a surprising source. The use of mobile phones has expanded in many African countries. This has given people in rural areas access to market information, so that they can make better judgements about what is a fair price for their produce. Mobile phone technology has also provided a way of handling transactions previously denied because of lack of access to the formal financial sector. This is in spite of the fact that relatively few people may own their own mobile phones. Entrepreneurs in some villages make a living from renting out their mobile phones or undertaking transactions.

Mobile phone use is on the rise in rural Africa

However, to what extent is the relative performance of emerging and less developed countries due to differences in the performance of the financial sector? The emerging economies had other factors working in their favour. The East Asian economies that developed in the 1960s and 1970s all had good social infrastructure to begin with, in the form of education and healthcare sectors that provided the foundations for developing human resources. They also developed in a period that favoured world trade, and when some of the advanced economies were moving towards a service orientation, leaving gaps for newly industrialising nations to fill. In the later wave, China had vast resources and a plentiful supply of labour to be mobilised. It was also able to channel funds into investment and maintain the competitiveness of its exports.

On this basis, the evidence seems to suggest that an effective financial sector is a necessary condition for economic growth and human development to take place, as it enables funds to be channelled to where they are needed. However, it may not be a sufficient condition to guarantee that success will be achieved.

Exercise 38.3

Analyse the importance of the financial sector for economic growth and human development.

Case study 38.1

Access to finance

Those living in rural areas in sub-Saharan Africa do not have access to the formal financial sector

In developing countries in 2014, only 53.1% of people aged 15 and above had an account with a financial institution. In sub-Saharan Africa, the figure was only 28.9% and in some countries it was even lower — for example, only 3.5% of people in Niger had an account and only 6.9% in Burundi. In October 2018, the World Bank noted that there were an estimated 1.7 billion adults worldwide (or 31% of adults) without a basic transactions account.

What this means is that any saving that takes place tends to be in the form of fixed assets, or money kept under the bed. Such savings cannot readily be transformed into productive investment. The lack of access to banking may be an impediment to the process of economic growth.

In the absence of branch banking, people in the rural areas do not have access to the formal financial sector. The commercial banks based in the urban areas do not have the information needed to be able to assess loan applications for rural projects. Furthermore, property rights are not secure, so it may be difficult to provide collateral against loans when ownership of land cannot be proved.

Follow-up questions
a Discuss the problems faced by a developing country when trying to mobilise savings for productive investment.
b Why should the lack of property rights be a hindrance to the provision of rural credit for small projects?
c How might the provision of rural credit for small businesses be improved in developing countries?

CHAPTER 38 QUESTIONS

A Multiple-choice questions

1 Which of the following is not a role of the financial sector?

    a To facilitate savings

    b To facilitate borrowing

    c To facilitate the exchange of goods and services

    d To facilitate taxation

2 Which of the following is not a reason for the existence of microfinance?

    a Informal borrowing often has high interest rates in developing countries

    b A lack of credit information about individuals in developing countries

    c Insecure property rights in developing countries

    d A high level of competition in developing countries' financial markets

B Knowledge and understanding questions

3 Explain the role of savings and investment in promoting economic development. [4 marks]

4 Explain the Harrod–Domar model. [3 marks]

C Stimulus response question

5 Microfinance has been an important part of the financial sector in many developing economies in recent years. This is particularly true where an economy is based on agriculture. Microfinance can provide funds for investment in small, but important projects that can increase the productivity of a farm.

    a Explain why microfinance might be needed in developing countries. [4 marks]

    b Evaluate the importance of the financial sector in promoting economic development. [12 marks]

D Essay

6 'Developed financial systems are the key to economic growth in developing countries.' Discuss. [25 marks]

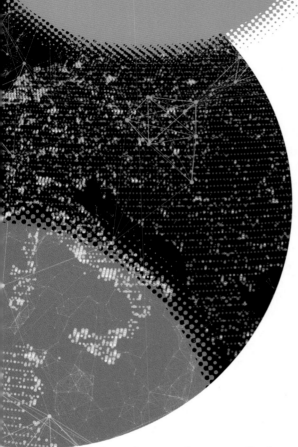

Chapter 39

The central bank and financial regulation

This final chapter explores the role of the central bank in the financial system, looking at the functions of the central bank, and the measures it has available to carry out those functions. Of particular importance are the provision of liquidity to the banking system and the role of an independent central bank in meeting targets set by the government. The need for regulation is examined, together with the way in which changes in the regulatory framework may have contributed to the crisis and its resolution.

Learning objectives

After studying this chapter, you should be able to:
- explain the role and functions of a central bank
- evaluate the effectiveness of different policy measures available to a central bank in targeting macroeconomic indicators
- explain the purpose and methods of financial regulation
- evaluate the importance of the regulation of financial institutions
- evaluate the role of the International Monetary Fund and the World Bank in regulating the global financial system

The functions of the central bank

All developed and most developing countries have a central bank that fulfils a range of roles, including having the responsibility for issuing currency. These roles may include:
- issuing banknotes and coin
- being banker to the government
- being banker to commercial banks and other financial institutions
- managing the government's borrowing
- managing the country's foreign exchange reserves
- being regulator of the financial system
- targeting inflation by influencing interest rates

Not all central banks fulfil all of these roles, and some have additional responsibilities assigned to them.

In developing countries, the central bank may have an important role in establishing and consolidating the domestic financial system in order to build confidence in the currency and financial institutions. It is worth being aware that in parts of sub-Saharan Africa, less than 20% of households have an account with a financial institution. This is not only because of the lack of bank branches (although this is clearly important), but is partly due to a lack of confidence in financial institutions. There

Knowledge check 39.1

What would be the principal effect of an increase in the rate of interest for the macroeconomy?

The problems in providing credit in rural areas in developing countries are discussed in Chapter 38.

may also be a developmental role in ensuring that credit can be made available for key development priorities.

In some cases, the central bank may be given responsibility for roles that support other objectives of the government. An example here would be the State Bank of Pakistan, which also has a responsibility for the 'Islamisation' of the banking system, to recognise the importance to the country of developing Islamic forms of financial instrument.

Extension material

Islamic banking

The key difference between banking as it is known in Western countries and Islamic banking is that Islam prohibits the use of interest (or usury, as it is known). This means that Islamic banks cannot charge interest on loans or pay interest on savings. Gambling is also prohibited.

A variety of financial instruments have been developed to allow banks to lend to firms or to households without charging interest. For example, a bank may agree a profit-sharing deal with a firm. The bank lends to the firm and then shares in the profits of the project. An alternative is a cost-plus-margin agreement. The bank purchases a given property at an agreed price, and immediately sells it to the buyer, stating the cost plus profit margin. The property is then treated as a commodity sold for money rather than an interest-based loan. The client pays in agreed termly instalments.

The Bank of England

As an example of central bank operations, consider the roles undertaken by the UK's central bank, the Bank of England. Its core activities comprise acting as banker to the government and financial institutions, managing the country's exchange reserves and supply of currency, and regulating the financial system. These have strong implications for the supply of money and credit in the economy. In addition, it has responsibility for meeting the government's inflation target.

The Bank of England, in central London

Issuing banknotes and coins

The issuing of notes and coins has long been a core function of the Bank of England, although it does not have a monopoly in the UK, only in

England and Wales. Commercial banks in Scotland and Northern Ireland can also issue banknotes, but the Bank of England regulates their issue. It is important to control the issue of banknotes in order to make sure that demands are met without leading to inflation. However, issuing notes and coins does not mean exercising control of the money supply because of the wide variety of other financial assets that are near-money.

Banker to the government

The Bank of England acts as banker to the government, in the sense that tax revenues and items of government expenditure are handled by the Bank, as are items of government borrowing and lending. In the past, the Bank of England also had responsibility for managing government debt by issuing Treasury Bills, but this was transferred to the Debt Management Office (an executive office within the Treasury) when the Bank was given independence to control the interest rate in order to meet the inflation target.

Banker to the commercial banks

The commercial banks and other financial institutions hold deposits at the Bank of England in the form of reserve balances and cash ratio deposits. The reserve balances are used as a stock of liquid assets, but also fulfil a clearing role, in the sense that they are used to equalise any imbalance in transactions between the major banks on a day-by-day basis. In normal times, the Bank agrees an average level of overnight reserves that institutions expect to require in the month ahead. If any institution holds reserves out of their agreed range, this attracts a charge. In other words, if a bank needs to borrow beyond its agreed average reserve level, it must pay a rate that is above bank rate. Deposits above the agreed average are remunerated below bank rate. This encourages institutions to meet their requirements in the interbank market, which helps to keep the interbank rate close to bank rate.

Managing the exchange rate

The Bank of England manages the UK's gold and foreign currency reserves on behalf of the Treasury. However, interventions have been rare in recent years, with the pound being allowed to find its own level in the foreign exchange market.

Monetary and financial stability

Apart from the functions outlined above, the Bank's main mission is 'to promote the good of the people of the United Kingdom by maintaining monetary and financial stability'. **Monetary stability** is interpreted in terms of stability in prices (relative to the government's inflation target). **Financial stability** means an efficient flow of funds in the economy and confidence in UK financial institutions.

The efficient flow of funds requires that there is sufficient liquidity in the economy. In other words, there must be enough liquidity for the financial institutions to conduct their business. The traditional way in which this was done was by the Bank acting as the **lender of last resort**, being prepared to lend to banks if they could not obtain the funds they needed elsewhere, albeit at a penalty rate. Although this was traditionally seen as a key role, events during the financial crisis made it untenable.

Knowledge check 39.2

Who sets the target for inflation in the UK, and what is the target that the Bank of England needs to meet?

Key terms

monetary stability a situation in which there is stability in prices relative to the government's inflation target

financial stability a situation in which there is a sufficient and efficient flow of liquidity in the economy

lender of last resort the role of the central bank in guaranteeing sufficient liquidity is available in the monetary system

Inflation targeting

In 1997, a significant change in the conduct of monetary policy was introduced by the incoming Labour administration. The Bank of England was given independent responsibility to set interest rates in order to achieve the stated inflation target set by the government. This represented a major change by taking discretion for monetary policy away from the government. This was discussed in Chapter 31, where it was pointed out that an important motivation for this change was to increase the credibility of government policy, in the sense that it could no longer try to use short-run policy measures to create a 'feel-good' factor in the economy. Instead, it was declaring a pre-commitment to controlling inflation, which it hoped would improve expectations about the future course of the macroeconomy.

The Monetary Policy Committee (MPC) has as its primary responsibility the maintenance of monetary stability by meeting the inflation target. However, it also has a secondary responsibility, as meeting the target for inflation is subject to supporting the economic policy of the government, including the objectives for economic growth and employment. In other words, the MPC cannot pursue the inflation target if this excessively endangers growth or employment.

The challenge of the period of inflation targeting has therefore been to balance the needs of monetary stability (meeting the inflation target) with ensuring financial stability (by ensuring the efficient and adequate provision of liquidity).

The advantage of having an independent central bank to pursue the inflation target is that it reinforces the credibility of the government's commitment to monetary stability, but the danger is that this could be pursued at the expense of the government's target for economic growth.

Not all central banks have been given this independent responsibility for meeting an inflation target. However, most developed countries have adopted this approach, which has been seen to be successful in maintaining a reasonable rate of inflation without hindering economic growth.

Synoptic link

Make sure that you are familiar with the way in which a change in bank rate eventually feeds through to affect aggregate demand and the rate of inflation. This is explained in Chapter 31 on monetary policy, which also introduced the MPC.

Exercise 39.1

Discuss the advantages and disadvantages of having an independent central bank dedicated to meeting an inflation target.

Summary

- The central bank of a country fulfils a number of important roles within the financial system to create monetary and financial stability.
- The central bank takes responsibility for issuing notes and coins — or at least for controlling the quantity in circulation.
- It may act as banker to the government and to other financial institutions.
- It also has a role in regulating the foreign exchange market.
- It may manage the government's debt position.
- In a number of countries, the central bank has been given independent responsibility for meeting government targets — for example, the Bank of England has responsibility for meeting the UK government's inflation target.

The effectiveness of policy measures in targeting macroeconomic objectives

Central banks have monetary policy as their prime responsibility, so do not have responsibility for all aspects of the government's macroeconomic policy objectives. For example, the central bank would not normally be concerned with ensuring an equitable distribution of income (which is more appropriately dealt with through fiscal policy), nor would it focus on ensuring environmental sustainability. A central bank may or may not have the responsibility of managing the government's debt.

For a country operating under a fixed exchange rate, the central bank's prime responsibility is to maintain the value of the currency, and it may have limited ability to do much else.

However, for most central banks the main focus is on creating a stable economy in terms of low inflation in conjunction with an adequate flow of credit, which in turn can encourage economic growth and high employment.

To illustrate how effective a central bank can be in meeting its objectives, we will explore the case of the Bank of England.

The effectiveness of policy measures available to the Bank of England

The Bank of England has responsibility for monetary policy, which is primarily intended to control inflation. This control is a key part of ensuring a stable macroeconomic environment, which in turn helps to encourage economic growth. However, in setting interest rates the Bank takes into account other aspects of the economy's performance, so there are occasions when the commitment to controlling inflation is tempered by the awareness of other macroeconomic indicators such as unemployment. In evaluating the effectiveness of policy measures available to the Bank of England, the main focus is on stability in financial markets.

Customers wait in line to remove their savings from a branch of the failing Northern Rock bank during the financial crisis of 2007

The financial crisis highlighted the need for central banks to enhance their roles in maintaining monetary and financial stability. This is well illustrated by exploring how the role of the Bank of England has evolved over time. In particular, there have been significant changes to the operations of the Bank of England in response to the introduction of inflation targeting and the financial crisis that began in the late 2000s. The crisis highlighted the need for closer monitoring of the financial system in order to ensure financial stability.

The pre-crisis period, 1997–2007

In 1997, the incoming Labour government delegated to the Bank of England the responsibility for meeting its inflation target. Specifically, the Bank was to keep inflation within 1 percentage point of the target, which was initially set at 2.5%, as measured using the retail price index (RPI). From January 2004, the target was reset in terms of the consumer price index (CPI), with its rate of change falling within 1 percentage point of 2%. The performance relative to the target from 1997 to 2007 is shown in Figure 39.1.

In the pre-crisis period, the Bank targeted inflation by using the interest rate. There are many different interest rates on financial assets, varying with the degree of risk associated with the asset, the length of loans and so on. However, they are interconnected, so the Bank can influence the rates of interest by changing the rate that it charges on short-term loans to domestic banks. This is known as bank rate. You can see how this moved around in Figure 39.1. These changes in bank rate affect the interest rates on other financial assets.

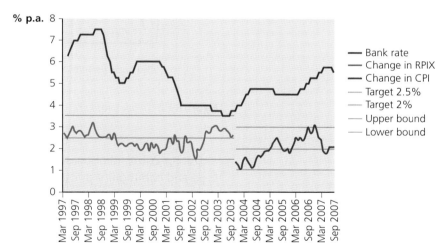

Figure 39.1 UK bank rate and the inflation target, 1997–2007

Sources: ONS, Bank of England

Key term

open market operations intervention by the central bank to influence short-run interest rates by buying or selling securities

Rates of interest also move around in response to market conditions, and the Bank of England can intervene to make sure that short-run interest rates are kept in line with bank rate. It does this by using **open market operations**, buying or selling securities in order to influence short-run interest rates.

Suppose there is a shortage of liquidity in the financial system. Financial institutions will need to borrow in order to improve their liquidity position. This puts upward pressure on interest rates, so there is a danger that interest rates will move out of line with bank rate. The Bank of England can intervene to prevent this by providing liquidity in the system by buying securities (Treasury bills or gilts) in the open market. Conversely, if there is excess liquidity in the system, interest rates may tend to fall, and the Bank can prevent this by selling securities in the open market.

This was a period in which policy appeared to be working effectively. Inflation remained within the specified 1 percentage point of its target, apart from one month when it dipped to 1.9% (April 2000), and one month when it rose to 3.1% (March 2007). Economic growth was steady during this period, and there were no obvious problems with liquidity.

Monetary policy from 2008

This period of stability was not to last. Figure 39.2 shows bank rate and inflation (measured by the percentage change in the CPI) from the beginning of 2008. You can see that the pattern here is very different from that in the period 1997–2007. Inflation moved out of its target range, and bank rate plummeted to an all-time low.

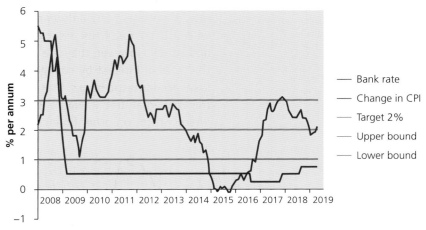

Figure 39.2 UK bank rate and the inflation target since 2008

Sources: ONS, Bank of England

During 2008, inflation accelerated. This partly reflected increases in food and commodity prices worldwide. The MPC took the view that this acceleration would not persist. Economic growth was expected to slow, and inflation was expected to move back below 2% per annum. Rather than increasing bank rate in order to put downward pressure on aggregate demand and inflation, the MPC reduced bank rate in August in anticipation of falling growth and inflation. In the following months, the financial crisis began to unfold.

Banks in difficulty

Even in 2007, it was becoming clear that a number of banks were facing difficulties, having expanded their borrowing substantially relative to their capital base. The response was to reduce lending, sell assets and look for new capital. Borrowing against property was one of the root causes of the problem, as the expectation that house prices would continue to rise had encouraged mortgage lending. When house prices in the USA stalled in

2005–06, defaults began to rise, putting pressure on lenders. The failure of some institutions prompted fears of recession, and one of the side effects of globalisation was that financial markets were interconnected across national boundaries.

A problem with bank failures is the effect it has on confidence in the financial system. As the crisis developed, it was perceived that some of the banks that were in danger were 'too large' to be allowed to fail. The demise of a large financial institution would have such an effect on expectations that the whole financial system might be called into question. Hence the moves by the UK and other governments to bail out banks that were in difficulties, in spite of the effect that this had on public finances (see Figure 30.2 on page 415).

Shortage of liquidity

In the UK, the crisis showed up in the interbank market, where a shortage of liquidity put upward pressure on the interbank rate. By March 2009, bank rate had been reduced to 0.5%, and this was seen as being the lowest possible, although it was subsequently reduced to 0.25% in late 2016 for a period. As the economy began to recover again, bank rate was raised back to 0.5% and then to 0.75% in August 2018. The Bank of England suspended the reserves averaging regime in 2009, as it could no longer be effective.

Instead, it introduced quantitative easing, a policy under which it created central bank reserves electronically, which were used to purchase high-quality financial assets such as government bonds in order to provide additional liquidity. This allowed the Bank to continue to influence interest rates, even with bank rate at such a low level.

Notice that the sudden fall in the public sector net debt (including financial sector interventions) in 2014 resulted from the reclassification of Lloyds Banking Group from the public to the private sector, following sales by the UK government of part of its shareholdings in the group. By early 2017, the divestment was complete, although net debt remained at a relatively high level.

Quantitative easing

This is essentially a way of increasing money supply. The foundations for this had been set in January 2009 by establishing the Asset Purchase Facility (APF), a subsidiary company of the Bank of England that carries out the necessary transactions. By mid-2018, the APF had purchased £435 billion of assets by the creation of central bank reserves. The level of quantitative easing is decided by the MPC as a joint decision with that on bank rate.

The problem faced by the Bank in this situation was that the rate of inflation had to be kept under control, but at the same time, the reluctance of banks to lend would affect investment and the growth of the real economy, which was heading into recession. Expectations were weak, threatening to prolong the recession. The UK was not alone in facing this combination of circumstances, and other central banks were adopting similar strategies to deal with the growing crisis.

Knowledge check 39.5

Explain why large-scale bank failures would be damaging to the economy.

Synoptic link

The notion of quantitative easing was introduced in Chapter 31.

543

Recovery was slow

Figure 39.3 shows the extent to which some other countries were following a common path for economic growth. Having badged the financial turmoil as being the worst since the 1930s, governments were anxious to avoid a repetition of the mass unemployment that had happened then. This was avoided, but you can see in the figure that the recovery was not rapid. It is difficult to disentangle the extent to which the recovery was a consequence of the policy stance adopted by the government and the Bank of England.

Knowledge check 39.6

Compare the performance of the UK economy with the EU19 in Figure 39.3. In which periods were there appreciable differences in performance?

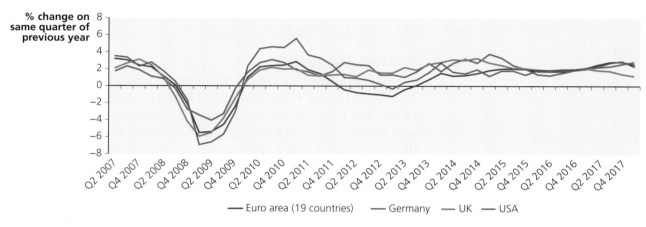

% change on same quarter of previous year

— Euro area (19 countries)   — Germany   — UK   — USA

Figure 39.3 Annual growth rate of GDP since 2007 (quarterly data)

Source: OECD (2018), Quarterly GDP (indicator). doi: 10.1787/b86d1fc8-en (Accessed on 19 June 2018)

Financial regulation

In recent decades, there have been rapid advances in technology that have transformed the way in which financial institutions can operate. Financial transactions have become so much simpler to undertake and to manage. Commercial banks and other financial institutions have adapted to these changes in a variety of ways, and new institutions have been established to take advantage of the new technology.

One direction in which institutions have developed is in devising new forms of financial assets that maximise returns. It proved difficult for existing forms of financial regulation to keep pace with these innovations. The danger of this situation is that financial institutions would take on more risk than they could handle. If things started to go wrong, this could culminate in the collapse of the whole system, once banks started to fail.

So, one of the key factors that led to the financial crisis of the late 2000s had been the inadequate regulation of financial institutions, which had allowed banks to build up portfolios of lending that carried risk beyond what could be covered by their capital. One way of viewing this is that, although central banks such as the Bank of England had structures to enable them to achieve monetary stability, the regulatory framework had not allowed the same degree of control over financial stability.

In the UK, a new regulatory framework came into operation in April 2013 to try to remedy this situation, and to avoid repetition of the financial crisis in the future. Two new statutory decision-making bodies were created that are part of the Bank of England. The **Prudential Regulation Authority (PRA)** is responsible for **microprudential regulation**, working at the level of the individual firm to promote the safeness and soundness of deposit-takers, insurers and major investment firms. The **Financial Policy Committee (FPC)** became responsible for **macroprudential regulation**:

> *responsible for identifying, monitoring and taking action to remove or reduce systemic risks with a view to protecting and enhancing the resilience of the UK financial system. And, subject to that, supporting the economic policy of the Government, including its objectives for growth and employment.*

Source: 'Changes to the Bank of England', *Bank of England Quarterly Bulletin*, 2013 Q1

In addition, the **Financial Conduct Authority (FCA)** was given responsibility for ensuring that relevant markets function well, and has responsibility for financial services firms that are not supervised by the PRA, including asset managers, hedge funds, many broker-dealers and independent financial advisers.

The intention of these arrangements is to improve the resilience and stability of the financial system by filling a perceived regulatory gap that had allowed the seeds of the crisis to develop. Other countries, including the USA and the EU, also established new bodies to perform similar tasks. This is crucial given the interconnectedness of financial markets following globalisation.

Notice that the FPC has primary responsibility for financial stability, but (like the MPC) it also has secondary responsibility for supporting the government's economic policy. This means that it must keep a balance between taking steps to stabilise the financial system and facilitating economic growth and employment.

The FPC has the power to make recommendations. For example, it can make recommendations to the PRA and FCA to take action to safeguard financial stability. The PRA and FCA need to comply, or to explain why this is not seen as appropriate. The FPC can also use the *countercyclical capital buffer*, under which banks, building societies and large investment firms can be required to hold additional loss-absorbing capital. The FPC can also impose *sectoral capital requirements*, under which firms need to meet additional capital requirements where the FPC perceives a risk to the stability of the financial system as a whole. A further power held by the FPC concerns the scope of regulation: in other words, it can recommend changes to the boundary between regulated and non-regulated activities.

The aim of these measures is to reduce the likelihood of future financial crises by monitoring activity more closely and having early warning of where problems may be building up. The FPC and PRA between them can then take action to mitigate the risks of a crisis. Given the impact of globalisation, it is recognised that there is also a need for international coordination of financial regulation. This is discussed in the next section.

Evaluation of the response to the crisis

The financial crisis highlighted the importance of the financial system for the real economy. Monetary stability is important because low and predictable inflation helps economic agents to form expectations about the future. This encourages firms to invest and allows households to plan their consumption. This in turn can promote economic growth and improvements in the standard of living. However, the crisis demonstrated that financial stability is also crucial, as this enables the flow of funds needed for firms to finance their investment.

The period before the crisis was characterised by monetary stability, with the inflation target being met, and economic growth proceeding at a steady rate. However, the inadequacy of regulation led to a build-up of pressure, which finally erupted in financial instability. This disrupted the financial system and had spillover effects for the real economy, resulting in recession and rising unemployment.

The main manifestations of this were in the failure of liquidity. The interbank market was unable to deliver the liquidity that was needed, and the Bank of England's role as lender of last resort could not be sustained with bank rate at 0.5%. In this situation, the Bank resorted to expansion of the money supply through the process of quantitative easing to supply liquidity while still keeping inflation within its target range.

The need for financial stability was tackled by the creation of new decision-making bodies with the responsibility for maintaining financial stability through enhanced regulation of the financial system and by monitoring developments in financial markets.

In seeking to maintain its primary objectives of both monetary and financial stability, the Bank needs also to maintain balance with its secondary objective of supporting the government's overall macroeconomic policy stance. This is no mean feat when the need to bail out failing banks has left a legacy of high public debt.

Summary

- There have been significant changes to the operations of the Bank of England since the financial crisis.
- The Bank had been given independent responsibility for the conduct of monetary policy in 1997 with a brief to meet the government's inflation target.
- This was to be accomplished through the Monetary Policy Committee setting bank rate.
- By setting bank rate, the rates of interest in other segments of the money market would also be affected.
- Open market operations were used to keep short-term interest rates in line with bank rate.
- In the financial crisis, banks faced shortages of liquidity and the interbank market could not cope.
- With bank rate at the lowest level that could be sustained, quantitative easing was introduced to supply liquidity to the financial sector.
- The crisis highlighted the need for greater regulation to maintain financial stability.

Study tip

Be clear in your mind about the distinction between monetary stability (low and predictable inflation) and financial stability (the efficient flow of liquidity). You should also be aware of the primary and secondary objectives of the Bank of England in terms of both monetary and financial stability.

The international context

It is important to remember that the financial crisis was not only a problem for the UK but affected most advanced economies. Indeed, some European countries faced more severe conditions than the UK. The actions of the Bank of England should therefore be seen in the context of the oversight of the international financial system by the multilateral bodies that oversee said system.

Along with globalisation has come the need to provide coordination of financial markets across countries. Deregulation increased the interconnectedness of financial markets, and the runaway advances in technology and the internet allowed financial transactions to take place smoothly and instantaneously. This improved the efficiency with which markets could operate, but also heightened the possibility for contagion — in other words, it increased the probability that crises could spread rapidly between countries.

There are three key organisations that contribute to international coordination of financial markets and regulation: the Bank for International Settlements (BIS), the **International Monetary Fund (IMF)** and the **World Bank**. Each fulfils a specific function in the global financial system.

At the end of the Second World War in 1945, a conference was held at Bretton Woods, New Hampshire, USA, to establish a system of fixed exchange rates. In addition to establishing the exchange rate system that operated until the early 1970s, the conference set up the IMF and World Bank to help to oversee aspects of the international financial system. A third organisation took responsibility for the conduct of international trade. This was the General Agreement on Tariffs and Trade, which was the precursor of the World Trade Organization (WTO).

After the collapse of the Dollar Standard in the early 1970s, the need for international cooperation in the operation of financial markets became apparent, and in 1982, G10 central bankers created the Basel Committee on Banking Supervision (hosted by the BIS), which was to play a key role in financial regulation.

The Basel Committee established a credit risk measurement framework that became a globally accepted standard. This has since been refined, the latest agreement being the Basel III agreement, which specifies internationally agreed capital adequacy requirements for banks. These are administered by central banks, so in the UK these Basel III capital requirements are built into the Bank of England's regulatory framework. The requirements are being phased in, and are due to be complete by 2019. This gradual phasing in of the new regulations is intended to avoid slowing the recovery.

In this way, it is hoped that the likelihood of financial instability spreading across countries will be reduced, as central banks will be imposing similar regulations on their respective financial systems.

The International Monetary Fund

The International Monetary Fund (IMF) was set up with a specific brief to offer short-term assistance to countries experiencing balance of payments problems. So, if a country were running a deficit on the current account,

Key terms

International Monetary Fund (IMF) multilateral institution that provides short-term financing for countries experiencing balance of payments problems

World Bank multilateral organisation that provides financing for long-term development projects

Synoptic link

The role of the WTO is discussed in Chapter 36.

it could borrow from the IMF in order to finance the deficit. However, the IMF would insist that, as a condition of granting the loan, the country put in place policies to deal with the deficit — typically, restrictive monetary and fiscal policies.

In the twenty-first century, the IMF continues to play an important role in maintaining the stability of the interconnected global financial system. In particular, it has provided loans to prevent default by a government. An example is the loan provided to Greece in 2010 (which is discussed in Case study 39.1 at the end of this chapter). The IMF has also provided loans to governments needing to bail out private banks that had become insolvent because of exposure to risky loans. Recent examples include loans to the governments of Hungary, Ireland and Latvia.

The World Bank

The International Bank for Reconstruction and Development was the second institution established under the Bretton Woods agreement. It soon became known as the World Bank. The role of the World Bank is to provide longer-term funding for projects that will promote development, rather than being directly involved in regulating the financial system.

The World Bank is especially important for developing countries, where internal financial markets are undeveloped or dysfunctional. It has a presence in most developing countries, being involved in a variety of projects to promote development and alleviate poverty. It has also undertaken research into ways of improving access to finance for people and firms in developing countries. Access to finance can be a substantial impediment for firms wanting to expand, and for households in need of small loans to improve their income-earning potential. This was discussed in Chapter 38.

Evaluation of the IMF and the World Bank

The Washington Consensus

The influence of the Bretton Woods institutions on economic growth and development has been considerable. In particular, the World Bank and the IMF have tended to impose conditions on countries in return for lending or debt forgiveness. These conditions were based on the prevailing views about how economies would respond to policy changes.

At a conference in 1989, John Williamson drew up a set of ideas about economic policy that he believed represented accepted views. These ideas became known as the *Washington Consensus*. The ten core policies were:

1 fiscal discipline
2 reordering public expenditure priorities
3 tax reform
4 liberalising interest rates
5 a competitive exchange rate
6 trade liberalisation
7 liberalising inward foreign direct investment
8 privatisation
9 deregulation
10 secure property rights

It was argued countries that adopted these measures would be able to initiate a process of economic development, and the list formed the basis of conditions imposed on countries. The measures reflect a market-oriented view of how economies operate. Although many countries did adopt some or all of these policies, it became clear that the consensus was not a complete solution. For example, China offered an alternative model, blending the introduction of market reforms with continuing state control.

It has also been argued that the set of measures neglects a number of key issues surrounding governance and the need to establish reliable and robust institutions to underpin the economy. In addition to the consensus measures, successful development also relies on improving the way that markets work, especially in terms of the need for flexible labour markets, and there needs to be targeted poverty reduction and social safety nets to bring together macro and micro aspects of the economy. This has led to initiatives centred on the notion of inclusive growth. Under this approach, it becomes important to ensure that growth provides genuine benefits for people.

Given the differing remits of the IMF and the World Bank, arguably the World Bank has been more successful in delivering its objectives in promoting development and poverty reduction than has the IMF in ensuring financial stability.

Globalisation has increased the interdependence of countries. This allows people around the world to share in economic success and gain mutual advantage through trade. However, it also allows financial crisis to spread more rapidly, and there is a need for international cooperation in regulating financial markets to reduce the likelihood of financial problems occurring.

The IMF and World Bank have contributed by providing a global framework within which financial markets can be coordinated, and common regulations agreed. However, this has not been not enough to prevent crises from occurring, such as the Asian financial crisis of 1997 and the global financial crisis of the late 2000s. In earlier years, the debt crisis of the 1980s gave warning that serious problems could occur when markets are not carefully monitored.

At the time of the 1980s debt crises, there was much criticism that the steps taken in response, such as the rescheduling of the debt of developing countries, were designed to safeguard the global financial system, but not designed to provide a permanent remedy to developing country debt. It was only with the HIPC Initiative that the World Bank agreed to allow debt forgiveness for developing countries — and even then under strict conditions. This may have impeded the development of some countries, especially in sub-Saharan Africa, where debt was putting such a strain on their resources. It is encouraging that some progress has now been made towards promoting growth and development in developing countries, and that measures are now being put in place to improve the stability of the global financial system in the future.

Exercise 39.3

Visit the IMF and World Bank websites to find out about their current projects and concerns:
www.imf.org/external/index.htm
www.worldbank.org/

Summary

- The process of globalisation has brought with it the need to coordinate the regulation and operation of financial markets around the world.
- The financial crisis of the late 2000s showed how rapidly a crisis could spread through global markets.
- Three organisations contribute to international coordination in financial markets.
- The Bank for International Settlements has produced standards for the conduct of financial markets that are accepted internationally.
- The International Monetary Fund (IMF) has moved on from its traditional role in providing loans for balance of payments purposes, and has made loans to prevent sovereign default.
- The IMF has also made loans available for national governments to avoid the failure of banks.
- The World Bank provides funds for key projects to promote human and economic development in less developed countries.

Case study 39.1

The bailout of Greece in 2010

In Greece, people wait in line to withdraw money from a failing bank during the 2010 global financial crisis

In May 2010 the EU and the IMF announced a €110 billion bailout loan for Greece. Traditionally, the IMF made loans to help a country to overcome a balance of payments problem or to stabilise its currency. But does that apply to this example?

In this case there was only one reason for the IMF to lend money to Greece and that was to prevent a Greek sovereign default. Prior to the credit crunch, highly indebted governments could borrow cheaply.

Governments such as the one in Greece took advantage of low borrowing costs by using debt to finance better public services. The recession that followed the crash of 2008 dented confidence. This led to an increase in the cost of borrowing. In Greece, the government debt servicing costs climbed, which created an even bigger fiscal deficit. The government was in a debt spiral, and a Greek sovereign default seemed imminent.

So, this was not a bailout for the people of Greece. Ordinary Greeks did not receive their share of the loan to blow recklessly on imported German BMWs. Instead, the Greek government used the borrowed money to pay its bondholders. These bondholders were French and German banks. According to research carried out by the Bank for International Settlements at the end of 2010, 96% of Greek government bonds were held by European banks. German banks alone held €22.7 billion of Greek debt. The Greek 'rescue package' was really designed to save the German and French banking system, which would have collapsed in the event of a Greek sovereign default. Most of the money lent to Greece spent no time in Greece — instead it was paid straight to French and German bankers.

Follow-up question
Discuss why it is so important to prevent sovereign default by a country such as Greece.

CHAPTER 39 QUESTIONS

A Multiple-choice questions

1 Which of the following is not a role of the UK central bank?

   a Banker to the government
   b Issuer of notes and coin
   c Managers of monetary policy
   d Managers of fiscal policy

2 Which body provides finance for long-term projects that will promote development?

   a The International Monetary Fund
   b The World Trade Organization
   c The World Bank
   d The Bank for International Settlements

B Knowledge and understanding questions

3 Explain **two** functions of a central bank.   [4 marks]

4 Explain **two** purposes of financial regulation.   [4 marks]

5 Explain the role of the International Monetary Fund.   [2 marks]

C Stimulus response question

6 PPI is payment protection insurance that may be sold to borrowers when taking out a loan. In the event of a borrower being unable to make regular payments, PPI can be used to cover these payments in the short term.

   The selling of PPI has been the basis for many compensation claims from UK bank customers. In many cases, customers were 'mis-sold' PPI when taking out a loan, as it was unnecessary for their circumstances.

   UK banks have already had to compensate customers more than £20 billion, and the deadline for claims was set as August 2019.

   a Explain how financial regulation might have been used to restrict the sale of PPI.   [2 marks]
   b Evaluate the benefits to the UK economy of increased PPI financial regulation.   [12 marks]

Acknowledgements

Photo credits

p2 Jeanette Teare/stock.adobe.comand; **p262** spainter_vfx/stock.adobe.com; **p7** Bloomberg/Getty Images; **p14** orestligetka/stock.adobe.com; **p15** Renate W/Fotolia; **p22** Image Source Plus/Alamy; **p26** andreykr/stock.adobe.com; **p31** René van den Berg/Alamy; **p49** ton koene/Alamy; **p54** Karen Mandau/stock.adobe.com; **p59** Timothy/stock.adobe.com; **p73** Steve Vidler/Alamy; **p74** Greg Balfour Evans/Alamy; **p87** Galina Barskaya/stock.adobe.com; **p93** geogphotos/Alamy; **p97** Probal Rashid/Getty Images; **p102** Kevin Britland/Alamy; **p105** BE&W agencja fotograficzna Sp. z o.o./Alamy; **p114** Franck METOIS/Alamy; **p122** Jeff Gilbert/Alamy; **p131** JEP News/Alamy; **p133** Kevin Britland/Alamy; **p137** Ian G Dagnall/Alamy; **p151** Robert Evans/Alamy; **p159** THANIT/stock.adobe.com; **p178** IB Photography/Alamy; **p188** Chris Pancewicz/Alamy; **p192** Piero Cruciatti/Alamy; **p195** dglimages/stock.adobe.com; **p196** Sergii Figurnyi/stock.adobe.com; **p200** Greg Balfour EvansAlamy; **p205** Fotomaton/Alamy; **p217** Tomasz Czajkowski/Alamy; **p229** Agencja Fotograficzna Caro/Alamy; **p233** kerkezz/stock.adobe.com; **p238** News Images/Alamy; **p246** Ed Reeve-VIEW/Alamy; **p252** Matthew Chattle/Alamy; **p255** Bloomberg/Getty Images; **p256** phonix_a/stock.adobe.com; **p266** keith morris/Alamy; **p273** MediaPunch Inc/Alamy; **p280** Dino Fracchia/Alamy; **p290** Stockr/stock.adobe.com; **p308** godrick/Alamy; **p315** Cliff Hide News/Alamy; **p316** Lou Linwei/Alamy; **p321** cristaltran/stock.adobe.com; **p324** Media Drum World/Alamy; **p333** blickwinkel/Alamy; **p337** Geoffrey Robinson/Alamy; **p349** islandstock/Alamy; **p363** Bloomberg/Getty Images; **p373** INTERFOTO/Alamy; **p388** Oleg/stock.adobe.com; **p401** Kai-Otto Melau/Alamy; **p404** Alexey Fedorenko/stock.adobe.com; **p413** Michael Kemp/Alamy; **p432** eye35.pix/Alamy; **p441** 67photo/Alamy; **p444** Jeff Gilbert/Alamy; **p459** Ian Schofield/stock.adobe.com; **p470** Bloomberg/Getty Images; **p473** KAZUHIRO NOGI/Getty Images; **p483** Africa/Alamy; **p486** Graham Prentice/Alamy; **p492** buhanovskiy/stock.adobe.com; **p497** Lucian Milasan/stock.adobe.com; **p505** Lazyllama/Alamy; **p509** Idanupong/stock.adobe.com; **p513** Mick Flynn/Alamy; **p526** FinancePix/Alamy; **p531** ZUMA Press, Inc./Alamy; **p533** erichon/stock.adobe.com; **p534** Godong/Alamy; **p537** KittyKat/stock.adobe.com; **p540** Peter Macdiarmid/Getty Images; **p550** Dimitris K./Alamy

Index

Note: **bold** page numbers indicate key term definitions.